HISTORY OF VATICAN II

HISTORY OF VATICAN II

General Editor

GIUSEPPE ALBERIGO

Istituto per le Scienze Religiose, Bologna

Editorial Board

History of Vatican II

Vol. II
The Formation of the Council's Identity
First Period and Intersession
October 1962 - September 1963

edited by

Giuseppe Alberigo

English version edited by

Joseph A. Komonchak

1997

ORBIS | PEETERS
Maryknoll | Leuven

Acknowledgment:

The Menil Foundation, Houston TX
The Rothko Chapel, Houston TX

Library of Congress Cataloging-in-Publication Data

History of Vatican II / edited by Giuseppe Alberigo: English version edited by
  Joseph A. Komonchak.
  XVIII-605 p., 24 cm.
  Includes bibliographical references and index.
  Contents: v. 2. The Formation of the Council's Identity
  ISBN 1-57075-147-1
  I. Alberigo Giuseppe. II. Komonchak, Joseph A.
  BX830 1962.H55   1996
  262'.52— dc20   95-42334
                                          CIP

CIP Royal Library Albert I, Brussels

History of Vatican II. — Vol. II
edited by G. Alberigo and J.A. Komonchak. — Leuven: Peeters, 1997

ISBN 90-6831-972-8 (PEETERS)
ISBN 1-57075-147-1 (ORBIS)
D 1997l0602l81

ORBIS BOOKS
PO Box 308
Maryknoll, NY 10545-0308

© PEETERS
Bondgenotenlaan 153
B-3000 Leuven
BELGIUM

TABLE OF CONTENTS

I. THE TUMULTUOUS OPENING DAYS OF THE COUNCIL
[ANDREA RICCARDI]

V. THE FIRST DOCTRINAL CLASH [GIUSEPPE RUGGIERI]

VI. THE DISCUSSION OF THE MODERN MEDIA [MATHIJS LAMBERIGTS]

VII. BEYOND AN ECCLESIOLOGY OF POLEMICS: THE DEBATE ON THE CHURCH [GIUSEPPE RUGGIERI]

VIII. THE DRAMA CONTINUES BETWEEN THE ACTS: THE "SECOND PREPARATION" AND ITS OPPONENTS [JAN GROOTAERS]

IX. EBB AND FLOW BETWEEN TWO SEASONS [JAN GROOTAERS]

X. THE CONCILIAR EXPERIENCE: "LEARNING ON THEIR OWN" [GIUSEPPE ALBERIGO]

PREFACE

With this volume the *History of Vatican II* launches into a description of the course of the conciliar event. The historiographical criteria applied in reconstructing what occurred and the literary criteria followed in the exposition have had to be radically changed from those used in Volume I. The preconciliar work of 1959-62 was done according to organized and quasi-prescribed methods and in the framework of the individual preparatory commissions and later of the Central Commission. The life of the great conciliar assembly, on the other hand, was marked by complex rhythms, a mass of subject matters, petitions, and sentiments, and interactions, sometimes chaotic, among the plenary assembly, the commissions, the Pope, the observers, the informal groups, the main residences of the bishops, the news centers, the press, and public opinion.

The task of providing adequate information about the elements of this collective phenomenon of quite unusual proportions while also being faithful to the daily development of the Council's work has posed considerable problems. The decision has been made to give priority to the real course of the conciliar experiment, even in its undeniable twistings and turnings, rather than to a thematic reconstruction that would certainly follow a clearer line but would also be less respectful of the concrete reality of the event.

For this volume, as for the first, it has been possible to obtain a broad and fruitful international collaboration, both during the preparatory investigations and discussions and in the construction of the narrative (although unfortunately no German collaborator was available). The differences among the viewpoints of the collaborators have been respected and constitute one of the values of the work.

The individual chapters are from the following authors: I, Andrea Riccardi (Rome); II, Gerald Fogarty (Charlottesville); III and VII, Mathijs Lamberigts (Leuven); IV, Hilari Raguer; V and VII, Giuseppe Ruggieri (Catania); VIII and IX, Jan Grootaers (Leuven); X, Giuseppe Alberigo (Bologna), who also is coordinating the entire project.

The acquisition of unpublished documents on the course followed by the Council has continued. These have come from numerous participants (fathers, experts, and observers) and have been collected and classified at the Istituto per le Scienze Religiose in Bologna. At the same time, inventories have been published of the various documentary archives, while Msgr. V. Carbone's gigantic undertaking, the publication of the official sources having to do with the work of the general congregations and with the functioning of the directive bodies, is almost complete.

By exploiting these new opportunities for access it has become possible to move beyond a chronicler's narrative and provide a hitherto impossible multidimensional understanding of the conciliar event that takes into account the multiple levels of the event. In addition to the impressive documentation on the general congregations and the directive bodies (Council of Presidents, Secretariat for Extraordinary Affairs, Coordinating Commission, moderators), other indispensable sources are the diaries, the minutes of the work of the commissions as well as notes on the meetings of informal groups, the informational material that circulated on the periphery of the Council, and the letters exchanged, especially during the intersession (information about them is given after the list of abbreviations). In dealing with the formation of tendencies and the redaction of the texts, the availability of such sources has played a decisive part in transcending the mechanistic idea that Vatican II was simply a series of debates held in the general congregations and ending with the voting of official decrees.

Only in this way is it possible to follow the development of the Council step by step, to weigh the influences that determined this development, and to account for the vast boiling up of ideas that took place not only during the period when the assembly was at work but no less decisively during the lengthy suspension of the Council during the 1962-63 intersession.

The first volume surprised some readers by its uninterruptedly historical treatment of the conciliar event. It seemed to us that the historical critical method ought to be followed faithfully even, and above all, in a case such as this, when the object of historical reconstruction is an event that by its nature claims to have a meta-rational dimension: the inspiration of the Holy Spirit. We are convinced that a rigorously historical treatment neither contradicts nor marginalizes that dimension, but respects it more than any pious, "domesticated" account would.

There are or will be at least six editions of the first volume: Italian (Il Mulino, Bologna); English (Orbis Books, Maryknoll, New York), Portuguese (Vozes, Petropolis, Brazil), German, (Grünewald, Mainz), French (Cerf, Paris), and Spanish (Sigueme, Salamanca); a Polish edition remains a possibility. Peeters of Leuven is coordinating all the editions. The reception given the work in the various cultural and linguistic areas has been very cordial and encouraging, beginning with a public presentation of the undertaking at Rome on December 1, 1995. During a private audience on December 2 the collaborators, accompanied by the publishers, were able to present the first volume to Pope John Paul II.

The research that lies at the basis of this history of the Council has been financed over the years by the Rothko Chapel and the Menil Foundation of Houston, Texas, and by other bodies and institutions to which we are most grateful.

Giuseppe Alberigo   Bologna, June 3, 1996

For the English edition, I must express gratitude not only to the translator, Matthew J. O'Connell, but also to William R. Burrows, managing editor of Orbis Books, and especially to Joan Laflamme, who provided invaluable editorial assistance.

Joseph A. Komonchak   Washington, July 4, 1997

ABBREVIATIONS

AAS	*Acta Apostolicae Sedis*, Vatican City
ACO	Archives du Conseil Oecuménique des Eglises, Geneva
ACUA	Archives of the Catholic University of America, Washington, D.C.
ADA	*Acta et Documenta Concilio oecumenico Vaticano II apparando: Series prima (antepraeparatoria).* Typis Polyglottis Vaticanis, 1960-1961.
ADP	*Acta et Documenta Concilio oecumenico Vaticano II apparando: Series secunda (praeparatoria).* Typis Polyglottis Vaticanis, 1964-1995.
Agende	A.G. Roncalli, *Agende 1936-1963*, unpublished
AS	*Acta Synodalia Sacrosancti Concilii Vaticani II.* Typis Polyglottis Vaticanis, 1970-
Attese	*Il Vaticano II fra attese e celebrazione*, ed. G. Alberigo. Bologna, 1995.
Beitrag	*Der Beitrag der deutschsprachigen und osteuropäischen Länder zum zweiten Vatikanischen Konzil*, ed. K. Wittstadt and W. Verschooten. Leuven, 1996
BPR	Biblioteca de Pesquisa Religiosa CSSR, São Paolo do Brasil
Caprile	G. Caprile, *Il Concilio Vaticano*, 5 vols. Rome, 1966-68
CCV	Centrum voor Conciliestudie Vaticanum II, Faculteit Godgeleerdheid. Katholieke Universiteit te Leuven.
CivCatt	*La Civiltà Cattolica*, Rome
CLG	Centre "Lumen Gentium" Faculté de Théologie, Université Catholique de Louvain. Louvain-la-Neuve
CNPL	Centre National de Pastoral Liturgique, Paris
COD	*Conciliorum Oecumenicorum Decreta*, ed. Istituto per le Scienze Religiose. Bologna, 1973
Commentary	*Commentary on the Documents of Vatican II*, ed. H. Vorgrimler 5 vols. New York 1968

Commissions	*Les commissions conciliaires à Vatican II*, ed. M. Lamberigts *et al.* Leuven, 1996
CrSt	*Cristianesimo nella Storia*, Bologna
DC	*Documentation Catholique*, Paris
Deuxième	*Le deuxième Concile du Vatican (1959-1965)*. Rome, 1989.
DMC	*Discorsi Messaggi Colloqui del S. Padre Giovanni XXIII*, 6 vols. Vatican City, 1960-67
DFenton	Diary of Joseph Clifford Fenton, Washington
DFlorit	Diary of E. Florit, Bologna
DOttaviani	Diary of A. Ottaviani, edited in E. Cavaterra, *Il prefetto del S. Offizio. Le opere e i giorni del card. Ottaviani.* Milano, 1990.
DSiri	Diary of G. Siri, edited in B. Lai, *Il papa non eletto. G. Siri cardinal di S. Romana Chiesa.* Rome/Bari 1993, pp. 301-403
DTucci	Diary of R. Tucci, Rome
DUrbani	Diary of G. Urbani, Venice
History	*History of Vatican II.* Vol. I. Leuven/Maryknoll, 1995
ICI	*Informations Catholiques Internationales.* Paris
Igreia	*A Igreia latino-americana às vésperas do concilio. História do Concilio Ecumênico Vaticano I*, ed. J.O. Beozzo. São Paolo, 1993
Indelicato	A. Indelicato, *Difendere la dottrina o annunciare l'evangelo. Il dibattito nella Commissione centrale preparatoria del Vaticano II.* Genoa, 1992
Insegnamenti	*Insegnamenti di Paolo VI.* 16 volumes. Vatican City, 1964-1978
ISR	Istituto per le Scienze Religiose di Bologna
JCongar	Journal of Y.M.-J. Congar, Paris
JDupont	Journal of J. Dupont, Louvain-la-Neuve
JEdelby	Journal of N. Edelby, Aleppo
JLabourdette	Journal of M.M. Labourdette, Toulouse
JS	Pope John XXIII, *Journal of a Soul*, revised edition. London, 1980.
Mansi	*Sacrorum Conciliorum amplissima collectio.* 32 vols.
NChenu	M.-D. Chenu, *Notes quotidiennes au Concile*, ed. A. Melloni. Paris, 1995

OssRom   *L'Osservatore Romano*, Rome
S. Paulo   *O Concilio vaticano II: as contribuições das
                    Conferências Episcopais latino-americanos e
                    caribenhas às quatro sessões (1962-1965) e
                    momentos decisivos da III sessão do Concilio*,
                    volume 3 of *Cristianismo na America Latina:
                    História, Debates, Perspectivas*. Petropolis, 1996
TJungmann   Diary of J. Jungmann
TSemmelroth   Diary of O. Semmelroth, Frankfurt am Main
Vatican II commence *Vatican II commence... Approches Francophones*,
                    ed. É. Fouilloux. Leuven, 1993
Vatican II Revisited *Vatican II Revisited By Those Who Were There*,
                    ed. A. Stacpoole. Minneapolis 1985
VCND   Vatican II Collection. Theodore M. Hesburgh
                    Library. University of Notre Dame, Notre Dame.
Vatican II à Moscou *Vatican II à Moscou. Actes du colloque de
                    Moscou, 1995*. Moscwa-Leuven, 1996
Veille   *À la veille du Concile Vatican II. Vota et réac-
                    tions en Europe et dans le Catholicisme oriental*,
                    ed. M. Lamberigts and C. Soetens. Leuven, 1992
Verso il Concilio   *Verso il concilio Vaticano II (1960-1962). Pas-
                    saggi e problemi della preparazione conciliare*,
                    ed. G. Alberigo and A. Melloni. Genoa, 1993
Vìsperas   *Cristianismo e iglesias de América Latina en
                    vìsperas del Vaticano II*, ed. J. O. Beozzo. Costa
                    Rica, 1992

SOURCES AND ARCHIVES

In the course of research on the history of Vatican II, access has been
requested and granted to many private collections of people who participated in the Council in various ways. These papers integrate and complete the documents of the Archives of Vatican II which, under the careful direction of Msgr. Vincenzo Carbone, Pope Paul VI wished to
remain distinct from the secret Vatican Archives and to be open to
scholars. Systematic use of such collections has been made in numerous
studies, in monographs, and in the colloquia which have prepared and
complete these volumes of the *History of Vatican II*. Two recent analyt-
ical reviews of these publications have been published: Joseph Famerée,

"Vers une histoire du Concile Vatican II," *Revue d'Histoire ecclésias-tique* 89 (1994) 638-41; and A. Greiler, "Ein internationales Forschungs-projekt zur Geschichte des Zweiten Vatikanums," in *Zeugnis und Dia-log: Die katholische Kirche in der neuzeitlichen Welt und das II. Vatikanische Konzil. Klaus Wittstadt zum 60. Geburtstag*, ed. W. Weiss (Würzburg 1996), 571-78.

The authors of this volume have made use of documents (original or copied) collected in the archives of various research-centers: Istituto per le Scienze Religiose di Bologna; Biblioteca de Pesquisa Religiosa CSSR, São Paolo do Brasil; Centre "Lumen Gentium" de Théologie, Université Catholique de Louvain, Louvain-la-Neuve; Centrum voor Conciliestudie Vaticanum II, Faculteit Godgeleerdheid, Katholieke Uni-versiteit te Leuven; Vatican II Collection, Archives of the Catholic Uni-versity of America, Washington, D.C.; Vatican II Collection, Theodore M. Hesburgh Library at the University of Notre Dame, Indiana.

In addition, many dioceses, libraries, religious houses, and families have given access, under various restrictions, to particularly valuable documentation: the Archdioceses of Chicago, Florence, Mainz, New York, and Paris; the Archives of the Jesuit Province of France, Vanves; the Berchmanskolleg, Munich; Bibliothèque du Saulchoir, Paris; Civiltà Cattolica, Rome; Couvent St. Jacques, Paris; Domarchiv, Cologne; Institut Catholique, Paris; Institut für Liturgiewissenschaft, Innsbruck; Pontificio Collegio Angelicum, Rome; Pontificium Consilium pro Laicis, Rome; Sankt Georgen Haus, Frankfurt a.M.

Many diaries have also been made available; on their use see A. Mel-loni, "I diari nella storia dei concili," in M.-D. Chenu, *Note quotidiane al Concilio: Diario del Vaticano II, 1962-1963* (Bologna, 1996). Other diaries of conciliar fathers and experts consulted are those of: J.C. Fen-ton, Washington; E. Florit, Florence; G. Siri, edited in B. Lai, *Il papa non eletto: Giuseppe Siri cardinale di Santa Romana Chiesa* (Rome-Bari, 1993); R. Tucci, Rome; Y.M.-J. Congar, Paris; M.M. Labourdette, Toulouse; J. Jungmann, Innsbruck; N. Edelby, edited in Italian transla-tion in N. Edelby, *Il Vaticano II nel diario di un vescovo arabo*, ed. R. Cannelli (Cinisello B., 1996).

Jan Grootaers has also made use of his own personal papers, Brus-sels; and the family of the late Cardinal G. Urbani granted access to his papers.

THE TUMULTUOUS OPENING DAYS OF THE COUNCIL

Andrea Riccardi

I. The Eve of the Council

An ecumenical council was no longer part of the Catholic Church's experience. Vatican I, which had been a very special kind of meeting in the list of the councils, was only a distant memory. Expectation of the new event was as great as the lack of experience of the dynamics and scope of a council. The memoirs of the fathers of Vatican II are unanimous in expressing a vague sense of expectation. Catholic public opinion displayed a diffuse sense of anticipation: prayer meetings in individual dioceses and documents which bishops addressed to their faithful heightened the sense that a major event in the life of the Catholic Church was about to take place. But, regardless of the role they might have played in the preparation of the Council and of their judgment on its results, which had reached the periphery of the Church during the summer, not even the future participants in the Council — the nearly 2500 bishops who would be its members, scores of theologians, and the countless people from the communications media[1] — were clear on what was about to happen.

Giuseppe Siri, Archbishop of Genoa and an influential cardinal during the reign of Pius XII, had concerns about the approaching Council. Not only did he fear that the work in hand was too complicated; he was also afraid of the logic of such assemblies. The dynamics of so large a gathering were dangerous because they could produce conflicts and confusions that would contrast with the clarity and simplicity which he wanted Catholicism to have in the modern world. The French and German bishops were among those he thought most likely to cause confusion: "They have never completely freed themselves from Protestant pressure and the Pragmatic Sanction. They are fine people, but they do not realize that they are the heirs of a mistake-ridden history." Accord-

---

[1] See J. Grootaers, "Informelle Strukturen der Information am Vatikanum," in *Biotope der Hoffnung zu Christentum und Kirche heute* (Olten, 1988), 268-81.

ing to an ancient Roman tradition of government, a balanced view of
history and the future could be had only at the center of the Church. Siri
thought that "the role of the Italians, the Latins, and of the Curia should
be to settle matters, whether by filling in holes or by correcting false
turns." He concluded: "Roman calm will help."[2]

But Rome was neither calm nor possessed of a single vision of the
course of Vatican II. Not a few thought the Council a risky undertaking
because of the centrifugal pressures that could develop. This was the
view of Pius XII's men, such as Siri, and it echoed the position they had
taken at the end of the 1940s when the possibility of holding a council
had been considered. Bishop A. Castelli, secretary general of the Italian
bishops' conference, for example, feared pressure against the Curia. But
not everyone shared that fear; others had received with respect and favor
John XXIII's proposal to revive the ancient conciliar tradition. Ever
since the preparatory work had begun, some Curial cardinals, Confalonieri and Cicognani among them, had shown their desire to support
the Pope's Council. In their view the imposing number of pages of
schemas — both those already sent out and those still being completed —
provided a safe way to bring Vatican II to a quick conclusion and to
avoid centrifugal developments.

A. The Fear of Disappointing the World

Outside of Roman circles, however, the atmosphere was mainly one
of concern and even pessimism regarding the material to be submitted
to the judgment of the bishops. M.-D. Chenu reported on a meeting
between Yves Congar and Hans Küng, both of whom were pessimistic.
When Chenu met Jean Daniélou, the latter launched into a severe criticism of "the doctrinal schemas, devoted to academic discussions and
lacking any evangelical perspective and any sense of the needs of the
present time."[3] In the preparatory material Karl Rahner saw nothing
that could be salvaged; Joseph Ratzinger thought it incapable of speaking to the Church. Edward Schillebeeckx was no more sympathetic
than the others,[4] and Henri de Lubac saw no room for intervention.

---

[2] *DSiri*, October 11, 1962, 356.
[3] See *NChenu*, 64-65.
[4] See J. A. Brouwers, *Vreugde en hoopvolle verwachting. Vaticanum II. Terugblik van
een ooggetuige* (Baarn, 1989).

Even Gérard Philips, Carlo Colombo, and Congar, who had been members of the Theological Commission, had not yet decided on a plan of action.[5] The concern of these men was not simply that Vatican II might prove to be a ceremonial council, intended to ratify what the preparatory commissions had produced, and thus a useless event. Their deeper fear was that the Council would utterly disappoint the expectations of the faithful, the other Christian communities, and public opinion. Then too, in light of their experience of the great parliamentary and constituent assemblies, people were asking how a council would operate, how it would turn out documents, what image it would present to the world.

In Congar's analysis, the eve of the opening was marked by "a lack of preparation." What image of itself would the Council give to the world? He found the journalists rather worried: "There are 700 journalists who are angry because while first-rate premises have been prepared for them, with up-to-date machines, no one is telling them anything."[6] No event of the Catholic Church, with the exception of the death and election of recent popes, had been given as much attention by the press. This attention was a sign of the renewed sympathy for the Church of Rome that had been engendered by the pontificate of John XXIII, and these hopes for the Council must not be disappointed. After the burdensome years of the Cold War and now that a period of detente was imminent, what was to be the significance of a gathering in Rome of so many bishops from every part of the world, under the leadership of this "extraordinary" pope, John XXIII?

Chenu realized this current of expectation and of sympathy toward Vatican II and suggested the Council prepare a message to humanity:

> It occurred to me that an effective response to the expectations of all would be an opening statement by the Council, a "message" to all people, Christians and non-Christians, which would explain the purposes and inspiration of the meeting, in a missionary perspective commensurate with the problems of the present world-situation, and would effectively respond to the sympathetic anticipations of people who will be frustrated if the Council begins with theoretical deliberations and denunciations of erroneous tendencies.

The idea which he expressed here was perhaps suggested in not dissimilar terms by others, but it was Chenu who urged it most convincingly.

---

[5] For the initial disquiet of theologians, see chapter 2, below.
[6] *JCongar*, October 10, 1962, typescript, 68.

In his view, two conceptions of the Council were becoming clear, "the inspiration of the Pope" and "the works of the doctrinaire people in the Theological Commission."[7]

B. To Rome Because Called

As a matter of fact, not many people were aware of these alternatives. Most of the Council fathers went to Rome simply because they had been called by John XXIII. They were not used to thinking of themselves as playing a part in the Church's major decisions, as a council requires of all its members. True enough, some bishops did have the experience of episcopal conferences, a common bond among the French assembly of cardinals and archbishops, the conference of German bishops, and many other episcopates, from Brazil to Poland, from the United States to South Africa, from Argentina to the Philippines. But not all bishops had had this experience, and there was certainly no thought about what it might contribute to the Council. The Italian episcopate, which encircles the Holy See and provided the conciliar assembly with its largest group, had never been constituted as a national episcopal conference and had never held a plenary meeting. Only during the previous ten years had the presidents of the Italian regional conferences periodically met under the leadership of Cardinal Siri. Nor did the experience of a few worldwide meetings of bishops, such as those on the occasion of eucharistic congresses or during the 1950 Holy Year or the one held for the proclamation of the dogma of Mary's Assumption, provide a real precedent.[8]

Great expectations, then, a lack of preparation, little experience, and, for most of the bishops — despite the impatience that showed in some of the *vota* — the habitual basic attitude that the *causae maiores*, the more important matters, were to be left to Rome, because it was thought that people in Rome saw the general problems of the Church more clearly and in a broader perspective. Well, it was Rome, the Pope, who had decided to call the bishops to a council!

[7] See *NChenu*, 60-61.

[8] See A. Riccardi, *Il potere del papa da Pio XII a Giovanni Paolo II* (Rome-Bari, 1992); on the Italian episcopate see F. Sportelli, *La Conferenza Episcopale Italiana (1952-1972)* (Galatina, 1994).

C. Expectations of the Bishops and Message of the Pope

What did the experience of the Council mean to the individual bishop who arrived in Rome during the first ten days of October 1962? The effect of the first contact with other bishops was an important one, as was the first contact with the Rome of the Council, quite different from any previous knowledge the fathers might have had of the city and the Curia.

A month before the opening of Vatican II, John XXIII addressed a radio message to the faithful of the entire world. He had been moved to give it by some very worried notes received from cardinals frightened by the idea of a rapid and mainly ceremonial council that would issue condemnations.[9] In the address the Pope spoke of "the great anticipation of the Ecumenical Council." For the bishops who were coming to Rome, this Council, in the Pope's mind, would be a way to renew the mission of the Church in face of the world's problems, poverty, and the desire for world peace. John XXIII set out a historical frame of reference that went beyond the limits of ecclesiastical chronology. He noted that the Council was to begin seventeen years after the end of the Second World War: "Mothers and fathers of families detest war. The Church, mother of all without distinction, will again raise that cry which rises from the depths of the ages and from Bethlehem...." To the bishops and faithful of countries on the periphery of the international stage John XXIII spoke in the ancient metaphor of the Church as a "Mother;" but he also spoke of a "Church that is and wishes to be the Church of all and particularly the Church of the poor."[10]

These words had helped to create a climate of "expectation" among the bishops. John XXIII was calling upon them to meet this "expectation" and grasp the new perspectives of the Church's mission in the world. But would the Council be a creative event or simply support some lines already set out from on high? To carry out the task given them would not be easy, especially for so vast a body of bishops unaccustomed to working collegially and as an assembly. The majority of the

---

[9] *DMC* IV, 519-28; on the importance of Suenens's suggestions on this point and on the proposal presented to the Pope in July, see L.-J. Suenens, *Souvenirs et espérances* (Paris, 1991), 65-80, and idem, "A Plan for the Whole Council," *Vatican II Revisited*, 88-105. On the petition initiated by Cardinal Léger, see G. Routhier, "Les réactions du cardinal Léger à la préparation de Vatican II," *Revue d'histoire de l'Église de France* 80 (1994), 281-301.

[10] For the subsequent use and importance of this phrase see D. Pelletier, "Une marginalité engagée: le groupe «Jésus, l'Église et les Pauvres»" in *Commissions*, 63-89.

fathers reached Rome in a state of uncertainty, not knowing what their own role was to be. Even the Apostolic Nuncios and Delegates with whom the bishops were in touch did not have a clear idea of what Vatican II was to be.

D. Last-Minute Uncertainty

As a result, many bishops in their uncertainty took refuge in a long-standing attitude of obedience not only to the pope but also to the Roman congregations. Few of them shared the contrasting concerns of a Siri or a Chenu, and for most of them the general problems of the Church and those of other countries were remote.

The varying moods were intensified by the difficulties in organizing so large an assembly. On the morning of October 10 the bishops crammed the offices of the General Secretariat on a side street off the Via della Conciliazione to acquire the needed documentation. The place was in chaos: the procedures for obtaining the documents had not been made clear, identification was a complicated matter. Cardinal Urbani noted in his diary: "Widespread feeling of improvisation on the part of the Romans."[11] This unpleasant feeling unfortunately spread also in other directions and surfaced in too many situations.

E. The Place

The waiting and the questions were accompanied by curiosity about the place where the Council was to be held. For the first time, the Council hall was to be the central nave of the Basilica of St. Peter and not the transept, as at Vatican I.[12] Some of the fathers could not wait and went beforehand to see the arrangement of the banks of chairs from which the bishops and others would take part in Vatican II.

For some, the inspection was prompted not simply by curiosity but by more substantive concerns. Maximos IV Saigh, Melkite Patriarch of Antioch and one of the leading personages of the Council, thoroughly inspected the Vatican Basilica and saw, as he had suspected, that the places for the Eastern patriarchs came after those of the cardinals in

---

[11] *DUrbani*, October 11, 1962.
[12] On the arrangement of the hall for Vatican II, see *History*, I, 481-83.

order of precedence.[13] Only a green cloth distinguished the place for the
Eastern patriarchs from that of the other council fathers. The choice had
therefore been made to follow Roman ceremonial, according to which
cardinals preceded patriarchs in seating at the Council as well as in all
the celebrations; but this was a step backward in respect to what had
been decided at the Council of Florence, which had acknowledged the
traditional role of patriarchs in the Church.

To the Curia the question of the place of the patriarchs seemed a sub-
tlety typical of the Eastern mind. As the body of papal advisers, the cardinals had to have the first places. After all, what was a patriarch? In the
Latin Church, where the sees of Venice, Lisbon, and Goa had for historical reasons been awarded the title, "patriarch" was simply an honorific
title that heightened the dignity of the see. And in concrete terms, the
Eastern patriarchs headed sees that were so much smaller in the number
of their faithful that a European bishop might have a larger number of
Catholics than an entire Eastern patriarchate. Thus in claiming for the
patriarchs a place immediately after that of the pope of Rome, Maximos
IV seemed to be defending formal privileges that lacked all substance.

If the Maronite, Chaldean, and Coptic-Catholic patriarchs quietly
accepted the place assigned to them after the cardinals, thus agreeing
with the Roman viewpoint, Maximos IV Saigh saw things differently.
Behind the question of the placement of the patriarchs he saw the problem of the non-Catholic East, of the Orthodox and non-chalcedonian
Churches which would be sending observers to follow the Council. The
Eastern patriarchs represented the major sees, after Rome, in the Christendom of the first millennium; and recognition of their role was a decisive step in the establishment of a dialogue. The pentarchy, that is, the
communion of the five patriarchal sees of the Mediterranean world, had
displayed the unity of the Church during the first millennium. An Eastern patriarch could not follow the cardinals and could not, during pontifical ceremonies, perform the ritual of obedience to the pope which
cardinals and bishops do. Despite the smaller number of faithful in his
Church, an Eastern patriarch represents a Church that is a sister to the
Roman Church.

This conception of things had no place in Roman ceremonial because
it had no legitimacy in Roman ecclesiology. The position of those uniates who were aware of their traditional role was therefore a difficult
one. What idea of the unity of Christians was Rome conveying to the

---

[13] See *JEdelby*, October 9, 1962, ff. 9-10.

Orientals? The placement of the Oriental patriarchs itself seemed to be saying that there is but a single Church, that of Rome, and that the Holy See saw no other way of reunion except complete absorption into itself. Did the Roman Church acknowledge that the patriarchal Churches had their own place and their own identity? The Melkite patriarch's question thus concealed a wider problem: ecumenism and relations with the Orthodox world.

As a matter of fact, Vatican II was giving attention to some of the "absent," that is, to non-Catholic Christians. But their location — material, but also symbolic — was also uncertain: on October 10 the Secretariat for Christian Unity was not yet sure where in the basilica the non-Catholic observers would be seated.[14] The presence of non-Catholics, even under the colorless title of observers, was an entirely new experience for a conciliar assembly, one whose ecclesiological meaning was rich, complex, and unfamiliar.[15] Those absent also represented a point of reference which the Council could not ignore in its work.[16] And while the Anglican and Reformed Churches could easily send a delegation, the presence of the Eastern Churches was a more complicated matter, and not only because of the political and diplomatic repercussions connected with the coming of two Russian Orthodox Churchmen carrying USSR passports.[17]

The Eastern Catholics, whom the Orthodox disparagingly called "Uniates," could not be unconcerned about the Christian world with which they had so much in common. The episcopates in union with Vatican II were not all of a piece. Some of them were, even in mentality, part of the Latin world and retained only the Eastern liturgical rite. Others, among them Maximos IV and his Melkites thought that they had to serve as a bridge between Rome and the Eastern world to which they at least to some extent belonged and which they wished to represent.[18] This

---

[14] Arrighi to Congar, in *JCongar*, October 10, 1962, typescript, 68.

[15] See G. Alberigo, *Ecclesiologia in divenire: A proposito di "Concilio pastorale" e di Osservatori a-cattolici al Vaticano II* (Bologna, 1990).

[16] Speaking on the schema *De Oecumenismo*, Maximos IV would argue that the Council must also remember the East that was not represented in the hall: "When we speak of the Orient, we must not think only of those who humbly represent it within the bosom of Roman Catholicism. We must also keep *a place for those who are not here*. We must not limit the compass of Catholicism to a dynamic and conquering Latinism, on the one hand, and to an often weak, assimilated, absorbed fraction of the Orient, on the other." See J. Grootaers, *I protagonisti del Vaticano II* (Cinisello Balsamo, 1994), 179.

[17] See the articles in *Vatican II à Moscou*.

[18] At their first meeting, in Jerusalem in 1964, Maximos IV would tell Patriarch Athenagoras: "I can tell you that every time I spoke at the Council, I was thinking of you.

seemed to realize an ancient dream, that of being a bridge between Rome and the Orthodox East, but a dream destined to be quickly smashed in the ecumenical dialogue of the ensuing years. But on that October 10, Patriarch Maximos was firm in demanding a proper and appropriate place, because he had the Orthodox in mind; a refusal to allow the patriarch his proper visibility meant that he must refuse to take part in the opening ceremonies.

This was a crack in the facade, which many perhaps did not notice amid the euphoria of beginnings and the impressive spectacle of the opening of the Council's work. But such oversight was the norm, not the exception, in this opening session when the revelatory events that were to determine and form the very fabric of the Council remained unknown to the majority. The absence of the best- known Eastern Catholic patriarch and the presence of the observers at the inaugural session were a sign of the contradictions that marked the start of Vatican II and that could not be resolved at a single stroke.

F. Awaiting "The Pope's Word"

Quite a few fathers, however, really thought that everything could and would be settled by the message and instructions of the Pope, who would resolve uncertainties and tell them what to do. This habit of mind, almost a spirituality, had been strengthened during the years of Pius XII whose words and instructions had guided the life of the Church, even at very concrete levels. From the Pope, then, the Council fathers expected orders, and not just general suggestions, about how the work of the Council was to proceed, on its duration, its objectives, and even on the task of the bishops.

Many bishops had no close experience of the parliamentary assemblies typical of Western democracy. The experience of democracy in Italy and in Germany was too recent for them to have assimilated its lesson in any depth; the experience was simply lacking in Spain, Portugal, Eastern Europe, not a few countries of Latin America, and in the young states of the southern hemisphere. Even though a Council is not a par-

I want to give the Council the most faithful possible witness to the authentic Eastern tradition." And the Ecumenical Patriarch replied: "You represent us all." Conversation between Maximos IV and Athenagoras, January 5, 1964, in *Ach-Chira*, March 17, 1964, cited in *Maximos IV*, ed. E. Inglessis (Paris, 1969), 72.

liament of the Church, a familiarity with voting methods, democratic systems, and the formations of majorities and minorities could have helped them grasp the dynamics of a large assembly that by tradition would be called upon to make choices by the votes of its members. Would the fathers express their will by votes, or would they simply have to follow the instructions of the Holy See? Vatican I had been governed by the votes of its members. Even the practice of the Roman congregations provided for voting by their members, although the results were subject to the decision of the pope. Would the Council be permitted to vote as it should?[19]

II. THE OPENING

The setting for the opening was a majestic one. The pictures transmitted by television showed a Council — and what an immense one! — to the general public for the first time. Italian state television, the RAI, joined some other European television networks in showing the Council live, and the pictures were also shown in the United States in the afternoon. It was a most impressive sight, enabling even the most distant observers to get an idea of what was happening and eliciting strong reactions.[20] The festive hope of the beginning became an image the whole world could see.

---

[19] The climate of expectation that the Council's convocation had created was stymied by the lack of a sure program. The most obvious program was represented by the schemas written during a preparatory period that was dominated by the Curia's experience and vision and by an expectation that the schemas would be rapidly accepted; see *History*, I, 44-49. Fear that "unedifying" disagreement and debate among the bishops might endanger Church unity had led to the postponement of the conciliar meeting suggested by Pius XII for 1950; see *History*, I, 63-65.

[20] This is confirmed by the *Carnets* of Louvain theologian Charles Moeller, who wrote: "Council on TV — Pope John tired, anxious, serious — His kindness written on his face. A spirit of profound grace visible in his entire person — The brief oriental part of the ceremony, making concrete the universality of the Church. But it must be admitted that the structures are indeed 'Latin of the Latins' — The patriarchs, for example, are placed after the cardinals. A choice heavy with consequences — The pope's address: excellent in its openness: explanation of the truth rather than condemnation; see the good aspects of the modern world (against the birds of ill omen) rather than only the bad — Very remarkable commentary by F. Colleye." On the problem of the media see M. Marazziti, *I papi di carta. Nascita e svolta dell'informazione religiosa da Pio XII a Giovanni XXIII* (Genoa, 1990).

A. The Procession and the Liturgy

The Council fathers came in a long procession down the *scala regia* from the apostolic palace and crossed the piazza to the Basilica of St. Peter — about 2500 in number. It took an hour for them to pass in rows among the faithful who filled the square. After the vexations of the morning, when it was found that there were no chairs for the cardinals in the vesting room, the fathers were moved at the sight of the procession. Their effort to maintain some recollection of spirit did not prevent their hearing comments and problems. The Orientals were aware of being noticed, and Cardinal Wyszynski commented on how bystanders whispered his name and exclaimed about how thin was the cardinal from "behind the Iron Curtain."[21] When they entered the basilica, the fathers, who did not yet have assigned places, sat down in a spontaneous order. In the same way, the periti crowded into their tribune without precedence or reservations.

John XXIII crossed the piazza in his gestatorial chair amid the acclamations of the faithful. He got down from his chair in front of the altar where he knelt before intoning the *Veni Creator*. Cardinal Tisserant, Dean of the Sacred College, celebrated the Mass of the Holy Spirit. The pope wanted the gospel to be read in Greek and the Byzantine *ectenia* (litany) to be recited, along with the *supplicatio orientalis*, in Greek, Arabic, and Old Slavonic. On the days that followed, the liturgy was celebrated at the beginning of the Council's workday in various rites, thus beginning to familiarize the overwhelmingly Latin majority of bishops with the existence of other ways of celebrating the liturgy and with other liturgical languages.

After Tisserant's celebration, the gospel, in a fifteenth-century codex belonging to Federico da Montefeltro, was enthroned, an act that would take place at every conciliar congregation. Finally, there was the ritual of obedience by the cardinals, the patriarchs, and the general secretary (Msgr. Pericle Felici), as two representatives of each category of fathers knelt before the Pope, seated on his throne. At the end of the ritual of

---

[21] In his diary Cardinal Wyszynski noted the course and atmosphere of the ceremony: the veneration, inaccurate pronunciations, the odd arrangement that seated an American prelate next to the cardinal from Soviet Armenia, ironic comments on his own thinness which "embarrassed the man from a materialist country," acts of devotion to the Queen of Poland (see S. Wyszynski, "By Cz owik pos any od Boga, a Jan mu by o na imi," in *Jan XXIII i jego dzie o. Praca zbiorowa*, ed. B. Bejze, B. Dziwosza, and W. Zió [Warsaw, 1972], 41-156 at 98-99; translated in *NChenu*, 30-31).

obedience, John XXIII made the profession of faith and took the oath, this last being repeated by the fathers; meanwhile, the creed was being sung by the basilica's choir, amid the silence of the bishops. Few people observed that, after the ancient Nicene-Constantinopolitan formula, the profession of faith was not expressed in the "new formula" that had been drawn up at the wish of the Holy Office as one of the preparatory schemas and was a synthesis of condemnations by the magisterium in the twentieth century.[22]

Congar was annoyed by the triumphalistic pomp that pervaded the opening ceremony;[23] and many liturgists were visibly upset by it. A leading spokesman for the liturgical movement, Joseph Jungmann, gave a pitiless analysis:

> The opening was not a pleasant affair for me. Still without an identity card, I had to make my way into the Vatican with my decree of appointment but without instructions on place and time. Wherever I asked, the only answer was: "Not this way!" Finally, after an hour of vainly wandering around, I reached the basilica and there was courteously led by an *assignator* to the places reserved for the experts, but almost none of these was to be found there (wrong side of the galleries). At any rate, from there I had a good view of the bishops' entrance and could hear everything very clearly. As a liturgical action indeed it was carried out correctly: good church music, excellent acoustic equipment, but the whole conception was in the style of Leo XIII. They learned nothing from the *statio orbis* in Munich. A high Mass without distribution of communion. Instead of integrating the open-ing actions (gospel in several languages, address of the Pope, profession of faith, intercessions...), all these gave the impression of being an appendage without any order. A *flectamus genua* followed the litany! The ugly prayer, *Adsumus*, to the Holy Spirit (as I was able to tell Bugnini, it comes from Pseudo-Isidore) at least was not recited by all but by an individual. — But most people there were pleased with it. Perhaps the idea was to make clear the *terminus a quo* in matters liturgical![24]

In his notebook, *Souvenirs Ie session*, Dominican theologian M.-M. Labourdette tells of watching the ceremony in the company of Father Rosaire Gagnebet:

> Solemn opening in St. Peter's.... We reach St. Peter's by way of the Museum. We have to look for our tribune. Finally: on the left, the closest tribune to the Confession of the Apostles, almost above the cardinals, fac-ing the bronze statue of St. Peter (clothed in pontifical vestments). An

---

[22] See A. Indelicato, "La *Formula nova professionis fidei* nella preparazione del Vat-icano II," *CrSt* 7 (1986), 305-20.

[23] See *JCongar*, October 11, 1962, typescript, 68-71.

[24] *TJungmann*, October 11, 1962.

unforgettable spectacle. The ceremony is marked by a gripping religious grandeur *despite mistakes*, e.g., a polyphonic singing of the creed instead of having the bishops sing it together. And what a fine occasion *for a concelebration!*[25]

And even a "little" bishop such as J. B. Musty, auxiliary of Namur, observed in his *Notes sur le Concile oecuménique Vatican II*: "October 11: Opening session. Imposing. Lack of liturgical participation. Everything in polyphony, including the creed. Communion not distributed. But impressive."

The Italians were rather satisfied with the ceremony. In recalling it, Msgr. Bartoletti waxes lyrical:

> At 8:30 the procession of bishops begins at the Sala dei Lapidi of the Vatican Museum. We enter St. Peter's: Here is the Church! Truly this is an epiphany of the mystery of the Church, unfolding as in a great liturgy. The mystery of the Church is at work, at its height of visibility. Nothing too external or secular here. The modern age has made a clean sweep of all the secular baroque in which the past delighted. This is already a good sign. The prayer "Here we are, Lord, gathered in your name," underscores the religious meeting of our assembly and reminds everyone of his own responsibility and of his own weakness.[26]

In the remarks he wrote down for the young people with whom he lived, even Cardinal Lercaro, the one Italian bishop in the liturgical movement, left out any criticism of the ceremony.[27]

---

[25] *JLabourdette*, October 11, 1962.

[26] Many of the bishops who wrote notes after the end of the morning were entranced by the rhetoric and emotion of the ceremonial. Enrico Bartoletti was among them, and in his manuscript "Quaderno" the opening address of the Pope and the words he uttered that same evening "in the moonlight" make their appearance: "Monday, October 11, 1962. Maternity of Mary / Solemn opening of the Council....The profession of faith made by the Pope alone before all the Church: marvelous! The faith is our real bond; and it is this faith that we all serve...the holy Church of God./ The pope — what a gift of God to his holy Church! — spoke simply and clearly. His optimism, his confidence in the new age, his faith in the Church, seem so rooted in his spirit that it would be very difficult for them to be drowned out by the voices of the Council. This is the line to take. Whether well or poorly, the Council will emerge safely./ Very beautiful words of the Pope to the crowd gathered in St. Peter's square in the evening for the torchlight procession: 'Fatherhood and brotherhood are equally gifts of God.'/ This man speaks to people as if they were really his children and his brothers gathered in his house. Whatever its future labors and conclusions, the Council has already borne its fruits. It has forced humanity to consider the mystery of the Church in its true light./ So many ideas are circulating and so many questions are being asked that they cannot fail to break through the general indifference and secularism./ God knows how to speak, when he wishes, to those who seek and wait for him."

[27] See G. Lercaro, *Lettere dal concilio* (Bologna, 1980), 62-63: "Well, the Council opened this morning; I am not going to describe the truly solemn ceremony for you, since

But within the liturgy the moment most awaited was the address of John XXIII, even if Latin was certainly not well understood by all, and there were a lot of tired people. (Few people became as impatient as Congar, who left the hall around 1:00 p.m., before the Pope's address.) This final act, despite the approximately seven hours of movements and ceremonies that had preceded it, was the central element in a day pervaded by an atmosphere of joy.[28]

B. *Gaudet Mater Ecclesia*: The Pope's Opening Speech

This address was in fact densely packed and not easily grasped. It was neither a program nor a merely celebratory discourse of welcome to the fathers. John XXIII's message departed from the models in which papal authority had hitherto found expression. He did not dictate a course the fathers of Vatican II must follow in order to emerge from the confusion and contradictions with which the Council was beginning. Instead, his approach was much more complex and would provide the basis that would liberate the work of the Council.

I imagine you followed it on TV. Moreover, it would be rather difficult for me, and certainly a lengthy business, to go over the series of rites performed. I shall tell you, instead, of some of my thoughts. And, first of all, that I certainly never felt so absorbed into the Church of God as I did today: the presence of the Pope, of the entire or almost the entire Sacred College, of the bishops of the entire world, around the altar that stood in the middle and on which the Sacrifice was first celebrated and the gospel was then enthroned; the gaze of the entire world fixed on what was happening, as was clear from the presence of delegations from so many nations and the presence of the separated Churches...; all this made me feel the vitality of the Church, its unity and variety together, its humanity and its divinity; and it created within me, who felt myself a member of it invested with special functions and powers, a deep feeling of joy and gratitude to the Lord. In the Council hall I found myself sitting between Cardinal Wyszynski (who was loudly applauded all across the courtyard, and the object of sympathy from the crowd) and Cardinal McIntyre; in front of me I had Cardinals Spellman, Ruffini, and Caggiano (Buenos Aires); a short distance away were President Segni with his entourage and Prince Albert of Belgium; almost directly opposite I saw the abbot and a monk of the Calvinist monastery of Taizé in Switzerland [sic] ...: all these were visible signs of the Church's effective presence in the world. I really felt how necessary it is that the Holy Spirit should guide this undertaking from which everyone expects so much; but the repeated prayer of the immense gathering, followed by the prayer of souls throughout the world, was a guarantee that the Spirit of the Lord will be with us in this work."

[28] Chenu, who was not admitted to the hall, listened to the address in the square (cf. *NChenu*, 68, note 1); although he was proxy for an absent Madagascan bishop, Chenu did not have an entrance ticket; only when the Council had begun would it be announced that proxies could sit in the hall during the public sessions (see *AS* I/1, 343).

The allocution *Gaudet Mater Ecclesia* is one of the most complete expressions of Roncalli's vision of the Council. The text of the discourse was due entirely to John XXIII,[29] who intended to give the fathers of Vatican II a personal and authoritative instruction that would link this assembly with the great conciliar tradition of the Church. For the Pope, the heart of the Council's work was "Christ...ever resplendent as the center of history and of life." The Council was convoked in order to bear witness of this truth to the contemporary world: "In fact, by bringing herself up to date where required, and by wisely organizing mutual cooperation, the Church will make individuals, families, and peoples really turn their minds to heavenly things." The call to *"aggiornamento"* (updating) reflected the Pope's turn away from a catastrophic reading of the situation of the Church and the world. This was not simple optimism but the manifestation of a departure from the culture of fear and suspicion that had led to predominantly defensive choices in the government and life of the Church in order to isolate it and to protect its truth from the dangers of contamination to which encounter with others and the world could lead. The Pope's rejection of this strategy was explicit:

> It pains us that We sometimes have to listen to the complaints of people who, though burning with zeal, are not endowed with an overabundance of discretion or measure. They see in modern times nothing but prevarication and ruin. They keep saying that as compared with past ages, ours is getting worse, and they behave as if they had learned nothing from history, which is nonetheless a teacher of life, and as if in the time of the preceding ecumenical Councils everything represented a complete triumph for Christian ideas and Christian life and for a rightful religious liberty. But We think We must disagree with these prophets of doom, who are always forecasting disaster, as though the end of the world were imminent.[30]

In the Pope's view, the age of the Catholic state and a Christian regime was no golden age of the Church in the history of the world, after

---

[29] There is ample documentation to verify John XXIII's claim to have written the address with "meal from his own sack," that is, entirely on his own. For a large part of the text there exists a continuous series of handwritten or typewritten drafts with written corrections in his own hand; for the final part there is a Latin version prepared by translators, in particular G. Zannoni, who worked directly with the Pope and whose notes were used in preparing the so-called "Italian translation" that appeared in *OssRom*. All of the drafts and a critical edition of the manuscript are in A. Melloni, "L'allocuzione *Gaudet Mater Ecclesia* (11 ottobre 1962): Sinossi critica dell'allocuzione," in *Fede Tradizione Profezia. Studi su Giovanni XXIII e sul Vaticano II* (Brescia, 1984), 223-83.

[30] See the ms in Melloni, "Sinossi critica," 253-54. [I am using the translation in *The Documents of Vatican II*, ed. W. M. Abbott (New York, 1966), 710-19, but have made some minor changes. — Tr.]

which Christian life had progressively declined. Consequently, the Church's ideal is not to restore that golden age. To read the present pessimistically would imply a policy that would hermetically close the Church to a world considered completely foreign, if not hostile, to it. Instead the Pope seemed to perceive, even amid many persistent problems, an improvement in the life of the world, "a new order of human relations." "It cannot be denied, however, that these new conditions of modern life have at least the advantage of having eliminated those innumerable obstacles by which, at one time, the children of this world impeded the free action of the Church."[31] Historically, ecumenical councils were "often held to the accompaniment of very serious difficulties and sufferings because of the undue interference of civil authorities." There were no such shadows over Vatican II as it began its work; the Church was "finally freed from so many obstacles of a profane nature such as trammeled her in the past." This did not mean — although the Pope made no reference to this point — that some governments were not very interested in what the Catholic Church would be doing at its ecumenical meeting and in gauging the concrete effects on earthly politics. But, in itself, the celebration of the Council manifested the freedom of the Church from civil authorities; the purposes of the Council were not subordinate to any political interest or the interests of any power. The eighty-six extraordinary governmental missions sent to the opening ceremony were simply a show of respect and not part of the dynamics of the Council. The "princes" — and this was something new — remained outside the realm of the Council's decisions. The Church of Vatican II had no privileged connections with politics or with any model of a state, although the assembly would have to face the question of what position to take in regard to communism, a problem made unavoidable by the forced absence of some fathers from Eastern Europe and the communist countries.[32]

To explain his own vision of the relations between the Council and the political powers, John XXIII cited the meeting of Peter with the crippled beggar in the Acts of the Apostles: What did the Church have to give to the world?

"I have neither gold nor silver, but what I have I give you; in the name of Jesus Christ of Nazareth, rise and walk" (Acts 3:6). In other words, the

---

[31] See Melloni, "Sinossi critica," 257-58.

[32] See A. Riccardi, *Il Vaticano II e Mosca* (Rome-Bari, 1992), and G. Turbanti, "Il problema del comunismo al Vaticano II," in *Vatican II à Moscou*, 237-86.

Church does not offer people today riches that pass, nor does she promise them a mere earthly happiness. She distributes to them the goods of divine grace which, by raising human beings to the dignity of children of God, are the most efficacious safeguards and aids toward a more human life.[33]

The Council therefore had to concentrate on what the Church could in fact give the world, namely, the ancient message of the gospel. Vatican II was called upon to communicate this "without any attenuation or distortion":

> Our duty is not only to guard this precious treasure, as if we were concerned only with antiquity, but earnestly and fearlessly to dedicate ourselves to the work our age demands of us....The salient point of this Council is not, therefore, a discussion of one article or another of the fundamental doctrine of the Church which has been repeatedly taught by the Fathers and by ancient and modern theologians, and which is presumed to be well known and familiar to all. For this a Council was not needed. But from renewed, serene, and tranquil adherence to all the teaching of the Church..., the Christian, Catholic, and apostolic spirit of the whole world expects a leap forward toward a doctrinal penetration and a formation of consciences.[34]

Such a leap forward by the Church in the world — and here the Pope was also speaking from a missionary point of view — was possible only in conjunction with a deeper penetration of the gospel and of the mystery of the Church. What was needed, then, was not a set of instructions for action, but the Church's reflection on revelation: "The substance of the ancient doctrine of the deposit of faith is one thing, and the way in which it is presented is another. And it is the latter that must be taken into consideration — with patience if need be — while weighing everything in the forms and statements of a teaching activity that is predominantly pastoral in character." This was an important methodological guideline, since it situated the work of the council fathers at the heart of the Christian message, while at the same time urging them to present this message to the world in an updated way.[35]

The pope's definition of Vatican II was formal: it was not to be a council of condemnation, even though the Church is opposed to errors now as in the past. But a new attitude must be part of the updating and rediscovery of the substance of the Church's life: "Nowadays, however,

---

[33] See the ms in Melloni, "Sinossi critica," 272-73.

[34] See Melloni, "Sinossi critica," 267-69.

[35] On the concept of the "pastoral" see G. Ruggieri, "La discussione sullo *Schema constitutionis dogmaticae de fontibus revelationis* durante la I^a sessione del concilio Vaticano II," in *Vatican II commence*, 315-28.

the Spouse of Christ prefers to use the medicine of mercy rather than severity. She considers that she meets the needs of the present day by demonstrating the validity of her teaching rather than by condemnations." This was something more than a program of work; it was the attitude which the Pope was asking the Council fathers to adopt, while leaving them free to be the active agents of the Council. He was asking them to plunge into the heart of the Christian message and at the same time to present it in a renewed form to a changed world. The Pope's allocution was the act, not of a "sovereign" imposing his will but that of the primate among Catholic bishops, providing authoritative suggestions about the path their work should take.

The Pope was aware of the importance of his allocution. "Every now and then," he confided in his secretary Capovilla, "I glanced at my friend on the right (Ottaviani)."[36] In his diary the Pope noted his own "great joy,"[37] even though he was aware that his conciliar undertaking would probably pass to his successor. John XXIII's address takes its place in the long series of his initiatives, the most important of which was the convocation of Vatican II.

C. The Impact of the Pope's Address

What impact did this address of the Pope have on the work of the Council? Congar noted two opposite interpretations, one offered by a headline in *L'Osservatore Romano* ("Chief Aim of the Council: To Defend and Promote Doctrine") and the other by one in *Le Monde* ("Pope Approves Research-Methods of Modern Thought"). In the view of *Il Corriere della Sera* for October 12, the papal allocution stated the program of John XXIII's pontificate. According to Fr. A. Wenger of *La Croix* it was the "real charter" of Vatican II. H. Fesquet of *Le Monde* went back to the text a few days later and observed that it was a real surprise for the Council.

A few grasped the important elements of the speech. After listening to it on television, Moeller elucidated the essential points, and Chenu immediately noted "its strong protest against the pessimists" and "its rebuke of discussions about established doctrines, the truth of which must of course be reasserted, but formulated to meet the needs of the age."[38]

[36] See A. Melloni, "Giovanni XXIII e l'avvio del Vaticano II," in *Vatican II commence*, 75.

[37] *Agende*, October 11, 1962.

[38] *NChenu*, 68.

But the address had little immediate effect in determining the direction taken by the fathers in the Council that was about to begin — and there is no need to suggest the "sabotage" which the Pope's secretary heard bruited around the Pope.[39] After the close of Vatican II Cardinal Garrone wrote that the opening discourse was one of the most important and decisive documents in the conciliar file: "The calm assurance of Pope John XXIII astonished and in the end almost irritated people.... He expected the Council to turn the work he thought urgent into a program."[40] But this was an awareness that arose only after October 11.

D. A "Brother Who Has Become a Father"

In reality, on that day, the most perceptive observers saw a great deal of uncertainty around them, and they felt the weight of a very long history. This was the case with Congar, who wrote his feelings down that very day. In his opinion, the opening ceremony had disclosed the Constantinian face of the Church of Rome.

> I see the weight, undenounced, of the age when the Church was dominant, when it had a temporal power, when the Pope and bishops were lords who had a court, protected artists, and laid claim to a pomp equal to that of the Caesars. The Church has never repudiated all that in Rome. Leaving the Constantinian era has never been its program. Poor Pius IX, who understood nothing of the movement of history, who buried French Catholicism in a sterile attitude of opposition, protectiveness, and spirit of restoration..., was called by God to listen to the lesson of events, those teachers God himself gives us, and to free the Church from the wretched logic of the "Donation of Constantine" and convert it to an evangelical outlook that would have enabled it to be less *of* the world and more *in* the world. He did just the opposite. A disastrous man, who did not know what the *ecclesia* is nor what tradition is....And Pius IX still reigns, Boniface VIII still reigns: they have superimposed him on Simon Peter, the humble fisher of men![41]

The great problem posed by the event of the Council, which fell outside all the standard rules of church management, was how to control this event and its work. Congar wondered whether the Council would be able to express itself without relying on the typical scholastic mentality that had become part of church government. His hope was that the individual bishops' experience of pastoral government would find expres-

---

[39] Cited by Melloni, "Giovanni XXIII e l'avvio del Vaticano II," in *Vatican II commence*, 87.

[40] G.-M. Garrone, "Témoignage," in *Deuxième*, 5.

[41] *JCongar*, December 11, 1962, typescript p. 71.

sion in new views. But they lacked a program, which the Pope did not
supply in his allocution. For Roncalli October 11 was not a day for programs.

   This attitude was confirmed by his address on the evening of October
11 at the end of the impressive torchlight procession in St. Peter's
square, in commemoration of the demonstration with which the Christians of Ephesus had greeted the third ecumenical council. The meaning
of the demonstration was suddenly changed by the second papal address,
which, at the insistence of his secretary, the Pope improvised at his window. This was the famous "moonlight" address: "Even the moon may
be said to have hastened on this evening." The address is well known for
the spontaneous greetings which the Pope gave to the people gathered in
the square: "When you return home you will find your children: Caress
them and tell them: 'This is a caress from the Pope.' You will find some
tears to dry. Speak words of comfort to the afflicted. Let the afflicted
know that the Pope is with his sons and daughters, especially in hours of
sadness and bitterness."[42]

   The "moonlight" address expressed in immediate and popular language how John XXIII experienced the opening of the Council. It was a
message of sympathy and confidence. Then the Pope described himself
as a "brother" who is a "father": "It is a brother who speaks to you, a
brother who, by the will of our Lord, has become a father. But fatherhood and brotherhood are both of them gifts of God. Everything is!
Everything!"[43]

   That was John XXIII's attitude during the opening of Vatican II, that
of a "brother" among the bishops, but one who had become a "father."
This brother-father, Bishop of Rome, primate, did not dictate a program
for what Vatican II should be. In all simplicity he told the people gathered
in St. Peter's square:

> It can rightly be said that today we are beginning a year that will bring out-
> standing graces. The Council has begun, and we do not know when it will
> end. If it is not to end before Christmas, because we shall perhaps not man-
> age to say everything by that time and to take up the various subjects,
> another meeting will be necessary....And therefore let these days go well;
> we look forward to them with great joy.[44]

   When these words were read as a reference to a program, the impression they gave was that the Pope meant to finish the Council in a single

---

[42] *DMC* IV, 593.
[43] Ibid., 592.
[44] Ibid., 593.

session. Cardinal Urbani noted with reference to the Pope's address: "Well-chosen words. Only the hint that he hopes to be finished by Christmas... left us puzzled."[45] John XXIII had indeed forecast a time for the course of the work, but the Pope's basic attitude was not to be concerned about how much time might be required. In the private notes he wrote down in his daily schedule-book, the Pope repeated that it would be his successor who would close the Council. In face of the contradictions and confusions that marked the beginnings the Pope was not worried but even looked forward to the coming days "with great joy."

Even in the improvised evening address we find ourselves in the presence of a text that is highly expressive of Roncalli's attitude to the problems of church government. To the awareness of the task he must carry out is added the serenity that comes from being unable to control events and being compelled to rely on the collaboration of others (in this case, the bishops of the Council) and having to trust in a "providential" guidance of history. It was not by accident that in this discourse the Pope reiterated one of his chief maxims of government: "In the meeting let us continue to lay hold of what unites and leave aside whatever might keep us in difficulties. We are brothers!"

These words certainly did not outline a set of rules for the assembly nor determine the time-frame for the work. They did show a basic way of looking at the dynamics of the Council and the relationship among the Council, the world, and Christians. At the end of the Council's first day, while concerns were mounting because of the uncertainties that marked the start, the Pope seemed to be distancing himself a good deal from the worry felt by some of his chief collaborators. He wrote:

> I will be prepared to give up the joy that marked these beginnings. With the same serenity I repeat "Thy will be done" with regard to keeping me in this foremost place of service through the whole time and all the circumstances of my humble life, and to knowing that I may be cut short at any moment so that the task of proceeding, continuing, and ending may pass to my successor. "Thy will be done, on earth as it is in heaven."[46]

---

[45] *DUrbani*, October 11, 1962, cited in Alberto Melloni, "Les journaux privés dans l'histoire de Vatican II," in *NChenu*, 44-45.
[46] *Agende*, October 12, 1962.

E. POLITICIANS, DIPLOMATS, JOURNALISTS, OBSERVERS, AND THE POPE OF
THE COUNCIL

On October 12 and 13, still in the setting of the Council's opening,
John XXIII received, in successive audiences, the eighty-four extraordinary missions, the journalists, and the non-Catholic observers. On these
occasions he delivered three rather pointed addresses which clarified his
views on these important groups at the frontier of the Council: the politicians, the world of the press, and the Christian Churches and communities.

In addressing the press the Pope emphasized the religious nature of
the Council: "You will be able to make people understand that no political intrigues are going on here." And he described himself: "It will be
enough for you to write, as a single honorary title for Us: He was a
priest in the sight of the Lord and the peoples, a friend of the nations."
The tone in which the Pope wanted to establish relations with the representatives of the press (who at the beginning of the Council were experiencing many difficulties in interpreting the event and finding channels
of information) was one of sympathy.[47]

The meeting with the Christian observers was a completely new experience. For the Orthodox and the ancient Oriental Churches there were
present at the beginning of the Council representatives of the Patriarchate of Moscow, the Coptic Patriarchate of Alexandria, the Syrian
Patriarchate of Antioch, the Ethiopian Church, the Armenian Catholicate
of Cilicia, and the Russian Church in exile. Among the Protestants were
representatives of the Old Catholics, the Anglican Communion, the
Lutheran World Federation, the World Presbyterian Alliance, the Evangelical Church of Germany, the Disciples of Christ, the Quakers, the
World Methodist Council, the International Congregational Council, the
World Council of Churches of Geneva, and the International Association
for Liberal Christianity.[48] Lacking among this impressive group were
any representatives of the Ecumenical Patriarchate of Constantinople, of
the Orthodox Churches of the Slavic and Mediterranean worlds, and of
the Reformed Churches, voids that would be filled later.

The presence of non-Catholic observers was one of the important
aspects of Vatican II. It marked the first collective meeting of non-
Catholic representatives with the pope of Rome. Cardinal Bea, President

---

[47] *DMC* IV, 599-603.
[48] *DMC* IV, 605-10.

of the Secretariat for Christian Unity, commented on the meeting in words that show how novel it was: "It is a miracle!"[49] The observers present likewise felt that they were leading actors in a transition.[50] John XXIII described the problem of unity to the observer delegates as he himself saw it. There was a movement toward unity that had not yet found its practical and theological formulations.

> Were you to read my heart, you would find there something more than finds expression in my words. How can I forget the ten years I spent in Sofia? And the ten years spent in Istanbul and Athens? They were twenty happy, very useful years during which I came to know many venerable personages and young people full of generosity. I considered them my friends.... Later, in Paris, which is one of the crossroads of the world,...I had many contacts with Christians belonging to various denominations. Never, to my recollection, was there among us any muddling of principles, any disagreement at the level of charity on the joint work which circumstances required of us in aid of the suffering. We did not negotiate, we talked; we did not debate but loved one another.[51]

The observers were still making their first contacts with the large world of the Catholic bishops and were perhaps for the first time taking part, from the inside, in a meeting of Catholic authorities. While they expressed reservations about some aspects of the start of the Council, this meeting with the Pope was important for their relations with conciliar Rome and with those Christians who were not represented in the Vatican Basilica. They could see a mature attitude of sympathetic attention by the Catholic Church toward their Churches, even if it was not clear what the work of the Council might mean for Rome.[52]

After the meeting with the Pope, during which the observers had been silent,[53] they continued to have a weekly joint meeting of their own, every Tuesday.[54] These meetings of the non-Catholic contingent at the

---

[49] S. Schmidt, *Augustin Bea: The Cardinal of Unity* (New Rochelle, 1992) 454.

[50] See M. Lackmann, *Mit evangelischen Augen. Beobachtungen eines Lutheraners auf dem Zweiten Vatikanischen Konzil* (Graz, 1963); G. Richard-Molard, *Un pasteur au Concile* (Paris, 1964); D. Horton, *Vatican Diary 1962. A Protestant Observes the First Session of Vatican Council II* (Philadelphia-Boston, 1964); K.-V. Selge, *Evangelischer Bericht vom Konzil. Erste Session* (Göttingen, 1965).

[51] *DMC* IV, 607.

[52] On the reports sent to the World Council of Churches see M. Velati, *Una difficile transizione. Il cattolicesimo e l'unità cristiana dagli anni Cinquanta al Vaticano II* (Bologna, 1996).

[53] Initially, they were asked for some words of greeting, to be given by K. Sarkissian, but this was cancelled for reasons of protocol; see L. Vischer to Visser 't Hooft, October 14, 1962, *ACO* 6 (Reports), I/8, 2.

[54] Meetings, usually from 4:30 to 6:30 P.M., were held on October 15 and 22, Novem-

Council, as well as preparatory or restricted meetings,[55] were a significant event. The Tuesday gatherings kept the observers from being transformed into "ambassadors" of their own confessions; as a result of
exchanging opinions and, in the end, combining their views, the
observers formed a group, united for work and in purpose, that could
express opinions which influenced the course of the Council. For members of the Secretariat, too, the Tuesday afternoon meetings were valuable and new. For the first time Christians of various Churches were no
longer participants only in a purely bilateral dialogue, in which the
emphasis on points of contact was matched by an emphasis, from others,
on points of divergence; here they engaged in a common exchange, as
equals. Several times, in discussion, correspondence, and diaries, there
would be an emphasis on the "ecumenical considerations" that called
now for the rejection of the schema on the sources of revelation, now for
a reconsideration of the schema on the Church, now for esteem for the
schema on the liturgy or the message to the world. One might, somewhat
maliciously, see in these "ecumenical considerations" a political dimension, a spiritual diplomacy that avoids difficult subjects and tries to find
a middle ground in rough territory. But the testimony of those involved
in the Tuesday meetings supplies a different interpretive key: "after centuries" different Christians were conversing simply as Christians.

On the eve of the first meeting there were strong suspicions that it
would be nothing but a boring worldly ritual; some were afraid that it
would be

> a modern cocktail hour, which is surely one of the most torturing attributes
> of our partly civilized world — everyone expressing polite banalities to his
> neighbor, ...a bubbling babel of almost complete meaninglessness. But this
> proved to be different, at least in part. Presently the cardinal [Bea] took his
> place at one end of the room and read in French a brief address of welcome
> to his "very dear brothers in Christ." The warmth which we had felt in our
> welcome from the beginning was not lacking here.[56]

ber 6, 13, 20, and 27, and December 4. Only beginning in the second session would a formal record be made of the meetings.

[55] On October 18 there was also a reception for the observers by the Waldensian Faculty, sponsored by the Federation of Protestant Churches in Italy (see Vischer's report,
over ten pages long, October 19, 1961, ACO, I/11). On October 24 there would be a gathering of the Internationaler Versöhnungsbund.

[56] Horton, *Vatican Diary*, 26 (October 15, 1962). Vischer's report of October 15,
1962, to the WCC (*ACO* 6, I/9, 1) likewise shows an appreciation of this tone, as well as
deep feeling at the presence of Thils, Hamer, and Congar: "How many times have they
been in danger! How much have they been suspected for their activity!...There was a
great joy about this meeting."

By the second meeting the atmosphere was so good that Lukas Vischer had to ask advice from the WCC as to whether the proposal made by R. Ullmann at the preparatory meeting on October 22, namely, that the observers support conscientious objection against military service, could be moved forward on October 24.[57] At the end of November it was through the observers that Willebrands obtained information on the situation in Rumania.[58] In November an Anglican prelate noted as the attitude of the "observers" his own and others' disappointment with the schema on the Church. When new observers from other Churches arrived a year later, they would find that the procedure for what was being called "our briefing session"[59] had been almost codified.

But let us return to the first days of Vatican II, when John XXIII also met with the missions which the governments had sent for the opening of the Council. Present at the opening ceremonies had been the President of the Republic of Italy (Segni) and the Grand Master of the Order of Malta. The missions from Italy and Ireland were led by the presidents of their respective councils, while Germany, Spain, and France, along with four smaller countries, sent their foreign ministers. High-ranking personages led the delegations from Belgium, Portugal, and Luxembourg. There also were delegations from Muslim countries (Syria, Egypt, Jordan, Turkey, and Indonesia), several Western European and Latin American countries, Japan, India, many African states that had recently become independent, the United States, and Formosan China (Taiwan). Not a single communist country was represented.[60] The presences reflected the picture of the Holy See's diplomatic relationship in the climate of the Cold War.

John XXIII spoke to the diplomats of the conciliar Church's commitment to peace, the perspective in which he located the contribution of Vatican II:

> This is the great peace for which all people are waiting, for which they have suffered so much. It is time to take decisive steps! The Church is committed to this peace: in its prayer, in its deep respect for the poor..., and by spreading its doctrine, which teaches brotherly love, because all human beings are brothers and sisters.

[57] October 22, 1962, *ACO* 6, I/14, 1.

[58] October 22, 1962, *ACO* 6, I/23, 3.

[59] Robert McAfee Brown, *Observer in Rome: A Protestant Report on the Vatican Council* (New York, 1964), 93 (October 22, 1963).

[60] On the Soviet attitude see J. Karlov, "Secret Diplomacy of Moscow and the Second Vatican Council," in *Vatican II à Moscou*, 129-36.

The Council would work to prepare the way for this new climate and to dissipate any likelihood of conflict, especially war, that scourge of nations which, in its present form, would mean the destruction of the human race.[61]

In these meetings, the Pope's intention was to make clear the Church's determination not to withdraw into itself but to take a position on the frontiers of worlds other than the Catholic. His words impressed his several audiences and sent a clear message to the Church, to Christians, and to the world. But the churchmen most concerned with the mechanics of governing the Church were wondering at the same moment how the Council could express this new position of Catholicism.

III. THE EXTRAORDINARY SECOND DAY OF VATICAN II

The fundamental choice that had to be made at the beginning of the Council was whether it was to govern itself. The will of the Pope and the direction adopted by some bishops converged to make this self-government a reality. After the opening ceremony on October 11, the fathers were given a list of those present at the Council, the conciliar regulations,[62] and other material that included the voting cards, which were to be scanned mechanically, and the cards for choosing members of the conciliar commissions. The latter cards were ten in number, one for each commission, and contained sixteen lines for listing the names of the fathers. Also given to those present was a list of the bishops who had served on the preparatory commissions.

Each bishop had, of course, the right to select other names from the booklet listing all the Catholic bishops, but it would have been easy simply to copy down the names of the members of the Preparatory Commission, since every father had to vote for 160 of his colleagues, and it was not possible for each voter to come up with his own list out of so many possibilities. Given the lack of knowledge of particular bishops, each would have ended up reproducing to a greater or lesser degree the list of men on the preconciliar commissions. The result would have been to establish a continuity between the preconciliar work and the Council itself, which would thereby have automatically accepted the schemas

[61] *DMC* IV, 597.
[62] *ADP* IV/I, 256.

already prepared. In this way, the choice made by the Curia during the preparatory phase would have been confirmed. Several testimonies regarding these first days brought out the dissatisfaction of a segment of the bishops with the prepared schemas; but it is not possible to generalize this feeling. According to the testimony of Cardinal Urbani, Cardinal Montini told his colleagues on the board of the Italian Episcopal Conference that "it would be better to put off tomorrow's meeting because we are not prepared."[63]

A. The Meeting on October 13

The first general congregation, held on October 13 and begun amid torrential rain, was to have been devoted to the election of the commissions. Cardinal Florit, Archbishop of Florence, celebrated the Mass. Msgr. Felici, general secretary of the Council, enthroned the gospel. The Council of Presidents, comprising ten cardinals and chaired by Tisserant, dean of the college of cardinals, took its place at a table in front of the papal throne. The general secretary asked the bishops to cast their votes for members of the commissions.[64]

According to some sources, a certain amount of planning had been done among the French, Belgians, and Germans.[65] Larrain and Câmara visited two churchmen who were involved in the operation of the French Conference, Villot and Etchegaray, and were given an attentive hearing.[66] Cardinal Ottaviani had taken a more effective step by circulating a "list of shadow commissions" with a set of appointees whom his Congregation regarded as "safe."[67] Rumor of this list, which was circulating in various conciliar circles, greatly disturbed some fathers, who read it as an attempt to steer the work of the commissions; it was also well known that Ottaviani had expressed very clear and personal views during the work, sometimes rather tense, of the Central Preparatory Commission.

---

[63] According to the notes of the Bishop of Modena, M. Bergonzini, *Diario del concilio Vaticano II* (Modena, 1993), 9.

[64] *AS* I/1, 107 and 207.

[65] The Melkites and some Africans were not part of this; see *JEdelby*, November 11, 1962, f. 15.

[66] See H. P. Câmara, *Les conversions d'un évêque* (Paris, 1977), 152.

[67] *DTucci*, October 13, 1962, f. 2; the same information about a list of the Holy Office is found in *DFenton*, October 13, 1962. See also G. Caprile, "La seconda giornata del Vaticano II 25 anni dopo," *CivCatt*, 138/3 (1987) 389, who says that Ottaviani's "purely personal" initiative aroused suspicions among many fathers.

There was great bewilderment in the Council hall at the announcement by the secretary general, "on order from the chairman," that the
election should begin immediately. As Montini would put it in a letter to
his diocesan clergy: "All the names, how are we to know them and how
are we to choose them?"[68] Some bishops used the masters of ceremonies to exchange private messages and to get advice from their colleagues. There was disorder in the hall. The process of writing down 160
names would have taken a good deal of time, certainly more than an
hour.

While the fathers were docilely getting ready to vote, Cardinal Liénart
of Lille stood up and spoke from the bench of presidents, of which he
was a member. The elderly cardinal, who had been created by Pius XI
and had great prestige among the bishops, read a short motion, in Latin,
on a point of order, asking that the voting be postponed for a few days
so that the fathers might have time to get to know one another and the
episcopal conferences might develop their own lists. His intervention
was interrupted by prolonged applause.[69]

Cardinal Frings, also one of the presidents, then spoke in the name
also of Döpfner and König and likewise from the presidential table, and
supported his French colleague's proposal.[70] After consulting with the
Council of Presidents, Tisserant announced that Liénart's proposal had
been accepted and that the voting was postponed until the following
Tuesday.[71] Since there were no other matters on the agenda, the meeting
was closed. The second working day of the Council lasted less than fifty
minutes and took place entirely at the presidential table.

B. Importance of the Postponement

This strange day, with its interventions by two members of the Council of Presidents, had a very strong effect on the assembly. Edelby noted
in his diary that Liénart's victory was regarded "as the first defeat
inflicted on the secretariat of the Council, which wanted to run the
Council with a rod." Siri viewed the incident with concern: "The par-

[68] See the letter to the diocesan clergy, October 20, 1962, in Giovanni Battista Montini, *Discorsi e scritti sul Concilio (1959-1963)* (Brescia, 1983), 181; for other information see *G. B. Montini arcivescovo di Milano e il I° periodo del Vaticano II* (Rome, 1988).

[69] See *AS* I/1, 207-8.

[70] *AS* I/1, 208.

[71] Replying to some questions from the fathers, Felici announced that cardinals, too,
could be elected to the commissions (ibid.).

ticipants went away in an atmosphere of obvious and excited uneasiness." The majority of the fathers were clearly pleased to have more time to decide who among them should be members of the commissions and that the interaction at the Council was to be determined by the dynamics of the assembly and not by some external direction. There was growing dissatisfaction among the fathers about the admittedly difficult task of organizing the work of such a large assembly.

While Liénart's action was interpreted by many bishops as a protest against any predetermination of the choices the Council would make, the immediate reaction in some Italian circles was more critical. An hour after the end of the first general congregation, Siri went to the palace of the Holy Office and had an informal meeting with Ottaviani, Msgr. P. Parente, the assessor, and Msgr. E. Vagnozzi, Apostolic Delegate to the United States. The problem was to get the more "consonant" episcopal conferences to agree upon a list. Vagnozzi offered to contact the North American bishops. Siri seems to have wanted to avoid the logic of blocs within the Council, whereas the others were persuaded of its necessity. "I think that we should not support a policy of blocs, unless it becomes strictly necessary for the defense of the Church. Above all, we ought not to see blocs everywhere. It seems clear to me that this was a maneuver directed more subconsciously than consciously by a certain antipathy to the Curia." For Siri behind Liénart's initiative lay the "eternal inferiority complex toward Rome" typical of "Northerners." The Holy Office people were somewhat puzzled by this overly benevolent interpretation; in their view there had been a very clear and organized maneuver to which they must react by joining forces with Spellman and the Latin American bishops. Siri suggested bringing in also the Africans, the Asians, and the Franciscans, headed by Father Balić.[72] In the eyes of these men, not yet aware that they would constitute a minority at Vatican II, this second day had revealed that there was a "Northern" alliance that wished to direct the work of the Council.

But was there so organized a directing body behind Cardinal Liénart's action? The sources record the incident as the result of a convergence, not of a conspiracy.[73] The previous evening, Cardinal Urbani had fore-

[72] *DSiri*, November 13, 1962, 361: "I am aware of how much balance is needed not to support either blocs or antiblocs, even when we have to face a situation of agreements that arise, in the final analysis, from the eternal inferiority complex which the Northerners have in their relations with Rome. But charity and peace are better! I feel a bit sad; the devil has had a hand in this."

[73] Chenu, for example, does not seem to have been aware of any maneuver and

seen "a little squall over the conciliar waters," although he had received a hint from Cardinal Léger about a possible procedural crisis.[74] Congar stressed the profound importance of the Council's first working day. In his view, this was the first substantive conciliar action, "a rejection of the very possibility of a prefabricated event."[75] The Council was choosing not to be a mere continuation of the preparation. For Msgr. B. Gantin, Bishop of Benin, "It was as if each of us were being told: You will no longer be *carried*; you will be a *carrier*. It is quite a different matter to have one's own ideas instead of being compelled to accept the ideas of others." And, he added, "It was a confrontation that opened the way to the spirit of collegiality."[76]

And in fact, Liénart's initiative did validate the importance for the Council of the intermediate bodies represented by the episcopal conferences, which immediately accepted the task of preparing lists. The bishops would no longer be regarded simply as individuals in the great mass of the fathers and, therefore, forced to choose between personal uneasiness and the directions of the organizing bodies. The council had intermediate bodies and areas that were useful in shaping a common will and in clarifying ideas and perspectives. But we are still at the beginning of a process that would take form throughout the first period of Vatican II.

C. The Background of Liénart's Action

Cardinal Liénart was certainly not the only one of the fathers who was looking for an immediate change in the election procedure. According to some, after the Mass Tisserant, dean of the cardinals and conciliar president that day, suggested to Felici, that the voting be postponed and that the episcopal conferences draw up their own lists. Cardinal Cicognani, Secretary of State, when consulted on the subject, declared himself in favor of an immediate vote, and Felici sided with Cicognani. When Tisserant communicated Felici's position to Liénart, the annoyed Bishop of

---

observed, with regard to Liénart's intervention: "The fact that the body of bishops was so unanimously and spontaneously ready to assert their freedom vis-à-vis the 'Rules of the Council' has provoked a sensation among the bishops themselves and all around them" (*NChenu*, 70).

[74] *DUrbani*, October 12, 1962.

[75] *JCongar*, October 13, 1962, typescript. 74.

[76] Interview with Cardinal B. Gantin, in G. F. Svidercoschi, *Inchiesta sul Concilio* (Rome, 1985), 13.

Lille decided to speak, followed by Frings, who had close ties with the elderly French cardinal.

This account of the facts, each element of which is separately verifiable, can be compared with a score or so of similar accounts, all of them partial, though not because of bad faith or disinformation. We have to recall how uneasy and uncertain the atmosphere was, so much so that each felt a "party" to the choices of others.

Behind Liénart's action lay a lengthy history. His action was not, as some claimed, the result of a sudden illumination given to the elderly cardinal; but neither was it the result of a plot of vast proportions, aimed at humiliating the secretary general and thereby the Roman Curia.[77] Liénart's intervention was located half-way between a personal commitment and the uneasiness of a small group of French bishops. He himself has related that a rumor was abroad that the secretariat of the Council had seen to the circulation of some lists of fathers to be voted for. The cardinal, like other Council fathers, was uncertain about the situation and realized that in the absence of alternative lists, the fathers would inevitably have reconfirmed the preconciliar commissions: "We had a duty therefore to accept our own responsibilities and not to trust in what existed before us." His decision to intervene was strengthened by the opinion of Cardinal Lefebvre, who asked him to speak in order *at least* to ward off any immediate elections and who provided him with a Latin translation of a petition, which Liénart would not have been able to improvise in that language.[78]

After the Mass in the basilica, when Liénart realized that they would in fact proceed immediately to voting, he turned to Tisserant, who was seated on his right at the presidents' table, and said to him: "Eminence, it is impossible to vote in this way, without knowing anything about the best qualified candidates. If you will allow me, I would like to speak." The dean of the Sacred College answered: "I cannot give that permission, since the program for this meeting does not include any discussion." At this point the Bishop of Lille decided to speak on his own

---

[77] J. Guitton, *Paul VI secret* (Paris, 1979), 96, speaks of seven cardinals, Montini among them. Câmara, *Les conversions*, names himself and Larrain, along with Villot and Etchegaray. Congar speaks of Garrone and Ancel; several sources speak of Martimort's role, at least in translating the cardinal's motion into Latin; and so on.

[78] According to Liénart's own account in *Vatican II* (Lille, 1976), 65-69, Lefebvre put the Latin text in Liénart's hands as he entered the hall on October 13. Tisserant himself had written to Felici the day before to complain of the lack of clear guidance for the election of the commissions (cf. *ADP*, App. Alt., 330-31).

without Tisserant's authorization,[79] and he was followed by Frings. The Bishop of Lille has always denied that there was any advance agreement with his German colleague, even though the press interpreted the successive interventions as a manifestation of a French-German alliance against the Roman management of the Council. The pope satisfied Liénart's request in the Council hall and granted the Council fathers three more days for consulting one another. Liénart claims that John XXIII later told him: "You have done right in expressing your thoughts aloud; that is why I have called the bishops to a council."[80] There was, then, no plot, but a concrete initiative resulting from widespread uneasiness.[81]

IV. THE CONCILIAR COMMISSIONS

A. A NEW ROLE FOR EPISCOPAL CONFERENCES

The stimulus was given to make use of the episcopal conferences, but the effort ran into organizational difficulties[82] and in addition raised a question of substance: if the conferences developed lists, would they not deprive the bishops of their freedom of choice and in a way take over the Council?

The question would not have been resolved if Msgr. Garrone, Coadjutor of Toulouse, had not been applying himself for several months to problems in the conciliar regulations, which he found rather full of gaps.[83] As soon as he read them upon their promulgation in August,

---

[79] There are vague indications that other bishops (e.g., H. Câmara) would have liked to ask that the voting be postponed, but we do not know who might have authorized them to speak. A distinction must therefore be made between the discontent of many at the procedure, and the organization of an effective procedural action.

[80] R. Aubert, "Lo svolgimento del concilio," in *La Chiesa del Vaticano II* (Storia della Chiesa 25/1; Milan, 1994), 229.

[81] As early as January 1962, Liénart had spoken to Felici about making use of the episcopal conferences in preparing lists for the Council. Jullien, Dean of the Rota, moved in the same direction some months later (although in October he was critical of the possibility of finding a new system of voting). At the meeting of the Subcommission on the Conciliar Regulations, May 28, 1962, the question had been raised of consulting the fathers in advance by sending them, along with the preparatory schemas, an invitation to present candidates for the commissions (see *ADP*, App. Alt, 159-70, and G. Alberigo, "La preparazione del regolamento del concilio Vaticano II," in *Vatican II commence*, 54-74; see also *History* I, 331).

[82] The *Annuario Pontificio* listed forty-two conferences, of which only seven had been erected by the Holy See; see G. Feliciani, *Le conferenze episcopali* (Bologna, 1985).

[83] On the similar dissatisfaction of Dossetti and H. Jedin, see Alberigo, "La preparazione del regolamento," 56-62.

1962,[84] he realized that the Council would find itself in difficulties when it came to the election of the conciliar commissions. Article 39 of the Regulations read: "In public sessions, general congregations, and conciliar commissions, a majority of two-thirds of the votes of the fathers present is required, except in elections, in which Canon 101, § 1, 1, of the *CIC* applies, and unless the Supreme Pontiff decides otherwise." The canon called for an absolute majority in the first two votings and a relative majority in the third.

Garrone realized the influence which the Regulations would have on the work of the Council. Among other things — to turn to a problem felt by the Melkites — the Regulations established the order of precedence even for interventions in the hall: the patriarchs followed the cardinals. Article 28 decreed that the language of the public sessions, the general congregations, the administrative tribunal, and the records of the Council was to be Latin. Only in debates within the commissions were interventions in the vernacular also allowed.

From the time of his arrival in Rome, Garrone was determined to work on the Regulations and in particular on the question of elections. He spoke with Cardinal Jullien, whom he found ill-disposed and who had him talk with Tisserant, according to whom nothing could be done (in fact, the French cardinal was himself perplexed by the Regulations and by the lack of a commission to deal with them). Liénart shared his younger French colleague's bafflement but made no decision as to what to do. Nevertheless, during the night between October 12 and 13, at the French Seminary, Msgr. Garrone and Msgr. Ancel, together with a few others, prepared a text to be given to Lefebvre that he might pass on to Liénart. In short, then, some Council fathers began to show an active interest in the mechanics of the Council. There was no mobilization of a whole sector of bishops, but rather an initiative taken, at various levels, by prelates who were sensitive and attentive to the dynamics of such an assembly.[85]

The meeting on October 13 was important both in itself and for its subsequent results. A bishop such as Liénart could express his opinion on the course of the Council's work and block an action of the secretariat. In contrast, Msgr. Felici's proposal that there be an immediate vote on the members of the conciliar commissions represented the idea of a Council that had already accomplished its purpose in the work done

---

[84] *History*, I, 326-35.
[85] See Ph. Levillain, *La mécanique politique de Vatican II. La majorité et l'unanimité dans un Concile* (Paris, 1975).

before it opened. In this view, the problem was to achieve a series of coherent, clear documents; it was much less important to make the most of the potentialities and impulses of the assembly. The driving force behind the work was to have been the secretariat and, ultimately, the Roman Curia. The assembly of bishops was a solemn and obligatory stage, but it contained no profound potentialities that needed expression.

This outlook derived from a consciousness and a well-established governmental practice that was typical of some circles in the Roman Curia and was now being applied to the Council. This "culture" had created a style of governing and a personnel who were, despite profound and sometimes painful disagreements, the very ones who had drawn up the preparatory *vota* of the Roman universities. It was not that they were unaware of the problems troubling the Church, but rather that they felt "called" and entitled to provide solutions for all problems. Felici represented this position.

Liénart's intervention, on the other hand, demonstrated the fathers' determination to govern themselves as an assembly. It was not a revolt against the Pope, as some newspapers wrote. Nor, at least, did it seem to mean a collision with the Pope's will as expressed in the allocution *Gaudet Mater Ecclesia*. On the other hand, it must be said, neither was it a direct application of what John XXIII had said. It simply voiced the uneasiness of the bishops with the electoral mechanics planned for that October 13. The stubborn initiative of a small group of French bishops, who were supported in the hall by a German, Frings, provided a way for this uneasiness to find expression.

An important result of Liénart's intervention was the entrance into the dynamics of the assembly of the episcopal conferences, which were to submit lists of fathers to the General Secretariat by October 15. This recognition of the existence of intermediate bodies in the assembly was less a matter of acknowledging "nations" or "languages" than a means by which the bishops became aware of the need to share responsibility with their nearest brethren if they were to participate fully in the great conciliar assembly. The preparation of the lists was only the beginning of a concerted effort that would reach a very high level in some episcopal conferences. They would not take part in the Council as isolated individuals over against the secretariat and the vast number of fathers unknown to them. Their more immediate point of reference would now be the episcopal conference.

The prejudice against national meetings of bishops, which had been very strong during Vatican Council I, was now finally being abandoned.[86] In fact, at Vatican I the Holy See was very concerned that the national episcopates, especially the French and the German, not play too independent a part. Msgr. Maret, a French bishop and a theologian opposed to infallibility, complained that the bishops were showing up at the Curia and the Council as isolated individuals, lacking any connection with one another and any joint preparation. But Rome took a negative view of concerted action among the episcopates, so much so that the bishops of the ecclesiastical province of Turin called off a meeting planned for that purpose.[87] Something of this distrust had clung to the Curia, as if its collective memory had transmitted an echo of the resistance of the French, German, and Austro-Hungarian episcopates to the proclamation of papal infallibility and primacy at Vatican I. In contrast, at the beginning of Vatican II the episcopal conferences found their role sanctioned through their formulation of lists: "One result of the Council," Congar wrote after the meetings to draw up the lists, "could be the birth of a well-structured, worldwide episcopal collegiality."[88]

In their concrete reality, the episcopal conferences differed in their functioning, in the scope of their work, and in their traditions.[89] Only since 1959 had the *Annuario Pontificio* listed the functioning episcopal conferences and acknowledged their official character; forty-two were listed, of which only seven had a constitution approved by Rome. They ranged from the Réunion annuelle de l'Épiscopat de Belgique to the German Episcopal Conference, which had begun in 1847, to the Assemblée des Cardinaux et Archevêques de France, which had at its service a very active secretariat. In recent decades, the Holy See itself had overcome the ancient Roman distrust of national organizations of bishops and begun to foster the formation of these groups (*coetus*). The pontificate of Pius XII was characterized by a particular push in this direction. In 1955 CELAM came into being as a body for co-ordinating the Latin-

---

[86] At Vatican I, Cardinal Antonelli, Secretary of State, had barred the national episcopates from concerning themselves with the "general council, which represents the whole Church and no longer the various national episcopates." Some bishops had intended to meet precisely for the elections; but Antonelli authoritatively advised the French bishops not to meet: "All nationalities will disappear in the ecumenicity of the Council." See G. Arrigoni, *Giornale del concilio Vaticano I*, ed. M. Maccarrone (Rome, 1966), nos. 8 and 9. (The stimulus for this publication was given in 1962 by John XXIII, to whom the manuscript, discovered by U. Betti, had been presented.)

[87] See A. Riccardi, *Neogallicanesimo e cattolicesimo borghese: Henri Maret e il Concilio Vaticano I* (Bologna, 1976).

[88] *JCongar*, October 15, 1962, typescript, 76.

[89] See G. Feliciani, *Le conferenze episcopali* (Bologna, 1985).

American episcopal conferences. Brazil, Bolivia, Colombia, Chile, Ecuador, Mexico, Peru, and Paraguay received approval of the statutes of their conferences from Pius XII.[90] In fact, in the vision of John XXI-II's predecessor, the episcopal conferences were an important pivotal point in the unitary structure of Catholicism.

Pope John XXIII, who was familiar with the functioning of the assembly of French cardinals and archbishops and played a part in the beginnings of the Italian conference, gave new stimuli to the collegial activity of the bishops by approving the statutes of still more conferences. On the eve of Vatican II, the subject of episcopal conferences was considered one of the subjects needing theological evaluation and legislative organization; and during the Council their status would be one of the important problems connected with the question of episcopal collegiality. But on that October 13 the episcopal conferences came on the scene more concretely as one of the players in the first choices which the Council fathers would have to make. For the first time, the secretaries of the episcopal conferences had talks and contacts not under the watchful control of the congregations.

B. The Lists of the Episcopal Conferences for the Elections

Many bishops remember the succession of meetings for the drawing up of lists. A European list took shape that included German, French, Belgian, Austrian, and Dutch bishops, but excluded the Italians and the Spaniards. The Oriental patriarchs tried to draw up a joint list, but the Maronites opposed the candidacy of Edelby for the Commission on the Orientals, with the result that the Melkites ended up endorsing the Northern European, North American, and African lists. The Holy Office gave the Italian and Spanish bishops a list for the Doctrinal Commission.

Even the Italian bishops, who until this point had never had plenary assemblies, were summoned to an assembly by Siri, the first time that all the bishops of the peninsula met together, preceding meetings of the Italian Episcopal Conference having included only the presidents of the regional conferences. With 430 bishops, the Italian episcopate was the most numerous at Vatican II, and to them must be added other Italian bishops engaged outside the country in the missions or working in the

---

[90] On the Latin-American episcopates see the papers of the Houston Colloquium in *Vísperas* and in *S. Paulo*.

Roman Curia. Connections were strong between the latter and the bishops of the Italian episcopal conference. On October 14 the Italian bishops all gathered in the Domus Mariae. Montini would describe this event as "historical" and identify the Council as the occasion for a maturing awareness that should foster "fruitful" relations "of mutual knowledge, harmony, and collaboration within the Italian episcopate," a result of the conciliar dynamics. Of the cardinals, Ruffini of Palermo, Urbani of Venice, and Lercaro of Bologna spoke, while Montini remained silent. Siri obtained from the assembly "an unqualified mandate... regarding negotiations and norms." The prevailing attitude at the meeting was one of respect for hierarchy; in other words, the cardinals determined the direction taken. An anonymous Italian bishop remarked: "It is not true that we were told how to vote, and no party line was imposed. But there has been a commandeering attitude...."[91]

Siri wanted "to compile a truly catholic list." Lercaro, who was committed to the liturgical movement, did not appear on the Italian list for the Liturgical Commission, but did find a place on the European list and on that of Madagascar, by means of which he was chosen ("by the votes of foreigners," he would observe with some bitterness[92]). Siri set to work diligently, making contacts with the Apostolic Delegate to the United States and with some Spanish bishops. The Italian list excluded the Germans and the French, while including some other, non-Italian names.

A few days later, the Italian Episcopal Conference, that is, the presidents of the regional conferences, decided to continue the plenary meetings of the Italian episcopate, opening them also to Italian-speaking bishops throughout the world; the Conference concluded that, while leaving each father his freedom, "we need a mutual enlightenment, in order to avoid forming pressure groups."[93]

After intense activity and much consultation thirty-four lists were presented.[94] The most complete was the one that Fesquet described, despite the absence of Italians, as "the list from the Common Market."[95] Austrians, Belgians, Germans, French, Swiss, Dutch, Yugoslavs, and Scandinavians were on this list, which contained 112 names for the ten commissions. Italy, which had tried to establish links with other countries,

[91] Rock Caporale, *Vatican II: Last of the Councils* (Baltimore, 1964), 62.
[92] Lercaro, *Lettere*, 81.
[93] See Sportelli, *La Conferenza Episcopale Italiana*, 52.
[94] The lists provided by the conferences were published in *AS* I/1, 40-75.
[95] H. Fesquet, *Drama of Vatican II* (New York, 1967), 27.

especially for the Doctrinal Commission, came forward in the end with 62 candidates who would presumably be backed by about 500 bishops. The British, Irish, and Portuguese bishops drew up three different, though rather limited, lists with names of their own. Outside of Europe, the United States episcopate offered 27 bishops as candidates for 9 commissions; the Canadians offered 12 candidates for 10 commissions; the Indian episcopate — the only one in Asia to offer a list of its own — proposed 38 candidates for all the commissions.

Of the Africans, only the bishops of Madagascar (33 candidates for the ten commissions) and Nigeria (14 names for 9 commissions) provided lists. The bishops of Oceania acted together: 19 names for all the commissions. Three lists came in from the Oriental Churches. The Latin American situation was rather complex: CELAM opted not to work up its own slate of candidates, while the Argentinean, Chilean, Colombian, Venezuelan, Peruvian, Bolivian, Paraguayan, and Uruguayan episcopates drew up lists of different sizes. People were surprised that the sizable Brazilian episcopate did not draw up a list of its own; neither did Ecuador. The superiors general handed in their own list. In addition, the council fathers still had available the list of the members of the preconciliar commissions from which to draw names in the coming election.

The lists were drawn up in great haste. Some candidates appeared in several lists, especially the lengthy "Common Market" list, while members of other episcopates (Brazil, Mexico, and Spain) found no place. Among the various poles represented by the lists the Council fathers could make their way by reference to various factors that are not always easy to track, such as links among Churches of the north and Churches of the south, fidelity to Rome, membership in religious congregations, bonds developed during studies. But membership in a common episcopal conference as a principal source of direction was a major identifying factor that should not be underestimated.

The voting procedures threatened to make the general congregation on October 16 very complicated. The vote would produce about 24,000 cards containing 400,000 preferences, which in fact it would take four days to count. No wonder, then, that the second general congregation opened with a debate over procedure. Ottaviani proposed that the system for counting the votes be modified, that the requirement of an absolute majority for election to a commission be dropped, and that a father be able to combine all the votes he received for all the commissions and thereby obtain a seat on just one commission.[96] The purpose was evi-

---

[96] *AS* I/1, 108-9 of the minutes; for Ottaviani's intervention, see pp. 211-12.

dently to reduce the voting to a single ballot and for that reason, according to some witnesses, the proposal seemed acceptable to the assembly. Although some suspected that such a procedure would favor the Italian candidates, it was an Italian cardinal, Roberti, president of the administrative tribunal of the Council, who objected to the idea.[97] The Council of Presidents was once again called upon to consult on the point, and in their name Ruffini announced that the regulation could not be changed without the Pope's approval. Tisserant was in visible disagreement with Ottaviani's idea and then, as president of the session, declared in his turn that they would proceed that day to the voting for the commissions and that the proposal for a simplification would be forwarded to the Pope only afterward.[98]

Felici then informed the fathers that the voting cards could be filled out at home but were to be handed in "personally, and not by messenger," by the afternoon of October 18. He also announced that the third general congregation would be held on October 20 and would begin the discussion of the schema on the liturgy. He also announced that the Pope had appointed four undersecretaries of the Council, Msgrs. Villot, Morcillo, Krol, and Kempf. (A few days later, the appointment of Msgr. Nabaa, a Melkite bishop, as a fifth undersecretary would be announced, an appointment requested of the Pope, it seems, by the Congregation for the Oriental Church in the person of Cardinal Testa.[99])

In his statement on the technical aspects, the secretary general had said that the vote did not have to be signed. Ottaviani then noted that an unsigned vote was contrary to the Council regulations, adding that the Church forbade one to vote for oneself. Acknowledging that his proposal had to be submitted to the Pope, he asked that the Council make its opinion known by an open vote on the subject. Tisserant paid no heed to what Ottaviani had said and ordered the election for the commissions to proceed. Edelby sensed among the fathers as they left the basilica that

---

[97] *AS* I/1, 212.

[98] *AS* I/1, 213-15.

[99] *AS* I/1, 218. According to Fr. Tucci, the Pope saved Felici by appointing the undersecretaries and thus secured Felici's loyalty. *DTucci* February 9, 1963, f. 130: "To which he observed that Msgr. Felici is a good and decent man, but limited in outlook; he knows Latin and Italian, and that's about all. It is true that he did not get the position for himself; Tardini suggested him for it without his knowledge; he is obedient and a good worker. But the Pope saved him (by giving him five undersecretaries), and Msgr. Felici knows this and is grateful to him." A few months earlier, John XXIII had spoken ironically of Felici, whom he kept from being discharged, as had happened at Vatican I, when the secretary, being unable to express himself in German, had had to be replaced (cf. *Diario di B. Migone* [in possession of the family], *Note d'udienza*).

day widespread dissatisfaction that the Council was getting nowhere, that nothing had been settled since the solemn opening on October 11. The same impression was shared by two observers from the ancient Oriental Churches: Father Zhakka Iwwas of the Syrians and Father K. Sarkissian of the Armenians of Cilicia.[100]

The weariness and bewilderment caused by the complicated voting process were factors not to be underestimated. The initial procedural quarrels seemed at odds with the spiritual approach being taken by many of those present. In his notes Florit grumbled that the very "practical" suggestions of Ottaviani had not been accepted.[101] He feared the formalism of the voting and that the press would be showing the world that there were divisions among the bishops. Discussion, voting, and division were part of the reality of all deliberative assemblies, but it would be impossible to hide the oppositions and divisions from the public, despite the strict secrecy.

On October 20 Tisserant would announce that, at the request of the Council of Presidents, John XXIII had decided that, along with those who had received an absolute majority, those having a relative majority would also be considered to have been elected.[102] To a degree, this decision moved in the direction of Ottaviani's procedural proposal (without, however, accepting it), but the events of the week gave the Pope's action a quite different character. The Pope was in effect accepting the assembly's suggestions for each list. Even members elected with a relative majority would become part of the commissions to take the places not filled by those elected with an absolute majority, who represented thirty-four percent of those elected. To obviate the need to repeat the voting process, John XXIII was making an exception to the Regulations, in particular to article 39, which provided for an absolute majority. (It could thus be seen that at least some parts of the Regulations were not practicable.) The pope would also grant a *sanatio* for irregularities in the elections. In this way, the different electoral preferences of the Council fathers were being accepted along with the vote on the commissions.[103]

[100] *JEdelby*, October 16, 1962, f. 24.

[101] *DFlorit*, October 16, 1962.

[102] *AS* I/1, 223.

[103] Four elected fathers would spontaneously refuse their election and would be replaced by the first of the nonelected; the most important of these substitutions was for Wyszynski, a member of the Commission for the Apostolate of the Laity (within which there would be a lengthy discussion of a possible new condemnation of communism);

C. THE VOTES

The results of the elections were less dramatic than the excitement over the procedure might have led one to expect; in the final analysis the organizational chart of the commissions retained some of the traits typical of the preparatory phase.[104] The areas of competence were similarly divided among the commissions, which retained the same titles, except for the "Theological" Commission, which was now called the "Doctrinal" Commission. We find once again, then, the following: the Commissions on Doctrine, on Bishops and the Governance of the Church, for the Discipline of the Clergy and the Christian People, for Religious, for the Sacraments, for the Liturgy, for Studies and Seminaries, for the Oriental Churches, for the Missions, and for the Apostolate of the Laity; and there was also the Secretariat for Christian Unity.

At the head of each we still find the head of the corresponding curial congregation, that is, Cardinals Ottaviani, Marella, Ciriaci, Valeri, Aloisi-Masella, Larraona, Pizzardo, A. G. Cicognani, and Agagianian. The only exceptions (but here again in continuity with the preparatory phase) were the leaders of the Commission for the Apostolate of the Laity and the Secretariat for Christian Unity, whose heads, Cardinals Cento and Bea, had an anomalous position, but one not without influence on the structure of the Curia.[105]

---

when appointed a member of the Secretariat for Extraordinary Affairs, the Polish primate gave up his election to the Commission.

[104] *AS* I/1, 225-29.

[105] Here, then, were the heads of the conciliar commissions:
> *Doctrinal*: Ottaviani, president; Browne, vice-president; Tromp, S.J., secretary.
> *Bishops*: Marella, president; McIntyre and Bueno y Monreal, vice-presidents; Governatori, secretary.
> *Discipline*: Ciriaci, president; del Portillo, secretary.
> *Religious*: Valery, president; Rousseau, O.M.I., secretary.
> *Sacraments*: Aloisi-Masella, president; Bidagor, S.J., secretary.
> *Liturgy*: Larraona, president; Giobbe and Jullien, vice-presidents; Antonelli, secretary.
> *Studies and Seminaries*: Pizzardo, president; de Barros Câmara and Staffa, vice-presidents; Mayer, O.S.B., secretary.
> *Oriental*: A. G. Cicognani, president; Quiroga y Palacios and Bukatko, vice-presidents; Welykyi, secretary.
> *Missions*: Agagianian, president; Labandibar, vice-president; Paventi, secretary.
> *Apostolate of the Laity*: Cento, president; Silva Henriquez and O'Connor, vice-presidents; Glorieux, secretary.
> To these should be added the Secretariat for Christian Unity and the Secretariat for the Press, which were to demonstrate rather different abilities to develop.

Europeans continued to dominate among the leaders and members of
the commissions, with two groups of electees particularly noteworthy:
the one represented by the so-called "Latins" (that is, the Italians and
Spaniards) and the other reflected in the "European" list of candidates,
of whom a good thirty-nine were elected, twenty-two of them by an
absolute majority. There were about the same number of members from
the North and South American episcopates. There was a very substantial
presence of Italians, with twenty-two elected.[106] Two other episcopates
experienced great success: the German (eleven elected) and the French
(sixteen), both of which had a representative in all the commissions
except the Commission for the Oriental Churches. The Spanish bishops,
who had not drawn up their own list, ended up with ten members elected
to the commissions.

The non-European bishops had fewer members elected to the commissions, although more than had served on the preconciliar commissions. Twenty-seven Latin-Americans were elected to the commissions
(of these 7 were Brazilians, even though their episcopal conference had
not presented a list). North America had 26 representatives on the commissions: the bishops of the United States were represented on all of
them (the only other episcopate in this position was the Italian). The
bishops of Asia and Oceania could count on 16 electees, of which 6
were Indian. The African bishops were poorly represented with 7
elected, while the Oriental Churches had 4, and the religious 3. Only in
the Commission for the Missions were there more members from the
southern hemisphere than from the northern (9 out of 16). Patriarch
Maximos IV was elected to the Oriental Commission with 1112 votes,
and Msgr. Edelby with about a hundred fewer votes; no Armenians,
Copts, Syrians, or Chaldeans were elected.

The numbers of those members elected to the commissions who had
not been part of any preparatory organization varied appreciably from
commission to commission. A first global picture of the trend showed
that 57 percent of those elected had been part of the preparatory phase,
while 43 percent were new and inexperienced in the work of the commissions. Some members of the preconciliar commissions would continue, but now on different commissions. The greatest number of new
members was found in the Commissions for the Liturgy (56 percent), for
the Discipline of the Sacraments (59 percent), for Studies and Seminar-

---

[106] The majority of these were elected from the Italian list supplied by the Italian Episcopal Conference; the episcopate of Italian origin was represented on all the conciliar
commissions.

ies (56 percent), and for the Oriental Churches (50 percent). On the other hand, the number of new members on the Commission for Bishops and the Governance of Dioceses was minimal: 13 members had served during the preparatory phase, and only 3 were new. On the other commissions at least a third of the members were new. In summary, then, on 5 out of the 10 commissions the Council re-elected at least half of the personnel from the preparatory phase (allowing for the displacement of bishops from one area to another).[107]

Moreover, in the Commissions for Religious, for the Oriental Churches, and for the Missions, the first one elected was a new man, who had not taken part in the preparation; the same was true of the second one elected to the Commissions for the Bishops, the Sacraments, and the Laity; the third one elected to the Commission on Discipline; the fourth elected to the Doctrinal Commission and the Commission on Studies; finally, on the Liturgical Commission the first new member was the sixth to be elected. Three new members — Schneider, McGucken, and Schäufele — had received over 1600 votes each.

The results of the voting and an analysis of the consensus show that there indeed existed a need to take over the future of the Council. The "maneuver" of the "Northerners" revealed a determination that extended beyond the sixty-four "new" people who, as a result of it, became part of the conciliar organizations.

---

[107] These are the new commission members, with the number of votes they received:

Sacraments (11): Schneider, 1673 (2nd of those elected); McGucken, 1602; von Strenge, 1497; Fonturvel, 1030; van Cauwelaert, 973; Renard, 963; Fleitas, 946; Puech, 931; Reh, 890; Arai, 854; Lallier, 788.

Liturgy (8): Grimshaw, 1515 (the 6th of those elected); Hallinan, 1347; van Bekkum, 1338; Lercaro, 1082; Pichler, 1023, Enciso, 835, Martin, 804, D'Amato, 795.

Doctrine (4): van Dodewaard, 1537 (4th of those elected); Dearden, 1189; Charue, 1138; McGrath, 1116.

Bishops (3): Schäufele, 1658 (2nd of those elected); Mathias, 745; Bueno y Monreal, 722.

Discipline (5): Jansen, 1315 (3rd of those elected); Lommel, 1174; Shehan, 1135; van Zuylen, 1107; Rossi, 1045.

Religious (4): Huyghe, 1804 (1st of those elected); Reetz, 1089; Daly, 1040; Cahill, 919.

Studies and Seminaries (9): Höffner, 1462 (4th of those elected); Daem, 1177; Klepacz, 1152; Cody, 1123; Bogarìn, 947; Cazaux, 927; Marchetti Zioni, 804; Pintonello, 802; Paré, 781.

Oriental Churches (8): Senyshyn, 1432 (1st of those elected); Perinciaro, 1264; Hoeck, 1167; Baraniak, 1116; d'Elboux, 1009; McEntegart, 754; Jansen, 753.

Missions (8): Zoa, 1403 (1st of those elected); Riobé, 1229; Escalante, 1002; Pollio, 871; Arellano, 860; Kerketta, 784; Platero, 744; Sevrin, 706.

Lay Apostolate (4): Ménager, 1530 (2nd of those elected); de Araùjo Sales, 832; Yü Pin, 783; Morris, 672.

D. Papal Appointments

By providing for the papal appointment of members to conciliar commissions the Regulations for Vatican II departed from those for Vatican I, where in fact all the members of the commissions were elected by the conciliar assembly, without any papal intervention. Originally the Pope was to have appointed eight of the twenty-four members on each commission, but he later decided to name a ninth member. The reason for this decision was never explained, although the rumor in Rome was that it was due to his having forgotten to appoint Msgr. Dante, secretary of the Congregation of Rites, to the Commission for Liturgy. In any case, John XXIII in the end appointed ninety fathers to the commissions.

Of the papal appointees, of whom a good twenty-seven were Italians, seventy percent had participated in the preconciliar activities.[108] It is difficult to determine the various reasons that led to the pontifical appointments. There seems to have been a clear desire to strengthen the presence of the under-represented episcopates, such as the Polish, Swiss, Irish, Portuguese, and African. Some countries acquired their sole representative by papal appointment. On the other hand, the Italian and Spanish episcopates saw their influence on the commissions increased by the papal appointments, the Spanish bishops thus acquiring a presence on every commission, like the Italians and the Americans.

With the constitution of what were now more balanced commissions, the Council could now begin. Contrary to the view that inflexible tendencies were forming in this process, the positions of the Council fathers were still rather in flux and would become clear only as individual subjects were taken up.

Another noteworthy decision of the Pope altered the overall structure of the commissions. On October 22 it was announced in the hall that the Pope was elevating the Secretariat for Christian Unity to the rank of a commission; this act formally established an eleventh commission of Vatican II. This Secretariat had already been concerned about its survival during the preparatory phase; but on December 13, 1961, John XXIII had told Bea that he himself, and not the conciliar assembly, would decide the future purpose and competency of the Secretariat.[109] In

---

[108] Doctrine, 3; Bishops, 1; Discipline, 3; Religious, 3; Sacraments, 2; Liturgy, 5; Studies, 3; Oriental Churches, 4; Missions, 1; Laity, 1. *AS* did not publish a complete list of those voted for, so that it is not possible to determine whether or not those appointed by the Pope had garnered votes.

[109] See Velati, "Una difficile transizione," 321.

the meantime, the conciliar Regulations had placed the Secretariat for Christian Unity among the "technical" organs of the Council, which would have greatly limited its field of competence. Bea delayed his response to this marginalization until the moment when the commissions were to be elected. If the bishop-members of the Secretariat were to be excluded from the essential work of the Council, they might seek places on other commissions, thus rendering purely decorative the function of the entity over which Bea was presiding.

The status of the Secretariat for Christian Unity was also discussed in the Secretariat for Extraordinary Affairs. Since his Secretariat had not been liquidated like the other preconciliar commissions, but, according to the Regulations, had kept its function, Bea asked whether its role was limited to helping the non-Catholic observers or instead also included the task of preparing schemas, as it had done in the preparatory phase. On the other hand, the members of the Secretariat for Christian Unity had not been elected like those of the other conciliar commissions. Could it, then, retain a function that would put it on the same level as a conciliar commission?

Bea requested the Pope to put his Secretariat on the same level as the other commissions. Despite the express opposition of Siri, John XXIII approved the request in an audience given to Cicognani on October 19.[110] The papal action, the result of negotiations between Bea and Cicognani, gave an "authentic" interpretation of article 7 of the Regulations, in virtue of which *all* the functions exercised by *all* the secretariats during the preparatory phase were extended into the conciliar period.[111] This interpretation meant that the Secretariat for Christian Unity retained its authority when it came to contacts with the non-Catholics and acquired the right to present schemas of its own in a general congregation, just like the other commissions. In addition, the Secretariat could play a role in joint or mixed commissions.[112] The connection between commissions and Curia, which had brought advantages to the latter during the preparation and which it did not wish to relinquish, was being weakened not only by the introduction of new personalities but also by this decision, which affected the very architecture of the Council. The Secretariat for Christian Unity was thus given an exceptional status among the conciliar commissions: it was the only one that had all its members in the preparatory phase confirmed in their posi-

---

[110] See Schmidt, *Bea*, 415-16.
[111] The change in the Regulations is in *ADP* IV/I, 256.
[112] The text, in four points, is in *AS* I/1, 78.

tion during the conciliar phase by the express will of John XXIII. Thus it was, paradoxically, an organ of the Pope that kept the ecumenical tension alive during the Council. While the Holy Office was losing its central role, as we have seen, the Secretariat for Christian Unity, despite its being a new organization, saw its role increased, and Bea would be able to continue at the Council the prodding role which he had been playing since 1961.[113] The importance of this action was evident, since the problem of relations with the non-Catholic Churches was to be a main concern in the work of Vatican II.

On the other hand, this decision of the Pope by-passed the Council. While it was clear that no one felt this act from on high violated the Council's prerogatives, there was a concern to keep this birth from on high of a new organ from weakening the Council's later functioning. The presence on the Secretariat of four new members, all from the former preparatory Commission for the Oriental Churches,[114] made it clear that Cicognani, Secretary of State and president of that Commission, had consented to the Pope's move. The problem was that objections might one day come from the Doctrinal Commission, which was in charge of the major schemas on revelation and the Church. Finally, there was the obstructionism of the General Secretariat, which until October 26 denied those members of Bea's Secretariat who had not been appointed experts in the first large batch the ticket that would have allowed them to be present at the morning's work. The fact that some of them (Thijssen, Weigel, Lanne, Duprey, Feiner) got around the ban by being appointed interpreters did not lessen the importance of the signal that was being given.

Is it possible that the assembly misunderstood the "elevation" of the Secretariat for Christian Unity and felt that the action limited its responsibilities? This was a concern that came up in a conversation that Thomas F. Stransky, an American ecumenist, had with the American press; he admitted that the provision made for the Secretariat gave the Council a commission of which no member was elected by the assembly, and he did not exclude the possibility of a vote in the hall to remove this anomaly.[115]

---

[113] *History* I, 263-66.

[114] I. Mansourati, Syro-Catholic chorbishop; T. Minisci, Archimandrite of Grottaferrata; A. Katkoff, a Greek Catholic; and A. Prinetto. It is therefore inexplicable that the *AAS* did not publish the appointment of the four members by papal letter, unless this was due to the climate of confusion at the beginning of Vatican II.

[115] Stransky glided over the fact that the Pope had appointed among its members four from the preparatory Commission on the Oriental Churches.

Was too much emphasis being placed on the role of the commissions? In fact, the commissions were not only still being steered by a staff that was the same as in the preparatory period, but they had not even met. The Doctrinal Commission had its first session on November 13, but during the preceding weeks Tromp continued to bring the former Theological Commission together in order to finish the last remaining schemas and — as was openly and unapologetically stated — to correct once again the texts that had been screened by the Latinists of the Secretariat of State, about whose accuracy the Jesuit theologian had his doubts.[116]

E. The Language of the Council

The problem of the language in which Vatican II was to be conducted was by no means a marginal one, even if in the first days of the Council it had been hidden by the more urgent problem of the election of the conciliar commissions. The Regulations provided for the use of Latin not only in the final documents of the synod, but also in the debates in the hall. The only exception allowed was in interventions in the conciliar commissions, provided that these were immediately translated into Latin. The status of Latin as the language of the Church had recently been confirmed by John XXIII in his letter *Veterum sapientia*.[117] The choice of Latin and the exclusion of simultaneous translation not only affected the ability of the fathers to understand what was happening; it also signified the choice of a mentality. In Rome's view, Latin expressed Catholic teaching in the best and clearest way and avoided the dangerous misunderstandings that the modern languages might introduce. Vatican II was expected to reaffirm the connections between the universality of Catholicism and Latin, links that had continually supported the use of this language, save for some exceptions in the liturgy of the Oriental Church.

But there were many problems of various kinds. One very concrete one was simply in understanding Latin as it was spoken with very different accents by various Council fathers, to the point that the addresses of some were almost unintelligible to others. The Italian pronunciation

---

[116] Tromp, Minutes of the Doctrinal Commission, A-Flo.

[117] See A. Melloni, "Tensioni e timori alla vigilia del Vaticano II: la costituzione apostolica *Veterum sapientia* di Giovanni XXIII (Febbraio 22, 1962)," *CrSt* 11 (1990), 275-307; *History*, I, 211-26.

of the Church's official language was quite different from that of the Germans or the English. Experience would show the difficulty the fathers had in making themselves understood in Latin in the large assembly hall. In part to meet this difficulty and to ensure that bishops understood them, practical announcements to the assembly of bishops were repeated in various languages, among them Arabic.

Another dimension of language was the question that would be addressed immediately after the elections to commissions when the schema on the liturgy would be discussed: the problem of preserving Latin as the language of the Roman liturgy. The liturgical movement supported the introduction of the vernaculars in sacred actions and in the sacraments, as was already being done in the majority of the Oriental Churches. The Pope had often emphasized the international make-up of the conciliar assembly as a mirror of the concrete catholicity of a Church that lives its life among so many different peoples. But should this international character be expressed in the historically sanctioned use of a single language, Latin, or in a plurality of languages? This was the problem, connected both with the liturgy and with the very life of the Church, that Vatican II faced. To insist on the primacy of Latin was to assert the privileged connection of the Church with classical culture, with the scholastic mentality, with a firm vision of law, and, at bottom, with certain countries, first among which was Italy. In addition, by using the language of the Curia, it said that Rome was the supreme synthesis of the Church's catholicity.

The need for greater international representation had determined the appointment of the five undersecretaries of the Council. Thus, alongside Secretary General Felici, an Italian, were Morcillo Gonzalez, a Spaniard, Kempf, a German, Krol, an American, Villot, a Frenchman, and, later, Naaba, an Arab. These were the first appointments, since the day when the Council was announced, that were made without reference to the parallel between conciliar functions and curial functions. The composition of the Council's Council of Presidents also followed the norm of international representation. But, despite the difficulties voiced by some, this internationalization did not extend to the language of the Council.

Not all the bishops of the Oriental Churches accepted the official language of the Latin Church. The Melkites, not feeling part of Latin Catholicism, particularly urged this challenge, even though the majority of them had known Latin ever since their studies. This request, which had been made and turned down during the preparatory phase,[118]

---

[118] *History*, I, 211-13.

appeared again with the opening of the Council. Some western bishops were also opposed to the use of Latin because, as we saw in the case of Liénart, they were unable to improvise in Latin and needed written texts. When König, who was in favor of using the living languages, asked Edelby to have Patriarch Maximos IV Saigh speak in French instead of in Latin, a gesture that might open the way to the use of the spoken languages, Edelby objected that the action might bring the patriarch a reprimand from the Council of Presidents.[119] König and Edelby sounded out the cardinal-presidents as to whether an address in French by the patriarch would be tolerated. A few days later, Tisserant in person told the patriarch that he could address the Council in French and that the General Secretariat would provide a Latin translation of his address.

This was an important precedent. As a matter of fact, other languages began to be heard during the third general congregation. Melkite Bishop Malouf spoke in French when he offered an emendation of the message to the world; he did so after excusing himself for not being able to express himself in Latin and for not wanting to use Arabic, which was unknown to the majority. His address in French was applauded. These addresses were a breach in the usage prescribed by the Regulations. With the exceptions allowed to the Melkites began a renewed discussion of the absoluteness of the norm; it showed, rather elliptically, that the entire Church was not Latin, if only because of the existence of the Oriental Churches.

The case of the use of Latin and of the vernaculars at the Council typifies the way in which John XXIII proceeded in directing the work. The Pope alone could have changed the strict use of the language of the Curia, but he did not do so, even though he clearly favored the use of the national languages. He neither pushed nor hindered the developing dynamics of Vatican II, but limited himself to preventing the Regulations from being interpreted so rigidly as not to permit exceptions. In fact, John XXIII noted in his own diary for the month of October: "The question of Latin certainly divides those who have never left home or Italy from those from other nations, especially in missionary lands, or who, although Italians, are living and sacrificing themselves in distant parts. On this matter of Latin in the liturgy it will be necessary to proceed *lento pede* [with slow steps] and by degrees."[120] This was another illustration of how the Pope intended to proceed in regard to the work.

---

[119] In fact, Hakim would be the first not to use Latin (see *JEdelby*, November 17, 1962, f. 68, and *NChenu*, November 17, 1962, 107).

[120] *Agende*, October 24, 1962.

The opening allocution, while not providing a program, did let the council fathers know of John XXIII's desire to effect an updating of the Church. And yet the Pope did not intend to manage the Council either directly or through the Curia or the organs of the Council. His presence at the work of the Council would be unobtrusive. By using his own powers sparingly, he would allow the Council to become aware of its responsibilities and the Council fathers to map out a direction of their own.

V. MESSAGES, PROGRAMS, AND PLANS

On October 20 Vatican II approved a "message to the world," *Nuntius ad omnes homines et nationes*.[121] This rather short text moves on two levels: one focused on the self-presentation of the Church and its mission, the second on showing the world the solidarity of Catholics in regard to the great problems of the age. Bishop Gantin of Africa would later observe: "The Council knew that the world was watching it. We were no longer in a shut-in place, in our own little huts."[122] One passage expresses the determination of the Council to be heedful of the world:

> We urgently turn our thoughts to all the anxieties by which human beings are afflicted today. Hence, our concern focuses first of all on those who are especially lowly, poor, and weak. Like Christ, we would have pity on the multitude weighed down with hunger, misery, and lack of knowledge. We want to fix a steady gaze on those who still lack the help they need to achieve a way of life worthy of human beings. As we undertake our work, therefore, we would emphasize whatever concerns the dignity of the human person, whatever contributes to a genuine community of peoples.

It was a message of interest to the world, especially in two of the points it made: peace and social justice. The conclusion echoed the citation from the Acts of the Apostles that John XXIII had used in *Gaudet Mater Ecclesia*: "We are lacking in human resources and earthly power. Yet we place our trust in the power of God's Spirit."

What is the significance of this message issued at the beginning of the Council, after the Pope's address and before the work of the Council had begun? The text was presented to the assembly by Felici as a proposal of the Council of Presidents approved by the Pope. The fathers could offer their remarks on it before proceeding to an open vote. The fewer

---

[121] *AS* I/1, 230-32. English translation (slightly modified) in Abbott, *The Documents of Vatican II*, 3-7.

[122] Interview in Svidercoschi, *Inchiesta*, 13.

than forty interventions that followed were the first conciliar debate on a text.

Significantly, some questions emerged that would accompany subsequent conciliar debates. Some were worried by the overly horizontal and irenic tone of the text; in his intervention, Msgr. Parente of the Holy Office, for example, expressed his concern that nothing was said about Catholic truth as a remedy for the evils of the present time. Archbishop Marcel Lefebvre complained that the message spoke too much of earthly and too little of supernatural well-being. Other fathers, among them Cardinal Ferretto (but not Wyszynski), Msgr. Fiordelli, Msgr. Heenan, Msgr. Hermaniuk, and others, regretted the absence of any mention of persecuted Christians. Msgr. Hamvas of Hungary begged the Council to avoid any reference to persecution in order not to aggravate a situation in which he could see some signs of improvement.[123] The problem that here began to emerge and would last until the very end of the Council was whether to condemn communism and offer solidarity with the "Church of silence." In fact, this emendation was not even put to a vote by the Council of Presidents, in whose view, significantly, the message to humanity was to contain no allusion to a serious problem for the Church and the contemporary world: the problem of communist regimes. This solution seemed to show a desire to avoid a condemnation of communism by the Council, something unacceptable to a considerable number of fathers.[124]

Some fathers, on the other hand, called attention to the absence of any reference to the Virgin Mary; a reference was later included at the suggestion of Msgr. Ancel.[125] Concerns about ecumenism and non-Christians were also expressed, along with complaints about the haste with which decisions about the text had to be made. Maximos IV reminded the fathers of the character of the Council message. Not intended to be a treatise on theology and spirituality, the patriarch observed, the message was a manifestation of "the new spirit which he [John XXIII] has spread abroad in the Catholic Church and which has the power in the end to bring the Churches together." The text was approved, with some finishing touches, as a message not of the Council but of "the fathers of the Council to all humanity," as Felici explained after it was voted on at the fourth general congregation.[126]

---

[123] *AS* I/1, 242-43.
[124] See Turbanti, "Il problema del comunismo."
[125] *AS* I/1, 243-45.
[126] *AS* I/1, 11 and 254.

It has to be said that the message did not receive a great deal of comment in the press and was quickly forgotten. The text nonetheless represented the need to show the Church's sympathetic attitude to the world outside itself. In some respects, therefore, it was also an effort to oppose the preparatory schemas, which had been prepared without any openness to the world. This point was grasped even by those who did not know the origin of the document, such as Edelby, who described it as a "splendid text, of clearly French inspiration, asserting that the Church has no desire to control anyone but to serve the entire world." *Témoignage chrétien* regarded it as clearly "incarnational" in character and attributed it to the work of Father Chenu: "Our readers will find in the text themes which he has defended in these pages."[127]

In fact, the document had a more complex origin and came into being in a setting of dissatisfaction with the preparatory phase of Vatican II and a fear that the Council would take its direction from that phase. The text approved by the Council was composed by four French bishops: Cardinal Liénart and Msgrs. Guerry, Ancel, and Garrone (in 1963 Guerry would himself claim the paternity of the document).[128] In fact, in the text which Felici presented to Vatican II Congar found nothing at all of what he had worked out with Chenu. He wrote as follows in his diary:

> The secretary announces that he will read a "message to be sent to all of humanity." I listen to the text, a project in which I played an active part. I transcribe here some remarks which I scribbled down on the spot: it is more dogmatic than Chenu's draft; at least it has prefaced the social part with a section on the Christian kerygma; it is more ecclesiastical; more biblical. It is too long. The interest in humanity is expressed to some extent in terms of concern. It is a happy call for the renewal of the Church and of Christian life, so that we may be more conformed to Christ.[129]

Only Congar notes the emphasis on the theme of renewal, a larger and broader question than the intent of the message might suggest. No one seems to have noted the appearance in the body of the message to humanity of some ecclesiological themes that would become supremely important during the Council. While it still lacked a theological formu-

[127] See *Témoignage chrétien*, October 26, 1962; see also *NChenu*, 53-54.

[128] See A. Duval, "Le message au monde," in *Vatican II commence*, 105-118.

[129] *JCongar*, October 20, 1962, typescript, 81; Congar's Papers, Paris (II/V, Dossier 25), include a correspondence between Chenu and Congar and the responses to the sending of a first draft (September 18-19, 1962) from Weber, Liénart, Marty, Suenens, Volk, Alfrink, Montini, Döpfner, and Charue. There is no trace of replies from Ghattas, Frings, Elchinger, Hurley, or König to the letter accompanying the draft.

lation of collegiality, the beginning does offer a description of the Church in Council as a gathering of the "successors of the apostles," who form "one apostolic body headed by the successor of Peter."[130]

A. CHENU'S DRAFT OF THE MESSAGE TO THE WORLD

It was, in fact, Chenu, with help later from Congar, who originated the conciliar message, in spite of Guerry's insistence on a considerable discontinuity between the approved text and the one offered by the two French Dominicans. Father Tucci likewise remarked that "the text approved by the Council does not correspond entirely to the one prepared by Father Chenu; the Council of Presidents changed it at some points, thus weakening it a bit."

In fact, Chenu's text, despite "being drowned in holy water," as he himself would complain,[131] played the very important role, as André Duval's study has shown, of *accentuating* the Church's expression of sympathy for the world. Several bishops were involved in Chenu's project, among them Liénart, who wanted the document to become part of the work of the Council. Agreement in principle also came from Cicognani, the Secretary of State; Confalonieri was informed of it on the morning of October 11 and mentioned it to Siri before the opening procession.[132] Parallel initiatives came from other bishops, among them Suenens, who sent the Pope a proposal similar to Chenu's. One sector of the bishops, identifiable on the European list for election to the commissions, felt the need of a declaration of this kind by the Council to contemporary humanity.

But we need to realize that this need arose also from dissatisfaction with the schemas drafted by the preconciliar commissions and from a determination to correct their direction. This attitude is clear in Chenu, who wrote of it in a letter to Rahner on September 4, 1962.[133] As the

[130] See A. Melloni, "Ecclesiologie al Vaticano II (autunno 1962 — estate 1963," in *Commissions*, 91-179.

[131] See G. Alberigo, *Le P. Chenu et Vatican II.*

[132] Confalonieri seemed to agree with the idea of a message to the world and told Siri of a "text" of "two short pages," adding, "There was little desire to throw it out." Siri commented: "I would have liked to ask him what could be said to the world in two short pages, but I judged it better not to continue the conversation. The incident shows that some people do not have a very elevated idea of an ecumenical council, which pains me. We ought not look to the world in order to offer it some agreeable feelings, but only to our Lord" (*DSiri*, October 11, 1962, 358).

[133] *NChenu*, 59-60.

French theologian saw it, the texts "were governed by an inflexible line of abstract and theoretical statements, whereas the Council has raised hopes of a pastoral consideration." As a result, Chenu notes, "the Council is becoming an operation of the intellectual police, within the closed walls of the School." In order to counteract this orientation, he said:

> The decisions of the Council should be preceded by a broad declaration in which the plan of salvation is proclaimed in the language of the gospel and in the prophetic perspectives of the Old and New Testaments.... A declaration addressed to a human race whose greatness and misery, beneath the failures and errors, represent a longing for the light of the gospel....A declaration proclaiming the fraternal unity of human beings — across borders, races, regimes — in a rejection of violent solutions, in a love of peace, which is a test of the kingdom of God. In this way, let the community of Christians share publicly in the hopes of humanity.[134]

Chenu's proposal grew out of dissatisfaction with the direction taken in the schemas; a similar attitude in other bishops gave support to his idea, which took form, during the month of September, in a text meant to be taken over by the Council. If the substantial changes made in it undoubtedly reflected the need to balance the excessive "horizontalism" of the original, the conciliar document retained the interest in and sympathy for the world with which Vatican II wanted to begin its work. A few days after the promulgation of the text, Chenu maintained, in *Témoignage chrétien*, that "the Council's message asks Christians, in their building of the world, to pay heed to the anxious and hope-filled appeals of humanity for peace, brotherhood, and the advancement of the poor," appeals which embody authentic "natural ideals" that are very closely connected to the "gifts of grace."[135]

B. PLANS AND PROGRAMS

While the message to the world was being drafted, two other documents raised questions about the overall direction of the Council. These were not public documents brought before the assembly, but letters addressed to the Pope and to Cicognani in his role as head of the Secretariat for Extraordinary Affairs, which had in its competence everything

---

[134] See Duval, "Le message au monde," 110.

[135] This interpretation would be confirmed by Paul VI on September 29, 1963, in his opening address for the second period of Vatican II, the first after his election as pope. See *Insegnamenti* I, 166-85.

not part of the order of the day. The letters, dated October 15 and 18, came from two prominent figures in the assembly, Bea and Montini, who both felt the need of defining clearly the goals and program of the Council but understood them in rather different ways.

Bea left the Pope a memorandum in which he defended and repeated the formulation of *Gaudet Mater Ecclesia*. The Council should give answers to the present day and should therefore place itself on the pastoral level, where the mere repetition of condemnations is not only out of place but inadequate to fulfill the historic vocation of Vatican II.[136] In terms of procedure this meant, according to Bea, reducing and rewriting the doctrinal schemas to make them consistent with the aims enunciated in the opening address to the Council, a discourse which the Jesuit cardinal regarded with the fervor of one who had found his own desires reflected in it. In his apprehension about the Council's start, Bea proposed a course of action that would exploit the themes set down by the Pope and expressed in the message to the world; his plan of conciliar activity would renounce any dealings with the preparatory organs and would seek a very broad maieutic role for the Secretariat for Christian Unity. It is perhaps not without significance that the October 15 memorandum was forwarded by the Pope to Cicognani along with the note that broadened the functions of the body over which Bea presided.[137]

Montini, for his part, formulated a plan that was strongly influenced by Suenens' "Plan" of the preceding summer.[138] It represents an effort to find a middle ground in face of the prospect of the shipwreck of the preparatory schemas whose imminence could not escape those who, like Montini, had an adequate knowledge of what was really going on. The Archbishop of Milan, who had not agreed to sign Cardinal Léger's petition in September,[139] realized that rigid adherence to the schemas, which the preparatory Theological Commission regarded as a necessity, was a

[136] See Alberigo, "Concilio acefalo? L'evoluzione degli Organi direttivi del Vaticano II," in *Attese*, 196-98; the text of the memorandum is on 219-24.

[137] The papal rescript, along with Montini's letter of October 18, would be passed on by Cicognani to the members of the Secretariat for Extraordinary Affairs; the rescript was apparently never to be published in *AS*; but the minutes of the fourth general congregation, October 22, 1962, which report the reading to the assembly of a papal rescript given at an audience with the Secretary of State (see *AS* I/1, 112), speak expressly of the *aequiparatio*. Now in an appendix of *DSiri*, 350-51.

[138] For Montini's letter, see *Giovanni Battista Montini Arcivescovo di Milano e il Concilio Ecumenico Vaticano II. Preparazione e Primo Periodo*, 420-23.

[139] See Routhier, "Les réactions du cardinal Léger" *History*, I, 424; and Suenens's testimony in *Giovanni Battista Montini Arcivescovo di Milano e il Concilio Ecumenico Vaticano II. Preparazione e Primo Periodo*, 168-87.

wrong choice. He proposed a "redistribution" of the material for the Council around a single conceptual center — the Church — that could support both the preparatory material and whatever would have to be integrated into it. Montini was critical of the prepared schemas mainly because in them, he felt, "there is no organic form to reflect the great purposes which the Holy Father has set for the Council." The Council lacked a plan and a direction to implement it; the result, declared the cardinal, might be dangerous or disappointing changes of direction.

While the analyses of Bea and Montini differ in many aspects, they both identify a lack of leadership and share the idea that it is up to Cicognani (after or before the Pope, depending on the view) to take the initiative. Perhaps, beyond the observations of the two cardinals, there was emerging in these first steps of Vatican II the need to identify a common path by which the bishops could be allowed to fulfil the function to which the Pope had called them.

VI. The Direction of the Council

Leadership of the Council in implementing the vision of Pope John was not very well defined. What were the organs appointed by the Pope to guide the work of the great assembly, to propose schemas, to organize the debates, and to deal with the pressures coming from various sides?

A. Who Was in Charge?

In the beginning, it appeared that John XXIII had entrusted this leadership role to the Council of Presidents. Although it had never met before the Council opened, its role seemed a considerable one. It rejected some emendations of the message to the world during the discussion of the text, and it was because he was seated at the presidents' table that Liénart was able to intervene and influence the work of the second day of Vatican II.

According to article 4 of the Regulations, the Council of Presidents, composed of ten cardinals appointed by the Pope, was to direct the discussions among the fathers and the running of the Council. On September 6 *L'Osservatore Romano* had published the names of the cardinals making up the board, all of them residential bishops, except for the Dean of the Sacred College, Tisserant. The board included only one Italian member, Ruffini, Archbishop of Palermo (he was one of several cardinals who for years had promoted the idea of holding an ecumenical council). The most important episcopates of the world were represented on the board, the aim being to emphasize the international character of the Church. Thus, along with Tappouni, an Oriental patriarch (Syro-Catholic), there were Gilroy, an Australian, Spellman of North America, and Caggiano of South America (Buenos Aires). Europe was strongly represented: Liénart, dean of the French cardinals, along with Pla y Daniel of Spain, Frings of Cologne, and Alfrink of the Netherlands. Since this membership did not correspond to that of the college of cardinals (where the Italians and the members of the Curia were far more numerous), was this membership a deliberate effort to put in charge of the Council a group that would be representative of an assembly made up in large measure of residential bishops? In any case, it showed quite concretely that the leadership of the Council was different from the governance of the Roman Curia.

Originally it had been planned that the Council of Presidents would have six members, but Pope John had changed the draft of the Regulations and increased the number to ten. This larger number "might have permitted a more representative structure, but it also encumbered the functioning of the board itself and therefore its ability to direct the work of the Council."[140] It is significant that after the experience of the first period the Council of Presidents would be set aside and four moderators appointed to direct the work of the Council.

By making this group broadly representative, John XXIII had intended to emphasize the point that the direction of the work was entrusted to the bishops of the world rather than to the representatives of the Curia. All the conciliar commissions, on the contrary, were led by the heads of the congregations. But, to help the directors of the Council function better, the Pope had added to the draft of the Regulations a Secretariat for Extraordinary Affairs of the Council, its task being to sift proposals made by the fathers. Secretary General Felici seems to have been opposed to the creation of this Secretariat, which he thought duplicated the Council of Presidents and interfered in the workings of the Council.[141] The composition of this Secretariat was highly significant. Its president was Cicognani, Secretary of State, who thus linked it at the

---

[140] See Alberigo, "La preparazione del regolamento," 68.

[141] See V. Carbone, "Il segretario generale del concilio ecumenico," in *Il cardinal Pericle Felici* (Rome, 1992), 70.

highest level with the most influential organ of the Curia; in addition, he would have the role of directly representing the will of the Pope, both because of his office and because of the constant access he had to the pontiff.[142] The members of the Secretariat for Extraordinary Affairs were among the most influential members of the Sacred College: Siri, Montini, Suenens, Döpfner, Confalonieri (secretary of the Congregation of the Consistory, responsible for the selection of bishops), and Meyer of the United States. To these cardinals, appointed on September 6, 1962, the Pope added Wyszynski, the only cardinal from Eastern Europe to be in Rome during the Council.[143] This appointment showed not only the sympathy which John XXIII had for the Polish primate but also his concern for the Churches of the East. All the attitudes present in the Council were represented at a high level on this Secretariat, as is clear from the presence of Siri, Montini, and Döpfner, and for this reason, too, it could become an important place for balancing and mediating the various pressures at work in the Council.

B. THE ROMAN PARTIES

If the Roman Curia was much better represented in the Secretariat for Extraordinary Affairs than in the Council of Presidents, its representatives were influential and unusual personalities. Confalonieri and Cicognani immediately showed that they intended to take a middle position in the work of the Council and thereby narrowed the space left for the "Roman party," of which Ottaviani was the most combative representative.

It was John XXIII who had promoted both Cicognani and Confalonieri within the Curia. The former had been appointed Secretary of State in 1961 after the death of Cardinal Tardini, the not very tractable collaborator of the Pope in the preparation of Vatican II. Having been Apostolic Delegate in the United States from 1933 to 1958, Cicognani had not shared in the vision of things that had developed in the Curia during those years and, in particular, in the idea of Rome as a "bulwark" against communism and on Italian matters. The Secretary of State wanted to make some changes, although discreetly, in his predecessor's

---

[142] No full study exists of Cicognani, who served as Secretary of State, president of the Secretariat for Extraordinary Affairs, and president of the Commission for the Oriental Churches.

[143] On him see C. Wyszynski, *Un évêque au service du peuple de Dieu* (Paris, 1968).

methods of government. He had confided to an important Italian church-man that he "preferred efforts to persuade individual authorities to noisy interventions," and he added: "The different methods of Pius XII and Cardinal Tardini were justified by a difference in situations and experi-ences." And when Father Lombardi urged him to act decisively against communism, the cardinal had answered: "We can only put in a few good words."[144]

Cicognani's moderate position had been made known during the work of the Central Commission, where he had stressed the repercussions of a possible condemnation of communism on the Catholics of the East and the dangers of a declaration on Judaism for relations with Muslims. Moreover, Mons. Lardone, Pro-nuncio in Ankara and a secret collabora-tor of Roncalli in the latter's first moves toward the East, was Cicog-nani's man, having been introduced by him into the diplomatic corps.[145] On the whole, Pope John's Secretary of State had shown a determination to remove from the attitude of the central administration of the Church the spirit of opposition that was Ottaviani's prescription for the govern-ment of the Church. He took seriously calls for renewal, especially those made by residential bishops, and he collaborated with the Pope much more closely than Tardini had. Of him the Pope noted in his diary, "I always get along quite well" with him.[146] Roncalli did not have an eccle-siastical staff linked to him whom he might bring into the central admin-istration of the Church as Paul VI would in his plan for a reform and a change of rankings. John XXIII promoted churchmen who were ready to adopt a balanced position.

It was not an accident, for example, that he called Confalonieri, at one time secretary of Pius XI, to succeed Cardinal Mimmi as head of the Congregation of the Consistory. John XXIII respected Pius XI's manner of governing as well as many of the personnel connected with him. In the Central Preparatory Commission Confalonieri had been sensitive to the solicitations of the residential bishops and did not align himself with the positions taken by Ottaviani.[147]

During the Council Ottaviani, Ruffini, Siri, and Browne formed a rather close-knit group, committed, according to Siri, to resisting pres-

---

[144] Cited in G. Zizola, *Il microfono di Dio: P. Riccardo Lombardi* (Milan, 1990), 440.

[145] A. Riccardi, *Il Vaticano II e Mosca*, 233-64.

[146] *Agende*, November 3, 1962.

[147] In addition, it was Confalonieri who would present the agenda for November 14 that ended the discussion of the schema on the liturgy and accepted the call for making "the various parts of the liturgy itself more vital and more formative of the faithful, in keeping with today's pastoral needs."

sures. This group attracted other representatives of the Roman Curia and various bishops throughout the world who had links with Roman institutions, such as the Lateran. They formed a real "Roman party" that stood for the traditional theology and believed that people in Rome could see the Church's problems with a depth and sureness not possible elsewhere. Because they thought they were interpreting the Roman point of view at the Council, they regarded themselves as something more than just another current of thought or party within the vast assembly of Vatican II. Not for nothing was the group spearheaded by Ottaviani, secretary of the Supreme Congregation of the Holy Office, whose task of defending the faith made it the most important congregation of the Roman Curia. This position led the Roman group, by tradition and setting, to consider itself not merely a part of Vatican II but its soul; its members felt called to carry out this task especially at moments of doctrinal confusion, a function they had exercised in the redaction of the doctrinal schemas during the preparatory phase.

The Holy Office and this group of "Roman" cardinals and bishops intended to provide guidance during the course of Vatican II and in the government of the Church. This attitude could be readily seen not only in the repeated interventions of that congregation in the conciliar debates but also in its reaction to the reform of the Curia that would later strip the Holy Office of its rank as "supreme congregation" and give the Secretariat of State first rank among the Vatican congregations. Ottaviani supposedly remarked after the reduction of his congregation's importance: "Until now, the supreme principle of Church government has been revealed doctrine, the preservation and correct interpretation of which has been entrusted first and foremost to the Pope, who made use of this congregation, which was therefore 'supreme.' Now I do not know what the guiding norm of Church government will be, but I am afraid that the criterion that will prevail will be diplomatic and contingent."[148]

According to the logic of the "Romans," it seemed that at the Council, because of pastoral concerns and ecumenism, "contingent" factors were taking the place of the defense of revealed truth. Beginning with the work of the Theological Commission, Ottaviani had been motivated by a concern to be an intransigent defender of truth that is destined to impose itself by its intrinsic power. In addition to the cardinals mentioned above, his positions were also adopted, with varying frequency,

[148] *DOttaviani*, 85.

by Pizzardo, Marella, and Aloisi Masella. In addition, there were all the disciples of the Roman school who had been promoted to the episcopate.

This rigorous attitude, which would require the Pope to intervene firmly even in the work of the Council, was not shared by all the curial cardinals. Important members of the Curia such as Cicognani and Confalonieri were convinced that a logic of opposition would be a mistake: their attitude was to take a middle ground, sometimes in irritation at Ottaviani's inflexibility. Moreover, even the "Romans" were not completely willing to cultivate the logic of blocs, because, among other things, they thought that their role was to be a central leader in the Council and not simply one party among others. After the second day of Vatican II, when Ottaviani brought up the idea of a co-ordinated organization of the fathers, Siri showed his opposition to a bloc-mentality. Ruffini agreed with Ottaviani's positions but opposed the idea of seeking consensus among the fathers. Urbani observed: "Not without some objections from Cardinal Ruffini there was agreement on the opportuneness of keeping in contact with and giving some guidance to the Italian episcopate."[149]

Even Msgr. Castellano, one of Pius XII's bishops, "advised that blocs not be formed." Moreover, at the plenary meeting of the Italian episcopal conference on October 14, Ruffini seemed to be on a different wavelength from Siri, even though on the whole both shared the same concerns. Their disagreement became publicly known and had a somewhat bewildering effect on the bishops linked to them.[150] Their divergence could already be seen at the general congregation on October 16, at which three cardinals of similar outlook acted publicly in contrasting ways. Ottaviani made a motion that the votes be counted; Roberti, speaking in the name of the administrative tribunal, declared this contrary to canon law; Ruffini rejected it in the name of the presidents. The more important leaders of the Curia or those connected with them, in short "the Romans," did not feel that they should descend to the level of a fight among "factions;" they possessed a confidence in their own authority and in the appeal to the power of tradition. Would not the authority of the Holy Office suffice to guide the fathers in their choices, especially those of a theological kind?

---

[149] *DUrbani*, October 14, 1962.
[150] Ibid.

C. THE GUIDANCE AND ORIENTATIONS OF THE COUNCIL

Although the Council of Presidents had the task of guiding the Council's work, with an authority ensured not only by the Pope's mandate but also by its broad membership, still, as was seen on October 13, it did not seem able to play an effective mediating role. Its first meeting came after the tumultuous second day of the Council, when it discussed duties and rights (Felici also took part in the meeting). It seemed already clear to Urbani that "the presidents were unprepared."[151]

At the Council of Presidents' second meeting, on October 15, 1962, some basic problems were raised. One was how to organize the work of the Council, that is, whether to follow the order of the schemas sent to the fathers during the summer or to put the schema on the liturgy first. The presidents were divided, with the majority in favor of discussing the liturgy (Tisserant, Liénart, Frings, Ruffini, Alfrink) and a minority against (Gilroy, Caggiano, Spellman, Pla y Daniel). At this same meeting the presidents decided to assign to Liénart the preparation of the text of the message to "humanity," to ban applause, to give technical information in the hall in the national languages as well as in Latin. John XXIII's view of the presidential council, according to what he wrote in his diary, was not negative: the meeting had been a "good" one, probably because of the decision to discuss the liturgy.[152]

But the problem remained of the organ that was to direct the Council. With the creation of the Secretariat for Extraordinary Affairs the Pope had already acknowledged that the Council of Presidents was not the only directive entity. As early as the third meeting of the presidents a conflict of competencies emerged between the Council of Presidents and the Secretariat for Extraordinary Affairs. Tisserant read the Secretariat's report on the norms for the discipline of the Council, a report already approved by John XXIII.[153] Felici did not attend the meetings of the Secretariat, despite the fact that he was the liaison between the Secretariat and the presidential Council. In a note in the margin of the minutes of the Council of Presidents Felici remarked: "There were, however, frequent disagreements between the presidential council and the Secretariat for Extraordinary Affairs; this often caused confusion."[154] Ruffini criticized the confusion between the two entities; in fact, at the third meet-

---

[151] Ibid., October 15, 1962.
[152] *Agende*, October 15, 1962.
[153] Report now published along with *DSiri*, 348-55.
[154] *AS* V/1, 21.

ing of the Presidents, he "vigorously demanded" that the competencies of the two be clearly defined so as to avoid conflicts. The presidential Council, however, was destined to see its role reduced; in fact, it held only two more meetings after the third (one to discuss a proposal similar to the one approved by the Secretariat; the other to accept John XXIII's decision with regard to the schema on revelation). There seems to have been no further meeting of the Council of Presidents after November 19.

In actual fact, the Secretariat for Extraordinary Affairs played a principal role in the direction of the Council. For example, its meeting on October 16 was held in the Pope's presence and in his library. Several problems had accumulated, such as the proposal of Suenens and Döpfner, seconded by Montini, to eliminate the Mass before the sessions and not to wear prelatial robes. After meeting with the Pope, they also met in the presence of the Secretary of State. Since no report of this was made, Siri's testimony is valuable:

> As usual, Suenens and Döpfner immediately want an audience: they are eager to influence the Council. Cicognani is unable to say no to their impromptu demand, and I, making my reluctance clear, go down with the others to the meeting room of the Secretariat of State. Another flood of requests: regulations, spiritual regulation (Suenens: a real obsession!), again the elimination of Holy Mass at the beginning of the sessions, except on Mondays. Montini would like this last to be decided immediately. Fortunately, the president gets off the point, and there is agreement only on calling for greater order at the sessions. Confalonieri is charged with drafting something to this effect.[155]

D. DYNAMICS OF A COUNCIL BEGINNING WITHOUT A PLAN?

The dynamics of the conciliar debates troubled the Secretariat for Extraordinary Affairs from its first meetings on. On October 19, Cicognani informed the assembled cardinals that the Pope had approved Bea's request but turned down the requests of Suenens and Döpfner regarding prelatial robes and the Mass. The latter were rather peripheral requests as compared with the decision to raise ecumenism as a problem at Vatican II (with a conciliar agency to see to it). The Secretariat for Extraordinary Affairs had to cope with the demand for a harmonious plan for Vatican II, a demand voiced first in Bea's memorandum and then in Montini's letter to the Secretary of State. Siri repulsed the attempts of

---

[155] See *DSiri*, October 17, 1962, 364.

the Archbishop of Milan and other cardinals along this line: "Cicognani goes away and I take over the presidency. With amiable words I arrange everything and reach the desired point: nothing definitive. I make the point that the Council can pass judgment only on limited matters. I do not understand how they can fail to realize that it is impossible to plan changes for a Council that has already begun."

Siri opposed the idea of changing the Secretariat into an organ for directing the Council and for preparing a plan for its work.[156] In the view of the other European cardinals the Council should not have to work in servile fashion on schemas drawn up by commissions under the control of the Curia; consequently, a new focal point for drawing up a plan had to be found. For the cardinal of Genoa, on the other hand, it was success that "nothing definitive" came out of the meetings of the Secretariat. The Council was important, but it was necessary to support the prepara-tory drafts and not to place excessive emphasis on an external directive role. On October 21, however, at an audience with John XXIII, Siri real-ized the place which the Secretariat for Extraordinary Affairs had in the Pope's vision. In fact, after having said that he was "edified" by the opposition of the Cardinal of Genoa to the requests of Suenens, Döpfner, and Montini for the elimination of Mass before the conciliar meetings, John XXIII explained his vision of the Secretariat in the working of the Council: "I realized that he intended the 'troublesome Secretariat' to be, as it were, the brain of the Council, because he is aware that the Coun-cil of Presidents is too much of a 'mixed grill.' But I let him know that our Secretariat is made up of *two* parts, which should put him on guard; and I advised him to have a very small group of personal consul-tants."[157]

In the view of Siri, as of Ottaviani and others, the duty of the Coun-cil fathers was to go along with the great stream of the Church's tradi-tion in theology and government, and to do it quickly and with brevity. Rome and the Curia were the best interpreters of that tradition. At most, the fathers should use their authority and experience to clarify and reformulate. While the activity of some leading figures at the Council, for example, some of the members of the Secretariat for Extraordinary Affairs, was interpreted as a determination to "pilot" the multitude of fathers, the "Romans" gave the impression of proceeding in a scattered fashion.

[156] Alberigo, "Concilio acefalo?" 202-4.
[157] *DSiri*, October 21, 1962, 366.

A week after the opening of Vatican II, Urbani observed that the first steps taken by the Council had included some mistakes in the conduct of the work on the part of the curial leadership. According to him, the reaction to the vote on the conciliar commissions should have been anticipated. In addition, anyone familiar with the *vota* of the fathers could see in them repeated, if polite, expressions of the problems residential bishops had with the governance of the Roman Curia and its impact on local affairs. The Patriarch of Venice wrote:

> The pope, wonderful in his addresses, especially to the non-Catholic observers, the journalists, and the diplomatic representatives; the General Secretariat, unprepared and confused, unable to control the assembly, and fully supported by the Council of Presidents, the latter itself lacking any cohesiveness and composed of persons well-known to be opposed to each other: Ruffini-Alfrink. Some currents are emerging for the first time. Naive to believe that the bishops have come to sprinkle holy water on what others have prepared. Psychological mistakes in proposing the old names and in circulating lists prepared by the Roman congregations. Impression prevalent among many fathers that apart from the Pope the Council has no responsible head — the Council of Presidents is at sea in the dark — that it has no definite plan, no detailed program, but is living from day to day. The choice of the liturgy as the first subject, for the reason that it is the easiest, suggests either a fear of tackling the substantial subjects or a desire to be obstructionist.... The appointment of undersecretaries, first four, then a fifth, seems to be an excellent corrective — as is the appointment of the Polish cardinal to the Secretariat for Extraordinary Affairs.[158]

Urbani, successor of Pope John in the patriarchate of Venice, had worked in Rome for many years and was well acquainted with the Roman Curia. Although a moderate, he could not fail to see the confusion amid which the Council was taking its first steps. If for Urbani, the Pope was the only point of reference, he knew that John XXIII could not dictate the entire mechanism to carry on of the work and that the assembly had won the right to make its own desires heard. Urbani also pointed out that two different trends were gradually taking shape among the fathers: "The trends are already forming: Curia and non-Curia, conservative integralists and progressive reformers; until now these words have only been in the newspapers, but there is a feeling in the air that they are not entirely inventions." Even Siri remarked in his conversation with John XXIII that the Secretariat for Extraordinary Affairs contained two "blocs" with different visions of the Council.

---

[158] *DUrbani*, November 18, 1962.

Did all this amount to an unseemly sight for a world that was following the work of Vatican II with some interest? If, as it seemed, the
Council was not to end with a single session, if the fathers wanted to
make their voices heard in the hall, this would lead to debates and oppositions. The work of the Council, therefore, was in large measure still to
be done, and subject to the dynamics of the assembly. Who would control the strings?

If the pope was the point of reference for the work of Vatican II, he
had no intention of acting as director of the Council's workings. John
XXIII had not exercised his role as head of the Holy See by acting as his
own Secretary of State, as Pius XII is said to have done. In the ordinary
government of the Church Roncalli gave general directions and made
good use of the people running things at the top of Catholicism, while he
himself concentrated on the extraordinary government, the highest manifestation of which was his convocation of the Council. John XXIII
believed in the Council and in the role which the bishops of the world
could play, along with the Pope, in the dynamics of the assemblies. If, as
in his opening allocution, he did not fail to express his deepest orientations, he wished the fathers to be able to express themselves freely.

While aware of this presence of the Pope in the life of the Council,
Montini's letter to Cicognani, Secretary of State, complained of the
absence of a coherent plan for the work. The plan that might be found in
the material prepared by the commissions under the direction of the
Curia seemed unsuitable to the Cardinal of Milan and to many other
fathers, which is why Montini proposed a plan for producing texts that
would speak of the renewal of the Church. Pope John did not have the
same interest in plans that his immediate successor had, nor did he have
the same sense of how to govern the Church that Montini had already
shown during his stay at the Secretariat of State. While the pope had his
own ideas and aspirations, he also believed that he had to let the bishops
do their work. This was the outlook he had earlier expressed at the meeting of the central commission and the subcommissions for the Synod of
Rome: "The possibilities of action do not always match one's desires
and will. But he consoled himself with the thought that he had always
faith in this plan of life: to let others act, to enable them to act, to prod
them to act."[159]

The holding of a Council was Pope John's great accomplishment. At
the outset of the Council's work he sketched the deeper perspectives

---

[159] Riccardi, *Il potere del papa*, 181.

within which the fathers were to act, and he saw to it that they would be able to conduct the Council themselves and be allowed to take up their own responsibilities. As a result, at the very outset of the Council an internal dialectic among the various positions began to take shape. The Roman position, which had Ottaviani as its point of reference, was one of those present in the Council hall, but it was no longer supreme. Unwilling to impose a plan on the Council from on high, Pope John believed instead that among the fathers there were ideas, problems, perspectives, conflicts, and experiences which should come to light as a result of a dialectic that in the end would produce results. The bishops also had to become acquainted with one another, because they did not have the slightest experience of links with bishops outside their own countries. The diaries and recollections of the fathers abound in signs of this growth of mutual familiarity. In the pages of Edelby's memoirs the stages of this familiarity are set down, as when, for example, on October 18, the Greek-Catholic prelate took part in a meeting of the African bishops, who asked him many questions about the Byzantine liturgy, which was completely unknown to them. The information gained did not fail to have its effects when the time came to discuss the schema on the liturgy.[160]

The dynamics of Vatican II began to operate even without guidance. Even the reception of the Pope's allocution varied widely. John XXIII himself knew that one sector of bishops "prefers to be silent" about his allocution. But instead of imposing anything, he had sought simply to grant freedom and reasons for speaking and thinking; he wrote in his notes: "It is I myself who ought to be most silent." In the Pope's eyes the Church was a complex reality — a "mystery," as it might be called in the language of theology — that cannot be reduced to a single traditional vision, however authoritative, or even to the Pope's vision of it. Thus John XXIII wrote in his diary a month after the beginning of the conciliar debates:

> Today also I listen with interest to all the voices. In large measure they are critical of the proposed schemas (Cardinal Ottaviani), for although these were drafted by many together, they reveal the dominant influence of the fixed ideas of one person and the persistence of a mentality that cannot free itself from the tone of a schoolroom lecture. The half-blindness in one eye casts a shadow on the vision of the whole. The reaction is a strong one, of course, sometimes too strong, but I think that good intentions will prevail in the end.[161]

[160] *JEdelby*, October 18, 1962, ff. 26-28.
[161] *Agende*, November 19, 1962.

CHAPTER II

THE COUNCIL GETS UNDERWAY

GERALD P. FOGARTY

I. FIRST CONTACTS AMONG BISHOPS AND THEOLOGIANS

Prior to the Council, the bishops had received preliminary schemas on the liturgy, on the unity of the Church, and on social communications drafted respectively by the Commission on the Liturgy, the Commission on the Oriental Church, and the Secretariat for Communications Media. Printed with these had also come four schemas prepared by the Theological Commission: on the sources of revelation, on preserving the deposit of faith, on the Christian moral order, and on chastity, virginity, marriage and the family.[1]

More than one participant in the Council noted the amount of material they were expected to read. Joseph Ratzinger later commented that while "the preparatory commissions had undoubtedly worked hard, . . . their diligence was somewhat distressing. Seventy schemas had been produced, enough to fill 2,000 pages of folio size. This was more than double the quantity of texts produced by all previous councils put together." In the beginning, he noted, "there was a certain discomforting feeling that the whole enterprise might come to nothing more than a mere rubber-stamping of decisions already made, thus impeding rather than fostering the renewal needed in the Catholic Church."[2]

---

[1] *Schemata Constitutionum et Decretorum de quibus disceptabitur in Concilii sessionibus. Series prima* (Vatican City, 1962); see *History*, I, 433-41. Only one of the four "dogmatic" constitutions in this first volume, the one on the sources of revelation, would be discussed in the first period, while the other three, "non-dogmatic" documents were all discussed. A second volume of schemas was distributed to the Council fathers only on November 23, 1962: *Schemata Constitutionum et Decretorum de quibus disceptabitur in Concilii sessionibus. De Ecclesia et de B. Maria Virgine. Series secunda* (Vatican City, 1962); the note of presentation bore the date November 10. Of these two only the text on the Church would be discussed in the first period.

[2] Joseph Ratzinger, *Theological Highlights of Vatican II* (New York, 1966), 5.

A. INITIAL ANXIETIES

Anyone in the Church who had great hopes for the Council experienced a sense of dismay when he encountered the results of the work of the preparatory commissions, especially the doctrinal schemas. Disappointment and dissatisfaction were particularly widespread in Central European circles and among many missionary bishops who had some contact with them. As Cardinal Alfredo Ottaviani himself would admit when he introduced the schema on the sources of revelation, among those who had sent in comments during the summer before the Council opened, there were "many" who had reacted negatively to the doctrinal schemas, particularly because of their lack of a pastoral character.[3] Reflecting this climate, *Études* noted, for example, how "in the judgment of many bishops, the theological schemas, especially the one on scripture and tradition, do not in fact correspond to the spirit of *aggiornamento* called for in [the Pope's] opening speech to the Council. . . . But it has to be recognized that the majority of bishops are not interested in these problems; unless they are theologians by profession, they have trouble in understanding the importance of the problems. In these conditions it would be desirable to postpone at least these schemas to another session."[4]

At the beginning, while many bishops and theologians were unwilling to work with the doctrinal schemas, they did not always agree on what to do about them. The Germans wanted to substitute a single alternative schema to replace all four of the schemas prepared by the Theological Commission. Although also negative, the reaction of French bishops and theologians was less rigid. Many bishops, especially, though not exclusively, non-Europeans, were annoyed that what they had thought would be the main point of the Council, the doctrine on the Church and the powers of bishops, did not appear on the agenda.[5] This was no minor complaint. Within the Secretariat for Extraordinary Affairs, which was quickly although at first imperceptibly to assume a central role in the conduct of the Council's work,[6] Cardinal Suenens, followed with grow-

---

[3] See *History*, I, 441-51. While the topic of "the pastoral" was raised by a bloc of German, Dutch, and French bishops, with significant agreement from Latin American and from "missionary" bishops, the terms of the problem were not yet clear. It would be the Pope's opening speech, *Gaudet Mater Ecclesia*, that would provide a reference for a common concept of "the pastoral," at least during the first period of the Council.

[4] *Études*, October 1962, 262.

[5] *JCongar*, October 21, reports the mood of the Brazilian bishops.

[6] G. Alberigo, "Concilio acefalo? L'evoluzione degli Organi direttivi del Vaticano II," in *Attese*, 193-238.

ing conviction by Cardinal Montini, led the way in arguing that the theme of the Church should be the unifying principle of the whole work of the Council.[7] To Cardinal Siri, however, it was clearly impossible "in that state of affairs to draw up such a plan in any proper order."[8] Even two weeks after the Council had begun, the same Secretariat could only express the desire that the schema on the Church be distributed to the fathers,[9] which, however, would happen only after November 10. The decision that the first of the doctrinal schemas to be discussed, after the one on the liturgy, would be the one on the sources of revelation, had already been communicated on November 7.[10] And because the text on the Church inexplicably was still not available,[11] the desires of the bishops could not be met, and they thus found themselves required to engage in the rather technical discussion of the sources of revelation.[12]

---

[7] See L.-J. Suenens, "A Plan for the Whole Council," in *Vatican II Revisited*, 88-105; and his remarks in *Giovanni Battista Montini arcivescovo di Milano e il Concilio Ecumenico Vaticano II. Preparazione e primo periodo* (Brescia, 1985), 178-87.

[8] *DSiri*, October 19, 1962, 349.

[9] *DSiri*, October 26, 1962, 351: "With regard to the order for discussion of the schemas, the Cardinals, recalling the need already expressed that the work should follow an organic and logical plan, proposed that the schema on the Church be distributed to the conciliar fathers as soon as possible, since that schema's topics constitute the principal and central theme of the various plans discussed."

[10] *AS* I/2, 291. The decision had already been made by the Council of Presidents on October 15, 1962, on the basis of the first series of schemas sent to the fathers. The decision was not unanimous. Arguing that the discussion of the liturgy would encounter fewer difficulties ("this schema would be discussed more expeditiously"), Tisserant, Liénart, Frings, Ruffini, and Alfrink barely prevailed over Gilroy, Caggiano, Spellman and Pla y Daniel. (One member of the Council, Cardinal Caggiano, was absent.) The decision was made not to follow the order of schemas in the printed volume sent to the fathers, but to begin with the schema on the liturgy, "after which the schema on the sources of revelation will be discussed" (*AS* V/1, 17-18). It is odd to see Ruffini agreeing with the Central European bloc. It is also odd that this decision was largely unknown until November 7. As late as November 6 Bishop Volk thought it more probable that the *De Ecclesia* and not the *De Fontibus* would be discussed after the liturgy (see *TSemmelroth*, November 6). Is it possible that Frings did not communicate the Council's decision? Or is this a sign of the total absence of direction in this phase?

[11] In his *Relatio Secretarii Commissionis Conciliaris "de doctrina fidei et morum,"* December 16, 1962, Tromp says that it was only on October 26 that he received the text, which, along with the schema on the Blessed Virgin, had been sent to the Latinists, that a final examination had been made (by whom?) of the corrections the Latinists had introduced, and that the whole was sent at the beginning of November to the General Secretariat for transmission to the printers. But it is also true that the Subcommission on Amendments had sent its suggestions for the *De Ecclesia* and the *De Beata* to the Theological Commission in June 1962. Any delaying tactics in the publication of the text would seem, then, to be excluded.

[12] On October 26 the Secretariat of the African Bishops sent the Council of Presidents a *votum* that after the liturgy, the first schema to be discussed should be the one on the

B. THE COMPLAINTS OF THE THEOLOGIANS

Aware of the age-old history of the literary genre of the *Gravamina nationis germanicae*, which, beginning in 1455, expressed German discontent with the way Rome was governing the Church, Semmelroth noted in his diary on November 10 that he had been working "tirelessly . . . on the redaction of the *gravamina* against the first schema put together by Rahner." But others besides Rahner were already engaged in the same task. In contrast to the later alternative schemas, these "annotations" to the schemas prepared by the preparatory Theological Commission did not represent a positive project but were intended to convince the bishops that the official schemas were inadmissible.

1. *Karl Rahner*

Since the end of 1961 Cardinal König had asked Rahner to examine the texts that the Central Preparatory Commission, of which König was a member, was reviewing for eventual submission to the Council.[13] On January 4, 1962, the Jesuit theologian sent the Cardinal of Vienna a first series of critical comments and proposals. The contacts continued throughout the first half of that year, and in April König asked Rahner to serve as a conciliar theologian for himself and for the Austrian and German bishops.[14] Rahner's comments were usually very severe, an effort to alert König.

As soon as it was decided that the Council would examine the *De Fontibus*, Rahner prepared a *Disquisitio brevis de Schemate "De fontibus revelationis."* [15] How widely this text was distributed is difficult to say; Rahner spoke of 400 copies.[16] In contrast to his later alternative

Church; P. Levillain, *La mécanique politique de Vatican II* (Paris 1975), 234; *JCongar*, October 21, documents the similar desire of the Brazilian bishops.

[13] See *History*, I, 477.

[14] "Karl Rahner in seiner mürrischen, aber herzlichen Art": Kardinal König über seinen Konzilsberater," *Entschluss* 43 (June 1988), 4-34, where several documents are abstracted. The texts were later edited by H. Vorgrimler in *Karl Rahner. Sehnsucht nach dem Geheimnisvollen Gott. Profil-Bilder-Texte* (Freiburg 1990), 95-165; see also R. Siebenrock, "Meine schlimmsten Erwartungen sind weit übertroffen," in *Beitrag*, 121-39.

[15] A copy may be found in the Vatican II Archives, ISR.

[16] Letter to Vorgrimler, November 12, 1962, the day the text was distributed. But this refers only to an initial action. On November 17 Semmelroth's diary speaks of yet another 500 copies, at the request especially of the American bishops. This shows that the number of bishops who wanted greater clarity increased as the debate on *De fontibus* heated up.

schema, he was careful here to use a theology accessible to the bishops. Rahner's text was in three parts: an introduction on the nature of conciliar texts and in particular texts of a pastoral council; general observations; particular observations. Rahner's criticisms — here he differs from Schillebeeckx — explicitly invited the fathers of the Council to set the schema aside ("if the Fathers agree, this text can simply be omitted") or to substitute another.[17]

2. Edward Schillebeeckx

Similarly in Holland Cardinal Alfrink had already involved a group of theologians in the examination of the texts presented to the Central Commission.[18] On September 17, 1962, sixteen Dutch-speaking missionary bishops gathered along with Bishops Bluyssen and Bekkers at the latter's residence in 's-Hertogenbosch.[19] Convinced that to accept the preparatory schemas would be fatal for the Council and the Church and that it would be useless to send their criticisms and suggestions to the Council's General Secretariat, they looked for a way to enter into direct contact with the world's episcopate. For this reason they decided to ask Dominican theologian E. Schillebeeckx for critical comments on the schemas, which would then be distributed to the conciliar fathers once they arrived in Rome. By the end of September Schillebeeckx had prepared his comments, which were then translated into Latin and English and mimeographed in anonymous form, without even being reviewed, because of lack of time.[20] Encouraged by John XXIII's opening speech, "which revived hope that the Council would succeed,"[21] the Dutch, thanks to the efforts of Jan Brouwers, secretary of the bishops' conference, distributed around 2000 copies of the *Animadversiones in primam seriem*

---

[17] For the doctrinal content of this *Disquisitio*, see chapter 5 below.

[18] See J. van Laarhoven, "In medio ecclesiae . . . Alfrink op het Tweede Vaticaans Concilie," in *Alfrink en de Kerk 1951-1976* (Baarn, 1976), 12-33; and J. Grootaers, "Une restauration de la théologie de l'épiscopat. Contribution du card. Alfrink à la préparation de Vatican II," in *Glaube im Prozess. Christsein nach dem II. Vatikanum* (Freiburg, 1984), 812.

[19] See J. A. Brouwers, "Derniers préparatifs et première session. Activités conciliaires en coulisse," in *Vatican II commence*, 353-68.

[20] This may be the reason why they are not "completely correct," as Semmelroth notes in his diary (November 11, 1962), probably referring to the statement that the encyclical *Humani generis* had followed Trent on the question of the "two sources." This is mistaken; the encyclical explicitly speaks of "sources of revelation" (DS 3883).

[21] Brouwers, "Derniers préparatifs," 356.

schematum constitutionum et decretorum de quibus disceptabitur in Concilii sessionibus.[22]

Schillebeeckx restricted himself to the most important questions. He began with a statement of method: it would be desirable for the Council, "following the example of Trent, to refrain from settling questions still debated among theologians, to avoid ways of arguing and of speaking that smack of the school, and to proclaim the Good News 'eagerly and positively.'"[23] These would become commonplaces in all the critical statements during the conciliar debate on the schema. Schillebeeckx lamented in particular that the schema on the "sources" omitted a prior treatment "on public revelation and on the Catholic faith" and that it made no reference to the proposals of bishops and of universities, something which had been done by the Liturgical Commission. Schillebeeckx suggested that this omission indicated partiality on the part of the Theological Commission. In his mind, the theory of two sources espoused by the schema was a function of the assertion that there are revealed truths not found in the scriptures but only in the oral tradition, a position that in turn is possible only on the assumption that revelation is nothing but a "communication of conceptual truths." Coherent with this presupposition was another implicit assumption, the nearly exclusive privilege accorded to revelation "in words" to the complete neglect of the revelation that occurs "in reality" itself.[24] It was not by chance, then, that the schema limited tradition itself to preaching, to the faith of believers, and to the Church's practice, while ignoring the tradition of the living *realities* of salvation and suggesting an absolute separation between scripture and tradition. Schillebeeckx's observations did not exclude the possibility that the text could be emended.

---

[22] See *History*, I, 447-48. The Latin translation is a text of forty-seven pages. The English translation, which does not exactly match the Latin and appears more accurate, is fifty-seven pages long, a difference explained largely by the type used. Jan A. Brouwers distributed the text, often by taxi, to the various residences of bishops. He found a good deal of interest among the European bishops and even more among the Africans and Americans. Some responses to his visit were more ambiguous. While one bishop residing at the Irish College said that he wanted nothing to do with "modernistic writings," a few days later an Irish bishop came to the Dutch College to ask for thirty-three copies of the text for his colleagues. A little later Brouwers received similar requests from Polish, Australian, and New Zealand bishops and from the missionary bishops of Oceania. Brouwers also established contacts with the Italian, Spanish, and Portuguese episcopal conferences, with the Oriental Catholic Churches, and with the bishops of Japan, Korea, Formosa, Vietnam, and Thailand (see Brouwers, "Derniers préparatifs," 355-58).

[23] For some reason the third of these premises is missing in the English text.

[24] The Latin text distinguished between "real" and "verbal" revelation, the English between "revelation-in-word" and "revelation-in-reality."

His analysis of the schema *De deposito fidei pure custodiendo* was more diffuse; it rejected the exclusively conceptual problematic, which arbitrarily equated "objectivity" with "abstraction and universality." This fault also largely vitiated the third schema, *De ordine morali christiano*, which would have to be rewritten "from beginning to end." As for the *De castitate, matrimonio, familia, virginitate*, Schillebeeckx granted that the Council would have to deal with chastity but also noted that other even more serious questions, such as war, were not discussed. The Dominican theologian reserved his only unqualified praise for the schema *De Liturgia*. Finally, for the *De instrumentis communicationis* he wanted a more modest language and tone; as for the *De unitate ecclesiae*, if it was good that it addressed the ecumenical question, its fault was that it restricted its interest to the Oriental Churches.

Schillebeeckx's effectiveness in identifying the weak points in the preparatory schemas was undeniable. Even when unable to appreciate all the nuances, the bishops who read his *Animadversiones*, distributed as they were with the clear even if non-official approval of the Dutch bishops, could not but be struck by the force of his arguments or by the suggestion that the Council's work should begin with the schema *De Liturgia*. His was also the most widely distributed text.[25]

C. CONTACTS AMONG THE BISHOPS

From the first days of the arrival of the bishops in Rome, mutual exchanges became possible whose importance should not be underestimated in the process that would lead to the new doctrinal balance achieved at Vatican II. The bishops at first did not appreciate this new and common awareness that would constitute the most important element of the conciliar event; their dominant initial sense was one of immense, almost impossible, work, of frustration, of solitude, and, at times, of confusion.

But the mere fact that contacts and encounters never experienced before were now possible counts more than reflective awareness of the fact. To explain the rapid development of events in the first period, then, the simple material fact of the conciliar event needs to be taken into account. Msgr. Marty had already recognized this the preceding April: "For decades we have lost a great deal from not seeing one another. We

[25] Brouwers, "Derniers préparatifs," 359-60.

will have to have regular meetings. And Msgr. Marty thinks that we are entering upon a conciliar era."[26] The event of the Council, their coming together, which theologians like to explain in its distinctive reality as a privileged presence of the Spirit, found concrete expression as bishops began to be liberated from a sense of frustration and to see the possibility of deeds that they would not have dared before. For a century they had been split from one another, each bishop in direct relation with Rome but with little sense of his horizontal links with other bishops. It was this link that would be theologically defined by the Council in terms of collegiality as a constitutive element of the Church's structure. As personalities especially alert to the deep dimensions of the Church, such as Congar and Semmelroth, would note in their diaries, episcopal collegiality began to be operative immediately, even before it came to be formulated. The bishops discovered by assembling and communicating that new and previously unheard of attitudes were created.[27]

But besides this, bishops would also begin to be "reimmersed" into a new sense of the people of God. The first weeks of the Council provided some, if not the majority, of the episcopates the opportunity for a "recovery," which might more exactly be called a "reception," by which they became aware of the great progress within the Church of the new approach to the Bible that had become more and more common among Catholics. In addition, their theologians helped the bishops to update themselves on the general progress of theology, from christology to ecclesiology.[28]

But this "evolution" occurred among the theologians as much as among the bishops, as can be illustrated in the regrets of a man like Congar, who frankly admitted that during the preparatory phase he had not thought there was much that he could do. On the one hand, he had seen himself "blocked" by the consensus that the antepreparatory *vota* of the bishops seemed to manifest. For example, with regard to the text of the *De beata Maria virgine*, discussed on November 22, 1961, he notes that in fact it contains "the minimum possible . . . , since so many bishops have even asked for definitions of the co-redemption of Mary the Medi-

---

[26] *JCongar*, 29.

[27] See *TSemmelroth*, November 14, for the changes in the Canadian bishops.

[28] See *JCongar*, 66 and 170, where he speaks of the change in the American bishops as a result of their contacts with theologians. The exegete Raymond Brown and then "two American priest-theologians of the bishops" tell him of this change and stress in particular the role of the conferences given by Passionist exegete Barnabas Ahern. This was not an isolated case; the German bishops scheduled weekly contacts, and the episcopates of Latin America, Africa, and Asia were particularly active.

atrix, Mary Queen, etc.!"[29] On the other hand, he applied to himself as much as to the bishops his remarks about the importance of milieu and about the decisive changes in the "general climate" from the preparatory phase to the Council.

> The general climate does a great deal: a pastoral climate, a climate of freedom, a climate of dialogue, a climate of openness. Then [during the preparatory period] it was the climate of the "Holy Office" and of the professors at Roman colleges. We were neutralized by a tacit but powerful code, by a very powerful social pressure to which we did not react until the point had been reached when we would have had to call everything into question.[30]

The bishops soon learned that the method Liénart had suggested for nominating members of the commissions was an apt way to prepare for the general congregations. The Spanish led the way. After drawing up their nominations for the commissions, they voted to meet on a regular basis and named three bishops to act as liaison with other episcopal conferences.[31] The Italian bishops met as a conference for the first time in history. Reporting the significance of this to his people back in Milan, Montini said it was "an historic date and evidenced a new canonical situation for the Church in Italy, preparing new developments in the consciousness and action of the Italian episcopal college." At a second meeting on October 27 at the Domus Mariae, chaired by Siri, the six cardinals and about three hundred archbishops and bishops recognized "the very great usefulness of such meetings" and voted to meet weekly.[32] Other national hierarchies were doing the same thing. Episcopal collegiality was clearly on the fathers' agenda, even if it was not yet under discussion.

On October 21 the American bishops met at the North American College and formally established a general committee to assist and coordinate their participation in the conciliar debates. One week later, Arch-

---

[29] *JCongar*, 51.

[30] *JCongar*, November 4, 1962. In this context, the attitude of the Louvain scholars, like Cerfaux and Philips, is indicative. From the beginning Tromp was concerned to have them take part in the preparatory work, during which they do not seem to have expressed any basic opposition. But their attitude changed during the first period of the Council. Philips began to act as Suenens' "operative," and Cerfaux established his own little independent center of studies on the *De fontibus*, for which he had J. Dupont and B. Rigaux come to Rome (*JDupont*, November 3, 1962).

[31] R. B. Kaiser, *Pope, Council and World: The Story of Vatican II* (New York, 1963), 120.

[32] *L'Osservatore Romano*, October 31, 1962, cited in Caprile, II, 67.

bishop Thomas A. Boland of Newark, chairman of this committee, summoned a meeting of the U.S. hierarchy. Archbishop John Krol spoke on
the conciliar procedures; Archbishop Paul Hallinan summarized the
work of the Liturgical Commission; and Father Frederick McManus
reviewed papal documents to show that the schema was in accord with
papal teaching.[33] The Americans then met virtually every week. While
they were clearly becoming organized and were taking advantage of the
presence of the experts, they spoke little during the first session. They
still tended to be dominated by the conservative influence of Cardinal
Spellman, one of the ten council presidents, and of Cardinal James F.
McIntyre of Los Angeles. One of the few who began to emerge as a
voice free of the domination of this conservative influence was Hallinan
(Atlanta), who spoke forcefully in favor of the schema on the liturgy.[34]

Meanwhile, other conferences were adopting similar organizations for
the Council. In Africa, for example, the fifteen conferences that either
had already been formed earlier or had come into existence for the purpose of suggesting names for the commissions formed a Pan-African
Secretariat under the presidency of Cardinal Rugambwa.[35] Such organization meant that at the general congregations one bishop could be designated to speak in behalf of a national group or of members of a
national group. The bishops were taking it upon themselves to stream-
line the procedures of the Council.

An effort was also undertaken to establish links among the episcopal
conferences. On November 9, representatives of episcopal conferences
began a series of meetings at the Domus Mariae, the residence of a number of Brazilian bishops, including Helder Câmara, the secretary of the
Conference of Latin American Bishops (CELAM). These meetings
reflected a cross section of the bishops from Latin America, Africa,
Asia, Canada, Europe, and the United States.[36]

D. PARA-CONCILIAR ENCOUNTERS

While German and French theologians agreed about the inadequacy
of the four doctrinal schemas, they began to develop strategies that, if

[33] Boland to "Your Excellency," October 25, 1962 (ACUA, Primeau papers).

[34] Xavier Rynne, *Letters from Vatican City. Vatican Council II (First Session)* (New
York, 1968), 119; see also Thomas J. Shelley, *Paul J. Hallinan, First Archbishop of
Atlanta* (Wilmington, 1989), 163-206.

[35] Carlo Falconi, *Pope John and the Ecumenical Council: A Diary of the Second Vatican Council, September-December 1962* (Cleveland, 1964), 189.

[36] "Domus Mariae," November 11, 13, 20, 1962 (ACUA, Primeau papers).

not quite opposed, were different enough to prevent them to the last from forming a compact front.[37]

1. German Initiatives

From their first days in Rome, the German bishops, with the agreement of Volk and of Frings, began to develop a strategy that was inspired by Karl Rahner, the theological adviser to König of Vienna and Döpfner of Munich. Rahner was living at the German College in Rome, the residence also of Volk and of Fr. Otto Semmelroth.[38] As the latter described it, on October 12 Rahner explained the broad lines of a strategy to "substitute a new schema for the present schemas of the Theological Commission. He is thinking of four parts, two on dogma and two on moral theology. To some degree the schema has to include topics found in the present schemas; but the whole text has to be shortened and presented in an entirely different way, more positively and organically."[39] To prepare the section on moral theology, the names mentioned were those of J. Fuchs, B. Häring, and J. Hirschmann; later W. Schüller of Frankfurt would become involved, making several journeys to Rome

[37] As early as September 27, Hans Küng, a young Tübingen theologian, just becoming known, visited Congar in Paris to seek his support for a strategy with regard to the four doctrinal schemas (the one on the Church was not yet known). Küng and several German theologians agreed on the need "to reject and not to correct them. If only corrected, they will remain substantially what they are, expressions of a school theology, that of the Roman schools. The public and, because of the media, half of the clergy will regard them as definitions of faith. This will mean a hardening in several ways, and it does not offer real possibilities for dialogue with contemporary thought. For there to be a chance of rejecting them, Küng says, we have to prevent these dogmatic schemas from being the *first* ones proposed; that would risk their being discussed under bad conditions and hastily. We should, then, see to it that the Council begins with the more practical schemas." Congar's reply expressed his fear that an isolated initiative by theologians would inevitably give "the impression of a para-council of theologians, determined to influence the real council of bishops." Although Congar and Küng did prepare the text of a letter to be sent to bishops, the initiative was not taken any further. See *JCongar*, September 27, 1962.

[38] Because of this proximity to Rahner and Volk, Semmelroth's diary is the best source available for reconstructing the events linked to the German strategy. Volk coordinated the Germans' theological work and the contacts with bishops and theologians from Central Europe.

[39] *TSemmelroth*, October 12. The schemas, which the Germans wanted to gather into a single schema with two parts, dogmatic and moral, were the texts on the sources of revelation, on the deposit of faith, on the moral order, and on chastity, marriage, family, and virginity. Initially, then, the German strategy did not include the schema on the Church, not yet known to them; later, however, an alternative schema on the Church would be prepared by A. Grillmeier, K. Rahner, and J. Ratzinger and distributed in December 1962.

for that purpose. But from the beginning it was difficult to get French-speaking theologians involved.[40]

On the morning of October 15, Volk, Rahner, and Semmelroth gathered at the German college for a discussion of the new alternative schema. They were joined by Frings's theologian, Joseph Ratzinger, who they discovered had already "written in Latin a first and basic chapter of a new schema which we liked very much. It simply has to be used as the initial section. Rahner, who also wrote a chapter of his own, will make typed copies of it so that we can discuss it tomorrow and the day after. Bishop Volk is also insisting that the themes of redeemed humanity in the world (peace, joy, hope) and the eschatological dimension also be included."[41] Two German projects were thus envisaged: the first would be based on the reflections of Rahner and Ratzinger, while the second, which was to be a preface to all the doctrinal schemas, apparently was to be written by Volk himself. Of these, Volk's project was soon given up, perhaps for political reasons.[42] Volk presented it at the first joint meeting with a French group. Semmelroth at one point preferred it to the preface to the Rahner/Ratzinger schema, which Congar had prepared; but in fact it never went beyond this restricted group.[43] There remained only the Rahner/Ratzinger project.

2. Meetings between the French and Germans

On October 19 an effort began to gain a wider audience for the German project. At the Mater Dei house, Volk organized a larger meeting, now including in particular, but not exclusively, French bishops and theologians.[44] The bishops present were Volk, Reuss, Bengsch, Elchinger, Weber, Schmitt, Garrone, Guerry, and Ancel; the theologians were Rahner, de Lubac, Daniélou, Grillmeier, Semmelroth, Rondet, Labourdette, Congar, Chenu, Schillebeeckx, Feiner, Ratzinger, Philips, Fransen, and

[40] In a conference at Santa Marta, organized by the Coadjutor Bishop of Dijon, Msgr. Charles de la Brousse, H. de Lubac warned the eight French bishops present against scattered criticisms of the schemas and against writing several counter-schemas that might compete with one another.

[41] *TSemmelroth*, October 15.

[42] It may be that the strategy to gain French support for the political tactics of the German bishops made it seem inopportune for the Germans to have a monopoly in the preparation of alternative schemas.

[43] *TSemmelroth*, October 21: "I pressed Bishop Volk also to prepare his schema. I would have translated it into Latin. Some points in his schema are better expressed than in Congar's. Above all, his schema is more kergymatic."

[44] The best accounts of this meeting are in the journals of Congar and Semmelroth.

Küng. The group was rather diverse and open. While Rahner was careful to include the Dominican Labourdette in the smaller working group
that would be formed to implement decisions,[45] he was unwilling to
move toward the Holy Office's group and thus excluded H. Schauf.[46] As
for the group's representative character, besides the Flemish theologians
Schillebeeckx and Fransen, there was the important Louvain theologian,
G. Philips. Encouraged by Suenens, Philips had already begun to rewrite
the schema on the Church, using for this purpose, since the final text had
not yet been distributed, an earlier draft he had received as a member of
the preparatory Theological Commission. The meeting thus brought
together for the first time some of the important representatives of the
thinkers who were advising the Central European bishops.

As Congar was to write, in a three-hour discussion, there will obviously be a whole series of nuances. But the differences were more than
nuances. Volk began by reading a sort of project for a statement that
would present the situation of the Christian in the world today and offer
a Christ-centered history of salvation in its anthropological, social, and
cosmological import. This was then completed by a largely similar proposal of Daniélou. The discussion that followed resulted in the decision
to write texts to be substituted for the official schemas. Despite this
common conclusion, the strategies were different and would remain different. This is how Congar saw them:

> Broadly speaking, the Germans are of a mind: 1) to reject the proposed
> dogmatic schemas (that is, the four already distributed, not the one on the
> Church); 2) to write a *preface* kerygmatic in content and form, rather in the
> style of Msgr. Volk's project; 3) to present it through the Commission on
> Extraordinary Affairs.[47] The French (Garrone, Guerry, Ancel) instead are

[45] *JCongar*, October 19: "At the last minute, Rahner invited Labourdette." But compare the note in Chenu's diary, October 19: "It was Garrone who asked that Fr. Labourdette come." In turn, Labourdette was uneasy at being involved in an initiative that was
calling into question his loyalty to the "quite different circle" to which he belonged; he
saw his role as one of "making links" (*JLabourdette*, October 19).

[46] See Rahner's letter to Vorgrimler, October 19: "Schmaus will not be there because
he's gone back to Germany; and we didn't invite Schauf" (see Herbert Vorgrimler,
Understanding Karl Rahner: An Introduction to His Life and Thought [New York, 1986],
155).

[47] This clearly showed a concern to work within the conciliar rules in order to get an
alternative project admitted that was both very problematic procedurally and foreign to
the mental universe of most bishops, even those French bishops who instead wanted to
follow a softer line. Interestingly, a note in Tucci's diary shows that even after the fall of
the schema *De Fontibus*, the evening of November 21, Congar expressed his conviction
that the schema "could be revised in a way that would satisfy everyone" (*DTucci*,
November 21, 1962).

thinking: 1) through very vigorous interventions by bishops from the main countries to convince the assembly that the schemas do not correspond at all to the pastoral goal of the Council defined by the Pope again in his opening speech, which ought to be the Council's charter; 2) after this, to get permission to revise the existing schemas in a kerygmatic and pastoral perspective. For this it would be good to have a text to propose.[48]

In the end it was decided to form a very small group of theologians to prepare substitute texts that would then be discussed in a larger group.[49] It seems also to have been decided that alongside the preface of Volk there would also be one by Daniélou. (In the end, however, neither of them would write this preface.)

When the smaller group met on October 21, Congar, Labourdette, and Daniélou represented the French, and Volk, Rahner, Semmelroth, and Ratzinger the Germans. Congar presented a draft of a preface and then, as he himself noted, "we discussed which one to choose: Msgr. Volk's, Fr. Daniélou's, or mine. In the end mine was chosen, and I was given the task of rewriting it in fifteen pages or so by next Sunday. In turn Ratzinger and Rahner, at Cardinal König's request, would work on the topics of the four doctrinal schemas; Fr. Daniélou is doing the same thing for Msgr. Veuillot."[50] From this point on, within the Central European group two alternate texts were being prepared: Congar's preface, which was supposed to clarify the spirit and context of the doctrinal texts of Vatican II, and a comprehensive doctrinal schema to take the place of the four official schemas (although only the first two were here in question).

But problems remained, above all the procedural questions: how to get the Council to accept these "external" documents and, should this effort fail, what the line of last resort would be. There was a further question, not addressed by this small group: how to redo the schema on the Church? It would be in terms of this text that the only tactic that would prove effective emerged; the one adopted by Suenens and Philips, which eventually involved also Montini's theologian, Msgr. Carlo Colombo.[51] Instead of writing an alternate schema, they would

---

[48] *JCongar*, October 19.

[49] The members of the group were Rahner, Daniélou, Ratzinger, and Congar, but the membership was rather fluid. As we have seen, Rahner in the end invited Labourdette and, a few days later, Semmelroth. It seems to have been taken for granted that Volk would also be a part of this group (*TSemmelroth*, October 21).

[50] Apart from the attribution to König of the alternative schema on doctrine, these remarks of Congar agree with those of Semmelroth.

[51] Among the theologians the Philips-Colombo tandem played the role of supporting

readjust the official schema to make it acceptable to everyone. This strategy's more general implications for the conciliar agenda were suggested in presentations made by Suenens and Montini at the meeting of the Secretariat for Extraordinary Affairs on October 19, a day after Philips had spoken of it to Congar in more technical terms as a way of preparing a more acceptable schema on the Church.[52]

Congar's notes for October 21, quoted above, with their reference to Daniélou's independent activity, show that Volk's group did not have much support apart from the Germans. When the French bishops met at S. Luigi dei Francesi on October 24, the discussion was on other wave lengths. Two opposing lines formed: the first and more rigid one, although favoring the "pastoral" perspective of John XXIII, claimed that they had to start with the official texts; the other, more ambitious, line was the one expressed by Msgr. Villot: anything was possible, including the rejection of the schemas proposed by the Theological Commission.[53]

The debate on the liturgy was to begin on October 22. Six days earlier, four of the most important members of the preparatory Liturgical Commission, Wagner, Pascher, Jungmann and Martimort, met to prepare amendments to the schema on the liturgy.[54] Jungmann had already given Karl Rahner a memorandum proposing corrections to the schema, and Martimort had already circulated a parallel but independent set of observations that repeated points of view already expressed in the preparatory commission. At the initiative of the French bishop, Elchinger, some bishops and experts, particularly from Central Europe, began to meet at Mater Dei. The bishops included Bengsch from Berlin; the Dutchmen Bekkers and Bluyssen; the Germans Volk, Nordhues, Reuss, and Schäufele; and the Frenchmen Martin and Pailleur. Among the theologians were Jungmann, Wagner, Pascher, Martimort, Gy, Jenny, De Jong, Semmelroth, and Schillebeeckx.[55]

Sometime before the debate in the Council began, Frederick McManus, professor of canon law at the Catholic University of Amer-

what the Suenens-Montini tandem was attempting within the Secretariat for Extraordinary Affairs.

[52] See *JCongar*, October 18, where he also gives Philip's outline.

[53] On this matter Congar's diary contradicts what is reported by Levillain, *La mécanique*, 242.

[54] *TJungmann*, October 17.

[55] Information taken from the section "Dietro le quinte del dibattito conciliare," in M. Paiano's study, in press, *Genesi storica della costituzione conciliare Sacrosanctum concilium*.

ica, a member of the preparatory Commission on the Liturgy and a *peritus* to the conciliar commission, informed Hallinan, the one American on the commission, of the situation. Jungmann had approached McManus on behalf of Martimort and Wagner about two concerns. First, they wanted to have "a spokesman, preferably a Cardinal, from the various countries on the vernacular Divine Office." McManus was already sounding out the possibility of having Cardinal Cushing or Cardinal Spellman address the issue. But the Europeans had a second and greater concern. They noted that the commission now was under different leadership from the preparatory phase and that there were no experts from mission countries. They feared "lest the S. Congregation [of Rites] proceed as in the past, calling on consultors as individuals rather than as a body, commission, or the like." McManus also urged Hallinan to arrange some contact "with the Austrian, German, French, Polish etc. group." At least one American bishop had shown McManus an "alternative schema," which, as will be seen, was then circulating. Urging König as "the best contact," McManus wanted to give the Americans some sense of "the non-Italian European views."[56]

The bishops of Brazil asked Cardinal Lercaro to discuss the significance of the liturgical schema in a meeting that took place at the Domus Mariae on October 19.[57]

Schillebeeckx's *Animadversiones* and Rahner's *Disquisitio* greatly influenced the orientation of public opinion in the first weeks of the Council, but many other analyses of the official schemas were also produced in other circles, on which we do not yet have complete information.[58] While they differed in size, authority, and value, they do indicate the interest provoked by the Council and the desire of the bishops for informed and active participation.

E. ALTERNATIVE SCHEMAS?

The collaboration between bishops and theologians meant wresting the Council away from the control of Ottaviani. Although they differed in tactics, the French and Germans were determined to support the Pope's purpose in convoking the Council — the papal emphasis on the

---

[56] McManus to Hallinan, Rome, n.d., but apparently before October 22, 1962 (ACUA, Hallinan papers).

[57] *Lettere dal Concilio 1962-1965*, ed. G. Battelli (Bologna, 1980), 78-79.

[58] Some information can be found in *NChenu* and in remarks prepared for Lercaro by G. Dossetti (ISR).

pastoral nature of the assembly was clearly at variance with the almost exclusively dogmatic orientation of the schemas prepared by the Theological Commission. The French and German group was creating a structure, parallel to the official commissions, that would finally prevail within the Council. But to follow the French agenda of mobilizing the larger hierarchies meant gaining the support of the Americans, among others, who were only beginning to become aware of the theological basis for their experience as an episcopal conference. But word of this growing opposition had reached the Holy Office. Speaking against the schema on the liturgy on October 24, Archbishop Pietro Parente, assessor of the Holy Office, would refer to himself and his co-workers as the "martyrs of the Holy Office."[59]

The German and French theologians began to extend their influence beyond Europe. Bishop Helder Câmara seemed to Congar to have the "vision" that was lacking in Rome. The Brazilian and many Latin American bishops were likewise in favor of rejecting the doctrinal schemas in favor of a more pastoral approach.[60] Helder Câmara later gave a homily at a Mass for journalists at which he said that the "unofficial meetings at which bishops from all the continents meet fraternally and talk" were as important as the formal discussions in St. Peter's.[61] Yet, some national hierarchies were still slow to take formal advantage of their theologians. While the German, Dutch, Spanish, and, to a certain extent, Belgian bishops held formal sessions to consult their theologians, the French as a group did not follow suit. The Americans, though they had a structure for theological discussion, were still under the conservative influence of Spellman.

On October 25 Philips presented his strategy to a small group that met at the Angelicum; besides Congar, Rahner, Ratzinger, and Semmelroth, Msgr. McGrath, Lécuyer, and Msgr. Colombo were present. At the center of Philips's plan was the doctrine on bishops, around which he wished to gather all the material on the Church.[62] Philip's text was slightly amended at this meeting, after which it was sent to Bea's Secretariat where it met the fierce resistance of Fr. C. Boyer, especially on the question of membership in the Church.[63]

---

[59] *AS* I/I, 425.

[60] *JCongar*, October 21, 1962, 87.

[61] Quoted in Peter Hebblethwaite, *Pope John XXIII: Shepherd of the Modern World* (Garden City, N.Y., 1985), 462.

[62] *TSemmelroth* and *JCongar*, October 25.

[63] *TSemmelroth*, October 31, along with *JCongar*, October 28.

It was also on October 25 that authorities superior to the theologians began to seek a wider audience for the German project. Frings assumed responsibility for the effort to ally bishops with the plans of the theologians; besides König, Alfrink, Liénart, Suenens and Döpfner, he also invited two Italian cardinals, Siri and Montini, members of the Secretariat for Extraordinary Affairs and men of great prestige, to a meeting held at S. Maria dell'Anima. After a conversation about the need for a pastoral inspiration in the Council and about the need for a thorough revision of the schemas, Frings introduced Ratzinger to outline an alternate schema. Ratzinger probably read the same text presented by Volk, Rahner, and Semmelroth on October 15, which later became the Rahner/Ratzinger schema. According to Siri, the reaction was enthusiastic, so much so that he thought it necessary to cool things down. In his mind the text could serve quite well for a later pastoral letter, in the style of the "Letter to Diognetus," but it was certainly not comparable to a conciliar document. Montini must also have been skeptical, since Siri notes that "he did well and helped dampen the enthusiasm, saying that right now we have to work on what's there and has already been well prepared."[64] If Frings's effort did bring the German project out of its semi-clandestine state, it did not succeed as a way of getting the project brought before the Council by means of the Secretariat for Extraordinary Affairs. While Siri and Montini had opposite strategies in mind, neither would agree to such an overthrow of the preparatory work. Indirectly, then, Frings's initiative helped strengthen the strategy of Suenens and Montini.

On October 28 Congar presented a completed text of his preface to the small group meeting at Volk's residence on the Gianicolo; his text was well received. As for the draft prepared by Rahner and Ratzinger as a substitute for the doctrinal schemas, Congar found it well done, especially on relations among Church, Scripture, and tradition, but he thought it too advanced in what it said about relations with the religions. Confusion also arose when Daniélou, also present for the meeting, continued to urge his own proposal. And then there was the question of how to get these alternate schemas through. Congar continued to be skeptical about the German strategy:

> I quite agree that substitute texts have to be prepared, or else we will get
> nothing done. But I think it is almost impossible to take so little account of
> the work already done, some of which is good and useful. We played "Per-

[64] See *DSiri*, 369-71.

rette et le Pot au lait." . . . Daniélou, who is preparing other schemas and wants to redo the whole council, agrees with me on this point. He sees everybody, speaks everywhere, says he's working at the request of four or five bishops. *Quid?* At the request of Cardinal Döpfner, Fritz Hofmann has been added to our little group; P. Cottier has been added at the request of Msgr. de Provenchères.

The small group was coming apart. It met again on November 4, with Cottier and Müller of Erfurt also present, and faced the impasse represented by the three projects of Congar, Rahner/Ratzinger, and Daniélou, all of them carefully constructed, which Volk vainly wished "to unify into a single usable schema."[65] Congar was even harsher: "Things got all mixed up. . . . I sensed a little desire for revenge on the part of the theologians who did not take part in the preparatory Theological Commission."[66] A day later Rahner wrote to Vorgrimler that "Daniélou has attempted to tailor a new garment from scraps of the official schemas."[67] In fact, the group preparing alternate schemas never met again. In all probability the Germans decided to go it alone.

Besides the weakness of the strategy envisaged to get them on to the conciliar agenda, serious objections could be raised against both texts: that of Rahner and Ratzinger, intended to take the place of the two dogmatic schemas on the sources of revelation and on the deposit of faith; and Congar's preface, designed to serve as an introduction to all the conciliar texts.[68]

1. *The German proposal*

The German text was quite dense. Its three chapters were to be preceded by a very brief preface, which would explain that while not claiming to offer solutions to the problems of society, the announcement of the gospel was designed to bring the "seeds of new life" also into this world. Moved by pastoral concern, the Church did not intend to present a theological system and still less to formulate new dogmas, but simply to place "the light of the Gospel on a lampstand . . . so that its serene light might shine upon all" — a clear reference to *Gaudet Mater Ecclesia*. But this preface appeared as an appendix, perhaps because the authors were aware that it duplicated Congar's preface.

[65] *TSemmelroth*, November 4.
[66] *JCongar*, November 4.
[67] Vorgrimler, *Understanding Karl Rahner*, 155.
[68] These texts are published in *Glaube im Prozeß*, 33-50 (Rahner-Ratzinger), 51-64 (Congar).

The three chapters of the text were in barely mitigated form a synthesis of the theology of Rahner. The first chapter spoke of the divine vocation of man, the second of God's hidden presence in human history, and the third of God's revealed presence in the Church's preaching. If the supernatural call is gratuitous, still, as "an obligatory end, it always touches man and pervades his whole nature, so that this nature, in its concrete historical condition, cannot be adequately understood in its totality without it." The text thus presented the themes of the apologetics of immanence initiated by Blondel, which had renewed theological anthropology in the first half of the twentieth century. It also reflected the reinterpretation which, starting with Rousselot and Maréchal, a dynamic Thomism had given when it stressed the "natural" character of the desire to see God. The result was a dynamic and profoundly unified conception of man, in that God "has constituted man's nature in such a way that out of love he may give him the free gift of himself." In addition, man was appreciated not only in his individuality but also in his constitutively social character, "in virtue of which the human race, one in principle and root but by divine ordering differentiated in the sexes and in peoples, progressively comes together in the course of human history so that it may be unified in the end in the eternal Kingdom of God."

On the basis of this anthropological vision, history was presented as the place of God's omnipresent, even if only implicit, manifestation. The text then attempted to combine Rahner's dynamic view of man as always open to hear the word with the anthropology of Vatican I, which revolved around the structural dependence of human reason on the uncreated Truth; this was an effort to combine the old neo-scholastic schema with an "immanent" vision of Christian revelation: "From the beginning, then, man was created in such a way as to be a fit subject of a divine revelation, in such a way also as to be able to hear the Word of God and to give it a reasonable assent." Within this general framework the text not only affirmed the presence of grace and therefore of salvation outside of Christianity, but also, without using the term, suggested a position rather close to Rahner's theology of "anonymous Christians":

> The end toward which the history of the human race is moving is already present in the man Jesus Christ. . . . Every action and every word of God which is addressed to this history, therefore, secretly speaks of him, tends toward him, finds in him its fulfilment. When one obeys the voice of God, then, even when he speaks in hidden ways, Christ and the salvation he effected are present and vice versa; when he is present, when one believes explicitly in him who speaks, when one lives in him, no element of the

truth ever given to the human race or ever reached by it is lost, but is rather brought to its full light.

This might be considered a successful synthesis. But, on the one hand, it said too little, as Semmelroth noted, because it failed to address some questions that concerned many people, such as the truth of the scriptures and the historicity of the gospels. On the other hand, it enclosed its teaching within a specific theological synthesis, largely taken from Rahner, which was rather foreign to the bishops. Also, they would have had considerable difficulty in adopting a text which was procedurally "external" to the Council.

2. A Global Preface

On the other hand, Congar's preface, not distributed at the time and thus unknown, in itself did not deserve a better lot. Although constructed as a symbol, a confession of the Council's faith (perhaps in this responding to the demand of those who during the preparatory phase had urged a new profession of faith), it was not very successful from a literary point of view. Among propositions presented as if they were formal confessions of faith ("We believe that . . . "), there were descriptive explanations that slowed the whole thing down.

The text began from the requirement that the exposition not separate truths about God from truths about the human "condition" in the world. Thus it stressed as a first aspect of the mystery of God the identity of this mystery with the love that has revealed itself to be at once "most high and most near." The love of the triune God is reflected in man, created in God's image not only individually but in human nature itself, which, while remaining one, exists in many and different people, called to live their lives in society. Human nature, as experienced in its concrete and actual condition contains both a principle of unity and the seed of divisions from which only Christ can liberate. Christ came to deliver us from the slavery of sin and to call us back to the truth that is at once about God and about our nature. Christ, true God and true man, is our peace, he who by his death established a new and eternal covenant between God and man and by his resurrection left us an inheritance which will never be destroyed and which remains thanks to "a sort of double and indissoluble vicarious action, that of the Holy Spirit internally and that of the Church externally."

In this text, which placed Christ at the center of the analysis of the human condition in its relationship with God, Congar successfully confirmed what Christ has revealed to us about God and about man, the true and paschal freedom that is victory over death and love for others and, therefore, peace. This powerful presentation, anchored in a dogmatic vision of the Christian mystery at its very center, effectively responded to the demand made by several people (by Volk when he presented his preface and by Bea in his document for the Secretariat for Extraordinary Affairs) that the conciliar agenda take into account the conditions of contemporary people.

The corresponding vision of the Church in Congar's preface was that of the "sacrament of salvation" for all, with the laudable attempt to develop a concept of the episcopal ministry that was organically related to Christian doctrine. Bishops appear as the heirs of the apostolic office to gather and to build the people of God in the economy of the new covenant, witness of the gospel to all. There was also an effort to go beyond a narrow vision of the old problem of belonging to the Church by a distinction between, on the one hand, external profession of the faith and communion with the hierarchical Church as a "sufficient" condition for remaining a member of the Church, and, on the other, a "full" condition, since "the Church does not fully exist except in true believers, converted to the Gospel." (This outlined a solution that after much debate would lead to the final formulation of *Lumen gentium*, a "full incorporation" whose first condition, even before visible links, is the gift of the Spirit.[69])

The problem of the salvation of non-Christians, who because of their "ignorance of the Church or even of Christ" are outside the Church itself, was addressed in a way that was at once weaker and more traditional than the one offered by Rahner. The mission of the Church was described as that of gathering into unity "all things that belong to Christ" with an ecumenical breadth that included not only people but all the "elements of the ecclesial sacrament," even those that, outside the visibile unity, "constitute the dissident Christian communities." And all of this is within an eschatological perspective of the Kingdom of God constituted by the people gathered from the four winds, as in the *Didache* (X,5); in this perspective the spectacle of the division of Christians is a scandal to non-Christians. Finally, there was a concern to distinguish between the Church's mission and the finality proper to the "world;" if the Church has her own distinct finality, that of eternal salvation, it also contributes to the purposes proper to human activity in the

---

[69] "They are fully incorporated into the society of the Church who, possessing the Spirit of Christ..." (*Lumen gentium*, 14).

world, since it brings the world hope in Christ. The final "consumma-
tion of the world" cannot in fact be reached merely by powers immanent
in the world, but only by the power of Christ, who does not cease to promote in our hearts truth, justice and peace, until the day he surrenders all
things to the Father and God is all in all.

Despite the differences between them, the alternate texts of Congar
and Rahner/Ratzinger had some things in common. Congar more discur-
sively and Rahner/Ratzinger more compactly tried to link the presentation of the Christian message to the exigencies of contemporaries,
including a consideration of human history in the presentation of the
mystery. The Germans' text was more successful in addressing some
claims of contemporary thought, Congar's in addressing the dramatic
problems of division and peace. The Council would take a different path,
dividing considerations *ad intra* from those *ad extra*, with the risk, visible above all in what would become the Pastoral Constitution, *Gaudium
et spes*, of a theological miscue. But the whole manner in which the
preparatory material had been addressed made it difficult to establish
links, and at least during the first phase of the Council, it was utopian to
think that the bishops could rapidly assimilate a more unitary vision.

In the meantime, the experts were also getting organized. The Pope
had appointed 201 of them, of whom 75 were Italian, 105 were diocesan
priests and 96 were religious. A good number had participated in the
preparation for the Council.[70] They covered a wide spectrum on the theological landscape. As the Council began its meetings, the experts
divided into two main groups. While the one composed principally of
those who had served on preparatory commissions tried to preserve the
schemas they had drafted, the other began meeting with groups of bishops in order to reject those schemas and draft alternative texts.[71]

A typical member of the group seeking to preserve the schemas of the
preparatory commissions was Msgr. Joseph C. Fenton of The Catholic
University of America in Washington, Ottaviani's principal ally in the
United States.[72] After taking the oath as a conciliar expert on October 8,

---

[70] Caprile, I, 15. Of the members of religious orders, Jesuits had 24, Dominicans 17,
Friars Minor 9, Friars Minor Conventual 4, Benedictines 6, Basilians of St. Jehosaphat 2,
Augustinians 2, Discalced Carmelites 2, Redemptorists 2, Oblates of Mary Immaculate 4,
Claretians 4, Oratorians 2, and Salesians 2. Other religious congregations were repre-
sented by only one member.

[71] Karl Heinz Neufeld, "In the Service of the Council: Bishops and Theologians at the
Second Vatican Council," in *Vatican II: Assessment and Perspectives*, ed. R. Latourelle
(New York, 1988), I, 74-105.

[72] For over a decade Fenton had attacked John Courtney Murray for espousing reli-

he lamented that "it is a crime that we did not take the Anti-Modernist Oath."[73] After Liénart's intervention at the first general congregation, Fenton spent his time faithfully circulating to his friends in the hierarchy Ottaviani's list of candidates whom the cardinal hoped could "be shoved in ahead of the candidates of the Blocco," as the cardinal termed the opposition he saw in France and Germany. Fenton was clear about his own reservations: "I always thought this council was dangerous. It was started for no sufficient reason. There was too much talk about what it was supposed to accomplish. Now I am afraid that real trouble is on the way."[74]

Fenton's diary provides a useful insight into the mentality of the conservatives. He recounted his contacts not only with Ottaviani, but also with Antonino Romeo and Francesco Spadafora, both professors at the Lateran University, who had been engaged in an assault on the Pontifical Biblical Institute. Romeo at one point informed him that Raymond Dulac, a French conservative who was not a conciliar expert, "was putting too much emphasis on Latin [in the liturgy], and was thereby harming the cause of integrism." For Ottaviani's men, *integrism* was a positive term — a return to the anti-Modernist crusade ended by Benedict XV. Fenton's own reaction to the schema on the liturgy was that its drafters "were stupid enough" to assert that "the Church is '*simul humanam et divinam, visibilem et invisibilem*' [at once human and divine, visible and invisible]." Dulac urged Fenton to use his influence with Archbishop Vagnozzi, the conservative apostolic delegate to the United States hierarchy, to prepare a reply to the French bishops who intended "very soon to propose that the Council pass up all the doctrinal schemas and settle for some 'pastoral' stuff."[75]

---

gious liberty. Once Murray ceased to write in 1955, Fenton and his cohorts leveled their attacks on biblical scholars and succeeded in dividing the faculty at the Catholic University (see G. P. Fogarty, *American Catholic Biblical Scholarship: A History from the Early Republic to Vatican II* [San Francisco, 1989], 260, 281-85, 287-98, 301-10).

[73] *DFenton*, October 9, 1962. The original of this is in the possession of Joseph Komonchak, who kindly allowed me to use it.

[74] *DFenton*, October 13, 1962.

[75] *DFenton*, October 19, 1962. Fenton further lamented that "since the death of St. Pius X the Church has been directed by weak and liberal popes, who have flooded the hierarchy with unworthy and stupid men. This present conciliar set-up makes this all the more apparent." What he confided to his diary during the Council was consistent with his earlier attacks on biblical scholarship. While claiming to adhere to the magisterium, he omitted any reference to Pius XII's *Divino Afflante Spiritu*. For Fenton, the papal magisterium ceased with Pius X. He also left no doubts about what he thought of some of his fellow American experts. One friend, "the only intelligent and faithful member of Bea's secretariat," had been left off the list, while "such idiots as [John S.] Quinn and the sneak

The flurry of activity among the experts came to the attention of Felici, the Secretary General of the Council, who announced at the eleventh general congregation on October 31 that "by order of the presidency, the Fathers of the Council are asked not to distribute among the Fathers in the Council hall private circulars without the consent of the presidency of the Council."[76] The next day Fenton paid a visit to Ottaviani and "found him shaken" at Alfrink's having cut him off when he exceeded his allotted time for speaking — "apparently it was one of A's more boorish actions," Fenton had commented at the time. As he entered the cardinal's apartment, however, he found him speaking with Bernard Häring, a moral theologian and one of two Redemptorist experts — "a bad man," Fenton commented, "but O [Ottaviani] seems to know about him." Ottaviani gave Fenton an English copy of Schillebeeckx's *Animadversiones* and asked him to have copies made and to write a commentary. Schillebeeckx's authorship at this time seems not to have been known to Ottaviani. Fenton commented that the author "does not know how to write in English, [and] seems to be completely unaware of the purpose of a conciliar doctrinal constitution." Fenton's model for a doctrinal constitution was the introduction to *Pastor Aeternus* of Vatican I, whereas Schillebeeckx "shows that he is talking about what he considers the theology of the last 30 years."[77]

During the following week Fenton made the rounds of Ottaviani's allies. The cardinal was "in terrible shape," he recorded, and both Dino Staffa, secretary of the congregation of seminaries and universities, and Parente said they "had been told not to talk." Staffa was "quite discouraged."[78]

In this early phase of the Council, however, the fathers faced a danger greater than that proposed by the Curia and its conservative allies. Within a week of the opening they faced the strong possibility of having to suspend the Council and return to their homes.

[Frederick] McManus have been put on. [George] Tavard is there as an American, God help us." (For Fenton's omission of *Divino Afflante Spiritu* and the Biblical Commission's letter to Cardinal Suhard, see Fogarty, *American Catholic Biblical Scholarship*, 183-84).

[76] *AS* I/2, 56. Brouwers notes that when Felici communicated the prohibition, "because the Dutch bishops were not directly involved in the composition and diffusion of the *Animadversiones*, they had no difficulty in giving silent approval" ("Derniers préparatifs," 359). It is rather difficult to follow the logic of this comment.

[77] *DFenton*, October 31-November 1, 1962.

[78] Ibid., November 9, 1962.

II. THE CUBAN MISSILE CRISIS AND THE PAPAL PEACE-INITIATIVE

The message to the world, approved on October 20, 1962, concluded with the prayer that "the light of the great hope in Jesus Christ our only Savior may shine upon this world which is still so far from the desired peace because of the threats engendered by scientific progress — marvelous progress — but not always intent upon the supreme law of morality."[79]

The fathers issued this statement at a moment when the world was closer to a confrontation between the superpowers, the United States and the Soviet Union, than at any other period in the Cold War. For some months the Soviets had been stationing fighter planes in Cuba. On October 18, a U.S. Navy fighter squadron had been moved to the southern part of Florida, from which it could easily attack the Cuban bases.[80] During the next few days the situation grew more tense. On October 16 President John F. Kennedy was shown evidence that the Soviet Union had also installed offensive missiles in Cuba, from which they could easily reach cities in the United States and Latin America, but he delayed revealing the presence of missiles in Cuba until he had more concrete evidence. On October 22 he addressed the people of the United States on television, showing high-level photographs of the missile sites and announcing the beginning of a naval blockade of all shipping to Cuba.[81] *Life*, the popular American journal, which had been ready to run its cover story on the Council, with a pictorial display of the pageantry inside, instead carried on its cover a picture of an American ship bearing down on a Soviet freighter, with the accompanying story inside coming immediately after the pictures of the opening of the Council.[82] The juxtaposition of the conflicting images captured the emotions of the day.

The Soviet Union's real objective was Allied withdrawal from Berlin, where the Berlin Wall had been in place for a year. Missiles in Cuba were a ploy to test the mettle of the young American president on the eve of American congressional elections. Nikita Khrushchev, the Soviet premier, also had to prove to his domestic opponents that he was strong in confronting the West.[83]

---

[79] *AS* I/1, 256.

[80] *New York Times*, October 19, 1962, 1:6.

[81] *New York Times*, October 23, 1962, 1:8 and 18:2. The texts of this address and other key U.S. documents in the Cuban Missile Crisis are given in Laurence Chang and Peter Kornbluh, eds., *The Cuban Missile Crisis, 1962: A National Security Archive Reader* (New York, 1992), 150-54.

[82] *Life*, 53 (November 2, 1962), 26-33. The story of the blockade begins on page 34.

[83] For a summary of Kremlin motivations, see Michel Tatu, *Power in the Kremlin: From Khrushchev to Kosygin* (New York, 1974), 230-97.

As Kennedy and Khrushchev began their diplomatic jockeying, a group of Soviet and American academics and journalists was assembling at Phillips Exeter Academy in Andover, Massachusetts, for the third in a series of discussions about the issues confronting statesmen of both nations. Both sides were getting acquainted on October 22, when they broke to watch Kennedy's address on television. After taking a vote, they decided to continue with their conference, despite the tension between their two nations. At this juncture, Father Felix Morlion, O.P., rector of Pro Deo University in Rome, joined the group as an observer. He proposed the possibility of a papal intervention in the crisis. With the encouragement of the members of both delegations, he phoned the Vatican and was informed that the Pope was deeply concerned about the crisis but wanted assurance that his intervention would be acceptable. In particular, Morlion's instructions were to ask if the Soviet Union would cease military shipping and the United States lift the blockade. Norman Cousins, heading the American delegation, then phoned Theodore Sorensen, General Counsel to Kennedy, who later phoned back to say that Kennedy welcomed the papal offer, but that it was imperative not only that military shipping to Cuba cease but that the missiles be removed.[84] Morlion conveyed this information to the Vatican. A member of the Soviet delegation then phoned Moscow and reported that Khrushchev would accept the Pope's proposal to withdraw military shipping if the United States lifted the blockade.[85]

In the meantime, direct negotiations between Washington and Moscow took place on several different levels. In addition to the official contacts between the two powers, Robert Kennedy, the Attorney General and President Kennedy's brother, had several meetings with Soviet Ambassador Anatoly Dobrynin, whom he considered a friend.[86] At the same time, Aleksandr Fomin, the KGB's station chief in Washington, met with John Scali, a correspondent for ABC news with personal connections with the State Department. With such back-door diplomacy, the Soviets were clearly intent on warding off a confrontation.[87]

[84] In a letter to the author, Sorensen recalled only speaking with Cousins after the crisis and had no recollection of a papal intervention in the crisis itself (Sorensen to Fogarty, New York, December 1, 1994).

[85] Norman Cousins, *The Improbable Triumvirate: John F. Kennedy, Pope John, Nikita Khrushchev* (New York, 1972), 13-18. Cousins, however, incorrectly gives the date of Kennedy's televised address announcing the blockade as October 21.

[86] Robert F. Kennedy, *Thirteen Days: A Memoir of the Cuban Missile Crisis* (New York, 1969), 65-66, 106-9.

[87] Chang and Kornbluh, *The Cuban Missile Crisis*, 81.

One problem for John XXIII was that the Holy See had diplomatic relations with neither of the superpowers. Relations with the United States government were strictly informal. Kennedy, the first Catholic president, had had to reject any intention of establishing diplomatic relations with the Vatican during his campaign and, once elected, he had to tread warily in regard to the Pope. In March 1962, however, his wife did have an audience with the Pope. On September 7, 1962, moreover, Vice President Lyndon B. Johnson had visited John XXIII to whom he presented a silver paperweight, a model of the American communications satellite Telstar. Inscribed on the base was a quotation from the Pope himself:

> Oh, how we wish these undertakings would assume the significance of an homage rendered to God the creator and supreme legislator. These historic events which will be inscribed in the annals of scientific knowledge of the cosmos will thus become an expression of true, peaceful and well-founded progress toward human brotherhood.

Quoting the inscription, Robert Kaiser, the correspondent for *Time*, the American weekly, commented that "ironically and to the shame of Johnson's aides, these words of Pope John were not those he uttered when the United States Telstar went into orbit," but were taken from the Pope's radio address on August 12 in regard to the Soviet Union's two cosmonauts making a simultaneous orbital flight.[88] Johnson's aides, however, may not have been remiss; they may have chosen the inscription deliberately as an informal American statement of appreciation for the Soviet achievement and a reiteration of Kennedy's earlier overture for future American-Soviet cooperation in space.

Despite Kennedy's need for caution in his dealing with the Vatican, he had joined other heads of state in congratulating John XXIII on the opening of the Council. The whole world, he said, found "renewed trust and encouragement" when the Pope said in his radio address of September 11 that the Council would address the "grave social and economic problems" that especially threatened "nations that were economically underdeveloped." His own hope was that the Council's decisions would "promote, in a significant way, the cause of peace and of international understanding."[89]

---

[88] Kaiser, *Pope, Council and World*, 48.
[89] Caprile, II, 28. The English text is in the *New York Times*, October 6, 1962, 3:1.

John XXIII's relationship with Khrushchev was more complicated and may well have surprised the West. In a little over a year Khrushchev had made several overtures to the Pope. First, in September 1961, only a month after the building of the Berlin Wall, the Pope had issued a plea for peace and disarmament in support of a similar plea issued at the first conference of the nonaligned countries in Belgrade. Khrushchev praised the Pope in a speech that he then had distributed in *Pravda, Izvestia,* and TASS.[90] Next, Khrushchev had congratulated John on his eightieth birthday, on November 25, 1961, and praised him for his contributions to "the accomplishment of peace on earth and to the solution of international problems through the means of open negotiations."[91] Much to the consternation of some of his advisers, John thanked Khrushchev for his greetings and expressed "on his part, to all the Russian people, cordial wishes for an increase and establishment of universal peace, through the felicitous agreement of human brotherhood."[92] None of this was reported in *L'Osservatore Romano.*

A final contact between the Kremlin and the Vatican occurred at the opening of the Council itself. For some time before the Council convened, the newly formed Secretariat for Christian Unity had been negotiating for the Orthodox to send observers. On September 27 Msgr. Jan Willebrands had flown to Moscow to see if the Russian Patriarchate would accept an invitation. Only on the day the Council opened did the Secretariat receive a telegram that the Russians would send two observers, Archpriest Vitalyi Borovoi and Archimandrite Vladimir Kotliarov. They were the only representatives of the Orthodox during the first session.[93] John XXIII, therefore, already had some indication of a changing Kremlin attitude toward the Church. Now he needed an occasion to intervene in the crisis.

With the assurance gained from the Andover meeting that both Kennedy and Khrushchev would welcome his intervention, John XXIII prepared his address. But first, he paved the way. On October 24 he spoke to a group of Portuguese pilgrims. In his conclusion he added what seemed to be an afterthought:

> The Pope always speaks well of all men of state who are concerned, here, there, and everywhere, with meeting amongst themselves to avoid the real-

[90] Giancarlo Zizola, *The Utopia of Pope John XXIII* (Maryknoll, N.Y., 1978), 120-21.

[91] Loris Francesco Capovilla, *Giovanni XXIII: Lettere, 1958-1963* (Rome, 1978), 337.

[92] John XXIII to Khrushchev, November 26, 1961, in Capovilla, *Giovanni XXIII: Lettere,* 336.

[93] Thomas F. Stransky, "The Foundation of the Secretariat for Promoting Christian Unity," in *Vatican II Revisited,* 79-80; see *History,* I, pp. 323-26.

ity of war and to procure a bit of peace for humankind. . . . Nevertheless, let it be well understood, only the Spirit of the Lord can accomplish this miracle, since, obviously, where the substance — true spiritual life — is lacking, many things cannot be imagined nor obtained.[94]

Here was the first signal to the two leaders. While upholding the need for "spiritual life," the Pope praised "all men of state" who sought to avoid war through negotiation. The Pope's next step was his formal address, dispatched ahead of time to both the Soviet and United States embassies in Rome. Speaking in French in an unscheduled broadcast at noon, October 25, the Pope made no mention of either Kennedy or Khrushchev by name, but addressed "all men of good will" to enter negotiations to end the conflict. An account of his address appeared the next day on the front page of the *New York Times*, right under a picture of Adlai E. Stevenson, U.S. Ambassador to the United Nations, presenting the Security Council photographic evidence of the missile sites in Cuba. The *Times* also carried the full text of the Pope's speech.[95] The same day *Pravda* published the following account on the page devoted to foreign news:

SAVE THE WORLD
Statement by Pope John XXIII
The Vatican. 25 Oct. (TASS) Pope John XXIII in Rome has made a plea for the defense of peace, "To All Men of Good Will." Speaking today in an unscheduled broadcast on Vatican Radio, he said his words came "from the very depths of a worried and saddened heart."

"Once again," said the Pope, "threatening clouds are gathering on the world horizon, bringing fear to countless millions of families." In this regard Pope John XXIII repeated his plea to the statesmen [the address he had given to the extraordinary missions sent for the opening of the Council]: "Let their reason come alight; let them heed the cry of distress arising to Heaven from all corners of the world, from innocent children and the aged, from individuals and all mankind: 'Peace, Peace.'"

"Today," he said, "we repeat the plea of our heart and invoke the heads of state not to be heedless of the cry from mankind. Let them do all in their power to keep the peace. Thereby they will be keeping mankind from the horrors of a war, the frightful effects of which no one can foresee. Let them go on negotiating."

"To agree to negotiations at any level and at any location to be well-inclined to these negotiations and to commence them — this would be a sign of wisdom and cautiousness that would be blessed by heaven and earth."[96]

---

[94] Zizola, *Utopia*, 7.
[95] *New York Times*, October 26, 1962, 1; the full text is given on page 20.
[96] *Pravda*, October 26, 1962, 5.

That *Pravda*, the official newspaper of the Communist Party, published anything of the papal overture was in itself significant; Khrushchev was watching and giving his approval to the Pope's words.

In the United States the *New York Times* briefly noted that TASS had distributed a dispatch on the papal address, the significance of which seems to have eluded the American press.[97] At the same time, incidentally, the American newspaper also reported that the five American cardinals — Spellman of New York, McIntyre of Los Angeles, Cushing of Boston, Joseph E. Ritter of St. Louis, and Albert G. Meyer of Chicago, joined by Archbishop Patrick O'Boyle of Washington — had issued a statement calling on American Catholics to observe the following Sunday, the Feast of Christ the King, "as a day of prayer to beseech God's blessing on our President and Government."[98] Meanwhile, the three Cuban bishops at the Council — Manuel Rodriguez Rozas of Pinar del Rio, Carlos Riu Angles of Camaguey, and Jose Dominguez y Rodriguez of Matanzas — denied reports in the Italian newspaper *Paese Sera* that they had made or intended to make any statement about the crisis.[99]

In the discussions over the crisis at the White House and in the American accounts written later, there was no mention of the Pope's speech or of *Pravda*'s reaction. Khrushchev's response, however, may reflect the influence of the Pope's plea. U Thant, acting Secretary General of the United Nations, had issued a plea calling for the United States not to interfere with peaceful shipping and for the Soviet Union not to attempt to ship armaments to Cuba. On October 26 Khrushchev addressed a personal letter to Kennedy. Stating his general agreement with U Thant's plea for negotiations, he asked Kennedy to guarantee that neither the United States nor any other nation would invade Cuba. He further proposed more general discussions on disarmament.[100] But then, the Soviet position seemed to harden.

On October 27 Khrushchev sent a second letter to Kennedy, broadcast ahead of its reception over Radio Moscow. He now introduced the question of Jupiter missiles in Turkey, "literally next to us." While still praising Kennedy's agreement to accept U Thant's mediation, Khrushchev now proposed the removal of the missiles from Turkey in exchange for the removal of Soviet missiles from Cuba. Both the Soviet

---

[97] *New York Times*, October 26, 1962, 20.
[98] Ibid.
[99] NCWC News Service (Foreign), October 29, 1962, 3 (ACUA).
[100] Khrushchev to Kennedy, October 26, 1962, in Chang and Kornbluh, *The Cuban Missile Crisis*, 185-88.

Union and the United States would then make statements "within the framework of the Security Council" pledging to respect the sovereignty and borders, respectively, of, Turkey and Cuba. While this second letter seemed to represent the position of the hardliners in the Kremlin more than of Khrushchev himself, there were, nevertheless, some indications that the Chairman was reflecting the papal appeal. Contrary to the usual Soviet policy, Khrushchev again called for negotiations. Specifically, he stated:

> Of course, for this we would have to come to an agreement with you and specify a certain time limit. Let us agree to some period of time, but without unnecessary delay — say within two or three weeks, not longer than a month. . . .
>
> If you are agreeable to my proposal, Mr. President, then we would send our representatives to New York, to the United States, and would give them comprehensive instructions in order that an agreement may be reached more quickly. If you also select your people and give them the corresponding instructions, then this question can be quickly resolved.
>
> Why would I like to do this? Because the whole world is now apprehensive and expects sensible actions of us. The greatest joy for all peoples would be the announcement of our agreement and of the eradication of the controversy that has arisen. I attach great importance to this agreement in so far as it could serve as a good beginning and could in particular make it easier to reach agreement on banning nuclear weapons tests. The question of the tests could be solved in parallel fashion, without connecting one with the other, because these are different issues. However, it is important that agreement be reached on both these issues so as to present humanity with a fine gift, and also to gladden it with the news that agreement has been reached on the cessation of nuclear tests and that consequently the atmosphere will no longer be poisoned. Our position and yours on this issue are very close together.[101]

The White House was now thrown into confusion by Khrushchev's two letters. After prolonged discussion, on October 27 Kennedy decided to respond only to the first letter and ignore the demand that the Jupiter missiles be removed from Turkey — a move that Kennedy himself had actually proposed several months earlier, since the weapons were in fact already obsolete and could be replaced by Polaris submarines. If the missiles were removed from Cuba, the President wrote, the United States would remove the quarantine and give its assurances against any invasion of Cuba.[102] On October 28 Khrushchev accepted Kennedy's

---

[101] Ibid., 197-99. For providing me with the interpretation of the plea for negotiations being a deviation from Soviet policy, I am grateful to William Burgess, who also provided the translations from *Pravda*.

[102] Kennedy to Khrushchev, October 27, 1962, ibid., 223-25.

terms, but not without providing a long list of grievances Cuba had against the United States. The communique was hardly friendly, but it made no mention of the missiles in Turkey. Kennedy acknowledged the message, and negotiations began at the United Nations.[103] Although tensions between the two superpowers remained high during November, as the United States negotiated for the removal of Soviet bombers as well as missiles from Cuba, the crisis had passed. The world moved back from the brink of nuclear war.

John XXIII's plea for negotiations had no obvious effect on the United States. While there is no available documentary evidence that Kennedy responded to the papal initiative, he is reported to have thanked the Pope through the United States embassy to Italy.[104] But the Pope's initiative did have an effect on Khrushchev. Although it is impossible to determine whether the papal plea actually influenced Khrushchev's response to Kennedy, it did set in motion a series of events that brought the Pope and the Soviet Union into more direct contact. During the Andover meeting, Morlion proposed to the Soviet delegates that they explore communications between the Vatican and Moscow. He informed the Soviets that Cousins would be acceptable to the Vatican and queried if he would also be acceptable to Moscow to undertake preliminary contacts. Late in November, Cousins received a call from Ambassador Dobrynin to say that Khrushchev would like to discuss the proposal with him on December 14. Cousins received Kennedy's approval for the visit and met with the President before departing for Rome on his way to Moscow. In Rome he was unable to see John XXIII, who was then being treated for the illness that would soon claim his life. He did, however, meet with Archbishop Angelo Dell'Acqua of the Secretariat of State and with Bea.[105]

Cousins's visit coincided with a delicate problem with which Bea was having to deal. On November 22 several newspapers, including *La Croix*, had published the draft of a statement from fifteen Ukrainian bishops at the Council stating their regret that the Russian Orthodox Church should have observers at the Council, while Metropolitan Josyf Slipyi, Archbishop of Lvov, remained a prisoner in Siberia. Willebrands

---

[103] Khrushchev to Kennedy, October 28, 1962; Kennedy to Khrushchev, October 28,. 1962, ibid., 226-29, 230-32.

[104] Zizola, *Utopia*, 9. Efforts to locate any information on this in the Kennedy papers were unsuccessful. It is possible that the communication to the embassy to Rome was oral, with no written record.

[105] Cousins, *The Improbable Triumvirate*, 20-29.

had to use a press conference to downplay this first display of anything but welcome for the Russian observers.[106] But the question of Slipyi remained. He was then seventy years old, and John XXIII had already named him a cardinal *in petto*. Bea suggested to Cousins that he seek Slipyi's release as a sign of the Soviet Union's desire to improve its relationship with the West. Bea and Dell'Acqua also proposed that Cousins discuss with Khrushchev the improvement of religious conditions within the Soviet Union, not only for Catholics but for all religious believers.[107]

In Moscow, on December 13, Cousins had a cordial meeting with Khrushchev, who noted the similarities between himself and John XXIII:

> We both come from peasant families; we both have lived close to the land; we both enjoy a good laugh. There's something very moving to me about a man like him struggling despite his illness to accomplish such an important goal before he dies. His goal, as you say, is peace. It is the most important goal in the world. If we don't have peace and the nuclear bombs start to fall, what difference will it make whether we are Communists or Catholics or capitalists or Chinese or Russians or Americans? Who could tell us apart? Who will be left to tell us apart? . . . [Turning then to the Cuban Missile Crisis, he recalled:] The Pope's appeal was a real ray of light. I was grateful for it. Believe me, that was a dangerous time.[108]

But Cousins found that the subject of Slipyi's release was more delicate. Khrushchev spoke at some length about the religious situation in Ukraine prior to 1947, especially the competition between the Ukrainian Catholic Church and the Orthodox Church and the power struggles within each. When Slipyi's predecessor, Archbishop Sheptytsky, died, he said, the circumstances indicated that "his departure from this earth may have been somewhat accelerated." While not directly implicating Slipyi in his predecessor's death, the premier did assert that the Metropolitan was imprisoned for his collaboration with the Nazis. He further feared that Slipyi would be used for propaganda purposes to show his harsh treatment by the Soviet government. After Cousins reminded Khrushchev that John XXIII had not denounced him or his government, the Premier offered to consider the matter of Slipyi's release. Cousins and Khrushchev then discussed other issues of concern to the Vatican, such as the Soviet treatment of the Jews.[109]

---

[106] Wenger, *Les trois Romes*, 174; see W. Dushnyck, *The Ukrainian-Rite Catholic Church at the Council, 1962-1965* (Winnipeg, 1967).

[107] Cousins, *The Improbable Triumvirate*, 29-31.

[108] Quoted in Cousins, *The Improbable Triumvirate*, 44-45.

[109] Ibid., 48-50.

Cousins concluded his interview with Khrushchev with a conversation about the proposal that the United States and the Soviet Union negotiate a treaty banning any further testing of nuclear weapons. As he made ready to depart, Khrushchev went to his desk to pen Christmas greetings to Kennedy and John XXIII. To President and Mrs. Kennedy, he simply sent his wishes for the holiday season. But to the Pope he wrote: "On the occasion of the Holy Days of Christmas, please accept these greetings and congratulations from a man who wishes you good health and strength for your abiding quest for the peace and happiness of all mankind."[110]

Back in Rome, Cousins personally handed the Pope the Premier's greetings. A few days later, John responded to Khrushchev's note:

> Thank you for your courteous message of good wishes. We return it from the heart with the same words that came to us from on high: Peace on earth to men of good will.
>
> We bring to your attention two documents for Christmas for this year invoking the strengthening of a just peace among people.
>
> May the good God hear us and respond to the zeal and sincerity of our efforts and our prayers. *Fiat pax in virtute tua, Domine, et abundantia in turribus tuis.*
>
> Best wishes for the prosperity of the Russian people and of all the people of the world.[111]

Had it been known at the time, this correspondence between the Pope and the Communist leader would probably have surprised a world still engaged in the Cold War. It set in motion a series of events that would not bear full fruit for almost thirty years.

In the meantime, both Italian and American diplomats were working for Slipyi's release. Although Cousins made no reference to Kennedy's concern about the Metropolitan, as he was leaving Rome Msgr. Igino Cardinale arrived with a Christmas present for the President, a silver icon, which the Pope's secretary, Loris Capovilla, said was "a sign of gratitude" for the President's cooperation in obtaining the release of Slipyi.[112] On January 25, 1963, Semeion Kozyrev, the Soviet Ambassador to Italy, brought Amintore Fanfani, President of the Italian Council, a message from Khrushchev announcing that Slipyi was to be released. On February 10, Slipyi, accompanied from Moscow by Wille-

---

[110] Ibid., 53-57; a facsimile of Khrushchev's message to John XXIII with an English translation is given opposite page 78. An Italian translation is given in Capovilla, *Lettere,* 439.

[111] John XXIII to Khrushchev, Dec. 21, 1962, in Capovilla, *Lettere,* p. 438.

[112] Cousins, 66; Capovilla, *Lettere,* 273n.

brands, arrived quietly in Rome.[113] His release was a major sign that relations between the Holy See and the Kremlin were beginning to improve. A short time later Khrushchev arranged for his son-in-law, Alexis Adzhubei, to be assigned as the Rome correspondent for *Izvestia*. On occasion of his receiving the Balzan Peace Prize, John XXIII received Adzhubei and his wife, Rada, in a private audience on March 7.[114] It was the beginning of a new relationship. When John XXIII died in June, Soviet Navy ships in Genoa harbor flew their flags at half-mast.[115] "Good Pope John" had made his impact on the Communist world.

John XXIII's willingness to take a risk, to move beyond the usual channels of communication, ran parallel to the desire of the bishops at the Council he had convoked. How decisive a role he played is difficult to determine, but his plea for peaceful negotiations in the midst of a council he envisioned as pastoral seems to have been the catalyst needed to ward off an impending nuclear holocaust. But the triumph of his vision in the Council was overshadowed by the growing rumors of his fatal illness.

III. THE POPE'S HEALTH

On November 29 *L'Osservatore Romano* reported that John XXIII would have to cancel his audiences on medical advice, because "the symptoms of gastric disturbance were getting worse; for some time the Holy Father has been on a diet and undergoing medical treatment that have led to rather severe anemia."[116] In fact, this was only part of the story. On September 23 the Pope had received the results of a series of X-rays and medical tests. Reflecting back on this, the Pope's secretary, Monsignor Loris F. Capovilla, recalled on October 9:

> It is fifteen days since we learned the news of the unexpected and worry-ing sickness that is affecting the Pontiff's life. He has gone on with a pro-gram of intense activity, interrupted only by consultations with eminent doctors. He seems calm when he asks for clarifications about the gastric disorders he is suffering from, and about the X-rays.

[113] Zizola, *Utopia*, 146-50.
[114] Capovilla, *Lettere*, 454-55; see also Andrea Riccardi, *Il Vaticano e Mosca* (Rome, 1992), 225, 249-50.
[115] *New York Times*, June 6, 1963, 18.
[116] Quoted in Hebblethwaite, *Pope John XXIII*, 458.

John had done more than remain calm. On October 4 he undertook a pilgrimage to Loreto and Assisi. "He was on foot throughout the journey," Capovilla recorded, "seemingly oblivious to the pain that went with him from early morning till his return to Rome in the depths of the night." On October 9 the Pope was determined to hold memorial services for the fourth anniversary of the death of Pius XII in St. Peter's, instead of in the Sistine Chapel. Capovilla remarked that "those who were beginning to guess something about his illness, remarked on his pallor and air of tiredness. But these were just the effects of having got up at 3:30 in the morning!" After a long day he handed a note to the Secretary of State expressing his concern on how to receive bishops from China, if they could come, and the "bishops from the *silenzio*."[117] On November 16 the Pope spoke with both Professor Pietro Valdoni and his new specialist, Dr. Pietro Mazzoni, who hinted to him that he had irreversible cancer.[118] Almost two weeks later *L'Osservatore Romano* made the first official mention of the Pope's health. The fathers of the Council immediately sent him a message of concern. At the thirty-first general congregation on December 1, Felici announced with "great joy" that the information on the Pope's convalescence gave cause for optimism and that he would impart his apostolic blessing the following day.[119] On December 5 the Pope seemed more robust and addressed the bishops and faithful gathered in St. Peter's Square from the window of his private study:

> My beloved children, providence accompanies us. As you see, from one day to another there is progress; we are not failing, but recovering, slowly. Sickness, convalescence: we are in convalescence. The joy of this present gathering is a cause of rejoicing; a hint of the power and strength that are returning.
>
> A new spectacle today: the Church assembled in its full representation. Here is the episcopate; here is the priesthood; here is the Christian people. So the family, the whole family, is present here: the family of Christ. My children, let us bless the Lord for this joy and in this unity. Let us continue to help one another, each one pursuing his own path.
>
> We are in the midst of the novena to the Immaculate Virgin. I do not want to leave you today without calling you all together back to our dear Mother; and with you to invoke her again as the powerful advocate and heavenly animator of our activity.

---

[117] Archbishop Loris F. Capovilla, "Reflections on the Twentieth Anniversary," in *Vatican II Revisited*, 108-9.

[118] Zizola, *Utopia*, 11.

[119] Caprile, II, 237.

> The Council will be suspended for some time: but we will always bear
> in our heart the sweetness, the gentleness, of such a perfect union of all;
> and not simply as representatives of the clergy and people, but as represen-
> tatives of the different human families, of the whole world, for the whole
> world was and is redeemed by our Lord Jesus Christ. To her, therefore, our
> Mother, let us recommend the Holy Church, our families, our lives, our
> health, because even this helps us to serve the Lord well.[120]

The Pope's invocation of the Virgin Mary may have been a gesture of
peace toward Ottaviani, whose separate schema on Mary, the Mother of
God and Mother of Men, had so recently failed. His emphasis on the
unity he perceived may also have been an allusion to the document on
the schema on the unity with the Eastern Church that also had failed.
This was Pope John's last appearance before the bishops he had helped
mold into a council.

The Council had opened with pageantry but in disarray. The multiplicity of documents alone, as Ratzinger commented, was enough to
daunt the most diligent of bishops or theologians. But it was their content and orientation that so many bishops found offensive, so much were
they at variance with the pastoral Council the Pope had announced.
While the conciliar commissions, except for that on the liturgy, did little
during the first session, the initial interaction between bishops and theologians was significant not only for making the bishops active participants in the Council but also for preparing the way for future sessions.
Suenens and others envisioned the Council dealing with the Church *ad
intra* and *ad extra*. Although the Council made no formal mention of the
Cuban Missile Crisis, the threat of nuclear war made real the need for
the Council not to limit itself to doctrinal matters. It had to be a voice for
peace among all nations. The bishops and theologians seemed to pick up
this theme as they took possession of the Council and developed their
own schemas, giving a model of the collaboration that should exist
between them. They had accomplished more than had been expected, for
the tide of the Council and of the Church had now turned. But when they
reassembled, they would be under the direction of a new pope.

---

[120] Ibid., 237.

CHAPTER III

THE LITURGY DEBATE

Mathijs Lamberigts

Introduction and Overview

The history of the schema on the sacred liturgy during the first session of the Council begins with the first meeting of the conciliar Commission on the Liturgy on October 21, the day before the Council fathers were to begin discussing the text in the hall. The Commission, which was to meet in twenty-one general sessions between that date and December 7, was chaired by Cardinal Arcadio Larraona, a Spanish Curial cardinal, prefect of the Congregation for Rites, who had served as the second chairman of the preparatory Liturgical Commission and had been appointed by Pope John XXIII to head the conciliar Commission on September 4.

At the first meeting Larraona named Cardinal Paolo Giobbe and Msgr. A. Jullien vice-presidents. The designation was something of a surprise, first because both individuals were members of the Curia and, second, because he passed over Cardinal Giacomo Lercaro, the only cardinal directly elected to the Commission by the general assembly and with a reputation as a specialist in the liturgy.[1] Larraona had yet another surprise in store. While the other conciliar commissions had designated the secretary of the respective preparatory commission to continue to co-ordinate the new commission's activities, Larraona replaced A. Bugnini with the Franciscan Ferdinando Antonelli, of the Congregation for Rites.[2] The reason for this substitution seems to have been that the prefect of the Congregation for Rites found Bugnini too progressive and considered him responsible for the spirit of the liturgy schema.[3] The choice was all the more surprising given that Antonelli had not participated directly in the activities of the preparatory commission,[4] although

---

[1] See A. Bugnini, *The Reform of the Liturgy (1948-1975)* (Collegeville, 1990), 30.

[2] Bugnini had other problems to deal with at the time; see his *Reform*, 30 n.4.

[3] It is quite possible that Ottaviani also had a role to play in getting rid of Bugnini; see M. Paiano, "Les travaux de la commission liturgique conciliaire," in *Commissions*, 7.

[4] See J. Wagner, *Mein Weg zur Liturgiereform (1936-1988): Erinnerungen* (Freiburg-Basel-Vienna, 1993), 61, who considered Antonelli a good choice.

it should be added immediately that he was not inexperienced in liturgical matters.[5] He was assisted in his work by Carlo Braga and Rinaldo
Falsini.

Although the experts were only officially allowed to intervene when
asked to do so, Larraona gave them permission from the first Commission meeting onward to intervene whenever they considered it necessary.[6] Questions of a juridical nature were the primary focus of attention
during the first six meetings.[7]

The conciliar discussion of the schema *De Sara Liturgia* began on the
following day, October 22, at the fourth general congregation.[8] The
liturgy schema was a test case for how the Council would function; as
the first application of the conciliar regulations and first test of the procedures, it no doubt would reveal difficulties to be dealt with. In his
introduction to the text Larraona emphasized the importance of adapting
ceremonies to the needs of individual peoples and nations.[9] Antonelli
then took the floor and gave a brief presentation of the schema.[10] In his
introduction he stated that a constitution on the liturgy was a proper
object of the Council's work for two reasons, to improve and adapt the
liturgical books, texts, and rites and to meet the pastoral demands of the
times. On the second point Antonelli noted that Christians had gradually
become silent spectators instead of active participants. The renewal and
nourishment of Christian life would profit greatly from a return to the

---

[5] See A. Verheul, "De leden van de conciliaire commissie voor de liturgie," in *Tijdschrift voor Liturgie* 47 (1963), 89.

[6] See W. M. Bekkers, "Het concilie over de liturgie," in *Tijdschrift voor Liturgie* 47
(1963), 81.

[7] At the first meeting, after deciding to meet every work day at 5:00 P.M., the Commission began discussing its precise task. There was some indecision as to what to do
with the written submissions concerning the liturgy schema. They apparently settled for
the following adage: "It is better for us to make the corrections and not leave it to the
whole Council to discuss them" (see Jenny papers, box 8, file 5, CNPL).

[8] For the discussion that preceded this decision, see *AS* V/1, 17-18; see also A. G.
Martimort, "La constitution sur la liturgie de Vatican II," *La Maison-Dieu* 157 (1984),
33-52, 43; idem, "Les débats liturgiques lors de la première période du concile Vatican
II (1962)," *Vatican II commence*, 297-98; see also G. L. Diekmann, "The Constitution on
the Sacred Liturgy," *Vatican II. An Interfaith Appraisal*, ed. J. H. Miller (Notre Dame,
1966), 17-30.

[9] *AS* I/1, 304.

[10] For the history of this text see H. Schmidt, *Die Konstitution über die heilige
Liturgie: Text, Vorgeschichte, Kommentar* (Freiburg, 1965); A. Bugnini, "De sacra
Liturgia in prima periodo Concilii," *EphLit* 77 (1963), 3-18; idem, *The Reform of the
Liturgy*, 14-38; "La Constitution liturgique de sa préparation à sa mise en application,"
La Maison-Dieu 39 (1982), nn.155-56; M. Paiano, "Il rinnovamento della liturgia: dai
movimenti alla chiesa universale," in *Verso il Concilio*, 78-86; *History*, I, 206-11.

sources of grace present in the liturgy and by the active and personal participation of the faithful in the liturgy. In this regard Antonelli referred to the wishes of Pius X concerning the role of the liturgical movement, to Pius XII's establishment of the papal commission in 1948, to the achievements of this commission, to John XXIII's announcement of the Council, and to the preparatory Commission for the Liturgy established in 1960.[11] In elaborating the schema the Commission had kept the following aims in mind: concern to preserve the Church's liturgical patrimony; elaboration of principles to guide a general renewal of the liturgy; derivation of doctrinally grounded practical and rubrical norms; concern that the clergy be better educated and more deeply imbued with the spirit of the liturgy, so that they would be able to serve as teachers and leaders among the faithful; and desire to lead the faithful into more active participation in the liturgy.

The schema itself consisted of a general Introduction, which spelled out the importance of the liturgy for the life of the Church, followed by eight chapters: I, on the general principles for the promotion and renewal of the liturgy; II, on the mystery of the Eucharist; III, on the sacraments and sacramentals; IV, on the Divine Office; V, on the liturgical year; VI, on liturgical furnishings; VII, on sacred music; and VIII, on sacred art.[12] Antonelli pointed out that of the eight chapters, chapter I was the most comprehensive and most important because it contained the doctrinal foundations of the liturgy and dealt with general principles decisive for the themes discussed in the subsequent chapters.[13]

The secretary explained that the first chapter had been subdivided into five sections. Section I, on the essence of the liturgy and its significance in the life of the Church, presented the theological foundations of the liturgy, the liturgy's unique place among the external activities of the Church, the spiritual life of the faithful, and pious extraliturgical customs of the faithful. Section II dealt with the liturgical formation of priests and laity and with the active participation of the latter and offered a number of provisions to attain these aims. Section III, on the renewal of the liturgy, was, Antonelli said, "of particular importance." He outlined five fundamental principles which would become the necessary

---

[11] *AS* I/1, 305-6.

[12] See *Schema constitutionis De Sacra Liturgia*, in *Schemata constitutionum et decretorum ex quibus argumenta in Concilio disceptanda seligentur* (Vatican City, 1962), 155-201; the text may also be found, with original pagination also indicated, in *AS* I/1, 262-303.

[13] See *Schema de Sacra Liturgia*, 159-74; *AS* I/1, 264-79.

guidelines for implementing the renewal: 1) avoiding unclarity in the
development of the rites; 2) balancing respect for liturgical tradition
with legitimate progress; 3) adapting the liturgy to the needs of the time
especially in mission territories; 4) accommodating, in light of the pastoral and catechetical nature of the liturgy, the structure of rites to the
intellectual capacities of the faithful so that there would be no need for
much further explanation and, in view of the instructional character of
the liturgy, supplementing the rites with didactic elements based on the
scriptures; 5) promoting the active participation of the faithful out of
respect for the hierarchical and communal character of the liturgy and its
dynamics.

Section IV, on the promotion of the liturgical life in the diocese and
in the parish, emphasized enhancing the community's awareness that it
is the family of God. Section V, on the promotion of liturgical action,
proposed establishing national and diocesan liturgical commissions
along with commissions for music and art. Antonelli ended his report
with a brief remark on the reform of the breviary that would be discussed in chapter IV.[14] The scene was set for the discussion to begin.

The debate on the liturgy lasted until November 13. During this
period there were 15 general congregations at which 328 oral interventions were made by 253 fathers, with another 297 interventions submitted in writing. Some of the fathers came to the podium more than once;
Cardinal Ruffini of Palermo intervened six times.[15] The majority of
interventions came from Europe (148) although the Americas also put
up a good show (49 — 14 from the U.S. and Canada, 35 from Central
and South America). Asia and Africa intervened 37 and 17 times respectively. Within Europe it was primarily the Italians and Spanish who
intervened on a regular basis, 46 and 30 times respectively, although
France also took the podium with some frequency (19 times). The
majority of addresses were given by bishops (154), but the conciliar regulations permitted cardinals and archbishops to take the podium with a
relatively high frequency (36 and 55 times respectively). Patriarchs
intervened on two occasions, religious superiors on nine. Speakers often
intervened in the name of their episcopal conferences,[16] and sometimes

---

[14] See *AS* I/1, 307-8.

[15] For an interesting survey see R. Laurentin, *L'enjeu du concile. Bilan de la première session* (Paris, 1963), 125.

[16] Archbishop McQuaid spoke in the name of the Irish bishops on October 24 and 30 (*AS* I/1, 414; I/2, 94); Bishop Kobayashi took the podium on behalf of his Japanese colleagues on October 27 (*AS* I/1, 525). On November 5 Bishop Bekkers articulated the posi-

even on behalf of an entire continent, as when Cardinal Rugambwa and Bishops Ramantoamina, Thiandoum, and van Cauwelaert spoke in the name of all their African colleagues.[17]

Examining the situation in more detail, item by item, we find that during the first two days (October 22 and 23) there were twenty-nine interventions on the text as a whole. On October 23 the discussion moved to the Introduction and chapter I, which dealt with general principles; this discussion lasted until October 29 and saw eighty-eight fathers intervene. A substantial amount of time was also devoted to the discussion of chapter II (the Eucharist), which began on October 29 and ended on November 6, after seventy-nine fathers had spoken.

Slowly it became clear that it would be impossible to spend this much time on a single document.[18] Having already advised the members of the Curia not to participate in the debates,[19] on November 6 John XXIII granted the presidents power to suggest to the assembly that a discussion be brought to a close if it was felt that, with respect to content, nothing more could be said on the matter.[20] The fathers would be free to accept or reject the presidents' suggestion. Voting would take place by standing or remaining seated; fathers prevented from speaking by this vote of closure were invited to submit their text in writing.

From that point on things ran more smoothly. The discussion on chapter III, which dealt with the sacraments and sacramentals, took less than two days (November 6-7), without the presidents having to suggest a closure. Forty-one fathers intervened.

Chapter IV on the Divine Office was discussed on November 7, 9, and 10, with forty-two fathers taking the podium. Chapters V to VIII (church materials, furnishings, decoration; liturgical music and art) were dealt with in three days (November 10-13), during which forty-nine fathers intervened. These last two discussions were closed on the suggestion of the presidents.

tion of the Dutch episcopal conference as well as that of the Indonesian bishops, a large number of whom were of Dutch origin (AS I/2, 129). Two days later Bishop Djajasepoetra intervened on behalf of the same Indonesian episcopate (AS I/2, 311). Bishop Perraudin took the floor on behalf of the episcopal conference of Ruanda-Burundi on November 5 (AS I/2, 122). Finally, Bishop Lebrum Moratinos spoke on behalf of the Venezuelan episcopal conference on November 6 (AS I/2, 177).

[17] See AS I/1, 333, 419, 526-27; I/2, 94.

[18] Letters reveal repeated complaints about the duration of the discussions; see, for example, Laurentin to Delhaye, October 29, 1962 (Delhaye papers, no. 160, CLG).

[19] According to Martimort, this was a consequence of the "counterproductive interventions" of Dante, Parente, and above all Staffa ("Les débats liturgiques," 301 n.34).

[20] AS I/2, 159-61.

The discussions on the liturgy schema took so much time because there was much repetition and because speakers often wandered off the point. The fact that the regulations granted the fathers the opportunity to speak either on the schema as a whole or on a particular part was the primary reason for lengthy and sometimes inappropriate deviations from the matter at hand. It will be no surprise that more than 100 of the fathers were regularly absent from the discussions and that the number of those present at the general assemblies decreased, albeit unspectacularly, the longer a particular discussion dragged on.[21] Moreover, along with Bishop Bekkers of s-Hertogenbosch, it could be asked whether those who intervened, especially the critics of the schema, were speaking in their own name or on behalf of a group.[22]

Before going into more detail on the individual interventions themselves, it is worth noting at this point the major points of discussion that occupied the fathers during the debate: Latin or the vernacular; concelebration; communion under both species; adaptation; the authority of bishops with regard to liturgical reform; the reform of the Breviary, the Missal, and the Ritual; and, finally, the anointing of the sick.

I. Comments on the Text as a Whole

From the very start of the debate, which began at the fourth general congregation on October 22, a remarkable number of fathers, even those from the missions, took a positive position with regard to the schema,[23] some openly describing it as the best of the texts they had received.[24] Its pastoral character[25] received as much praise as its moderateness and bal-

---

[21] See the survey in R. Laurentin, *L'enjeu du concile*, 56-57.

[22] See *AS* I/1, 441.

[23] See, for example, J. Frings (Cologne, Germany); Lercaro (Bologna, Italy); R. Silva Henríquez (Santiago, Chile), who spoke on behalf of a number of colleagues; L. Rugambwa (Bukoba, Tanganyika); A. Devoto (Goya, Argentina), who spoke on behalf of four colleagues; H. Volk (Mainz, Germany); J. Landázuri Ricketts (Lima, Chile); Maximos IV Saigh (Antioch, Syria) (*AS* I/1, 309, 311-13, 323, 333, 524, 355-56, 375, and 377 respectively).

[24] See J. Döpfner (Munich, Germany): "I am glad to accept and to commend the Constitution on the Sacred Liturgy presented to us; of all the schemata given to us it provides the best way to begin the work of the Council" (*AS* I/1, 319); see also D. Hurley (Durban, South Africa) (*AS* I/1, 327).

[25] See, for example, G.-B. Montini (Milan, Italy) and R. Silva Henríquez (*AS* I/1, 313-14, 323, respectively).

ance.[26] The schema plotted a well-chosen middle path between renewal according to personal judgment and without respect for tradition, on the one hand,[27] and the changeless character of the rites, on the other.[28] It preserved the essence of the liturgy while leaving room for changes in its form, although such changes had to be made with the utmost care and prudence.[29] It established, moreover, a sound relationship between liturgy and faith[30] while clearly expressing the fact that the liturgy as such is the very heart of the Church's life and of the mystical communion between God and humanity.[31]

Third-world representatives expressed their delight that the schema gave an opportunity for non-western cultures to celebrate the liturgy and to give instruction in their own ways. Rugambwa, for example, was elated that the episcopal conferences were being offered the chance to make the changes in worship needed to make it conform more to the unique character and traditions of various peoples.[32] In the same vein the Chilean bishops expressed their satisfaction that room had been created for the use of the vernacular; they pointed out that the Church had not insisted on the preservation of Aramaic or Greek when they were no longer understood by the people.[33] There was also much praise for the biblical character of the schema[34] and joy at the fact that it would contribute greatly to the promotion of active participation in the liturgy.[35] Finally, there was satisfaction in some circles that the schema furthered the study of the liturgy.[36]

From the very beginning the proponents of the schema were quite aware that there would inevitably be some opposition. Anticipating criticisms of the schema's apparent lack of theological foundations, Ler-

[26] See Montini, AS I/1, 314.

[27] On two occasions it refers to the Ambrosian rite, the second of which contains an explicit statement on the preservation of traditions: "Those who follow the Ambrosian rite are particularly desirous to remain faithful on this point" (AS I/1, 314); with regard to respect for tradition, see also Hervás y Benet, AS I/1, 339.

[28] Döpfner, for example, also points to the moderateness of the schema (AS I/1, 319 and 321).

[29] AS I/1, 313-14.

[30] See A. Fares (Cantanzaro, Italy), AS I/1, 353.

[31] AS I/1, 309; see also Döpfner, AS I/1, 319; and Hurley, AS I/1, 328.

[32] See AS I/1, 333-34; also, for example, Tatsuo Doi (Tokyo), AS I/1, 323.

[33] AS I/1, 324.

[34] See, for example, Döpfner, AS I/1, 321, written addition to his address; Hervás y Benet, AS I/1, 339.

[35] See, for example, Döpfner and Doi, AS I/1, 319 and 323 respectively.

[36] See Hervás y Benet, AS I/1, 339.

caro, for example, stressed the fact that the theological principles that lay at the basis of the constitution were clearly present in the Introduction and chapter I; on the other hand, the fathers should not expect a sort of scholastic theological treatise but rather a firm foundation for the renewal and advancement of the liturgy. Lercaro also emphasized the fact that the schema only offered a *summa* of the theological principles, in other words, a description of the essence of the liturgy, an approach that followed the method of the encyclical *Mediator Dei*.[37] The cardinal also noted that the general norms (nos. 16-31) were the logical outcome of this theological basis and that what was said about adapting the liturgy to the national character and the traditions of the various peoples was quite in line with what had been stated by popes since Benedict XV. The world's peoples today were striving for cultural and civil progress, which deserved to be realized without reserve.[38]

Lercaro continued that the concrete description of norms in chapters II to VIII was certainly open to comment and correction. He suggested, however, that even here things had been done in line with the Apostolic See, especially from Pius XII onward. What the schema proposed was in complete agreement with the renewal that had been approved and even encouraged by the Holy See. The proposed adaptations were also necessary for a more conscious, active and fruitful participation of the faithful in the sacred mysteries.[39] The basic tenor of appreciation, as Montini noted, centered on the fact that the liturgy is for the people and not the other way round.[40]

A number of speakers in favor of the schema criticized certain changes that had been made in the text, alterations that were becoming public knowledge thanks to a list Martimort had drawn up of the differences between the original text discussed at the Central Preparatory

---

[37] *AS* I/1, 311-13. For Lercaro's intervention, see *Per la forza dello Spirito. Discorsi conciliari del card. Giacomo Lercaro* (Bologna, 1984), 73-78; for an interpretation of this address, see G. Alberigo, "L'esperienza conciliare di un vescovo," ibid., 14-15. On the relationship between the encyclical *Mediator Dei* and the constitution, see Y. Congar, "L''Ecclesia' ou communauté chrétienne sujet intégral de l'action liturgique," in J. P. Jossua-Y. Congar, *La liturgie après Vatican II* (Paris, 1967), 268-76.

[38] A similarly positive understanding of the theological level of the text can be found, for example, in the speech of Hervás y Benet (*AS* I/1, 339).

[39] With some clarity Lercaro added at this point: "They do not proceed from some sterile archeologism or from a senseless itch for novelty, but from the daily urging of pastors and from pastoral exigencies, since, as St. Pius X said, active participation in the Liturgy is the first and indispensable source of the Christian spirit" (*AS* I/1, 313).

[40] "The Liturgy was instituted for men and not men for the Liturgy" (*AS* I/1, 315).

Commission and the now official text.[41] In the first place, it was repeatedly requested that the text which had been sent to the Central Commission by the preparatory liturgical commission be reprinted, together with
the clarifying *Declarationes*, so that whatever seemed vague or indefi-
nite could be explained.[42] Speakers also saw an opposition between the
introductory nota at the beginning of the schema,[43] which in effect
placed all decision-making power in the hands of the Holy See, and no.
16 of the schema, according to which the revision of the liturgical books
was to be the work of specialists from every part of the world.[44] It was
also pointed out, for example by Frings, that in the passages relating to
liturgical language, which had been approved by the Central Commission, the right had been reserved to the local episcopal conferences, in
agreement with bishops from neighboring regions, to determine how and
within what limits the vernacular would be introduced, with the Holy
See simply reviewing the decisions already made.[45] But in the schema
before them, everything had been reduced to the presentation of suggestions, the execution of which was now in the hands of the Holy See.[46]
This complaint made clear that certain circles were annoyed by this centralizing addition to the schema and deplored the absence of the *Declarationes*.

Of course, a number of speakers criticized the schema for going too
far. Msgr. Dante of the Congregation for Rites boldly declared that the
Council ought to concern itself only with general principles, the imple-

---

[41] See Martimort, "Les débats liturgiques," 293, n.7; *History*, I, 313-17.

[42] This complaint returns time and again; see, for example, Döpfner (October 22),
Bishops S. Méndez Arceo (October 23), Jenny (October 27), Spülbeck (October 29) (*AS*
I/1, 319-21, 359, 513, 578, respectively); see also Schmidt, *Die Konstitution*, 74-77.

[43] "The intention of this Constitution is to propose only general norms and 'loftier
principles that concern the general liturgical renewal,' leaving it to the Holy See to implement the individual matters" (*AS* I/1, 263). The removal of this note was repeatedly asked
for (see, for example, J. Le Cordier, Auxiliary Bishop of Paris [*AS* I/1, 476]).

[44] "Within a few years the liturgical books are to be revised with the help of experts
drawn from the whole world" (*Schema constitutionis de Sacra Liturgia*, no. 16; *AS* I/1,
269).

[45] "The episcopal conferences in individual regions, after consultation, when appropriate, with the bishops of neighboring regions using the same langauge, are to establish
the limits and the way in which the vernacular language is to be admitted into the liturgy;
their acts are to be reviewed by the Holy See (see can. 291)" (*ADP*, III/2, 21). Silva Henriquez emphasized the importance of granting special authority to the episcopal conferences. Indeed, he urged that "the so-called exaggerated 'centralization' which weakens
pastoral efforts be avoided" (*AS* I/1, 324); see also Tatsuo Doi, *AS* I/1, 323.

[46] The text under discussion in the Council hall had changed the word "*statuere*"
[establish] to "*Sanctae Sedi proponere*" (propose to the Holy See) (*Schema constitutionis
de Sacra Liturgia*, no. 24, 167; *AS* I/1, 272).

mentation of which should be left to experts in the liturgy. He also used his intervention to point out that episcopal conferences or individual bishops were limited to offering suggestions, while approval of any changes had to be left to the Holy See.[47] While Dante's intervention focused, in a certain sense, on a question of procedure, others questioned the very content of the schema. There were complaints about what was seen as an overindulgence of the spirit of renewal, which carried dangers for clergy and people alike.[48] Some even warned that there was too great an emphasis on the participation of the faithful.[49]

The schema was criticized as rather "verbose," more poetical and ascetical than theological, more a liturgical treatise than a conciliar document. Theologically, vague formulations and lack of precision caused some unease.[50] For this reason the doctrinal part of the schema should be submitted to the Doctrinal Commission before being presented to the fathers for their decision.[51] Ottaviani argued for a complete revision of the entire constitution.[52] In his opinion, too much weight was being given to the liturgy.[53] Ideas such as communion under both species and concelebration were dismissed.[54] The scripture texts used in the schema should be examined to see if they were being employed in their actual biblical meaning.[55] Other complaints focused on the fact that the schema did not mention reform of the cult of saints or of the processes involved with beatifications and canonisations, relics, and the cult surrounding them,[56] and the Eastern rites and their need of reform.[57] Msgr. D'Avack (Camerino, Italy) found that the schema did not sufficiently explain the relationship between the sacrifice on the cross, the sacrifice of the mass, and the daily life of Christians.[58] A final and theologically justifiable

[47] Dante, *AS* I/1, 330-31.
[48] Spellman, *AS* I/1, 316-17.
[49] Spellman, *AS* I/1, 316.
[50] Vagnozzi, see *AS* I/1, 325-26; see also Parente, *AS* I/1, 423.
[51] See Vagnozzi, *AS* I/1, 326.
[52] *AS* I/1, 349-50.
[53] See *AS* I/1, 349-50.
[54] Dante, *AS* I/1, 331.
[55] See Fares, *AS* I/1, 354.
[56] Dante, *AS* I/1, 331; see also García Martinez, *AS* I/1, 332.
[57] Dante, *AS* I/1, 331. It should be noted here that the general norms for the liturgy as found in the schema were also considered to be applicable to the Eastern rites and that these rites were also in need of liturgical renewal and adaptation. It is evident, nevertheless, that the remark of G. Amadouni (Exarch for the Armenians, France) in this regard implied something other than Dante intended (see *AS* I/1, 361-62).
[58] *AS* I/1, 359-61. D'Avack also called for a revision of the mass prayers from the offertory to the communion.

complaint concerned the insufficient attention devoted to the Holy Spirit in the schema, a complaint which was in no way a condemnation of the schema as a whole.[59]

Meanwhile, the Liturgical Commission met for a second time on October 22 amid indications that its members were already beginning to feel that they were wasting their time. Larraona was difficult to understand, and people were still not clear on the commission's *modus operandi* although they were eager to get on with their job.[60] Upon Martimort's initiative, it was proposed and accepted that a subcommission should draw up a set of internal regulations. The subcommission, which consisted of Martimort, Jullien, Jenny, Bonet, and McManus, worked out a five-page *Ratio procedendi commisionis conciliaris de Sacra Liturgia* [Procedures for the Conciliar Commission on the Sacred Liturgy],[61] which was to prove valuable to other commissions also.

II. THE RIGHTS OF EPISCOPAL CONFERENCES AND THE USE OF THE VERNACULAR

COMMENTS ON THE INTRODUCTION AND CHAPTER I

After the comments on the schema as a whole had concluded at the assembly of October 23, the discussion moved to the Introduction and chapter I.[62] Most attention was given to nos. 16 (the revision of the liturgical books) and 24 (Latin and the vernacular), although nos. 20-22, which dealt with the adaptation of the liturgy to local traditions, elicited some contrary reactions.[63] No. 16 and no. 24 were a sort of test case in the struggle between supporters and opponents of the decentralization of

---

[59] Silva Henriquez, *AS* I/1, 324, also requested that the constitution offers a synthesis of biblical and patristic teaching on the spiritual priesthood of the faithful.

[60] See Jenny papers, box 8, file 5, CNPL; see also Martimort, "Les débats liturgiques," 307.

[61] See Jenny papers, box 8, file 5, CNPL; Bekkers papers, document 390 (Archives of the diocese of 's-Hertogenbosch); see also Martimort, "Les débats liturgiques," 308, and Caprile, II, 98-101.

[62] Before continuing, however, Felici announced that for those fathers who, for a serious reason (such as pastoral obligations), intended to leave the Council, a simple message to the Secretariat to that effect would suffice.

[63] Most of the objections to the various changes stemmed from former or still active members of the Curia. Critical vocies were also heard from representatives of the English-speaking world.

authority and the use of the vernacular,[64] although the former turned out to be far more nuanced than the latter.[65]

Before taking a more detailed look at the interventions, it is perhaps worth noting that a number of the criticisms were rather general,[66] suggesting, for example, that a text should be shorter, clearer, and more efficiently formulated.[67] Some felt that the schema lacked a precise definition of the liturgy as such,[68] while others complained that it did not always deal with the nature of the liturgy in a logical fashion. Still others thought it insufficiently explicit on the relationship between liturgy and spiritual life.[69] Problems also arose about the use of words such as *instaurare, instauratio* [to renew, renewal], etc., which gave the false impression that the Council intended to reform everything having to do with the liturgy.[70] Such remarks, which were in line with the critique expressed by Dante and Ottaviani on the schema as a whole, were supported by, among others, Staffa's intervention, which stated that the schema's encouragement of an ecumenical spirit should not proceed at the cost of the truth and the faith, the content of which, it was clear to all, he understood well.[71]

On the other hand, a number of fathers were glad that the Introduction stated that the schema did not intend to issue dogmatic definitions but gave priority to the renewal of the liturgical life as such, apart from any theological debates.[72] Several speakers pointed out that the Introduction

[64] R. Kaiser, *Pope, Council and World: The Story of Vatican II* (New York, 1963), 136.

[65] In this regard see Fares, *AS* I/1, 364, for example, who appealed for the use of one single language, namely Latin, but added immediately that additional explanations could be given in the vernacular.

[66] The complaints were in fact made by people who may be considered rather conservative (see F. M. Stabile, "Il Cardinal Ruffini e il Vaticano II. Le lettere di un 'intransigente,'" *CrSt* 11 [1990], 83-176).

[67] Ruffini with regard to I/1-3.5-6; see *AS* I/1, 364.

[68] Godfrey (Westminster); *AS* I/1, 374.

[69] Van Lierde (Rome); *AS* I/1, 412.

[70] See Ruffini, *AS* I/1, 364.

[71] *AS* I/1, 428-29. The intervention closed with the clever proposal that the whole schema on the liturgy be remanded to a mixed commission, composed of members of the Doctrinal, Liturgical, and Sacramental Commissions. If the proposal had been accepted, the liturgical reform would have been postponed *sine die* and would have been returned to the competency of Ottaviani. Montini understood this immediately and suggested, through C. Colombo, that a vote of general approval of the schema be proposed immediately (see M. Paiano, *Genesi storica della constituzione conciliare Sacrosanctum Concilium*, in press).

[72] Among others, J. De Barros Câmara (Rio de Janeiro), W. Godfrey (Westminster), V. Garcias (Bombay), W. Bekkers ('s-Hertogenbosch) (see *AS* I/1, 367, 373, 400-1, 441).

stated quite clearly that the purpose of the liturgical renewal is eminently pastoral; the sacraments exist for the sake of the people.[73] Where liturgical changes were being proposed, priority should be given, therefore, to those based on pastoral rather than historical arguments.[74] The Eucharist was considered the way par excellence through which the word of Christ and the voice of the Church could be heard.[75]

Discussions of no. 16, which dealt with the revision of the liturgical books by an international group of specialists, reflected great tensions. A number of speakers felt that this number needed an addition; namely, that the Congregation for Rites was to keep the revision under its control.[76] In his address on October 24 Parente complained about the way in which a number of speakers had spoken of the Holy Office, but he himself did not hesitate to call those advocating renewal "*novatores*" [innovators].[77]

Others insisted that the episcopal conferences should also be consulted for the revision of the liturgical books[78] and that any decisions on the matter should be swiftly put into practice, precisely because of pastoral need.[79] Bishops from mission territories, who had positively received this part of the text because it met their pastoral needs,[80] also requested that the group of specialists who would carry out the revision of the liturgical books consist of people familiar with the local cultures;[81] people from the mission territories themselves should also be included in the group because they were the ones more aware of specific local needs. From their perspective it was vital that the diverse particular cultures be integrated into the universal patrimony of the Church.[82]

Fireworks went off when it came to nos. 20-22, which gave the local bishops and the national episcopal conferences greater jurisdiction at the level of the administration of the sacraments, sacramentals, liturgical

---

[73] See, for example, Léger, AS I/1, 371.
[74] Godfrey, AS I/1, 374.
[75] Léger, AS I/1, 371.
[76] See Ruffini, Parente, AS I/1, 365, 425.
[77] See AS I/1, 425.
[78] See W. Bekkers, AS I/1, 387. His contribution is a good example of an intervention that was the result of comprehensive consultation and profound reflection within a particular episcopal conference, in this case that of Holland. (See Bekkers Papers, Archives of the Diocese of 's-Hertogenbosch, nos. 375-78).
[79] Léger, Vielmo (Chile), D'Agostino (Italy); AS I/1, 372, 553, 590, respectively.
[80] See, for example, V. Gracias (Bombay), AS I/1, 400-1.
[81] For Africa: Ramanantoanina (Madagascar), AS I/1, 419.
[82] See Ramanantoanina, who spoke on behalf of the entire African episcopate, including the bishops of Madagascar and the other islands (300 bishops), AS I/1, 419-20.

language, and so forth.[83] For Ruffini it was quite clear that this was simply not appropriate.[84] The only way forward was to keep in line with the Holy See.[85] In contrast, others felt that the latitude given by the schema was a positive thing because it gave the local episcopal conferences sufficient authority to set about their task in an adequate fashion.[86]

The discussions surrounding the use of liturgical language dealt with in no. 24 seemed endless: no fewer than eighty interventions focused on this topic.[87] The African bishops requested the removal of the adjective "western" from the phrase "in the western liturgy," since the word suggested too close a link to the culture and history of Western Europe, a problem during a time when aspirations for emancipation were rising in Africa.[88]

Arguments for maintaining the use of Latin in the liturgy were numerous and reflected a certain wariness and fear, as was the case with Cardinal McIntyre, who argued, "The Sacred Mass should remain as it is. Serious changes in the liturgy introduce serious changes in dogma."[89] There was also a fear that the use of the vernacular would endanger the unity of the Christian peoples, symbolized in the unity of the liturgy.[90] Some asked whether the fathers were aware that unity of faith presupposes one liturgy and one language.[91] If the Council were to take a different line would this not run counter to tradition?[92] Did the use of Latin not transcend the limits of nationality and in so doing reveal the

---

[83] Concerning the theological background of this tension, see for example, R. Rouquette, *La fin d'une chrétienté. Chroniques* (Unam Sanctam, 69a; Paris, 1968), 236-37.

[84] Ruffini found that the restrictive phrase *"actis a Sancta Sede recognitis"* [with the acts reviewed by the Holy See], was insufficient since jurisdiction in this matter belonged entirely to the Pope. The bishops, therefore, had absolutely no right to make decisions on their own (*AS* I/1, 366); see also Browne, *AS* I/1, 377. Landázuri Ricketts pointed out the dangers that such freedom might create for the unity of the rite (*AS* I/1, 375).

[85] Godfrey, *AS* I/1, 374; see also Bacci, *AS* I/1, 410.

[86] See Gracias, *AS* I/1, 401.

[87] See *AS* I/1, 285; for the broader background of the discussion, see A. Wenger, *Vatican II. Vol. I: The First Session* (Westminster, Md., 1966), 60-63.

[88] See *AS* I/1, 420.

[89] See *AS* I/1, 371. McIntyre's intervention made the quite surprising argument that as early as the fourth century the councils had fixed the doctrines and dogmas of the Church in precise Latin formulations! (see *AS* I/1, 369). Spellman was in all respects an enthusiastic ally of his American colleague (see *AS* I/1, 318).

[90] Ruffini, McIntyre, Bacci, Calewaert (member of the Liturgical Commission), *AS* I/1, 366, 369, 409-10, 474, respectively.

[91] Fares, *AS* I/1, 354-55; see also McIntyre, *AS* I/1, 370.

[92] See Bacci, *AS* I/1, 408-9, who pointed out that the use of a national language in the Eucharist had already been condemned in the person of Rosmini and was also diametrically opposed to the decisions of the Council of Trent, which are cited in *Mediator Dei* and *Veterum Sapientia*.

Church's political neutrality?[93] Reference was likewise made to the superiority of Latin at the intellectual level; no other language could provide such a clear, precise, and categorical medium for the formulation of the Church's teaching.[94] Continued use of Latin would also better preserve the liturgy's sense of mystery.[95]

Supporters of Latin did recognize that it was not understood by everyone. Their solution was to provide missals with adequate translations of the Latin texts.[96] Not everybody considered this a desirable solution. Bacci, for example, was of the opinion that, given the low intellectual level of many of the faithful and the danger of temptation lurking in certain biblical narratives, it made no sense to multiply translations.[97] Ecumenical arguments also received little sympathy within this group. Some of the fathers pointed to the situation in the Protestant Churches, where the vernacular was already in use; not only had it led to endless fragmentation,[98] but it could hardly be considered a success given the poor attendance and paucity of Church membership among them.[99] It was also claimed that the introduction of the vernacular in the missions would lead to problems, given the multiplicity of languages and tribes in these territories.[100]

Opposed to those who would countenance no changes whatever, a large number of speakers called for a more widespread use of the vernacular in the liturgy, without wishing to minimize the importance of Latin. These fathers proposed a variety of degrees of use ranging from the *via media*[101] to the complete discontinuance of Latin in the liturgy. A number of arguments were presented, pastoral concern being the chief one. The introduction of the vernacular in those parts of the liturgy intended for the people would lead to more active participation by the faithful.[102] The majority of people, and not only in mission terri-

[93] McIntyre, *AS* I/1, 370.

[94] McIntyre, *AS* I/1, 370.

[95] See Parente, *AS* I/1, 426.

[96] See Spellman, *AS* I/1, 318, who favored greater latitude in the use of the vernacular in the administration of the sacraments and pointed out that this was already happening in practice; Dante insisted that the use of the vernacular be restricted to preaching and catechesis (*AS* I/1, 331).

[97] Bacci, *AS* I/1, 409.

[98] McIntyre, *AS* I/1, 370.

[99] Godfrey, *AS* I/1, 374.

[100] Godfrey, *AS* I/1, 373, who was of the opinion that the matter should be handed over to the episcopal conferences.

[101] See A. Meyer (Chicago); Barrachina Estevan; Bekkers; *AS* I/1, 411, 584, 442.

[102] See, for example, Feltin, Ramanantoanina, *AS* I/1, 369, 420. Even Bacci, for whom

tories,[103] were unfamiliar with Latin.[104] Latin was an obstacle to the prayer life even of the clergy.[105] For people in mission territories there was the additional problem that they had no affinity with the Latin language.[106] A country like Japan, or even a whole continent, as in the case of Africa, also expressed reservations on the continued use of Latin. If the intellectual elite of these lands did not understand Latin, let alone the ordinary man and woman in the street, was its maintenance in the liturgy not a grave mistake?[107] The African bishops requested that local authorities be given the right not only to make suggestions with regard to the use of the vernacular but also to make decisions in the matter and that this be added to the conclusion of no. 24 in the schema.[108]

Other interventions underlined that from the earliest times the liturgy had been the locus par excellence of catechesis.[109] Those who desired to give the faithful a more active role in the liturgy or to nourish them with the grace of God by means of the liturgy were constantly confronted with the impediment of language.[110] In this regard Descuffi asked why permission to use the vernacular in the administration of the sacraments, which had already been granted in a number of places, could not be widened to include all the nations.[111] As a matter of fact, with Rome's assent, the liturgy was already being celebrated in the vernacular in a number of places.[112] The fathers who knew the Church's history better than others presented arguments from history in favor of the translation of the liturgical books into the vernacular.[113]

The frequently raised argument that the introduction of the vernacular in the liturgy would endanger the Church's unity of expression was fre-

the use of the vernacular in the Eucharist was unacceptable, appealed for its use in preaching, catechesis, and the sacraments and sacramentals (see *AS* I/1, 410).

[103] J. Descuffi (Smyrna) notes, for example, that even the Church in the West found itself in a missionary situation in several places (*AS* I/1, 416).

[104] See, for example, Feltin, Descuffi, *AS* I/1, 368, 415.

[105] See, for example, Feltin, *AS* I/1, 369.

[106] Feltin, Gracias, *AS* I/1, 368, 402-3, respectively.

[107] See Schmidt, *Die Konstitution*, 88-90; *La Croix*, October 30, 1962.

[108] They proposed returning to the original language, using *statuere* instead of *proponere* (*AS* I/1, 420).

[109] See Feltin, *AS* I/1, 368.

[110] Feltin, *AS* I/1, 368. According to Feltin, Latin was sometimes used as an excuse not to take the faith seriously.

[111] *AS* I/1, 415.

[112] See Gracias, Descuffi, *AS* I/1, 402, 415.

[113] Tisserant discussed a number of examples from the Church's history (see *AS* I/1, 399-400). Together with those of Bea, Tisserant's examples were received with much appreciation (see Koslowiecki, [Lusaka], *AS* I/1, 422).

quently commented upon. It was pointed out that too great a stress on the use of the Latin language in the liturgy might give offense to the other liturgical languages.[114] Koslowiecki noted that it was possible to be a very good Christian without using Latin in the liturgy. True unity, moreover, lay in the realization that we are all members of the one body and not in a common language.[115]

The problem of intelligibility was not restricted to the Latin rite. The Armenian Bishop Zohrabian pointed out that his people were spread out over the entire globe and that those outside his own land no longer understood Armenian. He appealed, therefore, for the national episcopal conferences to be able to provide translations so that liturgical texts would be made intelligible.[116]

Speaking in French on October 23, Maximus IV Saigh offered something of a synthesis of the arguments raised by a number of the supporters of the introduction of the vernacular in the liturgy.[117] The Patriarch felt that from the perspective of the Eastern rite it was strange that the presider in the liturgy would use a language that differed from that of his congregation, who in turn had to pray in a language they did not understand. A living Church has no use for a dead language. Since it is the instrument of the Holy Spirit, language should be living. Saigh proposed that the statement, "The use of Latin in the western liturgy is to be preserved," be replaced by "Latin is the original and official language of the Roman rite." Episcopal conferences should have the right to define the extent to which a living language is employed in the liturgy.

Maximos IV Saigh concluded his address by asking if it was possible to provide simultaneous translation for the Council fathers, precisely because those who had come from the East were not obliged to know Latin.[118] This remark touched on a sensitive point. Many of the bishops, for whom Latin was not a medium of communication, did not understand what was being said in the council hall. Even minor procedural instructions were only given attention when they were translated. It can be stated, without exaggeration, that the observers, for whom translation

---

[114] See Koslowiecki, *AS* I/1, 421.

[115] *AS* I/1, 422. A good summary of the arguments in favor of the vernacular is found in the intervention of L. La Ravoire Morrow (Krishanagar), who made a plea for the vernacular because of pastoral and ecumenical reasons (see *AS* I/1, 467-69). F. Simons (Indore) intervened in a similar fashion (see *AS* I/1, 586-87).

[116] *AS* I/1, 508. Zohrabian's praise of Armenia was not appreciated by Ruffini, who was the president of the day (see 507).

[117] See *AS* I/1, 377-80.

[118] See *AS* I/1, 377-79.

was provided, were able to follow the debate much better than many of the bishops.

Because of the many repetitions, the debate on the Introduction and chapter I could only be brought to a conclusion on October 27. Seven more chapters remained to be treated.

During the debate on the first chapter, the Liturgical Commission continued its activities, but, as Lercaro remarked on October 23, without being sure of its right to begin discussing a schema that had not yet been approved in general by the Council. Larraona replied that the fact that the discussion of the Introduction and chapter I had already begun meant that the schema had been accepted de facto, and, therefore, the Commission could get on with its job. The rest of the meeting that day was devoted to a discussion of how the Commission should operate, in conformity with the conciliar regulations.[119]

At the meeting on October 26, Larraona announced that he had set up a theological subcommission headed by R. Gagnebet.[120] The majority of the subcommission's members were dogmaticians from Rome. Besides Gagnebet, Masi and Van den Eynde were also appointed to the Commission, which was then strengthened by Vagaggini and Martimort. Apparently the reason behind this move of Larraona was to avoid the setting up of a mixed commission.[121] As we shall see below, a total of thirteen subcommissions would be established, each with eleven members.

It is clear from the meeting of October 26 that the members of the commission were still not sure about how to proceed. This is apparent, for example, from the discussion of the episcopal conferences. While Larraona was of the opinion that these had not been clearly defined juridically, Martimort argued that they already had juridical existence in fact. Stalling for time, Larraona replied that it was not the Commission's role to deal with the law, but Wagner replied that in any case it would have to formulate a text, should the bishops' conferences come up for discussion.[122]

---

[119] Since the items discussed in this meeting were to find expression in Martimort's *Ratio procedendi*, we do not deal with them here.

[120] Not everybody was happy with Gagnebet's inclusion in the Commission (see Jenny to Delhaye, November 2, 1962): "And they have put Gagnebet and Masi on the commission; they are afraid the style will be too 'biblical,' not scholastic enough" (Delhaye papers, no. 161, CLG).

[121] See replies submitted to Jenny that refer to the fact that there was talk in the aula of the establishment of a mixed commission (Jenny papers, box 8, CNPL).

[122] See Jenny papers, box 8, CNPL.

The following day Martimort presented the document of his ad hoc subcommission on the Commission's working procedure. The first part dealt with the Commission's structure and included an outline of the particular task of the Commission and the competence of the chair and the secretary;[123] it also discussed the role of a reporter and the possibility of setting up subcommissions. Part 2 explained the way the Commission should set about its business. Broadly speaking, the Commission would begin by discussing the corrections and comments of the fathers on the basis of a report. Each member would have the right to contribute to the discussion, which would end with a vote. The corrected text would then be presented to the general congregation, during which the commentator would explain the criteria used by the Commission in dealing with the corrections. After a vote in the general congregation, the approved corrections would be included in the text, while the rejected corrections would come back to the Commission, and the whole procedure would be repeated. The same procedure was also to be followed for the *modi*.[124] Apparently Martimort's text was approved without much discussion.[125] The Commission had its regulations but no work to do yet, because the Council was still discussing the use of the language in the liturgy and the juridical status of episcopal conferences.

III. COMMUNION UNDER BOTH SPECIES AND CONCELEBRATION

THE DISCUSSION ON CHAPTER II

The general congregation on October 29 began with Felici's announcement of the names of the fathers whom the Pope had designated members of the conciliar commissions; he then asked that the final speakers on the question of liturgical languages refrain from repeating what had already been said, an indication that the leaders of the Council were also impatient at the slow progress of the discussion.[126] What was

---

[123] In fact, the document simply described matters that were de facto already operating; Jenny noted subtly on the margin of page 2 that the Commission had not yet done any work! (Jenny papers, box 8, CNPL).

[124] Jenny papers, box 8, CNPL.

[125] This can be deduced, at least, from the minimal number of notes on Msgr. Jenny's copy of the document (Jenny papers, box 8, CNPL). Apparently more time was devoted to the way in which incoming texts should be dealt with (see the written notes on page 3 of Msgr. Jenny's copy).

[126] AS I/1, 563. After the discussion of language ended, Felici read to the assembly the Pope's reply to a telegram the fathers had sent him two days earlier (AS I/1, 597).

to prove to be a lengthy discussion on chapter II, "The Mystery of the Holy Eucharist," then began.[127] The lion's share of the debate on this chapter centered on communion under both species (no. 42) and concelebration (nos. 44-46).

As was gradually becoming the norm, the discussion was opened by a number of heavyweights, namely Spellman, Ruffini, and Léger. Spellman protested no. 37, which proposed revising the order of the Mass; in his view "this opens the door to all sorts of innovations."[128] The following day Ottaviani returned to no. 37, which he considered far too vague[129]; it made him wonder if the fathers were planning to launch a revolution.[130] In his opinion the proposal to revise the order of the Mass, as a whole and in its parts, should be dropped from the schema altogether; otherwise the faithful, whom the liturgical movement had made familiar with the structure of the Eucharist, would be led into confusion.[131] Ottaviani had so many difficulties with the chapter as a whole that he overran his allotted time and had to be interrupted by Alfrink who, with the assistance of Villot, was chair for the day. Alfrink's interruption and the great applause that followed it left Ottaviani so enraged that he did not show his face at the general assemblies for two entire weeks.[132] While Ottaviani provoked one kind of commotion, an earlier intervention by Cardinal Gracias from Bombay had also made a profound impression on the fathers. He expressed his anxiety, and that of his seventy-one colleagues, about the political situation in his country, which had made him ask whether the bishops should not be with their people at this time, when India was under the threat of a Chinese invasion.[133]

---

[127] The material entitled *Animadversiones in schema Constitutionis de Sacra Liturgia. Caput II. De Sacrosancto Eucharistiae Mysterio* totaled 218 mimeographed pages; there is a copy in the van den Eynde papers, CCV.

[128] *AS* I/1, 598. It should be noted that a substantial number of speakers had reservations about the introduction to this chapter. Some felt that the sacrificial character of the Eucharist had not been sufficiently emphasized while others complained that the two-part structure of the mass, liturgy of the Word and liturgy of the Eucharist, had not been stated clearly. Still others objected that the distinction between sacrament and sacrifice had not been sufficiently elaborated (see, for example, Bea, Browne, Florit, Trinidade Salgueiro, *AS* I/2, 22, 26-27, 28, 39, respectively).

[129] Bea made the same remark (*AS* I/2, 22).

[130] "Do people want a revolution in the whole Mass?" (*AS* I/2, 18).

[131] Ibid.

[132] *AS* I/2, 20; it was a fairly ordinary occurrence for speakers who had gone over their time to be interrupted, but Ottaviani, given his position, was no ordinary speaker; see *DOttaviani*, 70.

[133] *AS* I/2, 13. On the same day, and purely by chance, a Chinese bishop was to request the inclusion of St. Joseph in the eucharistic prayer (see *AS* I/2, 31).

Despite Spellman's and Ottaviani's substantial reservations about no. 37,[134] it has to be said that the schema's emphasis on the active participation of the faithful was on the whole quite positively received.[135] The process of renewal had already made substantial ground, partly under impulse from Rome, and should be continued in conformity with the wishes of the pope.[136] The process itself was absolutely necessary if the Church was going to appeal to young people through the liturgy.[137] Rausch (Innsbruck) testified from his own experience how much fruit had been derived from the permission given in 1942 for use of the "dialogue mass" and readings in the vernacular.[138]

A substantial amount of interest was shown in the homily, which was treated in no. 39 of the schema[139] Almost everyone felt that the homily should not only be recommended, as a significant part of the liturgy, but that it should even be required,[140] especially on Sundays and feast days.[141] In a time of growing ignorance, some noted,[142] the homily was the moment par excellence to instruct the people.[143] The discussions on the homily also focused on its content: preaching ought to be systematic

---

[134] Spellman and Ottaviani were not alone in their conviction that the canon of the mass should be left untouched and that the active participation of the faithful would only lead to distraction. See Fares, who appealed to the Council of Trent (AS I/2, 116). The bishops' ignorance of the facts is sometimes quite shocking. According to Msgr. C. Saboia Bandeira de Mello (Palmas), for example, the Roman rite went back to Peter himself, one of the reasons why it should be left untouched.

[135] Appreciation of this fact was aptly expressed by F. Melendro on October 30 (AS I/2, 30-31).

[136] Compare the thoroughly documented intervention of Lázló, AS I/2, 112-13. In his intervention on October 31, Elchinger noted subtly, with reference to the so-called revolution, that if the Declaratio on no. 37 had been added to the text instead of dropped it might have prevented a great deal of unnecessary commotion: "That explanation presented us not with a revolution but with an evolution, a pastoral evolution, and one that is healthy and prudent" (AS I/2, 80); compare also Jenny's intervention on November 5, which was, even in its very choice of words, a frontal attack on Ottaviani's address of October 30 (AS I/2, 121-22).

[137] See Elchinger, AS I/2, 80-81.

[138] AS I/2, 35.

[139] At least thirty-four bishops intervened on this point; see Animadversiones in schema Constitutionum de Sacra Liturgia. Caput II. De Sacrosancto Eucharistiae Mysterio, 98-110. Judging from the remarkable number of repetitions, some of the fathers were clearly determined to stick to their prepared text.

[140] See Bea, Florit, A. Fernandes, AS I/2, 23, 28, 45.

[141] On this point one notices the particular accents of the various "tendencies;" see, for example, Spellman, AS I/1, 316-19; and A. Gianfranceschi, F. Jop (rather juridical), and C. Himmer, AS I/2, 228, 60-61, 92-93.

[142] As one among many, see F. Tortora, AS I/2, 277.

[143] See A. Franco Cascon, AS I/2, 224.

and theologically well founded.[144] Those who felt that the homily should be kept short for practical reasons[145] or who wished its recommended use relaxed in regions suffering from a shortage of priests were few and far between.[146]

Relatively few speakers felt called upon to intervene with regard to the prayers of the faithful. Pildain's intervention on November 6, in which he considered the point thoroughly and made a well-reasoned and warm appeal for a prayer on behalf of the poor, is thus all the more remarkable.[147]

The discussion of no. 41, which dealt with the use of the vernacular in certain parts of the mass, again raised the thorny question of language. Although new arguments were scarce,[148] Hallinan's intervention on October 31, in which he spoke on behalf of a significant number of U.S. bishops, deserves special mention. While he did not introduce anything really new into the discussion, his intervention was important because it showed the assembly that figures such as Spellman and McIntyre had not been speaking for the entire American Church and that a substantial number of the fathers from the United States disagreed with them.[149]

As already noted, a great deal of attention was given to no. 42, which dealt with communion under both species.[150] Those in favor presented a variety of arguments. For Alfrink, communion under both species was completely biblical; both eating and drinking belong to the very essence of the meal.[151] The Lord himself had commanded it, and from an evangelical and apostolic perspective it had been the normal practice.[152] The early church had respected this tradition,[153] and there were sufficient

---

[144] Helmsing, *AS* I/2, 46.

[145] See Godfrey, *AS* I/2, 10.

[146] See A. Hage, Superior General of the Basilians of St. John Baptist, *AS* I/2, 231-32.

[147] See *AS* I/2, 157-58. This intervention on behalf of the poor in the Church elicited strangely little response from commentators at the time.

[148] See G. Dwyer (Leeds), *AS* I/2, 38; McIntyre (against the use of the vernacular), *AS* I/2, 108-9. A rather remarkable call for appreciation of the work done by the preparatory commission on the liturgy together with an appeal for the introduction of the vernacular based on his own experience came from Zauner, *AS* I/2, 151-52.

[149] See *AS* I/2, 75-76; see also T. J. Shelley, *Paul J. Hallinan. First Archbishop of Atlanta* (Wilmington, 1989), 167-68.

[150] More than sixty interventions touched on this issue: see *Animadversiones in schema constitutionum de Sacra Liturgia. Caput II. De Sacrosancto Eucharistiae Mysterio*, 139-72; forty-four fathers were in favor of permitting communion under both kinds, although it should be noted that eleven of them had little sympathy for the idea of extending this permission to the laity (see, for example, Iglesias Navarri [Urgel], *AS* I/2, 62-63).

[151] *AS* I/2, 16-17.

[152] See N. Edelby, *AS* I/2, 85-86.

[153] Ibid., 85.

examples in the later history of the Church to show that the practice had been permitted in certain Churches even after Trent.[154] In eastern-rite Churches communion under both species remained the norm,[155] and its resumption in the West would therefore promote ecumenism.[156] Supporters were not blind to the possible practical problems the practice might bring, admitting that in circumstances where the people were too numerous it might be impossible; but such difficulties, they felt, should not be allowed to constitute an obstacle in principle.

The counter-arguments, which were partly theological and partly practical, testified to the creativity of the proposal's opponents. First of all, it was argued that if the Council acceded to the request for communion under both species, it would go against the tradition of several centuries. More than this, it would run counter to the Council of Constance; to the Bull of Leo X which condemned Luther; and ultimately to the definitions of the Council of Trent.[157] Ruffini argued that any decision on changes in this matter belonged not to the Council fathers but to the Pope.[158] Godfrey, conscious perhaps of the Anglican Church in his own country, felt that the introduction of communion under both species might give the impression that the Church had been mistaken in the past.[159] Ottaviani claimed that the proposal to restore the practice had been almost unanimously rejected by the Central Commission.[160] Communion under both kinds, it was felt, would be dangerous to administer and perhaps even unhygienic,[161] especially in a time when lipstick was the fashion.[162] Others pointed out that the fathers had not taken sufficient account of the fact that wine was very difficult to obtain in certain places.[163] What would happen in places where the people did not drink wine,[164] and how much wine would be needed when large crowds came to com-

---

[154] Bea, *AS* I/2, 23-24.

[155] Edelby, *AS* I/2, 85.

[156] See Alfrink, Bea, Weber, *AS* I/2, 17, 24-25, 79-80.

[157] See Ruffini, *AS* I/1, 600-601; Bea countered this argument on October 30 with an appeal to certain concessions granted by the pope in 1564 to several German provinces (*AS* I/2, 23-24).

[158] Ibid. This could make one wonder why the bishops were in Rome.

[159] *AS* I/2, 11.

[160] *AS* I/2, 20.

[161] See, for example, Ruffini, *AS* I/1, 601; Gracias, *AS* I/2, 12.

[162] Godfrey, *AS* I/2, 11.

[163] Gracias also noted that the drinking of wine was against the law in India (*AS* I/2, 13).

[164] Godfrey, *AS* I/2, 11.

munion?[165] Such a practice, some opined, would make the mass too long.[166]

As early as October 29 Léger had defended the introduction of concelebration. His speech was primarily a request for the restoration of the positive arguments in favor of concelebration that had been present in the original schema.[167] In the days that followed, the restoration of concelebration (no. 44) was repeatedly praised. In a remarkable intervention Elchinger stressed that in *Mediator Dei* the Pope had provided a theological justification for the practice of concelebration, which was also the norm in the Eastern Church.[168] Maronite Archbishop J. Khoury (Lebanon) expressed his appreciation for the fact that the Council wished to promote concelebration, but he regretted that the text was so limiting and argued that theologically and historically this manner of celebrating the Eucharist deserved preference.[169] The monastic communities also wished to see it restored.[170] Speaking on behalf of his 262 fellow bishops, Msgr. J. van Cauwelaert (Inongo) concluded by pointing out that concelebration as a concrete expression of unity was highly esteemed in cultures in which community was an important aspect.[171]

Critical voices were, of course, not absent from the discussion. Ruffini, for example, held fast to the one-priest-one-mass rule and proposed that if daily mass was impracticable because of an overabundance of priests then they might say mass every other day.[172] It was also claimed that overemphasis on concelebration might give the impression that the private mass was somehow inferior.[173] Critics also raised the problem of stipends. If the faithful gave a stipend for a mass, they did so for personal motives and in the expectation that the mass would be celebrated by one priest only.[174]

[165] Godfrey and McQuaid (on behalf of the Irish bishops), AS I/2, 11, 44.

[166] Godfrey, AS I/2, 10-11.

[167] Helmsing (Kansas City) was of a similar mind (AS I/2, 45). Léger's position was also supported by S. Kleiner, Abbot General of the Cistercians, who spoke on behalf of his fellow abbots (AS I/2, 47); see also Ramanantoanina, in the name of the African bishops (AS I/2, 267).

[168] AS I/2, 82.

[169] AS I/2, 83-85; the Melkite Archbishop Edelby followed Khoury on the podium and expressed complete agreement with his Maronite colleague.

[170] See B. Gut, Abbot Primate O.S.B., who spoke on behalf of the entire Benedictine family (AS I/2, 127).

[171] See AS I/2, 94-95.

[172] AS I/1, 601.

[173] Ottaviani, AS I/2, 20.

[174] Godfrey, AS I/2, 11. Ottaviani remarked with cynical humor that if the clergy were to see the financial implications of concelebration, their desire for it would soon fade (AS I/2, 20).

Since several of the fathers had complained that the text before them had been tampered with, Confalonieri felt compelled to intervene on November 5 with an official statement on the matter to deny the circulating claims and rumors. The head of the Central Commission's Sub-commission on Amendments stressed that the former had performed its duties in conformity with the motu proprio *Superno Dei nutu* (June 5, 1960),[175] duties which had been confirmed by the Pope and approved in the *Normae* of September 1961.[176] According to Confalonieri, the schema that had been sent on the Pope's orders to the Council fathers was the result of the observations made by the Central Commission together with the responses of the Liturgical Commission to those observations. Where there appeared to be disagreement between the observation and the response, his subcommission had made its own decision on the basis of reasoned argument and only after careful consideration of the responses received. The schemata at hand were under discussion, not the former texts.[177]

Boredom and fatigue began to take their toll, and bishops and experts alike were finding their way to the coffee bars ever sooner and more frequently. Fortunately the Pope intervened on November 6 and gave the presidents permission to draw the discussion of a particular chapter to a close if it considered the matter to have been given sufficient treatment. The message came from the Pope at 10:00 A.M., and the debate on chapter II was immediately terminated!

Meanwhile, the activities of the Liturgical Commission, which had not yet begun to discuss the text itself, quietly continued. The impression gradually surfaced that certain individuals were simply stalling for time. Dante's appointment on October 29 provided Larraona with a partner in his delaying tactics. It also seems that Larraona himself was very confusing and without method in the way he worked.[178] Because the conciliar discussion on the Introduction and chapter I had lasted until October 29 and the General Secretariat was not yet ready to set the remarks in order prior to the meeting planned for October 31,[179] a real start on the text could not be made until November 5[180] on the basis of a

---

[175] See *ADP* I/1, 93-98; *AAS* 52 (1960), 433-37; *DC* 57 (1960), 706-10.

[176] *ADP* II/1, 424-25.

[177] See *AS* I/2, 106-8; see also Bugnini, *Reform*, 37-38.

[178] Msgr. Jenny complained of this to his friends as early as October 26 (see *JCongar*, 98).

[179] See Antonelli's letter to the members of the Commission dated October 30 (De Clercq papers, CCV).

[180] It ought to be underlined, however, that the Commission's secretary, Antonelli, his assistants, and a convent of Franciscan nuns had done a great deal of work up to that

dossier sent out on November 3, which contained the comments of the fathers on the schema as a whole and on the Introduction.[181] The Commission immediately established a total of thirteen subcommissions. Three of them occupied themselves with more general questions: one theological, one juridical, and the third examining general comments.[182] The eight chapters of the schema were entrusted to the other subcommissions, chapter I being treated by no fewer than three and the remaining chapters by one each.[183]

Lercaro's subcommission, which was to deal with the general comments, met at 4:30 P.M. on November 6 in Domus Mariae. They worked until 7:45 P.M. and were able to present a report to the Commission on the following day.[184] They were of the opinion that the prefatory note to

---

point. In a short period of time they had typed out the incoming comments, copied them, and supplied them to the Commission in a total of twelve volumes. During the meeting of November 5 the comments on chapter I were already available.

[181] See Antonelli's letter to the members of the Commission (De Clercq papers, CCV).

[182] The juridical subcommission, which, like the theological subcommission, fulfilled an advisory role with regard to the other subcommissions, was chaired by E. Bonet, with F. McManus, A. Stickler, C. De Clercq, and J. Fohl members. Lercaro chaired the subcommission on general comments, the other members being A. Pichler, N. Ferraro, J. Wagner, and A. Bugnini.

[183] Subcommission IV, chaired by A. Martin (assisted by H. Rau, Salmon, M. Righetti, and A. Dirks), examined the comments on the Introduction and chapter I, 1-9. Subcommission V, chaired by F. Grimshaw (assisted by J. Malula, C. Egger, H. Cecchetti, and J. Nabuco), dealt with the comments on chapter I, 10-15 and 32-36. Subcommission VI, chaired by C. Calewaert (assisted by B. Fey Schneider, A. G. Martimort, A. Stickler, and G. Martinez de Antoñana), treated 16-31 of the same first chapter. Chapter II on the mystery of the Eucharist was the subject of study of subcommission VII, with J. Enciso presiding; the other members were H. Jenny, J. Jungmann, J. O'Connell, and D. Van den Eynde. Chapter III on the sacraments and sacramentals was entrusted to subcommission VIII under the leadership of Hallinan, assisted by F. Jop, R. Masi, F. McManus, and C. Vagaggini. Chapter IV on the Divine Office was entrusted to subcommission IX, under the leadership of A. Albareda; the other members were W. Bekkers, Salmon, C. Egger, and P. A. Frutaz. The liturgical year, subject of chapter V, was studied by subcommission X under the leadership of F. Zauner, assisted by Schweiger, H. Cecchetti, J. Wagner, and C. De Clercq. Chapter VI, on the sacred furnishings, was submitted to subcommission XI with O. Spülbeck in the chair, assisted by R. Masnou, N. Ferraro, A. Bugnini, and A. Dirks. (Spülbeck was unhappy with his appointment as chair. At the meeting on November 7, he remarked that he had more important things to do than discuss this particular topic.) Chapter VII on sacred music was given to subcommission XII, chaired by C. d'Amato, assisted by J. Prou, H. Anglès, J. Overath, and J. Wagner. Finally, subcommission XIII occupied itself with chapter VIII on sacred art under the chair of C. Rossi, assisted by H. Van Bekkum, M. Righetti, P. A. Frutaz, and J. Wagner. Subcommissions IX-XIII did not meet during the first session.

[184] See *Relatio exhibita a III subcommissione circa animadversiones generales in schema constitutionis de S. Liturgia*, three pages (Van den Eynde papers, CCV).

the schema should be dropped.[185] They also felt that the fathers' request to have the explanatory *Declarationes* included in the text should be accepted. As for the coordination of material which might be the subject of discussion in other commissions, the advice of the juridical subcommission was followed: distribution of all the schemas to the fathers; coordination of overlapping schemata by the Council presidents; informal contact between commissions such as those for the Oriental Churches, the missions, or the Secretariat for Christian Unity. At the same time Lercaro's subcommission proposed that, given the rather uneven advice from the fathers,[186] the existing text should be voted upon. They did not agree with the suggestion to include liturgical principles because they were of the opinion that the text before them already expressed these with sufficient clarity. As for the requested theological revision of the text, it was thought that this should be handed over to the theological subcommission. On the question of episcopal conferences, the subcommission proposed that these should be understood as "the body of bishops of a whole nation."[187]

Lercaro's subcommission, then, was of the opinion that the broadly positive appreciation of the schema deserved to be respected, that the complaints of the fathers about the prefatory note and the missing *Declarationes* should be taken seriously, that any criticism of the theology of the schema should be treated within the Commission itself, and that by interpreting the episcopal conferences as assemblies of bishops within a given country, the reservations expressed with regard to their juridical status would be overcome. It was clear from the discussion that followed that much emphasis was being placed on the fathers' right to have the *Declarationes* at their disposal. While the theological and juridical subcommissions supported this position,[188] Larraona continued to have reservations.

---

[185] This was the note that limited the scope of the constitution to general principles, leaving the execution to the Holy See. The same advice came from the juridical subcommission, which also gathered on November 6, although a little earlier (3:30 P.M.), in the building of the Congregation for Rites (see Bonet report, 1, in Van den Eynde papers, CCV).

[186] Some found the text too long, others too short; still others thought it excellent (see *Relatio*, 2).

[187] A number of more minor points were treated after this (see *Relatio*, 3).

[188] See the reports of Gagnebet, 1, and Bonet, 2, in Van den Eynde papers, CCV.

IV. Sacraments and Sacramentals

Comments on Chapter III

The permission the Pope had given to the presidents, providing for votes of closure, was beginning to have its effect. Discussions on the relatively long chapter III, which dealt with the sacraments and the sacramentals, took less than two days to complete (November 6-7).[189] Forty-one fathers took the podium in the aula,[190] while a number of fathers who had wanted to speak waived their right to do so. From Felici's announcement on November 7 that chapters V and VIII would be discussed together, it was clear that the administration was intent on speeding things up.[191] The discussions on chapter III caused little commotion, except with respect to nos. 55 (confirmation) and 57 (anointing of the sick), where a genuine difference of opinion was apparent. The remaining interventions, some of which were full of praise,[192] limited themselves to requesting a more accurate title for the chapter[193] or a more careful formulation of this or that paragraph. Some called for a clearer distinction between sacraments and sacramentals.[194] From a pastoral perspective others requested that any revision of the rites should be kept short and to the point, and that their social dimension should not be overlooked. Some suggested a distinction between rites for adults and rites for children.[195] Finally, some of the fathers warned of the need for prudence in the event of any changes.[196]

---

[189] It should be noted that Cardinal Tappouni, who chaired the discussions on November 6, kept a tight rein on the proceedings and interesting speakers were sometimes rather abruptly cut short (see AS I/2, 190-92).

[190] Several who intervened did so on behalf of their colleagues: Hengsbach (Essen); Alí Lebrún Moratinos (Valencia, Venezuela); Botero Salazar (Medellín, Columbia); A. Djajasepoetra (Djakarta, Indonesia); Bekkers ('s-Hertogenbosch, The Netherlands); Malula (Leopoldstad, Zaire); and Romo Gutiérrez (Torreón, Mexico).

[191] See AS I/2, 291.

[192] See Bekkers, H. Sansierra (San Juan de Cuyo), J. Sibomana (Ruhengeri), who was delighted by the fact that no. 49 gave permission to introduce local elements into the rite of initiation, and Malula, AS I/2, 313, 302, 309, 323.

[193] See the interventions by Bekkers and Jaeger, who rightly pointed out that the sacrament of the Eucharist had already been dealt with in chapter II and that the title of chapter III should therefore read "On the Other Sacraments" (AS I/2, 314, 369).

[194] See Ruffini, A. Del Pino Gómez (Lerida), AS I/2, 162, 306-7.

[195] In this regard see, for example, interventions by M. Pham-Ngoc-Chi (Quinhon), M. Maziers (Lyon), T. Botero Salazar, A. Barbero (Vigevano), AS I/2, 172-73, 174, 178, 187-88. See AS I/2, 168.

[196] See, for example, Browne, AS I/2, 165.

Msgr. D'Souza (Nagpur, India) made a much-remarked intervention in which he asked how one should interpret the statement, "Particular Rituals, adapted to the needs of individual regions, are to be prepared by episcopal conferences as soon as possible" (no. 47). Did the statement mean that the episcopal conferences had the power to adapt the entire sacramental liturgy or was their competence limited to the introduction of the vernacular? D'Souza himself proposed that the episcopal conferences have broad competence for both the adaptation of the liturgy and the use of the vernacular. In justifying his appeal he pointed out that the administration of the sacraments in his own and in other countries was not properly understood by the faithful and that local sensitivities should, therefore, be kept in focus. He also argued that if the sacraments were intended for the spiritual welfare of the faithful, they ought to be administered in the language of the faithful. If this was not done, then the spiritual effect of the sacraments would leave the faithful untouched.[197] Other speakers expressed the same pastoral concern[198] and invoked their own experience in the matter.[199]

The bulk of the fathers' attention, however, was devoted to the sacraments of confirmation and anointing of the sick. On confirmation, it was pointed out that there was a relationship between this sacrament and the apostolate of the laity, and that interaction between the two commissions competent in these matters was therefore essential.[200] While some called for raising the age for confirmation so that the person receiving the sacrament would be fully able to take up his or her responsibility as a Christian,[201] others were of the opinion that there should be freedom to administer the sacrament to the very young, as was the case in the Eastern rite, since the three sacraments of baptism, confirmation, and Eucharist formed a unity.[202]

Some speakers, particularly from Latin America, were not in favor of administering confirmation during the Eucharist but felt that the sacrament would be more appropriately administered during a pastoral visit;

[197] See AS I/2, 318-19. In his intervention D'Souza delivered an implicit yet sharp critique of the Roman Congregations who were frequently nothing short of intransigent in this matter.
[198] See, for example, J. Arneri (Sibenik), AS I/2, 168.
[199] See Garkovic (Zadar), AS I/2, 185-86.
[200] Hengsbach, AS I/2, 167.
[201] See A. Faveri (Tivoli), A. Djajasepoetra, I. Fenocchio (Pontremoli), AS I/2, 303, 312, 363-63; see also, however, T. Botero, AS I/2, 178, contradicted by Isnard, AS I/2, 300.
[202] See, for example, A. Scandar (Assiut), AS I/2, 379.

they also pointed out that there was too little time on Sundays and feast
days because of other pressing activities.[203] Others were even inclined to
request that the possibility of a collective administration of the sacrament be considered when large numbers were involved.[204] While the
Latin American continent on the whole was not in favor of the administration of confirmation during the Eucharist, some Latin American bishops nevertheless considered no. 55, which dealt with this question, to be
an excellent idea.[205] It was clear that practical reservations and theological considerations were here clashing.

The discussion of the numbers which dealt with the anointing of the
sick included a remark from Browne, who regretted the fact that in no.
57 the name "Extreme Unction," which could boast a long and richly
attested tradition, had been changed to "the Anointing of the Sick."[206]
While Archbishop D. Capozi (Taiyüan) argued that the sacrament
should be requested and administered frequently,[207] Msgr. Kempf (Limburg) was unreservedly against repeating the sacrament, as no. 60 proposed.[208] He was supported in this by Ruffini, who noted that repeated
anointing went against tradition and wondered why some wished to rein-
troduce it; true comfort was rather to be found in frequent confession.[209]

Counter-arguments were proposed among others by Msgr. Rougé
(Nîmes), who pointed out that the change from "Extreme Unction" to
"Anointing of the Sick" was in line with the latitude offered by the
Council of Trent. In addition, such a change was faithful to the evangelical tradition and the practice of the early Church, in which there was a
close relationship between this sacrament, Christ's ministry of love to
the poor, and the mission of the apostles, a fact which Trent had clearly
confirmed.[210] It was also pointed out that at the moment of administer-

---

[203] See, for example, E. De Carvalho (Angral), L. Cabrera Cruz (Luis Potosi), *AS* I/2,
180, 181-82. See also the written comments of V. Brizgys (Kaunas) and A. De Cunha
Marelim (Caxias do Maranhao, Brazil), *AS* I/2, 349, 355.

[204] F. Romo Gutierrez (Torréon), *AS* I/2, 324; see D. M. Gómez Tamayo (Popayán),
who wanted the rite to be shortened because of the scarcity of priests and with an eye to
the duration of the service for children (*AS* I/2, 366).

[205] See Isnard, *AS* I/2, 300.

[206] *AS* I/2, 164.

[207] *AS* I/2, 170.

[208] *AS* I/2, 297 (supported by a thorough written explanation on pages 297-300); see
also other protests from German bishops, such as Jaeger and Volk, *AS* I/2, 369-70, 381-82.

[209] See *AS* I/2, 162.

[210] See *AS* I/2, 292-93 (scientifically founded); similar ideas were to be heard from
Botero, for example, who spoke on behalf of the Columbian bishops; see also D. Capozi,
AS I/2, 170, 179.

ing the sacrament those who received it and their families were frequently in such a state that they did not wish it to be repeated.[211] A positive response to the change of name was also to be heard in pastoral
quarters.[212] In a remark on no. 60, Rougé pointed to the fact that the
anointing of the sick was traditionally a repeated event and that permission to repeat it was more than defensible.[213]

Several speakers requested that the reform of the rite of anointing of
the sick be left to the episcopal conferences, in light of the different traditions and the varying conditions of those receiving the sacrament. Proposed reforms of the rite would then be submitted to the Holy See for
approval.[214]

Finally, with reference to no. 64 (revision of the sacramentals),
Kozlowiecki, Archbishop of Lusaka (Rhodesia), called for permission to
employ lay people, especially catechists, to administer the sacramentals
where there was a scarcity of priests. He saw this as a way to integrate
experience with faith, thereby ensuring that faith would have the chance
to permeate the entirety of a person's life.[215]

V. THE TENSION BETWEEN PRAYER AND ACTION

DISCUSSION OF THE BREVIARY (CHAPTER IV)

Anyone who had hoped that the discussions would quickly move to
their conclusion was doomed to disappointment. Several of the comments on chapter IV on the Divine Office reflected different spiritual
and pastoral options. It will come as no surprise that priests were repeatedly called upon to pray their Breviary with the greatest of care;[216] but
pleas that greater weight be given to the New Testament in the Breviary
were due in great part to such choices.[217] Both the multitude of detailed

---

[211] Rougé, *AS* I/2, 293.

[212] See, for example, F. Angelini, A. Mistrorigo, A. Tagle Covarrubias, *AS* I/2, 294-
95, 305, 326.

[213] *AS* I/2, 293; see Botero, for example, who expressed similar thoughts, *AS* I/2, 179.

[214] Rougé, *AS* I/2, 293.

[215] *AS* I/2, 171.

[216] The principle of Breviary prayer and choir office was never called into question.
The text itself was convincingly and thoroughly praised by Döpfner, for example, see *AS*
I/2, 401; see also Weber (Strasbourg), speaking on behalf of a substantial number of his
French colleagues, *AS* I/2, 409.

[217] See Bacci, J. Corboy (Monze), F. Garcia Martinez (Spain), *AS* I/2, 409, 423, 439.
The same proposal met with some resistance from the Benedictine Prou; see *AS* I/2, 446.

remarks[218] and the renewal of the debate on language made it difficult to keep the debate focused.[219] On top of this, a great deal of attention was devoted to the obligation to recite the Divine Office. Who was obliged and in what measure? It was even questioned whether there was any need to revise the Breviary.[220]

The discussion was opened on November 7 by Frings,[221] whose address set out several of the directions which were to be followed in the forthcoming debate. After calling for a Latin version of the psalms in conformity with the language of the Church Fathers,[222] he asked for a wider use of the scriptures and the Church Fathers in the Breviary and requested greater balance between the psalms and the scripture readings, particularly at Matins. In light of the fact that knowledge of Latin was clearly on the wane among the younger generations, Frings concluded his address with a plea on behalf of the German bishops, including those in the missions, that bishops be permitted to dispense priests from praying the Office in Latin.[223]

A pastoral request to ensure that any renewal of the Divine Office should take the actual situation of the modern-day clergy into account was made, among others, by Spellman.[224] Comments on no. 68, on the sequence of the hours, repeatedly pointed out that those involved in pastoral ministry would be unable to fulfill this obligation and, that the

Also worth mention is the call for a reduction in the length of the patristic texts, which accompanied an appeal for greater respect for the authentic explanations these texts had to offer (see, for example, Corboy, *AS* I/2, 424).

[218] It was partly for this reason that the entire discussion of this chapter came across as tedious and time consuming; see the pertinent comments of Bea, *AS* I/2, 411-13 and the bitter commentary in *JCongar*, 131-32.

[219] No fewer than thirty-eight interventions had to do with the use of Latin in the Divine Office.

[220] Fifty-six fathers commented on the question of obligation alone. The dossier entitled *Animadversiones in Schema Constitutionis de Sacra Liturgia. Caput IV. De Officio Divino (nn. 68-78)*, which the competent subcommission had to study, totaled more than 200 pages. Surprisingly enough, none of the fathers had anything to say about no. 75, which dealt with the participation of the laity in the Divine Office.

[221] Other speakers repeatedly praised this intervention as well as that by Léger. See, for example, A. M. Aguirre, who spoke in the name of several bishops from Argentina, Uruguay, and Paraguay (*AS* I/2, 427).

[222] The speaker received support on this point from a variety of corners (see Bacci, Prou [on behalf of a number of monastic orders], Guano [Livorno], Carli [Segni]), *AS* I/2, 410, 445-46, 458, 463. The existing translation of the psalms had pleased very few and was experienced as an impoverishment in the liturgy (see J. Schiphorst, "Eensgezindheid over de noodzaak van brevier," in *Het concilie. 1e periode (1962)*, in *Ken uw tijd* 12 [1963], 61); but there also were voices against change (see V. Costantini, *AS* I/2, 472).

[223] See *AS* I/2, 327-28.

[224] Spellman, *AS* I/2, 391.

order of the Divine Office should be brought into line with pastoral life of today,[225] at least with regard to the "minor hours."[226] Some insisted that where the Office is recited in the vernacular, the so-called imprecatory psalms, among others, should be dropped because nuns and lay people did not have sufficient training to understand their correct meaning.[227]

The discussion on the precise levels of obligation with regard to the recitation of the Office was quite lengthy, partly because of the different expectations people had of priests with pastoral functions. According to Léger, who praised the spirit of renewal in no. 73, it was sufficient for those not bound to choir office to pray lauds, vespers, and the *lectio divina,* as was stipulated in no. 71. In defense of this he pointed out that for priests active in pastoral ministry, as opposed to monks, it was impossible to pray all day.[228] The quality of prayer should be preferred over its quantity.[229] Others pointed to the need for clear guidelines that would take actual pastoral situations into account.[230] Msgr. B. Yago (Abidjan)[231], stressed, at the same time, that any revision of the Breviary should be such that it would stimulate the clergy's taste for prayer.[232]

Of course, not everyone was happy with the idea of a reduction in the Divine Office. Wyszynski highly praised the Breviary, saw little reason for making changes, and was upset by the fact that the time-argument had been used, a fact he considered a slur upon good and pious priests. Action without prayer could not bear fruit.[233] A Spanish bishop, who dismissed any argument of a pastoral nature, felt that the obligation to the Breviary as it currently stood should remain unchanged and that those who did not fulfill it were committing a grave sin.[234]

---

[225] See, for example, M. Gonçalves Cerejeira (Lisbon), *AS* I/2, 390-91.

[226] See Döpfner, *AS* I/2, 398; in the same context, Landázuri Ricketts alluded to the (omitted) *Declaratio,* which had contained a reference to the pastoral situation (see *AS* I/2, 408).

[227] See Ruffini. That he was speaking yet again was not appreciated by those present, and there were disapproving murmurs as he took the podium (see *JCongar,* 125; see also Bacci, J. Corboy [Monze, Rhodesia], *AS* I/2, 329-30, 409, 423). Other positions were also voiced, for example, by Prou, *AS* I/2, 446.

[228] See his comments on no. 68, *AS* I/2, 334-35. Interventions from Weber, Reuss (Mainz, Germany), and Garrone ran along similar lines (*AS* I/2, 409, 448, 455).

[229] See *AS* I/2, 335-36.

[230] See, for example, Gonçalves Cerejeira, *AS* I/2, 391.

[231] Yago spoke on behalf of his West African colleagues, *AS* I/2, 467.

[232] See *La Croix,* November 13, 1962; see also *AS* I/2, 466. The Indian Gracias was clearly on the same wavelength (see *Dokumente,* December 1962, 442).

[233] See *AS* I/2, 393; see also Godfrey, Lefebvre, J. Flores (Barbastro, Spain), Carli, *AS* I/2, 395, 396, 436, 463.

[234] See *AS* I/2, 468.

With regard to language, significant figures such as Léger proposed with reference to no. 77 that the clergy be granted permission, with the approval of the local episcopal conferences, to use the vernacular even in private recitation, in order to avoid formalism because they did not understand the language.[235] Döpfner used the occasion to point out that the original text had proposed that where knowledge of Latin was wanting and there was little hope of seeing it improve, the episcopal conferences had the right, in conformity with no. 24, to promulgate norms with regard to the language to be used.[236] Cardinal Meyer, while admitting that the lack of Latin was partly responsible for the current appeal to use the vernacular, urged the latter for the sake of greater piety.[237] But appeals for the continued use of Latin in the seminaries and for official prayer were still to be heard. Carli, who openly referred to Döpfner's address, was not convinced by the suggestion that candidates for the priesthood, who had been educated in public schools, no longer knew Latin. He pointed out that the same candidates were also ignorant of philosophy and theology, yet no one would even think of ordaining them until they had satisfactorily completed their study of these subjects. He proposed that such candidates, who were to be examples to the laity, should make the effort, for whatever reason, to learn a foreign language. Priests should study Latin in order to be able to draw from the rich sources of Church Latin.[238] In addition, Wyszynski pointed out that if priests were no longer obliged to pray in Latin, they might no longer be motivated to learn the language, and this unifying bond would disappear.[239] Godfrey appealed to *Veterum sapientia* to urge that the study of the Latin language be encouraged.[240]

As is apparent from the volume of written comments submitted on this chapter, the debate could have gone on for many more days. In

---

[235] "So their minds can understand what their lips are pronouncing," *AS* I/2, 336; see also Weber, Reuss, *AS* I/2, 409, 448. Léger was supported *nominatim* in this by Döpfner who also referred to Frings's speech (see *AS* I/2, 399); see also Garrone, *AS* I/2, 454-55. Spellman even proposed that everyone be free to choose on the matter, which was something of a surprise to those present, considering his vociferous defense of the use of Latin in the Eucharist (*AS* I/2, 392); see also V. A. Yzermans, *American Participation in the Second Vatican Council* (New York, 1967), 136. The fact that the American bishops were not "Latin-minded" when it came to the Breviary is evident also from interventions by Connare, S. Leven (San Antonio), and J. Marling (Jefferson City), *AS* I/2, 415-16, 452-53, 455-56.

[236] *AS* I/2, 398-99.

[237] *AS* I/2, 404.

[238] *AS* I/2, 463-64; Costantini followed a similar line of argument, *AS* I/2, 473.

[239] *AS* I/2, 394.

[240] See *AS* I/2, 395.

essence, the entire discussion turned around the following points: openness to change, adaptation to the contemporary pastoral situation, the vision of the priesthood, and the place of Latin in the spiritual life of the clergy — all of them themes that focus on the relationship between the priest as pastor and the priest as man of prayer. Fortunately the presidents intervened on November 10. Ruffini, chair for the day, noted on behalf of the presidents that nothing new was being contributed to the discussion and proposed a closure to the debate, which the assembly then ratified.[241]

Along with the fathers, the members of the liturgical commission had the feeling that they were wasting their time. Larraona, who had already expressed reservations about including the *Declarationes* in the reports to be presented to the fathers, returned to the question on November 9, having asked the advice of Confalonieri, who apparently told him that the explanatory notes had no official value. After some discussion it was decided, nevertheless, that a positively worded *votum* should be submitted to the presidents on the following day.[242] The remainder of the November 9 meeting was partly taken up by an appeal from Egger to review the Latinity of the schema.[243] At the same time, after some discussion,[244] it was decided to replace the word "western" with "Latin" in line with the advice of Lercaro's subcommission; the proposed namechange with respect to the episcopal conferences was followed, although with some hesitation. On the same day, partly under pressure from Hallinan's motion (which we will examine more closely below), it was possible to move on to the votes.[245]

In the meantime the malaise surrounding the Commission's slow progress was growing.[246] Irritated by Larraona's maneuvering,[247] Halli-

---

[241] *AS* I/2, 474. Because the fathers frequently broke into applause, sometimes when the Curia was being criticized, Ruffini found it necessary at the beginning of the assembly to call for an end to both applause and criticism in order to prevent a rift in the proceedings (see *AS* I/2, 436).

[242] Apparently this note was actually despatched; see the secretary's announcements during the meeting of November 12 (see Jenny papers, box 8, CNPL).

[243] See Jenny papers, box 8, CNPL.

[244] Ibid.

[245] The advice of Lercaro's subcommission was also followed on the remaining questions.

[246] Martimort mentions an angry outburst in this regard from Malula during the Commission's seventh meeting ("Les débats liturgiques," 307); according to Jenny's report to the French bishops at S. Luigi on November 10, both Rossi and Spülbeck had also expressed their displeasure at the slow pace of progress (see Jenny papers, box 8, CNPL). See also the *pro memoria* of Lercaro, edited by G. Alberigo in *Par la forza dello Spirito*.

[247] See Shelley, *Hallinan*, 168.

nan worked out a proposal to be presented for discussion at the meeting of November 7 in the hope that a genuine start to the work might be made.[248] Since Hallinan wanted to appeal his case directly to Secretary of State Cicognani he was unable to be present at the meeting and for that reason he had given his text to Grimshaw. Grimshaw, however, did not read out the proposal but showed it to Larraona prior to the meeting, thereby causing something of a stir. But during the general congregation on November 9 Hallinan sought out 13 members of the Commission[249] and was able to convince them to sign a petition which proposed a faster procedure for the activities of the Commission.[250]

[248] Hallinan proposed that each time the general congregation had dealt with a particular chapter, the Commission would then go to work as follows: In the first place, each article from a specific section would be treated by the Commission in consecutive order on the basis of the report of the subcommission. If few or no changes were being proposed for a specific article, the Commission should accept it as stated in the schema. If proposals had been made with regard to a specific article or significant corrections, the Commission should vote on every change in the usual manner. If the result proved positive for a particular change or correction, the Commission should accept the corrected version of the article. If the result was negative, the Commission should pass the matter on to the general congregation together with a corrected schema containing both the original article and the corrections proposed by the fathers but rejected by the Commission. In this event the general congregation needed only to vote in order to solve the problem. Once a section was corrected the Secretary General should present it to the fathers for a vote. The new text should include (1) the articles on which there were no proposals; (2) the articles which had been corrected and approved by the Commission; and (3) the specific proposals of the fathers not approved by the Commission. Hallinan used the following arguments in support of this procedure: (1) It is in line with the conciliar and commission regulations; (2) an orderly procedure is necessary because the specific votes on a particular section deserve to take place together with the discussion on that section and this both in the Council and in the Commission; (3) psychologically, it makes better sense to combine the fathers' legislative task during the votes with their deliberative task during the discussions in the aula; and (4) individually organized votes would have the effect that the Council's discussions would be reasonable and limited. (See Calewaert papers, box 4, document 8, Archives of the Diocese of Ghent; Jenny papers, box 5, CNPL; Bekkers papers, document 780, Archives of the Diocese of 's-Hertogenbosch).

[249] Grimshaw, Van Bekkum, Zauner, Rossi, Calewaert, Jenny, Spülbeck, Malula, Pichler, Rau, Jop and Martin (see Shelley, *Hallinan*, 321).

[250] Hallinan proposed the following: "In order to avoid taxing the work of the Council with an overly detailed and drawn out discussion the undersigned fathers, members of the commission for the liturgy, request: 1. that immediately, i.e. at the beginning of today's meeting, the commission on the liturgy should vote on the proposals of the Lercaro subcommission; 2. that then, following the report of the subcommission on the Introduction and a short discussion of each correction, during which the members and, if desired, the experts *in ordinem* should have their say, the commission should move on to the vote; 3. that consecutive corrections reported by the respective subcommissions, after a short discussion and vote according to the sections of each chapter, should be sent, without further delay, to the secretariat; in order to avoid future procrastination and to

The proposal was accepted, and there were even three votes on the report of Lercaro's subcommission on the same day. Larraona, however, would not submit. He proposed that there was no need for haste in sending the results to the General Secretary. For that matter, the fathers should not vote on the various changes until the entire schema had been completely revised by the Commission. In order to reinforce his authority he announced that there would be no meeting the following day.[251] Not about to admit defeat, Hallinan, on November 10, sent a letter to Cicognani in which he stressed that the bishops were ready to vote and complained that, while the Pope and the bishops genuinely desired an *aggiornamento*, precious little of this spirit and concern was at work in his own Commission.[252]

The situation changed only on November 11, when Lercaro sent a note to the Secretary of State in which he outlined the difficulties.[253] It also appears that Cicognani had mentioned the Commission's procedural problems to the Pope, and that Felici was concerned with the question. Together the various interventions produced results.[254] The very next day, November 12, the Commission members received an *Ordo agendi*,[255] and from then on things started to move a little faster. This was indeed desirable since the debates on the scheme were coming to an end.

VI. A CHAOTIC END

COMMENTS ON CHAPTERS V-VIII

On November 10, after the presidents' intervention closing the previous debate, the assembly moved to the discussion of chapters V-VIII.[256]

---

fulfil the wishes of the Council fathers this proposal is presented for a vote" (Calewaert, box 4, file 1, document 11, Archives of the Diocese of Ghent).

[251] See Shelley, *Hallinan*, 170.

[252] Ibid., 170, 321.

[253] In Lercaro's *pro memoria* one will find an excellent survey of the problems: many meetings, few results (16-17). Others, including Martimort, had made similar efforts but without success (Martimort, "Les débats liturgiques," 307).

[254] See Shelley, *Hallinan*, 170-71.

[255] See Calewaert papers, box 4, file 1, document 13, Archives of the Diocese of Ghent; C. De Clercq papers, CCV.

[256] Chapters V-VIII were quite well received on the whole and no serious controversies emerged after this point (see A. Plaza [La Plata], L. Raymond [Allahabad], *AS* I/2, 477, 616; see also 645, 647).

During this and the next two general assemblies (November 12 and 13),
the discussion focused primarily on the liturgical year (chapter V),
although the liturgical vessels and furnishings (chapter VI), sacred music
(chapter VII), and sacred art (chapter VIII) were also the subjects of a
number of interventions.[257] Because four chapters were now being discussed at once, an already drawn-out debate now became chaotic as
well.[258] The survey which follows attempts to make some sense of the
chaos by examining the interventions chapter by chapter.

With regard to the liturgical year, Spellman's short intervention
started the proceedings: revise anything that will genuinely benefit the
pastoral ministry.[259] At the same time, the cardinal felt that the establishment of a fixed date for Easter, which had been requested, partly on
ecumenical grounds, in no. 85, ran counter to the tradition of the Roman
Catholic Church, which he saw no reason to change.[260] Msgr. Nabaa
(Beirut), on the other hand, was a clear supporter of a fixed date for
Easter, seeing in it an opportunity to overcome the scandalous division
of Christians.[261] Nabaa was supported by Cardinal Feltin, who, although
acknowledging that to celebrate Easter on a fixed date did go against tradition, pointed out that the people did not understand why a historical
event was celebrated on a different day each year. Seeing both pastoral
and social advantages in the choice for a fixed date, he concluded by
supporting Nabaa's proposal that the question be further discussed in a
mixed commission.[262]

Representatives from the mission territories also made a number of
interesting proposals with respect to the liturgical year. Msgr. S. Hoa

[257] It should be noted that almost every number of these four last chapters could boast
at least one intervention. It is remarkable that the "big names," with but a few exceptions,
did not take the podium in this debate, but American, African, and Asian bishops were
well represented.

[258] On November 13 Felici found it necessary to remind the fathers to speak briefly
and to the point (see AS I/2, 631).

[259] AS I/2, 475. With regard to the introduction of a fixed liturgical calendar see also,
for example, Bafile (Nuncio to Germany), A. Baraniak (Poznan), C. Zohrabian (Armenian), AS I/2, 593-96, 599-600, 607-8. On another matter, there was a call for a greater
liturgical emphasis on Advent and Christmastide (A. Jannucci [Penne-Pescara], L. Bere-
ciartua Balerdi [Siguenza-Guadalajara]), and for a recognition of the social dimension of
sin (S. Hoa Nguyen-van Hien [Dalat], AS I/2, 608-9, 612, 614).

[260] See AS I/2, 475.

[261] See AS I/2, 475-77.

[262] See AS I/2, 590-91. Among the other proponents of a fixed date for Easter who
shared the ecumenical concerns expressed in the text were J. Khoury (Tyre of the
Maronites, Lebanon), and A. Sapelak (vicar apostolic for the Ukrainians in Argentina),
AS I/2, 604-5, 660; but see also L. Raymond, AS I/2, 616-17.

Nguyen-van Hein asked on behalf of the Vietnamese bishops that episcopal conferences be permitted to introduce liturgical feasts on certain
civil feast days in order to give them a Christian dimension and to show
nonbelievers that Christians respect ancestral traditions. He also
requested permission to celebrate the birthdays of numerous Oriental
martyrs with a liturgical feast in order to hold them up as models for the
faithful and to stimulate Christian religious feelings.[263] Requests such as
these made it clear that the third-world countries were also striving to
give the Church local characteristics.

Some fathers called for greater simplicity and soberness in celebrating
the liturgical year, while others asked that more weight be given to feasts
such as the Epiphany or the Ascension, which were frequently celebrated in the mission territories on working days and did not, therefore,
receive their due attention.[264]

Archbishop Castellano of Siena noted, with some justification, that
chapter VI would be better combined with chapter VIII since both chapters dealt with the same subject.[265] With regard to these two chapters, it
was regularly requested that, in response to the much-regretted abuses
already noted in the Introduction, the liturgy should be characterized by
a much greater evangelical simplicity without thereby doing injustice to
the fact that worship as an act directed to God deserved to be beautiful.[266] The Chilean bishop E. Larraín Errázuriz reminded the fathers that
the liturgy was a celebration of the paschal mystery of Christ and that
justice could only be done to this fact if the poverty praised in the gospel
were respected. The gospel was to be proclaimed to the poor. According
to the words of St. Augustine, he noted, the liturgy did not celebrate the
splendor divitiarum (the splendor of wealth) but rather the *splendor ver-
itatis* (the splendor of truth), the revelation of God's love in Christ. The
Church was obliged, therefore, to show both in word and deed that it
took the side of the poor while ensuring at the same time that its riches
did not give offense in places dominated by poverty.[267] It was a question

---

[263] *AS* I/2, 613-14.

[264] J. Cheng Tien-Siang (Formosa), *AS* I/2, 668.

[265] See *AS* I/2, 619; see also 630. Gouyon (Bayonne) also proposed that the two chapters be treated together (*AS* I/2, 628); we also are treating them together here.

[266] See Gouyon's appropriate remark in *AS* I/2, 626.

[267] *AS* I/2, 621-23. Larraín Errázuriz spoke on behalf of a number of South American
bishops. He addressed a word of explicit welcome to the non-Catholic observers, as
Soares de Resende from Mozambique had done before him (see *AS* I/2, 600). The authenticity of his witness was supported by the fact that he had turned his episcopal palace into
a home for the poor.

of pastoral sensitivity: a Church which preaches poverty cannot afford
to give the impression of wealth and pomposity in its liturgical manifestations when these are often the only avenue for nonbelievers to come to
know Christianity; rather it should take the child of Bethlehem as its
example.[268] It was noted, furthermore, that in the liturgy genuine beauty
and true simplicity were perfectly reconcilable and that such a combination frequently delivered the best results.[269]

The intervention of Yoshigoro Taguchi (Osaka), should not go without mention.[270] He pointed out that the splendor of the liturgical vessels
gave offense in Japan precisely because the Japanese love simple, taste-
ful, and measured colors. He noted, in addition, that his people had trouble understanding certain Western elements, unknown in the East, such
as the putting on and taking off of the miter, kneeling to kiss the bishop's ring, and so on. He also proposed that a passage be added to no. 88
in chapter VI to stipulate that liturgical vestments should conform to the
customs and tastes of the local people, and he concluded by warning,
with regard to no. 99, that adaptation should not be a bland imitation of
local art.[271] The remarks of L. Seitz (Kontum, Vietnam), speaking in the
name of the bishops of his country, ran along similar lines. Sacred art, he
noted, was in the service of the liturgy of the people of God and ought
to be marked by simplicity, integrity, and poverty.[272] From a similarly
Asian perspective, some fathers pointed to the fact that indigenous art
could express the sacred in a genuine and worthwhile manner.[273] Msgr.
Gasbarri (Velletri, Italy), among others, drew attention to the importance
of modern art in the experience of the sacred.[274] It was noted, in conclusion, that schools should be established for the promotion of sacred
art.[275]

With regard to sacred music (chapter VII), the fathers were unanimous in their belief that the laity (*and* the clergy) should be able actively
to participate in it, which implied that they should also understand what

---

[268] See Gouyon, *AS* I/2, 627-28. The theme of liturgical sobriety returns again and
again (see J. Urtasun [Avignon], H. Golland Trinidade, *AS* I/2, 632, 645). A dissenting
voice could be found, for example in Zelanti, who made a distinction between personal
attitude and liturgical usage (*AS* I/2, 640-41).

[269] See Golland Trinidade, Badoux (Saint Boniface), Ancel, *AS* I/2, 645, 666-67, 682-
83.

[270] *AS* I/2, 630-31.

[271] See *AS* I/2, 651.

[272] *AS* I/2, 661-62.

[273] See *AS* I/2, 669.

[274] *AS* I/2, 623-25.

[275] See *AS* I/2, 639.

they were singing.[276] It was also asked that recent advances in musical education, both in schools and because of radio and television, be taken into account and that the Church should give an adequate response to this in its liturgy.[277] Volk reminded the assembly that for the separated brethren communal singing was an essential part of the liturgy, and Catholic liturgy might profit from this fact.[278] In addition, de Barros Câmara (Rio de Janeiro) stressed the fact that music was an integral part of the liturgy and that candidates for the priesthood should receive good musical training.[279] At the same time, Rugambwa, among others, requested the freedom to integrate sacred music with indigenous African music, which plays an important role in the life of the faithful, so that the liturgy could take on some of the unique characteristics of the African people. He also requested that the commissions devoted to sacred music include members familiar with the music of Africa.[280]

During the debate on November 13, a day before the vote would be taken on the whole schema, Cicognani announced that, at the request of a great many fathers,[281] the Pope had decided to introduce the name of St Joseph into the eucharistic prayer directly after the name of Mary. This would be a tribute to the saint under whose patronage the Council was meeting.[282] The decision came as something of a surprise[283] and left

[276] See A. Fustella (Todi), C. D'Amato, H. Volk (who emphasized that everyone should be able to join in the singing and called for songs in the vernacular), and Baudoux, M. Dario Miranda y Gómez, who found that the tone of the schema might inhibit progress in the field of music), AS I/2, 636, 636-37, 662-64, 667, 669-70.

[277] See De Smedt, AS I/2, 697-700.

[278] AS I/2, 664.

[279] AS I/2, 588-89. Kempf made a similar intervention (AS I/2, 659).

[280] AS I/2, 592-93. In his written intervention Rugambwa made a similar appeal with regard to sacred art. Raymond appealed along similar lines from an Indian perspective (AS I/2, 616-17).

[281] On November 5 Cousineau (Haïti) had appealed to the support of more than 500 individuals and institutions in favor of St. Joseph; see also the interventions of Cule (Mostar, Yugoslavia), A. Tedde (Ales), AS I/2, 479-80, 483. Others poked fun at the "Josephologists;" chairing the assembly on November 10, Ruffini rather cynically said to Cule: "I ask Your Excellency to conclude your very pious sermon. I can assure you: we all have the greatest devotion to St. Joseph." Soon after, he told Tedde not to preach to preachers (AS I/2, 480, 483). Other saints also had their zealous supporters among the fathers; see the intervention of Marling in favor of Bl. Eymard and St. Gaspar of Buffalo (AS I/2, 598-99).

[282] AS I/2, 644. Not every liturgist was equally taken by the proposal (see Schmidt, Die Konstitution, 93-94).

[283] See R. Laurentin, Bilan de la première session, 108; H. Fesquet, The Drama of Vatican II (New York, 1967), 68-69; A. Wenger, Vatican II: Volume I: The First Session, 68-69.

some with the feeling that the Council was wasting its time. Others felt that the action might harm ecumenism or was at least redundant.[284]

On November 14 it was time to vote on the schema as a whole. Three groups may be distinguished. The first was a small group, systematically opposed to any significant reform, that included individuals who had been (e.g., Ruffini) or continued to be active members of the Congregation of the Holy Office, the Congregation for Rites or the Congregation for Seminaries, as well as a part of the English-speaking episcopate, such as Spellman, McIntyre, and Godfrey. A second and quite numerous group was in favor of moderate adaptation to the times. A third group, consisting primarily of bishops from the Third World, included perhaps the most radical of the Council fathers and called for a more thorough and fundamental adaptation of the rites to local situations and mentalities. This latter group enjoyed extraordinary support from the professional liturgists.[285]

When Tisserant proposed that the assembly move to the vote,[286] the fathers were presented with two motions, the text of which had been composed under the direction of Confalonieri.[287] The first ran as follows in the official English translation:

> The Second Vatican Ecumenical Council, having seen and examined the schema of the sacred Liturgy, approves therein the general directives which, with due prudence and understanding, tend or aim to make the various parts of the sacred Liturgy more vital and more instructive for the faithful in conformity with the pastoral needs of our day.

The second motion read:

> The changes proposed in the conciliar discussions, as soon as they are examined and compiled in due form by the conciliar commission on liturgy, will be submitted with due care to this general session, so that by their votes the Fathers may assist or direct the commission in preparing a definite, revised text, which again will be submitted to the general session.[288]

Since a substantial number of the fathers had expressed rather negative opinions of the schema, the vote, the Council's first, was awaited with a certain amount of tension. The surprise was enormous when the

---

[284] See Laurentin, *Bilan*, 27. Congar, *ICI*, December 1, 1962; idem, *Vatican II: Le Concile au jour le jour* (Paris, 1963), 53-55, 122-25; *JCongar*, 137.

[285] See Rouquette, *La fin d'une chrétienté*, 235-36.

[286] *AS* I/3, 10-11.

[287] See Martimort, "Les débats liturgiques," 304.

[288] See *AS* I/3, 9-13 for this text, which was read out in Latin, Spanish, English, French, German, and Arabic.

schema was approved by 2,162 of the fathers out of a possible total of 2,215. Only forty-six participants voted against the schema (seven votes were invalid). Barely 3 percent of the fathers lay behind all those dissenting voices which had either rejected the schema, proposed radical changes in it, or wanted to remand it to the Theological Commission because of its alleged theological or pastoral errors. A large majority had emerged which could no longer recognize itself in a liturgy that was no longer up to date.[289] The fathers had clearly opted for a different, more vital liturgy. The interventions themselves leave no doubt that genuine pastoral concern was the motive for their choice.

VII. The FURTHER ACTIVITIES OF THE CONCILIAR COMMISSION FOR THE LITURGY

At the commission's meeting on November 12 the discussion of Lercaro's report was brought to a close,[290] and Lercaro was designated reporter for the general comments. Although there were some objections to the decision to vote on this report, Wagner, among others, pointed out the need to learn what the fathers thought of the whole matter.[291] At this point in the proceedings the reports on the Introduction by Martin's subcommission IV and by the theological and juridical subcommissions were heard. It became apparent from Martin's six-page report that his subcommission, which had met on November 8, had reasonably disposed of the most important objections[292] to the content of the Introduction without being blind to the better-grounded emendations.[293] Gagnebet then gave the report of the theological subcommission which had met on November 6 and 8 in the Angelicum.[294] Although Gagnebet's

---

[289] See Kaiser, *Pope, Council and World*, 129-30; Schmidt, *Die Konstitution*, 86-87.

[290] Dante's proposal to introduce a section in the schema on the process of canonisation was not followed (see Jenny papers, box 8, CNPL).

[291] Ibid.

[292] Martin's report, 1-3, C. De Clercq papers, CCV. For example, criticisms of the use of the words *instaurare, instauratio* were rebutted with the help of numerous papal and other documents.

[293] See ibid., 3, where the suggestion of several of the fathers that the phrase "while it declares that it does not intend dogmatically to define anything in this Constitution" be dropped from chapter II, 25-26 was considered and accepted, on the basis of advice from Cardinal Silva, who had spoken on behalf of the Chilean bishops and whose argument had been very well received; his advice was also followed with regard to chapter II, nos. 29-33.

[294] In the first part of the first meeting the specific task of the theological subcommis-

subcommission had looked into the minor amendments proposed by such critics of the schema as Parente, Browne, and Staffa, the subcommission had chosen to retain words such as *instauranda*, defending themselves with a number of papal documents.[295] Bonet followed Gagnebet with the report of the juridical subcommission, where apparently no difficulties had arisen. Both remarkably short reports were briefly discussed without raising any major differences of opinion.[296]

On November 14 Antonelli was in a position to read out the corrected text, which was then approved after a few minor alterations. At the beginning of this meeting it was announced that Lercaro's report on the general comments was ready. After a brief exchange of thoughts on both the value and content of the report, it was decided to present it in the aula.[297]

At this point Martin's report on nos. 1-9 was heard. Because no concrete improvements had been suggested, the subcommission had brushed aside the complaint of some of the fathers that the language of articles 1-9 was insufficiently clear. The subcommission also thought that other proposed changes were insufficiently grounded.[298]

Gagnebet then spoke on behalf of the theological subcommission, which had met for three hours on November 10 and 13 to discuss the same material.[299] At their first meeting it had already been decided to reject proposals for a thorough revision of this section, partly because such a revision was not the subcommission's job and partly because it did not seem necessary.[300] With regard to chapter I, no. 1, line 19, it was proposed, after a long discussion, to replace the word *cause* with *instrument*, a term that could boast a rich tradition and was accepted among theologians, although there remained some discussion as to its precise content.[301] Comments on nos. 1 and 2 focused primarily on matters of

---

sion was discussed: theological advice and the revision of the scripture texts (see Gagnebet's report, 1, Van den Eynde papers, CCV).

[295] Ibid., 2. Further comments on the Introduction from this subcommission were minimal. See Jenny's notes as a member of the subcommission, from which it is apparent that the subcommission considered the renewal movement as achieved: "'instaurare' [to renew] is a consecrated word" (Jenny papers, box 8, CNPL).

[296] See Jenny papers, box 8, CNPL.

[297] See Jenny papers, box 8, CNPL.

[298] The suggestion to give the Holy Spirit a place in chapter I, nos. 1 and 2, was followed, however. The theological subcommission also supported this change (see Gagnebet report, 1, Van den Eynde papers, CCV).

[299] See the reports in the C. De Clercq papers, CCV.

[300] See Gagnebet report, 6.

[301] Ibid.

detail, although this subcommission did agree to introduce a mention of the Holy Spirit in no. 2, line 20.[302] Gagnebet reported that his subcommission had devoted much time to the discussion of no. 3, lines 16-25, which dealt with the various ways in which Christ is present in the liturgy.[303] To meet the fathers' wishes, a new text had been composed which described more clearly the various forms of Christ's presence.[304] With respect to nos. 4-6 only minor changes were made in order to make the text more intelligible.[305]

Bonet then presented the report of his subcommission. With respect to chapter I, he insisted that it was of the utmost juridical importance that the authority of the various ecclesiastical organs at the level of the liturgy be carefully outlined.[306] The meeting then proceeded to the discussion but got no further than no. 2, line 25 on that particular day.

It was agreed, however, that the theological subcommission and Martin's subcommission should meet the following day at 10:00 A.M. to go through the text from no 2, line 25 to no. 9. From Gagnebet's extremely detailed report[307] it is clear that a great deal of time had once again been devoted to the question of Christ's presence. It was decided to adopt the changes already proposed by Gagnebet's subcommission. In addition, Van den Eynde apparently had difficulties with the expression "under sensibly perceptible signs which, each in its own way, effect what they signify," (page 160, line 30), because it implied more than what was actually effected in the sacraments, sacramentals, and other liturgical activities. At Vagaggini's suggestion, it was decided to change the text to make it more clear how the perceptible signs effect the sanctification of the human person.[308] Other changes were simply for the sake of clarification.

The commission met again on November 16, devoting all its time to the further discussion of nos. 2-9. Since no fundamental objections to the subcommissions' proposals were made,[309] Martin was in a position to present the completely revised text, in which the comments of the Latinists had been incorporated, to the meeting on November 19. Appar-

---

[302] Ibid.

[303] Ibid., 10-11.

[304] See Martin's well-reasoned report, discussed below.

[305] See Gagnebet's report, 12-13.

[306] *Subcommissio iuridica-Continuatio*, Van den Eynde papers, CCV.

[307] See Gagnebet, *Relatio a Subcommisione theologica et de Cap. I (nn. 1-9) una simul concinnata*, 5p., De Clercq papers, CCV.

[308] Ibid., 3.

[309] See Jenny papers, box 8, CNPL.

ently the proposed changes in the Latin of the text did not always meet
with the approval of the fathers, since a number of these were changed
once again.[310] Moreover, the addition of the word *sacrifice* to no. 2, line
25, which had been suggested by the mixed subcommission of November 15 "to make the teaching more complete," was presented once more
for discussion.[311] Finally the text was approved.

Msgr. Grimshaw then took the floor and read the report of his subcommission on nos. 10-15 and 32-36. It was evident that they had had
few difficulties with their part of the text since they had met only once.
The report itself caused little trouble, although it was the subject of discussion on November 21 and (briefly) 23.[312] On November 21 there was
a long discussion on the place of the liturgy in theological formation in
the seminaries and theological faculties (no. 11),[313] a discussion which
ultimately resulted in the acceptance of Antonelli's proposal that the
liturgy should be considered "necessary" in seminary formation and
"important" in university training.[314] The remaining material appears to
have been accepted without further ado. Approval of chapter II was
delayed, however, until after the discussion on the episcopal conferences, a discussion which belonged to the work of Calewaert's subcommission.

If one considers the amount of time that could be spent on minor
points such as the above, it will come as no surprise that, as early as
November 19, Hallinan, now accompanied by Grimshaw, had proposed
a new document entitled *De Modo Procedendi*. The document asked
whether the theological difficulties and the *"nugacitates Latinae"* [tri-
fling matters of Latin] ought not to be talked through by the competent
subcommission and whether the chairman of a particular subcommission
should not be responsible for the clarity of formulation when presenting
a specific part of the text. In order to speed things up, the document also

---

[310] See Jenny's notes in *Textus capitis I, nn. 1-9. Emendationes a commisione et a peritis linguae Latinae propositae*, 5p., Jenny papers, CNPL.

[311] See Jenny's notes, ibid., 2.

[312] See the *Ordo agendorum* for these three days, De Clercq papers, CCV.

[313] Jenny noted laconically: "We spent an hour on no. 11" (Jenny papers, box 8, CNPL). A relatively large amount of time was devoted to the change from "among the principal disciplines" (no. 11, 163) to "among the necessary and more important disci-plines," a change which Grimshaw felt would give greater weight to the study of the liturgy without thereby placing it on a par with dogma (see Grimshaw report, 1, De Clercq papers, CCV).

[314] It is evident from the votes that 19 fathers supported part I (liturgy in seminaries) and 21 fathers supported part II (liturgy in theological faculties); see Jenny papers, box 8, (CNPL).

proposed that a subcommission's corrections should only be submitted to the Commission after they had been reviewed by the subcommissions dealing with language, theology, and juridical matters. In addition, the text should be presented in such a way that the Commission could move immediately to a *placet/non placet* vote. Only after it was evident that a majority was not in favor of the change should the matter be given over to discussion. When all of this had taken place, the secretary of the Commission should prepare a text in three columns, the first of which would give the original text, the second all the corrections presented by a subcommission to the Commission whether approved by the latter or not, and the third a new text in line with the decision of the majority of the Commission.[315]

In the meantime, and in order to increase the pressure, Hallinan wrote a short text in which he stressed that the bishops of the United States still wished to vote on chapter I of the schema during the first session. Bishops Tracy and Connare had recruited enough votes to support this proposal during the November 26 meeting of the U.S. bishops. One hundred and thirty-two bishops signed the petition, while McIntyre and Hurley of St. Augustine refused.[316] The following day the petition was passed on to Spellman who was to hand it over to the Council of Presidents. Spellman probably never did so.[317]

Others in the commission were also anxious to get on with the votes. On November 23, Jenny suggested that the discussion on chapter I be completed as quickly as possible in order to present it in its entirety for voting prior to December 8. If this did not happen, the bishops would have to return home empty-handed, a situation which would not do the reputation of the Council or the Church much good.[318] The atmosphere at that moment was apparently not very good. During the meeting Larraona and Pichler fell afoul of each other, the latter accusing the Cardinal of not doing his duty.[319] This meeting and those that followed (November 24, 26, 27, 28, and 30) were to deal with the most sensitive points of the discussion: the power of the episcopal conferences and the use of the vernacular.

The report of subcommission VI was read out by Calewaert. Subcommission members had gathered on November 15, 18, 19, and 22 but had

[315] See Calewaert papers, box 4, document 19, Archives of the Diocese of Ghent.
[316] Shelley, *Hallinan*, 173, 321.
[317] See Shelley, *Hallinan*, 175, 322.
[318] Jenny papers, box 8, CNPL.
[319] Shelley, *Hallinan*, 173, 321.

only completed their task on the previous day.[320] At the first meeting it was agreed, on Martimort's suggestion, that the order of chapter I, nos. 16-31 should be changed.[321] Instead of the former A (general norms), B (guidelines for adaptation of the liturgy to the particular character and traditions of the peoples), C (guidelines derived from the didactic and pastoral nature of the liturgy), D (norms based on the communal and hierarchical nature of the liturgy), the subcommission opted for a new order: A,D,C,B, with the Introduction remaining in its place. In addition, no. 28, which dealt with authority in liturgical matters, was given first place among the general norms and divided into three paragraphs.[322] Finally, although with some hesitation, a passage was added to no. 16 on composing a liturgical code.[323] When subcommission members met for a second time, on November 18, they now had at their disposal the advice of the theological and juridical subcommissions, which had met on November 16 and 17 respectively.[324] In light of the fact that the subcommission had decided for a while to set aside the vexed questions of nos. 20-22 and 24, the meeting proceeded to a discussion of no. 28 (now 16), into the second paragraph of which the text of the juridical subcommission had been inserted,[325] and nos. 18-19 (minimal changes). During the general congregation, article 16 (revision of the liturgical books) had caused much commotion because some felt that it gave the impression that the Council was imposing something on the Pope. The subcommission decided, nevertheless, to leave the text as it stood with the exception of a few significant word changes.[326]

---

[320] The very comprehensive report totalled twenty-two pages (see De Clercq papers, CCV).

[321] The original suggestion came from Msgr. Vielmo (see Martimort, "Les débats liturgiques," 310).

[322] Paragraphs 1 and 3 contained the original but now divided text. The advice of the juridical subcommission was asked for paragraph 2, where a juridical text was required.

[323] See Calewaert report, 2-3.

[324] The advice of the juridical subcommission with regard to former no. 28 § 2, ran as follows: "In virtue of power conceded by law, the governance of liturgical matters, within the stated limits, also belongs to various kinds of legitimately established competent territorial groups of bishops" (see Bonet report, 7, De Clercq papers, CCV). The subcommission also advised that in no. 24, lines 16-19 should be changed to: "The competent territorial ecclesiasical authority, having consulted, where necessary, with the bishops of neighboring regions . . . " The remaining comments dealt with matters of detail. The suggestions of the theological subcommission also dealt with minor matters and offered no suggestion whatsoever with regard to the much-controverted nos. 20-22 and 24 (see Gagnebet report, 3p., De Clercq papers, CCV).

[325] The subcommission proposed to change "only the hierarchy may change anything in the liturgy" to: "the competent authority in governing the liturgy."

[326] The addition of *"episcopis"* included the bishops, while the change of "from the

Changes to the remaining numbers were also minimal, thus permitting the subcommission to proceed to a discussion of nos. 20-22, to which a phrase had been added which offered the chance to integrate local cultural elements into the liturgy.[327] In addition, no. 21b was made a new number which gave the local authorities the opportunity to establish (*statuere*) adaptations. The term "episcopal conferences" was changed to "competent territorial ecclesiastical authority" in no. 22.

On November 22 the subcommission moved on to the discussion of liturgical language. Considering the variety of different perspectives on this point, the subcommission opted for the *via media*, which had also received much support in the aula. In response to requests from the African bishops, among others, the word "western" in the first paragraph was replaced by "Latin." With the addition of "with due respect to existing particular law," account was taken of those who were already celebrating the liturgy in the vernacular with the Holy See's permission.[328] As for the second paragraph, the suggestion that the use of the vernacular should either be clearly limited or permitted without limit was not followed, and the text was left unchanged, with the exception of a few minor clarifications. "Episcopal conferences" in paragraph 3 was also replaced with the phrase mentioned above. It was stated that the local bishops could issue stipulations with regard to the use of the vernacular, although these were to be reviewed by the Holy See. Finally, it was suggested that a new paragraph be inserted which would state that the translation of Latin texts into the vernacular should be approved by the competent local authority.[329]

The whole Liturgical Commission was to follow the broad lines of the subcommissions' proposals. There was some protest with regard to no. 16 (the revision of the liturgical books) because it was felt that this took over the work of the Congregation for Rites, but Larraona pointed out that it was evident that this Congregation would also have to be involved in such a revision.[330] At Larraona's suggestion the phrase about the Holy See's reviewing (*actis...recognitis*), in the disputed no. 21b, was replaced by the statement that they were to be "approved or confirmed"

---

whole world" to "from the various regions of the world" guaranteed the international Church its place in the revision (see Calewaert report, 6).

[327] Calewaert report, 13.
[328] See Calewaert report, 16-17.
[329] See Calewaert report, 20-23.
[330] See Jenny papers, box 8, CNPL.

(*probatis seu confirmatis*) by the Holy See.[331] All that remained for the meeting of November 27 was the discussion of the language-question, a discussion which continued into the next day. In spite of the resistance, among others, of Dante — who had to be silenced by Larraona at one point because he was screaming[332] — to the use of the vernacular in the Eucharist, the draft text of Calewaert's subcommission came through the discussions pretty well unscathed.[333] After reading and approving with some minor changes the "Report to the Fathers," mostly Martimort's work,[334] on November 30, the Commission was ready to send everything to the printer. Grimshaw's report on nos. 32-36 was quickly approved and, after the *Relatio ad patres* was read on December 3, this part was also ready to go to the printer.

The Commission had at least managed to complete one chapter and had thereby fulfilled the wishes of many of its members. On the whole, the activities of the Commission had certainly become more efficient after Lercaro's intervention on November 11 and Larraona's subsequent turn-around. The theological subcommission, which had initially been feared as something of a "watch dog," had cooperated very constructively. The juridical subcommission, whose comments were short and to the point, gave no evidence of desiring to throw a spanner in the works. The various subcommissions had either worked with speed or, where Calewaert's subcommission was concerned, had prepared the dossier so thoroughly that even on points of conflict, such as the competence of the episcopal conferences or the use of the vernacular in the liturgy, consensus was reached relatively quickly.

During the last days of the first session the Commission was able to buckle down to work on the report of Enciso's subcommission with a clear conscience. This group, which had been entrusted with the revision of chapter II on the mystery of the Eucharist, met with some regularity. At their first meeting on November 15 they were able to deal with the comments on the chapter as a whole and establish which of them fell under their sphere of activity and which did not.[335] During their second

---

[331] See Martimort, "Les débats liturgiques," 312. The fact that Dante continued to express his dissatisfaction with this formula on December 4 indicates that not everyone was pleased with it (see Jenny papers, box 8, CNPL; Martimort, "Les débats liturgiques," 313).

[332] Dante apparently had difficulties with the fact that such a delicate question had been given over to the Council and not to his own Congregation for Rites (see Shelley, *Hallinan*, 174).

[333] See Jenny papers, box 8, CNPL.

[334] See Martimort, "Les débats liturgiques," 312.

[335] See Enciso report, 1-2, De Clercq papers, CCV.

meeting, on November 17, they focused on the detailed comments on the introduction to chapter II and proposed a number of changes which were intended to give a clearer picture of the mystery of the cross, death, and resurrection within the context of the Eucharist.[336] On November 20 the subcommission discussed the comments on no. 37 (on the renewal of the order of the Mass). The members were of the opinion that the already mentioned criticism of this number did not deserve to be taken into account. After due consideration, they decided to insert Bea's suggestion that the rites should be simplified and that historically rooted duplications and insufficiently understood matters should be dropped.[337] On November 22, the subcommission devoted its time to nos. 38-40. After an examination of the comments, no. 38 remained unchanged. With regard to no. 39, which dealt with the homily, the subcommission followed the wishes of many of the fathers and endorsed the need for a sermon on Sundays and feast days. As far as the common prayer was concerned, a formulation was chosen which, following Pildain's request, did justice to the needs of all, including the poor.[338] Nos. 41-43 were discussed on November 24.[339] After carefully weighing all the arguments for and against the use of the vernacular, Léger's proposed formula, that the vernacular could be used in the readings and *some* of the prayers and hymns, was chosen. At the same time, an addition was made to the effect that care should be taken that the faithful be assisted to sing the Latin hymns of the ordinary mass with greater ease.[340] Communion under both kinds (no. 42) was then considered, and it was decided, over many objections, to endorse the arguments in favor of the practice — with an explicit appeal to Trent.[341] At the same time, the subcommission was aware of various practical considerations (for example, large crowds of communicants) and offered a number of suggestions as to appropriate occasions for distributing communion under

---

[336] The influence of the theological subcommission is perhaps evident on the formal level in the text eventually presented to the Commission, but on the level of content it is hard to detect a change; see Gagnebet report, 14, together with the corrected text submitted to the commission (Van den Eynde papers). It should also be noted at this point that in its discussions, the theological subcommission made relatively few changes in content on the basis of interventions from the fathers.

[337] Ibid., 7-8.

[338] See Enciso report, 11.

[339] One should be reminded that nos. 41 (vernacular) and 42 (communion under both species) caused something of an uproar during the meetings in the aula.

[340] See Enciso report, 14. The addition accommodated the *desiderata* of Bea, Florit, and Calewaert, among others.

[341] See the proposal of the theological subcommission, dated November 25, page 23 (Van den Eynde papers, CCV).

both kinds.[342] The discussions on chapter II were brought to a close on November 26 with the treatment of nos. 44-46, the last two of which remained unchanged. With regard to no. 44, however, Léger's proposal in favor of the promotion of concelebration, as an expression of unity, was included in the text. At the same time, the subcommission returned to the original text of the preparatory commission for the liturgy in which concelebration was called for in the conventual mass and in the most important mass in the parishes.[343] In so doing the subcommission had clearly chosen to integrate the ideas of the liturgical movement.

This subcommission's suggestions were followed by the whole Commission almost in their entirety,[344] although a vote on chapter II was not reached during the first session.[345]

VIII. The Initial Conciliar Votes

Before they began voting on the Introduction and chapter I, the Council fathers heard an explanation from the chairmen of the subcommissions and received eleven fascicles containing the old text and the corrected text placed side by side in two columns.[346] These fascicles also contained discussion of several remarks and observations, even of some that had ultimately been rejected by the Commission. In addition, the fathers were given the *Declarationes* from the original liturgy schema. They were thus able to form a relatively good picture of the Commission's work.

---

[342] The rather strange phrase "having removed danger to the faith" was dropped in conformity with the wishes of several of the fathers.

[343] See Enciso report, 17.

[344] See Enciso report together with *Commissio conciliaris de sacra liturgia. Caput II Schematis: De sacrosancto Eucharistiae Mysterio. Textus a Subcommissione, iuxta disceptationem in Commissione habitam, emendatus* (Lercaro papers, ISR). According to Bonet's report the juridical subcommission appears to have placed nothing in the way of Enciso's Commission (Bonet report, 10-11); see Van den Eynde papers, CCV.

[345] The *Ordo agendorum* of December 4 reports that the meeting was to continue discussing Msgr. Enciso's report; see also the *Ratio agendi in commissione conciliari de Sacra Liturgia congregationibus generalibus concilii oecumenici vacantibus, id est a die 8 dec. 1962 ad diem 8 sept. 1963*, 1; Jenny papers, box 8, CNPL; De Clercq papers, CCV. Since Hallinan's subcommission VIII, after meeting on November 27 and 29 and December 2, 3 and 5, was only able to finish its discussions on chapter III at the very last minute, the fathers received a copy of their report only as they were about to depart. For this reason it can be left aside at this point.

[346] *Emendationes a Patribus conciliaribus postulatae a commissione conciliari de sacra Liturgia examinatae et propositae*; these may be found in *AS* I/3, 114-15, 693-701; *AS* IV, 166-70, 266-77, 322-26.

When voting on the proposed corrections the fathers could express their agreement (*placet*) or disagreement (*non placet*) in written form. (It ought to be mentioned that no single correction was rejected by a majority.) When voting on the individual chapters, the fathers had a third possibility (*placet iuxta modum*).

The proposed corrections based on the general observations were presented by Lercaro to the twenty-first general congregation on November 17.[347] Martin then gave an overview of the corrections to the Introduction (1-4).[348] The result of the voting revealed that the fathers were for the most part satisfied with the work of the commission. The votes were as follows: on no. 1: 2181 *placet*, 14 *non placet*; on no. 2: 2175 *placet*, 26 *non placet*; on no. 3: 2175 *placet*, 21 non placet; on no. 4: 2191 *placet*, 10 *non placet*.[349]

During the thirtieth general congregation, on November 30, Martin presented the changes for chapter I (nos. 1-9, now 5-13), noting in his introduction that the Commission had not considered it necessary to undertake a suggested thorough revision of the text. The Commission had also judged it inopportune to draw the text doctrinally closer to the encyclical *Mediator Dei*, since a conciliar document was of a different literary genre than an encyclical.[350] The Commission had taken up the suggestion that the Holy Spirit should be given more weight and had

---

[347] Lercaro started his presentation by noting that the request of a number of fathers to have the *Declarationes* placed at their disposal had been passed on by unanimous agreement of the Commission to the Council of Presidents. On the differences between Lercaro's official presentation in the general congregation, AS I/3, 116-19, and another duplicated text, see Paiano, "Les travaux de la commission liturgique conciliaire," 9-10.

[348] To avoid confusion, it should be noted that in the text being presented at this stage even the Introduction had been numbered (1-4) and that a choice had also been made for a continuous enumeration. In practice this meant that no. 1 in chapter I, for example, was now no. 5. Our references will follow the latter numeration (see AS I/3, 695). Concerning the corrections, the following should be said. In no. 1 the most important alteration was the change from the use of "separated brothers" to "all who believe in Christ." In no. 2 the expression "visible and invisible" was replaced by "visible and endowed with invisible realities." An addition was made at this point: "vigorously active and yet making space in its life for contemplation," by which the rather flat "Church of action and contemplation" was given a more dynamic character. The phrase in no. 3 in which it was stated that the Council did not intend to formulate dogmatic declarations in this constitution was dropped. References to western and eastern rites were changed to Roman and other rites (see AS I/3, 114-15; also Schmidt, *Die Konstitution*, 98).

[349] For the four paragraphs there were respectively 11, 1, 7, and 3 invalid votes.

[350] Besides, the Commission was of the opinion that the definition of liturgy, as it had been formulated in the document, was sufficient, and therefore did not need to be made more precise, especially since agreement on a precise definition would have been difficult to achieve among the experts at that moment.

made three additions in this regard.[351] Before going into more detail on
the changes to the text, Martin pointed out that this section had received
fifty-nine alterations of which nine were of some importance, forty were
of a stylistic or linguistic nature, and the remaining ten had nothing to do
with content but simply clarified the intent of the text. He suggested that
to save time only the nine serious changes should be the subject of a
vote.[352]

The most important change to no. 5 was the replacement of the word
"cause" in the phrase "the cause of our salvation" with the word
"instrument," a term already in use among the Fathers and accepted by
all theologians.[353] At the end of no. 6 the words "by the power of the
Holy Spirit" were added in order to elevate the role of the Spirit.[354] No.
7, which dealt with Christ's presence in the Eucharist, underwent extensive surgery, but in terms of content the new text was the same as the
old.[355] The various forms of Christ's presence were described in the new
text as follows: Christ is personally present in the Eucharist in the person of the priest, in the eucharistic elements, in the power of his sacraments, and in the word, since it is he himself who speaks when the holy
scriptures are proclaimed in the Church.[356] Finally, Christ is personally
present whenever the Church prays or sings.[357] The changes in no. 8
were limited to two linguistic alterations.[358] The statement, "In its cen-

---

[351] Namely, in nos. 1 and 2; see *AS* I/3, 703.

[352] See *AS* I/1, 703.

[353] It is quite possible that the too scholastic connotations of the word *cause* had a role
to play in this alteration (see Bugnini, *Reform*, 33). The word "sacraments" in no. 6 was
altered to "through the Sacrifice and the Sacraments," in order to give more weight to the
Eucharist (see *AS* I/3, 704).

[354] See *AS* I/3, 696.

[355] To justify these formal changes Martin recalled that many of the fathers had
requested that the schema include the various distinctions found in *Mediator Dei*. In addition, a significant number of the fathers had expressed their reservations with regard to
the use of the phrase "and is explained." In doing so, the schema had given the impression that Christ's words in the scriptures and the homily that followed were on an equal
footing, which was obviously false. Finally, a substantial number of fathers had suggested
changes with regard to the sacrifice of the mass. For all these reasons, the decision had
been made to write a new text which would reflect the spirit of *Mediator Dei* and which
would give pride of place to the sacrifice of the mass (see *AS* I/3, 705).

[356] The phrase which referred to Christ's personal presence in the explanation of the
scriptures was dropped "as being a doctrinal development not sufficiently advanced for a
conciliar document" (Bugnini, *Reform*, 34).

[357] See *AS* I/3, 697. The following was added to the next paragraph: "[The Church]
invokes her Lord and through him offers worship to the eternal Father." This was in order
to make mention of worship of Christ, which is not mentioned elsewhere.

[358] See *AS* I/3, 697-98.

ter, which is the divine sacrifice of the Eucharist, [the liturgy] is at once the summit toward which everything should tend and the source from which everything proceeds," was removed from no. 9 and placed in no. 10 in an altered form: "The Liturgy is at once the summit toward which the activity of the Church tends and the source from which all her power flows." The relocation gave this important passage more weight since it was now placed in the number which dealt specifically with the eucharistic sacrifice as the Church's source of life.[359] The changes to nos. 11 to 13 had hardly any effect on their content.[360] Here, too, approval of the corrected texts was virtually unanimous except for no. 6,3, which received 150 negative votes, and no. 10,7, which found 101 fathers opposed.[361]

Msgr. Grimshaw took his turn on December 3 to present the changes to chapter I, nos. 14-20, to the thirty-second general congregation. He thought only two of these changes worth mentioning, the rest being elucidatory or literary in nature.[362] By the addition of "in virtue of baptism," no. 14 placed greater emphasis on the fact that the active participation of all the faithful was rooted in baptism and not in Church authorization.[363] No. 16 pressed the point that liturgy ought to be included in the list of courses required in seminaries and study houses of religious orders and congregations.[364] Here also these limited changes were accepted by the overwhelming majority of the fathers.[365]

Msgr. Calewaert presented the changes to chapter I, nos. 21-40, to the thirty-fourth general congregation, on December 5. Apparently the fathers had not remained in their places during the previous rounds of votes, for in his introduction Felici expressly requested that they remain in their places during the votes.[366] Calewaert, emphasizing that he spoke in the name of all the members of the Commission,[367] opened his very

---

[359] AS I/3, 706; see also Bugnini, *Reform*, 34. The remaining changes to this number were simply elucidatory.

[360] See AS I/3, 699-700. By the addition of the introductory sentence "The spiritual life is not limited to participation in the liturgy alone," no. 12 gave more weight to the personal piety of the faithful.

[361] The closest other negative result was on no. 5,1: present: 2145; for: 2096; against 41; invalid: 8.

[362] See AS I/4, 170.

[363] See AS I/4, 167, together with Grimshaw's clarification on 170-71.

[364] AS I/4, 167.

[365] The result of the vote on no. 14 was as follows: for: 2096; against: 10; invalid: 7; on no. 16: for: 2051; against: 52; invalid 6 (see AS I/4, 213).

[366] See AS I/4, 266.

[367] What is remarkable in Calewaert's report is the regularity with which the fathers' remarks and criticisms are mentioned and followed by a positive or negative reaction.

thorough report[368] by referring to the guidelines for the implementation of the liturgical renewal, the main subject of this part of the schema. Since this part of the schema had been substantially changed, Calewaert first gave the reasons the Commission had rearranged the text. So that these highly important matters would not be overlooked, the norms derived from the liturgy as a hierarchical action and as a community action (formerly D, now B),[369] together with those derived from the didactic and pastoral nature of the liturgy (C), were placed before the guidelines for its adaptation to the unique situations and traditions of peoples. In this way the guidelines for adaptation were provided with a clearer framework within which the changes should take place "so that there can be no doubt about them."[370] The following numbers dealt with respect for tradition and openness to legitimate progress on the one hand, and the biblical spirit of the renewal on the other (formerly nos. 18 and 19, now nos. 23 and 24). Only at this point do we find the paragraph which dealt with the revision of the liturgical books (formerly no. 16, now no. 25). In section B, the former no. 17, now no. 31, which dealt with the need to pay special attention to the ordering of the role of the faithful, was placed in the rubrics. By placing the former no. 27 (dealing with the active participation of the faithful) after nos. 28-29 (dealing with the place of each individual in the community celebration), the Commission intended to give the new nos. 30-31 a certain coherence, precisely because both numbers had to do with the laity. Section C remained more or less as it had been with the exception that the former no. 24 (on liturgical language) was now placed after the section dealing with the reading of the scriptures, the sermon, and the liturgical catecheses (without real motivation for the relocation). What was section B now became section D without any changes to the numerical sequence.

Calewaert then focused on the individual sections. He pointed out that the former no. 28 had been brought forward as no. 22. The relocation

---

[368] See *AS* I/4, 278-90; with regard to the commotion surrounding the fact that the emended text was relatively long in coming, see Shelley, *Hallinan*, 175-76.

[369] The former title, "Norms from the Communal and Hierarchical Nature of the Liturgy," now read "Norms from the Nature of the Liturgy as a Hierarchical and Communal Action."

[370] Within the various subdivisions of the text a number of individual numbers were also shifted. While no. 28 of the schema ("Only the hierarchy has authority to change anything in the liturgy"), for example, could formerly be found among the guidelines arising from the communal and hierarchical nature of the liturgy, it was now moved to first place among the general norms (no. 22), thereby clearly defining the legitimate authority with regard to the liturgy (see *AS* I/4, 278-79).

was prompted by the fact that the liturgical renewal had, for the most part, to be realized by the bishops in their different regions and on the basis of a variety of different conditions. In addition, several of the fathers had expressed various difficulties with the expression "episcopal conferences." At the suggestion of the Commission's canonists, therefore, a completely new paragraph had been inserted in this section. It stated that the ordering of the liturgy was, within defined limits, under the authority of the various legally established episcopal conferences (nos. 22 § 2).[371] An addition was also made to the number dealing with the revision of the liturgical books stating that this should be done by experts in consultation with the bishops.[372] In addition, without pinning themselves down to a specific date, the Commission had inserted a phrase stating that the revision should take place as soon as possible.[373] It was evident that the various relocations, additions, and changes gave more importance to the bishops' role in the realization of the liturgical renewal.

The third part of Calewaert's explanatory remarks dealt with the norms derived from the liturgy as a hierarchical action and as an action of the community. A new sentence had been added to no. 27 in which the public and social value of the Eucharist and attendance at the sacraments was emphasized. In addition, the phrase "while preserving customs to be approved by the Ordinary of the place," which weakened the concept of the fundamental equality of all the faithful in their participation in the liturgy, was dropped.[374] The remaining changes were small and did not touch on matters of fundamental importance.

The guidelines derived from the didactic and pastoral nature of the liturgy were then explained. Here, too, the majority of changes were intended as elucidations and were hardly spectacular. In no. 35 (formerly no. 25), however, a paragraph was inserted in which the desire was expressed that in places where there was a shortage of priests, religious services celebrating the word of God should be organized on specific occasions.[375]

---

[371] Calewaert added that since the phrase, "by the power granted by law," did not imply a juridical or theological statement, enough room was left for the text to be filled out in the future (see AS I/4, 280).

[372] See AS I/4, 270; see also the Commission's reasons on page 281.

[373] See AS I/4, 270, together with the commentary of Calewaert on page 282.

[374] See AS I/4, 271.

[375] See AS I/4, 273; the eve of the major feasts, certain weekdays in Advent and Lent, along with Sundays and feast days, were proposed.

Although strictly speaking a part of section C, a separate section in Calewaert's explanatory remarks was devoted to language, the endless discussions about which were surely still fresh in the memories of his audience.[376] Calewaert emphasized that, as the fathers had requested, the Commission had taken a middle way on the language issue, in which both Latin and the vernacular were given their due place. Quite a lot had been changed in this new no. 36 (formerly no. 24). In paragraph one, where the original schema had spoken of "western" liturgy, it was now stipulated that Latin ought to be the language of the *Latin* rites. This change met the desire of, among others, the African bishops to have the word "western" dropped; and by using the plural "rites," recognition was given to the fact that besides the Roman rite other rites such as the Ambrosian had a right to exist in the Church. Since Rome had already permitted liturgical celebrations in the vernacular in various local churches in the past, the phrase, "preserving particular law," was inserted.[377] It was further specified that the use of the vernacular could often be extremely useful for the people, especially for readings, exhortations, and certain prayers and hymns, consonant with the guidelines on the matter, which were set down separately in the chapters that followed. In conformity with article 22 § 2, the phrase in the third section, in which territorial Church authorities were only permitted to make suggestions to the Holy See, was changed to one that strengthened their role: they have the right to make decisions about the use of the vernacular and the extent of that use. In this way the Commission met the desire of a number of the fathers to give greater competence to the episcopal conferences. It was added, however, that these decisions had to be approved by the Holy See, approval here having the meaning of "confirmation." This would remove the ambiguity of the word "*recognitis*," employed in the schema, and would express the fact that the lower authority established the law while the superior authority added a new juridical value by its confirmation.[378] A completely new fourth paragraph proposed that, to prevent a proliferation of translations, the vernacular versions of the Latin texts should be the responsibility of the territorial authorities mentioned in nos. 36 § 3.[379]

---

[376] Once again ample attention was given to this point, more, in fact, than to any other item in chapter I (see *AS* I/4, 285-88).

[377] See *AS* I/4, 286.

[378] See *AS* I/4, 273, 288.

[379] See *AS* I/4, 288.

Calewaert concluded by discussing the guidelines for adapting the liturgy to the unique characteristics and traditions of peoples.[380] The votes on this occasion, which were spread over two days, provided no difficulties.[381]

The following day, December 6, Grimshaw presented the corrections to chapter I, 32-36 (now 41-46), which discussed the promotion of the liturgical life in the dioceses and the parishes together with pastoral-theological activities. He pointed out that with regard to the material on the bishops, the Commission had accepted some proposed amendments but rejected others on the ground that they either were matters of canon law or were adequately dealt with elsewhere in the text. The text was offering general principles and should not be weighed down by exceptions or particular aspects.[382] At this point he briefly explained three amendments.[383] In the vote that followed his remarks, the overwhelming majority, as before, voted in favor of the proposed corrections.[384]

---

[380] An addition to no. 37, in which respect for local traditions had already been recognized, stated that these traditions could be taken up in the liturgy as long as they were compatible with the basic principles of the true and genuine liturgical spirit. No. 39, which dealt with the limits of the adaptation, was thoroughly revised at a formal level by the Commission (AS I/4, 289). The introduction to no. 40 (dealing with the adaptation of the liturgy) was rewritten for the sake of clarity and to meet the desire of a number of the fathers (see AS I/4, 274 and 290); the mention of the Congregation for Rites was dropped from paragraph three of this number in order to give the Pope complete freedom in choosing the modus operandi.

[381] We follow the order in which the emended texts were presented. The results were as follows: no. 25: for: 2087; against: 14; invalid: 9; no. 37: for: 2083; against: 21; invalid: 10; no. 39: for: 2044; against: 50; invalid: 15; no. 36: for: 2033; against: 36; invalid 5; no. 36: for: 2011; against: 44; invalid: 17; no. 36: for: 2016; against: 56; invalid: 10; no. 36: for: 2041; against: 30; invalid: 8; no. 35: for: 1903; against: 38; invalid: 145; no. 27: for: 2054; against: 22; invalid: 6; no. 22: for: 2037; against: 37; invalid: 4; no. 32: for: 2023; against: 31; invalid: 4. The number of invalid votes under no. 35 can be explained by the fact that several of the fathers had already left the hall to pray the Angelus with the Pope, who had been ill for a couple of days (see Bugnini, Reform, 34).

[382] AS I/4, 326.

[383] He noted that the phrase in which it was stated that baptism, confirmation, first communion, marriage, and burial could only take place outside one's own parish for serious reasons (old no. 33, new no. 42) had been dropped because such a regulation would be difficult to realize in practice and had no basis in law. A change had also been made to no. 34 (new no. 44), which dealt with the establishment of national liturgical commissions. Once again, in conformity with articles 22 §2, it was decided to replace the phrase "In individual national episcopal conferences" with "By the competent territorial ecclesiastical authority," since it was not yet clear what sort of juridical status would be granted to the episcopal conferences. Finally, since the interdiocesan commissions spoken of in no. 45 (former no. 35) had no juridical status but were only consultative bodies, the words "after consultation" were added in order to clarify the absence, for the time being, of that juridical status (see AS I/4, 324 and 326-27).

[384] I, 42: for 1916; against: 115; invalid: 6; I,44: for: 1981; against: 22; invalid: 11.

Speaking on behalf of the presidents, Felici proposed on December 6 that in light of the majority votes in favor of the changes to the Introduction and chapter I that the amended text be voted on as a whole the following day.[385] The fathers accepted his suggestion, and the vote took place on December 7. The total number of fathers who participated in the voting was 2118. Of them 1992 gave their *placet*, 11 voted *non placet*, while 180 voted *placet iuxta modum*.[386] This very positive result safely anchored the basic principles of the Council's liturgical renewal.[387]

In his speech at the end of the first session, Pope John XXIII expressed his satisfaction with this initial result:

> It was no accident that the first *schema* to be considered was the one dealing with the sacred liturgy, which has to do with man's relationship with God. This relationship is of the utmost importance which must be based on the solid foundation of revelation and apostolic teaching, so as to contribute to man's spiritual good and to do so with a broadness of vision that avoids the superficiality and haste which often characterize human relationships.[388]

---

[385] See *AS* I/4, 361-62.
[386] See *AS* I/4, 384; five votes were invalid.
[387] See Schmidt, *Die Konstitution*, 97.
[388] See *AS* I/4, 645; ET in *The Pope Speaks* 8 (1962-1963), 400.

CHAPTER IV

AN INITIAL PROFILE OF THE ASSEMBLY

Hilari Raguer

On balance, the preparatory period had disappointed hopes for the Council. As Hans Küng was to comment later,

> It is not giving away any secrets to say that morale on the eve of Vatican II, even in Rome itself, was none too good, Optimism was not in evidence. There was nothing but problems, worries and questions in all directions: How is anything going to work, with these delegations and these schemata? Is not the "open" element only an insignificant minority amidst this multitude of over two thousand bishops? What is it possible to achieve here? Hasn't everything really been settled and finished in advance by all that anything-but-reassuring process of preparation? The ghost of the Roman Synod walked again, and there was talk of a *concilio lampo*, a lightning council with no real discussion.[1]

As one of the more important chroniclers of the Council wrote when describing the opening procession,

> Not all of the bishops were smiling as they passed. Many believed that the Council had been convoked simply to rubber-stamp previously prepared documents. Some United States bishops had intimated that they would put in a token appearance for two or three weeks, and then go home. And all the bishops of Paraguay had been informed by a high ecclesiastical dignitary that everything had been so well prepared in Rome that the Council would soon be over.[2]

If we regard the *vota* of the bishops as a reflection of the universal episcopate, the resultant picture shows some Council fathers who were concerned — if anything at all concerned them — with trivialities and lacked much awareness of the deep problems of the Church and contemporary society.[3] The work of the preparatory commissions, which was firmly controlled by the Curia, had only confirmed this general view of things. The voices of dissent, that is, in favor of renewal, were impor-

---

[1] Hans Küng, *The Council in Action: Theological Reflections on the Second Vatican Council* (New York, 1963), 67.

[2] Ralph M. Wiltgen, S.V.D., *The Rhine Flows into the Tiber* (New York, 1967), 13.

[3] See the study of the *vota* in *History*, I, 55-166, and the various analyses cited there.

tant, but very few, and had been expressed privately. When Cardinal Döpfner asked Cardinal Montini how many Italian bishops he thought could be counted on, the latter replied: hardly 30 out of 344. And, according to the testimony of the future Cardinal Jubany, at that time Auxiliary Bishop of Barcelona, the Spanish bishops who supported a renewal by the Council were exactly 11 out of 78.

Despite all this, hardly had the Council taken its first steps when the multitude of the world's bishops began to come to a sense of themselves. The general opinion that took shape and the face which the assembly presented became radically different, to the point where "majority" and "minority" changed their meaning within a very short time.[4] The two positions began to form during the discussions of the introduction to the schema on the liturgy, of the use of the vernacular, and of the faculties to be allowed to the episcopal conferences instead of the Roman Congregations. During the intersession Joseph Ratzinger would say that "the great, surprising, and genuinely positive result of the first session" had been the inability to approve any document, which demonstrated "the strong reaction against the mentality behind the preparatory work" and represented "the truly epoch-making character of the Council's first session."[5]

How did this reversal of positions and forces come about? This is the focus of interest in the present chapter. After explaining the make-up of the assembly, we shall look at the part played by some groups to which the Regulations of the Council assigned no competence, that is, the episcopal conferences above all, but also some informal groups. We shall also look at the role of the news media, which not only conveyed more information about the conciliar events than had ever been done before, but also in turn influenced the Council fathers themselves. We must also speak of the people of God, who were not simply spectators at the show but through the news media also acted as a sounding board, with undeniable results. Undoubtedly, however, the key to the reversal of majority and minority was John XXIII, who was the great catalyst for the few

---

[4] At the very beginning of the debate on the schema on the liturgy, a Melkite bishop, Msgr. Neophytos Edelby, realized that the ratio had changed: "Two trends can be perceived in the assembly: a conservative trend, represented above all by the Italians and the North Americans, and a reform trend, though a moderate one, represented by the rest of the Europeans and the bishops from the missions. This second trend must, it seems, carry the day" (*JEdelby*, October 22, 1962, ISR). In fact, the terms "majority" and "minority," in the sense which I am giving them here, made their appearance only in commentaries of a somewhat later date.

[5] Cited by Wiltgen, *Rhine*, 59.

reform-minded bishops; he had been able to excite the people of God and world opinion with his plan and, at the same time, he found, in the universal sympathy which his person and his Council aroused, the moral strength to overcome the opposition that reigned in the Curia against the ideas of a council of renewal.

I. COMPOSITION OF THE ASSEMBLY

The first and most visible external characteristic of Vatican II was the large number of participants; the second was their variety. In this section, after providing some statistics, I gather some details, selected from the rich fund of stories about the Council, which I trust will be more than merely picturesque and will help to sketch the face which the assembly presented. Let us look first at the men who made up the assembly.

A. The Council Fathers

The Regulations said nothing new about those being summoned but simply referred to the Code of Canon Law and the Code of Oriental Law.[6] The norms given in the 1917 Code for ecumenical councils (now applied for the first time) were contained in canons 222-229 and established that the following were to be summoned, with the right to a deliberative vote: (1) cardinals, even if not bishops;[7] (2) patriarchs, primates, archbishops, and residential bishops, including those not yet consecrated; (3) abbots and prelates *nullius*; (4) the abbot primate,[8] the abbot superiors of the monastic Congregations, and the superiors general of the exempt clerical Orders, while the superiors of the other religious congregations were expressly excluded, unless the Pope should say otherwise in his bull of convocation. As for titular bishops, it seems that Pius IX, who in his management of Vatican I was less authoritar-

---

[6] The Regulations, art. 1 § 2, cite canon 223 § 1, of the Code of Canon Law and canon 168 § 1, of the Code of Oriental Law.

[7] Six months after opening the Council, in his motu proprio, *Cum gravissima* (April 15, 1962), John XXIII ordered that all cardinals were to possess episcopal rank; as a result all cardinals who did not have it were consecrated bishops.

[8] The reference was to the Abbot Primate of the Benedictine Confederation, which Leo XIII had established in 1893 with the intention of unifying to some degree the various Congregations of the Order of St. Benedict and of centralizing their relations with the Holy See.

ian than is usually maintained,[9] was initially doubtful about summoning them to his council, but he eventually did call them and also the major religious superiors, having in mind Abbot Prosper Guéranger, founder of Solesmes and a distinguished ultramontane.[10] In a somewhat reserved manner, the Code of 1917 took over this practice, although it left open the contrary possibility when it said that "titular bishops, if summoned, will also have a deliberative vote, unless the bull of convocation expressly orders the matter differently." Finally, it envisaged the invitation of theologians or canonists, but with a merely consultative vote.

The papal bull convoking Vatican II complied with these norms:[11] "Our beloved sons the cardinals, the venerable brother patriarchs and primates, archbishops and bishops — both residential and titular — and also all those people who have the right and the duty to attend the Council." But the Regulations, art. 3 § 3, expressly excluded "theologians, canonists, and other experts" from the number of the Council fathers, denying them even a consultative vote and relegating them to the role of "assistants" to the fathers, more or less like the auxiliary personnel: "notaries, promotors, ballot-examiners, scribe-archivists, readers, interpreters, translators, stenographers, and technicians." According to art. 10§1, these could be present at the general congregations but could not speak unless they were asked; they were indeed present, but no expert was ever invited to speak in the council hall.

The work of these collaborators — both the conciliar experts strictly speaking and those brought to Rome by episcopates or some individual bishops — was nevertheless very important. The talks or round-tables to which many episcopal conferences and centers of ecclesiastical studies invited them were occasions for the Council fathers to meet and converse with them, and it was in this setting that many fathers began to change their theological outlooks.

The "progressive" experts were much more sought after than the "conservative" ones, perhaps because the latter said nothing new, nothing that was not contained in the manuals which the bishops had studied. In his personal diary Father Congar complained that despite his poor health he had to comply with countless requests, which it distressed him to turn down. Even some conservative bishops were curious to find out precisely what Schillebeeckx, Rahner, and Congar were saying. An

---

[9] See René Rémond, preface to Philippe Levillain, *La mécanique politique de Vatican II. La majorité et l'unanimité dans un Concile* (Paris, 1975), 10.

[10] See Roger Aubert, *Le pontificat de Pie IX* (Paris, 1948), 313.

expert called by the Spanish episcopate, Father Adalbert Franquesa, a Benedictine monk of Montserrat, refers in his personal diary to the almost daily meetings which the liturgists invited by the Spanish episcopate held during the debate on the liturgy schema; at these meetings they decided on the *vota* which they thought should be presented, and they outlined them so that the bishops could defend them. The diarist also tells of the important meetings which these liturgists held at the Hotel Columbus with the main liturgists of the other episcopates (Martimort, Gy, Wagner, and so on) and at which they decided on a common strategy to be adopted.

A year later (July 6, 1963) Paul VI extended the right to participate in the Council, with a deliberative vote, to the Prefects Apostolic, even though these were not of episcopal rank. There were some eighty of them.

Some 2500 bishops and other Council fathers took part in the first session;[12] in addition there were the experts, observers, and auxiliary personnel. Recall that the first ecumenical council, the one that gathered in Nicea in 325, was traditionally called "the great and holy synod of the 318 fathers" and that in fact the fathers there numbered barely 220. And the last council held, Vatican I, despite the availability of means of transport far superior to those of earlier centuries, brought together for its opening session on December 8, 1969, only 642 prelates with a right to vote; still Bishop Ullathorne was led to exclaim: "Never, before today, has the world seen such an assembly of prelates!"

According to an official Vatican report, those who had a right to attend the first session of Vatican II numbered 2904, although only 2449 (89.34%) were actually present.[13] According to unofficial statistics circulating among the reporters at that time,[14] those summoned to the Council numbered 2778. Of these 87 were cardinals and patriarchs (3.4%); 1619 were archbishops and residential bishops of dioceses

[11] Apostolic Constitution *Humanae salutis* (December 25, 1961), in *AAS* 54 (1962), 5-13; ET in Walter M. Abbott, S.J., ed., *The Documents of Vatican II* (New York, 1966), 703-9.

[12] According to a mimeographed document distributed in Rome, 2681 bishops had a right to be summoned; *Bilan du Monde* gives the number as 2693.

[13] *I Padri presenti al Concilio Ecumenico Vaticano II*, published by the General Secretariat of the Council (Rome, 1966). According to information at the ISR, there were 2443 participants in the first session.

[14] J. L. Martín Descalzo, *Un periodista en el Concilio. Primera etapa* (Madrid, 1963), 107-14. This Roman document was also used in the dossier published in a special issue of *ICI* on the Council, October 1, 1962.

(58.%); 975 were titular or auxiliary bishops (35%); and 97 were general superiors of religious Orders or Congregations. There were 939 religious (38%), the rest belonging to the secular clergy. They came from 116 different countries: 849 from Western Europe; 601 from Latin America; 332 from North America; 256 from the Asiatic world; 250 from black Africa; 174 from the communist bloc; 95 from the Arab world; and 70 from Oceania. Western Europe, with 33.70% of the world's Catholics, had 31.6% of the Council fathers, while Latin America, with 35.53% of the world's Catholics, had only 22.33% of the fathers. Relatively overrepresented were black Africa, with 4.08% of the world's Catholics and 9.30% of the fathers; the Arab world, with 0.51% of the Catholics and 3.53% of the fathers; Asia and Oceania, with 6.71% of the Catholics and 12.10% of the fathers; and North America, with 8.69% of the Catholics and 12.36% of the fathers.

As far as the age of the fathers was concerned, J. L. Martín Descalzo calculated, on the basis of the statistics already mentioned, that 60% of the fathers were not yet 62 years old. The largest bloc had been born in the first decade of the present century, and 59.12% between 1900 and 1920, so that they were between 42 and 62, as can be seen from the following distribution according to date of birth:

Before 1871	9
Between 1871 and 1880	124
Between 1881 and 1890	418
Between 1891 and 1900	521
Between 1901 and 1910	981
Between 1911 and 1920	604
After 1920	24.[15]

We must not be too hasty in drawing conclusions from this age distribution. Cardinal Ottaviani, the energetic leader of the conservative group, was 71 years old at the beginning of the Council, and one of the most charismatic of the fathers turned out to be an ancient of 84 years, the Melkite Patriarch of Antioch, Maximos IV Saigh.

It was to be anticipated that, especially among the 40 percent of the Council fathers who were over 60, there would be absences due to death or sickness, while at the same time other newly appointed bishops would join the Council. The Archbishop Emeritus of Salisbury, Rhodesia, and Titular Archbishop of Velebusdo, Aston Chichester, S.J., died suddenly in the very atrium of the basilica an hour before the beginning of the

[15] Martín Descalzo, *Un periodista*, 109.

sixth general congregation on October 24. Alfonso Carinci, an Italian, Titular Bishop of Seleucia in Isauria, who as a boy of 7 had been an acolyte at Vatican I, reached his hundredth birthday on November 9. When, in his absence, Cardinal Frings announced the occasion during the general congregation of that day, the man was loudly applauded by all the Council fathers in a standing ovation. At the end of the working day Msgr. Felici read out the telegram which the Council had sent to Carinci, congratulating him and wishing him many more years of life. Present at most of the general congregations of the first session and at some of the second, Carinci died on November 6, 1963, and thus could not take part in the third and fourth sessions. The youngest of the fathers, at 34, was Peruvian Alcides Mendoza Castro, Bishop of Abancay, who used to collect the elderly Carinci at his residence so that they might go together to the Vatican.

A definitive list of all the Council fathers has been difficult to establish, even from official documents, but the data base begun by the Istituto per le Scienze Religiose in Bologna makes it safe to say that 3054 was the complete number of Council fathers, although some were present only at the beginning and others only at the end. Of the 3054 in the complete count, 2443 fathers took part in the first session; only 1897 in all four.[16] Vote counts reveal that the number of those present at general congregations during the first period dropped from 2381 at the general congregation of October 16, the day of the election of the commissions, to 2086 at the thirty-fifth general congregation on December 6.[17]

In addition to these numbers of participants at one or several sessions, account must be taken of the fact that more than a few bishops did not stay in Rome for the whole session but rather came and went; this was especially true of the Europeans, whose dioceses were not very far away. After all that they had said and written to their faithful during the period of preparation about the importance of the Council, these men could not simply leave it, but once they realized that the Council would last far longer than they had imagined, they had to take steps for the proper governance of their dioceses. In some cases those who had auxiliary bishops accompanying them to Rome sent them back home to watch over the diocese, while they themselves remained in the Eternal City. Anticipating what would happen, the Holy See had granted bishops coming to the Council the faculty to delegate for the administration of the sacrament of confirmation.[18]

[16] Calculation of the author on the basis of the data at the ISR.

[17] See the statistics and the graph showing the curve in René Laurentin, *Bilan de la première session* (Paris, 1963), 56-57.

The Holy See had also instructed the nuncios to inform the episcopates that large cities should not be abandoned for a long time and that where there was more than one prelate, it was expedient that one of these bishops remain there, at least when there was question of a lengthy period.[19]

Art. 41 of the Regulations repeated verbatim canon 225 of the Code of Canon Law and canon 170 of the Code of Oriental Law, according to which no one could leave the Council without authorization from the President. The norm had in mind the possibility, absolutely unthinkable in 1962, that a group of bishops might boycott the celebration of the Council. In the case not of leaving the Council but simply of not being present at one or other of its public meetings or general congregations, there would be no need to ask permission; it would be enough, according to art. 42 of the Regulations, to let the Council of Presidents know, through the Secretary General, the reason for the absence. Secretary General Felici reminded the Council fathers of this regulation a few days after the Council had begun, but he added that there would be no need to wait for an answer from his Secretariat.[20]

After the numbers, the first thing that strikes one in looking at the assembly is its variety. Pictures of the event, the reports of the journalists, and the recollections of those who were there agree in calling attention to the spectacle afforded by bishops from all parts of the world. But over and above the picturesque anecdotes and superficial impressions, the Council enabled an authentic spiritual experience of an intensity hitherto unknown. Even before the opening Msgr. Garrone had proclaimed:

> The Church today is experiencing what might be called the physical reality of its universality. We believed in this, we proclaimed it in our Creed; now, for numerous reasons, *it has come home to us* in a sensible way. Distant peoples, who used to be only names on the map to us, something we remembered, are in many cases acquiring a face and coming very near to us: it used to be a country, now it is a group of human beings. Suddenly and forcefully we understand what it means to say that Christ is King of the universe, for this universe is there before our eyes. At the same time, however, the Church grasps with a kind of amazement the real limits of this kingdom: Haiti, Goa, Katanga, Kuwait are no longer mere ideas but human beings for whom Christ died; and yet very close to us, right beside us, we feel that Christ is absent! Here you have the soul of the Council.[21]

---

[18] Decree of the Sacred Congregation for the Discipline of the Sacraments, October 4, 1962; in *OssRom*, October 11, 1962, the opening day of the Council.

[19] Interview with Cardinal Morcillo, *Ecclesia* (Madrid), October 17, 1962.

[20] October 23, 1962 (see *AS* I/1, 364).

[21] *ICI*, February 1, 1962.

But this spectacle was not a triumphalistic manifestation of a Church turned in on itself; instead, the deployment of the mass media at the Council reminded the bishops of the reality of the human race that is the reason for the Church's existence. On the eve of the opening Congar wrote: "Today the gospel must be preached to a world in which one person out of four is Chinese, two out of four do not have enough to eat, one out of three lives under a communist government, one out of every two Christians is not a Catholic."[22] Never had a council had so many participants; never had a council been so aware of the problems of humanity; never had humanity been so interested in a council.

The quantitative leap which Vatican II represented in comparison with all previous ecumenical councils brought with it a qualitative change. It is probable that there had never been another deliberative assembly of this size, whether ecclesiastical or civil (except perhaps for the Chinese assembly, but its role is to acclaim, not to deliberate). In the first vote taken by the Council on October 16 to elect the 160 members of the ten commissions, the large number both of voters and of posts to be filled required the verification of over 400,000 nominations and therefore the postponement of further sessions until October 20. At the Eucharist in the Ambrosian rite, which Montini celebrated in the council hall on November 4, the Holy Father delivered a homily in which he described the event as "unsurpassed in the history of centuries past, and difficult to surpass in the future," and he took delight in the presence of "your vast choir of 2500 bishops."[23]

According to what Felici told the assembly at its thirty-fifth general congregation (December 6), 587 fathers spoke during the first session and another 523 gave their remarks on the schemas in writing. It was obvious that the method for the work had to be quite different from that of previous councils if the legitimate role of the bishops and their freedom to intervene were to be maintained and, at the same time, the work was to be done efficiently. The methods for inspecting the schemas, counting the votes, proceeding during the general congregations, and studying the schemas and emendations in the commissions proved inadequate, and it was necessary to turn to the model afforded by modern parliamentary practice and, more generally, the working method used at congresses and assemblies, including those with fewer participants than the Council had.

[22] *Le Monde*, September 6, 1962.
[23] *OssRom*, November 5-6, 1962.

The activity of the Council fathers was not limited to interventions during the debates. Contacts with bishops from the same country and with other episcopates, often at the bar next to the hall, were very important for the outcomes of these debates, while the conversations that went on in the side spaces of the basilica, to both sides of the central nave where the rows of seats had been erected, inspired some one jokingly to give the Council the name *Lateranense VI*.

The various residences, mainly the national or international colleges (some ninety in all[24]), in which the Council fathers were lodged, also played a decisive part in forging agreements, drafting texts or *modi*, and deciding votes. But those who lived together in these residences were not grouped strictly by nations. An example, at first glance anecdotal but surely illustrative, is given us by the diary of a young prelate (41 years old when the Council began), Msgr. Neophytos Edelby, a member of Basilian Fathers of Aleppo, Titular Bishop of Edessa in Osrhoene, and adviser to the Melkite Patriarch of Antioch.

At Salvator Mundi, where Edelby resided with Patriarch Maximos IV and the other Melkite bishops, there happened to be, among other groups of various nationalities, a dozen or so North American prelates from the ecclesiastical province of Milwaukee; these were very different from the Arabs in many respects, and yet they got along wonderfully with them. One of the Americans, William Patrick O'Connor, Bishop of Madison, celebrated both his birthday and his jubilee of ordination on October 18, and he provided a party for all of them. "Rarely have I seen a bishop so cheerful and also so good. Every time he met us," said the Melkite prelate, who like all Orientals was very sensitive to manifestations of respect, "he showed his friendliness in the little French that he knew. The patriarch and he embraced at least once a day and clapped one another vigorously on the shoulders." The Melkite bishops joined the party singing in chorus the hymn *Eis polla êti*. Mgsr. Nabaa addressed some words in Arabic to Bishop O'Connor, and Msgr. Hakim some in Hebrew, none of which the North American understood, but they left him visibly moved. The party ended with a large supper, and the Americans and Arabs ended the evening by singing "Happy birthday," while the guest of honor cut a large cake. Edelby wrote that night:

> We have been very touched by the simplicity and cheerfulness of the American bishops. I also think they have taken a liking to us. One of the great benefits of the Council is that it makes possible these contacts among

[24] Caprile, II, 287.

the bishops of the entire world. For us Orientals, in particular, how important it is to make our Church known! People have nothing against us, but they know nothing about us!.[25]

Later on, these Melkites were able to count on the support of the North Americans in defending the rights of their patriarchate. For the first time in centuries, they felt important. On the eve of the vote for the commissions, when the exchange of lists was in full swing, Edelby wrote:

We have received no fewer than 50 visits. The four bishops and two secretaries of the patriarch's entourage have not stopped receiving, introducing, and assisting. The French, African, and Brazilian bishops are asking for the list of our own candidates. We give the list of six of our people, along with His Beatitude. . . . We feel increasing sympathy from those around us.[26]

When John XXIII made his historic decision to reject the schema on the sources of revelation, Edelby wrote the following description of the reigning mood in his house: "At Salvator Mundi everyone is rejoicing, for it must be said that in this residence everyone is in the avant garde of the progressives: Americans, Germans, Africans, and Orientals."[27]

General congregations lasted from 9:00 A.M. to 12:15 P.M. Before they began, since concelebration was not then possible, the bishops and other Council fathers celebrated Mass, usually in the chapels of their various residences, sometimes at temporary altars, and serving one another as acolytes. Afternoons and weekends were for rest, letter-writing, study, drafting or revising Council documents, contacts and interviews, attending lectures or press conferences. They were also used for devotional or cultural visits to the churches and monuments of the Eternal City and its surroundings.

Transportation from the residences to St. Peter's and back was by special buses, hired by the Council organizers from two Roman firms; these buses had fixed routes that covered all the residences. The cardinals made the trip in luxurious automobiles with SCV (Sacra Città Vaticana) license plates; some of the cars were Mercedes, to which the sharp Roman wit applied the gospel saying: "*Iam receperunt mercedem suam*: They have already received their reward (*mercedem*)." A few bishops had personal automobiles at their disposal.[28]

---

[25] *JEdelby*, October 18, 1962.

[26] Ibid., October 12, 1962.

[27] Ibid., November 21, 1962.

[28] Early in the Council, N. Camels, Abbot General of the Premonstratensians, wrote to his monks: "How do the Council fathers spend the day? First of all, and this will not surprise you, the cardinals, bishops, prelates, abbots, general superiors, and, in short, the

B. THE NON-CATHOLIC OBSERVERS AND GUESTS

Although they were not fathers of the Council, we cannot forget the presence of the observers sent by other Churches. They were not passive spectators at the conciliar event but had a positive influence on the definitive text of various conciliar documents. The Spanish Ambassador to the Vatican told his Minister that "ecumenism is henceforth the characteristic mark of this Council and of the Pope's outlook."[29] "The presence of the thirty-seven observers from the non–Roman Catholic Chris-

twenty-five hundred fathers of the Council, must rise early in order to reach St. Peter's on time. The sessions begin at nine o'clock. This is not a very early hour, but there is Mass to be celebrated, although those who wish may celebrate it in the evening. Time also has to be allowed for traffic jams, for the inconsiderate telephone call at the last minute (when you're putting on your hat), for the trifling things that keep you from leaving on time, and for remembering the confrere who rides in the same vehicle as you and has a genius for noticing, only after he has settled in, that he has forgotten his skullcap. . . . On Thursday, October 11, for the first time in the history of the Church, all the bishops of the world rose at the same hour on the same day, dressed in the same garb, meditated on the same thought, before going to the same assembly with the same program. From the time they awoke, the fathers of the Council were 'one.' . . . Little by little, step by step, alone or in groups, the fathers of the Council enter, and the places fill up. All are robed in violet or purple or the habit of their religious Order; the Orientals are in black. Over their soutanes they wear the lace rochet, covered in turn by a mantelletta of the same color as the soutane, with the pectoral cross standing out against this background. There's a liturgical air about God's parliament. Some prelates, the ones who are always exactly on time, arrive right at 9.00, not a minute before, not a minute after; those who have gotten used to not being punctual (this, too, is an acquired habit), 'sit quietly' in an empty place; they seem more at ease, especially if by chance the place is near the entrance. . . . At nine on the dot a bell chimes, Holy Mass begins. It is celebrated by an archbishop or bishop at a small altar set up facing the audience, a little in front of the tomb of St. Peter, at the head of the central nave. All the fathers answer the prayers at the foot of the altar and during the Mass. When Mass is over, Msgr. Felici, Secretary General of the Council, or someone else, solemnly carries in the famous evangeliary (manuscript Vat. Urbinate lat. N° 10, fifteenth century) and places it on the altar between two candles, on the same stand that served to display it during Vatican I. It remains on display throughout the meeting. Thus the Word of God presides over the words of men and guides them. After this, the cardinal-president of the conciliar meeting recites the prayer *Adsumus*, composed in 619 by St. Isidore of Seville for a council held in that city. Sometimes, as the newspapers have told you, the sessions have lasted only for a short time. But if the congregations in St. Peter's are short, they are followed by various meetings in different locales, and at these people work hard and for hours — you always know when they begin, but never when they will end. . . . There are always more meetings. Some days are so crowded that it is difficult to find time to look at the calender and find out what day of the month it is. No one, unless he wishes, has time to relax or to go for a walk....After the Mass, Msgr. Felici gives the order *Extra omnes*. Only the fathers, the experts, the officials, and the delegated observers may remain in the basilica; all others must leave" (*La vie du Concile* [Forcalquier, 1966], 31-33).

[29] Report of Spanish Ambassador Doussinague, February 26, 1963 (Archivio General del Ministerio de Asuntos Exteriores [AGMAE], R 7190/2).

tian Communions," said Congar, "is one of the important elements in the conciliar situation."[30]

The arrival of the non-Catholic observers at the Council had behind it a complex and surprising history,[31] but the fact was that they were there. In a special tribune in the Vatican hall sat fifty-four non-Catholics, of whom forty-six were "observers" in the proper sense, that is, official delegates of their respective Churches in response to an invitation sent them by the Secretariat for Christian Unity. Eight were "guests;" that is, non-Catholic personages invited or admitted on their own count, because of their sympathy for Catholicism (for example, Roger Schutz, Prior of Taizé, and Max Thurian, theologian of the same community) or for their work for Christian unity (for example, exegete Oscar Cullmann).[32]

Etienne Fouilloux remarks that some of these personal invitations served to fill vacancies left when some institutions turned down the invitation. For example, Msgr. Cassian Bezobrazov and Father Alexander Schmemann, leaders at the two most prestigious theological institutions of the Russian exile, were under the Patriarchate of Constantinople, which was officially absent. The Baptist World Alliance was the only major Protestant confederation that did not accept the Vatican's invitation,[33] but its President, Joseph H. Jackson, was present as a guest and on December 21, 1961, had been received by the Pope at a private audience. Another American Baptist, Walter Harrelson, of Vanderbilt University (Nashville, Tennessee), had himself accredited as a journalist at the Council.

Some of the announced observers did not come; others had themselves replaced; and as happened among the Council fathers, the number of observers actually present varied in the course of the Council, the overall trend being an increase in the numbers. According to Fouilloux's calculations, fewer than thirty (give or take a few) attended the first session from beginning to end. Some of those who came later proved afterward to be very important for the ecumenical dimension of the Council; in this context Fouilloux mentions Argentine Methodist José Miguel

[30] Y. J. Congar, "Bloc-notes," *ICI*, no. 182 (December 15, 1962), 2.

[31] See *History*, I, 318-26, 402-4.

[32] See *Observateurs, délégués et hôtes du Secrétariat pour l'unité des chrétiens au deuxième concile oecuménique du Vatican* (Vatican Polyglot Press, 1965), 11-15, cited with commentary by É. Fouilloux, "Des observateurs non catholiques," in *Vatican II commence*, 235-61. The number of the personages present and the label given to each (observer or guest) differ according to various lists. The list in *OssRom* for October 15-16 contains only thirty-nine names, instead of the fifty-four on the official list.

[33] Resolution passed at the meeting in Oslo, August 20-24, 1962.

Bonino, Italian Vittorio Subilia of the Reformed Church, and Hungarian Lutheran Vilmos Vajta. Although theologian André Scrima, personal envoy of Patriarch Athenagoras, did not officially represent his Church and was not an observer, he maintained important contacts on the periphery of the Council.

Also in Rome were some who had wanted to be invited and were not. Lukas Vischer reported that Max Lackmann and Peter Meinhold had tried to arrange an invitation, and the Secretariat for Christian Unity did consider at least the second of these two, but the official observer delegated by the Evangelical Church in Germany, Edmund Schlink, let Cardinal Bea know that the two did not really represent German Protestantism and, furthermore, that "the Secretariat should not invite anybody who is known for his openness towards Rome."[34] Vischer himself told Father Roberto Tucci of his concern about the prominence being given to Lackmann's movement by an interview on Vatican Radio; he even said that if this trend continued, the Evangelical Church in Germany might feel obliged to withdraw its observers.[35] In practice, however, there was no difference between the two kinds of persons present. According to a confidential report of the observers, "the difference between 'Observers' and 'Guests' appears to be merely nominal, their status being for all practical purposes the same."[36]

The group who came was not representative of the totality of the Christian Churches, either geographically or confessionally. The refusal of the majority of the Byzantine-Slavic Churches meant that the Protestants were much better represented, since only the Baptists were missing: there were fourteen Oriental Orthodox Churches as compared with forty Anglican and Protestant Churches. The Orientals, because of their showy attire, drew more attention from the photographers; the Protestants, however, were not only more numerous but also had more important roles.

Even within the Oriental Orthodox the representation was unbalanced: six delegates from the Monophysite Churches, which Msgr. Willebrands had visited (the Armenian Church of Lebanon, the Coptic, Ethiopian, and Syrian Churches), compared with eight Russian dele-

---

[34] L. Vischer, cited by Fouilloux, who remarks that by that reasoning the two Taizé monks, Schutz and Thurian, should not have been invited, since they were by no means representative of French Protestantism and were notoriously sympathetic to Catholicism (in fact, Thurian later became a Catholic) ("Des observateurs non catholiques," 239).

[35] *DTucci*, November 13, 1962.

[36] *Report of Observers at the Second Vatican Council*, No. 1, *strictly confidential*, cited by Fouilloux, "Des observateurs non catholiques," 238.

gates, but from three different and even antagonistic jurisdictions and without any representative from the Byzantine-Slavic area. Bezobrazov and Schmemann had long been involved in the ecumenical dialogue through their connection with the Istina Center of the Paris Dominicans. In contrast, the Patriarchate of Moscow had just barely emerged from its isolation; only a year before, in 1961, it had joined the World Council of Churches, where it was represented by the same Vitalij Borovoi who was now its observer at the Council. The third group was from the Russian Synod in exile, which, because of its concern for legitimacy and its conservatism, did not have very cordial relations with the other two. All, however, were drawn in by the atmosphere of positive cordiality and ecumenical hope in the Rome of those days, and the envoy of the World Council of Churches observed with amazement that there were no confrontations between the three rival groups: "Even the Russians from Moscow and the Church in Exile speak now friendly to each other."[37]

Fouilloux asked whether the observers formed a group or were simply a collection of individuals. In support of the second hypothesis, he cited two of the testimonies collected by Rock Caporale. One said: "We lived together, but we never attempted to identify ourselves as a distinct group;" and the other: "We held no meetings, or common discussion for us alone, to present a common front. It would have been very difficult for us to do so, because of our varying theological outlooks."[38] Some, however, did try to establish some minimal structure, at the urging especially of Schlink (who, as Vischer reported to Geneva, thought that they should not give the impression of being divided, since this was just what the integrists expected of them). On the day the Council opened, October 11, the observers met, on the initiative of Anglican Canon Bernard Pawley, for an attempt to organize themselves into a group. Despite the absence of the six Orientals, they agreed to meet regularly and appointed a small committee that would prepare for the meetings. There were also prayer meetings, proposed by the Reformed observers, to pray for the success of Vatican II. On Monday and Friday mornings they celebrated their own religious services in the Methodist chapel near Ponte Sant'Angelo. On October 14 Vischer told the Secretariat for Christian Unity of these celebrations and invited its presence; we do not know whether the invitation was accepted. Not all the participants had good memories of these services:

[37] Fouilloux, "Des observateurs non catholiques," 241.
[38] Rock Caporale, *Vatican II: Last of the Councils* (Baltimore, 1964), 166; see Fouilloux, "Des observateurs non catholiques," 243.

"They were more expressive of a suffering, a neediness, a humiliation than of a real measure of 'communion' among Christians separated from Rome."[39]

A sign that the group had a collective personality was the fact that it had a common spokesman in some official actions, something that had not been entirely easy to achieve. At the first meeting held, Schlink, a German Evangelical, succeeded in getting the group to accept a common spokesman, despite the opposition of Anglican Bishop Moorman. At the papal audience on October 13, Karekin Sarkissian, an Armenian of Lebanon, was to reply to the Pope, but he was not allowed to do so for reasons of protocol, which the observers deplored. At the reception hosted by the Secretariat for Christian Unity, Schlink was the one who responded to Bea. At the reception, which the Secretariat of State hosted for them on December 8, at the end of the first session, it fell to Lukas Vischer to reply to Cardinal Cicognani.

The mere fact that the observers were present was already very significant; it stirred the emotions of an old battler for the ecumenical cause, Congar: "I was on the verge of tears when I met the observers for the first time, here!"[40] But the proof of the success of John XXIII's attitude or method was that from the first moment the observers felt very welcome and that their number continued to increase throughout the celebration of the Council.[41] Beginning in the first general congregations, when some of the speakers referred to the observers present, loud applause rose in the council hall. During the first session (1962), the number of non-Catholics present reached 54 (among them 8 guests); at the second (1963), the number rose to 68 (including 9 guests), at the third (1964) to 82 (with 13 guests), and at the fourth (1965) to 106 (of whom 16 were guests). Altogether there were present at Vatican II, for one or more sessions, 192 non-Catholic observers or guests.[42]

[39] Hébert Roux, cited by Fouilloux, "Des observateurs non catholiques," 244-45.

[40] Congar in *ICI*, November 1, 1962. In his personal diary he spoke more openly: "The event has happened. 'They' are in Rome, received by a cardinal and an organization dedicated to dialogue; and *Chrétiens désunis* appeared 25 years ago."

[41] Nevertheless, Vischer complained to Tucci that too much was being said and written about the observers being satisfied and even enthusiastic, without explaining that this referred only to the welcome they received and not to the teaching set forth at the Council. Tucci said: "I will try to warn our reporters and even to set up a meeting between them and L. Vischer himself, since he seems open to this" (*DTucci*, November 13, 1962).

[42] Alberigo, *Ecclesiologia in devenire: A proposito di "concilio pastorale" e di Osservatori a-cattolici al Vaticano II* (Bologna, 1990), 6, n.7.

C. THE COUNCIL MEETINGS

The Regulations provided for two kinds of Council meetings in St. Peter's Basilica. The more solemn were the public sessions over which the Supreme Pontiff would preside in person and at which the fathers would vote on texts discussed at the Council and, if the Pope judged it opportune, he would voice his own opinion and order the promulgation of the texts (art. 2). The opening of the Council was also a public session and was even broadcast live by many television and radio networks. The ordinary, or working, meetings were to be called "general congregations," perhaps to distinguish them from the work of the commissions. "At the general congregations that precede the public sessions, the fathers will, after discussion, decide on the formulation of the decrees or canons" (art. 3). The meetings of the Council commissions were also acts of the Council, with this difference, that they were not held in the hall of St. Peter's and that during them the use of Latin was not obligatory, although all that was said had to be translated into Latin later (art. 20§2, and arts. 28-29).

Only occasionally did the Regulations mention what was intended to be the high point of the conciliar sessions and congregations, or, to use the words the Council itself would later adopt, their *culmen et fons* (summit and source): the Mass.[43] At the meeting of the Technical-Organizational Commission on June 7, 1962,[44] Testa suggested that the first, solemn meeting open with a pontifical Mass, "but it would be more practical to begin the other meetings simply with the singing of the *Veni Creator* and pertinent prayer, instead of a Mass, even a read Mass." Dante objected that the Commission for Ceremonies had decided always to begin with a mass, to which Testa replied that "that committee does not decide anything, since everything will be put before the Holy Father, along with the opinions of the Eminences present here." Traglia voiced his apprehension that "it might make a bad impression if all meetings did not begin with the celebration of Holy Mass, as was done at Vatican I," but Montini, who had published valuable pastoral letters on liturgical spirituality, pointed out that "the speakers at the coming Council will be

---

[43] Art. 54§3, of the Regulations says who is to celebrate the opening Mass of the Holy Spirit.

[44] With Cardinal Testa presiding and Cardinals Quiroga y Palacios, Montini, Richaud, Döpfner, Traglia, and Di Jorio taking part; also present were Msgr. Dante for the Commission on Ceremonies, Felici as Secretary General, and Undersecretaries Casaroli, Guerri, and Igino Cardinale.

far more numerous than those at earlier councils, and it is important to ensure that they have an opportunity to speak, since the spoken word is an essential expression of the Council; but this would not be easy if an hour had to be subtracted from each day for the celebration of Holy Mass." After this, "the Cardinals agreed with the view of the president."[45] Fortunately, the Pope rejected this innovation and held to the original plan of the Commission for Ceremonies, with Mass at the beginning of each general congregation.[46]

The initial form taken by the liturgy at the Council was not very positive. Apart from the fact that concelebration was not possible, the participation of the Council fathers did not reach even the degree attained in "participated Masses" or "dialogue Masses" held in many parishes sensitized by the liturgical movement. The more devout prelates used the time to recite the Breviary or the Rosary. Others conversed with their neighbors to right and left. A confused murmur could be heard, to which the auxiliary personnel of the secretariat contributed by taking advantage of the opportunity to distribute conciliar documentation to those present. Complaints from a group of bishops who were pressured by the liturgists accompanying them caused this last abuse to be quickly corrected, but the conciliar liturgy, far from being a model, was a noisy testimony to the need for reform. The singing of the Sistine Choir, directed by Bertolucci, contributed an aesthetic richness, but was quite peripheral to the liturgical action. The day after the opening of the Council, at a reception in the French embassy, Cullmann commented to Congar on the way in which the sacred rite had been carried out, "*That* is your liturgical movement?" Congar replied: "Unfortunately, it hasn't made it through the bronze doors."[47]

The liturgical celebrations in the hall, and the Eucharist in particular, should have given a meaningful picture of the face which the Council was presenting to the Church and the world. They are not secondary or merely conventional, nor even a simple prayer begging the help of God for the work of the Council; a synod or council has not only a canonical but also a liturgical dimension, and the latter is more important than the former. Five years earlier, when he opened the Synod of Venice, then

---

[45] *Methodus servanda in prima sessione Sacri Concilii Oecumenici Vaticani II*, meeting of the Technical-Organizational Commission, June 7, 1962, ISR, Lercaro papers.

[46] The problem also arose in the Secretariat for Extraordinary Affairs on October 16, as Siri recorded (*DSiri*, pp. 363-64). On the liturgy at the Council see H. Schmidt, *Die Konstitution über die heilige Liturgie* (Basel, 1965), 81-85.

[47] *JCongar*, October 12, 1962.

Cardinal Roncalli had appealed to the *Liber Pontificalis*, describing it as "my liturgical and pastoral guide."[48] Paul VI would say later on that the Church has many aspects, but it is never so much itself as in its liturgical celebrations.

The celebrations of the Eucharist in the magnificent oriental rites elicited favorable responses from the western fathers of the Council; and as the Council progressed, the celebrations in the Roman rite also improved. Father Franquesa took the initiative of sending a letter to the Pope asking that at the papal mass that would close the first session on December 8, instead of the Sistine Choir's polyphonic singing, the entire assembly should sing in Gregorian chant. Franquesa had first obtained the approval of all the Spanish bishops, and many others added their names. For lack of time the petition did not reach all the residences, but none of the bishops asked refused his signature, and the Pope granted the request.[49]

A particularly significant rite was the one with which each congregation began: the solemn enthronement of the gospels. At the end of the opening ceremony, Congar noted: "I know that they will immediately install the Bible on a throne, that it may preside over the Council. But will it speak? Will they listen to it? Will there be a moment for the word of God?"[50] Although the official communiqués spent more time on a bibliographical description of the codex than on an explanation of the theological meaning, this rite proclaimed the supremacy of the word of God in the life of the Church and over all the conciliar debates. It thus

---

[48] Address to the Thirtieth Diocesan Synod of Venice, November 25, 1957, in A. G. Roncalli, *Scritti e discorsi*, III (Rome, 1959), 318.

[49] The document, dated "Rome, the fifth day before the Kalends of December, 1962," was written in calligraphy by Abbot Pedro Celestino Gusi, the Abbot General of the Subiaco Congregation. A photocopy of the document (but including only the first page of signatures) is kept in the Archive of the Abbey of Montserrat. Maestro Bertolucci took this move very badly and had it in for Franquesa. According to Franquesa himself (from whom the preceding information comes), there was pressure to end the second period with a concelebration of all the Council fathers, with the Pope presiding. Here the agreement was not unanimous, with the French bishops the ones most in favor and many Spaniards unwilling to endorse it. Although Paul VI received the proposal favorably, it could not be implemented since the rite of concelebration had not yet been approved. The third session did end with a concelebration, but not according to the rite proposed by the Consilium (Franquesa had been secretary of the commission on concelebration), but according to the rite demanded by the traditional pontifical masters of ceremonies, Dante, Capoferri, and others (note of Father Adalbert Franquesa, attached to the letter addressed to the Pope in December of 1962 [Montserrat Archive, ArxLit c. 009, doc. 37]). On Franquesa's action see A. G. Martimort, "Les débats liturgiques lors de la première période du concile Vatican II (1962)," in *Vatican II commence*, 300.

[50] *JCongar*, October 11, 1962.

anticipated one of the most important statements of Vatican II: "The magisterium is not above the word of God but at its service."[51]

D. QUESTIONS OF PRECEDENCE

The seating-arrangement of the fathers in the council hall was significant. The seats of honor, closest to the great statue of St. Peter and bedecked with red cloth, "dressed in the style of Boniface VIII,"[52] were those of the cardinals. Next came, almost without distinction, except that the cloths were green, were the places for the patriarchs, archbishops, and bishops. Within each of the four orders precedence was by seniority in office, the oldest being closer to the main altar and the newest in the back near the door. The same norm of precedence was applied to the order in which speakers might intervene. The result of this seating arrangement was that the Council fathers could not choose a seat near others whom they preferred or who were of the same mind; the places were strictly assigned them, and they had to sit with people unknown to them and with whom they could communicate only by means of a little Latin and a great deal of good will. This arrangement also explains why, since the youngest bishops, who were in principle the most progressive, were relegated to the back of the basilica and were farthest away from the presidential table, it was there especially that applause at interventions showing an open mind and signs of displeasure at statements conservative in tone broke out. Nor did these bishops pay any great heed to the repeated reminders of the president of the day that such reactions were prohibited.

An authentic ecumenical spirit should have begun by showing greater consideration for the Oriental Catholics who were in communion with Rome. In accordance with the Regulations for the Council, the patriarchs were relegated to places behind the cardinals, even the cardinal deacons. To the oriental prelates, very sensitive as they were to the importance of history and symbols, it seemed an insult that those venerable sees with their long tradition, some of them regarded as of apostolic origin, should be preceded by the cardinals, who were originally nothing more than the domestic clergy of the Bishop of Rome (even if more recently they had been turned into "princes of the Church" and given the prerogative of

---

[51] *Dei Verbum*, 10.
[52] *JCongar*, October 11, 1962.

electing the pope). This painful situation could not have been very encouraging to the delegates of the separated Churches and the desired ecumenical climate.

II. THE EPISCOPAL CONFERENCES

The Regulations of the Council completely ignored the episcopal conferences, because, among other things, few were functioning at the beginning of the Council, while the over forty that were in existence were basically meetings for discussing common pastoral problems but lacked any power to make decisions. The oldest episcopal conference seems to be the German: the Fulda Conference has been meeting since 1847. But the Irish claim that their conference was the first to hold a "formal" meeting, in 1854, and the first to have its statutes approved by the Holy See, in 1882. Between 1917 and 1940 eighteen episcopal conferences had been established, and another fourteen after 1940. The *Annuario Pontificio* for 1962 listed forty-four episcopal bodies. Of these, some were regional or included more than one country (CELAM, South Africa, French Africa, Portuguese Africa, Central America and Panama [CEDAC], and the British Antilles). Some did not have the name "episcopal conference" (Conference of Ecclesiastical Authorities of South Africa; Réunion annuelle de l'Épiscopat de Belgique). Others were restricted to the major prelates (Assemblée des Cardinaux et Archevêques de France; Conferencia de Metropolitanos de España). Among the episcopal conferences in that Vatican catalogue were the National Catholic Welfare Conference of the U.S. bishops (statutes approved as early as 1922) and the Catholic Welfare Organization of the Philippines.

In the very first days of the Council Congar predicted that the surest and most promising result would certainly be the formation of a structured and well-organized episcopate. A council is essentially a gathering of bishops, but some people expected these prelates to form a huge amorphous mass that would receive appropriate direction from the Curia, supposedly in the name of the Pope. Although the Church's social teaching, here differing from classic liberalism, placed great stress on intermediate bodies, without which individuals are left helpless before the state, this doctrine was not applied to the Council, within which no provision was made for the episcopal conferences, the obvious intermediate ecclesial bodies between the diocese and the universal Church. The conferences would therefore have to emerge as if by spontaneous generation.

In his sociological study of Vatican II, Rock Caporale proposed and validated the hypothesis that the Council laid the foundations for an unprecedented intensification, and even a structural modification, of the pattern of communication among the bishops, and that this change was the source of many other changes that have begun to appear in the Church. In his opinion the preconciliar conferences lacked a solid theological foundation, and the model for the postconciliar conferences does not much resemble the preconcilar. An important difference is that since the Council *all* the bishops take part in the assembly, something that previously had not been a frequent occurrence. Another advance is in the frequency of the meetings. Of the thirty-nine conferences he studied, twenty-one met once a year before the Council, six twice a year, five every two or more years, one had never met, and six did not specify. During the Council five met twice a week, one once a week, and twelve irregularly, when need arose.[53]

During the first weeks of discussions, when the work came to a halt because speakers were repeating the same ideas, the Council fathers were urged to let one person speak in the name of several who held the same views. The result was to encourage interventions in the name of episcopal conferences. But perhaps the first official recognition of the new situation was in the papal norms for the intersession, which were communicated to the assembly by Felici at the thirty-fifth congregation (December 6) and which announced that the text of the schemas would be sent to the bishops through the presidents of the episcopal conferences. (The text of this communication was significantly shortened when it appeared in *L'Osservatore Romano*.[54])

Oddly enough, in this area the Churches of the Third World were ahead of the those of the First World. As Houtart and Goddijn wrote at the end of the Council: "In Europe comprehensive pastoral care developed in a diocese or a particular town. The pastoral projects, however, of Africa and Latin America mainly used the framework of the episcopal

---

[53] Caporale, *Vatican II*, 49-70.

[54] "As soon as the individual schemas have been drafted and have obtained the general approval of the Holy Father, they will be sent to the bishops *through the presidents of the episcopal conferences, in cases in which this method seems the most expeditious; the bishops themselves then* are asked to study them and send them back to the general secretariat of the Council within a certain period that will be determined *from time to time, but that will in any case be a short one*" (Caprile, II, 257). According to Caprile, the italicized passages were in the original Latin but were omitted in *OssRom*.

conferences." According to these authors, the phenomenon was due not to doctrinal positions but to concrete situations and to the very inferiority of those Churches: "The rapidity of social changes and the weakness of diocesan organization in the developing countries called for common action on a higher level, often even before any more modest experiments had been launched. This was the case in Chile, the Congo (Leopoldville), and a large part of Brazil." In these countries and others of the Third World, the pressure from institutions is less and the resources available to each bishop in isolation are more limited, so that it is easier, and even necessary, to develop pastoral plans at the level of the national episcopal conference. The European episcopal conferences, on the other hand, "have been mainly concerned with coordination, and collegial action, in the full sense of the word, has been rare (as in the case of the Mission de France)."[55]

The most important example of unified action by the episcopates of the Third World was the Pan-African group, important both because of the number of bishops involved and because of their repeatedly unanimous votes at the Council, which gave interventions in the name of the group an immense influence. This group organized a "General Secretariat of the Episcopal Conferences of Africa and Madagascar at the Second Vatican Ecumenical Council." According to the answer which its General Secretary, Father Joseph Greco, S.J., gave orally to an inquiry by Gómez de Arteche during the third session, this group had been the first one formed at the Council, having come into existence during the first eight days. Its influence was already felt in the lists for election to the commissions. It included the following subgroups: French-speaking Africa, North Africa, French-speaking West Africa, Equatorial Africa — Cameroon, the Congo, Rwanda-Burundi, Madagascar, Nigeria, South Africa, Rhodesia, and East Africa. Only Somalia and the Sudan failed to participate.[56]

In 1962 the Italian bishops were still without a conference in the proper sense. There did indeed officially exist an Italian Episcopal Con-

---

[55] F. Houtart and W. Goddijn, "Problems of Pastoral Organization," in *The Pastoral Mission of the Church*, Concilium 3 (Glen Rock, N.J., 1965), 24-42 at 28.

[56] See Salvador Gómez de Arteche y Catalina, *Grupos "extra aulam" en el II Concilio Vaticano y su influencia* III, Appendix II, 118-49 (three volumes in nine parts, totaling 2585 pages; an unpublished doctoral dissertation; Biblioteca de la Facultad de Derecho de la Universidad de Valladolid). Étienne Fouilloux, who told me of the existence and importance of this work, tracked it down and was able to consult it in the library of the World Council of Churches in Geneva. By the author's kindness, there is also a copy at the ISR.

ference, which was established in 1951-52 and met for the first time in Florence, but the only ones who met were the presidents of the episcopal conferences of the various Italian ecclesiastical regions, joined by the nuncio, the military ordinary, and the bishop in charge of Catholic Action; it was thought impossible in practice to bring together almost 400 prelates for a functional working meeting. The Council showed that this was not true, and the Italian bishops ventured to meet in a plenary session for the first time in history on October 14, at 10.00 A.M., in the Domus Mariae. After this meeting Siri proposed that the Italians continue meeting in order to decide on a course of conduct in the decisions to be made by the Council, to keep one another informed, "not to lag behind other rather active groups," in this way to avoid the formation of pressure groups, and, finally, "to protect the freedom of the Council fathers."[57]

A second meeting of the Italian episcopate took place on October 27, and a third on November 13, but its members did not succeed in presenting a united front at Vatican II. According to Caporale, "the few times when Siri was delegated to present the position agreed upon, the intervention was carefully worded in the name of '*fere omnes*' [almost all], a convenient Latin expression that took into account the 'dissidents,' who might have been more numerous than at first apparent."[58] The negative role which the powerful Siri endeavored to assign to the Italian episcopate was clearly reflected in what he wrote in his diary on the eve of the opening of the Council:

> I am afraid that at this Council we shall feel the influence — not for good — of a habit of activism that causes people to think little, study even less, and cast into the shadows the great problems of orthodoxy and truth. A pastoral outlook is taken to be a necessity, whereas, even besides being an inferior method, it is an erroneous intellectual position. In the second place, the cross, if I may use the word, will come as usual from the French and German worlds and from the underbrush of each, because they have never completely freed themselves from Protestant pressure and the Pragmatic Sanction. They are fine people, but they do not realize that they are the heirs of a mistake-ridden history. I believe, therefore, that the role of the Italians, of the Latins along with the men in the Curia, should be to settle matters, whether by filling in holes or by correcting false turns. Roman calm will help.[59]

---

[57] *DSiri*, 191-92.
[58] Caporale, *Vatican II*, 62.
[59] *DSiri*, 183.

The stay in Rome helped the Orientals, too, to hold meetings which, for various reasons, they had not been able to hold in their home areas. On the evening of November 2, in the house of the Maronite Fathers of Aleppo, at St. Peter in Chains, the first general meeting of the oriental hierarchy took place, with the patriarchs, including Cardinal Tappouni, presiding and about fifty bishops in attendance. "It was not easy to reach a decision on meetings, but we finally succeeded," said Edelby.[60] It was decided to appoint a committee of twelve bishops — two for each of the seven communities: Armenians, Chaldeans, Copts, Melkites, Maronites, Syrians, and Ethiopians — who would be responsible for calling further meetings and for their agendas. This committee met for the first time on November 7, the sole absentee being the Ethiopian representative, who excused himself. The members decided to gather every Tuesday evening in the residence of each of the seven communities in turn. They would endeavor to study the schemas, especially the points affecting the Orientals as a whole, so that they might develop common views and decide on interventions to be made at the general congregations in the name of all.

The bishops of the United States had been meeting in conference since 1919, in the form of the National Catholic Welfare Conference (NCWC).[61] These bishops constituted one of the largest hierarchies in the Church; 246 took part in the Council. They held their annual meeting in October, but Msgr. Paul Tanner, their Secretary General, informed them on October 11 that "the Holy See prefers that national groups not hold meetings in Rome." Cardinal Cicognani, who had been Apostolic Delegate in the United States, granted permission for the annual meeting to take place at the North American College, but he required that "no communiqués be provided to the Catholic or lay press and that none of the bishops discuss the call to the annual meeting with the bishops of other countries."[62] It is clear, then, that at the beginning of the Council Cicognani was attempting to keep the emerging episcopal collegiality under control.

---

[60] *JEdelby*, November 2, 1962.

[61] The United States episcopal conference was established in 1919 under the name of the National Catholic Welfare Council. At the beginning of 1922, due to the opposition of Cardinals William H. O'Connell of Boston and Dennis Dougherty of Philadelphia, the Congregation of the Consistory condemned the organization and ordered its dissolution. The action elicited protests from the great majority of the bishops. They asked Pius XI not to let the organization be dissolved, and he agreed; it later changed its name to the National Catholic Welfare Conference (see Douglas J. Lawson, *The Foundation and First Decade of the National Catholic Welfare Council* [Washington, 1992], especially 45-178).

[62] Tanner to "Your Excellency," Rome, October 11, 1962, ACUA, Primeau papers.

On October 18 the United States bishops held a meeting at which they adopted a proposal, initiated by Bishop Ernest Primeau (Manchester), aimed at making their participation in the Council more effective. Primeau had observed that at the end of only one week all had realized the need of a better organization. "Surely we Americans do not want to join Cardinal Cushing in the 'Church of silence.'" Primeau proposed "the creation of an instrument that will help the bishops to consult with one another, to coordinate their efforts, and to draw up a schedule of interventions. Clearly, this will help them make their voice heard at the Council in a structured way." In explaining how such an organization could coordinate the efforts of the United States bishops with those of the Secretary General of the Council, he reminded them that Archbishop John Krol of Philadelphia had recently been appointed an assistant to the Secretary General. He then went on to sketch the structure of the organization whose creation he was proposing.[63] Whatever may have been the reservations of the Curia regarding meetings in Rome of the national groups of bishops, the Americans did as the other hierarchies did and ignored them.

The United States bishops unanimously adopted Primeau's suggestion and appointed a committee to draft concrete plans for the organization. The committee — comprising Lawrence Shehan, Archbishop of Baltimore; Francis F. Reh, Bishop of Charleston; and Primeau — met that same day and prepared a plan which the bishops subsequently adopted. It provided for the establishment of a "general committee," composed of a presidential board of five bishops elected by the episcopate with a president elected by the five from among themselves; a secretariat of three bishops elected by the episcopate to assist the presidential board; and ten committees corresponding to the conciliar commissions, each composed of seven bishops elected by the episcopate and meeting whenever the discussion of the conciliar agenda made it necessary.

From the viewpoint of procedure, the general committee made substantial progress in promoting collegiality among the American bishops. The bishop at the head of the board of presidents had authority to convoke "general meetings of the bishops once a week or when he judged useful." The board of presidents was to meet when the bishop presiding over it judged necessary and could "select for their own work and the work of the secretariat theologians, exegetes, canonists, liturgists, and Latinists from the list already distributed to the bishops, or any other

---

[63] Ibid., message to the United States bishops.

expert of their choice." The secretariat was to meet every time its own president or the one presiding over the board of presidents considered it necessary. The task of the secretariat was "the collection, filing, and presentation of summaries of interventions to the secretariat of the Council at the request of the bishops." Each committee was to meet when its chair or the one presiding over the board of presidents judged it necessary.[64]

The Spanish episcopate exerted no small influence on the assembly as a whole, not only because of its size but also because of its close historical, cultural, and pastoral relationship with the Latin American Church. While the latter received financial help from Germany, it looked to Spain and from it received many priests and religious men and women. An expert in the service of the Spanish episcopate noted:

> The Spanish bishops met this evening at six o'clock, and Cardinal Larraona spoke to them of the need to remain united in defense of Rome and not to let themselves be won over by the people from Central Europe, who often go to extremes. He spoke of the dangers of episcopal conferences. . . . He obviously wants to set up a defensive bloc! Today he spoke with various bishops as they were leaving, and some of them were impressed by what the cardinal said to them.[65]

According to the same informant, Larraona said they had to treat the Council as they did the rain: open the umbrellas and hope it will pass.[66] A sector of the Spanish bishops proved loyally devoted to the Curia, but, despite the efforts of Larraona and, indirectly, of the Spanish embassy to the Vatican to move them in that direction, the general atmosphere of the Council and the clear attitude of the Pope in favor of *aggiornamento* led almost all of them to associate themselves, out of conviction or a desire not to be different, with the positions and votes of the great majority of the universal episcopate.

Toward the end of the first session a group of Catalan Catholics drew up a statement of opposition to the Franco regime because of its dictatorial character and its suppression of nationalities; they distributed it to all the bishops, experts, observers, and auditors of the Council. The doc-

[64] Ibid., first draft of the general committee.

[65] A. Franquesa, unpublished diary, October 29, 1962, Archive of the Abbey of Montserrat.

[66] It was Larraona who later composed the harsh letter which a group of Spanish bishops addressed to Paul VI, asking him to keep the subject of religious freedom from being voted on by the Council. The present writer was told this, in an interview on October 24, 1990, by José L. Martín Descalzo, a priest and member of the Spanish Press Office at the Council, who had a great deal of access to the Spanish bishops.

ument, said Martín Descalzo, "seemed disastrous to the great majority
of the Spanish bishops,[67] especially to Morcillo and Cantero Cuadrado,
who composed a very harsh reply and delivered it to Iribarren, Director
of the Spanish Press Office, for publication. Alarmed by this reply, Iribarren met with Montero and Martín Descalzo, members of the same
office, and they agreed that the reply should not be circulated. They
were at the residence of Enrique Pla y Daniel, Cardinal Primate of
Toledo, and they asked his advice. Pla, who was elderly and very infirm,
was no longer attending the general congregations, but with the energy
that had always marked him, he told them that, on his responsibility,
they were not to publish the reply, since, first of all, the document of the
Catalonians was anonymous and such documents are never to be
answered, and, further, the reply was presented as coming from all the
Spanish bishops, "and I am the primate, and they said nothing to me."[68]

III. THE FORMATION OF INFORMAL GROUPS[69]

We could draw up a long list of churchmen who, afraid of exaggerat-
ing the human dimensions of the Council, have insisted that a council is
not a democratic parliament. But we could also cite an abundant literature, by authors who have written about Vatican II, that justifies the
application of the methodology of political science and group sociology
to a study of the Council. There even exist references, even from the
main characters at the Council, to the model provided by secular political institutions. Thus Msgr. Julián Mendoza, Secretary General of
CELAM, explained that this important organization had been structured
on the model of autonomous departments that had been adopted by the
Organization of American States. And Father Gustave Martimort was
able to begin his detailed report on the work of the Liturgical Commission by comparing it with parliamentary practice.[70]

---

[67] Of the seventy-eight Spanish bishops, sixty-four had been appointed since 1936,
that is, with Franco using the right of presentation which the Holy See had allowed him.

[68] Conversation of the author with J. L. Martín Descalzo, in Madrid, November 12,
1990. According to this priest, Iribarren's failure to obey Morcillo in this incident led to
his being removed as editor of *Ecclesia*, the official organ of Spanish Catholic Action and
the unofficial organ of the episcopate (see Jésus Iribarren, *Papeles y memorias, Medio
siglo de relaciones Iglesia-Estado en España* [Madrid, 1992]).

[69] The phenomenon of groups at the Council is the subject of the monumental and practically exhaustive study by Gómez de Arteche, *Grupos "extra aulam."* Because of its immense
size this work has never been published, but I shall refer to it frequently in this section.

[70] A.G. Martimort, "Les débats liturgiques," in *Vatican II commence*, 291-314, especially 291.

Applying the methodology of the North American school of sociology or psycho-sociology, Rock Caporale came to the view that the formation of these groups had a threefold significance. First, it called attention to the need for more limited groups in which participation would be easier and more effective, as compared with the large general sessions in the hall. Second, it provided more capable leaders with a large field of action in which to channel and use their energies so as to have a greater influence in the Council. Third, it brought cohesion and support, since the members of these groups were homogeneous, were there by their own free choice, and shared fairly similar outlooks. These groups thus avoided the quite rapid disintegration of minorities, so that by their opposition they compelled the majority to deepen and clarify its own positions.[71]

A. THE "*COETUS INTERNATIONALIS PATRUM*"

This was the most important, both in size and in effectively organized action, of all the groups that were conservative in tendency. In addition to the members expressly appointed to it, it was always open to sympathizers. While its members and sympathizers always responded with great loyalty to the instructions issued by the group's leaders, this discipline was due not to any internal rules but to shared convictions.

Although it was especially alert to juridical questions and matters of procedure (it usually called for a rigid application of the Regulations in order to hinder the approval of texts it regarded as wrong), it was one of the groups which Gómez de Arteche describes as having a "global ideology;" that is, the group was formed not to influence a particular question but so that its conservatism might find a voice in all the areas or subjects under deliberation at the Council. "It represented the *conservative line* in all its purity, both in its fundamental attitudes (zeal for the precise formulation of truth; a suprahistorical or *triumphalistic* outlook, and therefore a mentality of caution in the face of change; scant interest in and even apprehension about ecumenism) and in its more important concrete choices."[72]

---

[71] Caporale, *Vatican II*, 74-75.

[72] Gómez de Arteche, *Grupos "extra aulam"* , II/3, 241; he bases the traits of this description on citations from conciliar interventions of Siri (nineteenth general congregation, November 14, 1962), Franić and de Proença (twenty-third general congregation, November 20), Lefebvre (thirty-first general congregation, December 1), Ruffini (thirty-fourth general congregation, December 5), Ruffini and Franić (thirty-eighth general congregation, December 1, 1963), and so on.

The founder and soul of the group was Msgr. Geraldo de Proença Sigaud, Archbishop of Diamantina (Brazil), a member of the Society of the Divine Word. He had links with the most reactionary elements and organizations in Brazil and abroad.[73] While still Bishop of Jacarézinho, his reply to Tardini's consultation on the conciliar agenda reveals his obsessive fear of revolution,[74] which led him to attack Christian socialists or democrats ("Maritainists," "disciples of Teilhard de Chardin," "Catholic socialists," "evolutionists," and so on) even more violently than he did the communists, because he saw the Christian clergy and people infected by revolutionary principles and devoting themselves to a "Trojan Horse strategy" in face of the silence of the majority of bishops.[75] He was convinced that under a Christian government it was much easier for God to win souls.[76] In 1965 he would be the chief promotor of a petition that the Council should condemn communism in schema XIII.[77]

Sigaud was aware that he was in a minority among the bishops of his own country[78]; for this reason, in his effort to have all the Council fathers consecrate their dioceses, Russia in particular, to the Immaculate Heart of Mary, he proposed that an ad hoc commission be formed, distinct from the National Commission of Brazilian Bishops (CNBB).[79] As he told Gómez de Arteche, from the very outset he saw clearly the need to organize scattered forces with a view to disciplined parliamentary action that could resist the conciliar majority, who were grouped by

[73] In Sigaud's archives there is an affectionate exchange of letters with Plinio Corréa de Oliveira and with Georges Bidault, former Minister of Foreign Affairs of France, a Christian Democrat who had begun his career pretty much as a leftist but had ended up on the extreme right, close to the members of the military in the Organization of American States; he had had to go into exile in Brazil. In a letter to Proença Sigaud (from Belo Horizonte, April 22, 1963), Bidault describes himself as an "outlaw" and expresses his gratitude for the welcome Sigaud had given him in the archepiscopal palace of Diamantina and for the books Sigaud had sent him with inscriptions (ISR, Sigaud papers).

[74] Dated: Jacarézinho, August 22, 1962; ADA, VII, 180-95. Original draft in ISR, Sigaud papers.

[75] "Rarely is a priest who attacks revolution elevated to the episcopate; frequently, those in favor of it."

[76] "In a revolutionary society God fishes for souls with a hook. In a Christian society one fishes for souls with nets."

[77] In Sigaud's personal archive can be seen the list of bishops from around the world who signed the petition. The leading group of signers was the Italian (104), followed by the Chinese (30 bishops who had been expelled).

[78] On the period of hope the Church of Brazil was experiencing on the eve of the Council see J. O. Beozzo, "Vida cristiana y sociedad in Brasil," in Vísperas, 49-81.

[79] Sigaud to Joâo Pereira Vanancio, Bishop of Leiria, Diamantina, February 15, 1963 (ISR, Sigaud papers).

nations or in the Central European bloc. During the first session he looked in vain for a group that would vigorously support this purpose and for some churchman who would volunteer to head it, but when he found no one he had to resign himself to taking on this role himself. The full title of the group designated a plenary assembly, but a "small committee," which met weekly, was the ordinary organ of government and action. This committee was set up either during the first week of the first session, according to Wiltgen,[80] or during the second half of that session, as Sigaud himself told Gómez de Arteche.

From the very beginning Sigaud's principal collaborator was Msgr. Marcel Lefebvre, Superior General of the Holy Ghost Fathers.[81] Lefebvre was especially distrustful of the "collectivist" principle which, in his view, lurked behind the advocates of episcopal conferences. But, as he explained to Wiltgen in an interview, he saw in some powerful episcopal conferences a threat not so much to the papacy as to the teaching authority and pastoral responsibility of each bishop; he could speak with authority on this point, because he himself had established the national episcopal conferences of Madagascar, Congo-Brazzaville, Cameroon, and French West Africa while he was Apostolic Delegate for French-speaking Africa from 1948 to 1959.[82]

Lefebvre also shared with Proença Sigaud the emphasis on ideology rather than on nationality in the formation and conflict of groups within the Council. But Proença Sigaud did not want his group to be based solely on doctrinal affinity; he thought that it would gain in vigor and size if it were based on pre-existing structures; "in other words, he was for a mixed ideological-national group, similar to the International Committees of the majority and the minority at Vatican Council I."[83] His idea was to establish a "Conference of Conferences" that would have as its supreme organ a "Conference of Presidents of Episcopal Conferences." To this end, he tried to recruit some presidents of episcopal conferences but was unable to convince a single one of them.

After Lefebvre, Proença Sigaud's principal supporter was Msgr. Luigi M. Carli, Bishop of Segni (Italy), who had already distinguished himself

---

[80] Wiltgen, *Rhine*, 89.

[81] Titular Bishop of Sinnada in Phrygia, former Archbishop of Dakar (Senegal); translated to the French diocese of Tulle with the personal title of archbishop, Lefebvre would end up heading a schismatic group that rejected the heritage of Vatican II and, more concretely, the postconciliar Missal of Paul VI.

[82] Wiltgen, *Rhine*, 89.

[83] Gómez de Artche, *Grupos "extra aulam,"* II/3, 243.

by his zeal for the strict observance of the Regulations of the Council.

Every week throughout the entire course of the Council the International Group organized meetings led by Council fathers, sometimes cardinals, in order to make known its viewpoint on the subjects being debated. These meetings provided an opportunity to get to know and be known by other Council fathers. In the beginning the text of the lectures was distributed to the Council fathers through the presidents of the episcopal conferences, but when the great majority of these presidents showed their lack of interest in the circulation of these documents, the International Group turned to distribution directly to the bishops. The Group also fostered and sought support for interventions in the council hall that favored its thinking. It even developed opposition schemas, as in the case of religious freedom.

The International Group "was perhaps the association within the Council that was most *aware* of its position as a parliamentary group," all the more so since, because of its *transnational* character, it lacked the support of existing institutions such as the national or regional conferences.[84] When the Group addressed itself to the fathers individually (for example, in its circulars), it presented itself openly as a collective entity, under its group name, but when it addressed itself to all the fathers together (the conciliar assembly or one of the official organs of the Council), it did not present itself as an established group but as a simple *collection* of fathers, with specific bishops, usually the most notable of the group, taking personal responsibility for the interventions or proposals.

Although some contemporary chroniclers described the Group as a "secret society," Gómez de Arteche denies this.[85] As for the extent of the Group, a distinction must be made between the members properly so called, who were few but very disciplined, and the mere sympathizers, who, to a variable but very large extent, followed the voting instructions of the Group. The members, properly speaking, may be regarded as those whose names appeared in the interventions of the Group during this first session.[86]

---

[84] Ibid., II/3, 247.

[85] Ibid., II/3, 250, note 19, where he cites *Katholiek Archief* and *Het Concile*.

[86] Gómez de Arteche has identified as early signatories, in addition to the three leaders (Proença Sigaud, Lefebvre, and Carli) the following: Antonio de Castro Mayer, Bishop of Campos (Brazil) and Pierre de la Chanonie, Bishop of Clermont (France). Later signatories were Luis Gonzaga da Cunha Marelim, Bishop of Caxias do Maranhao (Brazil); João Pereira Venancio, Bishop of Leiria (Portugal); Carlos Eduardo Saboia Bandeira de Mello, O.F.M.Cap, Bishop of Palmas (Brazil); Jean Rupp, Bishop of

Although the International Group of Fathers was the catalyst for the so-called minority, not all the fathers of the minority belonged to it in a strict sense, and some even sought to make it quite clear that they did not belong to the group. The Spanish bishops who agreed with the Group in its opposition to the Declaration on Religious Freedom and, to a large extent, in its demand for an explicit condemnation of communism, expressly declared that they had no connection with the Group. The episcopates most influenced by the propaganda of the Group were the Italian, the Spanish, the Philippine, the Latin American, and the French. The Group had as sympathizers the two groups formed to defend the confessional state, classified by Gómez de Arteche as "statist groups." It had links with a group of missionary bishops (*Vriendenclub*) through Father Schütte, Superior General of the Society of the Divine Word (to which Proença Sigaud also belonged), who would later be the reporter (*relator*) of the schema on the missionary activity of the Church.

As for support from outsiders, mention must be made of the Lateran University (where Carli had been trained) and the Roman Seminary. At a greater distance, but with significant influence on more reactionary French intellectuals, was *La cité catholique*, which from the beginning supported the International Group and its men. Also of service in the Group's campaigns was the press agency of the Society of the Divine Word, the Divine Word News Service; the founder of this agency, Father Ralph M. Wiltgen, whom I have so often cited, belonged, like Proença Sigaud, to the religious congregation, and both men were staying at its Generalate in the Via dei Verbiti. The Group had well-known connections with rightist political organizations that wanted a religious ideological cover, such as the Property, Family, and Tradition Movement, which was of Brazilian origin but was implanted in more conservative and counterrevolutionary circles throughout Latin America and also in Spain,[87] and which had Proença Sigaud as its mentor. The Group

Monaco (Monaco); Xavier Morilleau, Bishop of La Rochelle (France); José Nepote-Fus of the Consolata Missionaries, Prelate Nullius of Rio Branco (Brazil); Giocondo M. Grotti of the Servants of Mary, Prelate Nullius of Acre y Purús (Brazil), just appointed to the Council (November 16, 1962); Auguste Grimault, a member, like Lefebvre, of the Congregation of the Holy Spirit, Titular Bishop of Maximianopolis, Palestine (a native of Canada and resident in France); Dom Jean Prou, Abbot of Solesmes, Superior General of the Benedictine Congregation of France; and Father Luciano Rubio, Superior General of the Order of Hermits of St. Augustine. Note that these sixteen fathers were primarily Brazilian or French. In addition, bishops and superiors general, some periti, and some members of the Curia belonged to the Group, but the leaders were always Council fathers.

[87] The official name of the Spanish organization is presently The Spanish Society for

had a foothold in the Secretariat for Extraordinary Affairs through Siri and on the Council of Presidents through Ruffini. The fact that Secretary General Felici was a native of Segni, Carli's diocese, explains the close relationship between the two men.

B. The Group of "the Church of the Poor"[88]

In his radio message of September 11, 1962, a month before the opening of the Council, John XXIII said: "Confronted with the underdeveloped countries, the Church presents itself as it is and wishes to be, as the Church of all, and particularly as the Church of the poor." These words became the banner of the group to which we now turn. But the group's foundational text was the intervention of Cardinal Giacomo Lercaro, Archbishop of Bologna, at the thirty-fifth general congregation (December 6, 1962).[89] Unlike the majority of Italian bishops, who were "enclosed in a presumption of self-sufficiency that often masked a fear of confrontation," Lercaro entered fully into the network of contacts between bishops and conferences that began to be woven as soon as the Council began. He did not limit himself to getting to know individuals in the field of liturgy, which would have been understandable in light of the route he had been following in the liturgical movement and of his present role in the preparation of the constitution on the sacred liturgy. He also gladly accepted the invitation of the informal working group that had been meeting since the end of October at the Belgian College under the inspiration of Father Paul Gauthier.[90]

---

the Defense of Tradition, Family, and Property (TPF-Covadonga). According to a propaganda sheet of the Spanish branch of the movement (1990), which describes itself as "the strongest civic-cultural Catholic-inspired anticommunist force in the entire world," "its point of origin was the city of São Paulo, Brazil, where in 1928 Professor Plinio Corréa de Oliveira, then a young law student, began to serve in the Marian Congregations movement. Under his leadership in the 1930s a Catholic group was formed that gradually spread its influence and later gave rise to the Brazilian TPF."

[88] See D. O'Grady, *Eat from God's Hand. Paul Gauthier and the Church of the Poor* (Derby, 1967), and Paul Gauthier, *E il velo si squarciò* (Torre dei Nolfi, 1988); also see D. Pelletier, "Une marginalité engagée: le groupe 'Jésus, l'Église et les Pauvres,'" in *Commissions*, 63-89.

[89] On this intervention see Giuseppe Alberigo, "L'evento conciliare," in *Giacomo Lercaro, vescovo della Chiesa di Dio (1891-1976)*, ed. Angelina Alberigo (Turin: Marietti, 1991), 116-23.

[90] See Paul Gauthier, *"Consolez mon peuple" : Le Concile et "l'Église des pauvres"* (Paris, 1965), with texts by J. Mouroux and Y. Congar.

The more remote spiritual roots of the group were located, first, in the French priest-worker experiment, begun in 1944 by Cardinal Emmanuel Suhard, Archbishop of Paris, and suppressed by the Vatican Curia in 1953, but which was now reviving in the free atmosphere of the Council. Second, and closer at hand, were what H. Fesquet called worker-priests, *Les Compagnons de Jésus Charpentier*,[91] a movement born in Palestine under the protection of the Melkite Church and its Patriarch, Maximos IV. Mention must also be made of "the vast stammering of the Third World, the immense disinherited collectivity that is tormented by hunger in the midst of the struggle between exploiters and exploited, the actors in which are entire continents."[92]

This group's great spokesmen at the Council would be Msgr. Helder Pessôa Câmara, who at the beginning of the Council was an Auxiliary Bishop of Rio de Janeiro but in 1964 was to be appointed Archbishop of Olinda y Recife, in the "hunger triangle" of northeastern Brazil, and Msgr. Georges Mercier of the Missionaries of Africa, Bishop of Laghouat (Sahara de Argelia), who spoke of the need for a "Christian Bandung." Finally, a strong influence seems to have been exerted by the fathers from the socialist countries, who were anxious to reply to the official propaganda that described religion as allied with capitalism for the oppression of the poor. To this end, they wanted to clear up the habitual confusion between Christian social teaching and a certain way of understanding private property that certainly could find no support in the earliest Christian tradition. In short, this group attacked and proposed to bridge the gap between the Church and the poor (not only those of the Third World but those also of the industrialized western world), a gap which they regarded as due to the Church's compromise with capitalism.

Georges Hakim, Archbishop of Akka-Nazareth (Galilee, Israel), had encouraged the writing, by Gauthier and the Companions of Jesus the Carpenter, of a first book, *Les pauvres, Jésus et l'Église*,[93] in which they gave voice to their suffering and their hope: "suffering because of the division between the Church and the poor and workers; hope because of the Council, which can heal this rent in the body of Christ."[94] Hakim and Msgr. Charles-Marie Himmer, Bishop of Tournai (Belgium), thought it useful to spread this work among the Council fathers, even before the Council began. In the early days of October they received

[91] See the dossier on them in *ICI*, no. 192, December 15, 1962, 17-26.
[92] Gómez de Arteche, *Grupos "extra aulam,"* II, 272.
[93] P. Gauthier, *Les pauvres, Jésus et l'Église* (Paris, 1962).
[94] Gauthier, *"Consolez mon peuple,"* 205.

replies from a series of bishops who upon reading the manifesto recognized it as representing their view of the question. This group, then, unlike the others, already had a rich history when Pope John XXIII opened the Council on October 11.

The first formal nucleus of this group met at the Belgian College, on the Quirinal, on October 26, 1962, at the invitation of Himmer and Hakim, with Cardinal Pierre Gerlier, Archbishop of Lyons, presiding. On this occasion Gerlier said:

> The duty of the Church in our age is to adapt itself in the most responsive way to the situation created by the suffering of so many human beings and by the mistaken idea, fostered by certain appearances suggesting that these human beings are not a primary concern of the Church. . . . If I am not mistaken, it seems that no room was allowed for this, at least directly, in the program of the Council. Now, the effectiveness of our work is bound up with this problem. If we do not tackle it, we leave aside some of the most relevant aspects of evangelical and human reality. The question must be raised. We must insist with the authorities that it be raised. Everything else is in danger of remaining ineffective if this problem is not studied and dealt with. It is indispensable that the Church, which has no desire to be rich, be freed from the appearance of wealth. The Church must be seen for what it is: the Mother of the poor, whose first concern is to give her children bread for both body and soul, as John XXIII himself said on September 11, 1962: "The Church is and wishes to be the Church of all, and particularly the Church of the poor."[95]

Mercier composed a note, entitled "The Church of the Poor," which raised three main problems: (1) development of the poor countries; (2) evangelization of the poor and workers; and (3) giving the Church once again its poor "face." To this end he advocated: (a) establishing the teaching on the social presence of Jesus to humanity and to impoverished humanity; (b) encouraging the practice of poverty in the Church; and (c) enlightening public opinion by means of simple gestures and a world congress.[96]

On November 5 another meeting was held at which over fifty bishops from many countries were present. This time Patriarch Maximos IV Saigh took the chair and once again invoked the well-known words of John XXIII:

> The Church and the poor: something has to be done everywhere to make the Church indeed "the Church of all, and particularly the Church of the poor." . . . Poverty is a matter of life and death for the Church; without

---

[95] Text cited at length in *ICI*, no. 180, November 16, 1962.
[96] Gauthier, "*Consolez mon peuple*," 209.

it it will lose the world of the workers. For the most critical problem is that in certain areas, especially in western Europe, the working population is slipping away from the Church. The problem is not so much one of rich and poor, but of the workers, who are the vital force in today's world.[97]

At the third meeting, held on December 1, some fifty Council fathers again turned up.

During the first session as many as five meetings of this group were held at which they dealt with the following areas: (a) circulation among the fathers of the document *Jésus, l'Église et les pauvres*; (b) making an ever increasing number of fathers aware of this problem; holding more limited meetings of fathers linked by similarities or language; examinations of conscience; reviews of life, and so on; (c) spreading these ideas to the public by taking advantage of the lively interest shown by the press; (d) a petition of November 21, addressed to Cicognani, Secretary of State and President of the Secretariat for Extraordinary Affairs, calling for the creation of a secretariat or special commission to deal with the following major subjects: 1. The exercise of personal and social justice, especially toward developing peoples; 2. The peace and unity of the human family; 3. The evangelization of the poor and the alienated; and 4. A call for an evangelical renewal of pastors and faithful, especially by means of poverty; and (e) a letter addressed to John XXIII in support of this petition.[98]

The last-named letter was to be delivered to the Pope by Gerlier, but the Pope excused himself on the grounds of illness from accepting it in person. He did, however, make clear his complete agreement with its contents, sent his blessing, and, as a sign of communion in the Spirit, presented Gerlier with a missal. Therefore, although this group did not succeed in achieving an official status (as would have been the case if the desired secretariat or commission had been created), it must be said that it was very favorably received both by John XXIII and by Paul VI, who himself had belonged to it. Nevertheless, this group always remained on the periphery of the Council, and even the step which Paul VI took in October 1963 of asking Lercaro, an active member of the group, to submit concrete proposals (which were presented a year later) had no results.

---

[97] *ICI*, no. 181, December 1, 1962.
[98] See Gauthier, *"Consolez mon peuple,"* 210.

C. THE "CENTRAL EUROPEAN BLOC" OR "WORLD ALLIANCE"

From the beginning of the Council the German, Scandinavian, French, Belgian, and Dutch episcopates (or, more accurately, a large majority of these bishops) adopted a common line. It is a curious fact that the name generally used for this group, Central European Bloc, had been given to it in a preconciliar pamphlet.[99] These bishops did not, however, close ranks within their own countries but from the beginning were open to bishops from other areas who shared their open-minded understanding of the Council. It was typical of this group of bishops that on the initial question of elections to the commissions, they were already asking other episcopates for the names of their candidates. At an audience the Pope gave to the French bishops on November 19, Cardinal Liénart said: "You know the French bishops too well to think of them as running the risk of acting in a partisan spirit at the Council or as pursuing their own course of action in the work of the Council."[100] And, in fact, many bishops from all parts of the world joined the group, so that it soon merited to be known as the World Alliance, which is what Wiltgen calls it.[101]

"Rather than a federation of more or less unified groups, this group resembled what. in the current vocabulary of politics, might be called a bloc, a front, an alliance, a cartel, an association, and so on: rather loose unions that lack any powers of their own and have no permanent organization." Gómez de Arteche, whose comment this is, compares this bloc to the *corpora*, "bodies," which were established or simply planned at Trent, and still more with the two "international committees," both embracing nations and half-nations, that were rivals at Vatican I. But he also understands that the Central European Bloc was not fundamentally like the majority of blocs known to us, a union of partisan or trend groups, but a union of national groups. Since the episcopates that made it up were, almost in their entirety (or in the case of the French, in a large majority), reform-minded, however, the group was at the same time "an ideological group that was open even in its regional limits."[102]

Msgr. Jean Rupp, Bishop of Monaco, said at the thirty-second general congregation (December 3, 1962) that the presence of this bloc at the

[99] Catholicus, *Il Concilio e l'assalto del Blocco Centroeuropeo*; see Gómez de Arteche, *Grupos "extra aulam,"* II/4, 9. The group was also known more familiarly as the "Common Market."

[100] *La Croix*, November 21, 1962.

[101] Wiltgen, *Rhine*, passim.

[102] Gómez de Arteche, *Grupos "extra aulam,"* II/4, 9-10.

Council made the catholicity of the Church shine out due to a spiritual decentralization that replaced the former "neo-latin" element that was dominant in the baroque period. He ended by saying "it is from the north that light comes to us today."[103] The influence of this group on the direction finally taken by the Council is also reflected in the title of one of the most widely known chronicles of the event: *The Rhine Flows into the Tiber*.[104] It is also reflected in the humorous name given the Council with seeming solemnity: *Vaticanum secundum, Lovaniense primum* (Vatican II, Louvain I),[105] or even *Concilium Lovaniense Romae celebratum* (The Council of Louvain, held in Rome).

A further reason for this group's growing influence was that the lack of famous experts from which some third-world episcopates suffered led them to seek the opinions of the Europeans. Thus Father Gustave Martelet gave a lecture to the bishops of French-speaking Africa on November 5; this was followed by another by Congar on November 7, and a third, by Martelet again, on November 10. Some bishops of Asian dioceses with historical and cultural ties with France (Indochina, for example) also approached this group, although "at first, the African-born bishops from former French African territories had been somewhat cool toward the French hierarchy, being anxious to avoid any semblance of colonial subservience."[106]

The superiors general of religious orders and the missionary bishops from the countries of the Central European Bloc likewise joined, as did the more open sector of the Latin-American episcopate, especially the prelates of dioceses that had recently benefitted greatly from the German organizations *Misereor* and *Adveniat*, which were controlled by Cardinal Frings. Some of these bishops took advantage of the Council as an opportunity to greet Frings in person and to thank him for the generous help of the German Catholics, and this cordial contact undoubtedly facilitated an agreement on positions before the debates began.[107] Especially

---

[103] *AS* I/4, 204-5.

[104] This is the title of Wiltgen's work, which has been cited so frequently here. As the author himself explains in his preface, the title was inspired by Juvenal's third *Satire*, which describes the influence of Antiochene Hellenism on Rome by saying that the Orontes has emptied into the Tiber. Commenting on Wiltgen's book, Congar wrote: "In short, the Rhine was in reality that broad current of vigorous Catholic theology and pastoral science which had got under way in the early 1950s and, with regard to liturgical matters and biblical sources, even earlier than that."

[105] See J. Perarnau, "Lovaniense I o Vaticanum II?" *AnalTar* 41 (1968), 173-79.

[106] Wiltgen, *Rhine*, 53-54.

[107] Ibid., 54.

close relations were established with the Melkite Church, between which and the bloc there existed a certain theological affinity.

Some bishops, distancing themselves from the conservative climate of the episcopate to which they belonged, "carried with them whole or half-nations," as, for example, the United States reformist Cardinals Albert G. Meyer, Archbishop of Chicago, and Joseph Elmer Ritter, Archbishop of St. Louis (both of German descent).[108] As for the charismatic Cardinal Paul-Émile Léger, Archbishop of Montreal, whom Gómez de Arteche describes as a "convert," it would be difficult to exaggerate the importance of his contribution from the very beginning, as can be seen from his correspondence with Cardinal Döpfner.

An important date in the expansion of this bloc was November 13, the eve of the start of the debate on the sources of revelation. At the meeting of delegates held that day there were present representatives of Germany, France, Italy, Spain, Africa, CELAM, Canada, Mexico, India, Ceylon, Burma, Japan, and the Philippines.[109]

"Beyond all calculation" were the connections made and the influence exercised through the experts from all of the countries of the bloc. The bloc also established connections with the main news centers or services (of which I shall speak further on in detail). The Dutch origin of *D-OC* shows that the Dutch bishops were in sympathy, but the bloc also established connections with the news centers of the German episcopate and of CELAM. These national news services, and others that were supranational, like KIPA or the *Katholiek Archief*, were the bloc's principal channels of communication with international Catholic opinion. The result was that a major part of the Catholic and, even more, the non-confessional press of the entire world came to endorse the positions taken by the Central European Bloc; this in turn influenced the views of not a few Council fathers. In addition, the contacts made at diplomatic receptions in the embassies of the member countries of the bloc would prove especially profitable.[110]

---

[108] Gómez de Arteche, *Grupos "extra aulam,"* II/4, 14.

[109] Ibid., 15, where the author is relying on Levillain, *La mécanique politique*. In Gómez's opinion, this universalization of the bloc was a "qualitative leap" that differentiated its status from that of other groups or subgroups and made it "a de facto rival of a legally established organization, the Commission for Coordination." Gómez goes so far as to say that "by the fact that the Committee of Delegates had an influence on the agenda proportional to that which it had on the appointment of candidates to the commissions (at the second election), the Central European Bloc, which opposed the Curia, would become, by the fact of its dominance within the Alliance, a shadow cabinet, and the Committee of Delegates, a shadow Parliament" (II/4, 16, and 15 n.13).

[110] Ibid., II/4, 16 and 19.

From the viewpoint of organization, the Central European Bloc, unlike the International Group of Fathers, had no leadership offices and no formal organizational structure, but we can speak, with Gómez de Arteche, of "levels of organization." The highest of these was a summit made up of the cardinal presidents of the episcopal conferences. They did not meet on set dates but only when a meeting seemed necessary to coordinate lines of common action; in addition, the number of participants varied. The very stable nucleus of this group was Cardinals Frings, König, Liénart, Suenens, and Alfrink, but occasionally the leaders of allied groups took part.

This looseness of the Central European Bloc's organization could not but detract from its effectiveness. This made Douglas Woodruff comment that the people from across the Alps, who were so powerful and full of ideas, seemed to think that these ideas would make their way on their own.[111]

D. THE CONFERENCE OF DELEGATES[112]

This organization arose as an agency for information and mutual relations among the meetings which the national episcopates were holding outside the council hall. It was also called the International Committee, the Committee of Twenty-eight, and the Interconference. "It was a current of awareness, without a moral personality," Msgr. Etchegaray told Gómez de Arteche. Gómez comments: "It was a loose union of national groups in which a reformist tendency dominated. It could be compared with a bloc, front, or cartel of parties, but with national parties replacing ideological parties." But in its turn, because of its broad base, it came to be "an authentic representation of the Council, a council in miniature," and it has even been said to have prefigured certain postconciliar institutions.[113] In answer to Gómez de Arteche's inquiry, Msgr. Cantero Cuadrado insisted that "the gathering in the Domus Mariae is not an

[111] "The Council's Second Month: Facing the Procedure Problem," *The Tablet*, no. 6390, 1070; cited by Gómez de Arteche, *Grupos "extra aulam,"* II/4, 21 n.22.

[112] I am profiting here from the information contained in replies to Gómez de Arteche's inquiry by Msgr. Pedro Cantero Cuadrado (Appendix I, 222) and Msgr. Roger Etchegaray (ibid., 223-25). See also Caporale, *Vatican II*, 67-70; J. Grootaers, "Une forme de concertation épiscopale au Concile Vatican II: La 'Conférence des Vingt-deux (1962-1963)," *RHE* 91 (1996) 66-112. P. Noël is about to publish a study of the group based on the papers of Msgr. Etchegaray.

[113] Gómez de Arteche, *Grupos "extra aulam,"* II/4, 29.

organ of the Council, either official or unofficial or private. It is a gathering of Council fathers from various episcopates, who come together
periodically, in a spirit of friendship and brotherhood, to exchange
impressions on the general progress of the Council."

Some Council fathers advocated the continuation of the group after
the Council, as an unofficial complement to the papal Senate. Another
cause of the formation of this conference was the almost unmanageable
size of the conciliar assembly. At the twenty-eighth general congregation (November 27, 1962) Msgr. Méndez Arceo proposed that during the
intersession a tenth of the Council fathers, elected by themselves, should
meet in Rome to study the schemas in greater detail and then let their
electors know the results. According to Cantero Cuadrado, during the
intersessions the members of this conference corresponded among themselves and exchanged news and especially articles in the press.

The discussions were held in French and in English, and the working
documents and minutes of the conference were composed in Latin. The
subject matter was regarded as secret. The Conference of Delegates did
not intervene as such in the Council, and no one spoke in its name or in
the name of its committee. It influenced the conciliar debates only indirectly, through the information and guidance which it passed on to the
Council fathers.

When the conference started, during the first session, it began its
activities with the declared purpose of providing mutual information. Its
purpose broadened as the number of its members grew, somewhat as the
Central European Bloc became the World Alliance. One of the first
things affected by this broadening of functions was the area regarding
which information was supplied. In addition to exchanging information
about one another, the need was seen to inform the journalists. As a
result, there came into being the Center for Coordination of Communications about the Council (CCCC). The exchange of information and
views, which in the beginning was limited to conciliar matters, was
extended later on to extraconciliar ecclesial matters.

In principle, each episcopal conference or group of conferences
appointed as its representatives a delegate and a substitute, both of them
bishops. Also represented were some groups of conferences, such as
CELAM and the Pan-African Conference. The two Canadian conferences had a single representative. The procedure for appointing representatives was left up to each conference. The delegate was often the
president of the conferences; thus one of CELAM's delegates was
always the president. By exception, some super-conferences sent more

than one delegate. Thus, during the fourth session the Oriental Churches (Melkites and Maronites) had two, CELAM had three, French-speaking Africa had three, and English-speaking Africa had two. The powers of the delegates were those which each conference granted them, and in principle the delegates could not legally bind those who sent them. As a matter of fact, there was no voting or formal agreements. There were not even fixed procedural rules.

The president of the Conference of Delegates had no authority, properly speaking, but acted simply as a moderator of the meetings and as a liaison between the conference and the episcopal conferences that sent the delegates. During the first session this part was played by Msgr. Miguel Dario Miranda y Gómez, Archbishop of Mexico City; in subsequent sessions it was played by Msgr. Pierre Veuillot, at that time Coadjutor Bishop of Paris. Msgr. Roger Etchegaray, a French Basque, at that time Director of the Pastoral Secretariat of the French episcopate, served as secretary throughout the Council.

The pace of the meetings was irregular during the first session, but beginning in the second the conference met regularly every Friday evening at the Domus Mariae. On the Wednesdays before,[114] the secretaries of the episcopal conferences would meet to prepare the meeting and agenda. Only the delegates of the various episcopal conferences could be present, and each conference was asked to send a delegate.[115]

E. THE ZEALOT FACTION IN THE CURIA[116]

According to Carlo Falconi, the general program of this group was "to prevent any lessening of papal prerogatives; to avoid a reform of the

---

[114] Wednesday according to Gómez de Arteche, *Grupos "extra aulam"* II/4, 36; Tuesday according to Wiltgen, *Rhine*, 130.

[115] See the list of the 21 delegates who took part in the first meeting and of the 22 at the first meeting of the secretaries of the episcopal conferences, in Jan A. Brouwers, "Derniers préparatifs et première session," in *Vatican II commence*, 367-68.

[116] I am here again following Gómez de Arteche's study. Although a great deal was said about the Curia during the Council and abundant reference would be made to it in contemporary chronicles and later historical studies, Gómez de Arteche first points out that the ensemble of dicasteries of the Holy See do not form a corporation with its own juridical personality. Second, among its members there were two sectors, opposed in tendency and of unequal importance, which Gómez describes as "factions," in the sense which Max Weber gives to this term. Nevertheless, while recalling the ancient distinction between *zealous* cardinals (*zelanti*), who pursue purely religious goals, and *political* cardinals (*politicanti*), who have an eye on what is politically advantageous, Gómez thinks that both factions in the Curia deserved to be regarded as *zealots*.

Curia itself by the Council; to check the increase of the bishops' powers; to resist the meddling of the laity; to moderate and apply gradually reforms of any kind."[117] It considered itself "the remnant of Israel," that is, the minority that was the trustee and interpreter of God's will.

Other general characteristics of the group were zeal for the proper and precise formulation of doctrine, and specifically its scholastic formulation; excessive caution, which might be summed up in Cardinal Browne's "Let us be on guard, fathers," with reference to collegiality[118]; a sense of the immutability and "happy possession" (*beata possessio*) of all that presently exists in the Church[119]; a deep appreciation of tradition (identified in practice with recent tradition[120]); the definitive and final importance of the magisterium;[121] the ahistorical triumphalism that led them to maintain, "as a cardinal rule of the Curia: never acknowledge faults, at least not publicly;"[122] an individualism that can be seen in the defense of the private celebration of the Mass;[123] and "essentialism," that is, "the predominance of abstract thinking."[124]

A complementary aspect of their program was an extreme "papalism" that found expression in an intransigent defense of what they called the rights or intangible privileges of the Holy See, which in many cases were simply the rights and privileges of the Curia. Thus, in the discussion of the liturgical schema, they rejected anything that might be interpreted as the Council telling the Holy See what to do.[125] For this reason, the greatest of errors, in their view, was the claim of episcopal collegiality, which they saw as an attack on the authority of the Curia. During the debate on the schema on the Church, Browne maintained that if collegiality gave the bishops the right to share in the government of the

---

[117] Carlo Falconi, *I Perché del concilio* (Milan, 1962), 174.

[118] November 8, 1963 (*AS* II/4, 627).

[119] Gómez de Arteche cites here the interventions of Vagnozzi on the liturgical schema (*AS* I/1, 325-36) and of Ottaviani with regard to the Order of the Mass (*AS* I/2, 18-20).

[120] Intervention of Msgr. Ferrero di Cavallerleone on the liturgical schema (*AS* I/1, 551-52).

[121] Interventions of Ottaviani, November 17, 1965; Browne, November 20, 1965; and Dante, November 21, 1965, all in the debate on the schema on religious freedom.

[122] Gómez de Arteche, citing X. Rynne, *The Third Session* (New York, 1965), 277.

[123] Intervention of Msgr. van Lierde, October 24, 1962 (*AS* I/1, 412-14).

[124] Gomez de Arteche, *Grupos "extra aulam,"* II/4, 52. A report (February 26, 1963) of Doussinague, the Spanish Ambassador to the Holy See, which was surely inspired by a Spanish churchman, described the Council as a struggle between "essentialists" and "existentialists."

[125] Interventions of Ottaviani and Browne, October 23, 1962 (*AS* I/1, 359-51, 376-77).

Church, the Pope would be obliged to respect it and therefore would no longer have a real primacy over the entire Church.[126]

The Curial zealots did not fail to display distinct marks of politicians. They were keenly interested in Italian politics and, by way of Catholic Action and the "civic committees," favored and tried to control the Christian Democratic Party, within which they supported the right wing and opposed the "opening to the left," that is, the pact with the socialists of Pietro Nenni. During the pontificate of Pius XII, this political outlook received its momentum from the top, but the situation had completely changed since the accession of John XXIII. In the area of international politics, the zealot faction in the Curia was characterized by its undiscriminating anticommunism, its identification of the Catholic cause with the so-called Western bloc (NATO), and its support for the foreign policies of the United States and for various authoritarian regimes of Europe, Latin America, and the Third World, some of which boasted of their superficial Christianity. "The purely negative anti-communism of the Curia was running up against the plan for universal dialogue of Pope John, who initiated conversations with the socialist countries and, more importantly, decided to bury the anti-communist policy and elevate the Church above the East-West confrontation, to be a source of peace and aid for the integral development of the world."[127]

This group saw from the start the danger that the conciliar event represented for its interests and for the political program just described, and it endeavored, by all the means at its disposal, to prevent the Council from being held or at least to delay it and rein it in. If, despite the efforts of the zealot faction of the Curia, the Council were to start, they would try to minimize it.[128] An outward sign of this attitude was the silence it often maintained in contrast to the enthusiasm of the rest of the Church and the lively solidarity of all of humanity.

Which fathers of the Council could be regarded as clearly members of this faction? A purely numerical list could be worked up by combining three main criteria: an important role in the Roman Curia; conservative interventions in the hall; and proven influence outside of it.[129] We find, first of all, the cardinals who were members of the Congregations, tri-

---

[126] November 8, 1963 (AS II/4, 626-27).

[127] Gómez de Arteche, Grupos "extra aulam," II/4, 54.

[128] Gómez de Arteche reports that a prelate, whose name he cannot reveal, told him that when Msgr. Felici was beginning his work, Cardinal Tardini said to him: "Hold, not a real council (concilio), but a miniature council (concilietto)" (ibid., 56-57).

[129] Ibid., 65-68.

bunals, and offices — above all, the Italians, "the only ones worthy of unlimited trust and the shared name of 'members of the Curia.'"[130] There were also the assessors and secretaries of the Congregations,[131] and the consultors.[132]

The Vatican Polyglot Press worked for the Council under orders from the Secretary General, but it was also used by some of the zealots of the Curia for their own documents. The Press published some circulars in support of conservative theses; these were distributed to the Council fathers as well as to other persons and organizations. In addition, thanks to his control of the Press, "Msgr. Felici was able, by hindering or limiting the distribution of texts, to influence the progress of the Council directly, but along the destructive lines already described."[133]

[130] Among the prefects, pro-prefects, and secretaries of the dicasteries were Cardinals Pizzardo (Seminaries and Universities) Ciriaci (Council), Ottaviani (Holy Office), Aloisi Masella (Sacraments). Confalonieri (Consistory), Marella (Venerable Fabric of St. Peter's), and, from the second session on, Antoniutti (Religious, successor to Valieri, who was opposed to the zealot trend). Among the simple members of the Congregations: Micara, the Vicar General of Rome, Bacci, and Ferretto. Among the foreign cardinals were Prefects Agagianian (Propaganda Fide); Tisserant, the Dean of the College (Ceremonies); and Larraona (successor to Cicognani in Rites). Browne was a simple member. Of the foreign cardinals, two, Larraona of Spain and Browne of Ireland, were regarded as "more zealous than the zealots."

[131] The following may be included in the group: Italians Parente (Holy Office), Carpino (Consistory), Sigismondi (Propaganda Fide), Staffa (Seminaries and Universities), Dante (Rites), Scapinelli di Leguigno (Oriental), and Palazzini (Council), and a non-Italian, Coussa (Oriental Church). Of the substitutes: Civardi (Consistory) and Giovanelli (Oriental).

[132] Italians: Piolanti (Rector of the Lateran University), Garofalo, Ciappi, Tondini (secretary of Letters to Rulers), Antonelli; non-Italians: Balić, Tromp, Martin O'Connor (rector of the North American College and secretary of the Pontifical Commission for Motion Pictures, Radio, and Television), Hudal, Bidagor, Goyeneche, and Gagnebet. Add: Msgr. Antonino Romeo, an official of the Congregation for Studies, who would distinguish himself for his attacks on the conciliar majority and the Biblical Institute.

[133] Gómez de Arteche, *Grupos "extra aulam,"* II/4, 93. He mentions, as an example of this tactic, texts on votes concerning the principle of collegiality, the schema of the declaration on relations with the Jews, and the declaration on religious freedom. But the most serious manipulation, according to Gómez de Arteche, was connected with the list of emendations (*expensio modorum*) for chapter III of the schema on the Church. In order not to sound an alarm among the majority, the clause specifying that the vote on these emendations was to be cast in the light of the "Prefatory Note of Explanation (*Nota explicativa praevia*)" was omitted from its proper place and published at the end as the result, supposedly, of a typographical error. At the fifty-second general congregation, Father Balić, a consultor of the Holy Office and President of the Pontifical International Marian Academy, who was charged with composing the text on the Virgin Mary (first a separate schema but later turned into a chapter of the *Constitution on the Church*) distributed to the fathers, in the council hall, a brochure, printed by the Vatican Press, publisher of the Council's official documents, in which he gave his personal commentaries on the proposed schema.

Let us look now at the groups which supported this faction as permanent or occasional allies. First, there were the national groups. The most important, logically enough, because of the mechanics of the Council as determined by the zealot faction in the Curia, was the Italian, which was "the Curia's geographical hinterland and historical prolongation, its closest and most loyal administrative clientele, and the principal beneficiary of the Vatican spoils system,[134] in the form at least of access to stages in the dicasteries with openings to offices of importance."[135]

The two great Italian prelates who stood out most for their adherence to the Curia and who carried many others with them were Giuseppe Siri, Archbishop of Genoa, and Ernesto Ruffini, Archbishop of Palermo. The latter gave public witness to his esteem for the Curia at the sixteenth general congregation (November 10, 1962), at which he was presiding; and in his intervention at the sixty-third general congregation (November 8, 1963) he thanked His Beatitude Ignace Pierre Batanian, Patriarch of the Cilician Armenians, for having spoken in defense of the Curia the day before. Also to be mentioned are Cardinal Giovanni Urbani, successor of Roncalli in the patriarchal see of Venice and president of the Italian Episcopal Conference, and Msgr. Alberto Castelli, secretary of that conference.

Of the few Italian bishops who were consultors to the Roman Congregations, mention may be made of Giuseppe D'Avack, Archbishop of Camerino (Seminaries), and Ermenegildo Florit, Archbishop of Florence (Biblical Studies). The many Italian bishops in the missions were usually loyal to their origins and therefore very close to the Curia. I mentioned earlier Montini's admission to Döpfner that very few Italian bishops possessed an authentically conciliar outlook.

Lesser groups that shared the zealot tendency included a number of Dalmatian bishops (belonging to the Yugoslav episcopate), headed by Msgr. Frane Franić, Archbiship of Split-Makarska, a member of the Istituto Pio V, founded by Ottaviani for the struggle against communism. Then there were also some Baltic, Cuban, Haitian, Chinese, Filipino, and Vietnamese bishops. More influential was the United States group, which to the tradition of Irish Catholicism had joined the influence of the prestigious Cardinal Cicognani, who was greatly respected during and after his twenty-three years as Apostolic Delegate there. This group

---

[134] In the political jargon of the United States the "spoils system" is the practice by which the winning party in elections distributes at its own whim public offices with their emoluments and advantages.

[135] Gómez de Arteche, Grupos "extra aulam," II/4, 100.

had as its main leaders Cardinals Francis Spellman (New York) and James Francis McIntyre (Los Angeles), "two firm supporters of the zealot group on the other shore of the Atlantic."[136] However, their partisanship and their maneuvers and violations of the Regulations led to an opposite reaction in a broad sector of Catholicism in the United States. In the English and Welsh episcopates the influence of Irish and Italian immigrants often showed in a Catholicism that was not only Roman but Curial. For very different reasons the Chaldean and Armenian prelates (unlike the Melkite) were devoted to the Curia.

Some religious superiors with ties to the Congregation for Religious were attached to the zealot faction in the Curia. I may mention Father Anastasio del Santissimo Rosario, Superior General of the Carmelites and president of the Union of Major Superiors, and Father Aniceto Fernández, Master General of the Dominicans and vice-president of the Union.

As for "ideological" groups, the only one openly connected with the zealots of the Curia was the International Group of Fathers,[137] which has already been described and which included Cardinals Larraona, Browne, and Santos along with Msgrs. de Proença Sigaud, Carli, and the latter's fellow townsman, Msgr. Felici, who exercised a great deal of executive and administrative authority in the General Secretariat of the Council.

On the other hand, as the Council began there were many conservative bishops who resented the haughtiness and centralism of the Vatican Curia, so that they lined up against it repeatedly.[138] At the same time, a number of churchmen belonging to the various Vatican organizations clearly separated themselves from the closed-mindedness of the zealot faction. Understandably, they belonged to those organizations that John XXIII or Paul VI were creating under the influence of the spirit of the ongoing Council. There was, then, a "new Curia," with some new men and a new mentality. They were a "fruit of the Council" and "symbolized the persistence of its spirit, just as the Sacred Congregation of the Council had symbolized the persistence of the Tridentine spirit."[139]

---

[136] Ibid., 103.

[137] "These two organizations joined together in all the controversies that marked the course of the Council," says Gómez de Arteche (ibid., II/4, 105); he refers especially to the great struggle over collegiality.

[138] See the forceful testimony of Schillebeeckx: "Many bishops were less concerned with a renewal of theology than with breaking the power of the Curia, which considered itself above the bishops. . . . I can confirm, from later years, that the bishops had serious grievances against the Curia, which understood nothing of what was going on in the Church and in the world" (*Je suis un théologien heureux* [Paris, 1995], 46).

[139] Gómez de Arteche, *Grupos "extra aulam,"* II/4, 117.

Most important were the secretariats. The first established, the Secretariat for Christian Unity,[140] served as a model for the later two, the Secretariat for Non-Christians and the Secretariat for Nonbelievers.

F. The French Group[141]

This group had its antecedents in the Assembly of the Cardinals and Archbishops of France and then in the Plenary Assembly of the French episcopate. It was, in itself, a discussion group within the French episcopate and the retired French missionary bishops, but it also held meetings that were open to all the bishops and experts of the world. It included the bishops of metropolitan France and also of the Antilles, the island of Réunion, and, in general, the overseas Departments and Territories, but on liturgical matters it collaborated with the Canadian, Belgian, Swiss, and French-speaking African episcopates. Its existence was limited to the time of the Council.

The group had no formal rules, but its practice can be described here. The most important characteristic of the group was its workshops (*ateliers*), which were coordinated by the authorities of the four secretariats of the episcopal conference and which acted as ad hoc organizations for the work of the Council. They were teams of volunteers, made up of bishops and experts, with a bishop responsible for each schema. Interventions in the hall in the name of the episcopate were prepared in the workshops. At each meeting of the group the workshops simply presented their reports, without any back-and-forth between the group and the workshops. The texts that had been worked up were not juridically binding. The bishops sought to come to agreement in advance in order to avoid repetitions. Especially important was the intervention of Liénart at the beginning of the Council when he asked that the elections be postponed.

The calling of meetings was up to the president. The meetings of the group as such (restricted to the French bishops) took place weekly, on

---

[140] Created by John XXIII in the motu proprio *Superno Dei nutu* (June 5, 1960). The Secretariat was confirmed as a properly conciliar organization in the motu proprio *Appropinquante Concilio* (August 6, 1962).

[141] Information based on the response of Msgr. Roger Etchegaray, secretary of the Pastoral Secretariat of the French episcopate, to the inquiry of Gómez de Arteche, *Grupos "extra aulam,"* Appendix I, 82-84. See also L. Perrin, "Approche du rôle des évêques de France," in *Vatican II commence*, 119-32, as well as the contributions of J. Famerée, Cl. Prudhomme, and Cl. Soetens on the French-speaking Belgian and African episcopates, in the same volume.

Wednesday; meetings open to other bishops and experts were held every two weeks. At the meetings of the group proper, votes were taken by raising hands; there was no voting at the open sessions. All were free to speak at the group's meetings, and a report was made of the meetings and afterward given in mimeographed form to the participants. Sometimes, while in Rome, the group dealt with questions referring to the Church of France.

The press emphasized the fact that "the French episcopacy wanted at all costs to avoid the formation of antagonistic camps." To this end, "they established numerous contacts with the bishops of other nations," Italian, Spanish, Dutch, Austrian, and so forth. As proof of their intention not to go it alone, they decided that their own meetings would be opened to whoever cared to attend, whatever his nationality.[142] At the same time, however, this group did have an especially close relationship with the Central European Bloc. At the meeting of the cardinals of this bloc, the French attended in the name of the group. Various bishops of the group also attended the meetings of other bodies. The connection of some bishops with the Secretariat of the Council was maintained in the name of the group, not of the workshops.

G. The Latin American Group

The classic councils of Lima and Mexico City in the sixteenth to the eighteenth centuries and the Plenary Council of Latin America celebrated under Leo XIII in 1899 were the distant but solid background of CELAM and therefore also of the Latin American group at Vatican II. (The canons of these councils had been in force until the promulgation of the 1917 Code.) In July and August of 1955 representatives of the entire Latin American episcopate (the archbishop of each ecclesiastical province and a bishop elected by the suffragans) met in Rio de Janeiro to form CELAM, which was approved by Pius XII on November 2 of that same year. At the Rio meeting the decision to establish the headquarters of the organization in Bogotá was approved by a majority of those voting. The first meeting of CELAM took place in Bogotá in November 1956; the group approved its statutes and appointed Msgr. Mendoza as its secretary general.

[142] *Le Monde,* October 17, 1962; see H. Fesquet, *The Drama of Vatican II* (New York, 1967), 24-25. On this point see also A. Wenger, *Vatican II* (Westminster, Md., 1966), 38.

According to this prelate, CELAM modeled its structure on a political organization: the Organization of American States (OAS), which also included North America and had its headquarters in Washington, D.C. Consequently, CELAM set up ten "Departments of Special Services (DES)," which reflected in Bogotá the Departments of Special Services of the OAS in Washington, but covering now the areas of the apostolate. The Holy See approved this decentralization and the creation of the DES, and recommended a review of the work.[143] The Latin American bishops applied themselves to this work of revision in twenty days of meetings, taking advantage of their being in Rome for the Council. During the Council this episcopate was able to play a quite important role, due especially to the initiative of Bishops Larraín and Câmara.[144]

H. THE RELIGIOUS SUPERIORS[145]

The immediate predecessor and institutional basis of this group was the Roman Union of Religious Superiors (URSR). "We did not act as a body with a distinct orientation or tendency," Father Aniceto Fernández explained. There were few meetings for discussion. In the course of the whole Council, this group organized only three or four conferences of theologians.

The group was made up of about ten Council fathers, including abbots. Although not all the religious superiors of the URSR were Council fathers, this group did admit even superiors general who were not members of the Council (including superiors of nonexempt orders and of societies with less than a thousand members), and these were given permission to speak on conciliar subjects at the meetings. Thus not only the Superior General of the Brothers of the Christian Schools, who was a member of the Council, was present at these meetings, but so was the Superior General of the Marists, who was not a member. There were

---

[143] Information based on the reply of Msgr. Julián Mendoza Guerrero, the Colombian Secretary General of CELAM, to the inquiry of Gómez de Arteche, *Grupos "extra aulam,"* Appendix I, 91, and on *Vísperas*.

[144] Câmara sent news of the Council daily to a group of correspondents in Brazil. These interesting letters are now being prepared for publication under the editorship of L. C. Marques. L. Baraúna has undertaken a comprehensive study of the contribution of the Brazilian episcopate to Vatican II.

[145] Information based on the response of Father Aniceto Fernández, Master General of the Dominicans and vice-president of the Roman Union of Religious Superiors, to the inquiry of Gómez de Arteche, *Grupos "extra aulam,"* Appendix I, 202-4.

subgroups according to the diversity of charisms (monks, mendicants, clerks regular, lay congregations, teaching religious, etc.), but they did not reach the point of studying questions in groups.

The governing or executive organ was the Permanent Commission or Council of the Roman Union, which had eight or ten members, elected by all the religious superiors of the Union. Father Fernández was vice-president. The Commission met almost every month. At the plenary meetings sixty or seventy members were at times present. These meetings took place once a month, or a little more often. There were no rules of procedure. In the beginning a vote was almost never taken; There were few interventions in the name of the group. There were no efforts to establish a common direction; all the members remained free, and the group could not even reach agreement on chapter 6 of the Constitution on the Church, which dealt with religious. Contacts with the organizations of the Council took place through the president of the group. The vice-president, Fernández, took part, in the name of the group, in some mixed committees of the Doctrinal Commission and the Commission on Religious. In general, the members did not take part in the meetings of other groups. Fernández never took part in the meetings of the International Assembly of (Religious) Bishops.

I. The Religious Bishops[146]

The official name of this group was the International Group of Bishops (*Coetus Internationalis Episcoporum*), but it was made up solely of bishops who were religious; they numbered between seven hundred and eight hundred. They sought to place the problem of religious in its proper light by taking account of the various religious orders represented and by drawing out the practical consequences of the subject under discussion.

The group, which began to operate during the second session of the Council, had no regulations or disciplinary norms. It never had plenary meetings but only meetings of study groups, which never voted and whose duration depended on the pace of the conciliar debate on the schema on religious life and on its parts. At times, experts took part in these meetings. The regular place of the meetings was in the Curia of the

---

[146] Information based on the response of Msgr. Enrico Romolo Compagnone, O.C.D., Bishop of Anagni, on December 3, 1965, to the inquiry of Gómez de Arteche, *Grupos "extra aulam,"* Appendix, I, 209-11.

General of the Jesuits. The discussions were generally carried on in Latin, and agreements were written up in Latin and Italian.

The only organizational structure was a limited group made up of a president, Msgr. Pacifico Perantoni, Archbishop of Lanciano; a secretary, Msgr. Richard Lester Guilly, S.J., Bishop of Georgetown (British Guyana); and some further collaborators, among them Msgr. Enrico Compagnone, who was a member of the conciliar Commission on Religious. The members of this groups made no formal interventions in the name of the group, but their influence was visible. They did not present alternative schemas, but did offer emendations (*modi*). Their list of candidates for election to the conciliar commissions was sent to the Holy Father for his information (in fact, the Pope appointed some religious bishops).

The group distributed some circulars, signed by Compagnone, intended for only some of the Council fathers, and sent through trustworthy individuals. The group never made protests to the official organs of the Council, nor did it submit any complaints to the administrative tribunal.

J. The Missionary Bishops (*Vriendenclub*)[147]

The source of this information, Msgr. Tarcisius van Valenberg, former Apostolic Vicar in Dutch Borneo, was the founder and leader of this group. He began by writing a letter, in Dutch, to various superiors general and some procurators general of Dutch religious institutes, and to some Belgians.[148] The predominant nationality of the members of the founding nucleus explains why they took the Dutch name *Vriendenclub* (Club of Friends). Those belonging to the group were usually members of the Council, some three hundred of them, "free men who have

---

[147] Information based on the reply of Msgr. Tarcisius Hendrik Jozef van Valenberg, O.F.M.Cap., Titular Bishop of Comba, in January, 1966, to Gómez de Arteche, *Grupos "extra aulam,"* Appendix, I, 212-15.

[148] C. de Flesinga, Superior General of the Capuchins; C. Heiligers, Superior General of the Montfort Fathers; J. van Kerckhoven, Superior General of the Missionary Servants of the Sacred Heart of Jesus (Belgian); S. Melsen, Procurator General and Assistant for the Netherlands of the Carmelites of the Ancient Observance; H. Mondé, Superior General of the Society of the African Missions; H. Systermans, Superior General of the Congregation of the Sacred Hearts, also known as the Picpus Fathers (Belgian); L. Volker, Superior General of the White Fathers; A. H. van der Weijde, Procurator General of the Order of St. Augustine.

worked together," both on the schema on the missions and in the post-conciliar period. The countries most heavily represented in the group were Belgium, Holland, France, and Canada. As for the missionary institutes represented, these were primarily the most progressive. In addition to bishops, there were some experts, the chief of whom was Father van der Weijde.

"We all want the good of the missions more than the good of our own institutes, even if this means that the institutes are no longer needed," said Msgr. van Valenberg to Gómez de Arteche. For this reason they wanted the group to continue once the Council was finished, "in order that the missions may receive their proper place in the new Canon Law and in the measures which the Congregation for the Propagation of the Faith takes by reason of it."

It was a loose structure, a study group more than anything else, without any organization, and regarded by the Curia as dangerous. The missionary bishops took part in meetings only during the sessions of the Council, but van Valenberg remained in Rome during the intersessions and continued doing necessary work. It was he who set the agenda and called the meetings, which had no set schedule but were called when thought necessary. They were often held in the house of the White Fathers, without rules of procedure, in great simplicity, beginning with a prayer and taking up the subjects over a cup of coffee and liqueurs. Votes were taken by raising hands. The languages used were Dutch and English. The secretary, usually van der Weijde, drew up minutes of the meetings.

The group held a discussion before the conciliar debate on each schema. Twice the group presented alternate schemas, a "Schema on the Missions" and "An Amended Text of the Schema on the Missions;" on many other occasions it formulated emendations. Suggestions that were accepted into the *Decree on the Missions* and that originated in this groups were: (1) a more theological foundation for missions; (2) request for more energetic activity on the part of the Congregation for the Propagation of the Faith; (3) dialogue with the non-Christian religions; and (4) reform of the Code of Canon Law to permit the missionary institutes greater room to work.

As for contacts and influence outside the group, each member asked the bishops of his own religious institute to espouse the proposals or emendations of the missionaries. They urged interventions by highly esteemed cardinals, such as Alfrink, König, and Zoungrana. These, as well as Carmelite Daniel Raymond Lamont, Bishop of Umtali (Southern

Rhodesia), spoke in the name of the group but did not mention this commission, saying only that they were speaking in the name of many superiors general. The group also tried to exert influence by means of short tracts and other printed matter. Each member of the group took some copies and passed them out to Council fathers and experts with whom he was familiar.

The group had no direct connection with the group made up of religious superiors, but the study group of the latter was aware that the missionaries were at work. At times the missionary bishops worked for the Congregation of Religious, but secretly. They had a good relationship with the Missionary Conference of the Netherlands and with that of Indonesia, located in the Foyer Unitas, but had no connections with the Belgian Missionary Conference. Msgr. van Valenberg was himself a member of the Church of the Poor group and a friend of Father Gauthier. They had no official connections with the official organs of the Council, but van Valenberg used to talk with Cicognani. Father Jan Schütte, Superior General of the Society of the Divine Word and the expelled Apostolic Pro-Prefect of Sinsiang (China), and the entire Commission on the Missions, talked with this group before presenting the schema in the hall. Fathers Xavier and André Seumois, who were brothers, were experts of the conciliar commission and also of the *Vriendenclub*, although not formally members of this. "There were no signs of any official recognition," said van Valenberg, "but the commission was very open in dealing with us." It treated the *Vriendenclub* like "His Majesty's Loyal Opposition," and Father Schütte frequently thanked the group.

IV. THE PRESS

Gérard Philips wrote that "by its nature the Council is an event rather than an institution."[149] But never before had an ecumenical council been so much of an "event," in the journalistic sense of the term, as Vatican II was. It represented a challenge both for the news media and for the Church itself, in terms of the attitude it would adopt toward journalists. One chronicler wrote: "I think it will be very easy to tack together some sets of phrases about the pope's affection for the press and for journalists. But our world gives increasingly less credence to words, and it is

---

[149] Gérard Philips, *L'Église et son mystère au IIe Concile du Vatican* (Desclée de Brouwer, 1967), I, 296.

asking how far the Church has accepted and assimilated the press and how far it simply tolerates it as a dangerous enemy."[150] *La Civiltà Cattolica*, a periodical published by the Jesuits but under the control of the Secretariat of State, began the first of its bulletins on the Council by reprinting the prefatory note written by its chronicler of Vatican I, ninety-three years before:

> The news presently having to do in one or other way with the council is so extensive that it fills the columns of the daily newspapers, but we have only a few pages twice a month for this varied information. If we wanted to assemble all of it, we would have to speak of nothing but the Council in the entire issue and thus change the nature of our periodical. We must, however, be satisfied to touch on only a few things, or, as they say, give a few generalities about each subject.[151]

On the eve of the Council some 900 accreditation cards had been issued to journalists by the Press Office, and as the first session went on, the number rose to 1255. One of the recipients, upon inquiry, learned that perhaps only one-third of these were professional journalists, since many Catholic publications had simply appointed as correspondent a priest or religious known to them and residing in Rome. Even so, the interest of the news media in the conciliar event reached an unprecedented intensity. In a letter to the editor of the less serious Italian magazines, a reader complained that she could not open any journal or magazine without finding page after page on the Council, which did not interest her at all.

The journalist mentioned above, Martín Descalzo, gave as the first reason for such expectation "the exceptional popularity of John XXIII throughout the world;" other reasons were the novelty of the Council, since this was the only one in the experience of the last few generations; the vast spread of the Catholic Church, implanted as it is in all corners of the planet; and an intuition that saw in the Council the world's hope for light and peace on worldwide problems.[152] Nevertheless, ecclesiastical news media could not bring themselves to accept the fact that the

---

[150] J. L. Martín Descalzo, *Prensa y Concilio: Del "muro del secreto" a las "puertas abiertas" en el Concilio Vaticano II*, 4-5. This work is a little thesis, never published and undated, but certainly written before the end of the Council, probably in mid-1963. Despite the fact that the author was afflicted with a serious illness, from which he died a few months later, he kindly granted me a lengthy interview on October 24, 1990, and allowed me to photocopy his work. His extensive library on Vatican II is now kept in the Madrid Jesuits' House of Writers.

[151] *CivCatt*, no. 2697, November 3, 1962, citing itself for 1870, vol. I, 356.

[152] Martín Descalzo, *Prensa y Concilio*, 40.

role of journalism is to spread not what is essential but what is news. As Henri Fesquet was to say, it is not news that thousands of bishops talk about God, but if one of them were to say that God does not exist, that would be front-page news.

A very strict and religious secrecy had reigned during the work of the preparatory commissions,[153] whose members could talk about the documents and deliberations only with other members of the same commission. Congar thought that the principle was a good one, since the indiscretion of the press and the interjection of public opinion could have disastrous effects; but at the same time, secrecy was "a means of atomizing and neutralizing all opposition. It reduces us, for practical purposes, to the condition of people who have direct relations only with Rome and not with each other. It means the destruction, in practice, of horizontal catholicity, to the profit of vertical catholicity alone."[154]

The problem arose in an analogous form when the Council began, since for the majority of the Council fathers the meetings outside the hall, the lectures, the circulation of documents, and, more generally, the communications media proved very useful, not to say necessary, in forming a solid opinion. In a famous address on public opinion as an indispensable element of the common good, Pius XII had said that it was needed even in the Church ("in regard, of course, to matters that may be freely discussed"), and he went so far as to state that "the Church, too, is a living association, and something would be lacking in its life if there were no public opinion, a failure for which both pastors and faithful would be to blame."[155] But this teaching had not been in fact applied to the life of the Church, especially during the last stage of Pius XII's own pontificate; and, as far as the Council was concerned, there was a positive interest in preventing the formation of a public opinion in order to give greater efficacy to instructions issuing from the Curia, a confirmation of Congar's remark.

To attend to the need of information about the Council, a Committee for the Press was set up. Its presiding officer was Martin John O'Connor, Titular Archbishop of Laodicea in Syria and President of the Pontifical Commission for Motion Pictures, Radio, and Television; he was assisted by fourteen bishops of different nationalities and from different continents, none of them Italian, with Msgr. Fausto Vallainc as secre-

[153] See *History*, I, 177-78, 462-66.
[154] *JCongar*, p. 8.
[155] Address to the International Congress of the Catholic Press, *OssRom*, February 18, 1950.

tary. The Press Office, which was more active, was created on October 5 and located at Via Serristori 12. It began its work a week before the beginning of the Council, with the same Vallainc as its director and seven others in charge of as many language sections: Gerhard Fittkau, German; Edward Heston, Secretary of the Congregation for Religious, North American; Frank Bernard, correspondent for *La Croix*, French; Cipriano Calderón, a conciliar peritus, Spanish; Francesco Farusi, S.J., Italian; Paulo Almeida, S.J., Portuguese (later on, Bonaventura Kloppenburg, O.F.M., a Brazilian); and Stefan Wesoly, Polish. Unlike the members of the Committee for the Press, the members of the Press Office were not conciliar fathers and had no right, unless by some other title, to be present at the meetings of the Council, even though their role was to inform the entire world about these meetings.

The key man in the entire organization was, of course, Vallainc, an Italian from Champorcher in the French-speaking area of the Valle d'Aosta, 46 years of age, with a good knowledge of the principal languages and with some journalism experience as editor of the *Settimana del clero* and as consultor to the press office of Italian Catholic Action.[156] He was directly under Felici and had to resolve an insoluble conflict: to channel information about the Council along the lines set down by Felici and, at the same time, to give the international press an impression of openness and freedom on the part of the Press Office. "The Press Office was pinned between the 'hammer' of the world press and the 'anvil' of conciliar secrecy imposed by the conservative forces in the Curia."[157] It seems that at one moment a despairing Vallainc threw himself at the feet of the Pope and asked to be relieved of this impossible task. In this respect, as in so many others, the first session was a laborious novitiate.

The first official bulletins given out by the Press Office disappointed both the religious journalists and many Council fathers, the former because the bulletins said nothing of interest and did not reveal who said what, and the latter because the little that was said was brazenly favorable to the conservative tendency. The communiqué on the general con-

---

[156] See F. Vallainc, *Images du Concile* (Rome, 1966). Written at the request of Paul VI, the book was published simultaneously in English, German, and Italian. It was not for sale but was distributed to the Council fathers in December of 1966. See also E. L. Heston, *The Press and Vatican II* (Notre Dame, 1967), and Ph. Levillain, "Il Vaticano II e i mezzi di comunicazione sociale," in *La Chiesa del Vaticano II (1958-1978)* I (Milan, 1994), 524-32.

[157] J. Grootaers, "L'information religieuse au début du Concile. Instances officielles et réseaux informels," in *Vatican II commence*, 218.

gregation at which the work of the Council actually began, with the first interventions in the general discussion of the liturgical schema, became famous: "Of the fathers who asked to speak, twenty intervened this morning, some to defend the schema, others to attack it."[158] Father Tucci, editor of *La Civiltà Cattolica* noted in his diary that many bishops (the Canadian bishops openly complaining) "are upset by the one-sided way in which the recent discussions at the general congregation have been described in the official bulletins, which openly side with the conservatives and distort the motives of those who want renewal, of the breviary for example. A certain pessimism is spreading among bishops and journalists."[159]

To present the needs and desires of journalists, Tucci arranged a meeting of a delegation of religious journalists and representatives from the various Council news centers with Casimiro Morcillo, Archbishop of Saragossa and one of the vice-presidents of the Council, in order to present the needs and desires of the journalists. Tucci wrote in his diary:

> He [Morcillo] received us with great understanding, saying that most of the requests are feasible: biographies of those who speak at the Council, greater expansiveness about the texts discussed, exhaustive and current information about more recent problems, and so on. He asked us to submit a short memorandum; he will speak about this in a meeting he will soon have with the Council of Presidents."[160]

Father Brêchet composed the memorandum, taking into account the explanation of the problem which Tucci, in the name of all, had given to Morcillo; Brêchet was aided by Haubtmann, Mejia, Rouquette, and Hirschmann, and he consulted some others as well.

On November 5, late in the afternoon, there was a meeting of the group of religious journalists at the Spanish Center for Conciliar Documentation. Tucci presided, and Msgr. Walter Kampe, Auxiliary Bishop of Limburg, who was in charge of the German news center, was also present. The visit to Morcillo had produced good results, but Vallainc had been offended. Kampe agreed to try to smooth relations by inviting him to meetings of the groups of journalists. Also present at this meeting was Father Ralph Wiltgen, S.V.D., whose presence meant that all the centers for conciliar documentation operating in Rome were now part of the group: the Dutch, Spanish, Italian, German, Argentine, North Amer-

---

[158] Official communiqué of the fourth general congregation, October 22, 1962.
[159] *DTucci*, November 12, 1962.
[160] Ibid., October 30, 1962.

226   CHAPTER IV

ican, and Divine Word. They were also in contact with the Secretariat of
the African episcopate by way of Dutch Msgr. Joseph Blomjous, Bishop
Emeritus of Mwanza (Victoria-Southern Nyanza). Kampe told Tucci
that one of the reasons for the difficulty with news was that in those days
nothing interesting was going on at the Council because of the many
repetitive interventions.

On the day after the meeting at the Spanish center, as Tucci was leaving the Vatican hall on his way to the Press Office, Vallainc asked to
speak with him, in order to complain about the memorandum submitted
to the Council of Presidents. Morcillo had evidently spoken of it as
though it were Tucci's personal work. The latter denied authorship,
telling Vallainc that the memorandum was the work of the entire group,
that he himself had not even seen it in advance, although he did himself
agree with it. He wrote in his notes: "Unfortunately, Vallainc is hyper-
sensitive and too 'Roman' to hold the post he has. And all he does is
criticize the pack of journalists! How can he possibly understand
them?"[161] On November 12 there was another meeting of the religious
journalists, which Vallainc, although invited, did not attend. Kampe,
who was in Germany, was represented by Heinrich Tenhumberg, Auxiliary Bishop of Münster, who told them that he was trying to organize a
concerted action of the presidents or secretaries of the various episcopal
conferences to obtain a better standing for the journalists from the Council of Presidents or, perhaps better, from the Secretariat for Extraordinary Affairs.[162]

The matter was not settled. On November 13 Vallainc telephoned
Tucci to complain of the criticisms of "one-sidedness" in favor of the
conservative tendency that had been leveled at his most recent bulletins
and also of the "closed-ranks opposition" he was meeting from his
seven direct collaborators (those in charge of the various language sections). He asked Tucci to help him on the following day to deal with the
points made by both groups as he composed his bulletin. Tucci declined
the invitation, saying that he lacked a journalist's ability to sum up
essentials in a short space ("and unfortunately," Tucci wrote in his
diary, "neither does Msgr. Vallainc have it, and perhaps doesn't know
it!"); what Vallainc has to do is "to win back the trust of his collaborators by obtaining permission for them to take turns in the hall in order to
check his impressions. Why not compose the bulletin collegially? A

[161] Ibid., November 6, 1962.
[162] Ibid., November 12, 1962.

good man, but completely out of place, unfortunately for him and, above all, for the journalists and, in the final analysis, for the Church itself."[163]

On the following day, in response to the proposal of Morcillo and Kampe, the Council of Presidents decided to allow those in charge of the language sections of the Press Office to be present at each general congregation, two at a time. Vallainc criticized this move at length to Tucci, for he was irritated by what he interpreted as a maneuver by his collaborators and as inconsiderateness on Felici's part for not telling him of it immediately.[164] Tucci suggested that he ask Felici and Morcillo that the texts of interventions be allowed to be seen the day before each general congregation (the speakers had to deposit these texts ahead of time with the Secretariat). As a result, Tucci was able to write on November 16: "At last, an 'objective' bulletin!"

But after a few days of bulletins less one-sided than the earlier ones, the conservatives became angry, and it appears that the Holy Office threatened to close the Press Office "for having violated the secrecy of the Council and thereby having broken the rules of the Council."[165] Emilio Guano, Bishop of Livorno, who confirmed this item of news, was indignant and said that "the Press Office is dependent on the Council, and the Holy Office has no authority to supervise the Council and the observance of the regulations for the Council."[166] On December 6 Vallainc attended a meeting of all the national centers of conciliar documentation. Tucci presided and later wrote in his diary: "Thank God! The most complete harmony and understanding on both sides!"[167]

Halfway between the official Press Office and the journalists or private press services came the centers for documentation and information of the various episcopates and religious congregations.[168] When the sessions began, two were already in operation: DO-C, the Center for Documentation of the Catholic Church in the Netherlands, which became international in 1963 and specialized in the compiling of excellent

---

[163] Ibid., November 13, 1962.

[164] Ibid., November 14, 1962.

[165] Confidential remark of Cipriano Calderón to Jesús Iribarren, who told Tucci of it (*DTucci*, November 23, 1962).

[166] Ibid., November 24, 1962.

[167] Ibid., December 6, 1962.

[168] I base my presentation of the national centers on the competent study of J. Grootaers, who was not only a journalist at the Council but also coordinator of the newspaper people ("L'information religieuse," in *Vatican II commence*, 211-334). At the end of this essay he publishes a list of the thirteen functioning centers, with their editors and others in charge.

monograph dossiers; and the CCC, the Information Center of the Canadian episcopate.

Given the regime of secrecy that reigned almost throughout the first session, the correspondents of the various journals became open competitors for news, while some accused others of taking less than serious approaches. "This deviation began in the Roman press: sensational titles, prolix and very vague commentaries, which also followed the most diverse lines," a French columnist wrote when the Council had barely begun.[169] Four days later he added: "The problem of secrecy in the Council keeps cropping up. The Italian press light-heartedly fails to respect it and has already published the essential content of the liturgy draft."[170] Commenting on this French charge, Caprile wrote: "We also regret the attitude of a sector of our press, but we would not want it to be held solely responsible."[171]

When Martín Descalzo, the most outstanding of the Spanish reporters, took inventory of the attitude of the international press toward the conciliar event, his view was that the various national groups had succumbed to their own peculiar temptations. While acknowledging the danger that his generalizations might be caricatures, he ventured to state five temptations. In his view the great weeklies had succumbed to the temptation of "externalism." The photogenic character of the opening spectacle enabled *Life, Paris Match, Epoca, Il Tempo, L'Europeo, Oggi,* and *Gaceta ilustrada* to print magnificent pages in wonderful colors.

> What a splendid impression of grandeur and magnificence! But what did it convey of the *religious event*, of the *problems* faced by the Council? Did it not give the impression of a triumphal Church rather than a Church humbly trying to reform itself? Did not these publications give an impression of the *triumphalism* which the separated brethren so often ascribed to us? Almost without exception these publications ignored the address of John XXIII, which was of infinitely greater historic importance than the best photographs, and most of them took much greater care with their photographs than with the written commentaries that accompanied them, or should have accompanied them, since many publications limited themselves to large photographs and brief captions.

The Italian dailies, for their part, were tempted to "politicization." Their task was doubly difficult for two reasons: (1) "the hyper-political atmosphere of Italy which causes everything to be seen in function of

---

[169] *La Croix,* October 16, 1962.
[170] Ibid., October 20, 1962.
[171] Caprile, II, 61.

politics, especially Church-matters, which Italians usually confuse with affairs of their country;" and (2) "the tendency of *Vaticanists* to see Church-affairs from the viewpoint of palace intrigues."[172] Martín Descalzo illustrates this judgment with a selection of headlines in papers dealing with the opening session. The fascist journal *Il Secolo* had emphasized the point that the Council "will demonstrate to the world the permanent validity of the teaching of its creator and redeemer." (The Spanish priest-journalist comments: "Note the typical rhetoric of all fascisms and its tendency to speak in grandiloquent sentences") and that "the Council has prayed for the Church of silence." The "philo-liberal" *Il Tempo* "did not allow its attitude to be seen so clearly in its headlines. Its anticommunism was more hidden, but it did appear." Four centrist journals (*Il Messagero, Corriere della Sera, La Stampa,* and *L'Avvenire d'Ialia*) "were in agreement in their eight-column leaders, all of them emphasizing a positive and confident outlook on the future and a faith and hope in our world."[173] Three leftist dailies (*Paese Sera, Il Paese,* and *Avanti*) laid stress on the optimistic and progressivist tone of the centrist journals. "The entire concern of the leftist Italian press during the Council will be to show that something is changing in the Church, which in its view means abandoning its old positions."

The peculiar temptation of the French press, says Martín Descalzo, was the temptation to "indiscretion," that is, to use "leaks." He acknowledges the quality of French reporting on Vatican II and the fact that France, along with the Netherlands, was the country that best succeeded in awakening interest in the Council among Christians. A month before the Council began, *La Croix* launched a campaign to win new subscriptions for the three months of the first session; the result was 53,400 new subscriptions for the main edition and 17,000 more for *La Croix du nord*, so that within a month it was printing 60 percent more copies. During the early conciliar congregations, *La Croix*, like the rest of the press, had to rely on the unsubstantial official bulletins, but starting with the seventh congregation it began to publish reports containing names and the particular content of the interventions of the fathers, "to

---

[172] Another major reporter of Vatican II, Robert Rouquette, S.J., agrees with this judgment: "One of the weaknesses of the Italians is that they are always looking for a political purpose behind religious acts" (*El Concilio Vaticano II*, in Fliche-Martin, *Historia de la Iglesia* 27 [Valencia: Edicep, 1978], 153). But it is possible to ask whether the temptation, which is not exclusively an Italian one, is not so much to *see* a political meaning in religious acts as to *read one into it*.

[173] In this emphasis on hopefulness, which was fully conciliar, the commentaries of Raniero La Valle in *L'Avvenire d'Italia* were outstanding.

such an extent that one could be sure either that its reporter was regularly in the council hall or that one of the French experts had been expressly commissioned by the French hierarchy to report to this journal." Martín Descalzo asks: "Was *La Croix* an indiscreet journal? All the uncompromising defenders of conciliar secrecy thought so, since, in light of *La Croix*'s information, secrecy had utterly disappeared." But he concludes:

> If I myself had to pass judgment on the facts and their results, I would completely absolve *La Croix* of this "sin," which was so immensely useful to bishops and journalists during the months in Rome and of decisive usefulness to all who are today writing the history of the first session of the Council. I would give a different answer if I were asked about the disadvantage which this dispensing of information to only one journalist caused to other French and to foreign reporters, simply because they committed the offense of writing in neutral journals or in the Catholic journals of hierarchies which took a different attitude toward secrecy. Every monopoly is unjust, and so is a monopoly on news when the exclusivity does not result from the skill or efforts of the reporter but from a privileged situation in which he is placed by circumstances or prejudice. And that is how *La Croix* became a small island in the invigorating world of companionship and mutual help that was established among the majority of journalists at the Council.

Very different was the attitude toward news of *Le Monde* journalist Henri Fesquet.

> His articles were undoubtedly the most sought after on the Roman newspaper stands; they went from hand to hand not only in the press room but in the council hall. . . . Fesquet's reports, which were lively, alert, penetrating, meaningful, came to be much more a means of exerting pressure than a news medium, so much so that one must ask whether, without realizing it, Fesquet was writing with an eye more on the life of the Council in Rome than on his Parisian readers. He gave his own views more than he conveyed information; he offered almost as many rumors as he did facts; his reports were more clever and purposeful than they were concrete; and he showed a much greater interest in what was happening outside the hall, in the corridors, than in what was happening in the sessions.

In contrast to the French press, the temptation to which the Spanish press had succumbed, in Martín Descalzo's view, was a "mediocrity" that was not able to retain the interest of the average Spanish reader. The causes of this failure as a news medium were the idea which the Spanish episcopate (unlike the French) had of secrecy; the shortage of special and skilled representatives; the tendency "to rehash the hardly informative official communiqués, the non-risky . . . and unjournalistic outlook, and the view that quantity rather than quality of information gives a newspaper the reputation of being 'a good Catholic' journal. In short, sins of omission rather than commission."

But Martín Descalzo's description needs to be nuanced by taking into account the political situation in Spain, with its dictatorial regime based on Catholic confessionalism and an alliance with the Church, a regime for which the winds blowing at the Council would help destroy. As a result, while the Spanish masses, lulled by the official propaganda, did not follow the conciliar debates in any depth, the sectors of the Spanish Church that were bent on renewal, as well as the political dissenters and the nationalistic irredentists, were passionately interested in Vatican II. This was true especially in the Basque country (Martín Descalzo was a reporter for *La Gacete del Norte* of Bilbao, which had a spectacular increase in subscribers, similar to that of *La Croix*) and in Catalonia.[174]

Finally, Martín Descalzo analyzes a few Russian journals, among which he inserts *L'Unità*, the Italian communist daily, which he thinks succumbed to the temptation of "incomprehension." They one-sidedly stressed the changes the Council represented, supported the view that the time of excommunications had passed, and contrasted the trends among Central European Catholics, with which they were in sympathy, with the Italian episcopate, which they accused of being boorish and ignorant.[175]

Wiltgen, whose account, *The Rhine Flows into the Tiber*, I have so often cited, skillfully found a way of extracting information from the bishops without their being accused of violating secrecy. Curtis Pepper, chief of the Rome bureau of *Newsweek*, recalled his experience of the World Council of Churches' meeting in New Delhi and told Wiltgen: "Nothing can substitute for interviews with important people." Robert Kaiser, the representative of another great American weekly, *Time*, said something similar to him: "What the press needs is access to bishops and theologians who have the freedom to speak frankly about something which is a human event involving intelligent men in dialogue." Many bishops avoided the press not only because of the secrecy imposed on them but out of fear that their words would not be faithfully reproduced. To protect secrecy, Wiltgen did not ask them what they had said in the hall but instead asked them to explain the needs and wishes of their dio-

---

[174] More details in H. Raguer, "L'Espanya de Franco i el Concili Vaticà II," in *Miscellània d'homenatge a Josep Benet* (Barcelona, 1991), 630-50; idem, "Bonzos incordiantes: Les católicos catalanes y el Concilio Vaticano II," *XX Siglos* 4 (1993), 88-97.

[175] Martín Descalzo, *Prensa y Concilio*, chap. 4: "La prensa mundial y sus 'cinco tentaciones' durante la primera sesión" (65-82).

ceses in relation to the subject being discussed at the moment. To overcome their fear of seeing their statements twisted, he composed his text
after the interview and submitted it to them for their comments.[176]

V. INTERACTION WITH THE PEOPLE OF GOD

I spoke in the previous section of the impact which Vatican II had on
the press and other communications media. However, the converse also
took place; that is, the communications media influenced the Council
fathers. When newspapers give time and space to a subject, it is because
they know what people consider important. John XXIII succeeded in
making "his" Council meaningful to the faithful and, in a way, to "all
men of good will." In addition to what the newspapers reported, many
bishops, especially the French and the Italians, published letters or
reports on the Council in their diocesan bulletins or religious weeklies,
thus following the example of the Pope, who took every available opportunity to speak of the Council and to ask prayers for its success. This
was what Martín Descalzo called "journalism clad in purple." Especially important were the *Lettere dal Concilio* which Montini published
in *L'Italia*.

In turn, it was the commentaries in the press and the lively response
of the public that finally convinced the bishops of the importance of the
Council. In addition, the bishops read the reports in the journals, which
helped more than one of them understand what was going on in the hall.
Not all of the bishops had a complete command of the Latin tongue, still
less of the way in which it was pronounced, and perhaps they had as little grasp of the depth of the problems being discussed.

[176] Wiltgen, *Rhine*, 33-34.

CHAPTER V

THE FIRST DOCTRINAL CLASH

GIUSEPPE RUGGIERI

I. A SCHEMA UNDER FIRE

With its vote of November 14, by which it overwhelmingly approved in principle the schema on liturgical reform, the Council ended its first month of work. It was a kind of honeymoon that had gone relatively smoothly and ended with a much larger consensus on the schema than anyone could have foreseen, especially since the course of the debate had given the impression that supporters and opponents of the text were evenly balanced.

Now, however, the Council faced a strictly dogmatic topic and one that was the subject of a still unsettled debate in Catholic theology: the relationship between oral revelation (the preaching of Christ) and its subsequent transmission (tradition), on the one hand, and, on the other, the New Testament; it also involved the very role of the ecclesiastical magisterium.

The common judgment is no exaggeration: the period from November 14 to December 8, and especially the week of November 14-21, which was devoted to discussion of the schema on the sources of revelation, represented a turning point that was decisive for the future of the Council and therefore for the future of the Catholic Church itself: the turn from the Church of Pius XII, which was still essentially hostile to modernity and in this respect the heir to the nineteenth-century restoration, to a Church that is a friend to all human beings, even children of modern society, its culture, and its history. This period proved decisive for the future of the Council, not because the Council fathers already knew all the decisions they would make later, but because in it the Council took possession of itself, its nature, and its purpose and attuned itself to the intentions of John XXIII, an attunement that had largely been impeded by the work of the preparatory commissions, especially the Theological Commission. The turn was no sudden flowering, but something that had been long desired and awaited during the decades after World War I and especially since things had begun to open with Pope John's announcement of the Council.

Even before November 14, when the discussion of the schema on the sources of revelation began, there had been considerable, even if inchoative, signs of the development that would lead to the turnaround. Three important episodes had already started the process by which the Council took possession of itself: the initial message to the world; the procedure adopted for the elections of the commissions, which dismantled the Curia's strategy for those elections; and, above all, the debate on the liturgical constitution.

I include this last not only because on seemingly more untroubled ground it revealed a pastoral and innovative orientation based on advances in scholarship and on the growth of the liturgical movement during the first half of the century, but also because it provided time and permitted the expansion of exchanges of which the preceding chapter has spoken. At the same time that discussion was in danger of wearing people down. Everyone knew that the clash had only been postponed. Many bishops whose conciliar expectations focused chiefly on ecclesiological themes were champing at the bit. Others were plagued by doubts. Two days before the debate on the first dogmatic constitution, Karl Rahner expressed sentiments that reflect the atmosphere of doubt and tension that marked the lengthy wait for the debate on doctrine that had begun with the sending of the preparatory schemas in the summer of 1962 and had grown ever more intense as the debate approached. "So this week the dogmatics is beginning here. I'm eager to see what happens; I don't have great hopes, but we will do what we can."[1]

The positive factors that would combine to make it possible to overcome all the others were essentially two, first, *Gaudet Mater Ecclesia* and, second, a kind of theological consensus, although the latter had not yet become clear before the week of the debate on the sources of revelation. For this consensus to take shape around a few doctrinal ideas and orientations, the bishops had to "go to school." To this end several national episcopal conferences (United States, France, Germany, and others) organized weekly meetings at which a trusted theologian or another bishop brought them up to date on progress in theological studies in the areas and on the topics on the agenda.[2] In forming their con-

---

[1] K. Rahner to H. Vorgrimler, November 12, 1962, in H. Vorgrimler, *Understanding Karl Rahner: An Introduction to His Life and Thought* (New York, 1986), 158-59.

[2] A first, still incomplete list of the lectures given by theologians during these weeks is given in X. Rynne, *Letters from Vatican City. Vatican Council II (First Session): Background and Debates* (New York, 1963), 130-39, 170-73, 185-87, 211-13, 235-39. Congar, Küng, Chenu, and Daniélou were among the most active lecturers. The Latin Amer-

sensus the bishops also took advantage of writings that offered a different approach than the conciliar documents. Before the bishops arrived in Rome, the circulation of these writings had been limited to some especially alert and eager bishops, but now the need critically to evaluate the first of the doctrinal schemas required bishops to look for material that might contrast with the official documents and so enable them better to understand the line taken in them.

The schema on the sources of revelation provided a target for bishops who during the 1940s and 1950s had developed a theological and doctrinal sensibility different from the one that had marked the era of anti-Protestant controversies and the scholastic restoration.[3] The schema was, in fact, a typical product of the scholastic mind. Produced by the sub-commission bearing the same name as the schema (*De fontibus Revelationis*), it reflected the classical positions taken in Catholic controversial literature. A first chapter was devoted to the "twofold source of revelation." The term *source*, which the Council of Trent had applied to the gospel, was here applied instead to the scriptures and to tradition, counterposed as the two originating fountainheads of revelation. In addition, the chapter said that tradition alone is the way in which some revealed truths become clear and are known.

The second chapter took up the problems of the inspiration, inerrancy, and literary composition of the scriptures. The personal, that is, non-collective nature of inspiration was explained, and the inerrancy of every statement in the Bible, whether religious or secular, was asserted. Chapter III, on the Old Testament, emphasized its relation to the New and stated that when the question of biblical authorship touched on the faith, only the Church could give a definitive answer. Chapter IV defended the historical truth of the "deeds" of Jesus narrated in the gospels and the substantial fidelity of the words they attribute to him. Chapter V, "Scripture in the Life of the Church," brought the schema to a close; it defended the Vulgate as an "authentic witness to the faith" and set down criteria for the reading of the scriptures by the faithful and by exegetes, who are obliged to follow "the analogy of the faith, the tradition of the Church, and the norms set forth by the Apostolic See on the subject."

---

icans and North Americans also had "their" theologians (Mejia, Ahern, etc.), while the Asian and African episcopal conferences were more eclectic. Also to be mentioned were the "external" interventions of Bea, which always drew a large audience, and, from the non-Catholic side, the strong impression made by contacts with the two Taizé monks who were present among the observers, Roger Schutz and Max Thurian.

[3] See *History*, I, 272-83.

The schema had been sent out to the bishops in the summer. A large number of theological evaluations of it soon appeared, which were distributed for the use of the bishops during the weeks preceding November 14. These critiques (*animadversiones*) enabled the bishops to move toward the new consensus on doctrinal matters that was to characterize Vatican II. But it must be emphasized once again that all this was possible only because *Gaudet Mater Ecclesia*, with the full authority of John XXIII's teaching office behind it, served as a catalyst for the theological ferment these critiques made available to all.

While French-speaking theologians (G. Martelet, Ch. Moeller, and others[4]) were among those most active, it is undeniable that the authority of Schillebeeckx and Rahner, along with the circulation of their texts (nearly universal for the first and quite extensive for the second), gave their critiques a very special weight.[5] Both men provided the bishops not only general reasons but also an abundance of data from advances in exegetical and theological studies.

Schillebeeckx, for example, in discussing the chapter on inspiration, emphasized the point that the schema, while correct in saying that inspiration in the narrow sense is a special and personal charism of the sacred writer, ignored the fact that the entire history of salvation, in both the Jewish people and the early Church, unfolded under divine influence and could therefore be said to be inspired, in a broad sense of the term. He went on to argue that the schema exaggerated in its criticism of the "history of forms" (*Formgeschichte*) method. If it is right to warn that the New Testament cannot be reduced to a simple expression of the faith of the original community, without connection with the historical Jesus, one cannot ignore that the original community interpreted the historical facts with the help of the Old Testament. Again, what was said about the authenticity of the Vulgate and Septuagint translations needed to be bal-

---

[4] See G. Martelet, *Rémarques sur la première série de schémas*, 56 pages (Léger Archive, 610); Ch. Moeller, *Animadversiones in schemata voluminis I*, 13 pp. (Léger Archive, 614). The same archive also contains a series of opinions on the schemas under the names of other French-speaking bishops (Maurice Baudoux of Canada, Jean Julien Weber of France, etc.), behind whom one may presume there were some trusted theologians. The presence in a single archive of a large number of such opinions shows that they were exchanged by various bishops or at least by the more diligent and authoritative among them.

[5] The text of Rahner referred to here is the *Disquisitio*, or set of *gravamina* (as Vorgrimler called them; see above, chapter 2), and not the alternative schema prepared by Rahner and Ratzinger. While the latter was intended to show how it was possible to think in a way different from that of traditional theology, the *gravamina* showed the internal weakness of the preparatory schema and perhaps played an even more decisive role.

anced by an assertion of the peculiar importance of the original Greek and Hebrew texts.[6] When the tumultuous first meeting of the Theological Commission was held on November 13, Schillebeeckx's text was on the table of the chair, Cardinal Ottaviani, as one count in his indictment.[7]

In addition to the observations mentioned above, Rahner effectively explained the difference between the conciliar magisterium and the ordinary magisterium of the Church. When a council issues a dogmatic decree, it does not issue a changeable law, but "is regarded by such a decree to be proclaiming the truth of Christ that remains forever." In addition, a council should consider not only whether, in the abstract, a doctrine is definable, but also whether a definition is opportune. Not content with this classic argument, Rahner also tried to link his thoughts with the spirit of the Pope's statements, especially in *Gaudet Mater Ecclesia*. He added that this second consideration, opportuneness, which the Church always bears in mind, should apply even more to a Council which the Pope wanted to be "pastoral" and which in the initial message to the world the Council fathers had proclaimed should be comprehensible to the people of our time. Let errors, then, be condemned, but only those that prevail in the hearts and minds of the faithful and not those limited to a few scholars. Questions requiring complicated explanations should be left to the ordinary magisterium and to papal encyclicals. Finally, the claim was invalid that the fathers ought simply to rely on the abilities of the preparatory Theological Commission, particularly since this Commission, unlike the liturgical, had not sought to link the teaching offered in its schema with the "proposals of the bishops and universities" and had thereby roused the suspicion that it was governed by scholastic disputes.[8]

In the general remarks contained in his *Disquisitio*, Rahner complained of four matters. First and foremost, he criticized the excessive length of the schema and its presumption in trying to settle controverted issues. Second, he objected to the lack of any pastoral orientation, a lack

---

[6] There was a difference here in the English and Latin versions of Schillebeeckx's text. The former did not counterpose the Vulgate and the Septuagint to the original texts, but the Vulgate alone to both the original texts and the Septuagint translation.

[7] See no. 4 of the *Relatio Secretarii Commissionis Conciliaris "de doctrina fidei et morum,"* composed by S. Tromp (prot. 15/62:19; ISR); hereafter cited as Tromp, *Relatio*.

[8] Schillebeeckx made the same point. They were calling attention to the different paths taken in the constitution on the liturgy, which reflected the Church's new self-awareness, and in the schemas of the Theological Commission, which had no relation to the Church of their own time.

already clear from the scholastic language used. This did not mean opting instead for the language of "a pious sermon from the pulpit." Between pious language and scholastic language there was a vast field in which there was room for language combining the need of doctrinal accuracy with a pastoral concern attentive to the mentality of contemporaries. To achieve a pastoral dimension it was not enough to cite passages of the scriptures as proof-texts; this reduced the scriptures to the role of supporting doctrine that was already known and certain on some other grounds "instead of being the primary source from which the truth to be stated springs."[9]

Rahner criticized, thirdly, the lack of a true ecumenical spirit. The truth is certainly to be proclaimed without ambiguities or reservations even to the separated brethren, but this should be done in such a way as not to awaken the suspicion that one is casting doubt on their true and authentic beliefs. The criticism applied especially to the whole question of sacred scripture, on which the schema prepared by the Secretariat for Christian Unity was to be preferred.[10] Thus, in speaking of inerrancy and historicity, the preparatory schema said things that only piled up causes of misunderstanding. Furthermore, there should have been a clearer insistence that the scriptures, as the inspired word of God, are the ultimate norm for the Church's magisterium, which, despite its infallibility, is obliged to go back to the preaching of the apostles. While the oral tradition of that preaching is mixed in with human traditions, the scriptures give us only divine tradition.[11] Furthermore, on the relation between scripture and the magisterium, Rahner's critique offered a formula that would later be echoed in the final text: "The infallible magisterium of the Church is not lord over the revealed word of God that is contained in the scriptures, but rather is at its service."[12] Fourth, the schema did not

---

[9] " . . . *tamquam fons, ex quo profluit primo ipsa veritas enuntianda.*" Note the slight slip in calling the scriptures a "source." Obviously, Rahner could have explained the word by saying that he meant a source for our knowledge of the revealed truth and not a source in an absolute sense. But the slip serves to show that the problem was not one of vocabulary as such, but had to do with the substantial weight given in the preparatory schema to "oral" tradition and with the resulting relativization of the normative character of the scriptures.

[10] Rahner was clearly referring to the Secretariat's schema *De verbo Dei* (*On the Word of God*) (see *History*, I, 283-85).

[11] The examples given, however, were not always obvious. Thus, as an example of human tradition mingled with divine tradition, the fact was cited that "for centuries the immediate creation of the human body from inorganic matter could seem to be part of divine tradition." But was not this conviction also based on the scriptures?

[12] See *Dei Verbum* 19: "The magisterium is not above the word of God but serves it."

explain the specific theological qualifications to be assigned to its individual statements but seemed to place everything on the same dogmatic
level.

Rahner's specific remarks dealt with eight points. First, the schema
should have begun with a discussion of revelation in general and not left
this to the schema on the deposit of faith. Second, to speak of two
sources of revelation was not consistent with Trent, which spoke of a
single source. It would be better to speak of the two ways in which revelation is passed on.

Third, Rahner maintained that it would have been more appropriate
to leave open the question, debated among Catholics, of the material
sufficiency of the scriptures. If it was commonly held that such truths as
inspiration and the extent of the biblical canon can be known only
through the authoritative preaching of the Church and through its infallible magisterium, these were in that respect unique cases, while all
other revealed truths have some basis, at least implicitly, in the scriptures. This question has never been decided, not even by Trent. There is
no dogma of the Church that can appeal only to oral apostolic tradition
rather than to written. If there are dogmas that at first sight are not
found in the scriptures, it is no less difficult to prove that they are found
in the tradition of the early centuries. It is easier to accept that oral tradition can render more explicit a truth contained only implicitly in the
scriptures. It would be better, then, not to go into this controverted
question.

Fourth, as for the nature of inspiration, Rahner's critique made essentially the same point as Schillebeeckx and explained that no "prudent
theologian" (*inter cordatos theologos*) had ever doubted inspiration to
be a personal charism of the sacred writer, but that it was also true that
the sacred writer was a member of the Church and in the service of the
believing people. Only if this fact is kept in mind does the connection
between inspiration and the history of salvation appear.

Also inadequate was the schema's section on inerrancy. It did not take
enough account of what Pius XII's encyclical *Divino Afflante Spiritu*
had said about the importance of literary genres. Now these literary genres are not easily identified, and modern exegesis had made great
progress in this area. As for the absolute inerrancy of the scripture in
secular matters, it would be better for the Council to stick to the status
quo, that is, the ordinary teaching of the Church, and not define anything
or give a higher theological qualification to the statements made in that
teaching. A great deal still remained to be clarified in the debate among

the exegetes. The very word *error* used in the schema did not, in fact, have an obvious sense.[13]

Sixth, the schema was not sufficiently cautious on the historicity of the scriptures. It seemed, in fact, to presuppose a univocal conception of history. But the historicity of the synoptics was not the same as that of the fourth gospel, and the "historical" literary genre of the stories of Jesus' infancy is not the same as that of the narratives of his death and resurrection. Furthermore, the purely negative, condemnatory language of nos. 21 and 22 of the schema[14] was inconsistent with the opening allocution of John XXIII and with what he said there about the medicine of mercy being preferable to the weapons of severity.

Seventh, the schema also seemed to introduce a break in the history of salvation, in the period between the sin of Adam and the Old Testament dispensation. God had not ceased to work the salvation of human beings even before "our fathers" had received the "prophetic oracles" of redemption. The eighth and last remark suggested that Chapter V, on the scriptures in the Church, be replaced by what was taught in the schema *De verbo Dei,* prepared by the Secretariat for Christian Unity.

Rahner's critique, unlike that of Schillebeeckx, expressly urged the Council fathers to set the schema aside ("if the fathers judge that the subject can be simply omitted") or to replace it. It is difficult to know which of these two critiques had more impact. In any case, the observations of both men provided precise and specific tools for those who were dissatisfied with the preparatory schema, and nearly all of the arguments found in their texts would be used during the discussion in the hall.

The critical arguments of Schillebeeckx and Rahner were confirmed by many of the theologians who during those days were setting the tone of the many meetings which the bishops held for their own updating. They were also in harmony with the line being taken by the Secretariat for Christian Unity. Back in the preparatory period the Secretariat had

---

[13] Rahner's critique limited itself to one example among many: according to Mk 2:26, the High Priest at the time when David ate the loaves of the Presence was Abiathar. But this is not consistent with 1 Sam 21, which says that the high priest was Ahimelech. It is not an accident that Matthew and Luke omit the name given in Mk 2:26. Is Mark in error? Exegetes are inclined to regard this *obiter dictum* as an error. If one adopts a different perspective and wants to avoid such a judgment, it is not enough to say, as the text of the schema does, that what the sacred writer seems to say in Mk 2:26 does not belong to those things "which he really meant as he wrote." In this case, what meaning does the word *error* have?

[14] "This sacred Vatican Synod condemns those errors that deny or reduce, in whatever way and for whatever reason, the genuine historical and objective truth of the facts about the Lord's life. . . . It condemns the errors that say . . . "

already approved the report of subcommission XIII, "On Tradition and Scripture,"[15] whose final *votum* was summed up in eight points and then sent on to the Theological Commission — too late, however, to be taken into consideration.[16] This *votum* was a summation of a theological consciousness that had left behind the climate of controversy and would in its substance be ratified by the Constitution *Dei Verbum*.

On November 9 and 16, 1962, the Secretariat met at the Hotel Columbus to organize its work for the upcoming debate.[17] The interventions of Bea and J. Feiner deserve special mention. At the first meeting Bea skillfully planned the strategy of the Secretariat. The schema offered by the Doctrinal Commission was not in harmony with the papal allocution of October 11 and did not square with the present-day position of the problem. Fearing a fight to the finish, Bea proposed the formation of various subcommissions to study each chapter of the schema and to be represented at the general congregations by a relator who would speak in the name of the Secretariat.

Among other speakers at the November 9 meeting was J. Feiner, who had been the relator for the document on Scripture and Tradition presented to the Theological Commission. He confirmed the principal intention of that document by appealing especially to the fifth point of the *votum*, which defended the legitimacy of the theo-

---

[15] The members of the subcommission were M. Bévenot, Ch. Boyer, J. Feiner, E. Stakemeier, and G. H. Tavard.

[16] In this *votum* the subcommission asked that the Council make clear: (1) that common and public revelation ended with the end of the apostolic age and that dogmas simply make explicit the truths contained in that revelation; (2) that Christ's revelation to the apostles is to be regarded as the sole source of the truth in which the Church believes and that scripture and tradition are simply two ways by which the Spirit communicates that revelation; (3) that Scripture and tradition are not two parallel ways, but are very closely united and permeate each other; (4) that the scriptures have a unique and irreplaceable function in the Church and that the Church depends on the word of God set down in the scriptures; (5) that expressions be avoided that would exclude the view of those who maintain that, except for the quite unique question of the canon, all revealed truths that are explicitly preserved in tradition are at the same time in some way contained or hinted at in the scriptures; (6) that the agent of active tradition is not only the magisterium but the entire people of God, who are animated and guided by the Holy Spirit, even though in submission to the magisterium; (7) that tradition is to be understood not as a mechanical transmission of truths known distinctly from the beginning, but as a living and life-giving process activated by the Holy Spirit, who gradually renders explicit the fullness of the truth revealed by Christ; (8) that the magisterium, even though infallible, does not replace the word of God, but is an authority which, with the assistance of the Spirit, safeguards and interprets the written and transmitted word of God and is subordinate to and in the service of the word of God that is to be preached and believed (see *History*, I, 276-77).

[17] See the minutes of the two meetings, Thils Papers, Archives LG, 0687 and 0689.

logical position, already present in the Church Fathers and fully developed in the modern period by M. J. Scheeben and many others, which claimed that all revealed truths, except for the canon, are somehow contained in the scriptures. This position was all the more legitimate and important for the ecumenical dialogue inasmuch as, while Protestant theology was abandoning the principle of *sola scriptura* or the formal sufficiency of the scriptures, Catholic theology was bringing out, better than it had in the time of controversy with the Protestants, the dignity and importance of the scriptures for the entire life of the Church.[18]

But Feiner's talk went beyond this reminder and expressed the desire of the Secretariat for Christian Unity, at this point in the Council's journey, to provide a point of doctrinal balance around which the theology of Vatican II could and should take form. In fact, Feiner used the several points of the *votum* as criteria for a detailed evaluation of the whole schema on the two sources of revelation presented by the Theological Commission. The first point of the Secretariat's *votum* (the completion of public revelation at the end of the apostolic age) was indeed adequately made in the schema, but Feiner complained of the absence of a discussion of revelation in general, without which almost any further statement would not make sense.

The second point (on revelation as the sole source of the truth known through scripture and tradition) was formally denied in the schema, which departed from the language of Trent and went along instead with the two-source theory of the post-Tridentine controversialists, a theory which not even Vatican I had accepted. As a result, as several Protestant observers had remarked, a new obstacle was being placed in the way of the ecumenical dialogue.

The schema was also weak on the third point (the connection between scripture and tradition). In fact, apart from a general assertion of this connection, to the effect that scripture cannot be understood apart from tradition, "it does not say scripture is nothing else than the original tradition of the early Church in written form and it says nothing about the continuing influence which scripture (as norming or primary norm [*norma normans*]) has exercised down the centuries on tradition and the entire life of the Church." For this latter reason, the schema was also lacking on the fourth point, the unique role of the scriptures in the faith and life of the Church.

---

[18] Copy of Feiner's report in Stransky Archive, 5.

On the fifth point, which Feiner regarded as central, not only does the schema speak several times of two sources of revelation, but it also explicitly states that tradition is the only way by which the Church comes to know certain truths (and not only the truths of inspiration, the canon, and the integrity of the scriptures). Then, too, nowhere does the schema say that the people of God in its entirety is the subject of active tradition (the sixth point). As for the seventh point in the *votum* (tradition as a living process of progressive understanding of revealed truth), although it was addressed in the schema on the deposit of faith, it was completely missing from the schema on the sources of revelation. Finally, the eighth point, on the sovereignty of the word over the magisterium itself, was also completely ignored.

Feiner's report was a genuine and open declaration of war. It did not originate in a group of theologians, nor did it express the views of only a few national episcopates or a cohesive sector of these; it expressed the attitude of the Secretariat, which at that very moment the Pope was declaring to be a conciliar commission of equal rank with the others. This recognition, combined with the principal argument in the Secretariat's strategy as formulated by Bea, namely, that the schema betrayed the Pope's intention that the Council have a pastoral character, provided a very strong institutional point of reference for all who were dissatisfied with the preparation for the Council. The result gave Bea enormous bargaining power, which he would use very shrewdly, as became clear in the final days of November during the work of the mixed commission that was called upon to rewrite the schema after the Pope's decisive intervention set it aside. Critical opinions of the preparatory schemas from Central European theological circles thus not only had the backing of the respective episcopates, but also squared with the attitude of an authoritative conciliar organization, the Secretariat, which was in a position to create and hold together a broad consensus.

Opposition to the critiques, of course, was not lacking. The Italian Episcopal Conference, for example, had its own experts prepare a short document containing *Animadversiones in schema de fontibus revelationis*, in which the preparatory schema was enthusiastically approved.[19]

---

[19] There is some information on these experts in a note dated October 22, *DSiri,* 367: "At 4:00 P.M. I summoned to the office of the Italian Episcopal Conference Msgr. Vagnozzi and the small group of collaborating theologians, Msgr. Fares and Msgr. Calabria. Msgr. Peruzzo also arrived, and I had him come in. The character of the group was set; it is a simple consultative tool of the presidency in preparing for the work in the office of the CEI and it remains *confidential*. Relations are being established with the

Some emendations were proposed that were compatible with what the document already said: the insertion of a prologue (the content of which was not described, except that it was to be "an introduction to so important a teaching"); the expansion of the section on tradition (to explain all its aspects; to reject the modernist view of the value and nature of tradition; to explain the role of tradition in safeguarding and effectively defending revelation; and to define more clearly the relation between revelation and dogma, between tradition itself and the Church's magisterium, both ordinary and extraordinary, by explaining more precisely the value of the documents of the tradition).[20]

The experts of the Italian Episcopal Conference also advocated a choice between the two perspectives that divided the field. On the one hand, there were those who simply stressed the idea of updating and therefore wanted the schema to offer only the common teaching of the Church in a form adapted to our time. But, on the other hand, there were those (and the Italian experts clearly agreed with them) who wanted to give even greater dogmatic force to the entire constitution, so that the Council might proceed "in a definitive way" against creeping errors. The experts, then, were supporting the preparatory schema in a way that tended to make it even more inflexible.[21]

American group, which is disposed to work for the success of the Council. These relations are at the level of mere friendly conversations. Any possible press releases of ours will be sent to them." The reference, then, is not to real "experts," theologians who were working with the Italian Episcopal Conference, but to a small group of bishops on familiar terms with Siri, who wanted to get in touch with a "group" of United States bishops of a similar mentality, through Msgr. Vagnozzi, Apostolic Delegate to the United States.

[20] Florit Archive, 335. In his note for November 12, Siri wrote in his diary: "In the office I complete the notes drawn up by the theological experts on the schema *De fontibus revelationis*. In fact, it seems to me that in the thirteenth point of Chapter I there are two major ambiguities. In this form the notes can go out and make their way tomorrow" (*DSiri*, 380). The view of the "experts," then, was also that of Siri, and it is obviously impossible to distinguish the various hands. We also learn that the document was distributed to the Italian bishops on November 13, the day of the meeting of the Italian episcopate to discuss the schema on the sources of revelation.

[21] Among the detailed suggestions the following also seem worthy of note: that episcopal succession to the apostles be traced back to the will of Christ himself; that the definition of biblical inspiration given in Leo XIII's *Providentissimus Deus* be repeated; that the statement about the extent of inspiration be strengthened — it was not enough to say, as the preparatory schema did, that "everything that the sacred writer expresses," but that "whatever the sacred writer expresses, asserts, insinuates, must be regarded as expressed (*enuntiatum*), asserted, expressed [*sic!* perhaps they meant "insinuated," *insinuatum*] by the Holy Spirit;" that human hermeneutical tools be clearly subordinated to those given by the Redeemer himself; that the historical character of the Old Testament be more explicitly reaffirmed; that there be greater emphasis on the vigilance of the Church over the reading of the scriptures.

Unlike the critical documents of Schillebeeckx and Rahner and unlike the position of the Secretariat for Christian Unity, the views of the Italian Episcopal Conference and those of other circles, whatever their character, do not seem to have found much echo or to have been circulated beyond the boundaries within which they were born. There were, then, two clear and contrary positions that as it were drowned out all other signals: on the one side, the preparatory schema itself and, on the other, the position taken by the Central European episcopates and the Secretariat. Others were left only with a choice. Mediating positions, which had surfaced in some circles within the French episcopate, would find no room in the conciliar debate that was to begin on November 14.

II. THE EVE OF THE BATTLE

"Tomorrow the discussion of the schema *De fontibus Revelationis* begins. The battles will be bitter,"[22] the gentle Father Semmelroth wrote on November 13. He was not the only person aware that day that he had to get ready for a struggle; everyone was more or less aware that the decisive point of the first session had arrived and strategies for interventions had to be outlined. November 13 saw various initiatives undertaken and various meetings held to plan what to do.

The most troubled meeting seems to have been the one held by the Doctrinal Commission at the little palace of Santa Marta, between 3:00 and 5:00 P.M., the very first meeting of this Commission. Even the phlegmatic report of Tromp, the secretary, had to say that the discussion was "confused and not without acrimony."[23] After a short introduction by the president, Cardinal Ottaviani, who told the group that he had chosen Cardinal Browne as vice-president, Tromp reported on the observations of the 160 bishops who had sent comments on the preparatory schemas. He did not hesitate to criticize them "in accord with the thought of the former Theological Commission,"[24] a remark that anticipated the introductory reports to be given the next day by Ottaviani and Msgr. Garofalo.

---

[22] *TSemmelroth*, note on November 13. Levillain thinks it an exaggeration to speak of an "eve of battle" (*La mécanique polique de Vatican II: La majorité et l'unanimité dans un Concile* [Paris, 1975], 246). But for November 13 he seems to know only of the meeting of the national episcopates, of which I shall speak below.

[23] Tromp, *Relatio*, no. 5.

[24] Ibid.

After Tromp, Msgr. Parente spoke.[25] He said that two schemas were
making the rounds: one composed by the Germans (he was referring to
the alternative schema of Rahner and Ratzinger) and circulated by the
episcopal conferences of Central Europe, and another document that
criticized the *De fontibus* and the *De deposito*.[26] According to Tromp's
report, the discussion then turned in a disorganized way around three
different topics: the right to propose new schemas; the freedom to speak
in the Council; the relationship between the Doctrinal Commission
elected by the Council and the preparatory Theological Commission.
Ottaviani maintained that the new Commission had a duty to defend the
old Commission's schema in the Council. But, besides this very serious
claim, which, if followed, would have blocked all interventions in the
hall by members of the Commission, the tone (Tromp's included) was
especially peremptory: "They talk of 'modern man': he does not exist!
They want to be 'pastoral.' But the first pastoral duty is teaching. After-
wards let the parish priests do the adapting. They talk of 'ecumenism.'
There is a great danger of minimalism."[27]

Cardinal Léger threatened to resign from the Commission if being a
member meant not being free to speak in the hall. Garrone intervened to
say that he did not accept the schema and would therefore not have
endorsed the introductory report to be given the next day. Msgr.

[25] H. Schauf's diary, November 15, relying on Tromp's testimony, makes Ottaviani
and Parente jointly responsible for the poor course of the meeting: "The day before yesterday, according to Tromp, the first meeting of the theological commission took place.
. . . He [Tromp] was to report on the schema. But then the cardinal [Ottaviani] decided on
Parente, without Tromp having known anything about it. Parente did so much sniping that
the atmosphere turned icy. . . . 'This is heretical; that is heretical. . . . ' Then Tromp made
his presentation. Afterward, Cardinal Santos congratulated him" (see the excerpts published in H. Schauf, "Auf dem Wege zu der Aussage der dogmatischen Konstitution über
die göttliche Offenbarung "Dei Verbum" N. 9ᵃ '*Quo fit ut ecclesia certitudinem suam de
omnibus revelatis non per solum sacram scripturam hauriat*,'" in *Glaube im Prozess:
Christsein nach dem II. Vatikanum* [Freiburg/Basel/Wien, 1984], 67.

[26] According to what Garrone told Congar (see *JCongar*, November 14), Parente said
that this second document was written in English but had been composed by a Frenchman, because its starting point was facts and not principles. Parente was referring to the
English version of the Schillebeeckx document, although some thought it had been composed by Congar. In his *Relatio*, Tromp wrote that on November 12 "two schemas
reached" the secretariat of the Theological Commission. The first was the one circulated
by the Austrian, Belgian, French, German, and Dutch episcopates (the Rahner-Ratzinger
schema). The second "contained, in Latin, a new redaction of the nine chapters of the
schema *De Ecclesia*, which at that point had not been distributed to the Council fathers,
and seems to have been written at the instigation of some Belgian bishops." The second
was obviously the schema Philips had been preparing. The Schillebeeckx document had
therefore reached Ottaviani and Parente in some other way.

[27] Garrone to Congar, as reported in *JCongar*, November 14.

Peruzzo, Bishop of Agrigento, arose to say that at the Council he some-times had the impression of being in a madhouse and that there is only one thing to do to with crazy people: lock them up.[28]

The discussion ended without a consensus. Even the proposal of Otta-viani, who said that he had been asked by the Secretariat of State to pre-pare a new and abbreviated version of the *De deposito* and suggested that this work be entrusted to a subcommission under the presidency of Browne, was not endorsed by a common decision.[29]

A few hours later, from 6:00 to 8:00 P.M., and a few kilometers away at the Domus Mariae, it was the episcopates of the world that met: the President of CELAM, the two Secretaries of the African epis-copal conferences, representatives of the episcopates of Japan, India, Ceylon, Vietnam, Burma, and the Philippines; from Europe, represen-tatives of the bishops of Germany, France, England, Ireland, Belgium, Spain, and Italy; from North America some representatives of the United States and Canada. Only the continent of Australia was not rep-resented.

This was not an ad hoc meeting, but the second meeting of the repre-sentatives of the episcopal conferences, the leading spirit being Helder Câmara, who spoke of it as a fraternal meeting of the entire world or ecumene.[30] The idea for the meetings had been born on November 4 dur-ing a meeting of R. Etchegaray, Secretary of the French episcopate, Helder Câmara of Brazil, and Larraín of Chile, these last two being Vice-Presidents of CELAM.[31] The purpose was to create an opportunity for communication among some representatives of the episcopal confer-ences, "not too many, but representative of the various conferences, although chosen according to an 'affective geography.'"[32]

At the first meeting, on November 9, representatives of thirteen con-ferences had taken part: one from Canada, five from CELAM, six from Asia, three Europeans (Beck for the Dutch, Höffner for the Germans,

---

[28] The interventions of Garrone, Léger, and Peruzzo are also reported here according to the testimonies of Garrone and McGrath, which Congar collected in his diary for November 14.

[29] See Tromp, *Relatio*, no. 5. The reference was evidently to the proposal, developed in the Secretariat for Extraordinary Affairs, to undertake a drastic reduction in the size of the preparatory documents.

[30] Helder Câmara, circular no. 31, November 13, 1962 (ISR, Câmara papers).

[31] Etchegaray Papers, 1.2; on this group see J. Grootaers, "Une forme de concertation épiscopale au Concile Vatican II: La 'Conférence des Vingt-deux' (1962-1963)," *RHE* 91 (1966), 66-112.

[32] Ibid.

Veuillot for the French), plus Etchegaray himself.[33] On that occasion
they had not only tackled problems of method in the Council's work, in
the hope both of speeding up the interventions and of preserving each
father's freedom to speak, but had also touched on the problem of the *De
fontibus*. Many were dissatisfied with the way in which it had been prepared and with its content, and the desire was expressed that after a general discussion the schema might be rejected.[34]

At the meeting on November 13, after voicing their concerns especially about the document on the Church, still unknown to them, the bishops turned their attention to the work which the Church of the Poor
Group was doing at the Belgian College. They also discussed conciliar
procedures. When they came to the *De fontibus*, "a representative of each
national group was asked to present the views of the various national conferences. Germany, Japan, India and Ceylon, the Philippines, Africa, and
CELAM declared their opposition to it. For many, a key question
remained what means were available for rejecting the schema. France,
while declaring the schema to be fundamentally bad, proposed, through
Veuillot, a two-stage procedure: first a general discussion and then a vote
to show the direction to be taken."[35] "Other episcopates, such as those of
Canada, Mexico, and Burma, were divided on the matter. Their criticisms
of the schema had not reached the point that they were considering the
need to reject it, and they thought that it was possible to revise it by way
of emendations. Italy, for its part, refused to voice an opinion, regarding
this as inopportune and illegitimate and falling back on the view that each
individual should, if necessary, decide in his heart (*in petto*)."[36]

---

[33] It was decided to make Helder Câmara the chairman of these meetings and to use
English and French, with Câmara himself acting as translator (see Câmara, 28th circular
[November 9/10, 1962]).

[34] Etchegaray Papers, 1.3.

[35] See Levillain, *La mécanique politique*, 245, who adds: "This procedure was not
foreseen in the Regulations of the Council and would be introduced only in September,
1963, after it had been acknowledged that there were a number of gaps in the conciliar
Regulations of 1962. As used on November 14 to end the discussion of the schema on the
liturgy, the step of taking a vote on the direction to be followed was at the discretion of
the Council of Presidents. Now, on that same day, during a meeting of the presidents, the
suggestion made by some that an orienting vote be taken at the end of the general interventions in order to decide on the rejection or acceptance of the *De fontibus* met with
implacable opposition from Cardinal Ruffini, which prevented a study of the question."
In the minutes of the Council of Presidents as given in *AS* V/1, there is no trace of this
meeting to which reference is made by Levillain, who does not cite his source. If Ruffini
did voice opposition to a vote of orientation, it would in any case be overcome later, at
the meeting of the Council of Presidents on November 19.

[36] Levillain, *La mécanique politique*, 245-46.

There was a story behind this opinion of the Italians. On that same day the Italian episcopal conference had also met. Siri wrote in his diary: "The Italian episcopate met today. What a rigmarole from Guano!" The strategy that emerged is recorded in Siri's diary, the one expressed in the advice of the Italian theologians: try to make the schema even more inflexible. The views expressed in the German schema were ridiculed, and fears of "new modernists" were expressed. Carli, Bishop of Segni and destined to play an important future role in the Council as spokesman for the conservative wing at the Council, intervened to urge the Italian bishops to vote for the schema presently being discussed, "so as not to leave the Council and the Church in the hands of the Germans."[37] Some, like Urbani, Patriarch of Venice, proposed that Siri be appointed to speak in the name of the Italian episcopate. Guano then stood up and remarked that to proceed in this way required discussion and a vote. Msgr. Carraro, Bishop of Verona, spoke against Guano. However, no formal decision seems to have been made.[38]

The meetings on the eve thus already prefigured the course of the coming debate in the hall: on the one hand, a determination to get the schema De fontibus rejected; on the other, a nervous closing of ranks in its defense.

III. DISCUSSION OF THE SCHEMA ON THE SOURCES OF REVELATION: THE COUNCIL CHOOSES A PASTORAL ORIENTATION TO DOCTRINE

Msgr. Salvatore Garofalo was the official reporter for the "Draft of a Dogmatic Constitution on the Sources of Revelation." But because Ottaviani, President of the preparatory Theological Commission and now of the conciliar Doctrinal Commission, spoke before him and anticipated

[37] DTucci, November 18, 1962.

[38] DTucci, November 24, reporting what Guano had told him. A more detailed source for a reconstruction of this meeting is a note of Dossetti, dated November 15 and found among the letters of Chenu; it seems, however, to go back to the same source, namely, Guano (see NChenu, 111). In his intervention on this subject in the Council hall on November 14, Siri seems to have exaggerated the degree of consensus achieved. The text reporting Siri's oral statement says: "I know that most bishops, at least those of Italy, whom I listened to yesterday, agree with what I have said." His written text says: "I know that most, indeed almost all the bishops of Italy agree with me" (AS I/3, 38-39). Urbani's diary has this comment on the meeting of November 13 (he says nothing about his own intervention): "Afternoon meeting of the Italian episcopate — Lengthy, tiring speech of Ruffini. Lengthy disquisition by Fares. Meeting inconclusive because no dialogue was allowed. And yet so little would be needed!"

what he was to say, there was a certain amount of repetition. Strangely, Ottaviani and Garofalo did not so much present the schema as defend it against anticipated objections; rather than initiating a debate, they were responding to a debate already begun outside the Council hall.[39]

Ottaviani first voiced his disappointment and his criticism of what was brewing in the "external" Council outside the hall; he then took up two objections to the schema and ended with an "appeal to the affections" (*motio affectuum*).[40] The circulating of alternate schemas to replace the official schema Ottaviani thought to be contrary to the prescription in the Code, can. 222 § 3, which reserved to the Pope the decision about material to be discussed at the Council. In addition, he knew "for sure" that the fathers would hear many "speak of the lack of a pastoral tone" in the schema, criticisms already expressed by many in the responses received during the summer.[41] Ottaviani also was aware that a reworking of the schema on the Church was underway.

The objection about pastoral orientation was the real enemy to be overcome. Although he thought the objection without basis, Ottaviani could not say this openly, given the stand taken by the Pope. To his own mind the objection ignored the fact that the foundation of pastoral practice is concise and clear teaching and that the conciliar style had been "stamped by the practice of centuries." Look elsewhere, not to a council, to find the pastoral expression of dogma. Without ever citing it, then, he could not have distanced himself more clearly from the Pope's opening speech. Another objection, which pointed to the lack of any "breath of the new theology," ignored the fact that the "breath" of a council is that of the centuries, and not of one or another theological school, which is here today and tomorrow may be "cast into the oven." His appeal to the affections at the end took the form of asking the fathers to remember that the schema was the product of two years of labor by bishops, theologians, and exegetes from around the world, as well as by the Central Preparatory Commission.[42]

---

[39] Garofalo's rather formal presentation of the text was a bare list of chapters and topics rather than a real explanation; it occupied barely twenty-five lines (see *AS* I/3, 30-31).

[40] *AS* I/3, 27-28.

[41] The written observations on volume I of the schemas, which had been sent out during the summer, are in *AS Appendix* (Vatican City, 1983), 69-350.

[42] The labor was real, but Ottaviani glided over the oppositions that had marked it and over the unscrupulous way in which he and the Theological Commission had dealt with these. The unscrupulousness would be recalled by Cardinal Döpfner (*AS* I/3, 124-25) and by Archbishop Denis Hurley of Durban, who, after Ottaviani's attempt to defend himself (*AS* I/3, 131-32), said: "In the Central Commission, as I now see, when we complained

Garofalo's introductory report was mostly repetitious of Ottaviani's remarks; his brief reference to the specific contents of the schema was hardly more than a table of contents, but he did make a rather disingenuous attempt to describe the text's restrictive statements and condemnations as responses to present-day needs. Thus he made the odd claim that what the schema said about the two sources called attention, first and foremost, to the historical development of the two Testaments, "so that Catholic teaching may be better adapted to the contemporary mentality;" what it said about scriptural inspiration "is in keeping with present-day research," and so on.[43]

As Ottaviani had, Garofalo juxtaposed the pastoral and the doctrinal, although he formulated it in terms of the more classical distinction between doctrine and discipline: "Our constitution is dogmatic, not disciplinary; and even though what is said occasionally reflects the circumstances of the time, it must nonetheless be valid for the ages, since doctrinal statements of councils, even if they may be made more complete, are irreformable."[44] He did attempt, however, to find a point of contact even with *Gaudet Mater Ecclesia*. "Although errors are here and there explicitly mentioned and condemned . . . , this is because they are among the things which, as the Supreme Pontiff said in his opening allocution, 'are so obviously in contrast with the right norm of honesty' and from their effects are easily seen by all to be erroneous."[45] Thus it was possible to reach the astonishing conclusion: "Finally, the constitution is to be described as *pastoral* in character, since the clear statement of doctrine and its safeguarding and defense are very closely connected with the pastoral task and provide any pastoral undertaking with the solid foundation it needs."[46]

---

about the unpastoral character of the schemas, we were voices crying in the wilderness" (*AS* I/3, 199). For documentation of these oppositions see A. Indelicato, *Difendere la dottrina o annunciare l'evangelo. Il dibattito nella commissione centrale preparatoria del Vaticano II* (Genoa, 1992), and *History*, I, 300-18.

[43] *AS* I/3, 32.

[44] Ibid., 31. On the scope and nature of a conciliar statement and on its special "dignity," Garofalo said nothing that was formally different than what had been said in the critiques of the schema. The latter, however, pointed out the contradiction in the use of scholastic language in the schema, while its defenders regarded scholastic precision as in keeping with the scope and nature of conciliar statements.

[45] The reference is to the passage in *Gaudet Mater Ecclesia* in which the Pope gave reasons for choosing the medicine of mercy rather than severity. Since this passage is clearly contrary to the spirit of the schema *De fontibus*, Garofalo's report seemed intended to suggest to the Council fathers a possible way of getting around the obstacle posed by *Gaudet Mater Ecclesia*.

[46] *AS* I/3, 31.

When one turns to the interventions that now followed, the first thing that strikes one is how generic the substantive discussion was. The problem of the two sources, to all appearances the most recurrent theme, did not seem to constitute the real difficulty. Frings did address the issue, speaking twice to clarify his thought (that there are two sources only in the order of knowledge; in the order of being, the gospel or revelation alone is the source); and many of what was to become the minority were not averse to accepting the terminology he proposed, namely, that the gospel or revelation alone is the single source of both scripture and tradition.[47] As for the question of the real extent of tradition, the interventions, at least those of the majority, kept to generalities. (Was this a clever tactic, or were people preoccupied by some other concern regarded as of higher priority?) Only Parente undertook a detailed exegesis of Trent, in which he essentially repeated Lennerz's critique of Geiselmann;[48] namely, that for interpreting the relations between scripture and tradition, the change from *"partim . . . partim"* in the earlier version of the Tridentine decree is irrelevant.[49] The majority limited themselves to insisting that the question was one legitimately debated among the theologians.

The main specific contents of the debate (relation between scripture and tradition, biblical inerrancy, new exegetical views on the historicity of some parts of the Bible) were thus opportunities for raising broader problems and, first of all, the problem of the very purpose of the Council. Of the eighty-five oral interventions, sixty-one made explicit and more or less extensive reference to the status of doctrine.[50] Without claiming absolute accuracy, since the references were sometimes not entirely clear, an analysis of the debate shows that twenty-two explicitly referred to *Gaudet Mater Ecclesia* and accepted its main points, while eleven repeated what the allocution said, but without explicit reference to it. On the other hand, twenty-two interventions defended what may be called the scholastic or textbook idea of Church teaching, and six did so while trying to interpret *Gaudet Mater Ecclesia* itself as backing their view.

---

[47] Ibid., 34-35 and 139.

[48] See J. R. Geiselmann, *Die Heilige Schrift und die Tradition* (Freiburg, 1962), who also gives information on the principal participants in the debate. As for Lennerz, see *"Scriptura sola?,"* *Gregorianum* 40 (1959), 38-53.

[49] *AS* I/3, 132-35.

[50] The picture in the written interventions was similar. Of these, Volk's was outstanding for its penetration (*AS*, I/3, 364-65).

It can be said that during the week of discussion of *De fontibus* the Council took possession of its purpose in the terms in which *Gaudet Mater Ecclesia* had described it. It was the decisive phase of a process that was clearly articulated in Bea's intervention on November 14: (a) The Pope has given the Council a pastoral purpose; (b) the Council has already made this purpose its own in its opening "Message;" and (c) the need now is consciously to ratify this purpose by rejecting a schema that runs counter to it. The clarity of Bea's vision of the real issue should not allow us to forget how passionate this debate was. H. Schauf, whose affections were with the preparatory Theological Commission, described the meeting of the German theologians on the afternoon of November 14 in extremely severe language: "It was a conspiracy and a political gathering rather than a theological conversation."[51] And during the debate some bishops tried to find a way not to split the Council and to reach a solution acceptable to all parties.[52]

One attempt at a compromise was that of Morcillo Gonzalez who on November 15 proposed satisfying the call for a pastoral approach by means of a suitable introduction, "which is to be desired and doubtless will be offered when the time comes." Quiroga y Palacios had already voiced the same idea the day before ("a general introduction . . . in which the pastoral intention of the Council is set forth"), and it would be voiced again by De Arriba y Castro and Martinez Gonzalez, Ruotolo (for the purpose of reaching "the harmony which some have called for in one way or another"), Carli, Klepacz (who seemed to have caught the idea on the wing, in his oral intervention in the hall, since it is lacking in the written text he had prepared), and Franić.[53] But this was to mistake the scope of the question of the pastoral character of the Council's teaching. The juxtaposition of a pastoral introduction with a scholastic exposition of the doctrine amounted to introducing a further dichotomy — the same claim made by those on the other side, who wished to return to the Tridentine

---

[51] Schauf, "Auf dem Wege," 67.

[52] This call for unanimity found strong expression especially in the intervention of Abbot Butler (*AS* I/3, 107-8), but, significantly enough, it was repeated not only by such men as Zoa (148-49), Pourchet (149-51), and Ancel (203-5), but also by men representing a different orientation, as, for example, Griffiths (181-83).

[53] In *AS* I/3, 61, 40, 163, 261-62, 201-2, 232, 215 and 218, and 246, respectively. This proposal must be carefully distinguished from that of the many who were asking instead for an introduction that would treat of the nature of revelation as such, before moving on to the relations between scripture and tradition. For this second kind of introduction, see, among others, Bea (49-50), Reuss (92), Garrone (189ff), and Ancel (204).

model, with its clear distinction between doctrinal decrees and reform decrees.[54]

The majority, however, had no hesitation in describing what was meant by pastoral teaching, and they could serenely, and authoritatively, appeal to the points made in *Gaudet Mater Ecclesia*. The teaching must be received "with new fervor by all in our own time;" it must therefore be addressed to the people of today and not to the schools of theology (Bea). There was a need to revitalize the life and strengthen the witness given by the faithful in today's world (Soegijapanata). Referring to the medicine of mercy, of which Pope Roncalli had spoken in *Gaudet Mater Ecclesia*, Silva y Henriquez distinguished between the mentalities of judge and pastor. Guerry articulated one of the clearest critiques of the schema in the light of *Gaudet Mater Ecclesia*:

> Our first duty as pastors is to teach our people doctrine that is complete and unadulterated, but in such a way that they can hear the word of God, understand it, accept it in faith, and, finally, put it into practice in every area of their lives. . . . It is not the teaching that must be adapted but the way in which the teaching is presented.

This was a paraphrase of the language of John XXIII. While a theologian might perhaps have some quarrel with this sharp distinction between the presentation of doctrine and doctrine itself, this was the position taken in *Gaudet Mater Ecclesia*. Garrone repeated the point that "it is the very concern for truth that forbids us to abstract from the human beings to whom the word of truth is addressed."

Hurley, cited earlier, was perhaps the bishop most conscious of the need to tackle and clarify, precisely from a doctrinal point of view, the essence of what "pastoral" meant.[55] He distinguished between those who thought that a council was pastoral to the extent that it safeguarded the truth (the version rejected in *Gaudet Mater Ecclesia*) and those who, besides safeguarding the truth, also wanted to preach and spread it. Even a bishop in favor of the schema, such as García Martinez, realized the need to deal with the obstacle represented by what the Pope had said about the "pastoral": "Therefore, according to these words of the pontiff it is not enough for pastoral teaching that a doctrine be true, although this truth is the underlying foundation of all authentic exercise of the teaching office; it is also necessary that the way in which it is transmit-

---

[54] See, for example, Cardinal Garibi y Rivera, November 17 (*AS* I/3, 122-24).

[55] On November 29, when the debate had ended, Hurley asked Congar for a paper that "would define the 'pastoral character' of a text" (*JCongar,* 182).

ted be truly pastoral, that is, better suited to win minds and effectively to move them."[56]

Following in the steps of Ottaviani and Garofalo, the group that would subsequently emerge as the minority in favor of the schema wanted to separate doctrinal proposition from pastoral adaptation. Some fell back on odd linguistic analyses: "pastoral" is an adjective, not a noun or substantive; doctrine is the substance by which the people of God are fed, while the pastoral element is a quality denoting all the activities of pastors in the Church (Cardinal Santos, and Fernandez, Master General of the Dominicans). Enrique y Tarancon linked definition of the truth to clarity, adaptation to the mentality of the hearer, and, therefore, the pastoral element to the phase of explanation. Others said that the main duty of pastors is to keep their flock from error and lead them to the truth of the gospel (Del Pino Gómez).

The debate, then, focused on formal aspects, the pastoral and ecumenical character of the schema. As far as the material content of the discussion is concerned, there is not much to add to the reconstructions of it that have already been undertaken.[57] One gets the impression, however, that in this phase of the conciliar debate there was a certain resistance to tackling overly technical problems of substance, which, at least for the moment, belonged rather to the "council of theologians" than to that of the bishops.[58] In addition, the debate was made more difficult and muddled by the fierce attack some Roman circles had unleashed against the Pontifical Biblical Institute.[59]

But a simple report on the debate in the hall, in the extremely concise terms in which I have summarized it, cannot enable us to understand the meaning of this week in which, in the felicitous expression of R. Rouquette in *Études*, "the era of the Counter Reformation came to an

---

[56] *AS* I/3, 214.

[57] U. Betti, "Storia della Costituzione dogmatica *Dei Verbum*," in *La Costituzione dogmatica sulla divina Rivelazione* (Turin-Leumann, 19674), 11-68; *La dottrina del concilio Vaticano II sulla trasmissione della rivelazione* (Rome, 1985), especially 45-50; E. Stakemeier, *Die Konzilskonstitution über die göttliche Offenbarung. Werden, Inhalt und theologische Bedeutung* (Paderborn, 19672); J. Ratzinger, *Commentary*, III, 155-61; and B.-D. Dupuy, "Historique de la Constitution," in *Vatican II. La révélation divine* I (Paris, 1968), 61-117. It should be noted, however, that in practice none of these reconstructions pays attention to what the pastoral aspect of doctrine really means. Much more alert to this point is the recent, extensive reconstruction of H. Sauer, *Erfahrung und Glaube. Die Begründung des pastoralen Prinzips durch die Offenbarungskonstitution des II. Vatikanischen Konzils* (Frankfurt a. M., 1993), 137-220.

[58] See Y. Congar, *Vatican II: Le Concile au jour le jour* (Paris, 1963), 64-65.

[59] On this attack, see *History*, I, 277-83.

end."[60] Back on November 14, with great clarity of vision, the Pope had written in his diary: "That disputes will arise can be foreseen. On the one hand, the draft [the preparatory schema] does not take into account the specific intentions of the Pope in his official discourses. On the other hand, a good eight cardinals, relying on these discourses, have discredited the main point of the draft. May the Lord help us and make us one."[61] Two points about this note are obvious: the Pope was clearly aware that his "specific intentions . . . in his official discourses" were at stake; at the same time, his aim was not victory at any cost; instead, playing down the disagreements ("disputes"), he adopted the higher perspective of a unity of intentions in which his own vision of the Council saw the highest good: "May the Lord help us and make us one."

Not everyone confronted the events with the gentle and far-sighted serenity of Pope John. H. Schauf's testimony has already been mentioned. The notes in Siri's diary begin with the presumption that he can control the situation but end with a tragic sense of a terrible calamity, the danger of a victory for heresy. On November 19, the eve of the vote, he wrote: "The situation is serious if the schema fails tomorrow! Lord, help us! Holy Virgin, St. Joseph, pray for us! You can obtain the victory: '*cunctos [sic] haereses sola interemisti in universo mondo [sic]*' ['You alone have overcome all heresies throughout the world!']"[62]

---

[60] *Études*, January 1963, 104: "We may think that with the vote on November 20 the era of the Counter-Reformation has come to an end and a new era, with unforeseeable consequences, has begun for Christendom."

[61] The Pope was referring to Cardinals Liénart, Frings, Léger, König, Alfrink, Suenens, Ritter, and Bea, who on the first day of the debate rejected the schema in very forthright terms. The cardinals who on that same November 14 spoke in favor of it were, in addition to Ottaviani in his introduction, Ruffini, Siri, and Quiroga y Palacios. The numbers were obviously disproportionate, and this explains why the diary notes of those opposed to the text were all gleeful at the end of the first day. But on the second day of the debate, November 16, the proportions were reversed: among the cardinals only Tisserant, Lefebvre, and Silva Henriquez spoke against the schema, while Gonçalves Cerejeira, de Barros Câmara, McIntyre, Caggiano, Rufinus I. Santos, Urbani, and Browne spoke in favor of it. To some extent it was the cardinals who set the mood, and this explains the highs and lows of their respective comments, depending on their starting points. On November 15 — but this was not known at the time — Döpfner sent a *votum* to the General Secretariat of the Council, asking for the schema to be reworked (see the text in Sauer, *Erfahrung und Glaube*, 222 n.3).

[62] *DSiri*, 382. As for the mistakes in his Latin text, since Siri does not seem to have been poor in Latin, it is hard to say whether they are typos or a sign of strong emotion. The note for that day does, however, contain the formulation of a *votum* in which the writer is thinking of measures suited to combatting "modernism" as a spreading error: "Great importance must be assigned to studies in 'historical propaedeutics,' not simply, however, as these are found, e.g. in Benigni, but with the addition of reflections on the

The people on the other side in the debate, if clearly they did not think of the contrary position as heretical, were considering what measures to take should the schema be approved. The principal agents in this activity were the bishops and theologians of Central Europe and the Secretariat for Christian Unity. The latter once again proposed its own strategy at a meeting on November 16.[63] Bea's address two days earlier had already set out a clear position, but it remained a personal stance; what was now needed was an official exposition of the ecumenical dimension of the problems raised by the schema. At the meeting on November 16, Bea repeated his negative judgment and spoke of the need for a mixed commission to prepare a new schema that would be more pastoral, more intelligible, and more ecumenical.

Some members of the Secretariat (Mansourati, for example) were puzzled at such a drastic rejection, which they thought was being dictated by the needs of the dialogue with the Protestants; consideration of the Orthodox would require taking into account the special place tradition has for them and would in fact call for approval of the schema *De fontibus*. This was a not very veiled criticism of the *votum* the Secretariat had offered during the preparatory phase and of the report given by Feiner at the meeting of November 9. In addition to Feiner, who had been personally challenged, Dumont, a Dominican, felt called to rebut this objection. As a matter of fact, the concept of tradition used in the schema did not capture the full wealth of the Orthodox concept, which was much deeper and broader than the one in the schema; for them tradition was not limited to the handing on of "doctrines" but was more "realistic," since they located tradition in the liturgy, which is the Christian mystery in act.[64] Dumont's position was supported by Bea, who recalled that even in the Central Preparatory Commission members had complained about the deficient concepts of revelation and tradition in the schema. Willebrands also defended Dumont's position, recalling that during the meeting of the Central Committee of the World Council of

pathology that affects theological studies when various methodologies derived from idealism, historicism, rationalism are introduced. For modernism is creeping in and is supported by historical criticism; but it will surely collapse if the measures mentioned above are properly taken." It is impossible to miss the objective link between this *votum* and the letter "against the errors and deviations of our age," which was signed by nineteen cardinals (Siri among them) and sent to the Pope on November 24 on the occasion of the establishment of the mixed commission. But it is not possible to establish a literary connection.

[63] Copy of the minutes in the Thils Archive, 0689.

[64] The minutes have "ministry" (*ministère*) but "mystery" (*mystère*) may have been intended.

Churches on Rhodes in 1959, the Orthodox expressed their dissatisfaction with the weak concept of tradition presented in the paper of Msgr. Chrysostom Constantinidis.

Another member of the Secretariat, Father Boyer, was unable to be present at the meeting but sent a note, which was read there, in which he said he was obliged to distance himself somewhat from the official position of the Secretariat. He clarified his only partial agreement with the *votum* that the Secretariat had submitted to the Theological Commission; he had accepted what was said in no. 5 of the *votum* (the section urging the avoidance of expressions that excluded some presence of all revealed truths in the scripture) only because the matter of the biblical canon had been formally excepted, an exception that for him was enough to justify the claim that "the deposit contains something not written." Moreover, Boyer went on, to deny that any truths were revealed "after the completion of the deposit" was not to exclude "unwritten traditions from the deposit." He also thought that Scheeben's position was a matter of debate.

At this point in the meeting it was realized that the need was not to go into details but rather to have the ecumenical problems posed by the schema explained at a general congregation. Since many fathers thought that ecumenism entailed a distortion of Catholic truth, it was necessary to present the ecumenical perspective in its proper light. Before the meeting closed, it was also decided to set up five subcommissions, each responsible for one of the chapters of the schema, with a view to reworking it.[65]

The reporter chosen to explain the ecumenical problems posed by the schema was Bishop De Smedt, who spoke at the general congregation on November 19. Here again, *Gaudet Mater Ecclesia* was the real point of reference, invoked to describe not only the pastoral but also the ecumenical character of teaching. De Smedt used essentially the same terms that Bea had, when the latter invoked the papal allocution to explain what pastoral meant. De Smedt's definition of ecumenical teaching did not differ much from that of pastoral teaching, except that in the former case the addressee was the separated Christians. Teaching is ecumenical

---

[65] The members of the subcommissions were: for the chapter on the "two sources": Jaeger, Stakemeier, Maccarrone, Feiner, and Tavard; for the chapter on inspiration, inerrancy, and literary composition: De Smedt, Höfer, Thils, and Boyer; for the Old Testament: Baum, Weigel, and Charrière; for the New Testament: Hamer, David, Dumont, Holland, and Deschamps; and for "Sacred Scripture in the Church:" Volk, Vodopivec, Thijssen, and Mansourati. For each, the first named was the chair.

when it fulfills the conditions required so that "our explanation of it can be accurately understood by noncatholics."[66]

De Smedt's address caused intense excitement. Congar's summary of De Smedt's speech is worth recording:

> He wanted to explain precisely what "ecumenical" means for teaching and its style. All Christians accept Jesus Christ, but they disagree on the means of going to him. For centuries, Catholics and others have thought it enough to give a clear explanation of their divergent teachings, but they both did it in *their* categories, which the other did not understand. The result: *nothing*. For some time now, a different method has been introduced: ecumenical *dialogue*. This involves paying heed to the *way* in which doctrine is expressed, so that it can be understood by the other. This is not a bargaining for unity, it is not an attempt to convert; but it is, on both sides, the giving of a clear witness which takes the other into account. It is this approach that our texts should take. It is not easy!
>
> There must be no watering down that would deceive the others. Nine conditions must be met, but for brevity's sake, he would give only the first four: 1) What is the present-day teaching of the Orthodox and the Protestants?[67] 2) What idea do they have of *our* teaching? 3) What are the elements that are not sufficiently well developed in Catholic teaching? 4) Is Catholic teaching being presented in the form required? Scholasticism will not do. What is needed is a biblical and patristic way of teaching.
>
> It is not enough, however, to express "the truth" for a text to be ecumenical. The members of the Secretariat offered their help to the Theological Commission; they proposed a mixed commission. But that Commission refused. People living in Protestant or Orthodox areas are the ones who have been saying that the schema lacks any ecumenical spirit. Should we not reflect on whether enough consideration has been given to a good method? The Secretariat, for its part, finds the schema "notably deficient in the ecumenical spirit." The schema represents not progress but regression. It will be a hindrance and a source of harm. On the other hand, the new method has borne fruit: the presence of the observers is a sign of it. If the schema is not rewritten, we will be responsible for the Vatican Council having disappointed a great hope (hearty applause from the bishops; no applause from the archbishops).[68]

On that same November 19, the Secretariat's subcommission on scripture in the Church met at Volk's residence in the afternoon. "We agreed

---

[66] *AS* I/3, 184-86.

[67] In De Smedt's exact words: "We must have a good knowledge of . . . "

[68] We may contrast the enthusiastic notes, for the same day, of Semmelroth and of Congar ("Text very well delivered and listened to with close attention. Rather strong emotion, arising not from sentimentality but from the heart of the truth. . . . Tears of the Holy Spirit, such as I wish for those who are obstinate in their dogmatic righteousness") with the laconic, almost irritated remark of Siri: "De Smedt of Bruges gave a jarring speech."

to recommend the possibility of suspending the discussion of the schema
De fontibus Revelationis so that the completed, though not yet printed
schema *De verbo Dei* could be discussed." But how could such a plan
be advanced? The Regulations of the Council made no provision for it.
Volk thought that Frings, with his authority as a member of the Council
of Presidents, might propose it in the assembly.[69] One has the impression
that there was no clarity, even within the Secretariat, on the appropriate
strategy to follow.

There was no greater clarity among the bishops of Central Europe. A
majority of the members of the French episcopate had already met on
November 14. About two-thirds were for rejecting the schema and one-
third for a half-way solution, correcting the present schema.[70] On
November 18, a strategy meeting was held, called by Volk, in which
well-known representatives of the German and French bishops and theologians took part.[71] It was suggested that, if the schema were accepted,
a group composed of theologians representing various tendencies and
nationalities should prepare a text to be distributed to the Fathers,
which would help them in detailed ways to emend the schema. Garrone,
too, proposed the idea of a mixed committee, on which he would speak
in the hall the next day, November 19. Rahner, for his part, had already
set to work preparing a petition that would, in case of a defeat, implore
the fathers at least not to define the existence of truths of faith that were
not somehow contained in the scriptures. At this meeting it was also
decided that, again in case of defeat, Rahner would be the one to
decide, point by point, the cases in which no compromise would be possible.

There was, then, great uncertainty on the part of the future majority,
which was not yet able to count its members, it being impossible to esti-
mate the degree of agreement with the two attitudes since the views of
the bishops themselves were still changing. For example, it was only on
November 21, when the turning point had been passed, that Congar
learned about the shift of opinion that was taking place in the United
States episcopate. The speeches in the hall did not permit one to grasp

[69] *TSemmelroth*, note of November 19.

[70] The numbers are not clear. Levillain, *La mécanique politique*, 250, speaks of 85
unqualifiedly opposed, 35 in favor of a complete rewriting, 3 in favor of the substance of
the text. In a diary note of November 14, Chenu speaks of 90 unqualifiedly opposed, 30
for the half-way solution, and only 1 for approval (but in parentheses he suggests three
possible names).

[71] See *TSemmelroth* for this day, and, for greater detail, Levillain, *La mécanique politique*, 251-52.

the real direction being taken by the Council; it was still in process of being determined.

During the days of the debate on the *De fontibus* there was an increasing number of meetings of bishops outside the hall, often in order to listen to the theologians. On November 14, despite having been invited to the meeting of the French bishops, Congar chose to speak to the Argentinean bishops about tradition. On November 16 he held a working meeting with some French bishops on the same subject.[72] The French episcopal conference had set up working groups, one of which was occupied with the relationship between scripture and tradition. Also on November 16, Mejia, a theologian from Chile, continuing his series of meetings with a group of Argentinean bishops, spoke on the historicity of the biblical narratives.[73] In his diary for November 16, Cardinal Urbani wrote that the meeting of the Italian bishops of the Triveneto had been unable to formulate a unanimous position on the schema. On November 19, B. Ahern, a Passionist exegete, continued his lectures at the North American College, speaking that day on literary genres and provoking the criticism of Apostolic Delegate Vagnozzi.[74] But the great majority of the American bishops now seemed to have been won over to the new exegetical trends.[75]

The preceding is not a complete list of the meetings and activities outside the hall, but it is enough to show how the episcopates, from Argentina to the Italian Veneto, from France to the United States, were being given rather intense training and how new balances among the fathers quickly took form. Urbani's note on the indecision of the Triveneto bishops speaks for itself and reveals that, while one may speak of blocs, they were blocs in course of internal movement.

The Doctrinal Commission seems to have been practically absent from all this activity. Tromp's *Relatio* mentions no other general meetings during the first period after the one held on November 13; after that turbulent experience, Ottaviani evidently did not consider it opportune to call any. Fenton, one of Ottaviani's right-hand men, however, does speak in his diary of an odd undertaking. Schauf, a faithful follower of

---

[72] See *JCongar*, November 14 and 16, 1962.

[73] Zazpe Archive, index card for a lecture of that date.

[74] See Fogarty, *American Catholic Biblical Scholarship: A History from the Early Republic to Vatican II* (San Francisco, 1984), 324-25.

[75] See *JCongar*, November 21. Semmelroth, in his diary for November 17, writes of the need to print another 500 copies of Rahner's critique of the schema, in which he, Semmelroth, and Father Pfister had a hand. The request for copies came chiefly from the American bishops.

Tromp, invited Fenton to a meeting on the afternoon of November 17 at Santa Marta's. The meeting was open only to the "faithful members of the old theological commission's corps of theologians." Present were Tromp, Schauf, Salaverri, Lio, Lattanzi, Trapé, Fenton, and two others whose names Fenton does not give. They waited in vain for Garofalo. Philips was deliberately not invited. What they talked about and by what right it is not easy to determine from Fenton's diary. In any case, at the end of the meeting, Fenton received some written notes from Tromp and from them, as a reminder to himself, he copied the notation that in *Gaudet Mater Ecclesia* the Pope had said that the first purpose of the Council was to "protect and promote doctrine."[76] The meeting was, then, probably intended to take a count of the conciliar experts who were ready to defend the conception of doctrine that had been basic in the preparation of the schemas.

On November 19, immediately after the general congregation, the Council of Presidents met and decided to have the assembly vote on a question which originally read: "Should, or should not, the discussion of this schema be continued?"[77] The minutes of the meeting, however, say in a note that the formulation was changed to: "Should the discussion be interrupted?" The change was decided on and communicated to the Secretary General by the president of the day, Frings, after an intervention of Ruffini.[78]

When, on the next day, Felici communicated the decision of the Council of Presidents, there was confusion in the hall. Obviously, many of the fathers did not understand the meaning of the vote, or at least some were worried that many did not understand it. A first clarification was therefore given by the Secretary, then another by Ruffini, who clearly explained that "interrupting" the debate meant "renewing," "redoing" the schema. Then, after an interval of eleven minutes, during which we may suppose that the majority of the bishops had

[76] *DFenton*, November 17. Fenton had been a member of the preparatory Theological Commission, was now a conciliar expert, and would be one of the experts chosen by Ottaviani for the mixed commission appointed to rewrite the *De fontibus*.

[77] *AS* V/1, 19-20.

[78] This note in the minutes is in agreement with what Caprile says (II, 176), although the latter, on the basis of a note of Msgr. Kempf, one of the undersecretaries, reports a fuller formulation, in which it is explained that an approval of the proposal for an interruption would lead ultimately to the preparation of a new schema. But this explanation, still according to Kempf (but this time in a press conference to the German-language journalists), was not read in the hall due to Frings's forgetfulness. Caprile correctly points out the contradiction in the statement of Kempf, since the text of the question was read in the hall not by Frings but by Secretary General Felici.

already written down their vote, there was still another clarification by Felici.[79]

The outcome of the vote, at first promised for the next day but then instead announced in the hall on that same day, was clear, even though the two-thirds majority required was not reached: 1368 voted for an interruption, 822 for continuing the debate. The required majority was 1473 votes out of the 2209 cast. Without resorting to unverifiable hypotheses, one may say that the simple size of the vote against the text showed that the positions of the majority had been adopted by large sectors of episcopates which, in the eyes of those unable to grasp the changes taking place during the first weeks of the Council, had been thought to be solidly aligned with the opposite position. Those in favor of renewal, then, were not reducible to the episcopates of Central and Northern Europe. Without seeking to play down the influence of these episcopates and their theologians, it is undeniable that broad sectors of the Italian, Spanish, United States, and Latin American episcopates, which had seemed impervious to calls for change, had now, even if only inchoatively, made their choice, all the more meaningful in that it meant the rejection of a schema "approved" by the Pope.[80]

The fact remained, however, that because of a shortage of 105 votes, a trifling percent of the total number of votes cast, the Council seemed destined to be plunged into a crisis from which there was no return. It

---

[79] AS I/III, 219-23. It is difficult to determine why the question was put in this way. The Regulations had essentially nothing to say about the possibility of a vote that could interrupt a discussion or even reject a schema proposed for discussion, although it did provide for the possibility of someone expressing himself on this point. But earlier, in connection with the discussion of chapter II of the liturgical constitution, the Pope had given the Council of Presidents "authority to propose to the general congregation that a discussion be closed when its subject had been at least adequately expounded and explained" (AS I/II, 159). May we then suppose that in coming to this decision the Council of Presidents simply made use of this authority and that for this reason the part of the question that spoke explicitly of a rewriting of the schema was omitted?

[80] Although it is inaccurate to say that the schemas had been "approved" by the Pope, this was the interpretation given by the defenders of the schema, who appealed to this argument in maintaining the impossibility of a global rejection of the preparatory schemas. See the interventions of Ruffini (AS I/3, 37), Quiroga y Palacios (39), de Barros Câmara (68), Fares (85), and others. Although perhaps persuasive to many, this argument was without basis. The Pope's consent had not been given to the contents of the schemas, but simply to their being sent out for discussion in the hall. This point was rightly emphasized during those days in a memorandum produced in Lercaro's circle; it recalled the precedent of Vatican I and the Apostolic Letter Multiplices inter (November 27, 1869), in which Pius IX explained that the schemas previously drafted by the theologians and canonists were presented for the fathers' consideration "without any approval of Ours being attached to them" (ISR archive, Alberigo papers, II/5).

took an extraordinary intervention of the Pope to rescue the Council
from this impasse. More than any others, two individuals influenced this
decision, Bea and Léger. Despite claims by many, it does not seem that
Bea had direct contact with the Pope on November 20. It seems instead
that he was contacted by the Secretary of State and that, having perhaps
gained the agreement of Frings and Liénart, he sent his view to the Pope
through Cicognani himself.[81]

It was Léger who saw the Pope directly, taking advantage of an audience granted to the Canadian bishops on the evening of November 20 to
ask for and receive permission to speak to the Pope in private.[82] At this
meeting, the Canadian cardinal, it seems, presented a written request,
which the Pope would later remember as a "letter," and spoke to him
"frankly about the situation." However, Léger received the impression
that the Pope had not decided to intervene, even though he admitted that
the majority's vote to reject the schema had faithfully interpreted his
own thinking. In fact, the Pope confirmed to him that his own opening
message had been rather clear: whereas Trent and Vatican I had determined the object of faith, it was the task of Vatican II to present the
Christian message to the modern world and the world of tomorrow. The
purpose was not to compose a handbook but to pave the way for a pastoral science of theology. Léger suggested the creation of a permanent
conciliar commission to supervise the rewriting of the documents during
the intersession, an idea that seemed to please the Pope.[83]

Although in the present state of our knowledge it is impossible to
determine who influenced the decision of John XXIII,[84] it is certain that

[81] *DTucci*, addition to the note of November 21, on the testimony of Schmidt, Bea's
secretary.

[82] Léger Diary, note of November 20. R. Aubert speaks of a "visit of Cardinals Montini, Meyer and Léger" to the Pope, but without any proof and with a "perhaps" ("Il concilio," in *La chiesa del Vaticano II [1958-1978]*, Part I [Milan, 1994] 238).

[83] Léger diary, ibid. That not only this last suggestion regarding the intersession, but
also the first one, asking for an extraordinary intervention, had an undeniable influence is
made adequately clear by the letter and the gift of "an old but valuable episcopal cross,"
which the Pope sent to Léger the next day. "I was thinking of our meeting yesterday
evening, of your very gracious letter, and of the conversation that followed" (John XXIII,
Lettere, 1958-1963 [Rome, 1978], 434-35).

[84] It may also be that John XXIII was influenced by the attitude which the various episcopal conferences displayed to him. On this point we may cite the audience given to the
French bishops on November 19. Liénart's address contained such statements as this:
"You know the French bishops too well to think of them as in danger of acting in a partisan spirit at the Council or of following their own line of action in its work" (see Caprile,
II, 155). We may add — but the reference is to November 24 — the special thanks
addressed to the Pope by the German bishops for his intervention regarding *De fontibus*.

in the hours that followed the Pope overcame his hesitation and that the next day, during the celebration of Mass which opened the general congregation, the Secretary of State gave Felici a document containing the Pope's decision.[85] The vote of the preceding day, said this document, was a source of concern. Although sufficiently revealing, it did not meet the standard set by the Regulations to settle the question. It would not be easy to resolve the opposition between the opinions that emerged in the discussion, and it was necessary to rid the schema of the defects that stood in the way of a "desirable conclusion." For this reason, and taking into consideration the reasons that were causing concern and "yielding to the wishes of many," the Pope had decided to refer the matter to a mixed commission made up of some members of both the Doctrinal Commission and the Secretariat for Christian Unity. It would be the task of this new commission "to emend the schema, shorten it, and make it more suitable, with an emphasis especially on general principles."

In this context, the Pope also reasserted the leitmotiv which he had long been repeating and which the now clearly defined minority had tended to ignore. Since the Council of Trent and Vatican I had already set forth the teaching given in the schema, the point now — though the Pope did not say this in so many words but left it to others to conclude — was to present this teaching to today's world. In the few days that remained (the Pope continued) there will be time "to consider other schemas as well or at least to sample (*delibandi*) them," that is, to take a position on their general characteristics.

The Pope's decision caught almost everyone by surprise. To fill up the working day somehow, the secretary announced that the fathers would continue the discussion of the first chapter, which had begun at the end of the preceding morning and had already seen interventions by Tisserant, Ruffini, and Jacono. The strange thing is that the speakers who had registered to speak did so, out of inertia and perhaps without caring that they were discussing a text that no longer existed, and only for future memory. A large number of the fathers, completely indifferent to the speeches being made, streamed into the side naves, where they exchanged impressions on what had happened. The enthusiasm of the

---

[85] *AS* I/3, 259. The incident is reported here on the basis of the clear recollection of the writer of these pages, who, from his post of observation, immediately behind the table of the secretaries, could see Felici's surprise as he withdrew to speak at length with the Secretary of State. The Pope's step caught almost everyone by surprise, especially the president for the day, Ruffini, who received from Felici the communication brought by the Secretary of State and with choking voice gave Felici the floor.

observers was also obvious. Some friendly bishops went to the observers' tribune to utter a friendly and ironic "Long live the Pope!"

Without its yet being put in writing, the Council had perhaps made one of the most important changes in the doctrinal development of the Catholic Church: the choice of a teaching that was "pastoral." That this had been clearly expressed in the interventions of the Pope did not mean that it had been equally clear to all. Bea had given an authoritative interpretation of what the term signified. Hurley, one of the most clearsighted as to the real heart of the debate, would speak again on the subject during the discussion of the schema on the Church. But in any case, an entirely new era was beginning.

What were the implications of the Pope's decision, a decision that was certainly his own and yet also so completely in line with the majority of the bishops that he would violate the prescription of "his own" Regulations in order to be in harmony with them? There were at least two such implications. One had to do with the very exercise of the primacy, the other had to do with the broader matter of balance in teaching. First, to a Catholic Church, accustomed for centuries to a quite different style, and to the representatives of the other Christian Churches, the decision gave clear expression to a way of exercising the primatial ministry that exalted not only its ability to take the initiative but also, and first of all, its ability to listen. It can be said, in still more relevant language, that the decision gave concrete expression to the synodal nature of the Petrine primacy.

The other implication of the conciliar turn-about ratified by John XXIII's intervention was that doctrinal formulas codified during the post-Tridentine period were becoming a subject for discussion. Nor were these formulas a minor matter; to meet the demands of controversial theology, some of them (e.g., on the relationship between scripture and tradition), had for centuries shaped the Catholic confessional identity and had been taken over by what had come to be called, since the 1760s, the ordinary magisterium. If the more thoughtful had concluded that the issue was to come up with formulas more faithful to Trent itself and, above all, to look beyond the formulas and recover a more traditional perspective, the fact is that up to this point the possibility of such a change had not been accepted and had, for the most part, been looked upon with suspicion.

The usual Thursday break helped the bishops to get over the shock of the vote on the previous Tuesday and the Pope's intervention on Wednesday. On Friday, November 23, at the twenty-fifth general congregation, they would begin the study of a minor schema that raised no questions of principle.

CHAPTER VI

THE DISCUSSION OF THE MODERN MEDIA

MATHIJS LAMBERIGTS

Compared with other schemata, the schema which dealt with modern communication media was granted only the briefest of treatments on November 23, 24, and 26, 1962.[1] The November 26 meeting only devoted half of its time to the schema. The schema had been prepared by the Secretariat for Communications Media under the leadership of Msgr. Martin J. O'Connor, who had already been chairman of the Pontifical Commission for Motion Pictures, Radio and Television for fourteen years. The secretary to both bodies was A. Galletto. O'Connor's preconciliar Secretariat had become part of the new conciliar Commission for the Laity and Communications Media, of which Cardinal Cento was president.[2]

Each part of the schema had a brief introduction and a number of chapters. A general introduction gave the reasons why the subject deserved the Council's attention and invited all people of good will to search together for the best ways to employ the various means of communication for the salvation of the world.[3] The first chapter of Part I dealt with the Church's right and duty to concern itself with means of communication; subsequent chapters dealt with the adequate means to protect the objective moral order and the duties of society and its citizens with respect to the media.[4] Part II focused on the apostolic value of the means of communication, especially for the proclamation of the Christian message, and on such resources as the Catholic daily and weekly newspapers, magazines, cinemas, and radio and TV stations. To facilitate the development of these channels of communication it was

---

[1] See *History*, I, 205, 364-65; E. Baragli's *L'Inter Mirifica. Introduzione — Storia — Discussione — Commento — Documentazione* (Rome, 1969) is probably the most thorough study dedicated to the decree on the media; for the period relevant to this article see pages 119-36. See also É. Gabel, "Le schema sur les moyens de communication sociale," in Y. M.-J. Congar, *Vatican II: Le concile au jour le jour* (Paris, 1963), 135-38.

[2] See Cardinal Cento, introduction to the meeting of November 23, 1962 (*AS* I/3, 417).

[3] See *AS* I/3, 374-75.

[4] *AS* I/3, 377-88.

suggested that an annual Media Day be organized on which the faithful would be given the chance to support Catholic media both spiritually and financially.[5] Part III dealt with the moral norms demanded of both laity and clergy alike in their dealings with the media. Special attention was paid to the role of ecclesiastical organs such as the Holy See, the episcopate, national church services, and international Catholic organizations.[6] Part IV treated each of the various means of communication separately: press, film, radio, and television.[7] The entire schema was rounded off with an encouragement of the faithful to promote a well-ordered progress in the use of the media.[8]

I. PRESENTATION OF THE SCHEMA

After a short introduction by Cardinal F. Cento, the schema was presented to the assembly by Msgr. R. Stourm, recently appointed Archbishop of Sens, who had been involved with the document's preparation.[9] In his introduction on November 23 Stourm noted with some humor that the fathers of the Council had been given this schema to discuss as an opportunity for relaxation after the previous rather heavily laden days. Stourm, nevertheless, was entirely convinced of the importance of the schema, the first time in the history of the Church that a council had been called upon to deal with such issues. To establish the seriousness of the matter he pointed to the fact that the press, film, radio and television industries combined were able to reach more than eighteen billion people per year.[10] Stourm continued by noting that all the means of social communication had a great deal to offer with respect to the proclamation of the gospel. In his opinion it was important that the Church take a positive and constructive stand on the issue and, in line with Pius XII's outspoken optimism, establish directives and explain the principles governing the material without being blind to the limits and dangers presented by the various dimensions of the media. Three impor-

[5] *AS* I/3, 389-94.
[6] *AS* I/3, 395-400.
[7] *AS* I/3, 401-15.
[8] *AS* I/3, 416.
[9] *AS* I/3, 418-23.
[10] Press: 8000 newspapers (300 million in daily circulation); 22,000 other journals (200 million in daily circulation); cinema: 2,500 films per annum, 17,000 cinemas, 17 billion viewers per year; radio: 6,000 stations (400 million listeners); television: 1,000 stations (120 million viewers).

tant issues had occupied those who had been prepared the schema: the Church as teacher,[11] the Church as mother,[12] and the role of the Church as coordinator on three levels: international, national, and diocesan. In this regard Stourm called for the establishment of a Communications Sunday on which the relevant issues would receive due attention throughout the world.

Stourm was not unaware that the schema would be open to criticism on a number of levels. A number of the Council fathers, for example, felt it was too long and too repetitious. Stourm noted that the length was intentional, since because so few people had any kind of familiarity with the material at hand and because there was a need for theological reflection on the question. If repetitions had found their way into the schema, it was evident to Stourm that they should be scrapped.[13] By way of conclusion, the archbishop referred once again to the enormous potential of the various means of social communication and to the challenge of technology facing the Church as a whole in its ongoing task of proclaiming the gospel throughout the modern world.

II. Discussion in the Aula

In spite of Stourm's support for the schema and his insistence on its importance for the Church, very few of the fathers, only fifty-four in total, felt called to speak on the question.[14] The vast majority of the interventions came from European bishops (34), followed by Americans (8),[15] Africans (5),[16] and Asians (4), to which must be added the three

---

[11] By this he intended the Church's role as educator in relation to the use of the press and other means of communication (AS I/3, 420-21).

[12] With the help of people of good will, the Church as mother intends to point to the importance of the various means of communication for the proclamation of the Christian message (AS I/3, 421).

[13] The archbishop warned that what might appear at first sight to be repetition might not in fact be such; AS I/3, 421-422.

[14] Another forty-three Council members submitted their comments in writing (AS I/3, 563-609).

[15] Five speakers came from Latin America and three from North America. Both Tagle (Chile) and Fernández Feo-Tinoco (Venezuela) spoke on behalf of the other bishops from their respective countries.

[16] Both Nwedo (Nigeria) and Parraudin (Rwanda) spoke on November 24 on behalf of the entire African episcopate (AS I/3, 468-69, 476-78). Although the sources I have consulted do not give an explanation as to why both spoke in the name of the African episcopate, it is probable that Nwedo spoke on behalf of the English-speaking bishops and Perraudin for the French-speaking bishops. In content both interventions are clearly on the same wave length.

interventions of members of the Curia. It is rather difficult to find any noteworthy interventions, and the speeches were not given much attention by the press, the very subject of the discussion, who had already been informed about the schema on November 21.[17] The lack of such attention is all the more surprising if one considers that, besides the frequently intervening Cardinal Ruffini, other important figures such as Spellman, Bea, Seunens, Godfrey, and Léger found it necessary to let their thoughts be heard on the matter. The impression remained that the subject under discussion had somehow been lost between the emotional debate on revelation and the discussions that, as Felici had announced prior to the presentation of the decree on the media on November 23, would soon begin on the decree on the unity of the Church and on the constitutions on Mary and on the Church. Given the general commotion surrounding these more "traditional" topics, it is hard to imagine that much attention would be devoted to an issue with which the Roman Catholic Church up to that point had had little experience and which, with a few notable exceptions,[18] was looked down upon by many.[19] Some of the Council fathers who considered the material important were critical of this apparent lack of interest.[20]

[17] The press had been notified at a press conference held by H. Baragli in the Council press office (see *OssRom*, November 23, 1962). The survey "Konzilschronik" in *Das Zweite Vatikanische Konzil* is quite revealing in this regard (vol. 3 in *Lexikon für Theologie und Kirche*, 632-33). Besides a brief communication on November 23 and a mention at the end of the debate on November 26, there is no further reference to the discussion. It should be added, however, that Msgr. F. Vallainc, head of the Council's Official Press Service, was not exactly enamored with the press. According to R. Kaiser, Vallainc had written to a journalist a few months before the Council: "We do not need the press" (*Pope, Council and World: The Story of Vatican II* [New York, 1963], 189). This attitude was not really in agreement with the task of the Ufficio Stampa (see "Pro memoria sull' Ufficio Stampa;" De Vet papers, Archives of the Diocese of Breda, unnumbered, undated).

[18] Kaiser mentions the Pope's secretary Capovilla, Secretary of State Cicognani, and Msgr. I. Cardinale besides the Pope himself (*Pope, Council, and World*, 189-90).

[19] The fact that Vallainc was not the only one guilty of fostering poor relations with the press is evident from R. Laurentin, "L'information au concile," in *Deuxième*, 364-68; and J. Grootaers, "L'information religieuse au début du Concile: instances officielles et réseaux informels," in *Vatican II commence*, 218-19. However, according to a report of July/August 1963 entitled *L'Ufficio Stampa del Concilio Ecumenico Vaticano II* (12 pages), "Comments on the efficiency of the Press Room and of the technical services have been universally favorable" (8), although further on in the report critiques by the press are recognized (9) (De Vet papers, Archives of the Diocese of Breda).

[20] Cf. Gabel, "Le schema sur les moyens de communication sociale," 136. On November 24, several speakers pointed out that the significance of the schema should not be underestimated (e.g., Léger, *AS* I/3, 460). Of primary interest in this regard is the remark that there was a need to avoid reducing the importance of the means of communication to their possible function in spreading the faith.

When one examines the content of the interventions on the schema, one is immediately struck by the fact that the fathers tended here to be less interested in detail than they had been in their interventions on the liturgy schema. Generally speaking, the fathers spoke very highly of the schema[21] and expressed their satisfaction that the Church was dealing with this important material[22] even though not everything had been fully explained at the philosophical and theological levels.[23] More than one speaker recognized that, given today's society, the document treated a theme that was of great importance to the Church.[24] This was certainly the case with regard to young people who lived in a world of images.[25] For adults also the various means of communication had an important role to play in their lives on a number of levels.[26] In fact, as Léger pointed out, people tended to understand more about this material than they did about questions of doctrine.[27] Several speakers stressed that the schema gave witness to a strong sense of pastoral motivation[28] The schema had earned its rightful place in the proceedings of the Council,[29] especially if one considered that the media had become the principal way by which information could be instantly disseminated.[30] There was also a call for the establishment of a Vatican press agency;.[31] at the very least efforts ought to be made to expand the existing papal commission into efficient international, national, and diocesan organizations for the spread of information and the formation of public opinion.[32] It was

[21] See, for example, Spellman, Ruffini, Bishop A. Sanschagrin (Amos), Bishop H. Bednorz (Katowice), Bishop V. Brizgys (Kaunas), Suenens, A. Perraudin (Kabgayi), Bishop A. Nwedo (Umuahia) (*AS* I/3, 423, 424, 427, 433, 449, 462, 468, 476).

[22] L. Lommel (Luxembourg) noted that the press and other means of communication were valuable in themselves apart from the opportunities they provided for the Roman Catholic Church. He proposed that this intrinsic value be properly emphasized in the document's introduction (*AS* I/3, 497). Cf. also Spellman (New York), *AS* I/3, 423.

[23] Léger, *AS* I/3, 461.

[24] E. D'Souza (Nagpur), *AS* I/3, 440.

[25] Cf. Bednorz, *AS* I/3, 434.

[26] Cf. Bishops A. De Castro Mayer (Campos), A. Renard (Versailles) (*AS* I/3, 445, 469-70).

[27] *AS* I/3, 460.

[28] Ruffini, G. Beck (Salford) (*AS* I/3, 424, 429). According to Suenens, it was necessary that the schema be pastoral and that it should be distinguished on this point from the doctrinal schemata, which called for a different approach (*AS* I/3, 462).

[29] See, for example, D'Souza, *AS* I/3, 440.

[30] F. Charrière (Geneva-Fribourg), *AS* I/3, 435.

[31] Bea, *AS* I/3, 466.

[32] A. Ona de Echave (Lugo) also called for the establishment of diocesan commissions on the means of communication that, in consultation with the international press service, would decide how to make the best use of the available options (*AS* I/3, 487-88).

politely added, nevertheless, that schemata such as that on the liturgy and on the Church were rightly recognized as being of greater importance.[33]

But there were some exceptions to the generally favorable judgements. A member of the preparatory Secretariat for Communications Media said that the Council was wasting its limited time deliberating this question, no matter how profoundly the subject had been discussed during the preparatory period.[34] Also by way of exception was the question from Godfrey, Archbishop of Westminster, as to whether the schema in question belonged at an ecumenical council; in his opinion it would have been better to publish it in a separate document.[35]

There was also some ambiguity in the statements of approval. Some praised the schema because, besides what it said about the preaching of the gospel, they saw in it a possibility to call a halt to what they considered to be dominant aberrations with respect to faith and morals.[36] It should be noted in this regard that the schema, next to various appeals for the establishment of the Catholic Church's rights in this material, was frequently hortatory in tone. Almost everyone agreed that the schema was too long. Even Spellman, the first speaker of the day, pointed this out. He felt that the schema went too deeply into certain very specific points, was very repetitious,[37] and should be considerably shortened.[38] Because the communications media were expanding and developing day by day, it made no sense to issue detailed guidelines.[39]

---

[33] Bednorz, AS I/3, 433.

[34] Beck, AS I/3, 429-31. Strangely enough, he felt that enough had been said on the matter by Pius XI, Pius XII, and John XXIII: "In these documents one can find not only all the principles to be observed in the use of the communications media but also what should be done in practice in order to avoid dangers and to spread the truth for the good of the whole Church." Ibid., 430). Along with the other preparatory commissions, he said with some humor, "We sinned by ignorance."

[35] AS I/3, 459.

[36] Ruffini, AS I/3, 424. De Castro Mayor's criticism concerning the moral indifference of the Catholic press and film organizations should also be noted. Even Catholic cinemas showed films that were not very uplifting (AS I/3, 446). Léger, for his part, found that matters were being presented too negatively where morals were concerned (AS I/3, 461).

[37] AS I/3, 424. Requests to shorten the schema as well as complaints about its long-windedness can also be found in the following interventions: Ruffini, Beck, Bednorz, Charrière, Fernández-Conde (Cordoba, Spain), D'Souza, de Castro Mayer, Godfrey, Léger, and Suenens (AS I/3, 424, 430, 434, 436, 437, 440, 445, 459, 461, 462).

[38] See also the interventions of Enrique y Tarancón (Solsona), Heuschen (Liège), Fernández Feo-Tinoco (San Cristobal, Venezuela; on behalf of his colleagues) (AS I/3, 425, 447, 522-23).

[39] See Enrique y Tarancón, AS I/3, 425.

One of the most important criticisms of the document pointed out that, although the laity were extremely successful in their dealings with the media, their place in the schema was quite minor. Archbishop Enrique y Tarancón of Solsona was one of those who made this criticism. He wondered whether priests had the competence to involve themselves in the area of the communications media. The laity had more of the competence and expertise required, and their experience should be drawn on.[40] Other speakers, in line with the exhortation in no. 41 to form priests, religious, and laity which respect to the media,[41] also pointed out the need to prepare experts on the matter and that priority in this should be given to the laity.[42]

In a noteworthy appeal, E. D'Souza attempted to encourage a more positive attitude toward the media. Other institutions besides the Church also had rights and responsibilities.[43] There was too much repetition of what had been said in the encyclicals, and the text gave the impression that it was not sufficiently aware of the extraordinary possibilities the use of the means of communication might offer in the contemporary world with regard to famine and disaster, for example. Were the means of communication not the instruments par excellence for showing people their responsibilities with respect to serious world problems?[44] D'Souza added here that the laity needed to be encouraged to make adequate use of the various media without expecting to be led by the clergy in every detail.[45] In his speech on November 24, Léger also underlined the importance of the treatment of the communications media for the welfare of the Church, but like D'Souza, he found that the document was too juridi-

[40] See Enrique y Tarancón, AS I/3, 426: "In this apostolic sense, I think this activity is more fitting for lay people than for priests;" cf. also Léger, Suenens, and Ménager (AS I/3, 462, 464, 467).

[41] AS I/3, 391.

[42] Heuschen, AS I/3, 447. Bishop Heuschen had little enthusiasm for the establishment of a Catholic institution: "We ought to enter into existing institutions, not create new ones. Otherwise we will often have to admit that our news came too late. In these matters a day's delay means a battle lost." See also, e.g., Suenens, Ménager, Kozlowiecki (AS I/3, 464, 467-68, 512). Ona de Echave requested a precise demarcation of territory between priests and laity; the Church's task of proclaiming the message was primarily given to the bishops and priests, and it was therefore also necessary to ensure that priests be given training in the matter (AS I/3, 486-88).

[43] In this regard see also the speech of Höffner; AS I/3, 505-506; Moro Briz also pointed out that the document contained much talk on the rights of the Church "while it is silent on the Church's duties"(AS I/3, 508).

[44] AS I/3, 440-442; Brizgys and Soegijapranata also saw positive opportunities for the Church (AS I/3, 450, 452).

[45] AS I/3, 441-42.

cal in nature and placed too much emphasis on the rights of the Church.[46] He would prefer that emphasis be placed on the pastoral concern of the Church in this material.[47] Many were convinced that the various forms of the media could be a splendid instrument for the Church. Spellman, for example, on the basis of his experiences in the United States, saw an opportunity in the media for cooperation between Catholics and non-Catholics with an eye to the sanctification of humanity and society as a whole.[48] According to Wyszynski, radio and television offered the only chance to proclaim the Christian message to those who were indifferent with respect to religion, especially in a time when people were reading less.[49]

A number of speakers complained that the schema did not sufficiently denounce the dangers associated with the means of communication.[50] They felt that the schema ought to have given a clearer warning against the disordered and widespread use of the media (words such as "naturalism" and "sensualism" were used) and that those involved in the media should be better prepared to resist temptation.[51] The faithful expected the Council to provide effective regulation with respect to such difficult material.[52] At the same time, the schema was too optimistic, since it dealt with material that frequently served less honorable and often unwholesome ends.[53] Some could not see how Catholics would benefit from the acquisition of expertise on the level of film or televi-

[46] Along similar lines, F. Simons noted that while the Catholic Church claimed its rights throughout the world it denied them to those under its own power (AS I/3, 523-24).

[47] AS I/3, 461. Léger received support in this position from, among others, Bea, Ménager, Bernacki, and Sana (AS I/3, 465, 467, 471, 521). Civardi found that too little emphasis was placed in part I,1 on the Church's duty to speak out with regard to the aspect of leisure associated with the media. While he thought the media frequently had a pernicious influence on users, he still maintained a broadly positive attitude toward the schema (AS I/3, 503-4). Cf. also Del Pino Gómez (Lerida), AS I/3, 518-19.

[48] Höffner made a similar remark (AS I/3, 506).

[49] AS I/3, 458. The Cardinal referred here to part IV,3: "On Radio and Television" (AS I/3, 410-13). Suenens also pointed out that the media could sometimes have a negative effect on the faithful because of their passivity; at the same time he called for a clear stipulation that the right to information should not affect the private sphere. Kozlowiecki expressed a similar wish (AS I/3, 463-64, 511).

[50] Fernández-Conde of Cordova said: "No one is unaware of the moral questions that arise from the use of these media" (AS I/3, 436). Cf. also Boudon, AS I/3, 453. With regard to the dangers associated with films see Llopis Ivorra (AS I/3, 432).

[51] De Castro Mayer (AS I/3, 446).

[52] Fernández-Conde, D'Avack (AS I/3, 436, 439-40).

[53] D'Avack, AS I/3, 438; cf. also the suggestive intervention of de Castro Mayer (AS I/3, 445).

sion.[54] The clergy, of course, were to maintain the utmost care where this material was concerned,[55] but great care in the matter was also expected from parents in raising their children.[56] Words of caution were also echoed among those who had spoken very positively about the schema. Besides all the positive opportunities the media provide, they threaten to substitute themselves for the personal judgment of their audiences, precisely because of the way they present their material.[57] It was also noted that the right to information, discussed in paragraph 21,[58] should not imply that the private lives of those in responsible positions may be placed in jeopardy.[59]

It would be a serious overstatement to suggest that the Vatican up to that point had been "switched on" to the media. The media rightly and repeatedly pointed to the lack of information from the international press service as well as the bungling of the official press service or in *L'Osservatore Romano*.[60] There was something tragicomic about the fact that on the first day of the discussion of the schema, the Canadian auxiliary bishop Sanschagrin announced in his long intervention that the Vatican needed to ensure a faster exchange of information with the bishops concerning decisions from Rome. In some places it took up to a month before the bishops were informed of a decision from Rome. Information prior to this came from the press and was so abbreviated and distorted that it was untrustworthy and confusing to the faithful. The bishops were starved for information.[61] At the moment when the press was complaining that it could get no information in Rome, bishops were complaining that the press was being given information before them — it was certainly a remarkable situation!

---

[54] D'Avack, *AS* I/3, 439.

[55] Cf. *AS* I/3, 439. De Uriarte Bengoa, for example, fulminated against the fact that priests frequently neglected their pastoral duties because of film and TV (*AS* I/3, 490).

[56] D'Avack, *AS* I/3, 439. According to Brizgys, the media have a greater impact on the education of children than their parents do (*AS* I/3, 450); Höffner also pointed to the importance of well-reasoned choices with regard to the use of the media (*AS* I/3, 505).

[57] See Charrière, *AS* I/3, 435.

[58] *AS* I/3, 382.

[59] Suenens, *AS* I/3, 463.

[60] Although held in the Council's press office, the press conference given by the Protestant Oscar Cullmann on November 23 was not reported by *OssRom* until November 25, and then only on page 4 under the hardly exciting headline, "At the Margins of the Council: The Statement of a Waldensian 'Observer.'" One might have expected better from an *ecumenical* council!

[61] *AS* I/3, 427-28. To illustrate his point Sanschagrin pointed out how the term *socialization* in *Mater et magistra* had sometimes been misused by the press as praise for socialism; it took weeks for the bishops to find out what the encyclical really said.

The debates on November 24 ran along similar lines. After sending a telegram to congratulate the Pope on his eighty-first birthday on November 25, twenty-four fathers took the podium to confirm and elaborate remarks that had been made the previous day. The significance of the means of communication was related to the proclamation of the good news;[62] the possibilities for universality offered by technology were to be employed in order to proclaim the good news throughout the world. At the same time, a positive opportunity to proclaim the teaching of the Catholic Church in an ecumenical spirit to both Catholics and non-Catholics was envisaged.[63] Priority was given, moreover, to the cooperation of Catholic laity with other Christians in using this material to influence public opinion by way of the media.[64] It was added here that one might rightly qualify the media as a gift of God in the sense that they offer opportunities for the creation of a new civilization and a new culture. The fathers did not neglect to add, however, that this gift should not be allowed to do any damage to Christianity. The media, it was noted, also provided an opportunity to create a front for the spread and defense of fundamental human values and human rights.

Frequent reference was made, particularly by bishops from third-world countries, to the applicability of the media to the proclamation of the gospel. Two interventions, both in the name of the African episcopate, pointed out that radio and television were among the most important avenues open to the Catholic bishops and that, at least in Africa, full use of these means of communication should be made for preaching the Christian message. The hope was also expressed that the wealthier parts of the world would assist the poorer communities in this endeavor.[65] Bishops from behind the Iron Curtain also spoke very positively with respect to the possibilities offered by the media for proclaiming the Christian message.[66] Charrière even noted that not only the entire world but individual families could be reached by means of the media. He felt, therefore, that the Church ought not to absent itself from the world of the

[62] Mentioned already on November 23 by Heuschen (AS I/3, 448); see also Ona de Echave (AS I/3, 487).

[63] Bea, AS I/3, 465-66.

[64] Bea, AS I/3, 466. Bea implied here that the ultimate purpose of this material ought to be cooperation among all people of good will.

[65] See the speeches of Perraudin and Nwedo, AS I/3, 468-69, 476-78; see also Duval, S. Soares de Resende (AS I/3, 506, 516).

[66] "We ought to remember this so that we can make a greater contribution to spreading Catholic teaching on this matter" (Bednorz, AS I/3, 434).

media, certainly if one were to take into account the fact that Christianity is a *revealed* religion.[67]

Besides the rather general remarks that characterized most of the interventions, there were also a number of comments on specific sections.[68] With regard to part IV of the schema, on the press,[69] reference was made to the importance of having a Catholic presence in press agencies.[70] These, for all the front-line information they possessed, were insufficiently familiar with Catholic issues. Frequent correction of their coverage of events gave a bad impression.[71] Finally, it was noted that the media offered opportunities for promoting cooperation with major world organizations.

The debate closed on November 26th. After a word of thanks from the Pope for the telegram sent on the occasion of his birthday was read and the announcement was made that the decree *Ut unum sint* would be next schema to be discussed, thirteen more speakers took the floor. There was not much new;[72] praise for the schema was repeated and the dangers associated with the modern means of communication were summed up once again. In addition there were appeals for the establishment of institutes for the Christian formation of directors and actors. It was noted, at the same time, that Catholics lived in a pluralist society and that they had a duty, therefore, to make correct choices when it came to newspapers and TV programs.

The following day the fathers moved on to the vote on the following three points:

1. The schema is approved in substance.[73]

2. On the basis of the remarks made by the Council fathers, the conciliar Commission should extract the essential doctrinal principles and

---

[67] Charrière, *AS* I/3, 435.

[68] See, for example, the tirade of Bishop J. Ruotolo (Ugento) against the positivism and idealism related to no. 22 of the schema, which dealt with freedom in art (*AS* I/3, 484-86).

[69] *AS* I/3, 401-6.

[70] Not everyone had equal faith in the international press agencies. It can even be deduced from the intervention of González Martin that Catholics did not always inform each other in an adequate way (*AS* I/3, 479-80). Gouyon found that nos. 80-82 of chapter IV, dealing with the Catholic press, did not explain its mission clearly enough. Duval pointed to the problems in setting up a Catholic press in countries where Catholics are in the minority (*AS* I/3, 482-84, 507).

[71] Cf. Heuschen, *AS* I/3, 447.

[72] Six of those announced as speakers on the shema did not even get the chance to take the floor (*AS* I/3, 502).

[73] This would be to recognize also that it is appropriate for the Church to exercise its teaching authority on a matter of such pastoral importance (*AS* I/3, 613).

the more general pastoral guidelines and then compose a shorter text, which preserves the basic material, and submit this to the fathers for voting.

3. Material on concrete implementation should be included in a pastoral instruction from the office mentioned in no. 57, with the help of experts from various countries.[74]

Of the 2160 fathers present at the vote, 2138 voted in favor, 15 voted against, and 7 votes were invalid. The schema was therefore accepted, at least in its essential aspects, and would now go to the Commission for the requested revision and shortening.

III. THE WORK OF THE COMMISSION

As regards the work of the Commission it is possible to be quite brief. It was rather late in beginning its task.[75] After an additional twenty-six written interventions were brought in on December 3, they set about the task of putting these comments in order. They were divided into four groups: the first included remarks praising the schema, the second included elements related, for example, to the functioning of *L'Osservatore Romano* or Vatican Radio, the use of airmail by the Holy See to inform bishops as quickly as possible of decisions from Rome, the promotion of an international conference for the defense of religious freedom, and so forth; the third included ten or so remarks of a more general nature; while the fourth included remarks concerning specific points in the schema. On the basis of this organization of the material the experts began the task of revising the schema between January 28 and 31, 1963.[76]

Elsewhere in this volume there is a more explicit treatment of relationships with the press, one of the dimensions of the subject dealt with in this chapter. By way of conclusion, let me note that the document on the media was treated as harshly as the media themselves were treated.

[74] It is apparent from this number that the Council fathers accepted the request of the preparatory Secretariat for Communications Media and that they petitioned the Pope to extend the authority of the Pontifical Commission for Motion Pictures, Radio and Television to all the means of social communication, including the press.

[75] This commission met for the second time only on November 26th (cf. letter from Cento to the members of the commission, De Vet papers, Archives of the Diocese of Breda, not numbered).

[76] Baragli, *L'Inter Mirifica,* 137-38; see also a handwritten text of De Vet for a press conference in Utrecht with regard to this revision (March 18, 1963).

Efforts on the part of the Church to improve relations with the press, such as the Eucharist in the church of S. Ivo alla Sapienza, at which Msgr. Helder Câmara presided,[77] were the exception. On the whole, relations with the press during the initial stages of the Council were shallow, disorganized, and amateurish.[78] The debate on the media itself did not receive high marks, probably the result of the way the press was being treated.

[77] See *OssRom*, November 26-27, 1962.
[78] Kaiser's description of the press office is devastating (see *Pope, Council, and World*, 189ff.).

CHAPTER VII

BEYOND AN ECCLESIOLOGY OF POLEMICS
THE DEBATE ON THE CHURCH

GIUSEPPE RUGGIERI

I. "AUTHORITY BEFORE ALL AND ABOVE ALL"

On the morning of November 23, as the discussion of the schema on the communications media was beginning, the much awaited schema on the Church was at last distributed. The schema that for almost all the bishops was the Council's reason for being was now in their hands.

Perhaps even more than the schema on the sources of revelation, the preparation of this schema had been marked by opposition and disagreements between the Theological Commission and the Secretariat for Christian Unity — and not on minor matters but on almost all the main points of the text.[1] Thus on the nature of the Church there was the conflict between a juridical conception of the Church as a society, reflected in the unyielding defense of the identification of the Catholic Church and the Mystical Body, and a conception of the Church that was more sensitive to its mystery. On the question of membership in the Church, Cardinal Bea, both in his public statements and by way of the Secretariat, championed the position that started from the efficacy of the means of grace found even outside the Catholic Church and on this basis claimed a *real*, even if incomplete, membership in the Church for non-Catholic Christians. The Theological Commission, on the other hand, adopted the position taken in *Mystici Corporis* and allowed only an *ordinatio*, that is, an orientation, of non-Catholic Christians to the Church.

As for bishops, while there was agreement on the sacramentality of episcopal consecration, positions diverged when it came to the origin of the episcopal power of jurisdiction. The Theological Commission made the pope the source of this power, while the Secretariat connected it with ordination.[2] Finally, in regard to the relationship between Church and

---

[1] *History*, I, 272-76, 285-300.

[2] The Subcommission for Amendments tried to reach a middle position on this point, saying that while the power of jurisdiction as such is grounded in episcopal ordination, its exercise depends on a mission received from the pope (ibid., 294-95).

State, the Theological Commission took its stand on the classical doctrine of thesis (the state has an obligation to support only the Catholic religion and to prohibit others) and hypothesis (tolerance when circumstances make Catholics the minority). The Secretariat pressed for the abandonment of this anti-modern perspective and the recognition of religious freedom based on the principle of charity.

The Central Preparatory Commission was unable to smoothe out these disagreements, both because it reflected them within its own membership and especially because the Theological Commission, regarding itself as sharing in the duties of the Holy Office as the supreme guarantor of orthodoxy, refused to acknowledge the right of anyone else to intervene in matters of doctrine. This somewhat conflictual situation would have disruptive consequences once there was a shift from tensions internal to the Curia or within the organizations of the preparatory period to the confrontation of views in the Council.

It has already been mentioned that, on the initiative of Cardinal Suenens, a subtle effort had begun win over to a middle position not only the more open bishops and theologians but also some influential moderates. This was the aim of the liaison between Suenens and Montini and their respective theologians, Philips and Colombo. On October 18 Philips told Congar that he had already been commissioned by Suenens "to revise, complete, and improve" the schema on the Church, and he also gave Congar an outline of his plan.[3] Suenens had chosen Philips

---

[3] According to *JCongar*, October 18, the plan contained six main chapters. Congar describes them as follows:

    1) The Church: People of God, Mystery, Mystical Body (bringing the authority of the bishops into the Lattanzi schema, from which it is absent.) I myself would like to see introduced into this first chapter the idea of the Church as missionary: a single entity that is constantly spreading.

    2) Members. Necessity of the Church. Adjust the Tromp schema.

    3) The bishops. Present them as successors of the college of apostles, according to the diagram: Peter/other apostles = pope/bishops. This chapter would have the following sections:

        — Bishops, successors of the apostles

        — Episcopal consecration a sacrament

        — Powers of residential bishops:

            — Teaching: their infallibility (gathered in council; separately)

            — Bring in here parts of the chapter on the magisterium and an explanation of the *ex sese*;

            — Governing (use the text of Pius IX, 1875);

            — Liturgical power;

            — Relationship to the primacy;

            — Collegial responsibility of the bishops.

    4) The laity

because the latter "embodied in his person a kind of *via media* that would not frighten either Cardinal Ottaviani or the man who wrote the original schema, Tromp (a Dutchman)."[4]

On October 25 a meeting at the Angelicum brought together, besides Congar and Philips, Colombo, Lécuyer, Rahner, Ratzinger, Semmelroth, and McGrath.[5] Half of these theologians had been, by a variety of titles, members of the preparatory Theological Commission. Congar observed that "we read and discuss Philips' version of the *De episcopis*, which, at least according to plan, covers the whole of the schema on the Church." Referring to this meeting, Semmelroth spoke of

> a schema prepared by the latter [Philips] on the Church and, included therein, on the bishops. We discussed this because it seems that a number of bishops would like to have this schema be the second one discussed, after the liturgical schema. This would be difficult to do, of course, since this schema is not yet available to the bishops. The work Philips has done in correcting the schema given to the central commission seems to be very good and acceptable. It would be nice if it went through.

At this point, then, using the preparatory text he had in his possession,[6] Philips "adjusted" the chapter on the bishops (chapter III of the

---

5) Evangelical perfection (goal for *all* Christians). Religious.
6) Ecumenism

Only after these chapters, which have to do with Christian existence, with the inner life of Christianity, bring in the chapters that have been prepared on Church and state, tolerance, and so on.

This plan reflected the organization of the material for debate at the Council around the distinction, dear to Suenens, between the Church *ad intra* and the Church *ad extra*. It may be noted that Philips was in fact quite reticent on the actual contents of this outline. Such expressions as "adjusting" Tromp's schema on the question of membership in the Church, a matter certainly central for the balance of the whole, show a minimal desire to make real changes.

For a reconstruction of the several not entirely clear stages through which Philip's schema went during this period, see J. A. Komonchak, "The Initial Debate about the Church," in *Vatican II commence*, 329-52; A. Melloni, "Ecclesiologie al Vaticano II," in *Commissions*, 91-179.

[4] L. J. Suenens, *Souvenirs et Espérances* (Paris, 1991), 114. In fact, even before beginning his work, Philips had Ottaviani issue him a kind of approval. In the Philips Archive (CCV, P.015.02) there is a note from Tromp to Philips, dated October 10, 1962: "I have just spoken to His Eminence. If the Constitution on the Church is not discussed before Christmas, he has decided that you may proceed as you think fit." Clearly even at that date (October 10), neither Ottaviani nor Tromp was able to appreciate the full power of the agreement Philips's undertaking was to win among the "adversaries." The events of the first weeks would throw quite a different light on the proposed adjustments.

[5] The meeting was rather resented by Dominicans such as Gagnebet and Labourdette, who lived at the Angelicum but were not invited (*JLabourdette,* October 26).

[6] Like the other members of the preparatory Theological Commission, including those

schema) that he had already presented to Congar six days earlier; he thus chose one of the less thorny themes, the one in which the middle way accepted by the Subcommission for Amendments (namely, that only the exercise of the power of jurisdiction depends on the Bishop of Rome) seemed to offer a practicable way of achieving agreement. Relying on what had been said at the meeting, Philips made further corrections and contacted Bea. The latter, according to Philips, made only some corrections of detail, whereas he seemed much taken up with the question, so central for ecumenism, of membership in the Church.[7] Within the Secretariat itself opposition to Bea's view was chiefly represented by Fr. Charles Boyer, who had also opposed the Secretariat's view on the relation between scripture and tradition.[8]

While Philips continued to weave his cloth by setting up valuable relationships that would make a consensus possible, Suenens concerned himself with procedure. The latter told a rather skeptical Congar that he planned "to introduce the revised text at the same time as the official text, using the services of the Commission [sic] for Extraordinary Affairs."[9] On November 12 Philips sent the corrected text of the schema on the Church to Tromp, who noted that he had received it not from the preparatory commission, "but from outsiders."[10] Before we can understand in what sense Philips's schema represented an alternative to the official schema, we must analyze the latter.[11]

---

closest to Ottaviani and Tromp, Philips did not at this point know the last emendations of the text on the basis of observations made by the Central Preparatory Commission and the revision by the Subcommission for Amendments (see Komonchak, "The Initial Debate," 332).

[7] See *JCongar,* October 28.

[8] "I wrote a text for Bishop Volk as a supplement to what he showed me yesterday. He had written something for Bea's Secretariat on the Church as fruit of salvation and as an institution for salvation. The occasion for this was a discussion in the Secretariat for Christian Unity on the question of membership in the Church; the discussion had been sparked by the new schema on the Church which Philips had submitted. It was Boyer especially who seems to have offered resistance on the question of membership in the Church. What Bishop Volk had written was quite attractive, but it ran into the difficulty that it uses an unusual terminology quite different from what the theologians are accustomed to. There is also the difficulty that the two levels of the Church are not sufficiently unified. It was in view of this that I wrote down something for him that would supplement the schema" (*TSemmelroth,* October 30). Semmelroth is referring to what Volk would say in the hall during the debate on the *De Ecclesia.*

[9] *JCongar,* November 6.

[10] Tromp, *Relatio,* no. 4.

[11] The official text appeared, along with the schema on the Blessed Virgin Mary, as the "*series secunda*" of the *Schemata Constitutionum et decretorum de quibus disceptabitur in Concilii sessionibus.* The date of the Pope's approbation was November 10, 1962. The schema is also in *AS* I/4, 12-91. For a reconstruction of the stages through which the text went before its publication see Melloni, "Ecclesiologie al Vaticano II."

The official text finally enabled the discontented to know what they would be opposing. Its characteristic elements were clearly stated: primacy of the Church's visible side (and therefore of the image of the Church as a "body"); determination of membership in the Church on the basis of acknowledgment of the authority of the Roman pontiff; this authority as "source" of all other jurisdiction in the Church; maximum extension of the subject matter of the authentic and infallible magisterium; inflexible safeguarding of the principle of authority; an ecumenical minimalism in relations with the other Christian confessions; an aggressive attitude toward all other kinds of religious experience found in society. There was also an explicit determination to cover all the points, based on the presumption that it was the privilege and exclusive task of the Theological Commission to determine the doctrinal principles of the Council's teaching, while "everybody else" could occupy himself with disciplinary and practical matters. This explains the sections on the religious, the laity, and ecumenism.

The text was divided into eleven chapters occupying eighty-two printed pages. In addition to the notes, the chapters on the laity and on the magisterium were accompanied by a "commentary" explaining the intentions of the redactors in language even more technical and scholastic than the already heavy language used in the text. It was not easy to grasp the unity of the overall structure. After the early chapters on the nature of the Church (I), membership in the Church (II), the episcopate (III), residential bishops in particular (IV), the states of perfection (V), and the laity (VI), the document suddenly went back to deal with the magisterium of the Church (VII) and with authority and obedience (VIII). Finally, the last three chapters spoke of relations between Church and State, the necessity of proclaiming the gospel to all peoples, and ecumenism, but without any logical order, since the inverse order would have been more obvious.

Chapter I was devoted to the nature of the Church militant and thus represented a careful choice, made, it seems, with a view to limiting the subject to a juridical and societal perspective. It grounded the institution of the Church in God's will to redeem human beings not individually but as persons who are "called out of the multitude" and are, by the power of Christ the head, not only "redeemed but redeemers as well." However, Christ does not sanctify and govern the people of God by himself alone, but "through leaders chosen by himself;" these he has appointed and adorned with the "offices of preacher, priest, and king, to be exercised under Peter." In other words, the Church makes its appearance not as a scattered crowd but as a "closely ordered host" (*ut confertum agmen*) due to unity in faith, communion in the sacraments, and apostolicity of government.

To this end and because of the clarity with which it expresses both the social and the mystical dimensions, the image of the body, among all the images that Christ and the apostles used to describe the Church, takes on an absolute value: "The image of the body holds first place." The controversialist ecclesiology of the Church as a society, with its echoes of Bellarmine, thus becomes the criterion for an interpretation of the Bible that makes one image emerge more clearly than all the others. The text also undertakes a "detailed explanation of the image of the body": visibility ("it is seen with the eyes"); links between unequal members (and therefore the socio-juridical dimension); vitality (also shown in the image of the vine and the branches); mystical union of persons (with quasi-monophysite hints: a union in which Christ is the head and the Spirit is the soul of the Church); intangible nature of its essential holiness (which is bestowed by the means of grace which the Church objectively possesses, despite the sins of individuals). The Church is thus likened, by analogy, to the incarnate Word, since the visible society and the mystical body of Christ are not two realities but only one, "which has a human and a divine aspect."

That the text was aiming ultimately at the identification of the Roman Catholic Church with the mystical body of Christ is confirmed by the definition that ends the chapter: the Council "teaches and solemnly professes that there is only one true Church of Jesus Christ, namely the one we celebrate in the creed as one, holy, catholic, and apostolic . . . which, after his resurrection, he entrusted to St. Peter and his successors, the Roman pontiffs, to be governed; therefore only the Catholic Roman has a right to be called the Church."

Chapter II connected the question of the members of the militant Church with the necessity of this Church for salvation. None can be saved unless he or she is a member of the Church or ordered to it by a *votum* (desire). The only "true and proper" members of the Church are those baptized persons who profess the true faith, acknowledge the authority of the pope, and are not separated from it by serious offenses (the reference seems to be to offenses that merit excommunication). Those who are "ordered to the Church by desire" include not only catechumens but all who sincerely seek the will of God. The state of catechumens is thus equated with that of non-Christians.

On the other hand, the state of "separated" Christians is described with considerable ambiguity: "those who do not profess the true faith or the oneness of communion under the Roman pontiff, but do desire it, even if the desire be unconscious."[12] The Church is linked to these people in various ways. Even if they do not possess Catholic faith, they do in fact have a loving belief in Christ as God and Savior; at times they distinguish themselves by their faith in and devotion to the Eucharist and by their love of the Mother of God; they share in the same baptismal consecration and, to some extent, also in the communion of prayers and spiritual blessings; and the Holy Spirit acts also in them. But they do not enjoy all the benefits enjoyed by those who "are really members of the Church," and for this reason the Church prays unceasingly that they may abandon their present state.

The text was thus not without some internal contradictions. The main one consisted in the fact that after having listed so many "objective" links, the text stubbornly insisted that non-Catholics are not "really" members of the Church, and seemed thereby to relegate them to the status of members "by desire." This was the iron cage created by recourse to the category of "member" in defining what it means to belong to the Church.

Chapter III was devoted to the sacramental nature of the episcopal office, which is "in the true and proper sense" the highest degree of the sacrament of orders. Simple presbyters, on the other hand, while they are "true priests" by reason of their sacramental consecration, and while they act "in the person of Christ" when they celebrate the Mass and the sacraments, do not have the power of jurisdiction unless it is bestowed on them, directly or indirectly, by either the pope or their own bishop.

Chapter IV, in keeping with the compromise reached by the subcommission for amendments, says that ordination gives bishops, in addition

---

[12] The text was not clear: "those who do not profess the true faith or oneness of communion under the Roman pontiff, but desire *ea* even with an unconscious desire." It is difficult to decide whether *ea* was a misprint and, if so, what the true reading was: *eam* or *eas*? If the word should have been *eam*, the text would be identifying "true faith" with oneness of communion under the pope; if the word should have been the plural *eas*, then the "or" between "faith" and "oneness" would in effect be adversative and true faith would be distinct from oneness of communion. In addition, in what follows, the text does not repeat "true faith" but has, instead "Catholic faith," which in note 15 is distinguished from "divine faith as such." Catholic faith, which is mentioned in reference both to the so-called Tridentine Profession of Faith of Pius IV and to the Constitution *Dei Filius* of Vatican I, is in its turn subdivided into objective (as explained, for example, by Pius IV) and subjective (as explained by *Dei Filius*). And, again in note 15 of chapter II, there is the lapidary statement that "baptism does not make one a member, unless subjective Catholic faith is added (*acedat* [*sic*])."

to the office of sanctifying, the offices of teaching and of governing
(jurisdiction consists of these), but it also states that the exercise of jurisdiction depends on a mission "from the supreme government of the
Church." The ways in which this mission is conferred are defined in a
flexible way: from local customs never revoked to direct papal conferral. The pope is also recognized as having the right to extend or restrict
the exercise of episcopal jurisdiction in virtue of the "immediate and
episcopal power of jurisdiction" he possesses over all the Churches and
each of them, over all the bishops and faithful and each of them.

The text then moved on to speak of relations between residential bishops and the Church as a whole. It said that these bishops constitute the
center, foundation, and source of unity in the local Churches to the
extent that in these and from these Churches (*in illis et ex illis*), which
are formed in the likeness of the universal Church, there exists the one
and only Catholic Church, whose center, foundation, and source of unity
is the successor of Peter. Individual bishops represent their own
Churches, but all of them, together with the pope, represent the entire
Church. Although the bishops, either individually or when united, even
in large numbers, do not have authority over the universal Church except
by participation in the authority of the supreme pontiff, they are
nonetheless bound to have an authentic concern for it. This concern does
not constitute a power of jurisdiction, but a "powerful solidarity" in fraternal communion.

In saying all this, the text does not, however, deny the proper reality
of the "episcopal college," which succeeds to the apostolic college and
which, "together with its head, the Roman pontiff, and never without
this head, is believed to be the single subject of full and supreme power
over the universal Church." Although this is an ordinary power, it is
legitimately exercised only in an extraordinary manner and in devoted
subordination to the pope, when and to whatever extent seems appropriate to him. Only residential bishops are members of this college by right.
The obvious contradiction between the several statements in the chapter
(an ordinary power cannot at the same time be a participation in another
power, nor can it be exercised only in an extraordinary manner) was not
grasped by the drafters of the schema.

Having reached this point, instead of proceeding, logically, to a further definition of the teaching office and authority of bishops, the text
succumbed, as it were, to the attraction of the section of the Code on
persons; it puts off to later chapters the discussion of these matters and
continues instead with a discussion of religious and the laity.

Chapter V was devoted to "the states for the acquisition of evangelical perfection." The viewpoint continued to be primarily juridical. Jesus did not leave us only precepts; to those who want them he offered the evangelical counsels of poverty, chastity, and obedience as an easier and surer way to attain to the fullness of charity. The counsels are therefore divine in origin and belong among the constitutive elements of the Church's mark of holiness. In order publicly to acknowledge that the observance of the evangelical counsels belongs to its life, the Church has issued rules or given the force of law to those proposed by outstanding men and women, so that those who observe this law may constitute "a state for the acquisition of perfection, and a chosen portion of the mystical body of Christ."

The state of perfection is not a state intermediate between the clerical condition and the lay condition but may be common to both. The observance of the counsels is by its nature a better thing if done in virtue of a vow instead of a promise and by perpetual rather than temporary commitment. The text condemns the view of those who belittle the obligation assumed before God and the Church or who maintain that the state of perfection hinders or diminishes the formation of the personality. And, just as it is for the hierarchy to judge the forms of a life consecrated to perfection, so too the pope, in virtue of his universal primacy, can remove from the jurisdiction of the bishops any institute of perfection whatsoever and its individual members. In thus linking religious life to a universalist and centralized vision of the Church, the document intended to give permanence to the conception of it that had developed in the Latin Church since the time of the Gregorian reform of the eleventh century.

Chapter VI of the text then took a further step away from the hierarchical center and turned to the subject of the laity. This was perhaps the chapter that, despite all its shortcomings, was most receptive to movements of church renewal in the twentieth century. The emphasis fell on the responsibility and duties that all the faithful have in carrying out the divine plan of salvation in the world. There was a reference to the common priesthood of the faithful, although it was emphasized that in the body of Christ it is the priests "properly so called" who offer the people the means of salvation and who speak the words of eucharistic consecration "in the name of Christ." In other words, there remained in the end a very dichotomous and negative vision of the state of ordinary Christians who are not called either to the hierarchic order or to a religious state that has been ratified by the Church.

However, as a result of the theological reflection and experience of the previous decades, the text did confirm the value of involvement in the world: the laity were those who, though being neither clerics nor religious, have a duty to attain to Christian holiness "by works, including those that are secular;" by following their Christian vocation they sanctify the world from within. No. 23 listed the rights and duties of the laity in a primarily sacramental perspective that was the most felicitous part of the document. The proper apostolate of the laity was further defined, chiefly in its religious setting, as a specific way of evangelizing and sanctifying. There was a passing reference to the reciprocal sanctification of spouses "by the power of the sacrament." Also mentioned as a task specific to the laity was the "consecration of the world;" that is, activity aimed at permeating every field of activity with the spirit of Christ without leaving the secular order as such.

A sharp distinction was made between the apostolate of the laity, undertaken in virtue of the universal baptismal mission, and the apostolate undertaken by a special mandate from the hierarchy; in virtue of the latter the laity "share in the hierarchical apostolate of the Church; this participation is known as Catholic Action." Also emphasized was the right of the Church to perform the spiritual and temporal works of mercy "publicly" and also through the agency of specialized institutions of religious or lay persons, as well as its right and duty to promote social works, especially when it is supplying for a lack. The laity were also urged not to withdraw from political responsibilities and commitments. Finally, the schema insisted that society is autonomous in the pursuit of its immediate end, which is the temporal common good; it exhorted Christians to avoid both a confusion between the religious and civil dimensions and an undue separation or opposition of a laicist and secularist kind, since society must always remain subject to the law of God.

After the chapter on the laity the schema turned back to the magisterium and the authority of the Church. Chapter VII, on the magisterium, was the more "technical" of the two and gave the impression of intending to specify and rigidify the teaching of Vatican I. The authentic magisterium was described as "the proximate source and perpetual means" of the universal Church's indefectibility in the truth. The prerogative of infallibility, which this magisterium enjoys, is different from "the charism of inspiration," since it exists not to give new revelations but to safeguard and transmit the integral deposit of faith in such a way that everything is constantly explained "in the same sense and with the same understanding."

The *object* of the authentic magisterium is divided in three. The primary object is the proclamation, safeguarding, and interpretation of what has been revealed. The secondary object is everything that, even if not explicitly or implicitly revealed, is nevertheless so connected with revelation that without it the deposit of faith could not preserved in its integrity, properly explained, and effectively defended.[13] The task and right of the magisterium is, thirdly, infallibly to interpret and declare not only revealed law but the natural law as well. The conclusion was, to say the least, striking: "There is, therefore, no area of human activity that can, in its religious and ethical aspect, be withdrawn from the authority of the magisterium instituted by Christ."[14] Finally, as a further area of competence, mention is made of the right to pass judgment on extraordinary religious phenomena that occur within the Church and outside of it. Logically one might have expected this to appear before the reference to the natural law.

The *subject* of the authentic teaching authority includes several persons and agencies, but the office itself is one and indivisible:

> The office of the authentic magisterium, which is endowed with the charism of truth and exists in the Church by divine institution, may be exercised by several persons and agencies but it is always one and indivisible. It has in fact been established by the sole supreme teacher, Christ the Lord; it is the representative of his authority and it is aided by the one and only Spirit of truth, in order that in the exercise of this office his [Christ's] truth may be taught.[15]

The teaching office is exercised, first of all, by the Roman pontiff, whose prerogatives are described in the language of Vatican I. The pope is the teacher not only of the faithful but of the bishops.[16] When he

---

[13] A note on this passage refers to the formulation of the secondary object of the authentic magisterium that Bishop Gasser had given at Vatican I (Mansi 52, 1226). The reference was rather inaccurate since it failed to recall a clarification made by Gasser. While he defined the secondary object of the infallible magisterium in the manner indicated, he also referred to a debated question on which the theologians were divided: that is, whether the infallibility of the secondary object was that of a "theologically certain" proposition (a proposition obtained by way of reasoning that arrives at a conclusion that is "new" in respect to revelation, thanks to the introduction of a nonrevealed term into the syllogism) or that of a true and proper dogma of faith. At Vatican I, it seemed to the fathers "by unanimous consent" that this question should not be resolved but should be left with the status it then had. This clarification was omitted in the schema, with the result that it took a more inflexible position than Vatican I had.

[14] No. 29 of the preparatory schema, referring to the teaching of Leo XIII, Pius XI, and Pius XII (*AS* I/4, 48).

[15] No. 30 (*AS* I/4, 48-49).

[16] As Christ is said to be the "supreme teacher," so the pope is said to be the "supreme teacher" of truth to the entire Catholic Church (no. 30, *AS* I/4, 49).

speaks *ex cathedra*, his assertions are infallible and irreformable, and they are such of themselves (*ex sese*) and not in virtue of the assent of the faithful or the other bishops. Even when he does not speak *ex cathedra*, his authoritative teaching requires a "religious compliance of the will and intellect." Mentioned as the means by which this authoritative magisterium is exercised are "some" apostolic constitutions, the encyclicals, and the more solemn allocutions. When the pope pronounces in these documents on a question hitherto controverted, the question can no longer be a matter for "public debate among theologians."[17]

Bishops in communion with the pope also exercise an authoritative magisterium. Although they are not individually infallible, they are, for their faithful, authoritative teachers of truth, whether they are scattered throughout the world or gathered in particular councils. The college of bishops, however, when gathered in council with and under the pope, enjoys the same infallibility that the pope enjoys when he speaks *ex cathedra*. In addition, the bishops enjoy the prerogative of infallibility when all, each teaching in his own diocese, are at one with the pope in teaching the same truth. Here again the schema was repeating what Vatican I had said about the so-called "ordinary" magisterium.

Finally, for the first time a council was called upon to clarify the doctrinal status of the Roman Curia. The Roman congregations and councils were described as subsidiary organs of the pontifical magisterium, since the pope "does not exercise his teaching office by himself alone but can partially entrust it" to them. These organs act with the aid of the Holy Spirit, who gives them his gifts "in keeping with the place they occupy in the Mystical Body," and they therefore deserve an interior religious obedience and assent of the mind.

The status of theologians was then explained. The document imagined a kind of medieval *res publica* or corporation of theologians and recognized them as having an authority specifically different from that of the bishops. Whatever the theologians set forth as "certain teaching" deserves a "deferential respect," as long as solid arguments do not prove differently (for example, the age-old interpretation of the first chapters of Genesis). Doctrines taught "with common and constant consensus"

---

[17] A reference is made in a note to the corresponding claim in *Humani generis*. It is the combination of the subject of *Mystici Corporis* (the unqualified identification of the Mystical Body with the Catholic Church) and that of *Humani generis* (the vindication of the authority of the magisterium against the new pluralist trends in Catholic theology) that perhaps best explains the spirit of the preparatory schema on the Church.

cannot be denied "without rashness or error in faith." The schema explained further, not in the text but in the commentary, that a special authority belongs to theologians who have received a canonical mission to teach in the name of the magisterium. This was a vision of theology that seemed to exalt its authority but in fact placed its function completely in the service of the magisterium rather than in the service of the Church as such.[18]

In this very lengthy chapter on the magisterium,[19] a place was made, finally, for "auxiliaries" of the magisterium at the pastoral level: priests who receive from the pope or bishops the duty of "teaching the word of God," but also clerics, religious, or lay people who are called upon to instruct others in the Christian faith and in religious education. A special role belongs to parents, who as fellow-workers of Christ and Mother Church have received the sweet burden of "engraving the elements of the faith on the minds of their children." In addition, experts in medicine, law, economics, the social sciences, and other disciplines should do their part in forming moral judgments on pertinent questions, so that these may be given answers inspired by Christian principles.

The final section of the chapter on the magisterium tightened the ranks, one last time, of the "closely ordered host" of which chapter I had spoken. None should too readily think themselves masters in theological matters, which are not to be judged by the standards of the secular sciences. Everyone should be obedient to the authoritative magisterium. Even lay people who have no official duty must be submissive to the magisterium when they apply themselves to sacred studies. All are also exhorted not to be ashamed of the gospel and to grow in knowledge of the faith, so that they may be ready to answer those who inquire into the reason for their hope.

There seemed no end to the concerns of the drafters of the schema with the question of authority. After acknowledging the authority of the Roman pontiff as the decisive criterion of membership in the Church (chapter II), after speaking of the episcopate "in union with the Roman pontiff and under his authority" (Chapters III and IV), and after further toughening the teaching of Vatican I on the magisterium in the very long

---

[18] This was a vision of theology not as a distinct charism of the Church and in the Church, but as a function completely exhausted by its relation to the magisterium. The commentary explained that it derived this conception of theology from the *votum* of the Lateran University.

[19] In a text of eleven chapters in eighty-two pages, this one chapter occupied almost twelve pages.

chapter VII, they still thought it necessary to add a chapter on the principle of authority itself.

Why? To understand what was going on we must keep certain facts in mind. The defense of the principle of authority had been the central point in post-Tridentine ecclesiology. Catholic apologetics had regarded the Protestant denial of the principle of authority as the cause of all the evils of the modern age. This view was eventually accepted by the Roman magisterium[20] and made official in the introduction to the Constitution *Dei Filius* of Vatican I. The schema prepared by the Theological Commission was in the line of this tradition and sought to perpetuate it. But, even from a merely quantitative viewpoint, the effect of this approach showed itself to be the reduction of every aspect of the Church to its relation to the central authority. The expressions used revealed the emotion behind this emphasis. The schema imagined a Church deeply disturbed by the crisis of authority: "strongly shaken by deeply felt anguish (*vehementi afflictione percellitur*)."

This state of mind determined the definition of "the true concept of authority": "All legitimate authority is from God (see Rom 13:1), and it has its power to bind consciences in the name of God not from the knowledge, prudence, or other gift required of leaders in the exercise of authority, but from the will of God."[21] The schema then applies this definition to the Church and explains how authority in the Church represents the royal power of Christ and has for its purpose to extend the blessings of redemption to all human beings. Therefore it rejects all the reasons given for avoiding obedience to authority (the dignity of the person and freedom of the children of God; special charisms; the lack of prior consultation; the imperfection or inopportuneness of a command).

This does not mean that superiors do not themselves have the duty of observing the divine law, of seeking advice where this is appropriate, and of not hindering initiatives coming from their subjects. The latter, in turn, must see their superiors with the eyes of faith, and they also have the duty of making their views known "through institutions appointed by the Church, if any are available." But once legitimate authority has

---

[20] Pius IX, Encyclical *Quanta cura* (*ASS* 3 [1867], 163).

[21] *AS* I/4, 60. For this definition of authority a note gives two references to the teaching of Pius XII: the allocution *Si diligis*, May 31, 1954, to the cardinals and bishops present for the canonization of Pius X (*AAS* 46 [1954], 314); and the allocution *Magnificate Dominum*, of November 2, 1954, to the cardinals and bishops present on the new liturgical feast of Mary Queen of Heaven and Earth (*AAS* 46 [1954], 673-74). The two passages cited do speak of the necessity of authority and obedience in the Church, but neither contains such a definition.

commanded something, there is no longer any room for criticism. Even the denunciation of evils in the Church should be made in accordance with the order established by Christ in Matthew 18:15-17 and can never be such as to cast doubt on the Church's essential indefectibility.

The schema then distinguishes public opinion in the Church from the *sensus fidei*. The latter comes from on high and is the consensus of faithful and pastors "in matters of faith and morals," whereas public opinion has to do with the "realm of action" and is a spontaneous reaction to what is happening. The manifestations of public opinion are therefore good or bad depending on whether or not they proceed from a real knowledge of things and from an authentically Catholic spirit. In any case, superiors are not always bound to consult public opinion, and no appeal may be made to public opinion in order to effect a change in the decisions of the hierarchy.

Chapter IX moves from relationships within the Church to relations between Church and State; chapter X takes up the necessity of proclaiming the gospel to all peoples; and chapter XI deals with ecumenism. Church-State relations are explained on the basis of the principles ratified in the public law of the Church: the Church has the right and duty of dealing with temporal questions to the extent that these play a part in the ordering of human beings to their supernatural end. But the state, for its part, cannot be indifferent to religion, inasmuch as it must help citizens to obtain more easily the goods that contribute to the living of a religiously human life. Not only that, but even if in the present order of things liturgical worship falls exclusively within the competence of the Church, the civic community must offer God a worship that is in some way social. The best way for it to fulfill this duty is for the state to grant complete freedom to the Catholic Church, while also excluding from its legislation anything that in the judgment of the Church hinders the attainment of the everlasting end. Only in the case of a non-Catholic society is the state not obliged to this recognition, but it must grant complete freedom to citizens who want civic life to be shaped by Catholic principles. And even if the principles in question need to be applied with moderation, the Church nonetheless condemns laicism, which is wholly bent on obscuring them.

Chapter X dealt with the necessity to proclaim the gospel to all peoples, a duty and right of the Church that originates in God and that no one may oppose. This right may not be opposed by appeal to the traditions of peoples, since the gospel does not reject anything that is not contrary to natural reason and divine law; the Church in fact wants whatever is honorable and beautiful in each nation to be preserved and even elevated to the supernatural order. The responsibility for carrying out this task belongs first and foremost to the pope and then also to the bishops. All, however, have an obligation to cooperate.

The final chapter was devoted to explaining the principles of ecumenism. While acknowledging the bonds that unite the Church to the separated brethren and above all to those of the Oriental "rites," the schema said that all these are insufficient to establish the unity willed by Christ. In fact, even the Eucharist is a sign of that unity only when it is accompanied by the profession of the one, true, and integral faith and celebrated in communion with a bishop who is himself united to the Roman see.

The Church looks with maternal affection on individual separated brothers and sisters and invites them to join her. The schema likewise acknowledges that these brethren are helped on the journey to unity by their mutual union within their "communities."[22] On the other hand, these communities retain within themselves the means and signs of unity, but in a way that is separated from the fullness of revelation and therefore actually provides them with reasons for dividing the inheritance of Christ. All the faithful are therefore exhorted to show by their words and example that the fullness of revelation is "maintained truly and purely" in the Catholic Church, so that if the separated brethren are united to us once again, they too can possess the fullness of Christ's inheritance.

The schema acknowledges the value of the ecumenical movement, which has arisen "in many parts of the world in separated communities that are detached from the chair of Blessed Peter." But those who mean to obey the will of Christ must draw ever nearer to the Catholic Church "in oneness of faith, government, and communion under the one Vicar of Christ."

The text then goes with great and complicated detail into "*communicatio in sacris*" or common worship, moving from a practical concession to a denial in principle and, conversely, from a concession in principle to a practical denial. If there is reason to rejoice that the ecumenical movement is growing even within the Catholic Church, the faithful must not run the risk of indifferentism and interconfessionalism.

---

[22] A note admitted that the term *Church* had always been used in dealing with the Orientals, but that in the text the less concessive expression "separated Christian communities" was preferred.

And since other sacraments besides baptism are validly administered in the separated communities, it is inherently possible that the children of the Church can and may ask for the administration of the sacraments from "separated ministers." Then, too, the separated faithful, "being duly baptized, are able . . . if they are acting in good faith, to receive the other sacraments fruitfully." In particular, the Church tolerates, though reluctantly, mixed marriages, in which the Catholic party and the non-Catholic party are the ministers of the sacrament; consequently, not every form of active assistance at worship "need be called intrinsically evil," although for the most part there are serious reasons for prohibiting this participation. In any case, it is the right and duty of the Church "to establish laws regarding common worship, for the good both of the children of the Church and of those who endure a painful separation from her."

The main obstacle in the way of liturgical communion with the separated brothers and sisters is the very nature of *communicatio in sacris*, since this is a sign of the unity given as a gift to the one and only Church, and a prefiguration and anticipation of heavenly unity in Christ. In it the faith of the Church is expressed; consequently, active participation in the sacred liturgy constitutes by its very nature a profession of faith. For this reason, the active participation of the separated brothers and sisters in Catholic worship and especially in the reception of the sacrament, and, conversely, that of Catholics in non-Catholic worship, cannot generally be allowed, because it is intrinsically contrary to the unity of faith and an exterior obscuring of the sign of unity in Christ.

When, however, there is no risk of indifferentism and interconfessionalism, as in cases of great spiritual need or advantage, the Church is to judge under what conditions it can bring the help of the sacraments to those who are not separated from her by "an individual act of their own" (*actu proprio*). Conversely, and always under the same conditions, the Church can allow its own faithful to ask a separated minister for the sacraments. At times, however, worship that is objectively true is accompanied by erroneous liturgical prayers or by erroneous preaching, so that it is very difficult to remove the danger of indifferentism and interconfessionalism. Finally, "the conditions required for liceity differ according to the nature of each sacrament."

The schema distinguishes, however, between "active participation" and the "mere presence" of separated Christians at the Catholic liturgy; the latter is always licit, as is the presence of Catholics at non-Catholic worship "for a reasonable cause, provided all danger is removed." On the other hand, the schema seems more open when it comes to the sacramentals, prayer, sacred places, funerals, and the like, "in which the doctrine of the oneness of the Church does not of itself demand a ban on sharing."

Finally, Catholics "can and ought" to cooperate with the separated brothers and sisters when it comes to practical collaboration in defending the principles of the Christian religion or of natural law. The schema ended here with a final exhortation to common prayer in the perspective of an ecumenism focused on the return of all to the one and only Church.

II. "What We Expect and Hope for"

How did Msgr. Philips's revision differ from the text just analyzed? From the very outset, his approach was very skillful. At first his schema was not really an alternative. Before the debate on the schema on the Church began in the hall on December 1, the document Philips was working on was very adaptable, being formulated at many points as *desiderata* rather than a complete text. It covered only five chapters: the mystery of the Church, membership in the Church, bishops, laity, and religious. But for the laity it referred to the preparatory text,[23] and for religious it was limited to some suggestions for improvement. In fact, Philips's revision was mainly a schema on the bishops, since on membership, the other central point in the first chapters, it tended to reflect what was being worked out at this same time in the Secretariat for Christian Unity. This limitation, however, had its advantage, since from the beginning it was a "work in progress" and therefore seemed practicable to everyone. Despite this, as long as the schema remained an unofficial undertaking, no one but Philips worked on it, although several offered advice that was often accepted.

In order better to understand this document "in progress," it will be helpful to compare three successive drafts of it. The first was the one given to Bea before October 28;[24] on the question of membership in the

---

[23] We must not forget that Philips himself had been responsible for the chapter on the laity in the preparatory schema. Not without a degree of mockery did Gagnebet reproach Philips for having saved only his own work when he composed his new schema (Gagnebet to Philips, November 23 [CCV, P.020.27]).

[24] Copy belonging to Msgr. De Smedt, in CCV, P.020.22.

Church it still displays the old terminology of the chapter *De membris*.[25] A second draft was distributed beginning probably on November 22/23.[26] The third was a French presentation entitled "What We Expect and Hope for from the Dogmatic Constitution on the Church."[27]

The draft given to the Secretariat for Christian Unity began with a declaration of purpose. The undertaking was justified as a response to the request of many bishops; the author stated that this was a new version, but only "in part" (*partim*), of the schema on the Church, and that he had proceeded "according to the guidelines set down in the allocution of the Supreme Pontiff on October 11," which he summarized as follows: (1) the teaching should not be repetitive, but should explain the points that are of greater importance "for a more intense life" of the Catholic Church, account being taken of advances in exegetical and patristic studies and in speculative thinking; (2) the approach ought to be positive and constructive and, while leaving intact all the condemnations of errors, must prefer the medicine of mercy; and (3) in this docu-

---

[25] Congar wrote: "Visit of Msgr. Philips; he tells me that the text *De Ecclesia* (=*De Episcopis*) that we corrected last Thursday has been given to Bea's Secretariat, which made only some corrections of detail. Msgr. Suenens is taking it upon himself to see it through later. Msgr. Philips tells me that the Secretariat intends . . . not to speak of 'members' and simply to describe, positively and in descending order, the ways of participating in the life of the Church: fully and in all respects for holy Catholics; incompletely for sinful Catholics; etc." (*JCongar*, October 28).

[26] In his November 23 letter to Philips, Gagnebet complains that he has seen a new Constitution *De Ecclesia,* which is meant to replace the official one. The letter is somewhat surprising. How is it possible that Gagnebet had not become acquainted earlier with Philips's schema, since Tromp says he had received this through unofficial channels as early as November 12? Is it possible that though Tromp mentions the schema and the date in his report, which was written some weeks later, he had in fact kept it for his personal use alone? And what is the relationship between the schema given to Tromp on November 12 and the one distributed beginning on November 22/23? For the latter, see *Constitutionis Dogmaticae Lumen Gentium Synopsis historica,* ed. G. Alberigo and F. Magistretti (Bologna, 1975).

[27] French title: "Ce que nous attendons et espérons de la Constitution dogmatique sur l'église." In a letter dated November 25 (CCV, P.020.26), Philips invites some people to a meeting to be held the next day, November 25, at 4 P.M. in the Belgian College, so that he may receive suggestions regarding this "article in French that gives the content of my Latin note on the schema on the Church, along with supporting explanations." Congar, who took part in the meeting only at the last moment, notes the presence of Rahner, Daniélou, Ratzinger, Onclin, Lécuyer, and others, and records that "Msgr. Philips is quite hopeful that his text will pass scrutiny" (*JCongar*, November 26). The French presentation was therefore distributed during the last days of November. Tromp's copy, of which I have a photocopy, has this notation on the upper right: "Msgr. G. Philips gave me this on November 19, 1962," and on the left, in Tromp's own handwriting, the notation that the author was Philips "at the urging" especially of the Belgian bishops, but that it was being distributed to other bishops who asked for it.

ment, the Church should be seen as "the very loving mother of all, kindly, patient, and merciful and good toward the children who are separated from her."

The statement of intention also criticized the lack of coherence in the preparatory schema. But the corrections it proposed were rather innocuous, being limited to the incorporation into a single chapter (the one on the bishops) of what the preparatory schema treated in two successive chapters[28]; placing the discussion of the laity before that of religious; and transferring to the end, as a final chapter, the chapter on Church-State relations. But, as already pointed out, his treatment dealt only with the first three chapters.

In regard to the first chapter of the preparatory schema, on the nature of the Church militant, Philips's text introduced a notable expansion of perspective by not limiting the discussion to the Church militant but taking in the entire mystery of the Church and bringing out in a balanced way both its earthly and its eschatological stages. As compared with the laconic list in which the preparatory schema cleared away the other images of the Church in the Bible, in order to give a privileged place to the image of the body, Philips made more room for the themes of the Church as people of God and as bride of Christ. The theme of the Church as body of Christ was linked with its roots in the Eucharist, but it was also explained for its role in the conception of the Church as an organized society. The Roman element was included in the description of the Church in its earthly phase: the heavenly Church, "ensouled, unified, and sanctified by the Holy Spirit, is a community of grace and love, namely the Catholic Church which is Roman. . . . " Thus, without succumbing to the rather Bellarminian exclusivism of the preparatory schema, this draft of Philips's schema included all its essential concerns.

The second chapter, on the necessity of the Church for salvation, addressed the question of the Church's members. The frame of reference remained that of the preparatory schema, but Philips avoided describing the membership of non-Catholics in the Church as a mere membership "by desire." Although in fact "they alone are really (and in the full sense) members of the Church who in addition to having received baptism maintain the bonds consisting in the profession of the true faith and in communion with the hierarchy," nevertheless, "other Christians, liv-

---

[28] That is, chapter III, on the episcopate as the highest degree of the sacrament of orders, and chapter IV, on residential bishops now became a single chapter III, on the ecclesiastical hierarchy and specifically on bishops.

ing outside the Catholic community, are linked to it by a variety of sacramental, juridical, and even spiritual ties."

In the third chapter, on the hierarchical constitution of the Church and in particular the bishops, the intention was to give expression to what Vatican I had been unable to voice because of its unexpected closing and thus to complete the doctrine of the primacy. Unlike the preparatory schema, the concern of Philips's text was to connect the episcopate with the institution of the Twelve "as a college." This is the most important novelty in the document. Not only did it seek to emphasize the sacramental nature of the episcopate (a teaching accepted in the preparatory schema as well), but it also made the entire concept of bishops revolve around the theme of collegiality. To this end it was of basic importance to assert the institution of the apostles "as a college under Peter." And since the ministry received by the apostles as an institution was to last until the end of the ages, then just as

> the power abides which the Lord gave to Peter individually as the first of the apostles and leader of the apostolic college and which continues in Peter's successors, so too there remains the apostles' duty of feeding the Church after its foundation, a duty to be carried out by the college of bishops under the supreme authority of the Roman Pontiff, who, as the visible head of the Church, strengthens the dignity and unity of all his brothers.

On collegiality Philips's text is less juridical than the preparatory schema. It omitted the details on the members of the college (according to the preparatory schema, residential bishops alone were de jure members), which presupposed a definition of the connections, or lack of them, between the bishops' power to govern and their ordination.

In the chapter on the sacramental nature of the episcopate, Philips's document repeated the preparatory schema almost verbatim, but, in making clear the superiority of bishops over priests by reason of the sacrament the bishops had received, it added, using primarily biblical language, a description of the ministry of bishops in the Church.[29] This was followed by a reflection on presbyters taken substantially from the preparatory schema.

Philips's document then dealt successively with the offices of teaching, governing, and sanctifying and concluded with a clarification of the relations between the primacy and the episcopate and between bishops

---

[29] This was an addition that would remain in the various revisions and become part of the definitive text, but as an introduction to the doctrinal assertion of the sacramental character of the episcopate (*Lumen gentium,* no. 21; cf. Alberigo and Magistretti, *Synopsis historica,* 90-91).

and the universal Church. The section on bishops in Philip's text was more coherent than the corresponding section in the preparatory schema;[30] in its extensive section on the office of governing, it successfully incorporated the doctrine on the magisterium that the preparatory schema had discussed in a separate chapter.

A close look reveals that the two documents did not differ greatly in content. Philips's schema was distinguished by more scriptural language, some emphases on authority or power in the Church as service, and a greater restraint when it came to the formula "of themselves and not by the consent of the Church" (*ex sese non autem ex consensu ecclesiae*) as applied to the irreformability of solemn papal pronouncements.[31] The power of governing, is said to be "ordinary, immediate, and proper to them, although the Roman Pontiff, as head of the Church, may in the final analysis control its exercise and place certain limits of it for the good of the Church."

This formula proved to be ambiguous and open to all sorts of interpretations. For example, although it did not say in so many words that the power of jurisdiction was received from the pope, those who defended the latter position found asserted here so indeterminate a right to "control" the exercise of this power that it could be interpreted in favor of their position. Also surprising were some nuances of vocabulary. For example, at the very time when talk of *sources* of revelation was being challenged, this word was used at least twice. Finally, there was one respect in which Philips's document was particularly distinctive; namely, its omission of details that most clearly showed traces of scholastic and juridical methods: the extensions of the primary and secondary objects of infallibility; the definition of the various forms of assent to the decisions of the magisterium; the omission of the section on the powers of the Curia.

On November 22, 1962, Philips began to circulate the Latin version of the document, which began with the words "The Council under the guidance of the Holy Spirit" (*Concilium duce Spiritu Sancto*). Apart

---

[30] Episcopate as sacrament; presbyters; dignity and office of bishops; primacy and episcopate; relation between bishops and the universal Church; college of bishops.

[31] On this point the preparatory schema had further toughened the formula of Vatican I by speaking of solemn pronouncements being infallible "in themselves, as being uttered in the name of Christ, and not from the consent of the faithful or the other bishops" (*AS* I/4, 49). Philips's document, on the other hand, repeated more faithfully the formula of Vatican I and applied it also to cases in which the college of bishops exercises the supreme teaching office together with the pope.

from some slight changes in wording and a change of the location of various parts, the important change is in chapter II, on the necessity of the Church for salvation and on belonging to the Church, where this version was influenced by guidelines from the Secretariat for Christian Unity. The noun *members* disappeared and was replaced by a form of words unconnected with the analogy of the members of a body: "In full actuality and without any restriction, there belong to the family of the Church" only those baptized Catholics who profess the true faith and the authority of the Church and have not been expelled because of their offenses, although this external belonging does not suffice for salvation for those who live in sin. The Church knows that it is united by various factors (faith in Christ, baptism, devotion to the Eucharist, and so on) with non-Catholics, even if they do not profess the faith in its entirety and are not in communion with the Roman pontiff. This perspective avoided overly abstract formulas and instead began from a concrete reflection on the faith and life of the Churches. In another important change, the term *college* was kept for the institution of the Twelve, but for the bishops the juridically vaguer term *body* was now preferred.

The French document, which was the final draft from this first phase of debate in the hall, emphasized by its style its character as a "suggestion" or "working hypothesis" for a new text. It began by repeating the criteria that had inspired the proposed new schema, but with some changes of emphasis as compared with the first declaration of purpose. There were now four criteria inspired by the opening address of the Pope, since a consideration of the theological qualification of the constitution was prefixed to the list: (1) there was no desire to impose an infallible and irreformable teaching, except in instances in which this intention was evident;[32] (2) scholastic language was to be avoided; (3) "pastoral orientation" was interpreted as meaning that the truth was to be set forth "in clear language that can lead to the assent of the intellect and the heart;"[33] and (4) "ecumenicity" is explained to mean not an incomplete presentation of the truth but a balanced presentation that could prevent misunderstandings and would show the Church to be the merciful mother of all.

---

[32] The document thus accepted the objections of those who had complained of the lack of any theological qualification for the preparatory schema.

[33] This was a weak interpretation of what Pope Roncalli had in mind, since, in his view, if a teaching was to be pastoral, there had to be an acceptance of historicity: "in the manner . . . which our era demands of us." Philips's interpretation, on the other hand, could be accepted by those who, during the discussion of the *De fontibus*, had given *pastoral* a didactic and sentimental meaning.

The French text had the same content as the Latin version but showed greater concern for didactic clarity. In particular, with regard to the problem of belonging to the Church, the text made clear, even to nonexperts, the strategic importance of abandoning the category "members of the Church."[34]

What, then, did the Philips document represent at this stage of the Council? Thanks especially to the Secretariat's contribution, it certainly helped to open the presentation of doctrine to horizons less scholastic and less tied to the ecclesiology sanctioned by *Mystici Corporis*. But its purpose was, above all, to form as broad a consensus as possible around the dogmatic constitution on the Church, the text which, in the mind of Suenens, who was claiming to control the strings of this operation, was to be the strong core of the Council.

To this end Philips thought it expedient to offer not an alternative schema but rather a set of central ideas around which to gather everything else. There were three of these ideas: (1) an expansion of horizons from the Church militant to the Church as mystery; (2) a way of determining who belongs to the Church that would break through the bottleneck set up by *Mystici Corporis*; and (3) a chapter on the episcopate that would be less rigidly scholastic and yet substantially the same as the preparatory schema.[35] Because of his official sponsorship by a sector of the episcopate and of his own commitment to moderation, Philips's emended version was suited to ferrying the old schema into more open theological waters, despite the fact that Gagnebet, the president of the subcommission that had drafted the *De ecclesia*, described the work of the Louvain theologian as an about-face.[36] In a reply in which he defended himself to Gagnebet, Philips gave the authentic interpretation

[34] "The suggested text deliberately abstracts from the theological debate over the term 'member of the Church.' Must we say that dissident Christians are completely lacking in the quality of 'member'? Or can we call them 'imperfect members,' whose right is incomplete, inchoative, or partially hobbled? All theologians agree on the objective data of the problem and on the real situation of the various categories envisaged. But some maintain that the quality of membership is indivisible and admits no degrees. Others prefer to speak of members in the full sense and members in a lesser sense. . . . In any hypothesis we must exclude the view that a person can belong to Christ or be linked to him without belonging or being linked in the same measure to his Church" ("Ce que nous attendons et espérons," 8-9).

[35] The reconstruction by J. Grootaers also stresses, in its own fashion, this mediating approach ("Le rôle de Mgr G. Philips à Vatican II. Quelques réflexions pour contribuer à l'étude de Vatican II," in *Ecclesia Spiritu Sancto edocta. Lumen Gentium, 53. Mélanges théologiques. Hommage à Mgr Gérard Philips* [Gembloux, 1970], 343-80).

[36] Gagnebet to Philips, November 23.

of his work: it was justified as a more explicitly biblical and more clearly pastoral presentation, in response to the request of the Belgian bishops and "of a certain number of others;" it made no claim to replace the commission's text but only to improve "its general organization and its editorial form."[37]

Far removed from the subtle tactics of Philips were the observations drafted by Schillebeeckx and Rahner. Schillebeeckx's notes began with a clear rejection: "The schema on the Church, except for the chapter on the laity (provided an exception is made within this for the treatment of so-called 'Catholic Action') . . . is unacceptable (*non placet*)."[38] The reasons for the rejection were: lack of organization, and confusion; the Church is regarded as an abstract essence and not as a concretely existing reality, so that the prevailing perspective is that of a "gift given" rather than of the "vocation" of the Church; as a result of this essentialist vision, the Church as "body of Christ" is not understood biblically, that is, in relation to the glorious body of Christ with which it is sacramentally identified, but in the derivative sense of a living organism comprising many members. Consistent with this deficiency is the lack of a sacramental view of the Church, so that the visible bonds of the Church and the bonds of grace and truth are dealt with separately. Consequently, from the ecumenical viewpoint, that is, the viewpoint of "the integral totality of the faith," the perspective adopted in the preparatory schema was extremely impoverished.[39]

With regard to the treatment of membership in the Church in chapter II of the preparatory schema, Schillebeeckx criticized the ignorance

---

[37] Philips to Gagnebet, November 26, 1962 (CCV, P.020.28).

[38] Edward Schillebeeckx, *Animadversiones in "secundam seriem" schematum Constitutionum et Decretorum de quibus disceptabitur in Concilii sessionibus De Ecclesia et De Beata Maria Virgine*. The mimeographed typescript bore the date of November 30. Brouwers says that it had already been distributed before December 1, before the discussion began in the hall ("Derniers préparatifs," *Vatican II commence*, 360). It appears that several thousand copies were made, the text having been mimeographed several times. In the archives of the ISR in Bologna there are various copies, each of which shows some differences. The copy that bears the handwritten notation "Copy no. 1" consists of ten typewritten pages; I shall be referring to this version.

[39] Note the different conception of ecumenism in comparison not only with the drafters of the schema but even with Philips. For the drafters of the schema there is simply the integrity of the truth, on the one side, and the perspective of a return, on the other. According to Philips, the problem is that of clarity and balance in the manner of presenting the truth. In Schillebeeckx's view, however, no one at any point in history possesses the integral totality of truth, because there are "truths which in the Church's past were explicitly present in Christian life but now, partly due to the refutation of the deviations of non-Catholic Christians, are as it were asleep in the bosom of the Church."

shown of the "traces of the Church" (*vestigia Ecclesiae*) that are present
in the communities of the separated brothers and sisters, and the use of
the distinction between members "true and proper" and members "in
desire only." This position was identical (he said) with the personal theology of Tromp (mention was made of a recent article of his[40]); it was,
however, opposed to that of St. Thomas, since it reduced non-Catholic
Christians to "merely potential members" of the Church, whereas St.
Thomas had said that the potential members of the Church were all
human beings.

But Schillebeeckx's severest criticism was devoted to the chapters on
the episcopate. In his judgment the schema did not discuss the subject
organically. It did not move from a theological reflection to a treatment
of the juridical aspects, but followed the inverse order, making the theological nature of the episcopate derive from present canonical discipline.
It restricted the authority of a bishop to his diocesan territory (this last is
a reality purely of ecclesiastical law), and in no. 15 it implicitly denied a
collegial government of the Church as a whole, since the collegial
dimension was reduced to a "vague concern." Furthermore, in no. 16
the schema identified collegiality with ecumenical councils as such,
though these are not part of the Church's essential structure. This
amounts to saying that apart from an ecumenical council collegiality is
simply a "name without a reality" and depends entirely on the whim of
the pope, who, as head, is not bound by collegiality. As a matter of fact,
the schema thus contradicted itself, since it also affirmed that even outside an ecumenical council the episcopal college, though scattered, can
exercise, under its head, the infallible teaching office.

Schillebeeckx did not limit himself to criticism but also offered an
alternative vision of episcopal collegiality. It is worthwhile here to present his vision with some completeness, since it represents the real alternative to the conception developed in Roman neo-scholasticism, and

---

[40] The reference was to S. Tromp, "De Ecclesiae membris," in *Symposium theolog-
icum de Ecclesia Christi Patribus Concilii Vaticani II reverenter oblatum*, published in
the journal of the Accademia Pontificia Teologica Romana, *Divinitas* 6 (1962), 481-92.
At the time, this review was the organ in which the wing most closely allied with circles
in the Holy Office were carrying on their theological battle. The first issue of the periodical for that same year carried a miscellany of articles dedicated to Cardinal Ottaviani;
they were divided into four sections: the unity of the Church; the existence and power of
the hierarchical Church; the devotion of the Roman pontiffs to the Sacred Heart and the
sacrament of the Eucharist; the authority of bishops and the exemption of religious. On
the politics of *Divinitas* see É. Fouilloux, "Théologiens romains et Vatican II (1959-
1962)," *CrSt* 15 (1994), 373-94.

would, through the entire time of the Council, be the enemy that the minority would seek to defeat or to which it would try to concede as little as possible.

With a rigorous systematic vision as his starting point, Schillebeeckx presented collegiality as having priority over the right of the individual bishop. In fact, the right of the individual bishop is grounded in the divine right of the episcopal college as such. The power of the college is an "ordinary power," and precisely because it is fundamentally and primarily the power of a college, it cannot be conceived in abstraction from the power of the head of the college itself. The head of the college, that is, Peter and his successors, does not have his power by himself alone and in opposition to the college of the apostles or bishops, but only insofar as Christ has appointed him head "*IN* this very college."[41] This apostolic college governs the entire Church independently of the assignment of territory to individuals. "The Supreme Pontiff, therefore, does not have his own (universal) province over against the bishops. Both the head and the members of the college, as members of it, have the same territory, namely, the entire Church, but they have it as head of the college and members of the college respectively."

Consequently, the episcopal college, in union with its head, has supreme authority over the whole Church, both within and outside an ecumenical council. The only difference here is the degree of visibility of the collegial government. The council is a solemn and in that sense extraordinary expression of the collegial government, which is also exercised outside an ecumenical council, but in an ordinary manner.

From here Schillebeeckx moved logically to an interpretation of Vatican I's formula "of themselves and not by the consent of the Church;" his interpretation differed from that in the preparatory text, with which Philips was in substantial agreement. According to Schillebeeckx, this formula should be referred not to the pope taken in isolation but to the supreme pontiff as such, that is, as head of the college; consequently, the expression "of themselves" implies the entire college in which the pope exercises the office of head.[42] But just as the pope cannot define a dogma apart from or in opposition to the college, neither can the college do anything apart from or in opposition to the pope. In either case, the collegial government that is of divine law would be diminished.

[41] The capitals and italics are in the text.

[42] Schillebeeckx found a proof of his claim in the Bull *Munificentissimus Deus* (on the dogma of the Assumption), in which the Pope appealed to the consensus of the bishops dispersed throughout the world, of all the faithful, and of scripture and tradition.

From the priority of collegial government it followed that every bishop is a bishop even if he does not have a territory, because he is primarily a member of the college and only secondarily the ordinary of a particular place. Furthermore, while Vatican I left unanswered the question of whether there is a double or single subject of supreme authority in the Church (that is, either the college together with the pope, or the pope alone), it follows from the collegial government of the Church that neither the pope separated from the college nor the college separated from the pope, but only the pope with his college (or only the college with its pope) is the single subject of this supreme authority. This is not the opinion of a few theologians, but the more or less implicit teaching of the entire Church, as can be seen, in addition, from canon 228 of the Code of Canon Law, which attributes this authority over the entire Church to ecumenical councils. If this were merely a canon of ecclesiastical or human law, it would contradict the dogma of the primacy. And, on the other hand, if the pope "alone" were the subject of the supreme authority, he could not abdicate this authority even during a council. One escapes the dilemma, then, by asserting that there is an exclusive and single collegial subject, head and members.

Having expounded this teaching, Schillebeeckx went on to explain a *votum* that of itself, despite never being accepted and indeed by the very power of its absence, was to mark the history of the Catholic Church in the years to come:

> Since this government that is collegial by divine law may become less visible outside an ecumenical council and since, therefore, it may, in the circumstances of modern times, be rendered less effective and even become almost a "name without a reality," it is highly useful that some organization be established, a kind of "central commission," the members of which speak for their conferences or groups of bishops. In this commission the voice of the entire episcopate will thus be heard in its own fashion. This commission must be the locus for deliberation by the bishops with the head of the college, that is, the supreme pontiff, so that the central government of the Church and its collegial government may be harmoniously combined.

The term "central commission" was certainly unfortunate, but not so the traditional call for synodal government of the Church that the *votum* was trying to express. Schillebeeckx saw in the assertion in principle of such a central commission the real task of the Council, since the issue was to give real effectiveness to government that is collegial by divine law. His

suggestion was not simply a pragmatic one but had practical consequences for the *dogma* of collegial government.[43]

Presbyters, in their turn, should not be regarded simply as collaborators of the pope or the bishops, in a canonical perspective connected
with exemption and incardination. From the dogmatic point of view
presbyters are collaborators of the college and therefore both of the pope
(even if they are not exempt) and of the entire episcopal order (even if
they are exempt). Incardination and exemption belong solely in the
realm of ecclesiastical law.

The Flemish theologian was more prudent, on the other hand, when
it came to the claim that the episcopate represents the highest degree of
the sacrament of orders. While he himself shared this view, he preferred that it not be defined, since it was a question still debated by
theologians.

He found fault with the chapter on the religious for its lack of eschatological sensitivity. And while sharing the views expressed in the chapter on the laity, he was uncertain about the meaning of the terms used.
The very term *lay person* was not being used with a theological meaning, since it served to identify not only nonclerical Christians but also
nonreligious Christians, and this in contradiction to what the schema
itself said about the states of perfection not being a state intermediate
between the clerical and the lay states. Furthermore, in regard to
Catholic Action, Schillebeeckx perceived in the schema a regression to
the positions of Pius XI, and rather than speak of "participation" in the
apostolate of the hierarchy, he would have preferred to speak of "collaboration."

Schillebeeckx criticized the lack of organic unity in the chapter on the
magisterium and thought it a mistake to make the magisterium alone the
"subject" of tradition. In fact, the entire believing Church plays an
active role in tradition and in the explicitation of the deposit of faith,
although never in separation from the magisterium. The schema itself
admitted this role of the Church in chapter VIII, and this was also what
the pastoral letter of the Dutch bishops in December 1960 had meant to
say. Here Schillebeeckx took the opportunity to reject the Roman criticism of that document.

---

[43] We may ask, however, whether Schillebeeckx's position was not in its turn the
child of a universalist ecclesiology that was possible only within the canonical development of the second millennium. In fact, the connection of the bishop with the Eucharist
was substantially absent from this perspective.

Next, to speak of a religious obedience not only of the will but also of the intellect to the fallible decrees of the magisterium implied that, as in the case of the condemnation of Galileo, one must give an intellectual assent to what is not true — morally a rather strange claim. The same observation applied to what was said about duties toward the subsidiary organs of the authentic magisterium, that is, to the Curia, in no. 31. As for what the schema rightly said about the need of a "respectful obedience" to a teaching commonly regarded by the theologians as certain, no one can be ignorant of the fact that in practice this demand was the source of various abuses, when, that is, the consensus of one theological school was turned into a universally accepted teaching. It was preferable, therefore, to say nothing about a subject so sensitive in practice.

Chapter VIII of the preparatory schema, on authority and obedience in the Church, should not have been made a separate chapter but should have been included in the consideration of the collegial authority of the Church, with an explanation of the deeper meaning of the relationship between the episcopal college and the people of God, which in this context is called "the laity."

Schillebeeckx was also harshly critical of chapter IX, on relations between Church and state. It presupposed an ideal state of affairs, according to which the entire world should be Catholic. Furthermore, by defending an intolerance in principle toward non-Catholics in states in which the majority were Catholics, and tempering this only by considerations of the common good, the schema contradicted the 1948 Declaration of the Rights of Man even though these rights can be regarded, from various points of view, as genuine preambles to the Catholic faith. The very presuppositions of the schema were mistaken. In fact the norm of human acts is not the truth in itself but only the truth as known, that is, the truth as mediated by human consciousness. For this reason, the statement that truth alone, and not error, has rights, is fallacious, since the person, and not an abstract right, is the real subject of rights. Tolerance, which is the state's duty to ensure to all citizens the objective conditions required for the exercise of their freedom of conscience, is not the same as indifferentism, since it implies that truth as recognized is the norm of action. Tolerance certainly has its limits, since the state must oppose those who want to get rid of freedom of conscience. The schema, however, is silent on all these points, being concerned solely to defend the freedom of the Church and placing its trust in the Church's position of power rather than in the power of the Spirit of truth. Finally, the schema does not seem to distinguish between laicism and the legitimate lay character of the state.

In chapter X, on the need to evangelize the entire world, the schema, in Schillebeeckx's judgment, was not concerned to deepen the understanding of the Church's mission but solely to defend the freedom to evangelize. As a result, it passed over in silence the freedom of other religions and of non-Catholic churches and offered no suggestions for meeting the difficulties that arise from the coexistence of all these religions and churches.

Schillebeeckx did not directly discuss the chapter on ecumenism, but simply said that it ought to be the result of collaboration between the Doctrinal Commission and the Secretariat for Christian Unity. Finally, after some remarks on the schema on the Blessed Virgin Mary, which accompanied the schema on the Church in the second volume of schemas distributed, Schillebeeckx proposed a new structure for the schema on the Church which was to have some success, especially in its suggestion of a final section that would be devoted to the eschatological dimension of the Church.

Two factors in particular differentiated Schillebeeckx's criticisms from Philips's proposed schema. Unlike Philips, Schillebeeckx, who did his work in organized collaboration with the Dutch Episcopal Conference, avoided any consideration of a "political strategy" for building a consensus around his suggested schema. At that point, after the victory that had been won in the rejection of the schema on the sources of revelation, all that he thought was needed was to repeat the same campaign against the schema on the Church. On the positive side, again unlike Philips, Schillebeeckx provided the elements for an effective ecclesiology freed from the rigid scholastic approach of the last two centuries and more attentive to all the data of the tradition.

A comparable spirit pervaded Karl Rahner's *Animadversiones de schemate "de Ecclesia,"* which were produced and distributed almost simultaneously with those of Schillebeeckx.[44] Rahner found fault with

---

[44] Semmelroth, who had collaborated with Rahner, says that Rahner's criticisms were mimeographed and distributed on November 30 (*TSemmelroth*). According to him, the document consisted of twenty pages. I myself have a copy containing thirteen closely typed pages. As with Schillebeeckx's text, Rahner's also appears to have been retyped several times. In a letter to Vorgrimler, December 5, 1962, Rahner speaks of approximately 1300 copies having been distributed. The psychological impact on the bishops, after the outcome of the debate on the sources of revelation and the confirmation of the "goodness" of the positions expressed by this group of theologians, was enormous. In the description to be given here I shall by and large limit myself to the general observations and leave aside the countless criticism of details, these being clearly distinguished in the document from the general observations.

the excessive length of the schema, its scholastic character, and the lack
of a pastoral dimension, which nowadays cannot be omitted from any
decree, even a doctrinal one. The schema lacked a catholic ecumenical
spirit; it reduced the scriptures to a series of proof texts; it was confused
and disorganized; it lacked any theological qualification; it did not take
into account the progress that had been made in the understanding of the
episcopate; it had an inflexible view of membership in the Church; it
minimized the role of the laity in the Church; it unduly exalted the role
of authority.

More specifically, in regard to the way in which the nature of the
Church was presented, the schema claimed to derive it by a logical
deduction (*enucleatio*) from the image of the body, as though this were
a logical concept and not a simple image that, as such, did not allow the
application of deduction.[45] In addition, the scriptures provide a whole
series of other images of equal weight and dignity that shed light on the
nature of the Church; for example, the image of people of God, to which
the schema alluded only incidentally. This image, like the others that
were not sufficiently considered (spouse, reign, and so forth), had the
advantage of emphasizing the difference between Christ and the Church,
of avoiding a kind of "ecclesial monophysitism," of making known the
spots and wrinkles of the Church, and of facilitating a proper reflection
on the laity. The phrase "Holy Spirit, soul of the Church" must be used
with caution. It is not biblical and cannot be put on the same level as the
phrase "Christ, head of the Church;" if used without discretion, it could
lead to a kind of ecclesial monophysitism or Apollinarianism. Moreover,
no one says that the Holy Spirit is the "soul" of a justified person, even
though the Spirit dwells and acts in that person.

On the other hand, in describing the nature of the Church the schema
omitted many essential elements: the place of the Church in the history
of salvation; its salvific function in relation to those who are not part of
it (the Church as sacrament for the world); the eschatological dimension; the twofoldness and, at the same time, oneness of the historical
("visible") and spiritual ("invisible") dimensions; the strict subordination of the Church to Christ; the relation between the institutional and
charismatic dimensions; the central place of faith as a constitutive element of the "society of the faithful" (*coetus fidelium*); and so on.[46]

---

[45] Rahner correctly noted, among other things, the coarseness of a statement claiming
that "the Church . . . by the very fact that it is a body, is visible to the eyes."

[46] Among the detailed remarks was the suggestion that the threefold division of the
office of Christ (a division dear to Protestant theology) be avoided and reduced (in keep-

Moving on to the second chapter, Rahner suggested that the question of the necessity of the Church be separated from that of membership.[47] In addition, the schema did not do sufficient justice to the doctrine that the necessity of the Church for salvation is a necessity "of means" (*medii*). Neither the scriptures nor the Fathers speak of a simple *votum* for baptism and the Church; the mature Augustine even expressly rejected such a doctrine. The schema should therefore not have spoken of a "merely subjective ordering," since the ordering is in some way objective. And if it wanted to speak of the Church as necessary, it should not have envisaged this necessity in the perspective only of the salvation of individuals but in a collective perspective: the necessity of the Church for the world. "For the Church is the root 'sacrament' of the human race, and therefore of those also who are saved without baptism." In addition, the schema should have shown greater prudence in tackling the question of infants who have died without baptism, a question that in the preparatory phase had still not received a satisfactory answer. As for the question of membership, Rahner expressed reservations substantially analogous to those of the Secretariat and of Schillebeeckx.

On the schema's teaching about the episcopate Rahner noted, above all, a point that would later be repeated successfully: the need to intro- duce the consideration of the hierarchy by a consideration of the people of God "whom authority in the Church serves." It is necessary to speak of the end before speaking of the means. In addition, the chapter should not have begun with the sacramental nature of the episcopate; it would be more logical to begin with a reflection on the fundamental nature of the ecclesial priesthood, which, at its highest level, fills the office that had belonged to the college of apostles; then to describe the institution of this office by Christ, the nature of the office, and its unity as estab- lished in Peter; and finally to set forth the truth regarding the succession of the college of bishops to the apostolic college.[48] Only after these

---

ing with a more traditional theology and with canon law) to a pair, prophet and priest, which is more consistent with the classical distinction between the power of orders and the power of jurisdiction. Also criticized was the minimalistic way in which the schema tackled the question of sin in the Church: while sin does not remove the essential holiness of the Church, neither is it an offense that is attached to the Church from outside as it were; no, it really affects (*afficit*) the Church.

[47] There is no point in noting the difference here, as almost everywhere else, from Philips's approach: the latter regarded the assertion of the necessity of the Church as an assertion of the principle that was the basis of the treatment of the members of the Church.

[48] Schillebeeckx had to some degree mixed together the college of apostles and the college of bishops; the division suggested by Rahner here seems more accurate.

points had been settled was it possible to assert the sacramental nature of
the conferral of the episcopal office and then to describe the functions
proper to the episcopal ministry.

At this point Rahner introduced another reflection, which implicitly
stirred memories of the bitter debates of the Jansenist era: Was it not
also proper to say something about the collegiality of the presbyteral
order? For presbyters are not only individual collaborators of the
bishop; they constitute as it were the bishop's senate. And in any case,
once the sacramental nature of the episcopate had been affirmed, it was
not possible to pass over the relation already existing between bishop
and priest at the sacramental level.

On the nature of the episcopal college, Rahner's position was substantially that of Schillebeeckx, although he did add to it the argumenta-
tive power that characterizes his theology. But his agreement with
Schillebeeckx had the merit of showing the solidity of a teaching that
was not at the stage of initial formulation, but claimed to represent what
was by now a universal tradition.[49]

Rahner criticized the fact that religious were given a separate chapter,
since it would have been more congruous to make them part of a single
section on the various classes of members of the Church. Above all, however, Rahner complained that the treatment of religious was not preceded
by a treatment of charisms in the Church's life that would apply to ministers and the laity. Such a treatment would bring out the quasi-institu-
tional character of the charismatic life, with the result that the "state of
evangelical perfection" would no longer constitute a third class of Christian between the classes of ministers and the laity. It would also have the
advantage of correcting the purely empirical conception present in the
schema. Biblically and theologically, the practice of the evangelical
counsels is already part of the Church's life prior to its organization into
"societies;" more adequate acknowledgment should thus be given to the
life of those who practice the counsels *outside* of religious communities.
In addition, the schema should have stated more clearly that the evangelical counsels are simply means of reaching the perfection of love to
which all Christians are bound. Only in this way is it possible to answer
the objection of the Reformers that the Catholic Church teaches the existence of two essentially different and separate classes of Christians.

---

[49] Even though it was difficult for many, at this point, to grasp the "traditional" character of the doctrine of collegiality, that would come gradually. The intervention of
Bishop Bettazzi on October 11, 1963, during the second session, would be important in
this regard (see *AS* II/2, 484-87).

In the chapter on the laity Rahner noted the exclusive focus on the laity as collaborators with the hierarchy and on the individualistic approach to their spirituality. The result was the omission of two essential points: a consideration of the lay life in itself, as a constitutive dimension of the life of God's people in itself and prior to any distinction; and a description of the specifically lay situation, that is, of secular life as such in the world. Instead, the schema conceived of this life in a solely clerical perspective.

In the chapter on the magisterium, Rahner emphasized the need to speak more explicitly of the role of the Christian people as a whole. In fact, indefectibility in faith belongs to the believing Church, in which there is not solely a passive acceptance, but also a positive influence of the Christian people on the magisterium. The distinction between "divine and Catholic faith" (the assent owed to a solemn statement of the magisterium on a teaching contained in revelation) and "ecclesiastical" faith (an assent to "definitive" statements of the magisterium that are not contained as such in revelation) is still a question debated among theologians and should therefore be left open. An explanation of the authoritative magisterium should begin with the episcopal college as the single and complete subject of the teaching office. A distinction also needs to be made, in the assent to non-irreformable decisions, between doctrinal and disciplinary aspects.[50]

The chapter on authority and obedience, in Rahner's view, did not reflect the spirit of fraternal cooperation that ought to exist in the Church between those who occupy different places in the hierarchic order. Christians are first of all united among themselves by a single faith and an identical love, even before any one of them is "subject" to another. In addition, the introduction to the chapter raised questions when it complained of a crisis of authority and exalted the authority of the natural law. No less serious, in fact, has been the damage caused our world by authoritarian and tyrannical systems. The historical forms (though not the substance) of obedience have been indebted to cultural developments that have not left even the Church unscathed. In addition, where the infallibility of the Church is not in question, subjects cannot excuse themselves from making (directly or indirectly) their own final practical judgment of conscience on the moral integrity of what is commanded.

---

[50] Rahner thus implicitly asked the same question that Schillebeeckx had asked when he emphasized the dubious morality of an intellectual assent to a possible error.

Rahner was especially severe in his judgment on the chapter dealing with Church-State relations. His evaluation was substantially that of Schillebeeckx, and he called for the Secretariat for Christian Unity to make its contribution on the problem of religious tolerance. His evaluation of chapter X, on the necessity of proclaiming the gospel to all peoples, and of chapter XI, which dealt with ecumenism, was likewise similar to that of Schillebeeckx. Instead of reviewing the text, he referred "to what has been said on this question by the Secretariat expressly established for the purpose."

Unlike Philips's work in progress, the criticisms of Schillebeeckx and Rahner were more useful for the discussion of the schema on the Church that was to begin on December 1. They provided a whole set of solid arguments to those who were now determined to continue on the path that had been opened for the Council during the week of debate on the sources of revelation. The texts of Rahner and Schillebeeckx could now appeal to the results of that week. Their aim was clear: the dismissal of the preparatory schema and of the spirit dominant in it. But although they and many others did not yet know it, the greatest obstacle to the attainment of this goal was not the preparatory schema, but Philips's compromise; it was this that allowed some of the positions in the preparatory schema to persist, rather contradictorily and with consequences that would be felt in the future, down to the so-called *Nota praevia*, "Preliminary Note."

But there is a second point to be noted. Because the documents of Schillebeeckx and Rahner enjoyed such a high standing in wide sectors of the episcopate, they completed the task of legitimating the central place of the Secretariat and therefore, inevitably, of its President, Cardinal Bea, to whom Pope John, for his part, had already given his backing. Thanks to a complex series of factors, the role of Bea and the Secretariat as a force for balance in the most sensitive doctrinal questions was thus being strengthened.

At the weekly meeting of the Secretariat on the very day on which the schema on the Church was distributed, Bea was already listing what he regarded as the sensitive points, those on which the position of the Secretariat clearly differed from the schema. These were found not only in the chapter on ecumenism, but also in what was said about belonging to the Church, the laity, relations between Church and state, and religious freedom.[51] Moreover, the chapter on ecumenism brought into play not

---

[51] The minutes of the meeting are in the Thils Archive, 0786.

only the Doctrinal Commission and the Secretariat, but also the Commission on the Oriental Churches. At this point Bea limited himself to saying that the question could not be treated separately by the three groups, and that it would be appropriate "to develop a text jointly."

This was a very ticklish area. The idea of a mixed commission, once it had been accepted for the *De fontibus*, seemed the most appropriate solution. Some representatives of the Oriental Commission, such as Welykyj, its Secretary, had already declared themselves in agreement on this point, at a meeting which had taken place at the Secretariat that same afternoon. Bea reminded all, however, that the principal difficulty in this matter was coming not from the Oriental Commission but from the Doctrinal Commission. Some, Maccarrone, for example, suggested that the question could be resolved procedurally with the help of the president of the Oriental Commission, Cardinal Cicognani, who as president of the Secretariat for Extraordinary Affairs would be able to submit the matter to the Pope.[52] Despite Bea's conviction, then, it did not seem that it would be easy to achieve a single schema on ecumenism, and, as we shall see, it was these very difficulties that would dictate a cautious attitude during the discussion of the *De unitate Ecclesiae* in the hall.

In addition, the Secretariat found itself involved at this time in a delicate task of mediation, which involved its relationship with the Orientals. The press had published a communiqué from fifteen Ukrainian bishops who disapproved of observers from the Russian Church being invited to the Council while their metropolitan, Slipyi, was languishing in a Siberian prison.[53] In accord with the Secretariat of State, the Secretariat prepared a printed communiqué that was read that very evening, November 23, on the premises of the press office, prior to a public lecture of Oscar Cullmann on the presence of observers at the Council.[54]

III. "THE MELKITES' DAY"

Meanwhile, November 26 saw the beginning of discussion of the decree on the unity of the Church: "That All May Be One," which had

[52] Ibid., p. 2.

[53] In Italy, the communiqué of the Ukrainian bishops was published in *Il Giornale d'Italia* for November 21, 1962. For a fuller account of the context of the problem see A. Riccardi, *Il Vaticano e Mosca* (Bari, 1992), 238-49.

[54] See *OssRom*, November 25, 1962. *OssRom* has the text but no explanation of the

been prepared by the Commission for the Oriental Churches, without consulting either the Theological Commission or the Secretariat for Christian Unity.[55] The Council was now to enter into a set of problems whose significance escaped a large number of the fathers. The schema did not deal with the unity of the Church as such or even with the more familiar problems connected with the Protestant Reformation; it dealt with relations between the Roman Church and Orthodoxy, and it took a position on the status of the Oriental Catholic Churches, a minority known to most of the bishops almost solely by their colorful garb and liturgical rites.

The discussion was to have a rather low profile. The energies of the fathers had been put to a hard test by the dispute over the sources of revelation and were now being saved for the impending confrontation over the schema on the Church. There was thus little psychological room for this seemingly minor subject. The entire episode is hardly mentioned in the diaries of Congar and Semmelroth. Congar does recall a meeting with the Melkite bishops, but he is not concerned enough even to describe what happened.[56]

The group of Melkite bishops was the only one that prepared a broad strategy; they knew that their own specific identity was at stake in the overall direction to be taken in the decree. While the decree indeed had for its formal purpose to point out the ways that would lead to the reunion of the Catholic Church with the Orthodox Church, it also brought up the status and significance of the Uniate Churches. This second aspect was mentioned unobtrusively, and almost incomprehensibly, in the final number of the decree: "In order, finally, to remove every

concrete context to which it relates. After its report on the general congregation of November 24, the Vatican daily printed a "Clarification by the Secretariat for Christian Unity": "The Secretariat for Christian Unity wishes to explain that all the observers and delegates were invited by the same Secretariat, which has been happy to receive them. All of them, without exception, have displayed a genuinely religious and ecumenical spirit. The Secretariat is grieved, therefore, at what has been published in contrast to the spirit that has inspired its sincere contacts, past and present, with the observers and delegates. The Secretariat can only dissociate itself from it."

[55] See *History*, I, 200-5. The time for beginning the discussion of the schema was uncertain for several days. On November 23 Secretary Felici had announced that after debate on the schema dealing with the communications media, the Council would discuss the schema on the Blessed Virgin and then the *De unitate*. But on November 26 he announced a new working order: first, the *De unitate* and then the *De Ecclesia*.

[56] On November 25 Congar was invited to lunch by Patriarch Maximos IV; afterward there was a lengthy meeting with all the bishops of the patriarchate (in addition to the short note in *JCongar*, November 12, 1962, see the even terser note in *JEdelby* for the same date).

doubt or unjustified suspicion, let no one presume to think that the present status of matters Oriental in the Catholic Church is definitive or completely unchangeable and cannot be better organized, nor should anyone think that they are an obstacle hindering a return to the Catholic Church."[57]

In his introductory report Father Athanasius Welykyj, Secretary first of the preparatory Commission on the Oriental Churches and now of the conciliar Commission, explained that the vague phrase, "status of matters Oriental," referred to uniatism, which he acknowledged was a subject of open complaint from the Orthodox Churches.[58] The schema was saying, then, that the status of the Uniate Churches was a result of historical necessities and could therefore change. The position taken in the schema was positive to the extent that it gave a historical dimension to this status, but at the same time it conveyed the tendency of the Latin Church to regard as a negligible quantity that part of the Oriental Church that it preserved within itself.

Within the Uniate Churches it was the Melkite Episcopate that accepted the responsibility for answering the Orthodox objection that the status of the Uniate Churches was unacceptable insofar as it prefigured the status of all the Oriental Churches in case of a reunion. These bishops saw in the schema a reiteration of the traditional policies of the Catholic Church in dealing with the Uniates. Clearly distancing themselves from the other Uniate Churches in this regard, the Melkite bishops thought of themselves as representing the Orthodox Church within the Catholic Church rather than as a manifestation of the Catholic Church over against Orthodoxy. This outlook was to be clearly asserted during the debate in one of the most interesting interventions, that of Archbishop Tawil, Patriarchal Vicar for the Melkites in Damascus. In his criticism of the schema he said:

> Our Oriental Catholic Churches will never find their full place within the Catholic Church unless they are looked upon, first and foremost, not only as what they now are but also as what they represent, namely, the Orthodox Churches not yet united. The provisional status given to the Oriental Churches, making them a kind of ecclesiastical "third world" that is neither Oriental nor Latin, and thereby abstracting from the ecumenical vocation of these Churches, has a false ring to it and ends up, in practice, by building a tower on sand. To the Orthodox, indeed, these Churches serve as a mirror in which they can see and experience what would happen to them, once union became a reality.[59]

[57] No. 52 (AS I/3, 544).
[58] AS I/3, 553.
[59] AS I/3, 660f.

The concrete example Tawil then gave, namely, that of the patriarchs, who in the Code for the Oriental Church saw themselves subordinated to the cardinals, the apostolic delegates, and even the Latin bishop of their own diocese, made eloquently clear the point he was making.

The Melkites therefore developed an entire strategy of attack that was fine-tuned at their regular weekly meeting on the afternoon of November 24. While not calling for a formal defeat of the schema, they did intend to offer a systematic critique of every point in it. As Edelby describes things, Patriarch Maximos IV himself was to fire the opening shot

> with general remarks on the schema as a whole. After him, Msgr. Nabaa will point out that union requires actions and not just words. Our bishops will then undertake to analyze the schema, part by part. I am responsible for a thorough critique of the ecclesiological basis of the schema's teaching on the unity of the Church; theologically, this basis seems to us to be utterly inadequate. It will be a tricky matter to get this across, but no one is better qualified than our Church to say it. Then six of our bishops will in turn offer minor amendments to the six parts of the schema.[60]

This Melkite claim to be the only Church in a position adequately to meet the need may appear presumptuous, but in fact it was a justified presumption.

The Melkites' most authoritative ally in carrying out the task might have been Bea, but the latter, as his intervention would show, had no desire to turn the *De unitate* into another point of disagreement between himself and Curial circles. This would have placed him in opposition to Cicognani, who was not only president of the Commission for the Oriental Churches but also Secretary of State and — a matter of much greater relevance to the conduct of the Council — president of the Secretariat for Extraordinary Affairs. In addition, these same days saw the difficult opening debate in the mixed commission charged with revising the schema on the sources of revelation.

Bea's Secretariat had also prepared its own schema on ecumenism, and Bea was preoccupied by the need to prepare a single future schema out of the three texts that had been prepared by his Secretariat, by the Commission for Oriental Churches, and by the Theological Commission. In his intervention he would therefore avoid tackling the problems head-on and would restrict himself to identifying only a few points that might cast doubt on the role of the Secretariat: the anticipated establishment of a pontifical council for coordinating ecumenical activities with

---

[60] *JEdelby*, November 24, 80.

the Oriental Churches; a new prayer for unity that would harken back to Leo XIII's proposal of a Pentecost novena; and so on.

In any case, nowhere else in Vatican II do we find an example of "autonomy" comparable to that given by these Melkite bishop-theologians who had to fight their "desperate" battle relying only on their own powers. When, on the evening of November 27, after the interventions of Maximos IV, Nabaa, Zoghby, Edelby, and Father Hage (Superior General of the Basilian Order of St. John the Baptist), Edelby wrote in his diary that in St. Peter's it had been "the Melkites' day," he was speaking the simple truth. But the Melkites were to pay for the choice they had made by being largely isolated within the Uniate Churches themselves. In fact, on the afternoon of that same November 27, the first meeting of the conciliar Commission for the Oriental Churches was held, and the two Melkite representatives, Patriarch Maximos IV and Msgr. Edelby, found themselves the object of an express attempt to deprive them of legitimacy, which would later be echoed in the Council hall. Criticisms came from all sides and on various points: the Melkites were not representative of the entire Oriental Church; they were wrong to criticize the Latin Church, since the Oriental Catholic Churches owed everything to the Latins; some even drew their attention to the fact that "at bottom the Latin Church was the Catholic Church."[61]

The discussion in the hall began with the introductions by Cicognani and Welykyj. Both acknowledged the limitations in the schema's perspective, since, on the one hand, it paid no attention to the Protestants and Anglicans and, on the other, it was unconnected with what was said in the chapter of *De Ecclesia* on ecumenism and with the schema of ecumenism prepared by the Secretariat for Christian Unity. However, Cicognani said, we are much closer to the Theological Commission and the Secretariat for Christian Unity than many people may think.[62] He explained in writing that "this schema had been prepared independently, not because there was disagreement or because it was not to be inserted at the right time into the treatise on the Church;" it was a document specifically devoted to the East "out of respect and in order to bring out the greater closeness between us."[63] In addition, the schema was offered

---

[61] In reporting this assertion in his diary, Edelby puts it in quotation marks and adds a "*sic.*" Patriarch Maximos and he decided not to reply to the attacks; they regarded it as much more important that everyone had been able to hear their point of view in the Council hall.

[62] *AS* I/3, 547.

[63] *AS* I/3, 548. These words were taken almost verbatim from Bea's intervention (*ibid.*, 709).

in continuation, so to speak, with the undertaking of Leo XIII in his apostolic letter *Orientalium dignitas* of 1894.[64] Anticipating attacks from more reactionary circles, which did not fail to come, Cicognani wanted to make it clear that although some might think that the schema leaned toward the outlook of the separated Oriental Churches, "it nonetheless expounded authentic Catholic teaching."

Welykyj, too, focused on justifying the document.[65] The schema was addressed to all Catholics and intended to speak only of the non-Catholic Orientals; it did not speak specifically of the Protestants in order not to go beyond its assigned limits; the composers of the schema had not been able to consult chapter XI, on ecumenism, of the Theological Commission's schema on the Church, or the Secretariat's schema on ecumenism, simply because these were not available.[66] The title of the schema was simply a signpost and not intended to give an exhaustive description of the question; in the first part (nos. 1-2), the unity of the Church was expounded solely insofar as it was a unity of government with its visible foundation in Peter; scholastic terminology had been avoided as far as possible; the term used in describing the Orientals was either "separated" or "dissident," with a certain preference for the latter as being "milder," in view of the fact that the separation from the Churches of the Orient had not involved "a formal and positive act" but had rather come about through a lengthy historical process.

Despite the reasons given by Cicognani and Welykyj, almost all the interventions found fault with the schema for its lack of connection with the work of the Theological Commission and of the Secretariat for Christian Unity. The aim of this faultfinding was not, however, to eliminate the schema as such but rather to have part of it (for example, the general introduction) inserted into the Constitution on the Church or else to have it become a special chapter, along with others devoted to the Anglicans and the Protestants, in a single decree on ecumenism. In the view of some fathers with ties to the minority, the schema was guilty of doctrinal minimalism and naiveté and was therefore doomed to failure, just as Leo XIII's attempt had been in its day.[67] Fathers representing the

---

[64] The notes of the schema bore eloquent witness to its debt to Leo XIII. Of the thirteen notes, ten appealed to Leo's teaching.

[65] *AS* I/3, 548-53.

[66] Without realizing it, Welykyj was here not only revealing the fundamental contradictions at work in the preparatory period, but also providing an argument to those who wanted to call into question the entire preparatory work.

[67] Thus Principi (*AS* I/3, 621f.). According to others, the decree succumbed to ireni-

opposite tendency, however, reproached the schema for its authoritarian character, which still reflected the vision of unity as implying the return of others to our own Church.[68] The question of repentance for past sins was one of the themes voiced with hesitation and displaying different nuances in each speaker.[69]

Prescinding from its possible insertion into and connection with the schema on the Church and the schema of the Secretariat, a wide range of conciliar fathers expressed substantial acceptance of the schema; almost all the cardinals, including Bea, were of this view (Liénart was the only one to reject the substance, without saying this in so many words[70]). In this general climate, the appraisal of the Melkites stood out for its clarity and decisiveness among the 141 interventions in the hall and the 65 presented in writing. This appraisal made it possible to grasp the important points of the question, points not easily understood in a document dominated by practical perspectives.

The Melkites faithfully followed the order of interventions decided on at their meeting on November 24. First, then, Patriarch Maximos IV was given the task of bringing to light the diseased musculature of the schema. His intervention came on November 27, the second day of the debate in the hall, after the interventions of Liénart, Ruffini, Bacci, and Browne on November 26 and that of de Barros Câmara on November 27.[71]

Maximos's seemingly moderate premise, that the schema could provide the basis for a sound discussion if the first part (the theological introduction) were radically revised and the second (practical) part improved, perhaps made his radical critique even harsher. It was aimed at the very starting point of the schema, which in the patriarch's view presented truths that were certain, but in a way that was unacceptable to those to whom it was addressed. This failure was due to the fact that the drafters were simply ignorant of fundamental historical facts. The

cism (Pawlowski, 623; Velasco, 662; and others, though less explicitly); the language of the schema did not make it clear that there is but one Church, and it spoke without justification of Churches in the plural (Fernandez y Fernandez, 636f., and others less decisively).

[68] Thus Liénart (AS I/3, 554). Mendez y Arceo complained of the excessively juridical and individualistic perspective of the introduction, which was preoccupied with the problem of the salvation of individuals and whose practical suggestions showed little openness to the ecclesial dimension as such (643ff.).

[69] Mention should be made here of the very profound intervention of Ancel on the humility of the Church (AS I/3, 682f.).

[70] AS I/3, 554.

[71] AS I/3, 616-20.

Church of the East does not owe its origin to the Roman see but is the firstborn of Christ and the apostles; its development and organization had been the work solely of the Greek and Oriental fathers. Furthermore, if the schema wanted to speak to this Church, it should have spoken first and foremost of something which this Church had preserved in its tradition, but of which the schema said nothing, the Catholic doctrine of the collegiality of the Church's shepherds. Only after this collegiality had been introduced was it possible to speak of the pope as "the central foundation of collegiality." But except for the Melkites, no one wanted to commit himself on this point, even though it was central to all the other statements to be made in a document on the Oriental Churches.[72] Even Bea preferred to say nothing on the question; perhaps he was awaiting a more favorable opportunity, after the discussion of the *De Ecclesia*, to take a more decisive stand in this direction.

After Maximos IV, and still following a logical line of attack on the schema, it was Nabaa's task to discuss the merits of the general observations made in the second part of the schema, the part devoted to practical measures.[73] To begin with, he pointed out the spirit that must be at the basis of practice: "toward the truth, in love." Only a prior fraternal understanding, only love, will bring the truth to light. It is love that even now suggests possible agreements: in solidarity, in the defense of rights, in the advancement of justice and ethical behavior. Love also calls for the celebration on the same day of the principal feasts, especially Christmas and Easter, and it can mitigate the norms governing mixed marriages. Moving on then to practical suggestions, Nabaa observed that the schema suffered from a one-way perspective: it was only the others who had to "return." Whatever the legitimacy of the word *return*, one thing should be clear: Catholics, too, had their faults and therefore they too must "return" to the separated brethren and speak with them.

Edelby was the third Melkite to speak.[74] His task was to criticize the theological basis of the first part. After criticizing the "neutral" biblical texts used in the explanation of doctrine in nos. 1-5 of the schema, he focused his remarks on nos. 6-11. In the theological section of the schema he saw a spirit of hostility which contradicted the spirit that animated the second part; in particular, he did not see the need to reproach all the Orientals for the idea that the state has a right to intervene in the governance of the Church; in addition, it was not historically correct to

---

[72] A notable exception was the intervention of Staverman (*AS* I/3, 733).

[73] *AS* I/3, 624-27.

[74] *AS* I/3, 638-40.

say that the Orientals had simply "removed themselves" from the authority of the Roman see, since both sides shared responsibility. Above all, however, the doctrine expounded in the schema was neither certain nor complete. No. 6 stressed the visible unity of the Church under the pope, but said nothing about collegiality; no. 7 did not acknowledge the ecclesial character of the Orientals, thus contradicting what the popes themselves had proclaimed at least a hundred times (*saltem centoties*); no. 9 did not speak of the relation of other Christians to the Mystical Body and stated, without making any distinctions, that they were deprived of "many of the means of salvation;" the schema even seemed at times to doubt the eternal salvation of the Orientals. Edelby concluded that it would be better to eliminate the first part and refer it to the schema on the Church or the decree of the Secretariat, and to keep only the second part.

After Edelby, Melkite Zoghby undertook to explain more fully the Oriental conception of unity.[75] The Oriental Church is a "source" Church, as original as the Latin Church, and even born before the latter; it is the sister, not the daughter, of the Latin Church. Consequently, it went through a "parallel" development in its theologies, especially its theology of the Trinity. In addition, the meaning of liturgical feasts is not identical in the two traditions. The two represent, therefore, two parallel directions that ought to enrich each other but not be confused. And, while the Oriental Churches with their emphasis on collegiality have evolved in the direction of an ever greater autonomy, the Latin Church has followed the opposite route. The unity of the two, therefore, can only be that of "*Churches* that remain distinct, but are united in *the Church*." If Latins justify their vision by appealing to a legitimate evolution, they should not fail to take into account those, namely, the Orthodox, who do not accept "our de facto evolution," since this would mean "dissolving their very being and their Churches into 'Latinism,' whereas unity is meant to enrich and not to impoverish."

Those responsible for the schema continued to gamble that a reduced form of the schema might save a document many criticized but no one really wanted to sink. On the second day of discussion, November 27, "to forestall objections," the Commission for the Oriental Churches had a statement read that made three points. The title, "That All May Be One," could very well be changed to show more clearly that the schema dealt only with the Orientals. The introductory section did not pretend to

---

[75] *AS* I/3, 640-43.

deal with the constitution of the Church, but was meant only to provide the few premises required by the practical section. The addressees were all the children of the Catholic Church.[76]

As noted earlier, the interventions of the Melkite Church did not receive the agreement of the other Uniate Churches. After "their day," the balance beam of the Oriental Churches seemed to incline to the other side. In fact, on November 28, while there were two more Melkite interventions, by Tawil and Assaf,[77] two Oriental Patriarchs, Tappouni and Cheikho, spoke in favor of the schema.[78] The vision of East and West as two "parallel" traditions was explicitly criticized several times.[79] Scandar, a Catholic Copt, gave a harsh speech in which he wondered about the orthodoxy of the Coptic Church of his native land, Egypt.[80] The opposition of the other Uniate bishops to the Melkites, which had emerged during the meeting of the conciliar Commission for the Oriental Churches, thus also found open expression at the general congregation.

When Bea intervened on the final day of the debate, November 30,[81] he began by accepting the "low-profile" vision of the schema that the official presenters had themselves given. He too was of the opinion that the schema had been written "to show respect for the Oriental Churches" and not to anticipate and deal separately with the general question of the unity of the Church. The intersecting questions would be brought into harmony later on, as would those questions that had been neglected.

Bea restricted himself, therefore, to a few remarks on a schema, "which," he said, "in general pleases me greatly."[82] On the question of the prayer for unity the Secretariat would have its say in its own schema, which was not yet printed. Recognizing the integrity of customs was

---

[76] AS I/3, 614-15. I have not been able to find any traces of the meeting that the Commission for the Oriental Churches held prior to November 27 and at which this intervention was approved. The statement was probably the work of Cicognani himself, who was determined to avoid a formal defeat of the schema.

[77] AS I/3, 660-61, 683-85; Assaf was especially critical on the question of rites.

[78] AS I/3, 654-55, 658-59.

[79] Khoury, a Maronite (AS I/3, 668ff.), Hayek, a Syrian (724ff.), and others.

[80] AS I/3, 679-80.

[81] AS I/3, 709-12. The Acta Synodalia erroneously gives November 29 as the date of the thirtieth general congregation. That was a Thursday, when, in keeping with the regulations, there were no discussions in the hall; the correct date, therefore, is November 30. Only during the final week was there a general congregation on Thursday (December 6).

[82] The words in quotation marks are lacking in the written text; Bea therefore chose to insert them at the moment of speaking.

more important than a simple "means of making prayers more effective;" it was rather an example of authentic Christian life that attracts others more strongly, the more it is conformed to the gospel. To understand the mentality of the separated brothers it was advisable to recall the distinction made in *Gaudet Mater Ecclesia* between the deposit of faith and the way of expressing it. The emended decree should be clearer about its purpose (doctrinal or practical) and about its addressees who, though comprising in the nature of things only Catholics, could not fail to include in some way non-Catholics as well. Finally, the body that Leo XIII foresaw and that was to be responsible for ecumenical relations with the Orientals had in fact already been revived by John XXIII in his establishment of the Secretariat, which now had two sections, one for the Orientals and one for the communities that had emerged from the Reformation of the sixteenth century. Bea's intervention was strikingly silent on the real questions at issue. It was obvious that, in his view, the real game would be played out elsewhere!

On November 30, at the end of the meeting, the president called upon the assembly to approve the termination of the discussion by rising or remaining seated. "All rose." On December 1 there was a vote on the proposition that the Council fathers

> approve the decree on the unity of the Church . . . as a document which sums up our common faith, and as a pledge of remembrance and good will toward the separated brethren of the East. However, after the proposed emendations have been taken into account, the decree is to be combined in a single document with the decree on ecumenism composed by the Secretariat for Christian Unity and with Chapter XI, on ecumenism, of the schema for the Dogmatic Constitution on the Church.[83]

The voting allowed for only two possibilities: yes or no (*placet* or *non placet*). The proposition was approved with 2068 in favor, 36 opposed, and 8 void votes.

We do not know if the Melkites were among those opposed. In any case, no one wanted to listen to them; perhaps the time for heeding their demands had not yet come. They were sadly isolated, like one of those ethnic minorities of the Near East whom the political wisdom of Westerners has left to its fate during the twentieth century simply because, from the standpoint of *Realpolitik*, the time seemed inopportune.

[83] *AS* I/4, 9.

IV. The Schema on the Church

For a whole week after the schema on the Church was distributed on November 23, it remained uncertain when the discussion of it would begin. On that day Secretary General Felici had announced that after discussion of the schema on the communications media, the Council would discuss the schema on the Blessed Virgin and then that on the unity of the Church. This was an obvious attempt, given the few days still available, to prevent a discussion on and defeat of the schema on the Church. But on November 26 Felici announced a new schedule for the work: first the schema on unity and then the schema on the Church.[84] Ottaviani tried to oppose this change in the schedule. Speaking on the unity schema on November 28, he expressed the wish that the assembly stick to the discussion of the schema on the Blessed Virgin. The schema on the Church, he argued, was too lengthy to be analyzed in a few days, while it would be a fine thing if the first session of the Council could end with the spectacle of the bishops' common love for their Mother.[85] The Council of Presidents, however, rejected Ottaviani's bid, and on November 30 Felici told the fathers of the decision, giving as a reason the suggestion made by the Pope in his intervention of November 21: to spend the few remaining days in "getting a first experience" of the general character of the schema, "so that after the views of the fathers on its general principles have been heard, any revision and adaptation of the schema, if such be needed, may be made at the appropriate time."[86] Despite the rhetorical hypothesis, "if such be needed," this statement presupposed that a revision of the schema on the Church was inevitable. This was a sign that, at least in the judgment of the Council of Presidents, the most important results of the preparatory work were not regarded as an adequate expression of the direction that had by now emerged in the Council.

In fact, that the schema would have to be redone was tacitly assumed from the beginning of the debate, and without any of the drama, any of the feeling of a life-or-death decision, that had accompanied the debate

---

[84] *AS* I/3, 501-2. The reason given for the change was the request made by many bishops: "For many fathers have earnestly and repeatedly asked that now, during this first session, the dogmatic constitution on the Church be studied." At this point, the schema on Mary was to be dealt with together with the schema on the Church, since Mary is the holiest member of the mystical body of Christ. In fact, there were to be few interventions on the Marian schema as such.

[85] *AS* I/3, 657-58.

[86] *AS* I/3, 692.

on the sources of revelation. There were even some who were still so affected by the stress of the preceding days that they thought they must lay down their arms.[87] Many of the speakers did not even feel it necessary expressly to call for the rejection of the schema as a basis for discussion or, on the contrary, for its simple improvement. Such moves evidently seemed superfluous or irrelevant.

In his introduction to the discussion Ottaviani spoke with bitter irony, saying that he expected the usual litany: the schema was not ecumenical, it was scholastic, it was not pastoral, it was negative, and so on. He could even let the fathers in on a "secret": the reporters for the schema would speak to no avail, "because the matter has already been prejudged." Even before this schema had been distributed, a substitute-schema was being prepared. "The only thing left for me, then, is to be silent, for sacred scripture teaches: Do not waste your words when no one is listening."[88] When, following Ottaviani, Franić, Bishop of Split, gave the opening explanation of the schema, he limited himself to the kind of summary a notary would make but added at the end a useless defense in which he appealed to the Apostolate of Prayer's intention for October 1962, "approved" by the Pope:

> All the questions in all the chapters are treated in a positive way through the explanation of Catholic teaching. Not without serious reason are errors listed and rejected in some cases so that "through the infallible teaching of Vatican Council II errors against and dangers to faith and morals may become clearer to all." This was the general intention for the Apostolate of Prayer in the month of October of this year, an intention approved by our Supreme and very loving Pontiff John XXIII, now happily reigning. That was our intention as well, namely, that through the denial of errors the truth might be seen in a positive and clearer light.[89]

---

[87] Semmelroth noted: "At lunchtime I had an opportunity to speak with Cardinal Döpfner about the schema on the Church. He and perhaps many other bishops as well seem to be somewhat tired and weary of the continual struggle. They are dangerously inclined to deal kindly with the schema. But in a twenty-minute conversation I was able to present the most important individual elements in such a way that he himself drew the conclusion that the appropriate vote had to be a *Non placet*" (*TSemmelroth*, November 30).

[88] *AS* I/4, 121.

[89] *AS* I/4, 125. On November 28 Gagnebet had given the French bishops a richer presentation of the schema. Having read Philips's schema, he was familiar with the main objections to the preparatory work, and he sought to anticipate the various difficulties. In his view, the schema was open-ended. "Our intention . . . was to offer the fathers an overview or outline of Catholic teaching, so that, having accepted this schema as a starting point, they themselves might be able to improve it and remove obscurities from it in the light of truth." He did not deny that it was possible to proceed otherwise. It was not

The debate lasted from December 1 to December 7, during which seventy-seven fathers spoke. Another eighty-five opinions, among them a joint one of the German and Austrian episcopates, which proposed an alternative schema of their own, were sent in during these days and in the months that followed. All possible variations emerged from the discussion, from the extremely negative views of the Secretariat for Christian Unity,[90] many bishops of Central Europe, and some bishops of Latin America and the non-Western world, to the extremely positive ones voiced especially by the Curial and Italo-Spanish bloc; the latter, however, was not completely united but saw such authoritative personages as Montini and Lercaro distancing themselves from the others. Above all, however, the debate brought out some requirements for the future prospects of the work and of the very image of the Council.

There were, then, those who expressed enthusiasm for the schema and, while asking for some emendations, called attention to its main

the Council's task to propose complete theological syntheses. For this reason he even regarded the disjointedness of the subjects and the lack of organization as in fact more appropriate, "as if we were dealing with different things, so that each may be judged on its own merits, in abstraction from the others." An organic synthesis could therefore be the task of a definitive redaction. In obedience to orders from on high, the traditional method followed by councils had been abandoned, namely, of producing "formal definitions and canons," and the task of determining the degree of certainty of the doctrines set forth had been left to their context. The constitution is a dogmatic one and should not descend to the level of disciplinary specifics. (Here Gagnebet was evidently referring to Trent's clear distinction between doctrinal decrees and "reform" decrees.) It was useless, therefore, to look to the constitution for guidelines for the functioning of episcopal conferences. Only after these premises did Gagnebet go on to explain the individual chapters. There is a copy of his presentation in the Gagnebet Archive (ISR), dated December 2, 1962. Here, however, I accept as accurate the date given by Congar (*JCongar*, November 28). In his diary, Congar acknowledges the clarity and objectivity of the text, as well as the skillful way in which Gagnebet prepared the bishops to approach the schema positively.

Congar himself spoke at the same meeting, proposing that work on the scheme be done in the light of three "major points": the general character of the schema, with its style and lack of organization; the ideas used in defining the Church, namely, people of God and body of Christ (the interpretation of which ought to take into account the discussion among the exegetes); the question of the bishops, which needed to be approached in a better way and to include something on the councils and the conciliar life of the Church.

[90] The Secretariat continued to act as a "channel" between the Council and the observers, and vice versa. It is therefore legitimate to inquire, as G. Alberigo does in his *Ecclesiologia in devenire. A proposito di "concilio pastorale" e di Osservatori a-cattolici* (Bologna, 1990), whether the usual way of interpreting the participation of the observers at Vatican II is not overly reductive from a theological viewpoint. On the especially lively meeting of December 2, at which the observers took a clear position, see Mauro Velati, *Una difficile transizione: Il cattolicesimo tra unionismo ed ecumenismo (1952-1964)* (Bologna, 1996).

controlling idea. For most of the group this idea was the emphasis on the juridical, social dimension and the identification of the Roman Church with the Mystical Body of Christ, with the concentration here on the Church militant. (Ruffini even said that the word "militant" might well be removed, "since this is the only Church of which the Council is speaking."[91]) Not all of those who opted for this emphasis called for the same degree of "Petrineness" (*petrinitas*) as did Bernacki, who asked for a separate chapter on the supreme pontiff and proposed that the Nicene-Constantinopolitan Creed be changed by the introduction of *petrinitas* among the marks of the Church.[92] But the reason why the supporters of the schema opposed any radical revision of it was clearly expressed by Siri: "The schema gives an excellent exposition of the truth about the visible Church that has been juridically established by the Lord himself, and this in light of the truth about the Mystical Body of Christ."[93]

In defense of the schema Archbishop Florit of Florence allowed a degree of historical relativity to some juridical structures — those of purely ecclesiastical origin — and therefore the acceptability of a few changes dictated by pastoral effectiveness. But he regarded as a very serious matter the tendency of many, among them even some priests, to deny that the Church "is by divine institution a visible society and therefore to be governed according to juridical norms."[94] Carli, for his part, defended the timeliness of a schema with a strongly dogmatic tendency.[95] And while some found fault with the presence in the schema of an aggressive conception of the Church as a "battle line" drawn up for conflict, others asserted, on the contrary, that we must not forget that Christ himself spoke of struggles and oppositions: "Therefore, in order to hold out in the battles of Christ, he set the battle line in order under Peter and established a hierarchical series of leaders who would lead the faithful into battle, carrying the standard of Christ."

The defenders of the schema also offered emendations. Ruffini asked that the chapters on the states of perfection, the laity, and ecumenism be removed, since they were to be dealt with in separate schemas, and that the text speak of the Oriental Catholic communities (which some "prefer" to call "Churches") but without creating the suspicion that there are

---

[91] *AS* I/4, 128.
[92] *AS* I/4, 138-41.
[93] *AS* I/4, 174.
[94] *AS* I/4, 298-303.
[95] *AS* I/4, 158-61.

several Churches.[96] Bueno y Monreal asked for a better explanation of
the relation between the vital (he called it "biological") and mystical
dimension of the Church and the juridico-social dimension; in addition,
along with many others who would come back to this point, he asked
that an explicit treatment of presbyters not be omitted.[97] Pawlowski and
others asked that the schema's description of Christians as "redeemers"
be corrected and that the term *ex sese* of Vatican I be explained. He too,
like Bernacki, wanted an explicit chapter on the pope.[98]

Cardinal Spellman asked for more attention to Catholic Action, as
Maccari, an Italian, would also do.[99] Siri asked for a fuller explanation
of the relation between the visible Church and the mystical body of
Christ, while Gonzalez Moralejo, a Spaniard, though approving the
schema, found fault with its lack of unity and proposed the elimination
of Chapters V, VI, and XI, as well as of chapter IX, which would be better combined with a schema on religious freedom.[100] Fiordelli, an Italian,
asked for the insertion of a chapter on marriage, since it is Christian
spouses who give the Church its increase.[101] Fares asked for the insertion of a preface that would clarify the fundamental idea of the schema;
McIntyre, from the United States, asked for a treatment of the lot of children who die unbaptized, a subject on which it had not been possible to
reach agreement during the preparatory period; and Kominek, a Pole,
complained of the absence of the motif of the cross.[102]

Critics of the schema were rather livelier than the somewhat repetitious defenders of the schema. Many of them focused on the need for an
inspiring central idea, which most of them considered to be the dimension of mystery in the Church's inner life. If the Church is essentially a
mystery, then language should be avoided that encloses it within the
bounds of comprehensibility, thereby "corrupting" it, said Liénart, who
by his seniority among the cardinals had the thankless task of firing the
opening shot at the beginning of each new discussion.[103] Marty in his
intervention likewise spoke of the central place of mystery and against
the prominence given to the juridical dimension in the schema; he also
wanted the missionary dimension to be pervasive in the treatment of the

---

[96] *AS* I/4, 128.
[97] *AS* I/4, 130-32.
[98] *AS* I/4, 151-56.
[99] *AS* I/4, 172-73, 242-47.
[100] *AS* I/4, 174, 242-44.
[101] *AS* I/4, 309-11.
[102] *AS* I/4, 346-49, 175, 189-91.
[103] *AS* I/4, 126-27.

Church.[104] Mels and Barrachina Estevan addressed the lack of the missionary perspective, the latter also developing the connection between the mystery of Christ and the Church as sacrament.[105] D'Avack, an Italian, insisted that the inner life of the Church be made central (as did Pluta in his statement), while van Cauwelaert, a missionary bishop, favored the motif of Christian fraternity.[106]

Of a more technical kind were the criticisms of those who were alert especially to the ideas set forth in the critiques of Rahner and Schillebeeckx. König asked for a briefer schema that would speak not only of the rights of the Church but also of its task of bringing the blessings of the gospel to all in a sincere involvement in the future of the non-Christian peoples; nor could the reflection on the Church pass over its eschatological dimension or over its charismatic dimension, which needed to be defined in its relation to the institution; it was also necessary to include the idea of the people of God as a fundamental image of the Church, and to make clear the necessity of the Church not only for the salvation of individuals but for the human race and the world as such, even the world of nonbelievers.[107]

In addition to complaining, like many others, of the schema's lack of organization and unity, Alfrink criticized its failure to integrate bishops as such into its vision of the episcopate, for it spoke only of residential bishops. Harking back to Zinelli's intervention at Vatican I and to the schema offered by Kleutgen, Alfrink also criticized the implicit inconsistency in asserting an exclusively extraordinary exercise of collegiality. Finally, he asked that the agency charged with the revision of the schema be the same mixed commission that had been appointed to redo the schema on the sources of revelation.[108]

---

[104] *AS* I/4, 191-93.

[105] *AS* I/4, 312-15, 351-53.

[106] The references for this paragraph are, respectively: *AS* I/4, 148-50, 305-308, 156-58.

[107] *AS* I/4, 132-34. Faced with the reemergence, here and in other interventions, of the people of God theme and of the charismatic dimension of the Church, Siri would comment: "It is time for the idea and term 'people of God' (three or four times already), which is becoming — how, I don't know — a source of some very serious matters. It is also time for the 'charismatic life' as something somehow constitutive of the Church. Everyone knows that we have to think about this and how the term conceals not only a danger but a new and scarcely catholic concept" (*DSiri*, December 3, 383). In a second intervention, on the second part of the schema König asked for the inclusion of the theme of peace, the need to help the mission countries, an extended reflection on natural law, collaboration among bishops, and the need to organize teams of priests for special missions (*AS* I/4, 369-70).

[108] *AS* I/4, 134-36.

Cardinal Ritter, for his part, brought out all the methodological defects of the schema, which made authority (*potestas*) the source of everything, whereas it is the source of only a part of the Church. As a result, the schema did not come to grips with the whole of the new conception of the Church, but instead took over partial conceptions from Trent and Vatican I. This explains the utter inadequacy of the schema, of which he gave three key examples: holiness was considered solely in the perspective of instrumental causes and not of formal causality, as the holiness of the entire Church; the task of preserving and explaining the truth was reserved to the magisterium alone; there was an absence in the description of Church-State relations of the perspective of the freedom of conscience, which is to be acknowledged as the right of all.[109]

Döpfner, also indebted to Rahner's observations, proposed that during the intersession a new schema be composed (something the Austro-German Episcopate was in fact to do), and he gave a complete critique of the schema as a whole and of its details. As a whole, he said that the lengthy structure lacked a fundamental idea; the use of scripture was superficial; the juridical dimension predominated; and there was no theological qualification given for the individual statements. Regarding details he noted that the teaching on episcopal collegiality was weak; it was not possible for the schema to resolve a disputed question such as the origin of episcopal jurisdiction; the language of authority took precedence over that of ministry; and the chapter on Church-state relations needed complete revision.[110]

Volk, who was a professional theologian as well as a bishop, criticized the weakness of the biblical foundation, not only in the language used, but also in the reduction of the theology of the Church to the theme of the "body" and in the inadequate attention paid to the theology of the people of God. In its conceptualist approach the schema ignored the pregnant character of the biblical motifs (Volk referred in particular to the theme of the anointing of Christ), which in their simplicity prove to be at once more comprehensive and more concrete. Another deficiency, in Volk's view, was the reduction of the Church to a means of salvation while passing over the fact that the Church is also a fruit of salvation that will remain forever. Finally, he complained of the lack of any pastoral dimension.[111]

---

[109] *AS* I/4, 136-38.
[110] *AS* I/4, 183-89.
[111] *AS* I/4, 386-88.

Frings also delivered a very effective intervention, for which one may presume a contribution from his theologian, Ratzinger. It was perhaps the most decisive intervention from a critical standpoint, since it demolished one of the central claims of the schema, that it was catholic. In Frings's view it represented only the Latin tradition of the past century; the Greek and the ancient Latin traditions were both missing. Frings gave detailed examples to support his claim: in the six pages of notes for chapter IV a single Greek Father was briefly cited twice, and there were not many more citations of the Latin Fathers and the medieval theologians; and even chapters VI-VIII had for their sources only documents of the previous century, except for one citation from Innocent III, one from St. Thomas, and one from Trent. "I ask whether this way of proceeding is proper, universal, scientific, ecumenical, catholic, which in Greek is *katholon*, that is, embracing the whole and with an eye on the whole. In this sense one may ask whether the procedure is catholic." This lack of catholicity had concrete consequences: the words of Paul, "we are one body, one bread," were given a reductive juridico-sociological interpretation, whereas in the Greek theological tradition the first and strongest bond of peace was found in the Eucharist and in the communion of Churches with one another and with the supreme pontiff. Frings saw similar defects in the separation of the treatment of the Church from the treatment of the bishops and in the conception of the Church's mission.[112]

The criticisms of the Orientals, who this time were pretty much in accord, were on the same wave length, although the sensitivities and language were different. Maximos IV complained above all of the schema's partiality, its failure to say the *whole* truth. The military-style triumphalism of the schema (the Church as "an army drawn up for battle") falsified the conception of the Church, which, as the body of the suffering and risen Christ, is called to join its head in completing, through faith and suffering, the redemption of humanity and of the entire creation. The foundation of diversity in the Church (no. 5) was located in the subjection of some to others, and the juridical character of this foundation falsified the true idea of the Church of Christ.[113] The juridicism of this conception of the Church meant that there was no room for titular bishops. But the place where the one-sidedness of the schema really became clear was in the treatment of the pope in separation from the bishops.[114]

---

[112] *AS* I/4, 218-20.

[113] Some Latins repeated this theme (see De Smedt, D'Souza, *AS* I/4, 142-44, 384-86).

[114] *AS* I/4, 295-97. Playing to the gallery, the patriarch also cited phrases from a book

The interventions of the other Orientals were similar to that of the Melkite patriarch. Rabban, a Chaldean, complained that the discussion of the members of the Church was removed from its natural context, the Mystical Body, and he criticized the omission of the diaconate. With regard to the teaching on the members he repeated the objection that could already be raised against the Bellarminian conception of the Church; namely, the absurdity of regarding Catholic criminals as full members while denying this status to holy non-Catholics. Finally he made his own the objection already raised by others, that it was impossible to assert that an ordinary power, such as that of the episcopal college, could only be exercised extraordinarily.[115]

In opposition to the separation of the power of orders from the power of jurisdiction, Doumith, a Maronite, appealed to the ancient conception of episcopal consecration as the source of all power.[116] Hakim, a Melkite, contrasted the realism of the Oriental conception with the juridicism of the schema and explained that, while the mystical reality of the Church certainly does take on concreteness and authenticity in a visible society with its powers and teaching office, this visibility never swallows up the mystical substance of the body of Christ. In like manner, the logic of the mystery of the Church requires that bishops not be defined by their jurisdictional authority but by the mystery, in which as a Greek hymn of the third century puts it, they are architects and leaders in virtue of their consecration.[117]

Finally, Ghattas, Bishop of Thebes, reproached the schema for not taking heed of the perspective of the Church as mother and for first reducing the Mystical Body to the militant Church, then the militant Church to members who acknowledge the hierarchy, and finally the whole to the Roman Church alone. The schema thus forgot that the focus of the ancient conception of the Mystical Body was the Eucharist; it was unable to conceive of Churches in the plural; and it had a defective conception of collegiality.[118]

From the West, too, especially from the French episcopate,[119] voices like those of the Orientals were being heard. One of them was Cardinal

by Bertetto, a Salesian, on St. John Bosco, in which he calls the pope "God on earth," and so forth.

[115] *AS* I/4, 236-39.

[116] *AS* I/4, 255-57.

[117] *AS* I/4, 358-60.

[118] *AS* I/4, 376-79.

[119] In this division of the various positions, constructed with special attention to the "subjectivity" of the various Churches, one may wonder what role was played, here more

Lefebvre, who said he was disappointed by the complete absence from the schema of the theme of the love of Christ. Another was Msgr. Ancel, who pointed out that, given the spiritual character of Christ's reign, only in the light of the gospel can the opposition between the juridical dimension and the spiritual dimension be made to disappear.[120]

Another important assault on the schema came, inevitably, from the sphere of the Secretariat for Christian Unity. The opening attack was launched in the rhetorically powerful discourse of Bishop De Smedt of Bruges. As in his earlier intervention on the sources of revelation, the emotional impact was considerable; it may have been to some extent irrelevant to the subject, but in any case it elicited some pointed replies from people of the opposite mind.[121] After beginning with polite praise of the schema, De Smedt offered a radical criticism of its triumphalism (a pompous and romantic triumphalism, he called it, like that habitual in *L'Osservatore Romano* and Roman documents), which was at odds with the real state of the people of God, which Jesus described as a humble "little flock." He then criticized the schema's clericalism, which conceived of the Church as a pyramid with dignity increasing as one reached the top, whereas the same fundamental rights and responsibilities ought to be in effect throughout the entire people of God. And he pointed out that its juridicism ignored the real theology of the Church and its motherhood.[122]

Bea's intervention aimed less at effect but was more profound and radical. He began by trying to locate the importance of the schema on the Church in historical perspective; the question of the Church, which had flared up in the sixteenth century and was not faced at all by Trent and only inadequately by Vatican I, now had to be given a satisfactory answer. While duly acknowledging the work that had been done, he could not fail to point out the deficiencies of the schema on essential

---

than elsewhere, by the distinct spiritual traditions of the Churches: the attention paid to spirituality in the French Church; the theological and doctrinal sensitivity of Churches that had to deal more directly with the Reformation; the middle way of the English, of which more will be said below; the juridical tradition of the Italian Church; the heritage of the Oriental Churches; and so on. It would be an anachronism to think here of the "nations" at the medieval councils or of the great regional subdivisions at the first ecumenical councils. But there did emerge here, in other forms, one of the characteristic traits of every conciliar experience. And while the voices of Africa and Asia were still weak, the face of the Latin American Church was beginning to emerge quite clearly.

[120] *AS* I/4, 371-73, 379-81.

[121] See Stella, an Italian, who devoted his entire intervention to a critique of De Smedt (*AS* I/4, 356-57).

[122] *AS* I/4, 142-44.

points, beginning with its reduction of perspective to the militant Church and its neglect of the Church that is to be made perfect and glorified, which was so central and deeply meditated on in the reflection of the Fathers.

The bishops had also expected, in vain, an explanation of the purpose of the Church — that is, its mission of proclaiming the gospel — in such a way that this would pervade every reflection on the means of achieving this purpose. Omitting these serious topics, the schema tried instead to resolve a controverted question, that of membership in the Church. In its discussion of the magisterium it inverted the order in the Bible, which would require speaking first of the college of apostles and then of Peter. Supporting the observations already made by Frings, Bea noted how little the schema looked to the entire tradition of the Church. In its exposition of the biblical metaphors for the Church, it concentrated unduly on the image of the body and generally removed the biblical citations from their contexts. Then Bea unhesitatingly identified as the root of all the defects of the schema its opposition to the spirit that prevailed in the Pope's opening allocution and in the Council's opening message to all of humanity.[123]

Another whole series of interventions, whether they agreed or disagreed with the text, called for important changes. Thus Blanchet asked that it attend to the present condition of the Church and move beyond the conception of bishops as "prefects" under the central authority. Guerry suggested a different order, a favorite theme of Suenens, which would separate reflection on the internal life of the Church from reflection on its relations with the outside world. Guerry also called for a more vital conception of the Church itself, with greater attention to the role of the bishop as father.[124]

Devoto, an Argentinean, asked for a description not only of the Church's essence but also of its concrete existence, giving new life to the idea of the people of God and emphasizing the simplicity and poverty of the Church. Vairo, an Italian, like so many others, wanted a deeper understanding of the relation between the pilgrim Church and the heavenly Church; a greater exactness in speaking of the hierarchical priesthood and the priesthood of the faithful; and a more accurate determination of relations between Church and State.[125] To the criticisms thus

---

[123] *AS* I/4, 227-30.
[124] *AS* I/4, 233-35, 240-41.
[125] *AS* I/4, 250-53.

far uttered, Hengsbach, a German, added others that were directed at the chapter on Church-State relations on which he also wanted the laity to collaborate.[126] Descuffi, the Latin-rite Bishop of Smyrna, and John Velasco, Bishop of Hsiamen, involved themselves in rather inconclusive reflections on the interpretation of the *ex sese* of Vatican I.[127]

Elchinger asked that pastoral considerations determine the aspects of the Church that needed to be emphasized at the present time. Gargitter criticized the adjective *improper* as used for the common priesthood of the faithful, the conception of the laity as subjects, and the inadequate treatment of the episcopate. Huyghe called for a greater adherence to the spirit of the gospel. Jubany Arnau tried to give his own theological qual-ification of the teaching of the schema. Rupp criticized, above all, the absence of consideration for the residential bishops. Koslowiecki asked for a christocentric explanation that would stress the eschatological dimension, the positive riches which the Church communicates, and the motif of charity. In addition to repeating criticisms already made by oth-ers, Mendez Arceo called for attention to the Jews and to the need of a more positive appraisal of freemasonry. Philbin of Ireland suggested that while maintaining the needed dogmatic accuracy there be a gradation of positions: concentrate on teaching being denied in the errors of our time and on the defense of the Church's rights (where such a need did not exist, it was better not to talk at length of the subject) and do not pull back from teachings that are now a common possession. Renard, a Frenchman, insisted again on the need to include a discussion of pres-byters. De Bazelaire de Ruppierre asked for a more nuanced discussion of authority.[128]

These positions, which I have collected here without attending to the order of the days on which they were expressed, testify to the evolution of the bishops' consciousness toward the end of the first conciliar period. If there was a certain degree of confusion, there was also an increased acceptance of responsibility. Cardinal Gracias's remarks, gen-erally favorable to the schema although asking for major improvements suggested by the special situation in India, with its need for a new encounter between Christianity and the Oriental cultures, included a common sentiment: "we have become habituated to the conciliar way of doing things."[129] Amid the wide range of their sensibilities, the bishops

---

[126] *AS* I/4, 254-55.
[127] For the preceding two paragraphs see, respectively, *AS* I/4, 257-59, 349-50.
[128] See, respectively, *AS* I/4, 147-48, 193-97, 201-6, 208-12, 338-46, 374-76.
[129] *AS* I/4, 176.

were responding much more fully and in greater depth than they had to the request for their views in the antepreparatory period.[130] As a result, an "ecclesial subjectivity" was emerging, at times strongly affected by the cultures to which the bishops belonged.

This was especially visible in some bishops from the Anglo-Saxon world. Thus Cardinal Godfrey, less in the doctrinal solutions he offered than in his remarks about dialogue with other Christians, mentioned the psychological characteristics often ascribed to the English and, quoting St. Paul, urged that the charity of the fathers *"non agit perperam,"* that is, not act unjustly. Abbot Butler asked above all for a positive tone, while Buckley, Superior General of the Marists, urged that attention be paid not so much to principles having to do with the essence of authority as to its exercise, in which the centrality of the person and personal freedom were to be kept in mind.[131]

In this final phase of the first period, when everything seemed to be involved in a turbulent process of transformations and new possibilities, it is perhaps wrong to limit to precise doctrinal alternatives the positions of most of the bishops, who were not professional theologians and could not avail themselves of the close collaboration with leading experts that was possible only to a few of them. Even in the case of a man such as Suenens, it was not then possible to see how very consistent his plan for the Council was with the "theological" plan produced by Philips. During these days, in fact, the Council was thinking less about particular doctrines about the Church than about its own future.

V. The Future of the Council

For many reasons that future seemed uncertain: the bishops had nothing concrete to bring home to the faithful of their dioceses; they had an immense mass of material still to study; the sense of a burdensome procedure caused them to anticipate lengthy periods ahead; the serious illness of the Pope made it uncertain whether the Council would even continue.[132] The conciliar agency that sought to give a concrete response to

---

[130] *History,* I, 97-132.

[131] *AS* I/4, 221-22, 389-91, 353-55.

[132] The beginning of the second period, originally set for May 1963, had been postponed to September 8, 1963. The Pope's decision, made on November 26 to comply with the request of many bishops for this postponement "for primarily pastoral reasons," was officially made known in the hall on November 17 (see *AS* I/3, 613).

these concerns was primarily the Secretariat for Extraordinary Affairs.[133] At its meeting on November 23, the Secretariat dealt not only with the question of having representatives of the Catholic laity participate in the Council's sessions as "observers,"[134] but also with the norms for determining "the order in which the conciliar schemas were to be discussed," with the result that the Secretariat was able to approve a new list at its meeting on November 30 and to distribute it to the bishops before they left Rome.

At the same meeting the Secretariat also formalized a proposal to be presented for papal approval: the establishment of a "directive committee that would have the task of coordinating and regulating the work of the conciliar commissions charged with sifting and reducing in number the materials to be submitted for the attention of the Council."[135] The committee was to be made up of seven cardinals chosen from among the members of the Council of Presidents and from the Secretariat for Extraordinary Affairs, with the Secretary of State as chairman. Another task of this directive committee would be to "keep the Supreme Pontiff informed in a timely way about the progress of the work and to see to the carrying out of the venerable instructions he might give." As a result of these decisions, on December 5 the bishops received a booklet containing the list of schemas from which subjects to be treated in the future were to be chosen.[136]

---

[133] Even apart from the agencies of the Council, people were thinking of initiatives for the future of the Council. One of these was the call from about thirty bishops of different nationalities in response to the suggestion of Helder Câmara to create a new "secretariat" to deal with problems of the contemporary world (see *NChenu*, November 29, 1962, 125f.). Suenens brought this proposal to the Secretariat for Extraordinary Affairs (copy in the papers of Cardinal Meyer, Archdiocese of Chicago). In his intervention in the hall on December 4, Suenens ended by suggesting the establishment of a "secretariat for the problems of the contemporary world" (*AS* I/4, 224-25). See also Suenens, *Souvenirs et Espérances*, 80.

[134] The question was suggested by the fact that there were lay people among the non-Catholic observers. It was explained, however, that Catholic lay people could take part in the Council not "by any right of theirs" but by a concession from the Church (*DSiri*, 354). A French layman, Jean Guitton, had been attending the Council since November 21.

[135] For both meetings see *DSiri*, 354-55.

[136] *AS* I/4, 265. The schemas were: divine revelation (text to be composed by the mixed commission); the Church; the Blessed Virgin Mary; the deposit of faith; the moral order (these last four texts already printed); the social order and the community of peoples; the Oriental Churches; clerics; bishops and the government of dioceses; states of perfection; the laity; the sacrament of matrimony; the sacred liturgy; the care of souls; the formation of seminarians; academic studies and Catholic schools; the social communications media (text already printed); the advancement of unity among Christians (in which the schema on religious tolerance was to be included) (cf. *AS* I/1, 90-95). Note the

In the hall, on the other hand, concerns for the future of the Council
were being echoed in proposals that dealt not only with procedure but
also, and above all, with content. On the one side were those who saw
the familiar and solid ground crumbling beneath their feet because of the
now-clear formation of a majority and the evident closeness of this
group to the outlook of the Pope. It was in this perspective that the proposal of Archbishop Marcel Lefebvre, Superior of the Spiritans, who
spoke immediately after De Smedt, was to be seen. His argument did not
lack logical consistency. Lefebvre argued that it was impossible to combine the requirements of the two goals of the Council — the doctrinal
and the pastoral — in a single schema; it would be better for each commission to produce two schemas on its subject, one doctrinal and the
other pastoral. Lefebvre did not deny that the characteristic peculiar to
this Council was the pastoral bent. (This was to be an idea that the
minority, too, would gradually make its own in order to deny the doctrinal rank of Vatican II; they would thereby interpret *pastoral* in a much
different sense than that intended by John XXIII.) According to Lefebvre, this doubling of the schemas and of the two relevant kinds of language would be a way of integrating the new pastoral element.[137]

Cardinal Bacci proposed an analogous position. Our disagreements,
he said to the bishops, are not on doctrinal substance but on form. Let
the latter, then, be adjusted, while the former remains firm.[138] Lefebvre's
proposal was explicitly supported by Bishop Holland and in particular
by Ruffini, who in his second speech, on December 5, also cited
Bacci.[139]

This desperate defensive effort required some quick thinking from the
other side, strengthened by the now-explicit support of the Pope, to
whom they openly appealed. The entire intervention of Léger, the man
who had played an important role in the solution of the difficulty raised
by the vote on the sources of revelation, was devoted to the need to support the Pope's desire for renewal and to provide for the work of the
intersession. Making his own the decision of the Secretariat for Extraordinary Affairs, he proposed a coordinating committee that would have
the responsibility of guiding the work of the other commissions and

absence from this list of the schema on the unity of the Church. As a matter of fact, this
last schema had already been approved in its general lines, although on condition that it
be combined with the chapters of ecumenism that had been prepared by the Theological
Commission and the Secretariat for Christian Unity.

   [137] *AS* I/4, 144-46.
   [138] *AS* I/4, 230-32.
   [139] *AS* I/4, 247-49, 290-91.

whose competence therefore needed to be determined. Léger's suggestion was, so to speak, a technical one and did not enter into the merits of
the questions, except to appeal to the guidelines given by the Pope.[140]
That same day, December 3, Hurley offered a critique of the schema that
did not simply look back to what had already been said but emphasized
the point so dear to him, namely, how important it was that teaching be
pastoral.[141]

December 4, however, was Suenens's great opportunity. The plan that
had been drawn up in accord with the Pope before the beginning of the
Council[142] and had then been explained to the Secretariat for Extraordinary Affairs was now presented in the hall to all the bishops.[143] Suenens
chose to appeal not to *Gaudet Mater Ecclesia* but to the Pope's address
on September 11, in which Suenens's suggestions had to some extent
been accepted. His problem was to determine a central theme around
which all the future work of the Council could circle. To this end he proposed a Council focused entirely on the Church, with two parts: the
Church in its inner life (*Ecclesia ad intra*) and the Church in its relations
with the outside world (*Ecclesia ad extra*).[144] The first part would be

---

[140] *AS* I/4, 182-83. It is worth noting that during these very days Léger received from
Moeller and the latter's fellow-workers "theological" suggestions for his intervention in the
hall (see the correspondence with Moeller and others in the Léger Archive). Léger left these
aside, however, and concentrated on the procedural problems of the immediate future.

[141] *AS* I/4, 197-99.

[142] See *History*, I, 411. In the Council hall Suenens had already manifested his concerns about the organization of the Council's work. Speaking on November 14 during the
discussion of the sources of revelation, after disposing of the matter of the schema with a
few remarks, he offered a whole set of procedural proposals aimed at making the discussions more expeditious: preliminary vote after an initial discussion, in order to determine
acceptance or rejection of a schema as a whole; the opportuneness of allowing only a
written intervention for all proposals having to do with particular points, while an oral
intervention to explain one's point of view could be given only in cases in which the commission had rejected the proposed emendations; in the meantime, all commissions should
set to work shortening the preparatory schemas as they saw fit; the immediate appointment of postconciliar commissions for putting into practice each schema that had been
approved; the names of those speaking in the hall should not be published in the press, so
as to induce bishops to present their proposals in writing and refrain from an oral interventions; simplification of formalities ("reverend brothers" instead of "most eminent and
reverend lords") (see *AS* I/3, 45-47).

[143] Suenens claims that he had asked for a prior assurance of the pope's agreement
with his address, and that he had received it by way of Msgr. Dell'Acqua (*Souvenirs*, 71).

[144] We may, however, ask whether the distinction was a very strict one, since the consideration of the Church as missionary was located in the part on the inner life of the
Church (*ad intra*). Suenens's outline seems rather to have proposed once again the idea
typical of the "theology of earthly realities," in which these earthly realities are the object
ad extra of the Church's activity, while "specifically" Christian realties belong in the *ad
intra* dimension.

devoted to explaining the Church as the mystery of Christ living in his Mystical Body. Once the nature of the Church had been expounded, on the basis of the principle that the kind of action follows the kind of being (*operatio sequitur esse*), it would be necessary to explain what a pastorally renewed Church ought to be doing today, according to the gospel saying: (1) *Going, therefore*: the missionary task of an evangelizing Church; (2) *teach them*: the Church's catechetical task; (c) *baptizing them*: the Church sanctifying by her sacraments; (d) *in the name of the Father*: the Church at prayer.

After this reflection on the being and actions of the Church in its inner life, the second part would deal with the Church in dialogue with the world. The points of the dialogue were defined in terms of what the Church has to say about the life of the human person, social justice, the evangelization of the poor, and peace and war.

Finally, Suenens defined three areas of ecclesial dialogue: (1) the dialogue of the Church with its own faithful (it would perhaps have been better to speak of dialogue within the Church or dialogue between hierarchy and faithful); (2) the ecumenical dialogue of the Church with those brothers and sisters who are not yet visibly united to her; and (3) the dialogue with the modern world.[145]

Suenens's address was received with great applause. Although not very rigorous theologically, it had the advantage of offering a plan of work with various chapters and sections. From this point of view it was reassuring, especially to those who, having lost the security provided by the former state of things, here had something concrete that was part of their mental world. In addition, it had the advantage of leaving no one "outside."

On December 5 Montini stated his agreement with Suenens's plan of action. For this most-favored of the *papabili*, the acceptance of Suenens's program was an implicit acceptance of the conditions for his own future election: a continuation of the Council with a middle-of-the-road program. But his "I cannot remain silent: it is inadequate," referring to the schema, also signaled an open distancing of himself from Curial circles — and in terms he had never dared use before. In addition to making his own the emphases already laid by others on the christological dimension and on the Church as a mystery, Montini repeated Bea's suggestions for a better structuring of the treatise on the bishops: begin with a chapter on the apostolic college; go on then to treat of the episcopal

---

[145] *AS* I/4, 222-27.

body as successor to the apostolic college; end with a chapter on the office of bishop and on the sacramental basis of this office. Nor did Montini fail to repeat the petition of those who wanted to move beyond a purely juridical description of the person of the bishop by emphasizing his role as father. As for chapter X, he proposed separating the discussion of the Church's task of proclaiming the gospel from the discussion of the rights of the Church, placing the former in the treatise on the magisterium and the latter in chapter IX.[146]

The final major programmatic address was that of Cardinal Lercaro on December 6.[147] After recalling, in general terms, the proposals of Suenens and Montini, he adopted a quite different starting point for his address by proposing to place at the center of the Council's attention the theme of a Church that preaches the gospel to the poor. His address brought together earnest solicitations and desires voiced in some circles that had come to Rome at this time in order to foster in the members of the Council a sensitivity to the problems of the Church's own poverty and of its presence among the poor.[148] Most of the persons in these groups were from the French-speaking world and Latin America; they had accepted the challenge of a book written by P. Gauthier in agreement with G. Hakim, Bishop of Nazareth,[149] and were now meeting, under the leadership of Cardinal Gerlier, in an informal study group at the Belgian College.[150]

Acting, therefore, as spokesman for urgent requests that were at this time making their way through the Church, from the East to Europe and Latin America, and to which John XXIII had shown himself especially receptive, Lercaro proposed in the hall that the dominant idea of the Council's ecclesiology should be "the Church of the poor," a phrase taken from Pope John's teaching.[151] This should not be just one motif among many, but rather "the sole theme of Vatican II in its entirety,"

---

[146] *AS* I/4, 291-94.

[147] *AS* I, 327-30. For a critical edition of this address and a placement of it within the broader conciliar involvement of G. Lercaro, see *Per la forza dello Spirito. Discorsi conciliari del card. Giacomo Lercaro* (Bologna, 1984); the text is on pp. 113-22.

[148] See P. Gauthier, *"Consolez mon peuple." Le Concile et "l'Église des pauvres"* (Paris, 1965); Lercaro, *Per la forza dello Spirito*, 19-22.

[149] P. Gauthier, *Les pauvres, Jésus et l'Église* (Paris, 1963), 47-78.

[150] Lercaro was invited to participate, but he sent as his representative G. Dossetti, who from this point on began an extensive collaboration that went well beyond this immediate setting (see G. Lercaro, *Lettere dal concilio, 1962-1965*, ed. G. Battelli [Bologna, 1980], 99).

[151] John XXIII, Radio message of September 11, 1962 (*DMC*, IV, 524).

"the synthesizing idea, the point that gives light and coherence to all the subjects thus far discussed and of all the work that we must undertake." Lercaro took the urgency of this perspective to be the urgency of history itself, which was raising the problem of poverty in a dramatic and inescapable way; this is "the hour of the poor." This situation ought to lead the Council to a deeper understanding of the gospel teaching on poverty as "an essential and primary aspect of the mystery of Christ." The most authentic and radical demands of the present time, including the hope of the reunification of Christians, would not be met, but avoided, if the Council tackled the problem of the evangelization of the poor as just one theme added to all the others. Lercaro asked, in particular, that there be a clarification of the very profound, even "ontological," link between the presence of Christ in the poor and the other two profound elements in the mystery of Christ in the Church: the Eucharist and the hierarchy.[152]

In the final part of his address Lercaro gave examples of some practical consequences of his idea for the life of the Church: a limitation in the commitment of material means in the organization of the Church; a general description of a new style and a new conception of the dignity of ecclesiastical authorities; a fidelity, not only individual but communal, of religious orders to poverty; the elimination of the historical developments that the patrimonial structures of the past had undergone.

Lercaro's vision, which was perhaps the most original and at the same time the most prophetic of this first period of the Council, was, as events would show, too advanced for the general consciousness of the fathers. In itself it was of a nature to make possible a real leap forward (to use Pope John's image) in the theological conception of the Church, but it proved to be only a stone thrown into a pond, causing merely a transient ripple of applause and agreement.

By strange timing, Lercaro's intervention was immediately followed by the reading of a schedule of work during the intersession, which the Pope himself had decided on December 5, "in accord with what long and diligent preparation has already produced and what we have learned from the very valuable use made of this first period."[153] The document stressed the goal of the Council, so often stated by the Pope and proclaimed in a special way in his opening address of October 11. The more important passages of that allocution were cited: on not repeating past

[152] This connection had been recalled in Gauthier, *Les pauvres*, 57-60.
[153] *AS* I/4, 330. For the text of the work schedule see *AS* I/1, 96-98.

doctrines already codified by Trent and Vatican I; on the pastoral nature of the magisterium's teaching; and on the motherhood of the Church, which is full of mercy and kindness toward her children. *Gaudet Mater Ecclesia* thus marked the beginning and the end of the Council's work; it was a true touchstone in the debates of the first period. More concretely, the Pope pointed out the need for careful selection from the vast sea of preparatory work and for a revision of schemas that would respect the goals of the Council. Subjects closely connected with the revision of the Code were to be left to the competent commission. Finally, the Pope accepted the suggestion of many and established a commission, with the Secretary of State as its president, to coordinate and direct future work. This papal intervention rendered it unnecessary to take a vote at the end of the discussion of the schema on the Church and marked the effective end of the work of the first period.

VI. THE RESISTANCES OF THE PAST

The outcome of the debates on the sources of revelation and on the Church should not make us think that events developed peacefully. In fact, the atmosphere outside the Council was rather disturbed. On the one hand, some more open circles, especially in the world of exegesis, managed to bank some gains. On November 22, the Pontifical Biblical Institute took the occasion of a defense of a doctoral dissertation — that of N. Lohfink on chapters 5-11 of Deuteronomy — to create "a show of sympathy on its own behalf." A tremendous number of people attended the defense, among them many cardinals and bishops; and Congar was able to say, rightly, that the affair was "a new victory for Cardinal Bea. The Council is Cardinal Bea's council."[154]

But other spirits were growing somewhat overheated. Fenton tells of a visit to an "angry" Ottaviani, who was convinced that, given the team he had to work with, he could not do anything more. And the men on this team were convinced that they were living in "the time of the devils."[155] A whole press campaign, in which it is likely that some Curial circles played a part, warned of the dangers of the turn taken at the

[154] *JCongar*, November 22.

[155] "I went up to see the old man in the afternoon. He was angry, and he talks about more action from our side. He is not going to get it with the bunch he has now. As I left, Paul Philippe was going in. He was crying. And he said that this was the time of the devils" (*DFenton*, November 23, 1962).

Council. Fenton himself found his thoughts confirmed in a publication representing extreme right-wing groups, written by Mario Tedeschi for the collection *I libri del Borghese*: that is, that the Council was an attempt by the United States and Moscow to create a "Christian International."[156] The American theologian thus realized "that some other people believe what I have thought for several months, namely, that John XXIII is definitely a lefty. . . . In the light of what Tedeschi has written, it is easy to see why O [Ottaviani] has taken such a bad beating in the Council and from the Pope."[157] Vagnozzi, the Apostolic Delegate to the United States, did not miss any of the meetings of the American bishops where he observed, constantly intervened, and tried to direct them along the lines of Holy Office policy.[158] But even the "moderate" secular press was tending to flatten the conciliar events and explain them in relation to two dangers: an opening to communism, on the one hand, and a return of the errors of Protestantism and modernism, on the other.[159]

---

[156] M. Tedeschi, *I pericoli del concilio*, published at Milan in October, 1962.

[157] *DFenton*, November 25, 1962.

[158] Testimony gathered in *JCongar*, November 25, but confirmed by *DSiri*, in which Vagnozzi plays precisely the role described.

[159] In particular, the articles of I. Montanelli in the most widely read Italian daily, *Il Corriere della sera*, caused a sensation (November 24, 25, and 26). The author sketched out the entire presumed strategy of Vatican II: John XXIII himself was an old man from the hills; he had skillfully caused Cardinal Tardini, with whom he had complicated relations of enmity and fear, to accept the idea of a council; the secretaries who had composed the texts in the preparatory phase were priests of the lower clergy (*sic*), who were impatient for reform and had ties with Montini. The key person in the whole business was, however, Cardinal Bea, who could deceive many because he had been the confessor of Pius XII; he had also been rector of the Pontifical Biblical Institute, the school that trained the modern exegetes who were casting doubt on the historicity of the conferral of primacy on Peter by Jesus. While Bea was the inspirer, Cardinal Alfrink was the most energetic anti-Roman activist. The work of the first period of the Council confirmed the tendency to introduce into the Church a policy of equal distance from the blocs (especially in the Council's opening message). The fight against scholasticism was in fact a fight against the philosophy that had made possible the victory over modernism and was therefore a sign of the return of modernism itself into the Catholic Church. The importance the Council wanted to give to episcopal conferences was a subtle way to get around the dogma of papal infallibility, and the room it wanted to give to the laity reflected the tendency to limit the powers of the hierarchy.

Montanelli's articles caused a great deal of comment in conciliar circles. Congar mistakes the title of the newspaper, changing it to *Corriere d'Italia*, but clearly grasps the ideological line followed by the writer: "liberal middle-class in philosophy and conservative in economics and politics" (*JCongar*, December 2, 1962). The articles also elicited an impassioned protest in the Italian Catholic press (see Caprile II, 183f.). It is undeniable, however, that the central theses of Montanelli's interpretation were hardly his own work; they are the same as those found in *DSiri*. While it is legitimate to attribute to the journalist himself the fear of the danger of an opening to communism and the rejection of

It is impossible to prescind from this oppressive atmosphere if we wish to understand the interventions of a now clearly defined conciliar minority during the debates of the final weeks and especially during the work of the mixed commission. This commission began and continued its work during the discussion of the *De unitate* and the *De ecclesia*.[160] The defeated minority used every possible form of resistance in an effort to thwart the new direction that had emerged in the discussion of the sources of revelation and was being confirmed during the final days. Tromp himself went around saying that the new schema on the sources would be a twin brother of the first.[161]

Brief mention has already been made of the letter sent to the Pope by some cardinals in order to hinder the development of events, especially after the crash of the schema on the sources. The principal organizer of the letter, signed by nineteen cardinals and dated November 24,[162] was Cardinal Ruffini.[163] The letter asserted that the Council must "affirm at least some doctrinal principles in order to defend the Catholic faith against errors and deviations that today are scattered about almost everywhere." In particular, it had to affirm that (1) revelation is an external, public, historically ascertainable event; (2) in addition to scripture, "divino-Catholic" tradition is a means of revelation; (3) tradition is necessary for guaranteeing the value of scripture and for interpreting it; (4) scripture and tradition are the remote norm of revelation, while the mag-

---

the idea of keeping equal distance from the blocs, it is at least problematic to acknowledge him as responsible for the emphasis on the connection between scholasticism and anti-modernism and on the dangers of exegesis. Again, a man like Montanelli was certainly capable of realizing on his own that the Council and its emphasis on the role of the episcopal conferences could mean a limitation on the primacy of the pope, but his almost obsessive identification of Montini as the "enemy" seems odd for such a man — but comes out clearly in Siri's letters. This does not necessarily mean that Siri himself inspired the articles, but only that circles of the same kind as that of the Cardinal of Genoa "suggested" some of the content of Montanelli's articles.

[160] In the first period of the Council, the first plenary meeting of the mixed commission took place on November 25, that is, on the eve of the debate on the *De unitate*; the second took place on November 27, the third on December 4, the fourth on December 5, and the fifth on December 7. I am referring to plenary meetings and not taking into account those of the subcommissions (see Tromp, *Relatio*).

[161] *JCongar*, November 26.

[162] The signers were Gonçalves Cerejeira, Santos, Godfrey, Heard, Copello, Concha, McIntyre, Siri, Bacci, Agagianian, De Barros Câmara, de Arriba y Castro, Caggiano, Ruffini, Wyszynski, Urbani, Traglia, Quiroga y Palacios, and Antoniutti. Regarding the date, however, it must be pointed out that in the note in his diary for Saturday, November 25, Urbani speaks of a meeting at 7:00 P.M. "with Cardinal Ruffini regarding this letter to the pope on 'biblical' dangers." The note may be an indication that the letter was delivered on the evening of November 25 or even later.

isterium is the proximate rule; (5) while it is legitimate to interpret scripture according to rational and literary norms, it is important, first and
foremost, to apply the principles of Catholic hermeneutics, which are
summed up in (a) the *sensus ecclesiae*; (b) the morally "unanimous"
interpretation of the Fathers, and (c) the analogy of faith; and (6) the
renewal of biblical studies must take place according to the criteria
established in the encyclicals *Providentissimus Deus, Divino Afflante
Spiritu,* and *Humani generis.* The letter then gave some examples of
authors and essays which proved that the errors to be condemned had
spread everywhere.[164] Finally, to strengthen their own arguments, the
writers cited some public statements of Cardinal Bea. On December 4
the Secretary of State sent the letter to the President of the mixed commission, Ottaviani, who passed it on the next day, prefacing it with an
interpretation of his own.[165]

[163] See F. Stabile, "Il Cardinal Ruffini e il Vaticano II. Le lettere di un 'intransigente,'" *CrSt* 11 (1990), 83-113. For the text of the letter, with a list of the cardinals to
whom it was sent for signing, see 124-26. It is interesting that some of these, such as
Spellman, Gilroy, and Brown, did not sign it. The Spellman papers in the Archives of the
Archdiocese of New York reveal that McIntyre had pleaded in vain for Spellman to sign
it. It is difficult to evaluate the significance of each signature. For example, in a diary note
for November 22, Urbani says that at the meeting at which the proposal to write to the
Pope was accepted, he tried to "moderate Ruffini's position," but thought it "expedient
to accept [the letter] precisely because it was the only way of bringing influence to bear
from within." It seems, then, that at that point Urbani had adopted the role of broker
within the most extreme position.

[164] The cardinals made a point of noting that the examples they cited were publications that carried the standard imprimatur. The works indicted were an article by Dubarle
on original sin from *Revue Biblique*; brief remarks by De Fraine on the history of the
patriarchs from *Nouvel Atlas historique et culturel de la Bible*; *L'Evangile de Noël* by F.
Neirynck; and an insufficiently critical review in *Rivista Biblica* of an article of H.
Schlier that had appeared in the Catholic journal *Biblische Zeitschrift*. The only author
whose name appears is Neirynck (misspelled as "Heirynck"!), professor at the major
seminary of Bruges; but the cardinals note that his book and the *Nouvel Atlas* bear the
imprimatur of Malines, Cardinal Suenens's diocese. The concern, therefore, was to draw
attention to the fact that these were publications authorized by ecclesiastical authority and
professors authorized to teach in ecclesiastical institutions. Among Ruffini's letters there
is one replying to Cardinal Döpfner, who in March of 1963 would send Ruffini a written
protest of his attack on Schlier (see Stabile, *Il Cardinal Ruffini*, 127-28).

[165] A copy of the Secretary of State's letter is in H. Sauer, *Erfahrung und Glaube. Die
Begründung des pastoralen Prinzips durch die Offenbarungskonstitution del II.
Vatikanischen Konzils* (Frankfurt a. M., 1993), 223 n.5. The oddity of the procedure
needs to be noted. Ottaviani was not the sole president of the mixed commission but only
its co-president along with Bea. Why, then, was the letter sent to Ottaviani alone? In any
case, the latter took advantage of Cicognani's action and interpreted it ("we can legitimately infer from it"), since it was "sent on . . . by command of the Supreme Pontiff," as
an invitation to take due account, in the work of the mixed commission, of the petitions
signed by the nineteen cardinals (see Ottaviani's text in Sauer, 224 n.6).

The mixed commission had Ottaviani and Bea as co-presidents, Liénart and Browne as vice-presidents, and S. Tromp and J. Willebrands as secretaries.[166] At its first meeting it was decided to change the title to *"On Revelation"* and that five subcommissions should be set up to match the number of chapters in the schema itself: the first on the relations between scripture and tradition (co-presidents: Frings and Browne); the second on inspiration, inerrancy, and literary composition of the scriptures (König and Santos); the third on the Old Testament (Meyer and J. Lefebvre); the fourth on the New Testament (Ruffini and Liénart); and the fifth on scripture in the Church (Quiroga y Palacios and Léger). Frings, seconded by Liénart, proposed that, as several fathers had requested in the hall, there be an introduction that would be pastoral and ecumenical in tone. Ruffini, for his part, proposed again the fundamental demand of the minority, which, in response to the objection that old condemnations ought not be repeated, claimed that modernism and its connected errors had emerged since Vatican I and that it was therefore necessary to take steps against them as new errors.[167] However, Frings's proposal was accepted and, with it, the nomination of Garrone as reporter (*relator*).

The same opposition surfaced again, unchanged, at the second meeting, on November 27. While Frings emphasized the Council's decision not to discuss the old schema any further, Ruffini maintained that this was too extreme a step and that it would be enough to revise the old schema as far as possible.[168] The decision taken was a somewhat tortuous compromise: to take the old text as a basis after it had been subjected to a radical revision. This was contrary to what had been formally decided at the Council, but the deciding factor was probably the subtle compromise offered by Bea, who, if we may trust Laberge's record,

---

[166] The make-up of the commission was reported in *OssRom*, November 25, which came out on November 24. For the composition of the five subcommissions and a description of their work see Sauer, *Erfahrung und Glaube*, 221ff.

[167] This attitude, which was somewhat paradoxical in light of the Pope's official explanation of the purpose of the Council, was connected with the already cited letter of the nineteen cardinals to the Pope. But, as we have seen, this letter had not yet been officially made known to the commission. Must we therefore suppose that the decision to send it on through formal channels was a last-ditch attempt to bring the commission to adopt this outlook?

[168] Sauer, *Erfahrung und Glaube*, 225, on the basis of the record made by L. Laberge. To this record, which is in the Archives of Vatican II, we owe our main information on the debate in the mixed commission. The substance of the record for the final meeting of the mixed commission, on December 7, has been published in Sauer, 678-83, who introduces it with the description, in parentheses: "Brief summaries of contents."

brought all the members into agreement by maintaining that "the revision will probably produce a new schema, but the latter will be the effect and not the basis" (of the work of revision).[169]

At the second meeting the draft of an introduction prepared by Garrone was also presented and discussed.[170] Under seven points this document developed an idea of revelation that attempted to combine with the neo-scholastic conception of it as the *locutio Dei* (the speaking/words of God) some gains made by contemporary theology: that God has given revelation to mankind in order to manifest the mystery of God's subsistence in three Persons and the "mystery hidden for ages in God." This revelation is inaccessible to human reason (no. 1), and has been communicated to us in Christ, who contains the whole of revelation (no. 2). But even at the beginning of the human race God did not leave humanity deprived of his testimony; in the Old Testament he foreshadowed and prepared the way for the revelation in the New Testament (no. 3). In Christ the final and complete revelation has been given; the position is condemned that makes of Christianity only a phase, the final one, in the religious history of the race (no. 4). Revelation takes place not only through words but also through the history of salvation. Christ, too, makes known his divinity not only through words but also through actions (no. 5). Revelation cannot manifest the mysteries of humanity's supernatural participation in the life of God without also affirming natural truths connected with those mysteries, thereby shedding light also on "the nature of humanity's life in time" (no. 6). The words of revelation are not simply an utterance but also contain a divine power that is more effective than a two-edged sword (no. 7).

This introduction was discussed again at the next meeting, December 4, where the request was made that it be further improved and discussed once more.[171] Browne reported on the conflicts and difficulties of the first subcommission, which was working on the relation between scripture and tradition. At the meeting on December 5 the other four chapters

---

[169] Sauer, *Erfahrung und Glaube*, 226 n.12.

[170] McGrath Archive, 5, 2, 21.

[171] On December 5 a first emended text of the introduction was submitted. It now began with the citation from the first letter of John that would remain in the final text; it had many more biblical texts woven into it; and the language was less scholastic. It avoided the formal language of condemnation for the conception of revelation that reduces Christianity to the final phase in the religious evolution of humanity (see McGrath Archive, 5, 2, 24). However, even this revision was not approved, and the request was made for another written consultation among the members of the mixed commission (see Tromp, *Relatio*, no. 7, p. 7).

were read and discussed, and the contentious issue of chapter I was post-poned until the meeting that would take place on December 7.[172]

Frings reported on chapter II,[173] which, in describing the nature of biblical inspiration, refrained from citing *Providentissimus Deus* verba-tim and referred instead to the patristic idea of the divine condescension.

> This divine speaking to humankind signifies both the condescension of God and the elevation of human beings. Condescension, because "God speaks through human beings, in the manner of human beings, for in thus speaking he is seeking us out" (Augustine, PL 41:537); elevation, because God has adopted human speech "in every respect except error." This action of God, which neither suspends nor diminishes the human process of speaking and writing, but whose end-result is nonetheless wholly the word of God, con-sists in a charismatic movement of the Holy Spirit, which we call inspiration.

Consequences of inspiration are the fact that the scripture contains in a special way the doctrine of salvation, but also that it cannot assert any-thing false. It is for the magisterium to give the "authoritative" interpre-tation of the scriptures. In questions not definitively answered by the magisterium account must be taken of the unanimous and dogmatic con-sent of the Fathers and tradition and of the analogy of faith. Since the scriptures are the words of human beings, all the linguistic sciences and the techniques for interpreting human language are useful. Therefore the use of textual, linguistic, and literary criticism, of archeology, philology, and so on is recommended.

Lefebvre and Scherer reported on chapter III. This chapter empha-sized the abiding value and importance of the Old Testament, since the latter shows the way in which God deals with human beings and how they ought to be related to God and neighbor. It therefore enjoys author-ity in the Church.

> For although some things in the Old Testament that belonged exclusively to the time of preparation have been abrogated in the New, yet the Old Tes-tament as a whole, having been taken over into the preaching of the gospel, has become a part of the one revelation and has acquired, and displays, a deeper meaning. The Church therefore reverently acknowledges the books of the Old Testament as its own scriptures.[174]

The text of chapter IV, which had essentially been composed by Cer-faux, was presented by Charue.[175] It asserted the apostolic origin of the

[172] In reconstructing what was done I am here following Tromp's *Relatio*.
[173] McGrath Archive, 5, 2, 23.
[174] Ibid., 5, 2, 18.
[175] *JDupont*, December 5; McGrath Archive, 5, 2, 19.

four gospels, inasmuch as the apostles themselves and other "apostolic men" recorded their teaching in them. The Church "has firmly and very constantly held and holds" that the four gospels really convey to us what Jesus did and taught. Although they reflect the form of a proclamation and do not have exactly the same purpose as historical writing in our time, "they convey to us a real and authentic history." It is the task of exegetes, under the guidance of the magisterium, to seek a proper understanding of passages of the gospel that are in need of a "sure and definite" explanation, so that in this way "the Church may reach a mature judgment" (with a reference to *Providentissimus Deus*). The other books of the New Testament are useful in confirming and giving a deeper understanding of the teaching of Christ and the saving power of his work.

Léger reported on chapter V. It urged the utmost veneration for the Old and New Testaments, and it aimed to promote the making of accurate translations that would give everyone access to the scriptures, although preference was given to the Vulgate as being "authentic in the juridical sense." The Church, instructed by the Spirit, "constantly seeks a deeper understanding of the scriptures and feeds the faithful with this understanding." Theology finds "its primary basis and subject matter" in the word of God and therefore it gains new strength and youthfulness from the sacred scriptures. The scriptures "in fact not only contain the word of God but are the word of God," and therefore they also feed and give power to the ministry of the word, that is, pastoral preaching. Ministers must therefore never cease to study the scriptures and have an obligation to communicate this spiritual treasure to the faithful, especially in the liturgy. The faithful in turn ought to approach the sacred text under the guidance of the magisterium, both in the liturgy and with the help of specialized institutions. It is the task of the bishops to guide the faithful in the proper use of the scriptures.

The discussion that followed these reports elicited no special reasons for tension. Tromp observed simply: "Some emendations were offered on all the chapters. His Eminence Cardinal Bea proposed that once the chapters were emended, their stylistic redaction should be entrusted to a special subcommission that would leave the doctrinal points untouched."

Things took a quite different course at the final meeting of the mixed commission on the afternoon of December 7, almost at the end of the Council's work.[176] Ottaviani and Bea presided. The subject was the rela-

---

[176] Our reconstruction of the meeting is based chiefly on the material in the McGrath

tion between scripture and tradition. Parente began by repeating the classical post-Tridentine Catholic interpretation: "It is certain that oral tradition originating in the apostles, who were taught either by Christ or the Holy Spirit, *is broader* (or *contains more*) than sacred scripture *in matters pertaining to faith and morals*; therefore, while revelation is one, it reaches us by two distinct means, which have customarily, and rightly, been called *sources* in the Catholic Church."[177]

In his comments on the text Parente said that the subcommission had not reached a real agreement on this point, which was, however, in his view, the common patrimony of post-Tridentine theology, except for a few contemporary theologians "motivated by ecumenical considerations," who were bent on exalting the scriptures as the sole and sufficient source of revelation. Parente claimed that his formula, "tradition is broader than sacred scripture," was in fact a toned-down formula designed to safeguard sound doctrine without offending the separated brethren.

Bea's intervention followed immediately and tried to assess the situation.[178] Relying on the Pope's opening address, he did not think a resolution of this question timely. Everyone, in fact, acknowledges tradition, but its extension is disputed among the theologians, and the Council ought to leave them freedom on the question. Ottaviani replied to Bea and voiced the opposite view.

When Bea then asked for a vote, Ruffini objected that it was impossible to proceed further, given the open disagreement between the two presidents. Heenan asked that the vote be secret. Ruffini spoke again to say that in his view the question of the greater extension of tradition as compared with scripture was a matter of faith and not a disputed question, since the point at issue was to know where "the full revelation" was located. Bea explained that the complete revelation is found "in scripture and tradition."

At a certain point in the debate the theologians present took the floor. Tromp maintained that the question "involves principles." It is certain that it is only by tradition that we know the canon of scripture. He cited the thought of several Fathers on the subject (Epiphanius and Augustine). He also cited the thinking of some Protestants and told of what had been said to him by an observer, Professor H. A. Oberman of Harvard,

---

Archive, Laberge's report published in Sauer, *Erfahrung und Gnade*, 678-83, and Tromp's *Relatio*.

[177] The italicized words are underscored in the typewritten original.

[178] Bea's intervention is in the McGrath Archive, 5, 2, 12.

who intended to write an article against Geiselmann's interpretation of Trent. It was not possible, therefore, Tromp said, to avoid taking a stand on the question simply because someone (read: Geiselmann) was singing apart from the choir.

Rahner replied to Tromp.[179] Apart from the canonicity and historicity of the scriptures, there is no need to maintain that there are truths that are not at least implicitly found in the scriptures. Even tradition has experienced the same process of explicitation that some statements in scripture have undergone. The testimonies of Epiphanius and Augustine cannot be regarded as settling the question. In addition, we may ask whether those Fathers intended to speak of a truth of faith in the real and proper sense or simply of a theologoumenon.

At this point, to address the interpretation of the Fathers, Ottaviani called upon a specialist in patristic thought, Father Van den Eynde, who in turn proposed what he regarded as a compromise formula: let it be said simply that tradition "is broader," but without giving examples, so that the question can remain open. Rahner said he was ready to accept the "is broader" formula, provided it was understood as referring to the canon of scripture and so on.[180] After these interventions the discussion unraveled completely. Bea tried to express the view that the only question was whether or not it was necessary to add anything to what Trent had already said, but by then no one was listening to anyone else. At the end a vote was taken on a formula of Bea that changed, to a large extent if not completely, Parente's original formula:

> The treasure of divine revelation is preserved not only in sacred scripture but also in sacred tradition, which began with the apostles, who were taught by Christ or the Holy Spirit, and has come down to us (Council of Trent, Session IV; Vatican Council I, Session III). In fact, certain revealed truths, especially those pertaining to the inspiration of the individual books, their canonicity, and the integrity of each book are known or become clear only through tradition.[181]

When put to a vote, the proposition received nineteen votes for and sixteen against, with six abstentions. Frings challenged the result, since

---

[179] The summary of his intervention in Laberge's report is not very clear.

[180] According to the summary Daniélou gave Congar of the meeting, Rahner expressly asked Tromp to make this point explicit, but Tromp did not reply (*JCongar*, December 11, 1962).

[181] Among those dissatisfied with this formulation was Frings, who justified his disagreement by pointing out that the adverb *especially* implied that there might be others as well, and that the formula therefore ended by implicitly condemning the position expressed by Geiselmann.

the majority was by no means absolute and a two-thirds majority was required. Ottaviani rejected Frings's objection but said he was ready to submit the matter to the Pope through the Secretary of State. Liénart attempted to throw water on the fire by saying that in the final analysis nothing had been decided but to offer a text for discussion in the following September.

The last part of the meeting found De Smedt protesting the letter of the nineteen cardinals and the "very serious" accusation contained in it. Ruffini explained that there was no question of an accusation but only of "an expression of our anxiety." When De Smedt also complained of the lack of secrecy attending that move, Ottaviani answered that if the Pope had not imposed secrecy, he himself could not have imposed it. This brought to a rather sad close the final activity of this instrument of the Council.

The next day, December 8, in his closing address Pope John XXIII gave his reading of the first period.[182] He saw it as marked by the hard work required to reach a consensus and as a demonstration to the whole of human society of the holy freedom of the children of God. He emphasized the happy choice of the liturgical schema as the opening subject; he also referred to the intersession and to the tasks of the new coordinating commission; and finally, he spoke of his hope of rich fruits for the life of the Church.

All in all, it was a modest farewell to Pope John's Council, which he would not see meet again. It was an address quite different from the opening allocution which had become the real stumbling block that had tripped up those who balked at his "*aggiornamento.*"

[182] *AS* I/4, 643-49.

THE DRAMA CONTINUES BETWEEN THE ACTS
THE "SECOND PREPARATION" AND ITS OPPONENTS

JAN GROOTAERS

I. UNCERTAINTIES AND CONFUSION

The 1962-63 intersession began amid uncertainties and a degree of confusion. It must be stressed at the outset that it would be a mistake to think that the self-awareness of the "majority" in the assembly developed gradually and continually during the fall of 1962 and the intersession. Chroniclers of the period used metaphors from meteorology (squalls, lightning, storm threats) or from physiology (bouts of fever, convalescence, depressions), which made it clear that it was only by fits and starts that the majority at Vatican II was able to gain and use its freedom at the Council. The process had its ebbs and flows. The most realistic of the fathers did not allow themselves to be caught up in the euphoria that marked the close of the session in December 1962; they were quite aware that the cause of renewal was still far from being won.

The suspension of the conciliar assembly's normal activities from December 1962 to October 1963 could easily have led to considerable retreat from results approached but not truly won. The intersession created a kind of void in Rome; the vigilant bishops had returned to their distant dioceses, and the inquisitive press had disappeared. For some in Rome this was the longed-for opportunity to regain lost ground both in the commissions, which were working behind closed doors, and with the guiding authorities of the Curia. The lot of those "Romans" who "had gone over to the barbarians" by choosing the side of the "northern Europeans" was not an enviable one; having lost all the protection afforded them by the Council, they had to traverse a lonely desert in which they were vulnerable to the Curial camp.

For the Council fathers who wanted an open council, the start of Vatican II had been a time of anxiety and uncertainty. It was the vote on the sources of revelation, taken on November 20, 1962, that first gave them a sense of confidence in the future, which lasted several weeks. In this

climate of joyful trust the leaders of the majority secured a reorganization of the future work and the establishment of a prevailing authority,
that of the Coordinating Commission [CC].

In a far-sighted interview early in November 1962, Father Edward
Schillebeeckx expressed the view that two possible routes lay before the
Council. On the one hand, the conservatives might succeed in making
the preparatory schemas acceptable, which would itself be a considerable victory that would guarantee the freedom of modern theology; on
the other hand, those of an open tendency might also succeed in having
their own draft texts admitted.[1]

But when, at the end of December 1962 and during January 1963 it
became apparent that many preparatory schemas that the fathers thought
had been scrapped were continuing to have an important influence, the
confidence of the majority was shaken. There were three kinds of
schemas: first, the texts on liturgical reform and on the communications
media, for which proceedings in the commissions were following a normal course; then the schemas that had been discussed in the hall but had
still to overcome certain obstacles in the commissions; and, finally,
preparatory schemas that appeared among those selected at the beginning of December but had not yet been discussed either in the hall or in
conciliar commissions.[2]

Two of the texts in the second group caused deep concern among the
majority. The confrontation over the text on the unity of the Church had
ended in ambiguity, and the turbulent debate on the schema on the
Church had not reached any formal conclusions. The majority would
have to wait until May 1963 to learn that pressure from the CC was
finally producing movement on the revision of these and other schemas.
This progress would give the members of the majority a sense that they
could at last move forward, watchfully indeed, but also with confidence.

It would thus be necessary to struggle, sometimes for several months,
for the abandonment of schemas considered disappointing and of little
use, an unpleasant work of negative criticism. This was followed by a
constructive phase in which the majority would have to go to work with-

---

[1] Jan Grootaers, "Twee concilie-theologie n," *De Maand* 5 (December 10, 1962), 606.

[2] In a widely known interview over Vatican Radio on January 31, 1963, Father Johann
Hirschmann distinguished two groups of commissions: those that worked on revising
texts on questions assigned them by the Council at a general congregation and after conciliar discussion; and those whose task was, on the basis of guidelines given during the
first period, to pare down, revise, and reassemble drafts composed by the Preparatory
Commission (see *DC* 60 [1963], 343-46).

out knowing initially just how far it could promote the trend to renewal without risking the possibility of setbacks. In addition, the limits of what was regarded as feasible were shifting; a compromise that seemed acceptable to a new redactional committee of bishops and experts in February they might well consider superseded three months later. Finally, it was necessary to move quickly and maintain a cohesive majority in the face of an opposing camp that was alert for the first signs of discord in order to impose a return to the heavily criticized schemas of the preparatory phase.

But besides such uncertainties, there was also a good deal of confusion. Although certain eminent members of the CC initially contributed to this confusion, in the long run the authority of this Commission would largely overcome it. The main cause of confusion was the overlapping of competing texts. The first period of the Council had ended with a degree of vagueness in order not to humiliate those who had directed the preparatory phase. The latter, however, had no great respect for this conciliatory spirit and would throw up obstacles in order to restore the preparatory schemas to the foreground. During the early months of this transition between the first two "acts" of Vatican II, some preparatory schemas were kept on the agenda, even while official replacement schemas were emerging. This overlapping of texts in circulation was to be seen at three levels: in the CC, in some conciliar commissions in Rome, and among the bishops in their dioceses or episcopal conferences.

Some members of the CC attempted to turn the clock back. At its very first meeting, Cardinal Cicognani declared that new schemas were not to be substituted for the material so carefully prepared during the preparatory period, which could, however, be amended.[3] Similarly, Cardinal Confalonieri spoke at length about the merits of the procedure followed in the preparatory phase.[4] To meet supporters of the preparatory schemas half-way, Cardinal Suenens himself assured them that the new schema on the Church reused sixty percent of the material in the preparatory schema. In March, Cicognani attempted to save the preparatory schema on the Oriental Churches,[5] and as late as July, Father Tromp, appearing before this Commission, was to regret the rejection of the preparatory texts.[6]

---

[3] *AS* V/1, 54-55.
[4] Ibid., 56.
[5] Ibid., 480.
[6] Ibid., 637.

The CC had a strong influence on the procedure followed in the inter-session. While John XXIII, particularly in his closing allocution and in his letter on guidelines, *Mirabilis ille*, of January 6, 1963, voiced his keen desire to associate the bishops with the work of the CC, the latter's work was not given the publicity needed to enable the fathers to follow from a distance the progress of the "second preparation" going on in Rome.[7] Msgr. Garrone expressed the wish that the bishops in the dioceses be informed of the new distribution of schemas, so that the CC would not be doing its work in vain.[8]

But the confusion was obviously felt more at the level of the conciliar commissions. There was first the question of the date by which the bishops had to send their remarks and amendments to the Secretariat of the Council for the use of the competent commissions. In early December the deadline for the schema on the Church was set for February 28, but a circular letter sent in late April changed it to July. Father Tromp, secretary of the Doctrinal Commission, did not miss the opportunity to wax ironic on the subject, not pointing out, however, that the first date concerned his version of the schema on the Church, while the second concerned Philips's version.[9]

As will be reported later, some commissions paid no heed to the elections by which the Council had updated their composition so as to make them truly *conciliar* commissions. Thus in November 1962, the preparatory Commission on the Lay Apostolate continued to work on its schema without summoning the members elected in October.[10] For its part, the preparatory Commission on Bishops turned a deaf ear to the instructions of the CC and never met in plenary session.

In December 1962 Tromp publicly praised the preparatory schemas, which he said reflected the diversity of the theological schools on which his Commission had already drawn before the opening of the Council.[11] But at the end of July 1963, after the Council's Doctrinal Commission

---

[7] In his working paper of January 18, 1963, Father G. Dossetti strongly emphasized this very point (see the Dossetti Archive I, 7 [ISR], under the title "Importanza e Criteri di Funzionamento della Commissione Coordinatrice," 8).

[8] *JCongar*, 227.

[9] These items of information are, however, supplied in a note in the *AS* II/I, 467.

[10] According to the Commission, the difficulty of working with the new members came from the fact that they had not participated in the preparation of the preconciliar schema and were unaware how that text had come to be (see the "Acta Commissionis conciliaris 'de fidelium Apostolatu,'" 2 [CCV, Philips Archive, no inventory number]).

[11] See the interview the Dutch Jesuit gave to the daily *De Gelderlander*, December 18, 1962, reprinted in *Katholiek Archief* 18, no. 5 (February 1, 1963), 108-15.

had worked for months on another draft, which had been entirely revised and already sent out, Tromp, the Secretary of this Commission, still preoccupied with the fate of the preparatory schema on the Church, composed and distributed a twenty-six page report synthesizing the remarks of 130 fathers on his schema, even though it had been removed from the agenda on March 5, 1963.[12]

The preparatory Commission on Catholic Schools and Universities, which had formally ceased to exist after October 1962, continued to function until December. A draft of a preparatory text on Catholic schools was distributed in 1963. The Subcommission on Mixed Matters, a preparatory body, continued its work until the end of 1962.

But it seems that it was at the level of dialogue among the bishops and the episcopal conferences that the confusion of circulating texts caused the most serious disadvantages and the most explicit dissatisfaction. In a circular letter of April 30, 1963, Cicognani told the bishops that he was sending a first series of revised schemas that had passed inspection by the CC and the Pope and on which the bishops' observations were expected in July at the latest. He was referring to twelve schemas, ten sent in May and two in July. One result of this lack of communication with the dioceses was that for a long time some Council fathers ignored the calendar and the activities of the CC and devoted their time and effort to schemas that would no longer be on the agenda.[13] For example, at the end of February 1963 the Dutch episcopate sent Cicognani a series of observations that mainly dealt with preconciliar schemas.[14]

Another good example of out-of-date discussion was seen at the North European meeting in Metz on January 29, 1963, at which six bishops and six experts discussed the schema *On Chastity, Marriage and the Family, and Virginity*.[15] This schema from Cardinal Ottaviani's prepara-

---

[12] S. Tromp, *Relatio de observationibus factis a Patribus Concilii circa primum Schema Constitutionis de Ecclesia* (typewritten) (ISR, Florit papers; CCV, Philips papers).

[13] The most alert bishops tried to make up for the lack of official information by personal contacts; see, in this regard, the correspondence of Msgr. Veuillot with Villot, the assistant secretary of the Council (Archives of the Maison Diocésaine, Paris) or of Suenens with Prignon, rector of the Belgian College in Rome (CLG). These examples could be multiplied.

[14] It is known that Father Schillebeeckx wrote critical commentaries of which the Dutch bishops made extensive use.

[15] The participants agreed in criticizing the lack of the pastoral openness commended by the Pope and the danger of Manicheism in dealing with conjugal life (see the Jan Brouwers Archive, carton 8, Archives of the Diocese of 's Hertogenbosch).

tory Theological Commission had been inspired by Father E. Lio and published in 1962 among the texts meant for the agenda of the first session.[16] Similarly, among the observations of the French bishops on the schema on the Church, two successive "waves" can be clearly distinguished: the first set were on the preparatory schema on the Church, while the second concerned the document on the Church written by Philips.[17]

The last in date of the schemas that caused confusion during the intersession was schema XVII, on the presence of the Church in the world, composed in September 1963 at the request of the CC and under the aegis of Suenens. The failure of this second version of the schema during the second session of Vatican II has often been attributed to the lack of information given to the bishops on the subject.[18]

These examples illustrate the confusion into which the bishops and many episcopal conferences were often thrown during the first six months of 1963. The instructions given at the beginning of the intersession had officially called for the collaboration of the episcopal conferences, but the latter fell victim to a deplorable lack of communication that would delay the revision of the schemas which would begin to be discussed in the autumn of 1963.

[16] This schema had been set aside at the beginning of the intersession; as a result of this action, Tromp, without the knowledge of the Commission on schema XVII, introduced a new rehash composed by Father Lio, which was again rejected in May 1963; still a third draft, dealing with marriage in schema XVII (first version), would be shipwrecked in the Coordinating Commission on July 4, 1963.

[17] The first series, February 1963, includes the criticisms of the bishops of the Paris region, some suggestions from the apostolic region of the East, from the regions of Angers and Bordeaux, from the bishops of Aix and Marseilles, and from Msgr. Elchinger, Coadjutor Bishop of Strasbourg. The second series, which for the most part dated from June 1963, contained observations from the apostolic region of Angers, the provinces of Aix and Marseilles, the Paris region (Paris, Versailles, Meaux), as well as the appraisals of Father Daniélou, who was present at many episcopal meetings (see the J. Daniélou Archive in the Jesuit archives at Vanves). Two comparable "waves" were to be seen at the Grand Séminaire of Montreal (Quebec) in the Archive of Cardinal Léger, nos. 731, 718, and 750, and in the Archive of Professor A. Naud. It would be easy to point out similar examples in the commentaries of German and Dutch bishops.

[18] I shall return to this point below in part III, section A. A witness to the event, Philippe Delhaye, wrote that several bishops who had worked on the preceding version, that of May 1963, and who had not had a part in the work of September 1963, were inclined to think that their texts had been set aside too quickly (see Ph. Delhaye, "Les origines du schéma et les premiers essais de rédaction," in L'Église dans le monde de ce temps [Unam Sanctam 65a; Paris, 1967], I, 227).

II. The Coordinating Commission

A. Coordination of a Second Preparation for the Council

At the end of the first period a very large majority of Council fathers keenly felt the need to ensure that the work of the conciliar commissions would continue during the intersession in order to reduce and revise the schemas that would be discussed during the second period of the Council. This meant, in fact, a second preparation for the Council, whose main characteristic, this time, would be an emancipation from the conservative influences that had controlled the work of most of the preparatory commissions in 1961 and 1962. How far this revision would go was a question deliberately left somewhat vague at the end of the first period.

It was a matter mainly of continuing the renewal of the Council's agenda along the lines the majority had promoted during the final three weeks of the opening period, that is, to preserve, at all cost, the dynamic momentum that had, however timidly, manifested itself. This desire had been expressed in their votes but also in the addresses of their leaders at the beginning of December; such men as Lercaro, Léger, Döpfner, Suenens, and Montini had deeply impressed the assembly as a whole. Behind the scenes people wanted the establishment of a "supercommission" that would continue the work while the bishops were absent.

At the beginning of December 1962 the pace of events speeded up. After the pleas of the leaders for a reorganization of the agenda, it was announced on December 6 that, on the basis of experience gained, the Pope had given instructions for the organization of the CC, which would henceforth have authority over the conciliar commissions in regard to the revision of the schemas. This step, as radical as it seemed, corresponded to the wishes and expectations of the council fathers.

1. *Norms, Guidelines, and Agenda*

The primary document that was the basis for the activities of the CC was an eleven-page pamphlet, distributed on the eve of the intersession, under the title *Schemata Constitutionum et decretorum ex quibus argumenta in Concilio disceptanda seligentur* (*The Drafts of the Constitutions and Decrees from among Which the Subjects to be Debated at the Council will be Chosen*). It listed the complete titles of the twenty draft texts chosen from among the undigested mass of seventy preparatory schemas that in theory might be presented to the fathers of the Council.

While the list gave each document in its "preconciliar," preparatory stage, without any indication of the discussion some of them had already undergone — the fact that the list was "limited" to twenty schemas could be taken as a concession to the majority in the assembly.

It was cause for suprise that this document was distributed on December 5, 1962, without any indication of its source. The General Secretariat of the Council was generally regarded as its source, a hypothesis not contradicted by the deliberations of the Secretariat for Extraordinary Affairs, over which Siri presided and the minutes of which have recently been published.[19] It was probably in accordance with guidelines provided by this Secretariat that Felici's collaborators made this selection of available schemas.

This was the first timid step that the authorities of the Council agreed to take in the direction of a more realistic conciliar agenda in accord with the views of the majority. But since the list once again provided a series of drafts that were entirely "Roman" in style and content, it was still quite insufficient for the purposes of the *aggiornamento* that was being proclaimed.

The next day, December 6, a second official document was distributed, this one promulgated in the name of Secretary of State Cicognani with the express approval of the Pope. It established as the *commissio princeps* or principal commission the much-awaited CC and provided it with its charter. The proximity of the two communications seemed to imply that the list of twenty schemas would provide the agenda for the new CC. But in fact, by the end of its first session, in January 1963, the CC had become familiar enough with the maze of proposed drafts that it could establish its own nomenclature for them. At the suggestion of Cardinal Urbani, a list of seventeen schemas, with a new numbering, was accepted as a working document and would remain the basis of the future agenda.

The main step forward in this new "guide" was the appearance in it of a project to bring together into a single schema various texts on contemporary society; by reason of its position at the end of the list it was called "Schema XVII" (baptized "Schema XIII" in the spring of 1964, it would be promulgated at the end of Vatican II as *Gaudium et spes*). Its official title at this point was *The Presence of the Church in the World of Today*, but the title would undergo numerous changes. While this list of January 27, 1963, set its agenda, the "supercommission" also consid-

---

[19] See *DSiri,* 349-55.

ered some other schemas that subsequently disappeared either through transfer or abandonment.[20]

2. The Charter of the Coordinating Commission

At the beginning of the general congregation of December 6, the next to last of the first period, Felici told the fathers of the steps that had been taken to ensure the continuation of the Council's work during the intersession. As the basis of his instructions for these months, John XXIII recalled his opening message of October 11, 1962, and especially the passage in which he had stressed the need of a renewed but serene adherence to the teaching of the Church and of an explanation of Catholic teaching that respected the research methods and literary forms of modern thought and responded to the needs of a primarily pastoral magisterium. The *Ordo agendorum* explicitly provided that the conciliar commissions were to receive the observations of the bishop, to decide whether or not to amend the schemas in accordance with them, and then to submit the drafts to a general congregation.[21] It was urgent, then, that the schemas be sent to the Council fathers as soon as possible.

Then there were the guidelines given by the Cicognani during the first meeting of the CC and the recommendations of John XXIII, read to the CC at the beginning of its second meeting, March 25, 1962.[22] In the directives the Holy Father said that he trusted the members of the CC to share their observations with the conciliar commissions and to supervise

[20] Here are the titles of the documents with the name of the reporter on it in the CC (nomenclature established by Urbani at the January 27, 1963, meeting of the Commission):

I. Divine Revelation (Liénart); II. The Church (Suenens); III. The Blessed Virgin Mary (Suenens); IV. Bishops and the Government of Dioceses (Döpfner); V. Ecumenism (Cicognani); VI. Clerics (Urbani); VII. Religious (Döpfner); VIII. Apostolate of the Laity (Urbani); IX. Oriental Churches (Cicognani); X. The Sacred Liturgy (Spellman); XI. The Care of Souls (Döpfner); XII. The Sacrament of Matrimony (Urbani); XIII. Formation of Candidates for Orders (Confalonieri); XIV. Catholic Schools (Confalonieri); XV. Missions (Confalonieri); XVI. Social Communications Media (Spellman); XVII. The Presence of the Church in the Modern World (Suenens).

Some schemas that were no longer in the list of January 27, 1963, but were nonetheless on the agenda of the CC: Deposit of Faith (Liénart); Associations of the Faithful (Urbani); Chastity (Spellman).

[21] The instructions appeared under the title *Ordo agendorum tempore quod inter conclusionem primae periodi concilii oecumenici et initium secundae intercedit*. *OssRom* carried a version shortened by the omission, among other things, of the part of a sentence that provided for the sending out of the revised schemas by way of the episcopal conferences (see Caprile II, 258).

[22] *AS* V/1, 200 and 260-61.

the implementation of the desired coordination. The Pope reminded the group of the need for dialogue with the cardinals who had been directing the work of their respective commissions during the previous two months. The subject of the Church should continue to be the main axis of the Council. Repetitions should be removed and the schemas shortened. Finally, the Holy Father said once again that it was not the job of Vatican II to resolve disputed questions; while doctrine was to be at the heart of the work, it was to be considered in function of the Council's pastoral goal and its practical applications.

3. The Inspiration of John XXIII

But we must look beyond these formal guidelines intended for the CC and dwell for a moment on the basic inspiration of John XXIII, who was looking for a way to dynamize the entire second preparation and wanted to involve the bishops, now back in their dioceses, as much as possible. The address that the Pope delivered at the close of the first session on December 8, 1962, was typical in this respect,[23] but his most eloquent exhortation was the letter *Mirabilis ille*, dated Epiphany 1963, and addressed "to all and each of the bishops of the Catholic Church."[24] The Pope reminded the Council fathers that it was their duty to propose, discuss, and prepare the decrees in the desired form. In saying this, he contradicted the arguments put forward by the Curial cardinals who during the first period of the Council had invoked the approval of the preparatory schemas by pontifical authority in order to limit the bishops' freedom of speech.

The Council required the diligent participation of every bishop: "For each of them this duty includes not only their presence at the coming meetings in the Vatican Basilica but also that during these eight months they remain spiritually united with their brothers in the episcopate and be faithful in replying each time the Commission presided over by our Cardinal Secretary of State makes some request of them." Finally, the cooperation of the clergy and the laity was also required. The unexpected stir that the Council had caused in public opinion was reason for

---

[23] "Today's ceremony, then, does not mean the cessation of the work; on the contrary, the work all of us still have to do will be of great importance; indeed, there has never been anything comparable to it in the intersessions of other councils. . . . Each bishop, despite the demands of pastoral government, will continue to study and enter more deeply into the schemas made available to him and everything else sent to him at the appropriate time" (*DMC* IV, 645-46; *DC* 60 [1963], 289-98).

[24] *DMC* IV, 499-501; *DC* 60 (1963), 289-98.

rejoicing, since the Council was something that concerned the whole of humanity.

The spiritual flame that burned in this letter bore witness to the personal involvement of John XXIII in the work of Vatican II. His emphasis on the urgency of progress in the second preparation was less a sign of impatience than the expression of a seriously ill man's awareness that his days were numbered. For this reason, some have even called this message the great Pope's "testament," and the Pope's words in *Mirabilis ille* were never absent from the background against which the work of the 1962-63 intersession was carried on.

Nor did the Pope forget those whom I am describing here as the "opponents of the second preparation." He was aware of their lack of understanding, and he suffered from their procrastination. Knowing the extent to which key sentences in his opening address to the Council had been sharply criticized in conservative circles, John XXIII took care to bring that address to the fore on many occasions. While he explicitly referred to it in the *Ordo agendorum* of December 6, 1962, and in his recommendations to the CC on March 25, 1963, it was in his Christmas address to the Sacred College on December 23, 1962, that he returned to it at length in order to assert once more the dynamic perspective in which Vatican II was to be located.[25]

B. COMPOSITION OF THE "SUPERCOMMISSION" AND THE DIVISION OF ITS WORK

The make-up of the CC was obviously very important for the success of the tasks entrusted to it and even more for the success of the second period of the Council.[26] The presidency of the CC was given to Cicognani, who could be thought of as representing the Roman pontiff. The members appointed to the Commission were Cardinals Liénart and Spellman (from the old board of presidents), Suenens, Döpfner, and Confalonieri (from the Secretariat for Extraordinary Affairs), and Urbani (Patriarch of Venice and representing the Italian episcopate). Msgr.

---

[25] *DMC* V, 54-57; *DC* 60 (1963), 99-102.

[26] Originally, during the first period, it had been thought that the general congregations would resume in May 1963. Next, the break in the full-scale activities of the Council was planned to be from December 7, 1962, to September 8, 1963, with John XXIII hoping the Council could end by Christmas 1963. After the death of the Pope, which caused the suspension of all the activities of the commissions for several weeks, the opening of the second period was set for September 29, 1963.

Felici, Secretary General of the Council, and his undersecretaries also took part in the meetings of the Commission and shared in the discussions.

The division of work was based on the list of twenty selected schemas that had been distributed on December 5, 1962. Each member of the CC was personally entrusted with some schemas for examination and improvement.[27] (The fundamental changes in the composition and functioning of the CC at the beginning of Paul VI's pontificate in September 1963 will be discussed later.)

C. LINKS TO CURIAL CIRCLES

It has often and rightly been said that institutional connections between the commissions of Vatican II and the corresponding departments of the Roman Curia had to a large extent hindered and often even prevented the development of the conciliar dynamics. In fact, the chairs of the conciliar commissions were generally the prefects of the Curial departments that had the same area of competence. Competition among these departments was to weigh very heavily on the conciliar commissions.

For example, the conviction of the Holy Office that it possessed a special authority within the administration of the Curia was inevitably reflected in the leaders of the Council's Doctrinal Commission. The repeated refusal of the president and secretary of this Commission to collaborate on a footing of equality first with the other preparatory commissions and then with the conciliar commissions is fully intelligible only when seen in the context of the functioning of the Roman Curia.

---

[27] Cicognani: (1) Oriental Churches; (2) ecumenism, and (3) missions (later given to Confalonieri); Liénart: (4) revelation, and (5) protection of the deposit of faith; Spellman: (6) the liturgy, and (7) chastity, virginity, marriage, and the family; Urbani: (8) the clergy, (9) the laity, (10) the social communications media, and (11) the sacrament of matrimony; Confalonieri: (12) seminaries, and (13) Catholic education; Döpfner: (14) the episcopate and the dioceses, (15) the care of souls, and (16) religious; Suenens: (17) the Church, (18) the Blessed Virgin Mary, (19) the moral order, and (20) the social order. At the first meeting of the CC (end of January 1963) the list was reduced to seventeen schemas and placed in a different order, to be discussed later (see AS V/1, 38-43). Spellman seems to have been placed at the periphery of the overall activity. He was reporter for a minor text on chastity that was quickly dealt with and for the schema on the liturgy, which had already made great progress at the general congregations and should not have been on the agenda of the CC. When the Commission for the Revision of Canon Law was set up, Spellman's name was omitted from the first list of members and had to be added in a later correction.

The major concern of Ottaviani and Tromp was not so much to gain a privileged position among the conciliar commissions as to preserve the special authority that the Holy Office had managed to acquire within the papal Curia, often in competition with other Curial bodies, especially the Secretariat of State. They feared that diminished prestige at the Council might inevitably weaken the Holy Office's position within the Roman Curia with serious consequences long after the temporary event of the Council had come to an end.[28]

Two other cases were significantly different. Cardinals Bea and Cento presided over two new and dynamic agencies that had no twins in the Curia, namely, the Secretariat for Christian Unity and the Commission for the Apostolate of the Laity. These cardinals did not represent Curial circles and soon became the objects of obvious hostility from some other conciliar commissions. Their new administrative bodies were in fact rooted in two preconciliar movements that had not previously been insti-tutionalized in Rome: the Catholic ecumenical movement and the World Congresses for the Apostolate of the Laity (and the corresponding con-ferences of international Catholic organizations).[29]

The difference between these two categories of conciliar commis-sions, the Curial and the non-Curial, is obvious. The administrative infe-riority of the non-Curial commissions immediately betrayed itself in their ignorance of precedents and of Roman procedures, in the difficulty they had in gaining access to those in authority, and finally in their lack of material organization.[30]

---

[28] Recall here the reaction of the Roman Curia when Vatican I was announced. Car-dinal Pitra exclaimed: "What? Call a Council? But the French and German theologians would come and drastically change our Congregations!" (see R. Aubert, *Le pontificat de Pie IX* [Paris, 1952], 312).

[29] There is room for a comparative study between, on the one hand, the Catholic Con-ference for Ecumenical Questions of Msgr. Willebrands (established in 1952) and, on the other, COPECIAL (Comité Permanent des Congrès Internationaux pour l'Apostolat des Laïcs, also established in 1952); Msgr. Glorieux soon became the ecclesiastical curator of the latter, and one of its mainsprings. These two organizations had some stable points of contact with Curial circles under Pius XII: Willebrands and Thijssen with the Holy Office of that period, Glorieux and Veronese with the Secretariat of State. These associations would be very useful to them from the beginning of the preparatory phase of Vatican II. Both the Secretariat for Christian Unity and the Commission for the Apostolate of the Laity would also be characterized by their call for outside collaborators, for the one the non-Catholic observers and, for the other, the lay auditors, both of which groups reflected unofficial relationships already established under Pius XII. This reliance on outsiders elicited very strong criticism from Curial circles and would continue to be resisted during the Council.

[30] Remembering these difficult beginnings, Glorieux commented: "Almost all the preparatory commissions were more or less paralleled by departments in the Roman

As for the conciliar commissions with ties to the Curia, it was somewhat as if the chairs añd personnel of a parliamentary commission were
chosen from among the civil servants in the cabinet offices to be
inspected, and as if the venues and the tools for the work of such a
commission were provided by the administrative services in power!

The connections between the makeup of the CC and that of the
Roman Curia have less often been analyzed.[31] And yet such an analysis
is obviously called for, since these connections shed a special light on
the attitude of some members of the CC. Thus Confalonieri, the executive head of the Congregation of the Consistory, was made responsible
for the schema on the bishops. Even more important, Cicognani simultaneously exercised several important and often obviously incompatible
roles. Although he had ceased to head the Congregation for the Oriental
Churches in 1961, he remained president of the Commission for the Oriental Churches during the Council. After the death of Cardinal Tardini,
Cicognani had been appointed to the very important post of Secretary of
State, and now he became, in addition, president of the CC for the crucial period of the first intersession.

The weight of these simultaneous roles held by Cicognani hindered
the functioning of the CC. This could be seen especially at the Commission's first meeting in January 1963, when he openly defended the value
of the draft texts from the preparatory period, and it was to be seen again
at the second meeting, in March 1963, when he was both judge and

Curia: they would therefore find venues and technical facilities for their work in the
palaces of the Congregations. There was nothing like that for the Commission for the
Apostolate of the Laity; and it was not without difficulty that the administrative offices of
the Holy See freed up two rooms . . . in the palace of the Chancery" (A. Glorieux, "Histoire du décret sur l'Apostolat des laïcs," in L'Apostolat des laïcs. Vatican II [Unam
Sanctam 75; Paris, 1970], 95).

[31] It will be useful to list here the Curial functions that important members of the CC
held in 1962-63 and combined with their participation in this guiding Commission. Confalonieri was Secretary (effective head) of the Congregation of the Consistory, which had
in its competence the appointment of bishops, the erection of dioceses and ecclesiastical
provinces, etc. Testa was Secretary (i.e., director) of the Congregation for the Oriental
Churches, of which. Masella, Cicognani, Agagianian, Cento, and Confalonieri were also
members. Marella was Prefect of the Congregation for the Discipline of the Sacraments,
of which Cicognani and Agagianian were members. Ciriaci was Prefect of the Congregation of the Council, which dealt with the discipline of the clergy and the laity, pastoral
activity, and catechesis. V. Valeri was Prefect of the Congregation for Religious. Agagianian was Prefect of the Congregation for the Propagation of the Faith, of which
Masella, Cicognani, Cento, Confalonieri, Marella, Suenens, and Ottaviani were members.
Pizzardo was Prefect of the Congregation for Seminaries and Universities, of which
Cicognani, Liénart, and Confalonieri were members. Marella was Prefect of the Fabric of
St. Peter's Basilica (see Annuario Pontificio 1963, 884-925).

judged in the appraisal of the schema on the Oriental Churches and tried to put a brake on the text on ecumenism.

As we read the minutes of the CC, it becomes clear that the non-Curial members were freer in voicing their judgments and more closely followed John XXIII's instructions for preparing the second period of the Council. We find examples of this in Döpfner as he judged the text on religious, in Liénart as he criticized the schema on revelation, and in Suenens as he advocated a recasting of the draft on the Church, and in all three when they refused to accept the schema on the missions. The position of Urbani, Patriarch of Venice, varied depending on cases; his open-mindedness in calling for the composition of a schema on the presence of the Church in today's world was not visible in other areas. In any case, it seems clear that the positions taken by the non-Curial members of the CC frequently led to conflicts with the leaders of commissions under Curial influence.

But there was another side of the coin. Cicognani and Confalonieri showed special consideration when reporting to the CC on a schema that had come from a commission under Curial influence. The benevolent attitude of Confalonieri as reporter for the schema on the missions (Agagianian's Commission) and the schemas on seminaries and on studies (both from Pizzardo's commission) was a clear example. As reporter, Cicognani obviously defended the text on the Oriental Churches even though it contradicted the instructions of the Council and of the Pope, because it came from his own Commission (Oriental Churches). In these particular cases we can, I think, see the cumulative negative effects of men who were resisting the conciliar renewal and the resolutions passed at the end of the first period of the Council.

D. THE ACTIVITY OF THE OPPONENTS OF THE SECOND PREPARATION

A study of events during the ten months of the intersession reveals that the opponents of the conciliar *aggiornamento* did not by any means lay down their weapons. During the first period of Vatican II they had revealed themselves mainly by their vigorous and sometimes stubborn defense of the preparatory schemas and of the positions they implied. During the intersession these same forces remained active but used other weapons; the defenders of the preparatory texts now became the opponents of a second preparation, something very clear in the CC.

There were at least two categories of opponents of the second preparation: those whose links to Curial circles would take on ever greater weight; and some important heads of large Italian sees, such as Siri (Genoa) and Ruffini (Palermo). (There was a difference between the latter, however; Ruffini had belonged to the Roman Curia from 1928 to 1945 and thus appears to have been closer to it than Siri, the "dauphin" of Pius XII.) During this first intersession at Rome, the activity of those linked to the Curia was clearly much more important than that of the diocesan prelates.

The opponents carried on this activity first of all in the area of procedure. Ottaviani continued to defend the special authority of the schemas prepared by his Theological Commission. As soon as the CC began to operate, he sent its President a lengthy note that ended with a vigorous defense of the fundamental incompatibility between texts of a dogmatic nature and those of the disciplinary order, the former being "supratemporal and irreformable," the latter variable because of "circumstances of place and time." Dogmatic and disciplinary decrees, therefore, must remain carefully separated.[32]

The typographical presentation of the series of seventy preparatory schemas in their original edition speaks volumes. Only the twenty-four red booklets coming from the preparatory Theological Commission carried the title *Theological Questions*. The booklets published by the other commissions did not have the right to use that adjective but were titled simply *Questions on Religious*, *Questions on Studies and Seminaries*, *Questions on the Oriental Churches*, *Questions on the Missions*, and so on. Ottaviani's position had as a corollary a consistent refusal to collaborate with the other conciliar commissions. The criticisms voiced on this point at the Council and the steps taken by John XXIII to multiply mixed commissions (the first being the one appointed after the debate on the sources of revelation) had done nothing to weaken the head of the Holy Office's unshakable conviction of his "superiority." When Ottaviani, with his back to the wall, could not in specific cases prevent a "mixed" activity, he sought a way out by preferring the policy of the "empty chair," that is, delegating an assistant, usually Cardinal Browne, and then trying to challenge the results produced in his absence!

The conflict between Ottaviani and Cento is one example of this characteristic. Following upon the CC's formal instructions at the end of January 1963, which called for a mixed commission, the heads of the Commission on the Lay Apostolate, Cardinal Cento and Msgr. Glorieux, foresaw a rivalry between their Commission and the Doctrinal Commis-

[32] *AS* V/1, 47.

sion. They were received at the Holy Office as early as the beginning of February, but Ottaviani claimed that he was too busy to see them and asked Browne to take his place. By the end of that month the team of Glorieux and Tromp had already succeeded in forming a "limited mixed commission" of eight bishops, which, under the presidency of Cento and Browne, rewrote the texts that would become schema XVII. This work was later continued with the consultation and with the participation of lay persons, called as experts, in one of the subcommissions.

But on the eve of the second meeting of the CC, it soon became clear that Ottaviani and Tromp would refuse to let the text of schema XVII be presented to the commissioners until the draft had been studied and accepted by the Doctrinal Commission. Not only would such a step have meant a delay of two months, but it was a direct attack on the dignity and authority of Cento's Commission. Cento refused to be thus humiliated and finally won his case before the CC at its second meeting, at which Suenens elicited an admission that Cento's Commission was not dependent on Ottaviani's and that the approval of a text by the mixed commission was enough.[33] In reprisal, Ottaviani and Tromp refused to attend the meetings of the CC, although they were invited and had an obligation to take part in the discussion of schema XVII.[34]

This typical incident caused all the more stir since this attitude of the leaders of the Doctrinal Commission applied to other more or less similar cases, and in March 1963 the whole of conciliar Rome was holding its breath because of the high stakes in the Cento-Ottaviani duel. Thus Willebrands feared that if the mixed commission for schema XVII came under Ottaviani's supervision, the same fate might await his own schema on ecumenism, which was likewise the work of a mixed set of redactors.[35] Cicognani, president of the Commission on the Oriental Churches, certainly did not want its schema to be subjected to a further examination by the Doctrinal Commission, since the latter had refused to cooperate with the Oriental Commission. In addition, following Otta-

[33] Ibid., 513.

[34] Tromp gives a different version. He says that Ottaviani and he had not been invited to the March 29 meeting of the CC (*Relatio*, March 13-September 10, 14). The agitation experienced in the commission for schema XVII due to the outrageous demands of Ottaviani and Tromp caused Cento to undertake a series of preliminary moves to plead his case; thus McGrath was delegated to visit Suenens in Malines and Griffith to visit Spellman in New York to argue in favor of the authority of the mixed commission.

[35] The two chapters that made up the draft on ecumenism at that time came from two different mixed commissions, both of which thought further examination by the full Doctrinal Commission unnecessary.

viani would have meant a considerable loss of time, since the date for sending the revised schemas to the bishops (around Easter, if possible) was already near. The decision not to give in to Ottaviani's demand made it possible to assert the CC's own authority over the second preparation.

Fathers Lio and Tromp, two authors whose preparatory schemas had been rejected by official authorities of the Council,[36] hoped to halt the second preparation by submitting a new redaction of some texts. Their move immediately elicited critical reactions from the leaders of the majority, and in the end, the Doctrinal Commission did not succeed in getting these counter-plans on the agenda of the CC.

The failure later of the so-called Malines text for schema XVII likewise had its origins in the activity of the opponents of the second preparation. Suenens had been given the assignment, by unanimous decision of the CC, to prepare from scratch a doctrinal introduction meant for the Commission on schema XVII.[37] The draft text that resulted was dated Malines, September 1963. For reasons never explained, this important decision of the CC was not duly communicated to the mixed commission for which the draft was intended. When, much later, the Malines text reached the mixed commission, the latter, not knowing its source or authority, decided to dismiss the schema. Whoever was responsible for the lack of communication, the failure of the schema again enables us to measure the weight and constancy of the influence of those who sought to undermine the decisions of the CC.

Opponents of the second preparation were also active outside the CC, as we will see when we speak of the history of the labors of the conciliar commissions.

E. MEETINGS AND INTERNAL DEVELOPMENT OF THE COORDINATING COMMISSION

In the course of the 1962-63 intersession, the CC held six meetings. (The death of John XXIII and the election of Paul VI inevitably caused a temporary break in its work.) It held its first meeting at the end of January 1963, the second at the end of March, and the third at the beginning

---

[36] Tromp's *De Ecclesia* was not considered at the decisive meeting of the doctrinal subcommission on February 26, 1963. Lio's schema *De ordine morali* was in effect buried when on January 26, 1963, the CC sent it back to be "re-organized."

[37] See *AS* V/1, 637.

of July. These first three meetings had a major influence on the course of the second preparation, while the last three served rather as a prologue to the opening of the second period of Vatican II.

Each of the first three meetings lasted several days, but the first two were the longest: January 21-27 and March 25-29, 1963. Minutes of these meetings enable us both to follow the main lines of the relatively rapid course followed by the leaders of this second preparation and to gain some idea of the tenacity of the opponents.[38]

The tone of the Commission's activity constantly changed during these six months. In the beginning it was those close to Curial circles who did the speaking, while the spokesmen for the majority sought to advance things prudently. As various commissions got moving and as public opinion and in particular Pope John XXIII himself showed the importance of the nascent *aggiornamento*, those in favor of a truly new preparation acquired greater authority. The election as pope of Montini, widely regarded as the candidate of the conciliar majority, provided a backdrop from which it is impossible to prescind as we read the minutes of the meetings from July on.

1. *Course of the Meetings*

With his usual clear-sightedness Suenens wrote to an adviser as the CC began its work: "Until now the negative battle has been taking precedence; the constructive part will come later, I hope."[39] The course of the transition made by the CC in 1963 corresponds exactly to this perspective. The "negative battle" consisted first of all in getting rid of the immense backlog of preparatory schemas and to do so gradually and with respect for the often very keen sensitivities of the persons involved. The second and "constructive part" would seek as much as possible to include old materials in the edifice of the second preparation. While this difficult process could not be rushed, it was also necessary to act quickly in order to finish all the work in eight months.

---

[38] *AS* V/1 presents not only the minutes but the reports and other documents of the CC. The accounts in *OssRom* give important details that are lacking in these published minutes, especially for the meeting in March 1963 (see *OssRom* for March 24, 27, and 31, and April 5, 1963).

[39] Letter of Suenens to Father Calvez, dated January 15, 1963 (Daniélou Papers in the Archives of the Jesuits Fathers at Vanves). The reader may recall that in his earlier correspondence with John XXIII in the spring of 1962 Suenens had used another dyad: "To like and dislike the same things" (see L.-J. Suenens, *Souvenirs et espérances* [Paris, 1991], 66-68).

In these circumstances the results could obviously not be fully satisfactory, and when the Council reconvened in the autumn of 1963 it would be obliged to work on an unfinished preparation. Nevertheless, without the ceaseless activity of a number of conciliar commissions, which had the support and encouragement of the CC, the second period of Vatican II would have had even great difficulty in functioning than it eventually did. It is the entire history of this period that we must skim through here.

While the start of the "negative battle" at the first meeting of the CC was much harder than the somewhat euphoric conciliar majority had imagined in December 1962, the second meeting brought a much more dynamic deployment of the subjects to be treated. It marked a second phase, which, thanks to joint meetings, made possible a direct dialogue between the CC and the leaders of the conciliar commissions. Finally, the third meeting, although very short, was able to attend to the most urgent matters and make progress in schemas dealing with the Church *ad intra* and the Church *ad extra*.

2. *January 1963*

The first meeting of the CC opened with Cicognani's reminder of the Commission's tasks. A hierarchy would have to be established between texts of greater and lesser importance; it was therefore necessary to reduce or eliminate texts, postponing some of them to the revision of the Code or leaving them to postconciliar commissions. Contacts should be made with the presidents of the conciliar commissions to ensure the needed coordination. Paradoxically and unexpectedly, Cicognani concluded his remarks by saying that the material that had been prepared for the Council was "substantially good and sufficient"; he was anxious to turn to good account the long process of preparation, first in the commissions, then in the Central Commission, and finally in the study that the Council fathers had made of it. This meant that the prepared schemas were not be replaced by new draft texts; at most proposed changes could be introduced into them. This argument in favor of the preparatory schemas was quite characteristic of Cicognani's ambiguous attitude. He did make one specific recommendation at the end: in regard to revelation and to the Church, the Council was not to answer questions that were still under study and which it would be risky to try to resolve.

During the first exchanges at this meeting, Urbani and Confalonieri, generally described as "moderate conservatives,"[40] set the tone: so that the revised texts might be sent quickly to the Council fathers, the Commission's work of reducing the number of texts would have to be finished by Easter. Then the observations sent in by the bishops for each schema would have to be discussed in the Commission before reaching the Council. Confalonieri and Felici used this tight timetable as an argument for limiting the number of texts as much as possible.

To come up with an order of priority in the presentation of the schemas of the second preparation, Urbani offered a list of seventeen schemas that would serve as an inventory of texts already revised or to be revised. This list differed considerably from the list of December 5 that had been drawn up by the General Secretariat of the Council and that had been based essentially on the titles of the preparatory schemas.[41]

The most tangible result of this first meeting was a set of fifteen propositions, promulgated in the name of the CC and intended for the various conciliar commissions. Each of them was the result of the Commission's discussion of the report presented by the designated member. In them it is possible to measure the progress made in some schemas, and also the stagnation in which others were stuck.[42]

3. March 1963

During five days at the end of March 1963, the CC succeeded in studying almost all the schemas that were on the agendas of the conciliar commissions. At the beginning of the meeting Cicognani, with the approval of the Holy Father, repeated the instructions for the Commission. Its function was to check whether the schemas had been revised in

[40] Urbani's name was among the nineteen signers of the famous letter of November 24, 1962, with its frontal attack on the Biblical Institute; the Patriarch of Venice was not afraid, by signing it, of choosing the conservative camp.

[41] *AS* V/1, 182 and again on 201; see above, note 20. This list should not make us forget that other schemata also came before the CC either before or after. The chief ones, with their respective reporters, were *On the Deposit of Faith* (Liénart), *On Associations of the Faithful* (Urbani), and *On Chastity, Virginity, Marriage and the Family* (Spellman). Some topics of the first would be transferred to the first part of schema XVII; the second text was referred to the Commission for the Apostolate of the Laity; the third would not be retained. The main topics of three other drafts, *On the Moral Order, On the Social Order,* and *On the International Order* (Suenens), would be found under the rubric of schema XVII in Urbani's inventory.

[42] For the fifteen propositions see *AS* V/1, 184-200. I shall return to them when I look in greater detail at the work of the conciliar commissions.

accordance with the corrections requested and whether or not they could now be sent to the bishops. The theme of the Church remained the primary subject of Vatican II. Two guidelines defined the work to be done: eliminate repetitions and shorten the schemas. Finally, it was stated once again that it was not the role of the Council to settle disputed questions and that the guidelines given by the Pope in his opening address were to be kept in mind.[43]

After having briefly considered giving each member of the Commission the task of "inspecting," on the spot, the work done by the conciliar commission in his particular area, the CC decided instead to summon the heads of each conciliar commission when its schema came on the CC's agenda. This procedure would permit the president of each conciliar commission to defend its work, but above all it was a way to strengthen the authority and control the CC was supposed to exercise over the conciliar commissions. It also gave the CC a better knowledge of the sharper conflicts among the competing conciliar commissions.

While the second meeting of the CC thus made progress, it also revealed more clearly the tensions between supporters and opponents of the second preparation. These tensions, which had previously remained under the surface, displayed an unsuspected depth and tenacity. The results of the March meeting were all the more important in that the death of Pope John was to cause a complete interruption of conciliar activities.

The exchange of views at the March meeting began with Confalonieri's laudatory report on the schemas dealing with seminaries and with Catholic education, after which the leaders of the relevant conciliar commission, Cardinal Pizzardo and Father A. Mayer, responded to his remarks. In the end it was agreed that the Commission would endeavor to take account of the remarks made, with a view to sending the texts to the Council fathers.

The same procedure was followed for the schemas on the clergy, the apostolate of the laity, the role of bishops, and the vocation of religious, each time in the presence of the heads of the pertinent conciliar commission. When the text on bishops came up for discussion, Cicognani registered a unanimous desire on the part of the CC that a commission be established for the revision of canon law, a wish that was immediately passed on to the Pope.

The schema on the Oriental Churches came up for review on the second day, but the official minutes mention only Father A. Welykyj as rep-

---

[43] *AS* V/1, 260-61.

resenting the competent commission, with no mention of the role of Cicognani, still president of the conciliar commission. Liénart's report on the schema on revelation did not succeed in freeing the text from the impasse in which it still found itself; it would have to be returned to the mixed commission on the doctrine of the faith and the unity of Christians. The Secretariat for Christian Unity was here represented only by Msgr. Arrighi, who found himself side by side with Ottaviani and Tromp, the spokesmen for the Doctrinal Commission.[44]

The next-to-last day of the meeting, devoted to the revised schema on the Church (Suenens reporting) and to the restoration of the permanent diaconate, was marked by a personal visit from John XXIII. He announced that a commission for the revision of the Code, as desired by the CC, was to be established immediately. When the Commission resumed its work, now in the presence of the Pope, the proposed text on ecumenism was next on the agenda.

According to the resolutions passed by the Council in December 1962, and repeated verbatim by the CC at the end of January, 1963, the revision of this schema was to be entrusted to a threefold commission involving the Doctrinal Commission, the Commission on the Oriental Churches, and the Secretariat for Christian Unity. The respective heads of these bodies, Ottaviani, Cicognani, and Bea, had met on January 3, 1963, but any agreement reached did not last long, as we shall see in describing tensions with regard to the schema on ecumenism. Cicognani, who reported on the ecumenism schema but who was also responsible for the schema on the Oriental Churches, wanted his commission to be able to treat of ecumenical relations with the Orthodox Churches; this ran contrary to the desire of the Secretariat for Christian Unity to reserve them to itself. The official minutes make no mention of a report from Cicognani on ecumenism, and this report was not included among the appended documents. There is no indication that the mixed commission was represented.[45]

When it came to the study of the schema on the Church in the world, the competent mixed commission was represented only by Cento and Glorieux, since Ottaviani and Tromp had decided to stay away from the meeting. The conflict of competencies that opposed Ottaviani and Cento

[44] According to a notice in *Katholiek Archief* Bea and Willebrands, President and Secretary of the Secretariat for Christian Unity, were in the United States at the time (*Katholiek Archief* XVII, no. 22, 530).

[45] But *OssRom* does mention the participation of Father A. G. Welykyj (Oriental Churches) and Msgr. J. F. Arrighi (Secretariat for Christian Unity) (April 5, 1963).

was evidently due to the desire of the Doctrinal Commission to make its own study of the orthodoxy of a text produced by a mixed commission of which the Doctrinal Commission was itself a part. The CC refused to be brought to a standstill by these procedural considerations.

4. *July 1963*

The meeting of the CC planned for the beginning of June was delayed for a month after the death of John XXIII and the ensuing conclave. The July meeting was short but very important for the schemas on the Church *ad intra* and *ad extra* destined to be on the agenda during the second period of the Council. The first item on the agenda was an exchange of views on the schema on the missions; it brought out the opposition between Confalonieri and Agagianian, who advocated presenting the text to the Council fathers, and Döpfner, Liénart, and Suenens, who had explicit and reasoned reservations. This tension persisted within the CC throughout the first intersession, reappearing during discussion of the text on mixed marriages and of a resolution that religious freedom be on the Council's agenda. The discussion of schema XVII ended nonetheless in the unanimous conclusion that Suenens be given the charge, of preparing, as soon as possible and with the help of five subcommissions, a new text to be submitted to the mixed commission on schema XVII.

Suenens's report on the revised schema on the Church made the extremely important suggestion, accepted in principle, that the section on the laity be divided into two chapters, the first dealing with "the people of God" and the second with "the laity," and, in addition, that the order of chapters be changed by placing the section on "the people of God" before the chapter on the bishops. It was decided, finally, to ask that chapters III and IV be sent to the bishops in their present form.

Two subjects of importance for the organization of the Council were discussed at the end of the meeting: improving the way the press was being treated and revising the regulations of the Council. Discussion of the first would lead to the establishment of a Press Committee headed by Msgr. M. O'Connor to improve the efficiency of the Council press office. And, in fact, starting with the second period of Vatican II, the quality and reliability of news about the Council did greatly improve, although the supervision hitherto exercised by Felici was not definitively removed.

As for the conciliar procedure, in the fall of 1963 a revised set of Regulations would endeavor to deal with the major problems caused by the unusual size of a deliberative assembly comprising 2700 members with rights to speak and to vote. The implementation and assessment of the "order of the Council" obviously belong to the history of the second period of Vatican II, but preparation for the revision was the work of the 1962-63 intersession.

Following upon the deliberations of the CC at its third meeting and upon the amendments the conciliar commissions had been asked to make, two new texts were published and, with the Pope's consent, sent to all the bishops around mid-July 1963. These were the draft of a decree on the sacrament of matrimony and the second part of a draft of a dogmatic constitution on the Church. The history of the second period of the Council will show the fate that awaited them.

The course of the last three meetings of the CC during the 1962-63 intersession bears the marks of the change that the Commission underwent under Paul VI some weeks before September 29, the date of the opening of the second period of the Council. The history of these three meeting belongs therefore in section VI, which is devoted to the first months of the pontificate of Paul VI.

III. The Conciliar Commissions at Work

Introduction

The activity of the conciliar commissions can be divided into three periods, each of them preceded by decisions taken by the CC at the end of January, the end of March, and the beginning of July. Each of the three periods was, in a way, activated by instructions from the seven cardinals of the CC, which provided the backbone of the commissions during the intersession. Besides the schedule to be followed (an important role, since only if delays were curtailed could the revised texts be sent in due time), it also determined the content of the revisions to be made by rethinking the issues, by shortening the texts, and by coordination and cooperation among those in charge of the schemas.

The first phase launched the commissions' work in February and March 1963. The second phase, following upon the meeting of the CC at the end of March and intended to cover only the months of April and May 1963, was prolonged by the death of the Pope and the vacancy of the pontifical see. After a month of mourning and conclave (June) the third phase, now under Paul VI, followed the meeting of the CC at the beginning of July and lasted until September.

In section A below I shall deal with the three schemas generally regarded as the most important: (1) revelation; (2) the Church; and (3) schema XVII on the presence of the Church in the world. For a correct understanding of these three texts I shall describe their development across the successive phases of the intersession. Next, I shall discuss two drafts that came to the fore (section B), the four failures of the second preparation (section C), and finally the texts I call "latecomers" (section D).

To appreciate the journey made and the results obtained by the conciliar commissions during the 1962-63 intersession or, more accurately, during the main activities that went on from the beginning of February to the end of August 1963, we might compare the titles of the seventeen schemas as adopted by the Coordinating Commission in January with the list of five schemas that it put on the agenda of the Council seven months later.[46] But comparison would not entirely suffice, since the schemas discussed during the second period of Vatican II constituted only a reduced selection, that is, texts chosen because they were "mature" enough for the assembly to consider.

Another point of comparison might be the collection of thirteen drafts sent to the bishops for their inspection: a first set in mid-May 1963, and a second in mid-July. But this series of thirteen would likewise be inaccurate, being this time too broad. Some of these schemas were found unsatisfactory and disappeared from the agenda, while others were soon absorbed into similar schemas. Finally, still another series of schemas discussed at length in 1962-63 did not really surface in the full assembly until much later, in 1964 and 1965. Two typical examples of this last series come to mind: the draft of a dogmatic constitution on divine revelation, and the draft of a pastoral constitution on the Church and the world.

The real dynamics of the intersession cannot, then, be measured either by numbers or by titles; it can really be appreciated only by an evaluation of all the texts discussed by commissions during this period. To carry out such an inquiry, I shall follow the order established in the list of seventeen schemas as accepted by the Coordinating Commission in January 1963. For the sake of clarity in such a complex historical development, I shall begin by describing in thematic fashion three prominent schemas that bring out in an excellent way the transitional character of the first intersession.

---

[46] *AS* V/1, 649-50 (meeting of the CC on August 31, 1963).

A. Three Important Schemas

1. *The Schema on Revelation*

It is no accident that the schema on revelation heads the list. During the first period of Vatican II the problem of "two sources," of relations between scripture and tradition, and of the "insufficiency" of scripture was the focus of the most basic controversy experienced by the Council in its first passage of arms. While the two main trends faced off in a number of areas: ecclesiology, ecumenism, the role of the laity, and so on, the controversy first crystallized around a critical point: biblical exegesis. The vote of November 20, 1962, brought the crisis to light, and John XXIII sought to resolve it by a new approach, the use of a mixed commission that would force the two camps to dialogue. This typically Roncallian method would be applied many times in the future, to the point that it gave rise to attempts at sabotage by the opponents of the second preparation, as we shall have further occasion to note.

The mixed commission on revelation held nine working sessions in all, but only the last four are part of the history of the intersession. Its activities followed a relatively simple timetable compared with the complicated development of other schemas, such as that on the Church in the world. The four meetings that interest us here, which took place at the end of February and the beginning of March, were marked by emotional confrontations similar to the violent discussions within the same mixed commission at the beginning of December 1962, conflicts that left the participants bruised and exhausted.

Nor was it by chance that in the CC Liénart was appointed reporter for the schema on revelation. On November 14, 1962, Liénart had been the first speaker to open fire on the preparatory text, "On the Sources of Revelation," and had emphatically called for its "complete revision."[47] In the report he presented to the CC on January 21, 1963, the Bishop of Lille summarized the serious difficulty still affecting the new schema offered by the mixed commission on revelation as a result of its meetings on December 4, 5, and 7, 1962.[48] At those sessions the mixed com-

---

[47] During that same nineteenth general congregation the Bishop of Lille had made three basic points: (1) the proposed decree passed over in silence the single source from which all the other sources emanate: the word of God; (2) in face of one of God's most wonderful gifts the schema spoke of sources in a completely Scholastic style; and (3) in an area so supernatural as revelation we ought to rely primarily on the teachings of the faith.

[48] *AS* V/1, 60-62. See also Cardinal Liénart, "Vatican II," *Mélanges de Science Religieuse* (Lille), 33 (1976), 87-92.

mission had accepted and unanimously approved the text of the Introduction and of chapters II-V of the schema, thereby ensuring considerable improvements. The one major difficulty that remained had to do
with chapter I, on scripture and tradition. The crucial point of disagreement was the question of whether or not tradition is more extensive than
scripture in matters of faith and morals. According to Liénart's report to
the CC, the thesis that would impose as certain that tradition contains
truths missing from the scriptures went far beyond the definitions given
in this area by the Councils of Trent and Vatican I. "The latter were content to say that scripture and tradition are two forms in which divine revelation has come down to us, without comparing the two to each other."

When the mixed commission had taken a vote on December 7, 1962,
a corrected text that claimed to tone down somewhat the strong position
regarding tradition had not, despite Ottaviani's claims, obtained the
required majority. Following the main lines of Liénart's proposals, the
CC gave instructions on the subject to the mixed commission on revelation: since the formula in chapter I dealing with the relation between
scripture and tradition had not won a two-thirds majority, it was to be
dropped and a new text capable of obtaining such a majority was to be
developed. If this were to prove impossible, it would be necessary to
return to the formulas of Trent and Vatican I.

Although these instructions were not unclear, they did not include a
"whereas" from Liénart's report which shed light on the roots of the
conflict: "Whereas the Council not only should not further alienate the
separated brethren but should instead endeavor to enlighten them and to
reunite them." Without here going into the details of a controversy that
would be given new impetus in 1964 and 1965 and was even to create a
climate of acute crisis in October 1965, I refer the reader to the positions
taken by the great French theologian Y. Congar, who on two occasions
at this time tried to locate the debate on its proper level.[49]

---

[49] A paper entitled "Observations sur le schéma de Constitution *De Divina Revela-
tione*," written by Congar, bearing the notation "Confidential," and dated June 29, 1963,
was distributed by the Dutch DO-C Center (no series number). In it the author lists the
three possible positions maintained at that time in the Catholic Church: (a) tradition is a
source independent of scripture, transmitting truths not contained in scripture (theory of
the two sources); (b) tradition is an interpretation and an unfolding of the content of
scripture, which is materially sufficient: everything is in the scripture, everything is in
tradition (Geiselmann); and (c) in regard to the essentials, the content of scripture and the
content of tradition are identical; tradition goes beyond scripture only in a relative and
subordinate way (J. Möhler, Scheeben, Newman, Franzelin). In Congar's view, the position that tradition is broader than scripture (*latius patet*) expresses something that is true
but not as understood by the promotors of the formula, which needs to be completed:

The result of these instructions from the CC was to be shown within a few days. While the Doctrinal Commission resumed its activities on February 21, 1963, in a very troubled atmosphere, the mixed commission on revelation met on Saturday, February 23, for the first time since December 1962. The renewed controversy had to do once again with the *latius patet* (that tradition is of wider extent than scripture). The minority spoke of tradition as having a constitutive function, while the spokesmen for the majority maintained that nowadays the problem was being posed differently than at Trent and that ongoing theological study should not be hindered by the present Council. Since no formula was found that would settle the matter, Bea managed to get agreement on a vote as to whether or not the Council really had to take a position on the problem of scripture and tradition. Of the votes cast, twenty-eight supported Bea and his refusal to settle a question that did not yet seem ripe; only eight were of a different opinion.[50]

This vote would often be cited thereafter, but at the meeting of the mixed commission on Monday, February 25, Ottaviani challenged the vote on the grounds that he had been absent when it was taken. But this attack by the Prefect of the Holy Office unleashed a "devastating storm," for by personally taking Bea to task and casting doubt on his fidelity to the Catholic faith and by wanting the bishops present to take an oath on the "two sources" doctrine, he inflamed even the most level-headed among the members. Charue, who was also challenged, was on the point of slamming the door behind him when Léger threatened Ottaviani with an appeal to the CC. As for Bea, he replied that the Secretariat for Christian Unity had a voice in the composition of the chapter and that there was no need to remind the bishops of oaths they had already taken. Léger's intervention calmed the turmoil of the majority. It was thus in an atmosphere of crisis that the mixed commission suddenly broke off its meeting without reaching any conclusion.[51]

"For if tradition contains more than scripture in extent, scripture certainly contains more than tradition in depth, being really inexhaustible" (Congar). The whole of the chapter in the mixed commission's text needed basic improvements, especially by defining what was meant there by *tradition*, by specifying that tradition includes the development of doctrine in the Church, and by stating that while the deposit of the word is indeed entrusted to the magisterium, it has also been entrusted to the Church as a whole.

[50] J. Feiner, "La contribution du Secrétariat pour l'Unité des Chrétiens," in *La Révélation divine*, ed. B. Dupuy (Unam Sanctam 70a; Paris, 1968), 150-51.

[51] This crisis, vividly remembered by the witnesses, had two different results: first, it led to informal meetings among the "stars" of the majority, who considered an appeal to the Pope; and second, it encouraged a more serene atmosphere at the next meeting of the Doctrinal Commission, which was devoted to the schema on the Church, since the main actors wanted at any price to avoid a repetition of personal attacks.

When the mixed commission resumed its activities at the end of that same week, spirits became heated once again. This meeting on Friday, March 1, began with the reading of a letter from Cicognani, who wanted the commission to end the present discussion. The end of the letter, which Ottaviani failed to pass on, said that if no agreement seemed possible, a meeting of the presidents would be necessary. It was at Léger's demand that this ending was at last read to the commission. After some procedural back and forth, a formula of Léger, which eliminated the *latius patet*,[52] was proposed for a vote by Bea; the result was thirty in favor to seven against.[53] Some chroniclers have claimed that this vote on March 1 was of historic importance, especially for ecumenical dialogue.[54]

But it was a forceful yet self-controlled and nuanced intervention by the very moderate Cardinal Lefebvre that was the great event of the day:

> Although I am not very expert on the very difficult questions that we must deal with here, I nonetheless make bold to raise my voice and express what many of us feel about the difficulties we have encountered at our meeting.
>
> Many are indeed saddened at how difficult mutual understanding is made by the fact that the opinions expressed are strongly opposed to one another. The deeper search for truth, which usually requires charity and effort on both sides, is seriously endangered when some want to impose their views, while others prefer to maintain their own opinions.
>
> It seems to me that there is no cure for our difficulties except to start from the conviction that each of us, whatever his rank, and solely because his consecration makes him part of the teaching Church, has the right and even the duty to give his opinion freely and cast his vote freely.
>
> On the other hand, all of us ought to be ready to accept fully and joyously the decision of the Sovereign Pontiff, whatever it may be. That is no doubt the desire of all of us, since our faith causes us to recognize in the person of the pope the Vicar of Christ.
>
> I would like to add that we feel admiration, respect, veneration, and, if I may say it, affection for the bishops who are the permanent assistants of the Holy Father in the Roman Congregations. Let me also, however, be allowed to ask them, respectfully, that they exercise in a more unassuming way the power to which they have inevitably (and quite understandably) become habituated, and that they set it aside at the Council in order to be

---

[52] "Sacred scripture and sacred tradition are related to each other in such a way that neither is external to the other." In the final version adopted by the mixed commission, the formula read: " . . . they [tradition and scriptures] are not alien, rather both are in close communication. . . . "

[53] Conversation with Father Naud at the Montreal Seminary, September 8, 1995.

[54] Feiner, "La contribution," 152.

bishops among their brothers in the episcopate, joining them, under the authority of the Sovereign Pontiff and with the help of the Holy Spirit, in the painstaking and fraternal search for the truth that frees and for the good of the Church. Let them deign not to impose their views in an authoritarian way but simply to express their opinions while leaving to the Holy Father alone the responsibility of making the final decision.

It is deplorable that during the first period of the Council many were deeply grieved — legitimately or not, I do not know — by the fact that the text of the schema was presented in the name of the Sovereign Pontiff as though it were being imposed on them, when, quite obviously, the Holy Father's intention was that it be offered for free discussion by all the fathers. It is from that action, unfortunately, that many difficulties and sometimes distressing words have flowed.

For these reasons, which I have perhaps stated too boldly, I ask the indulgence and good will of all of you. I have spoken simply and freely without any intention of offending anyone. My desire was solely to find a way that would allow us to do our work in tranquillity and fraternal charity. "Where charity and love are found, God is present."[55]

This address made a very deep impression on almost all the members of the commission.

The ninth and last meeting of the mixed commission on revelation was held on March 4. The discussion focused mainly on the *sensus fidelium*, mentioned in the sixth paragraph. Discussing scripture, tradition, and the magisterium, the paragraph said at the end: "These three together cooperate for the salvation of humanity, and the submissive assent of the faithful also contributes to this." But, when shortly afterward Liénart gave his report on the work of the mixed commission, he had to point out that the text presented to the Coordinating Commission had been manipulated: the second clause in that sentence had been erased. Liénart made an effort to restore the authentic version of the mixed commission.[56]

Apart from this minor oral remark, Liénart's written report had to do mainly with his evaluation of the text as revised by the mixed commission. This evaluation was in fact much more positive than that of theologians

[55] Translated from Lefebvre's Latin text, previously unpublished, found in the Léger Archive, no. 801, in the Grand Séminaire of Montreal.

[56] When Congar attended a conciliar commission for the first time, it was the March 4 meeting of the mixed commission on revelation. He spoke in favor of a degree of active contribution of the faithful in the passing on of the faith, and he proposed the introduction of the phrase "agreement of pastors and faithful" (*conspiratio pastorum et fidelium*). Ottaviani saw to the rejection of this proposal because in his view it was not relevant (see *JCongar*, 224). But the final text of *Dei verbum* (no. 10) contains the formulation the French theologian had proposed two and a half years earlier.

regarded as experts in the matter. In his report of March 27, 1963, the Bishop of Lille thought that the disputed question of the relations between tradition written down in the holy books and oral tradition had been settled: "After lengthy discussions the mixed commission has approved a text for chapter I of the schema that is in agreement with the thought of earlier councils. I propose, therefore, that our commission declare the work of the mixed commission to be praiseworthy and approve the schema of a constitution on divine revelation in its present form."[57] We shall soon see that some spokesmen for the majority did not share the optimism of Liénart's report. Subsequent events would prove him wrong and them right.[58]

It has been said that the wishes of the Secretariat for Christian Unity had been fulfilled inasmuch as the term "two sources" had been abandoned, the idea of the "material sufficiency" of the scriptures had not been condemned, and the exact relationship between scripture and tradition was left to the free investigation of theologians. But the representatives of the majority trend were anything but enthusiastic; and the conciliar experts in this area said they were discouraged by so distressingly impoverished a theological compromise. And, in fact, the real stakes in the Council, as expressed during the discussion of November 1962, required a broadening of the debate, something for which the mixed commission turned out to be, in the final analysis, incapable. As Fr. G. Dejaifve wrote in 1963:

> The point is not to distort the position of the problem but rather *to enlarge the data of the problem*, for *from the ecumenical perspective in which the conciliar discussion is being carried on*, this is the real issue: behind the term "sacred scripture" the Reformation focused on the word of God, and it is the primacy and sufficiency of this word that is being defended both by the Reformation and by the ecumenical theologians who are trying to show that in the Catholic Church the authority of the scripture is total and its witness normative.[59]

The majority at Vatican II wanted to get away from an outdated anti-Protestantism. The vote on November 20, 1962, had expressed the Council's solidarity with the biblical renewal and the liturgical movement, with a return to the sources that would bring with it a re-centering on the Christian mystery.[60]

---

[57] *AS* V/1, 445.

[58] See Feiner, "La Constitution," 152.

[59] G. Dejaifve, "Révélation et Église," *Nouvelle revue théologique* 85 (1963), 563. Italics added.

[60] On this subject see Father Congar's report "La question débattue du rapport entre Écriture et Tradition," *DO-C*, no. 150, dated June 12, 1964.

In these circumstances no one was surprised that the schema on reve-lation, as revised by the mixed commission, was not put on the agenda for the second period of Vatican II. For another schema, composed from scratch, to surface in 1964, it would be necessary to wait for the exhor-tations of Paul VI on the subject in his address at the end of the second period, the efforts of a new working group, and the involvement of the Doctrinal Commission.

The failure in March 1963 also had an institutional aspect we cannot pass over in silence. In the spring of 1963 the Doctrinal Commission on faith and morals had not sufficiently freed itself from the heavy-handed supervision of the Holy Office to make progress, and this was one case on which the opponents of the second preparation were not disposed to bend! The institutional climate of the Council would gradually change during the second period: through the appointment of four moderators the very harsh debate on the Holy Office at the beginning of November 1963, and, above all, the further elections that at the end of the second period would alter the balance of power within the Doctrinal Commis-sion. *Tantae molis erat.* . . .

2. *The Draft of a Text on the Church*

While during the first period of a Council that was still feeling its way, the set of themes having to do with revelation had unexpectedly become the main issue around which two currents of opinion crystal-lized, the schema on the Church had drawn the attention of the theolog-ical schools ever since the Council was announced in 1959.

The discussion on the relationship between scripture and tradition raised problems of faith with a direct bearing on the very way of doing theology and on the overall way of presenting the message; and for this reason the Constitution *Dei Verbum* was regarded in the end as the most fundamental of the sixteen texts produced by Vatican II. The issue was quite different for the projected constitution on the Church. Starting as it did from doctrinal foundations anchored in the dogma of the Trinity, the revised draft on the Church sketched the main lines along which the ecclesial community should be organized and from them deduced its main structures.

While the ecclesiological problem was, in a way, secondary by com-parison to the central questions of the Christian faith, still it caused the greatest agitation at Vatican II. This phenomenon can be explained. Once a Church assembly begins to discuss the renewal of its own structures, it touches on the exercise of power within it, and the tension that is inevitable between those who hold the levers of authority in their hands and those who would like to be in that position, makes compromise especially difficult.

It may be said, then, that the revised and radically renewed version of the schema on the Church became the basic document of the 1962-63 intersession, along with, of course, related schemas such as those on ecumenism, on bishops, and on the lay apostolate. The renewed version of the schema on the Church would continue to dominate the second period of the Council in the autumn of 1963.

a. The First Phase (February-March 1963)

1) *Starting Points*

To avoid anachronism we must beware of thinking that the primary concern of the promoters of *aggiornamento* was to draw up a complete treatise on the Church. Back in September 1925 Father Lambert Beauduin, a precursor of genius, during a lecture in Brussels, had reminded his listeners that the work of the Vatican Council of 1869-70 had not been completed: "Let us not forget that it was only suspended, and let us pray that it will soon take up its work again and provide us with a 'second dogmatic constitution,' this one on the powers of the teaching Church and of bishops." At that time Dom Lambert believed that in order to do away with the ambiguities of the undue emphasis on papal infallibility, "it would be enough . . . to take the schema provided by the theologians" in order to recover "the harmonious proportions and wise counterweights which a one-sided exposé can cause to be lost from sight."[61]

It was to this task that the best-informed bishops and theologians devoted themselves from the moment Vatican II was announced. In the view of the "avant garde," the real starting point was a concern to provide a complement to the First Vatican Council, which because it had suddenly to be interrupted, had left its work unfinished and therefore unbalanced. In addition to the promulgated texts on pontifical primacy and infallibility, that Council had in its program other drafts on the proper role of the episcopate, but circumstances did not allow it to finish its agenda. In well-informed circles, then, the first concern, when a

---

[61] L. Beauduin, in *La Revue Catholique des idées et des faits* (Brussels) (October 23, 1925), 10-13; and in *Église et Unité* (Lille, 1948), 23-29.

council was announced in 1959, was to seize the opportunity to set out a fuller theology of the episcopate and so to complete a conciliar task that had lain untouched since 1870.

One of the first men alerted was the Flemish theologian Schillebeeckx, who had just been appointed lecturer at the University of Nijmegen (Holland). Barely fifteen days after the announcement of the Council, he published two insightful articles on the significance of the announcement.[62] The young theologian outlined the main issues that would concern the coming council: relations between pope and bishops, the meaning of episcopal collegiality, the importance of the laity in the Church's life, and, finally, the urgent need to complement Vatican I by freeing "pontifical infallibility" from the doctrinal isolation in which the interruption of the 1870 Council had left it.

A pastoral letter signed by all the bishops of Holland and published at Christmas 1960 developed the same set of themes. To the great surprise of its signatories, this declaration, intended only for Dutch Catholics, was translated into numerous foreign languages and had wide international circulation.[63] This concern of many bishops and theologians for a restoration of the theology of the episcopate was the background for the preparatory phase of Vatican II and for the first months of the actual assembly.

When at the beginning of the Council certain alternate schemas began to appear, their starting-point was often a desire for a better definition of the functions of the bishop and of the episcopal college; and some authors even limited their texts to considerations on the episcopate.[64] But to gain favor and carry authority, alternate schemas would have to offer a complete set of ecclesiological themes. Any that were limited to a single aspect of ecclesial communion, would have had a very weak strategic position, all the weaker, indeed, since the official schema on the Church from the preparatory Theological Commission had eleven chapters, a fact which seemed to give it great weight.

---

[62] E. Schillebeeckx, "De genade van een algemeen concilie," *De Bazuin*, February 7 and February 21, 1959.

[63] See my study, "Une restauration de la théologie de l'épiscopat. Contribution de Cardinal Alfrink à la préparation de Vatican II," in *Glaube im Prozess. Christsein nach dem II. Vatikanum. Für Karl Rahner*, ed. E. Klinger and K. Wittstadt (Freiburg — Basel — Vienna, 1984), 804-6.

[64] See in particular the text of Bishop Ghattas (Egypt), which at that time was considered to be a schema, and the text from Cardinal Feltin and his colleagues of the Paris Region; both of them, presented in February 1963, dealt only with the episcopal college (see S. Tromp, *Relatio de observationibus factis a patribus concilii* [July 26, 1963], 5).

In short, the various substitute texts that were the objects of meetings held at the end of 1962 and the beginning of 1963 in Rome, Germany, France, Spain, Chile, and elsewhere endeavored to offer a more or less complete and balanced ecclesiology. Yet the impression persisted that for these drafts the real point of departure, in many instances, was not their first and more general chapter but the chapter on the role of the episcopate. To "fill out" the chapter on the episcopate, the theological motif of the laity presented itself quite naturally as another point at which to anchor a renewed ecclesiology. The role of the lay apostolate, which had been on the agendas of the Catholic Church ever since the success of Catholic Action (1925-35), had been a subject of work by some well-known writers, such as Émile Mersch, Karl Rahner, Yves Congar, Gustave Thils, Gérard Philips, and many others. Some of them were present at the Council as official experts and felt quite at home in this particular area to which no past council had ever given its attention.

These substitute schemas on the Church were already being prepared before the official schema on the subject was finally officially distributed on November 23, 1962. In fact, however, it had already become well known and had been quietly circulated by some cardinals of the Central Preparatory Commission, and especially by the efforts of Suenens, Bea, and perhaps Alfrink.[65]

The official schema on the Church, written by the Theological Commission, was discussed at the Council only during the very last week of the first period, at the beginning of December 1962. The disappointment of the majority current was great, and the belated discussion was extremely critical of a text whose authors were increasingly on the defensive.[66]

Despite this, the official schema on the Church remained for some time the obligatory point of reference. But if at the first meeting of the CC at the end of January the members still felt obliged to pay it lip-service, things had already changed by the time the same Commission met at the end of March. At the first meeting of the CC, Suenens, who was the reporter on the subject, drew up a comparative list of the material in the preparatory schema, still viewed as the reference text, and the con-

---

[65] From a detailed analysis of the texts J. A. Komonchak has concluded that Philips used an earlier version of the preparatory schema on the Church and not the one later distributed to the fathers (see his article, "The Initial Debate about the Church," in *Vatican II commence*, 347 and 351 n.56).

[66] See Ottaviani's introductory address with its grating humor, December 1, 1962 (*AS* I/4, 1f.).

tents of an alternate schema. The comparison allowed Suenens to show that the material in the second part of the preparatory schema could well find a place elsewhere and was by no means "lost;" he could thus justify the new structure of a rewritten schema on the Church.[67]

As we have seen, the main task of the CC was to see to it that the wishes expressed by the Council during its first period were respected and that the conciliar commissions set to work according to the directives they had received on the preparation for the second period. Because the conciliar debate on the Church in December 1962 ended without any vote or resolution, it was up to the CC to make up for this lack and draw upon the discussion at the Council in undertaking the second preparation. The official resolutions of the CC at the January meeting give interesting guidelines for the schema on the Church and these in particular: the schema in question was to be revised in order to show clearly the close connection between Vatican I and Vatican II; after recalling what Vatican I had promulgated on pontifical primacy, this teaching was to be set in a pastoral and ecumenical framework. It would therefore be necessary to explain in a more detailed way the bond connecting the head of the Church and the apostolic college in order to forestall the danger of misunderstandings among the Protestants and the Orthodox. This doctrine would make it possible to establish the proper role of episcopal conferences. The meaning of the episcopate as such would help produce a balanced teaching on the Church. Finally, it would be necessary to clarify the relationship with the ministry of priests and to explain the place of the laity in the Church.[68]

We should not imagine, however, that these resolutions of the CC were carried without difficulties. In fact, they were preceded by impassioned discussions on the part of the defenders of Roman centralization, who did not wait for a real exchange of views but declaimed against the risks of confusion and against the perilous consequences that a dangerous "episcopalism" might have.[69]

---

[67] According to Suenens's report, the new chapter 2 would correspond to the old III and IV, together with parts of the old VII and VIII; the new chapter III would correspond to the old VI and some parts of the old VII and VIII; the new chapter IV would match the old V; as for the old chapters IX-XI, some parts would be used elsewhere (especially in the schema on ecumenism), and other parts would be salvaged in various ways (see AS V/1, 95). Tables comparing the Philips schema with the preparatory schema on the Church are in A. Acerbi, *Due ecclesiologie. Ecclesiologia giuridica ed ecclesiologia di communione nella "Lumen Gentium"* (Bologna, 1975), and U. Betti, *La dottrina del episcopato nel Vaticano II* (Rome, 1968).

[68] For more details see AS V/1, 185-86.

[69] See the minutes of the CC, in which a feeble echo may be heard of this debate behind closed doors (AS V/1, 99-100).

It was these directives of the CC that the Doctrinal Commission
would now have to deal with, a Commission that was still, and would
long be, under the sway of the major backers of the preparatory schema
on the Church. The atmosphere would remain tense until May 1963. At
its plenary session on February 21, 1963, the Doctrinal Commission met
for the first time in two and a half months. Many ticklish subjects were
on its agenda. On the occasion of the "re-openings" of February 21 and
March 5, Tromp was called upon to take stock of past events; in nostalgic tones this reporter deplored the developments of the first conciliar
period without even mentioning the rejection of the preparatory commission's work by the vote taken on November 20, 1962. He fulminated
against the alternate German schema on the Church, which had been distributed the previous November, and he expressed pessimism about the
future.[70]

After beginning by appointing a special subcommission of seven
members for the schema on the Church, the plenary meeting on February 21, 1963, was completely devoted to the schema on revelation and to
preparations for the mixed commission on the subject, which was to
meet in the ensuing days. Only after this work on the schema on revelation did the full Commission turn to the schema on the Church (March
5). Meanwhile, the subcommission on the Church played a decisive role
by preparing the ground for a revision of the schema. This subcommission had seven members: Browne, appointed chair by Ottaviani (with
Gagnebet as his expert), Léger (Naud, then Lafortune), König (K. Rahner), Parente (Balić, then Schauf), Charue (Philips), Garrone (Daniélou,
then Congar), and Schröffer (Thils, then Moeller). The miraculous thing
about this subcommission of "the Seven" and the teams of experts that
assisted them was its unexpected composition, which gave five votes to
the reformers and two to the conservatives (Browne and Parente). The
make-up of the commission was unexpected because it reversed the ratio
of forces within the full Commission, where the conciliar minority was
large enough (one third plus one) to block the plans of the majority.

At its first working meeting on Tuesday, February 26, 1963, the
Seven heard Cicognani express his wish, "Let nothing new be done,"

---

[70] Although Tromp's semi-official report mentions only some procedural points, we
know from the recollections of a close collaborator of Léger that when the Secretary of
the Doctrinal Commission was asked to report on what had happened, he deplored at
length the dismissal of the work of the preparatory phase and was carefully discreet about
the marginalization at the Council itself of the preparatory schema on the "two sources"
(conversation with Father André Naud, September 8, 1994, in Montreal).

which meant that the Commission should not undertake to draft a new schema; it was, however, authorized to rearrange the most worthwhile parts of the preparatory text.[71] Despite the authority of Cicognani, this imperative but ambiguous wish was given the broadest possible interpretation by the Seven. The latter discussed the choice to be made among the five alternative schemas they had before them: the Parente schema, a French schema, the famous schema in German, the Philips schema, and a very lengthy text from Chile. Most of these were texts recently composed; the Philips schema was the only one to have circulated rather widely during the first period of the Council.

The question has been asked whether the so-called Belgian team had tried, since the fall of 1962, to have the Philips schema (an alternative text) introduced into the official agenda of the Council during its first period. Evidence on the subject differs greatly. Philips himself believed that his draft had been offered to the Council of Presidents at the end of the session. Msgr. Heuschen hoped, but in vain, that Philips's "working paper" could be taken into account and voted on before the end of the 1962 session. On the other hand, Moeller was convinced that Philips's draft of November 1962 had been rejected by the authorities in charge of the Council.[72] Congar's testimony is conclusive: when he questioned Suenens on this subject, he learned that the Cardinal intended to introduce the Philips schema into the Council by way of the Secretariat for Extraordinary Affairs. Thanks to the study of Joseph A. Komonchak, we know that Suenens's request was made and that it was rejected at Felici's entreaty.[73]

What, then, were the main characteristics of these texts that were on the agenda of the Seven? When the discussion began, the camp repre-

[71] "That nothing new be done, but that the best material contained in the Constitution on the Church be organized differently, shortened . . . " (Tromp, *Relatio Secretarii Commissionis*, February 21 — March 13, 1963, III, 13).

[72] Jan Grootaers, *Diarium*, Cahier 5, for Philips (January 24, 1963); ibid., for Heuschen (January 11, 1963); ibid., Cahier 7, for Moeller (May 1, 1963). The last-named, due to a slip that further complicates the question, spoke of the "Coordinating Commission," although this did not yet exist in November 1962.

[73] *JCongar*, 122. This, then, was Suenens's intention at the beginning of November, but the minutes of the Secretariat for Extraordinary Affairs at that time contain no trace of such a step or of a possible refusal. But Komonchak was able to consult the journal kept by Henri Denis, who tells of a conversation between Villot and Felici from which it emerges that Suenens did in fact make attempts to have the revised schema on the Church put on the agenda of the Council after the close of the debate on the liturgy. His proposal was rejected by the Secretariat for Extraordinary Affairs, in which Felici argued that such a step was impossible since the official schema on the Church had not yet been printed (see Komonchak, "The Initial Debate about the Church," 336).

senting the conciliar majority was not homogeneous. Thus Léger, under the influence of his personal adviser Father Lafortune, seems initially to have preferred the French schema; later he joined the majority group.[74] The five members in favor of renewal quickly rallied to the Philips schema because of its conciliatory character and international origin. As a result, a majority of five very quickly decided in favor of the Belgian text, while the two representatives of the minority chose Parente's text. It was then agreed to consider the Philips schema as a base text, but without excluding contributions from Parente's schema and possibly from other sources.[75] This decision was quite different from the Secretary of State's instruction: "Let nothing new be done"!

On that same February 26, the seven experts were already meeting for a first working session during which the participants chose Philips to direct the work. That work began immediately and proceeded very rapidly, so much so that a week later, on March 5, the full Doctrinal Commission was already studying a revised text of chapters I and II.[76] If Ottaviani and his close collaborators were using every means to slow down the work of the Commission in the hope that the revision would not be finished by September, the bishops of the majority were speeding things up in order to finish the schemas and send them to the Council fathers in due time. We should not forget that John XXIII himself, aware

[74] A working note that Moeller composed at the last minute for Léger's use seems to have tipped the balance in favor of the Philips schema. Among the arguments invoked for this move, Moeller referred to the fact that the Philips text was in a way the source of the French, German, and Italian texts; its starting point was the Trinitarian aspect of the Church and it was thus ecumenical, and it brought out fully the ministerial aspect of the hierarchy, as the CC had requested (CCV, Philips Archive, P.019, 11).

[75] Since some have challenged this important resolution it is worth reproducing here the document reporting the vote of the Seven: "Commission of the Seven. 26/02/63. The work which the experts are to undertake according to the mandate received from the Theological Commission: (1) They are to draft a new schema; (2) In drafting a new schema they are to look: a) first, to the schema of Msgr. Philips, which is to be the basis of their work; b) second, they are immediately to have recourse to what is contained in the schema of His Excellency Parente; c) they are also to take from other schemas whatever appears useful. (3) If the experts are not in agreement, let them note down the parts on which they differ, along with a statement of the various opinions" (CCV, Philips Archive, P.021.28).

[76] These quick decisions and rapid work can only be explained in light of the preparation that preceded the meeting of March 26. Without here going into the many contacts Suenens and Msgr. Charue had been making since January, we must at least note that the five open-minded bishops on the subcommission of the Seven had a preliminary meeting on the eve of the official meeting. As for the experts, on Monday, February 25, they had already met at the Belgian College to study the Philips schema, which at that point had not yet been officially chosen as the base text. It was at that meeting that they learned by telephone of the official appointment of a subcommission on the Church.

of his illness, constantly hounded the authorities of the Council to have the new schemas sent by Easter at the latest. Despite Felici's promise to the Pope that the schemas would be sent in April, some texts would not go off until May, only a few days before the Pope's death.

2) *The Range of Available Texts*

After the Council it was generally thought that when the Doctrinal Commission met in February 1963, it found seven substitute schemas on its working table — as many drafts on the agenda as there were members on the new subcommission on the Church! This "sacred" number soon became part of the "oral tradition" of Vatican II. Today, as we look back from a distance and have gained access to many archives, things look rather different.

In Tromp's report (devoted to the observations of the bishops and ending with July 26, 1963) we find a list of ten alternative texts, of which seven were complete and three partial. Father U. Betti's chronological history notes that among the proposals of the bishops "there are, above all, about fifteen schemas new in substance or in form."[77]

In this wide range of texts, nine schemas were given special attention. A first series of five drafts was presented to the Doctrinal Commission on March 26:

1. Parente, close collaborator of Ottaviani (eighteen pages).

2. Schröffer (thirty-two pages), a schema in German, prepared at the end of January 1963 by a group of German theologians and discussed in Munich at the beginning of February by a conference of German-speaking bishops; the text reached Rome several days too late to be in circulation at the moment when the CC held its first meeting at the end of January.

3. D. de Cambourg, a French schema with five chapters, drawn up by some well-known French theologians from whom the French bishops had asked for observations on the official draft.

4. Silva Henriquez and McGrath, a schema from Chile, with twelve chapters in eighty-nine pages; the length of the text was a drawback for this undertaking by Latin American theologians.

5. Philips (thirty-six sections), the first in time, the draft having been prepared as early as October 18, 1962, radically revised on November

---

[77] U. Betti, "Histoire chronologique de la Constitution," in *L'Église de Vatican II*, ed. G. Barauna (Unam Sanctam 51b; Paris, 1966), 13. In addition to the ten cited, Tromp also lists six other proposals for rearranging the material on the Church.

25, and completed on January 12, 1963; this so-called Belgian schema was in fact composed by an international working committee, although the initiative came from the Belgian episcopate.[78]

A second series of alternative texts comprised four schemas that were less developed or else came in later:

6. Elchinger (twelve pages), a schema in French that included a prologue and five chapters (it reached the Doctrinal Commission in mid-March 1963).

7. Barbado (eighteen pages), a schema in Spanish, composed by consultors to the Spanish bishops under the leadership of Sauras, a Dominican; the text had nine chapters.

8. Ghattas, a schema containing a single chapter (three closely written pages), devoted to the college of bishops, the primacy, and bishops.

9. Feltin and the bishops of the Paris Region (five pages), dealing only with episcopal collegiality.

The content of the various lists of new drafts derived from the criteria chosen for a "schema." Despite some great differences, the five schemas of the first series had some common characteristics that reflected the circumstances of the moment. Most of them were careful not to ignore completely either the structure or some concerns of the official preparatory schema on the Church. These texts were also characterized by borrowings from all sides: the French schema contained extensive extracts from the Philips schema (as a result, in particular, of an exchange of letters between Daniélou and Philips); the Philips text, whose author took part in the German-speaking meetings in Rome and in Germany, borrowed from the German schema, which in turn at times was inspired by Philips's text; the Parente schema showed similarities with the Philips text. All focused on some watershed issues: the question of the episcopate and its collegial character, the situation of the laity in the Church, the meaning of the "states of perfection." All were concerned, to one or another degree, to renew the overall image of the

---

[78] The genesis of the Philips schema is not easily summarized: I. In mid-October 1962 the Louvain professor worked with an international group of experts in Rome which comprised, among others, Congar, Rahner, C. Colombo, Semmelroth, McGrath, perhaps Ratzinger, probably Lécuyer, and, of course, Philips (with advice from Cerfaux and Onclin). This text was in Latin. II. A second version, this time in French and in a diffuse style, was sent to a broader group of theologians with a view to a meeting at the Belgian College on November 26, 1962; a supplement was composed by a smaller team at Louvain on January 12, 1963, for the CC, which met for the first time at the end of that same month. III. A synthesis of these texts, which from February 26 on served as a base text for the subcommission on the Church and, from March 5 on, as a revised schema for the full Doctrinal Commission.

Church (*Kirchenbild*) through a return to the biblical, liturgical, and patristic sources of the Christian faith.[79]

The question remains why the subcommission on the Church so quickly chose the Philips schema. To explain this choice we must go back to the situation and atmosphere in the spring and summer of 1963, both of which would be radically altered from October-November on. In February-March 1963 the controlling factor was a keen sense that things were at a dangerous impasse: in circles of the recently formed "majority" people were torn between the hope of overcoming the difficult obstacles that confronted them and the fear of utter failure. The principal asset of the Philips text was not primarily that it took the preparatory schema into account, since others in the series of five texts offered had done the same, but that it had sought a *via media*, involving some compromises, between the old schema and the calls for a new approach. In addition to his vast knowledge of modern theology and his personal experience of the Roman milieu, Philips felt called to be a reconciler.[80] He often felt inclined to take on the task of interpreter, translating into language accessible to bishops of every tendency the established results of the contemporary renewal movements. While these had inspired the majority-current at the Council during its first period, many authorities in Rome did not know even the ABCs of these movements. This labor of translation also involved the art of using expressions that toned down "without altering content."[81]

Given the very tight calendar of the proceedings, it was another advantage of the so-called Belgian schema that it had a head start. This was the result of a general strategy that since October 1962 had constantly taken account of the delays imposed by events. The core of the minority group was still convinced that the dispersal of forces and ideas among the majority members would prevent the latter from rallying in due time around a single alternative text; the minority expected a failure that would compel the "progressives" to return to the schemas of the preparatory phase as the only solid basis on which to save the Council

[79] Descriptions, sometimes detailed, of the reciprocal borrowings between the proposed texts may be found in the following authors: U. Betti, *La dottrina sull'episcopato del Concilio Vaticano II* (Rome, 1984), 76-80 and 85-91; H. Schauf, "Das Leitungsamt der Bischöfe," *Annuarium Historiae Conciliorum* (1975), 76, 80, 93; A. Acerbi, *Duo ecclesiologie*, 183-84. According to Betti, the three schemas that were considered (Philips, Parente, and the German text) took into account the preparatory schema and the other texts (*La dottrina*, 71).

[80] *ICI*, interview of May-June 1962.

[81] Schauf, "Das Leitungsamt," 78.

from chaos. It was therefore a matter of great urgency for the majority members to agree on a single substitute text; they had to "concentrate" in order to counter the preparatory schema.[82]

By its reasonable tone and very clear content, the Philips schema was able in these moments of dangerous crisis to serve as a rallying point for an unconfident majority. Its very existence refuted the negativism of the minority, whose leaders had taken the initiative during the preparatory phase and were not at all ready to surrender their position of prominence, even if it meant a policy of despair. Furthermore, in these circumstances the choice of the Philips schema seemed better suited to win the support of a great many votes than was the maximalism of some radical currents that argued for a complete replacement of the old schema with entirely new texts with no relation to the schemas of the preparatory period.

In this setting the work first of the seven experts and then of the seven bishops was able to begin without any loss of time and even to finish in record time (four working days according to the chronology of Tromp[83]), to the great surprise of the full Commission, which was able to meet as early as March 5 to discuss the rewritten chapters I and II.

The subcommission was quite aware that the president of the Doctrinal Commission would not agree to have a discussion based on another text than his own preparatory schema without a final attack — and indeed Ottaviani made a gallant last stand. The entire first part of the meeting on Tuesday, March 5, was taken up by an attack of the president and secretary of the Doctrinal Commission on the work done by the subcommission of the seven, who, according to them, had gone beyond the limits of its mandate and rights when it took a new text as the basis of its discussion. Resistance to the storm required the very sharp reactions of Browne, who had to remind the attackers that the mandate given to the subcommission included the possibility of a new schema, and the protests of Charue and other bishops.

A second attack was aimed at belittling the schema revised under Philips's direction, which was criticized as dangerous, pompous, and

---

[82] In a letter dated January 29, 1963, and therefore before the meetings at the end of February, J. Daniélou wrote to G. Philips: "Could we not get the German bishops to abandon this [German] draft and concentrate on yours? In any event, that will be the position of the French bishops" (CCV, Philips Archive, P 015.16).

[83] According to Tromp's *Relatio*, the meetings of the experts (with or without the bishops being present) took place on February 26 and 28 and March 2 and 5. According to the working notes of Philips, the experts continued to work on revising the chapters on the episcopate on March 8 and 9.

"relativistic." After these troubled preliminaries, of which the experts were mute witnesses, the full Commission was able at last to listen to the introduction by Philips, the reporter, and to begin its discussion of chapter I on the mystery of the Church.

There had been rather lively discussions among the experts, especially between Daniélou and Philips, about the theological starting point of the revised schema on the Church. It was finally agreed that the Philips version should start with the *Ecclesia de Trinitate*, "the Church as originating from the Trinity," and not with the spiritual aspects of the Church. The great concern of the Louvain theologian, who henceforth served as reporter, was to have his schema accepted as a base text, so that the discussion could make real progress. To the surprise of some members of the Commission, he succeeded by showing himself open and receptive to suggested changes while at the same time emphasizing the need to respect the majority current at the Council.

The theme of the Mystical Body gave rise to sharp tensions (Philips and Congar were criticized for playing down its organizational aspects), whereas the question of belonging to the Church no longer caused the same difficulties as in the past. For some, the idea of the Church as a "sacrament" was an unheard of and unacceptable innovation.

The foundation of the second chapter (on the hierarchical Church) was the idea of episcopal collegiality. This idea initially gave rise to very strong tensions; Moeller would later speak of a "terrible fight." But the storm subsided more rapidly than expected.[84] Ottaviani himself soon seemed impressed by the style of the ongoing discussion, and in the end he resigned himself to a text other than his own occupying the foreground.

The discussion of chapter II, however, still had to face major difficulties: (1) the idea of the Twelve as foundation of the Church, since "by right" Peter alone is the rock on which the Church is built; (2) the idea of the college of scattered bishops (outside a council) as supreme authority was a problem for some; and (3) finally, the need to explain the concept of papal infallibility according to Vatican I's formula, *ex sese et non ex consensu Ecclesiae*, caused the reporter to be accused of Modernist tendencies. The connection between a priest and his bishop would require explanation, and the question of married permanent deacons had to be shelved for the time being.

---

[84] The relaxed atmosphere that began to be felt around some very controverted ideas was attributed by Philips himself (in his notes on the meeting) to his own calmness, his constant concern not to have "either victors or vanquished," his facility in improvising in Latin, and also to a skill in debate that a lengthy parliamentary life had taught him.

On Wednesday, March 13, the first two chapters of the new schema were reviewed and duly amended.

3) *The Coordinating Commission*

This first part of the text had to be submitted immediately at the CC's meeting at the end of March so that it could be approved and sent to the bishops. The result of these deliberations, which marked a turning point in the history of the schema on the Church, was the subject of a report that Suenens gave at the second meeting of the CC, on March 28. He urged the acceptance of the two chapters of the new schema on the Church: "The new text avoids questions controverted among the theologians; it expounds authentic doctrine in an irenic, coherent, and balanced way."[85] Suenens's recommendation was well received by the Commission.

He concluded with some brief recommendations about the next chapters on the laity (chapter III) and the states of perfection (chapter IV). The latter would have to be placed in a larger perspective than that of the preparatory schema, namely, the call to holiness of *all* Christians. In the exchange of views that followed, Tromp said again that it would be desirable to distinguish, with regard to the laity and to religious, between dogma and discipline, in such a way as to make it clear that in these two chapters the schema on the Church would deal only with the dogmatic aspects. The remark was approved by the reporter and the CC. The difficulties that Tromp pointed out here were to resurface every time it was necessary to divide this material between the chapters on the laity and on religious in the schema on the Church and the separate decrees on the lay apostolate and the renewal of religious life.[86] Ottaviani insisted once

---

[85] *AS* V/1, 463; but the reporter criticized the fact that chapter II refers to the Supreme Pontiff as many as twenty-four times, even though the subject was the episcopal college.

[86] The appointment of mixed commissions to deal with these two borderline cases (something the CC had asked for in January 1963) was not enough to overcome tensions and conflicts over competencies. The Commission for the Lay Apostolate often felt that some of the best contributions to its draft decree had had to be handed over to the Doctrinal Commission for the chapter on the laity, where they sometimes simply disappeared. Glorieux, a very important witness and participant, would later write, not without some bitterness: "No document of Vatican II is expressly devoted to the family. On many occasions, lay people brought in as consultants expressed a desire for such a document, and the chapter of Schema XIII on 'marriage and the family' gave them hope that their desire might be met; but marriage, and all its familiar problems, occupied the attention more and more. The Commission on the Apostolate of the Laity had prepared some good chapters on the family when the mixed commission and the Doctrinal Commission were working together on the chapter on the laity in *Lumen gentium*; they were given over for

again on the need to highlight the prerogatives of the pope as head of the Church who alone carries out the tasks of the vicar of Christ.

From this exchange of views in the CC it became clearer that Suenens had committed himself to supporting the development in process and that he wanted it to be completed in due time.[87]

b. The Second Phase (April-May 1963)

The Doctrinal Commission resumed its work on May 15. The agenda for this two-week session was overloaded and the work intense. It was undertaken in a setting very different from that of the work in March.

After the uncertainties and confusion of January-February 1963, the schema on the Church was given a new basis in March, and the commission had agreed to a different working method. In face of a conservative group that had lost none of its confidence, despite the way things had developed, the representatives of the majority felt that the impasse had been overcome and that they were now beginning to construct a new schema that corresponded more closely to the Council's expectations.

The principal themes of the schema on the Church that were on the agenda in May seemed less explosive than those of the first two chapters, but they were also less homogeneous. Not only were the laity and the religious also the subjects of other schemas composed and discussed in parallel commissions that wanted to be autonomous;[88] but this material had also been scattered among members of the CC, with Suenens responsible for the schema as a whole, Urbani for the lay apostolate, and Döpfner for the religious.

The greatest difference, however, between the discussions on the Church in March and in May was due to the very crowded calendar for the latter session. The urgent need to recast the six chapters of schema

---

inclusion in the latter Constitution, but they were never used there" (A. Glorieux, "Les étapes préliminaires de la Constitution pastoral *Gaudium et spes*," *Nouvelle revue théologique* 108 [1986], 388-403, at 398). The frustration of the Cento-Glorieux Commission was renewed when it had to surrender still other material to the group that was composing schema XVII.

[87] After the composition of the notes for chapters I and II, which took until April 18, this first part of the new schema on the Church was sent to the bishops of the entire world in consequence of an official decision of the Secretary of State. The decree was dated April 22, 1963, but it seems that it was actually sent in May.

[88] The reason for saying that these subjects *seemed* less explosive is that the "religious vocation" would give rise to strong tensions at this meeting and to memorable "explosions" in the future.

XVII before the beginning of the third meeting of the CC upset the agenda. It was difficult for the writers of the schema on the Church to get some scraps of the full Doctrinal Commission's time. The work of the subcommissions would attempt to resolve this problem of time to some degree.[89]

The small group of bishops and theologians who had in the past actively supported the Philips schema was sometimes called the Belgian squad, even though it also included eminent French, German, and sometimes Italian, Dutch, and other personages.[90] This little group took great care in preparing the texts of the schema on the Church that the Doctrinal Commission was to consider at its May meeting.

1) *Chapter III, on the "Laity"*

The revision of the chapter on the laity went through three quick stages: the decision of the full Commission to improve the proposed text; the undertaking of this work by a redactional subcommission; and finally the approval of the amended version by the full Commission.

In the Philips schema, the chapter on the laity was the only one that corresponded almost completely to the text of the preparatory schema on the Church, which, we should recall, had in large part been written by Philips.[91] (The Louvain professor belonged to the group of theologians who, well before the Council, had already been striving to develop a theology of the laity.) Chapter VI of the original schema had emerged from

---

[89] Schema XVII occupied both Commission and subcommission from May 16 to May 25; the chapter on the laity in the schema on the Church was allowed several full days (May 15, 16, and 25), and the chapter on religious had some time on the agenda on May 16, 27, and 28. The subcommission on the laity worked on May 17-18, the subcommission on religious on May 29, 30, and 31. As a result of the death of John XXIII on June 3, the CC had to postpone its meeting.

[90] The composition of this "team" varied according to the schemas in questions; among the non-Belgians can be named, first of all, Congar, who was a permanent member, then K. Rahner, C. Colombo, R. Tucci, J. Lécuyer, R. Laurentin, and others. The notes for the first two chapters of the schema on the Church, not available in Rome, were composed at Louvain in April 1963 by a working group made up of Philips, Thils, Moeller, and Cerfaux. (These were mainly liturgical, biblical, patristic, and conciliar references; see letter of Moeller to Léger, April 12, 1963, in the Léger Archive in Montreal, no. 48a.) Philips sent to Rome a new version of the chapter on the laity and consulted Congar on the subject. The Louvain "laboratory" worked to expand the perspectives of the chapter on religious so as to take as the starting point the common Christian call to holiness (see letter of Philips to Congar, April 26, 1963, Congar Archive in the Couvent St-Jacques in Paris).

[91] CCV, Philips Archive, P. 008.04 and following numbers.

a subcommission of the preparatory Theological Commission on which specialists such as Congar, Tromp, Philips, and Schauf had worked and confronted one another. These same experts found themselves together once again in May 1963 to recast the ecclesiology of the laity; this time, however, they were pressed for time and were working in a noticeably different setting.

At the beginning of the Doctrinal Commission's work, several plans for revising the chapter on the laity cluttered the work table; in particular, there was competition between a new plan of Schauf (dated March 7, 1963) and various amendments by Philips (dated March 20, 1963), the latter intended mainly to restore passages which Schauf's revision thought should be abandoned. The revised text that was to serve as the basis for discussion was the one Msgr. Florit presented in the name of the subcommission entrusted with this task.[92]

One of the thorniest issues in the discussion was once again how to lay hold of so fluid a concept as "lay person" and how to succeed in defining it. Neither canon law nor attempts to derive a theological concept satisfied the Commission, which had to be content with a pragmatic approach and a simple description.[93]

The revision begun in the full Commission was completed by Florit's subcommission, which gave Philips the task of drawing up the amended version. This last was the subject of a thorough discussion at a plenary meeting of a mixed commission on May 25, with Cento presiding.[94] The

[92] The subcommission over which Florit presided with the assistance of Betti included Spanedda and Franic and had been able to collaborate with Cento's Commission on the lay apostolate (see Tromp, *Relatio 15-31 maii 1963*, 12). It was at Léger's request that Philips was appointed henceforth secretary of this subcommission.

[93] The difficulty in handling the idea of "lay person" was even to cause controversy over the name of the competent Commission, of which Glorieux was the watchful secretary. The latter was very anxious to retain the title Commission for the Apostolate of the Laity, while some in Curial circles had tried to change the title and make of it Commission for the Apostolate of the Faithful. Twenty years later, Glorieux explained: "Let me point out that in the appendixes to his letter and in almost all the correspondence that follows Cardinal Cicognani gave our commission its proper title of 'Commission for the Apostolate of the Laity," whereas a year earlier, in the list of commissions, the word 'laity' was replaced by 'faithful,' without consulting the president and even without advising him or giving any explanation. At the same time, the Doctrinal Commission was preparing a chapter on the 'laity' in the constitution on the Church; as for our commission, it had reserved the word 'faithful' to designate any baptized person (layperson, priest, religious, bishop) and given the name 'layperson' to one who does not embrace the religious life and does not enter the clergy" (Glorieux, "Les étapes préliminaires," 389 n. 5).

[94] This revised commission brought together members of the Doctrinal Commission and of the Commission for the Lay Apostolate. The latter was represented, on this occa-

principal subjects discussed were, once again, the definition of a *lay person*, the Christian people's sense of the faith, the idea of the universal priesthood, the significance of the "profane" world, and the relations of the laity with the hierarchy.

2) *Chapter IV, on "Religious"*

The revision of the draft-chapter on religious followed a less peaceful course than the debate on the laity. A new version of the schema accompanied the letter of May 3, 1963 in which Ottaviani called the meeting. The revised version was itself the product of a mixed subcommission of the Commissions on Doctrine and on Religious, which worked on it on March 6 and 7. The draft was now entitled "On Those Who Profess the Evangelical Counsels." The constant changing of the chapter's title illustrates the great difficulties encountered in its revision.

By comparing chapter V of the preparatory schema, "On States for the Acquisition of Evangelical Perfection," with chapter IV of the schema on the Church at the end of May 1963 entitled, "The Call to Holiness in the Church," one can easily measure the enormous distance traveled in a short time in an area that is at the heart of the Church: religious life.[95] The most dynamic current of thought at Vatican II had, from the beginning, sensed in the preparatory schema's chapter on religious a spirituality that sought to remain "above the struggle," not only the struggle of simple lay folk but also the struggle of diocesan priests. These critics were not inclined to accept the sense of superiority it felt in a text built on "states" of "perfection."[96] The thinking of the majority — which had already rejected a pyramidal Church and argued for collegiality and for a Church as people of God — would also reject a spiritual ideal that involved levels, with "religious" at the highest level of the pyramid. Advocates of renewal wanted not only to change the pro-

---

sion, by only a half-dozen bishops. In the absence of Florit (who was ill), Franić had the task of introducing the draft text in the name of the subcommission. The discussion of each number was introduced by Philips.

[95] The revision at the end of May 1963 was, obviously, not yet the final state of *Lumen Gentium*, but it did represent a historic development that seemed revolutionary. The sudden developments still to come, which produced the definitive text of chapters IV and V of the Constitution promulgated in 1964, did not really change that basic fact.

[96] Read, for example, the end of chapter V of the preparatory schema on the Church: "Thus the Sacred Synod exhorts each of those who are called to evangelical perfection to have the strength to follow unwaveringly in their actions what St. Paul says: 'Imitate me, brothers and sisters, and observe those who live according to the example you have in us' (Phil 3:17)."

posed text but also to open up new perspectives by placing the universal call to holiness in the foreground; from this call would then flow particular forms of holiness, all of them equally valid.[97] This, in my view, was what was at stake in the deliberations at the end of May. And, in fact, the CC had already opened the way for this revolution.[98]

The liveliest debates on this chapter's openness to new basic perspectives occupied the greater part of the Commission's meeting on May 27. The "improved" version of the chapter that was set before the commission was unable, however, to satisfy the majority. On the other hand, the mere change of title was unacceptable to the conservative wing.[99] But representatives of the majority — among them Charue, Garrone, and Huyghe — threatened to appeal to the conciliar assembly to win their case. The next day Charue invoked the formal support given to his position by the episcopates of Holland, Belgium, and Germany. Spokesman for the most advanced "episcopalist" positions, he refused to have religious considered under the "structures" of the Church, since the latter included bishops, clergy, and laity, while religious were a special class that cut across these three categories.[100]

---

[97] The universal call to holiness was brought into view as soon as the new text of May 1963 tackled the practice of the evangelical counsels: "For all and for each, then, whatever their state or order, whether they live in the world or in religion, there is only one Christian holiness. This begins with faith and baptism, and with the unmerited help and inspiration of God's grace grows and produces abundant fruit, as the history of the Church and the life of the saints make luminously clear. Therefore, let all Christians tend toward perfect love and develop the powers they have received according to the measure of Christ's gift, in order that by following in his steps they may devote themselves with their entire soul to the glory of God and the service of the neighbor" (Schema *De Ecclesia*, no. 29; a draft text given to the Council fathers and dated July 19, 1963, 18; also in *AS* II/1, 269).

[98] In Döpfner's report at the first meeting of the CC, he had asked that the revision of the text be entrusted to a mixed commission (Doctrine and Religious), which would lay down the doctrinal foundations of spirituality. At the conclusion of his report he asked that the title of the chapter be changed to "The State of Imitation of Christ through the Evangelical Counsels" (see *AS* V/1, 192-93). The title Suenens proposed at the May 27 meeting of the full Doctrinal Commission was more trenchant: "Holiness in the Church."

[99] When the supporters of the title "Holiness in the Church" invoked the authority of the CC, Tromp observed in his notes that this new title did not result from a decision of the CC as such but was only desired by some of its individual members. See Tromp, *Relatio 15-31 maii 1963*, 33, note 1. Suenens immediately sent a letter to the CC to defend the title.

[100] This precise point was to become the subject of one of the major disputes in 1963-64, with Charue and his supporters opposed to Daniélou and his followers. The division of the former "On Religious" into two chapters would be regarded by Daniélou as a victory, but the final text, which refused to recognize religious as part of the structures of the Church, would be taken by the other camp as a vindication of its views.

The always ticklish question of "exemption" was also on the agenda. With its patience exhausted, and in order to get out of the impasse, the CC resolved to establish a mixed subcommission (Doctrine: three bishops and two experts; Religious: three bishops and two experts) to complete the revision of the text. But time was running out, and the subcommission had to finish the revision posthaste. The contributions of Charue, McGrath, and Fernandez (Master General of the Dominicans) were central to its work.

The basis of the revision was a new draft, "The Call to Holiness in the Church," which came from Thils, who had published widely translated and circulated treatises on spirituality — in particular, on the spirituality of diocesan priests. This text was intended to be a first section of the schema, while the old schema would supply a second section dealing with institutes of evangelical perfection. Taking as its starting point the universal call to holiness, the new text described the manifold practice of this holiness, the means used, and the importance of this call for the life of the Church, the authority of which must be respected.

It is not easy to determine precisely why this little mixed commission did not have the makeup it was meant to have.[101] The Commission for Religious would later say that it had not been represented on this redactional committee, and during the second period of the Council it would successfully carry out a campaign against the revision made at the end of May 1963, which over 600 bishops judged unacceptable.

The text inspired by Charue and a limited group of collaborators probably represented an extreme version of a kind of "episcopalism" that did not take sufficiently into account the atmosphere in the conciliar assembly, in which the number of fathers belonging to religious orders was immense. The criticisms the majority had once leveled against the work of the preparatory commissions were now turned against some representatives of that same majority.

In any case, in July 1963 this text, revised on May 29, 30, and 31, was part of the second booklet of the schema on the Church that was approved by the CC and sent to the bishops with a view to their return in the fall.

---

[101] The collaboration of Fernández and other religious such as Häring and Gagnebet, the presence of Msgr. Šeper, and the approval of Browne all helped to create an atmosphere of consensus. It should be noted that Fernández and Šeper had been members of the preceding mixed commission (end of February, 1963) and ensured a degree of continuity. The influential Gagnebet devoted himself to winning the agreement of the Commission on Religious. On the other hand, Ottaviani once again disapproved of the procedure followed.

c. The Third Phase (July-September 1963)

The meeting of the CC planned for the first days of June could not be held until the beginning of July, because Vatican II was interrupted by the death of good Pope John and the conclave held in June. The third meeting of the CC took place on July 3-4, and, despite its brevity, was to have a major impact on the schema on the Church.

After asking and obtaining the approval of the CC for the two recently revised chapters on the laity and on religious, Suenens submitted to the Commission a radical change in the entire schema on the Church. He proposed not only to alter the division of the materials in chapter V on the laity but to change the entire arrangement of chapters. A new chapter II would take over the general material on the laity with the rest of the material remaining in a new chapter IV on the laity. The new division of the Constitution that Suenens proposed would thus be: (I) The Mystery of the Church; (II) The People of God in General; (III) The Hierarchical Constitution of the Church; (IV) The Laity in Particular; (V) The Call to Holiness in the Church.[102] The restructuring meant a fundamental reorientation of ecclesiology that would put an end to the pyramidal vision of the Church. It showed that bishops, laity, and religious were all part of the people of God, the description of which took precedence over the chapter on the episcopate.[103] The first two chapters laid the foundations for membership in the Church in a spiritual dimension in which all members are equal by reason of their baptism, prior to any differentiation by the functions described in the next two chapters.

It is obvious that the discussion of this new proposal by the CC could not have been an easy matter.[104] While it was not rejected, because it had not yet been passed by the Doctrinal Commission, it was left for the second period of the Council. It was also a fact, however, that as early as July Cicognani agreed to let the Council fathers know immediately of

---

[102] AS V/1, 594.

[103] As happened often at Vatican II, innovative ideas were "in the air;" thus the idea of such a division of the material was to be found in Germany, Holland, France, and Canada; the credit for having actually suggested it to Suenens at the moment when the latter was going to join the CC belongs to Msgr. A.´Prignon, Rector of the Belgian College in Rome and a very effective "liaison officer" during Vatican II.

[104] While Browne and Tromp were favorable to Suenens's proposal, Morcillo and Urbani expressed reservations, the latter's opinion being that the views of the Council fathers should be heard first (see AS V/1, 635). Later on, Paul VI showed himself to be quite reserved toward this new division of the chapters, but after an exchange of views he told Suenens that he was willing to leave "the question open for free discussion at the Council" (see Suenens, Souvenirs et espérances, 115).

the CC's decision to propose a new distribution of the chapters. The communication was made on the first page of the chapter on the laity that was revised in May 1993 and sent to the bishops for their comments on July 19, 1963. When the Council reopened in the fall, the Doctrinal Commission, some members of which felt they had been bypassed, would demand an examination in proper form of Suenens's proposal.

Meanwhile, those pushing for the new division of the material were not inactive. At the time when the Malines text, which had to do with the revision of schema XVII (see the next section), was being prepared, a nucleus of people working on the schema on the Church got together to prepare for the debate that was shaping up at the Council and in the Commission on the new division of the material. This group met twice at the Archbishop's residence in Malines (first on September 6-8 and again on September 17), and it was during the first meeting that the group members prepared the new chapter on the people of God, which they anticipated would be considered during the coming period of the Council.

3. *Schema XVII*

None of the sixteen texts promulgated by Vatican II went through as slow, as long, and as complex a development as the schema that, last on the list on the CC's agenda in January 1963, was therefore called schema XVII. This odd bestowal of a purely numerical title is by itself enough to show the anonymity that marked a draft text that one group refused for a long time to study. It would be put on the agenda of the full assembly of Vatican II only in the fall of 1964 and then only after lengthy hesitation on the part of Paul VI. Countless attempts were made to eliminate this anonymity and give the schema a name, but they all failed during the intersession that we are studying here.[105]

---

[105] Here are some examples of these suggestions: "The Presence of the Church in Today's World" (Urbani); "The Principles and Activity of the Church in Promoting the Good of Society" (official title given by Cicognani in January 1963); "The Presence and Activity of the Church in Today's World" (official name in May 1963); "The Church and the Human Person" (Suenens); "The Effective Presence of the Church in Today's World" (official name in July 1963); "The Active Presence of the Church in the Building of the World" (September 1963). Opposition to the schema could also find expression in the choice of title; this was the case with Tromp, who, at the end of April 1963, after four months of work in the Commission, persisted in calling it "The Social and International Order" in an attempt to preserve a direct connection with the preparatory schemas (see Tromp, *Relatio 21.II. 1962 — 13.III.1966. Pars IV*, 29f.). An analogous picture could be painted of the succession of chapters and the structuring of the text in the course of five stages running from January 1963 to December 1965.

This uncertainty reflects how unready this vast project was, something that the opponents of this second preparation for Vatican II would not fail to criticize and on occasion exploit. No other conciliar text was so lacking in coherent preparatory work, and no other conciliar commission was so late in becoming aware of the extent of the problems handed to it.[106] Finally, the relatively homogeneous character of what we have been calling the majority was not enough to withstand the differences of theological perspective regarding schema XIII which became clear in 1965 but were already having an influence as the work began in 1963.

a. The First Phase (February-March 1963)

The birth, or more accurately, the conception, of what was to become schema XVII, resulted from a confluence of several currents of thought and several plans from different sources. In retrospect, perhaps the earliest was Suenens's ideas on the *Ecclesia ad extra* (see his correspondence on this subject with John XXIII; the Pope's message of September 11, 1962; and Suenens's statement to the Council on December 4, 1962), and then the discussions in the conciliar Commission for the Lay Apostolate in December 1962 and on January 17, 1963. From these very important meetings came the proposal of Hengsbach and De Vet to set up a lasting collaboration between this Commission and the Doctrinal Commission. This mixed commission was to draw up a joint schema that included the social documents of Ottaviani's Commission and the fourth part of the schema on the lay apostolate, the part dealing with the social involvement of the laity.[107] Hengsbach's suggestion was immediately adopted by Urbani, who won its acceptance by the CC at its first meeting. At this same meeting at the end of January, Suenens was commissioned to report to the CC on the three "social" schemas originating in the preparatory Theological Commission. In this area as in others, the goal was to clear the ground while at the same time dealing tactfully with the sensitivities of the authors of texts that were being sacrificed.

Suenens's reports, prepared with the assistance in particular of Father J.-Y. Calvez and Canon F. Houtart,[108] dealt with:

[106] A. Glorieux, *Historia praesertim sessionum Schematis XVII seu XIII de Ecclesia in mundo huius temporis* (no place of publication, no date), 2.

[107] Ibid., 1-2.

[108] The report given by Suenens to the CC repeated, in its entirety, except for some details, and in French, the critical commentary Jean-Yves Calvez had drawn up at Suenens's request. In a letter addressed to the latter (January 11, 1963) Calvez wrote: "In my opinion, however, entirely new problems concerning growth and development in all

1. The schema on the moral order, chapters I and IV of which, Suenens said, could be re-used in the new schema of the new mixed commission.[109]

2. The schema on the social order, which the reporter subjected to a radical critique: it took too little account of new subjects (socialization and developing countries); it read too much like an abstract scholarly exposition and lacked the open style of *Mater et magistra*; it focused on Western European society; the teaching set down did not correspond to the expectations voiced by the Pope in his opening address to the Council. It was therefore desirable that the text be examined by the new mixed commission and be made both to look beyond the borders of the West and to take account of *Mater et magistra*.

3. The schema on the community of the nations, the literary genre of which was criticized by Suenens as that of a handbook of moral theology and as lacking in the persuasive power of the Holy Father's addresses. He also complained of the draft's complete silence on some important subjects and of the static, juridical way in which other matters were discussed.

The second piece of this "puzzle" is the contribution of Liénart at this same meeting of the CC, in his report on the schema on defending the deposit of faith, a text that even in the preparatory period had provoked sharp disagreements. Liénart's report was extremely critical. Not only the vocabulary but even the general conception of the schema were judged unacceptable; for example, in twelve sections, the schema denounced twenty-one different errors! Referring expressly to the opening address of John XXIII and to the pastoral concern of the majority of the fathers throughout the first period of the Council, the Bishop of Lille

countries are cropping up at the present time, and it is in relation to these great projects of human groups that the Church ought to take a position today through its Council. Or, rather, it ought to locate these within its own mystery, its own anthropology. It is even possible, in this respect, that problems which are seemingly more political — the plans of the major political systems, the desire for a classless society, the hopes for democracy — would profit by being treated jointly with social and economic problems. Without going too much into less useful technical details, the Council might thus come to grips with the ambiguous, sometimes atheistic, expectation that is at work in the human race today; it could say under what (religious) conditions humanity in search of a future could effectively attain to a truly human future in which human beings are not in danger of being sacrificed" (see the file "Église dans le monde de ce temps," in the Daniélou Archive, Archives of the Jesuit Fathers at Vanves). It is possible that Suenens's report on the international community, which was likewise given in French, had as its source François Houtart, whom we know for certain to have been consulted by the Cardinal at this same period.

[109] *AS* V/1, 144-47, 162-63, and, for the other two schemas, 148-52 and 153-59.

judged the text to be unacceptable and suggested that some parts of it be distributed among other schemas.[110]

When Liénart drew the attention of the cardinals of the CC to a general theme that might be isolated from some chapters of the text — namely, a doctrine on the human person, its origin and destiny, its norms of action, its rights and duties — he stirred a lively interest. Confalonieri and Urbani both spoke in favor of a schema *De homine* that would deal with the human person as natural and supernatural and with a person's life in the Mystical Body and in the family and society; this text could follow the text on revelation and precede that on the Church. At the end of the discussion and at the request of the President of the CC, Liénart gave the synthesis described above, which the Commission immediately approved; it was destined to become part of the schema on the presence of the Church in the world.[111]

The contribution of Urbani and of his report on the lay apostolate provides a third factor in the origins of schema XVII. The preparatory text on the lay apostolate had four parts, devoted to (1) general ideas; (2) activity for the Kingdom of Christ; (3) charitable activity; and (4) social activity in the lay apostolate, a subject that itself occupies four chapters. After observations on the division of the material, Urbani proposed shortening the fourth section and inserting parts of it into the text on the Church in the world. Urbani stressed the special importance of this latter text, and the proposal to establish a new mixed commission from the Commissions on doctrine and on the laity was accepted by the CC.[112]

Through these alluvial deposits, so to speak, from rather different perspectives,[113] flowed a common current which had still to flow a long distance and pass through many locks before emptying into the sea. The navigation of this lengthy course was entrusted primarily to the new mixed commission, an initially shaky alliance of two unequal partners, the Doctrinal Commission, long accustomed to dominate, and the Com-

---

[110] Liénart, *Vatican II*, 83, 88-91. He proposed that chapters I, IV, V, and VI be put in the schema on the Church, that X be eliminated, and that II, III, VII, VIII, and IX be made part of a doctrinal decree "on the human person."

[111] *AS* V/1, 68-69, 97.

[112] *AS* V/1, 108, 133, and 194.

[113] The proposal of Hengsbach and De Vet aimed at concrete guidelines for the activity of the laity in meeting the urgent needs of society. Liénart, who had an illustrious past in the area of Catholic social action, was concerned mainly to clarify the great principles of social action in the Church. Suenens wanted to formulate answers of the Church to some specific problems of Christians in the modern world: conjugal morality and action for peace (what the popular press called "the pill and the bomb") (see G. Turbanti, "La Commission mixte pour le Schéma XVII-XIII," in *Commissions*, 217-50).

mission on the Lay Apostolate, which was modest, inexperienced, and somewhat looked down on by Curial officials who had grown gray in the harness.[114] After the months of apprenticeship during the 1962-63 intersession, this alliance would finally acquire a well-defined profile with the reorganization that took place at the end of November 1963.

Objectivity requires, however, the acknowledgment that the difficult and hesitant start of the mixed commission on schema XVII was due also in considerable measure to the additional burden of work that weighed on each of the commissions during March and May of 1963 and kept them from giving the time needed for the work.

In these difficult circumstances the first phase of the work on schema XVII, after the meeting of the CC in January 1963, produced only the preliminaries to a preparation. The outline of the schema to be developed already existed in the letter from the CC; all that remained, then, was to carry it out.[115]

First of all, a limited group of experts composed a provisional version of the introduction and the six chapters.[116] After the revision of this version, which was done with Cento and Browne presiding (the latter appointed by Ottaviani), a limited mixed commission was set up on February 18 and met on February 28 and March 1.[117] This entrance of bishops with the responsibility for drafting the text was accompanied by the arrival of new and weighty experts: Daniélou, Medina, de Riedmatten, Tucci, Prignon, and Ligutti. Cardinal König was to preside.

---

[114] I have already spoken of the conflicts over autonomy and competencies that had long created opposition between Ottaviani and Cento. A typical example of the burdensome supervision exercised over the Commission on the Lay Apostolate could be seen when the latter organized a first consultation with lay experts; the entire process took place in the greatest secrecy, and this despite the official encouragement and formal instructions given by the CC. Some leaders of the commission were also wary of frightening bishops who had not been consulted.

[115] In March-April 1963 schema XVII contained six clearly demarcated chapters, the subjects of which would, in general, be maintained to the end, despite further radical alterations in the structure of the text. These subjects were (1) the wonderful calling of the human person; (2) the human person in society; (3) marriage, the family (and demography); (4) human culture; (5) the economic order and social justice; and (6) the community of peoples and peace.

[116] Glorieux gives the names of these experts and the distribution of the work: the experts were mainly Pavan, Ferrari-Toniolo, Sigmond, Tromp, Lio, Hirschmann, and Guano. I must emphasize here the irreplaceable value of the detailed chronicles that we owe to Glorieux, who was himself the workhorse of the entire effort (see his *Historia* and "Les étapes préliminaires").

[117] This limited commission was made up of König, Griffiths, Pelletier, McGrath (all of the Doctrinal Commission), Hengsbach, Guano, Blomjous, and Kominek (of the Commission on the Lay Apostolate); not all were able to be present on February 28.

The days of mid-March were decisive for sizing up the situation and marked the turning point for this limited mixed commission. Tromp and Lio were in effect replaced by McGrath and Daniélou, who formed a team; the last named was given charge of the first chapter, which until that point had been Lio's. The redactors of the preparatory schemas were thus replaced by theologians of the conciliar majority.[118]

Even before things had reached this point, the spokesmen for the majority were perfectly well aware of efforts to apply the brakes that were being made behind the scenes by some who were nostalgic for the preparatory schemas. For example, in notes taken during a meeting of the Commission Léger asked: How is it that the text of the Commission contains new reflections of Father Lio?[119] Alluding to the work of Lio for the future schema XVII, Suenens told a confidant: "Yes, we too have our Father Tromp."[120]

While acknowledging the good points made by Lio, McGrath wanted to take into account the directives given by John XXIII: a scholastic discourse is of no value in dealing with the Church in the world. According to Daniélou, it was necessary to abandon the distinction made in the schema on the deposit of faith between "natural" and "supernatural" vocations, and it was advisable to base the chapter dealing with anthropology on the creation of human beings in the image of God, and this in the perspective of the history of salvation.[121] Thus, even though this was not fully realized during the initial approaches, the issue was the basic direction to be taken by the new text, the desire to liberate it from the burden of the schemas composed before October 1962.[122]

[118] There was a certain parallelism at work: as Tromp had been replaced by Philips for the schema on the Church, so Lio was replaced by Daniélou for schema XVII. The two events took place at the beginning of March. Philips was brought in by Charue, and Daniélou by Garrone. Daniélou was replaced by Congar in the subcommission for the schema on the Church.

[119] See the Léger Archives at the Grand Séminaire of Montreal, no. 27; the notes are dated November 23, 1964, but are in a series from 1963; in addition, the document to which the Canadian prelate is referring carries the date of May 9, 1963; the latter document is in the same archives under no. 1300. It seems to me probable that the notes should have been dated in 1963.

[120] Letter of Moeller to Léger, April 12, 1963, in the Léger Archive, Grand Séminaire of Montreal, no. 849.

[121] Not to be forgotten, however, is the fact that Lio, in a preparatory schema that did not survive the reduction of schemas in December and January, had been the apostle of procreation as the primary end of marriage. The chapter on marriage in the new schema XVII had initially been returned to Lio through the efforts of Tromp; Lio rewrote it without the knowledge of the Commission on the Lay Apostolate, but later this text also was set aside.

[122] See Turbanti, "La Commission mixte."

This episode sheds light especially on the procedural conflicts between Cento and Ottaviani. As happened often at Vatican II, incidents involving procedure were directly connected with the substance of the discussion. By combining into a "limited mixed commission" some dynamic bishops and experts from the Commission on the Lay Apostolate with some supporters of renewal from the Doctrinal Commission (where they were usually kept under a watchful eye), the CC was able to set out in a progressive direction. This is why Ottaviani and Tromp so strongly and stubbornly claimed that texts originating in a mixed commission were subject to the theological oversight of the undiluted Doctrinal Commission!

b. Second Phase (April-May 1963)

When the cardinals of the CC met for the second time at the end of March, they found on their working table a pilot study for schema XVII that had not been examined even by a plenary meeting of the new mixed commission. Cento acknowledged this in an accompanying letter and added: "However, it seems appropriate to send you some texts that will allow you to see what point the work of the mixed commission has reached."[123]

This meeting of the CC was notable for the absence, although they had been invited along with Cento and Glorieux, of Ottaviani and Tromp, who unable to gain theological control of the Cento-Browne pilot project, had decided to sulk.[124]

As for the proposed text itself, the reporter judged it, despite the improvements made, to be still inadequate and in need of being amended further in order to be made consistent with the guidelines given by the Pope and the wishes both of the Council fathers and the present-day Church. The explanation of doctrine was still too defensive and superficial. A more positive and more pastoral exposition was wanted.[125]

---

[123] Cento's letter to Cicognani, March 21, stressed the point that the revised text had just been sent to all the members of the mixed commission with a request that they send in their observations before Easter (see *AS* V/1, 505).

[124] "Ottaviani and Father Tromp are not present because the schema has not yet been submitted to the judgment of their commission" (*AS* V/1, 513). This is the statement in the official minutes. Defending Cento, Suenens, the reporter, made the point that the schema was to be judged by the mixed commission, whose judgment did not depend on the Doctrinal Commission.

[125] *AS* V/1, 506 and 514. Suenens's report then set forth a series of detailed remarks on each of the six chapters, except for the one on economic and social questions. He also returned to the claim that the schema on religious freedom, which had been prepared by the Secretariat for Christian Unity, should no longer be excluded from this schema (some

In mid-April 1963 an important event occurred that would subsequently have a significant influence on the development of the schema on the Church and the world, the publication by John XXIII of the encyclical on social and international relations, *Pacem in terris*, "on peace between all the nations, a peace based on truth, justice, charity, and freedom." This document, dated April 11, 1963, would awaken a surprising echo in international public opinion and have lasting effects on the work of Vatican II, especially on the writing of schema XVII.

During the second half of this same month of April, another event made it possible to recast the schema. Following the wish of the CC, a call was issued, for the first time officially, to a group of experts, eminent lay people, well-known both in international Catholic organizations and at the World Congresses on the Apostolate of the Laity (1951 and 1957). Their evidence, given both to the subcommission and the plenary commission, on April 24 and 26, 1963, made it possible to revise the schema at several points.[126] They also opened the way for lay auditors at the Council, who in March 1964 would begin to participate in the Commission on the presence of the Church in the world.[127]

The most important moments of this second phase were the convocation (April 30), the chapter-by-chapter preparation (May 16), and the meetings of the whole mixed commission (May 20-25). This new stage was aimed toward the meeting of the CC scheduled for the beginning of June 1963. It represented the end of what Glorieux calls the "prehistory" of *Gaudium et spes* and the entrance of the mixed commission into the normal course of the conciliar proceedings.

To clear the ground, the plenary meetings of the mixed commission were to alternate with the meetings of the five mixed subcommissions on schema XVII, which worked every morning without respite. In the course of seven plenary meetings, from May 20 to May 25, the five chapters of the draft were revised. Right from the start of the discussion of the "vocation of the human person," Karl Rahner criticized the text

time later it would find a place in the schema on ecumenism). Finally, Suenens insisted that lay people should have a part in preparing schema XVII. This proposal was accepted on condition that their role be purely consultative.

[126] R. Tucci, "Introduction historique et doctrinale à la Commission pastorale," in *L'Église dans le monde de ce temps* (Unam Sanctam 65B; Paris, 1967), II, 42.

[127] Rosemary Goldie, widely known for her pioneering work in the field of the lay apostolate, published one of the best summaries of the active participation of lay persons in Vatican II (see R. Goldie, "La participation des laïcs aux travaux du Concile Vatican II," *Revue des sciences religieuses*, 62 [1988], 54-73).

for its lack of clarity on a point that was essential and decisive for schema XVII as a whole, namely, the relationship between nature and grace. This central theme was the first on which the mixed commission showed its internal divisions.

The exchanges on chapters III (marriage) and IV (culture) gave rise to similar oppositions. In chapter III the issue in the discussions was the order of priority among the ends of marriage, and, in chapter IV, the relationship between religion and culture as well as the evolution of the world toward the new creation, a point on which the majority camp itself proved to be less united. Chapter V (the community of people and peace), which was introduced by König, made it possible for de Riedmatten in particular to show the need to study the demographic problem. Each of these chapters was allowed only one session of discussion during a single day or even half-day. Some of the participants were scandalized; Congar, for example, complained of work being "rushed."[128]

It was unlikely from the outset that a commission with so many members would be able to deal with such new and complex matters in so short a time.[129] As Glorieux himself remarked, "A good many bishops had acquired only a hasty knowledge of a document that was new to them; as a result their remarks were generally cautious."[130]

The schema submitted to the plenary mixed commission at the end of May was over sixty typed pages in length, and any discussion of it would be rather heavy going. The work done was finally approved, but only in principle and with serious reservations. Tucci, who witnessed this episode, tells us: "One had the impression that the majority of those present did not regard the text as ready for presentation to the Council fathers and that the editing of the text ought to continue."[131] It was during these difficult discussions that doubts began to be expressed about the advisability of having a council discuss matters that are so concrete and in constant flux, more suited for treatment in an encyclical. The idea of two texts emerged: a short doctrinal exposé of the vocation of the human person, and a longer text dealing with contemporary problems and not involving the authority of the Council in as formal a way. This idea was soon accepted by the CC.

[128] *JCongar*, May 22, 1963, 249. Congar feared the consequences: "This is not taking things seriously. This won't work at the Council!"
[129] With its approximately fifty bishops and the countless experts who assisted them, the mixed commission was, from this first meeting on and to the end, a mini-parliament.
[130] Glorieux, "Les étapes préliminaires," 400.
[131] Tucci, "Introduction," 43.

c. Third Phase (July-September 1963)

Amid this dissatisfaction and uncertainty, which would long accompany the difficult birth of the schema, the CC studied this amended version of schema XVII at its meetings on July 3 and 4. Suenens was called upon, as reporter, to give an evaluation of the text. His opinion of it, taken as a whole, was negative: "The text given to me is certainly an improvement on the earlier version, and contains some excellent sections; but it is not yet fit to be presented to the Council."[132] Chroniclers and historians of this schema often present this criticism as something isolated; they neglect the fact that the other cardinals of the CC spoke in equally negative terms.[133] Urbani, for example, suggested dividing the material into two parts, one doctrinal, the other instructive in style, like a "social catechism."

Although Suenens approved of making the theme of the human person as image of God the guiding thread of the schema, he thought it insufficient to give real unity to the various chapters. What was lacking was a balanced synthesis of data from the natural law and from the gospel message. Suenens also disliked seeing general principles and secondary applications mixed in together. In conclusion, he proposed that a special commission compose a new and shorter text that would set forth the general principles governing the relations between Church and world and would take biblical and patristic teaching into account. As for particular problems (marriage, culture, social life, international community), commissions of specialists should be appointed for each of them.[134]

Suenens's report offered remarks on each of these individual problems. In his proposal he suggested that the doctrinal statement to be drawn up derive its inspiration from the present chapter, duly corrected, on the vocation of the person. He proposed, however, that the conclusions of the specialized commissions, after receiving general approval, be published in the form of "instructions."[135] The exchange of views in

[132] Ibid., 630.

[133] The official minutes of this meeting, unavailable to earlier chroniclers, show that Browne, Urbani, Confalonieri, and Döpfner also offered critical appraisals (see AS V/1, 636-37).

[134] Ibid., 633.

[135] The reader will realize that in formally proposing two categories of texts, with the more concrete half of the picture having an inferior status, the CC seemed to be returning to the distinction between "doctrinal" and "pastoral" that Ottaviani and Tromp were constantly invoking.

the CC ended with an intervention of Confalonieri, who proposed that the task of developing a new text be entrusted to Suenens, who would pass it on to the mixed commission. Confalonieri probably wanted to give some gratification to the cardinal who had been the first to launch the idea of a Church not only *ad intra* but also *ad extra*. The proposal was seconded, first by Döpfner and then by all the other members.[136]

1) *Preparations for Malines*

The especially important mandate that the CC gave to the Belgian archbishop was implemented without delay.[137] Thus began what might be called the adventures of the Malines text, composed as a revision of schema XVII. In the entire complicated maze from which *Gaudium et spes* finally emerged in December 1965, the Malines text probably did not play an essential role, but in the history of the 1962-63 intersession with which we are dealing here the episode was especially significant. It can show us the extent to which the route of this second preparation was strewn with snares and obstacles and also the extent to which the opponents of the second preparation sometimes still had a decisive influence on the control of procedures.

The preparation of the Malines text had in fact already begun in May, two or three weeks before the CC decided to have a new draft made. This paradox is easily explained when we realize that the team of experts who prepared Suenens's report to the CC were at the same time taking the first steps for the meetings the Archbishop of Malines would organize during the first half of September.[138]

The remote and proximate preparations for the Malines meetings were of concern to Congar. As early as mid-May the French theologian drew up a series of "general criticisms" of the schema on the presence and activity of the Church in the world and sent them to Suenens, Léger, Garrone, Browne, Cento, and some people at Louvain.[139] About ten days

---

[136] *AS* V/1, 637.

[137] The day after the CC's decision, Prignon, received his first instructions from Suenens, to the effect that he should form a working team that would have for its task to develop the conciliar part of schema XVII (see CLG, Prignon Archive, no. 236).

[138] The reader should not forget that in May it was already anticipated that Suenens would make a report to the CC at the beginning of June. As a result of the death of John XXIII and the interruption of the Council, the Cardinal would not be able to give his report until the beginning of July, a delay that could not have been foreseen in May.

[139] The critical observations were dated May 17 and were therefore compiled before the meetings of the large mixed commission at the end of May. Congar thought that the schema, in part made up of fragments from earlier schemas, lacked organic unity and did

later he took part, with Philips and Moeller, in a working session to prepare the critical report that Suenens would soon have to present to the
CC.[140]

In reply to a message from Carlo Colombo, Congar shared with him
some key issues he was raising with regard to schema XVII: (1) Chapter I (version of end of May 1963) was overly philosophical and should
be linked to the key idea of the human person as the image of God; and
(2) if the Council were satisfied simply to enunciate some great moral
principles but give no concrete applications, the world would be terribly
disappointed.[141]

At the beginning of August, after receiving an invitation from Suenens to join the team that would revise schema XVII, Congar realized
that this invitation was in line with the criticisms he himself had
offered in May. "This is a serious and important business," he wrote
in his *Journal*.[142] Encouraged by this mark of confidence, the theologian who in the recent past had so often tried to shed light on the theology of Church-world relations sent Suenens three closely written
pages entitled "Propositions for the Required Revision of Schema
XVII" in which he made use of the triad Community-Service-Wit-
ness.[143] This text was sent to Suenens four days before the beginning
of the team's work in Malines. Congar was probably the best prepared
person there, and he was to have a very profound influence on the
text.[144]

---

not live up to its fine title. The spirit of the gospel was not sufficiently present in it and
the style was too abstract. In addition, the schema ought to have given at least a description of the presence of the Church in today's world and should have said that this can
only be a missionary presence.

[140] *JCongar*, 257 (May 28).

[141] In reply to a message from Colombo, Congar wrote to him on June 22, 1963, to
report on the work being done in the Commission (see the appendixes in *JCongar*, 293).

[142] *JCongar*, 262.

[143] See Y. Congar, *Jalons pour une théologie du laïcat*, chap. III: "Royaume, Église,
Monde," 85-145; idem, *Sacerdoce et laïcat*, Part II. "Pour une Église servante et pauvre."

[144] It is clear that the Louvain people did not remain inactive, but except for Philips,
their preparations seemed rather scattered. Moeller composed a number of notes, from
which two pages of "General Observations" were sent to Léger and others (Léger
Archive, Montreal, no. 1366); a group from Louvain compiled a radical critique of chapter III on marriage, a move that presaged the conciliar debates in October and November
1965 (Léger Archive, Montreal, no. 15424); P. Delhaye wrote a lengthy commentary for
the use of the French episcopate on the subject of the first chapter: the vocation of the
human person (General Secretariat of the French episcopate, *Études et documents*, no. 16,
dated July 24, 1963).

424 CHAPTER VIII

2) *The Malines Text*

In a reminder sent to Moeller eight days before the meetings began, Prignon spoke of "our usual group of theologians."[145] This team of experts would in record time discuss a provisional draft of a text by Philips, prepare individual reports, and receive an amended text for their examination. This stage of the work they got through in less than three days, September 6, 7, and 8, 1963. The definitive revision was approved during a second stage, at the meeting of September 17 (in Malines), this time after a meeting with Suenens.

The starting point for this work was the presentation by Philips of a set of themes in the form of three chapter headings: (1) The Church that has for its purpose to proclaim the gospel; (2) Human society and its goal; and (3) The influence of the Church on society.[146] During the first day and in the absence of Congar, who arrived a day late, the main interventions were those of Delhaye, Thils, Rahner, and Dondeyne. The last two joined in a critique of the proposal, which they regarded as insufficiently radical.[147] The next day Congar's gave his very influential support to the perspectives suggested by Philips. The latter had also insisted that the final part of the schema take for its structure the trilogy used by the World Council of Churches and emphasized by Congar: *martyria* (witness), *diakonia* (service), and *koinônia* (communion).[148] Finally,

[145] Moeller Archive, no. 02905, CLG. A look at the list published by some chroniclers shows the following names: Prignon, Philips, Delhaye, Thils, Tucci, Congar, Rahner, Dondeyne, Cerfaux, and Rigaux. It was possible, therefore, to describe the "working group" as international. Thus Delhaye spoke of "theologians representing other countries": K. Rahner for Germany, Congar for France, Tucci for Italy, Delhaye himself for Canada, all of whom joined the Louvain group (see P. Delhaye, "Histoire des textes de la Constitution pastorale," in *L'Église dans le monde de ce temps* I, 224). It should be noted that later on, after Malines, when seeking to soothe the bad humor of Garrone, who was dissatisfied with the Suenens undertaking, Philips would appeal precisely to the international make-up of the September working group in order to legitimize the Malines document (see CLG, Prignon Archive, no. 514). In October and November 1962, during the preparation of a revised version of the schema on the Church, Philips was already fond of emphasizing the international character of the team assisting him.

[146] In preparation for beginning their work the participants received (a) a note from Suenens; (b) Congar's "Propositions for the Required Revision of Schema XVII" (CLG, Prignon Archive, no. 238); and (c) the remarks Liénart made to the CC (*AS* V/1, 638-39).

[147] I am relying here on the handwritten notes taken during the meeting by Prignon, principal organizer of the Malines discussions (see CLG, Prignon Archive, nos. 239-42).

[148] At the Third General Assembly of the World Council of Churches, in New Delhi, 1961, the main theme that inspired and organized the discussion was based on this trilogy, which at that time made a deep impression on Congar; for more details see the acts of that assembly, the first that involved the participation of five official observers from the Roman Catholic Church (see *Nouvelle Delhi 1961. Conseil oecuménique des Églises.*

Philips drew some initial conclusions, gave a very detailed list of the main articulations of the schema, and went on to "distribute" the work to be done the next day, the last of the meeting.

On Sunday afternoon each of the participants offered his personal observations. Congar wanted to reduce the number of chapters to three. In his final remarks Philips suggested reducing the length of the schema and explained how he would try to include the various suggestions in the base text, which all the members of the team would receive for a new reading on September 17.[149] Another interest of the Malines meetings was the fact that they provided a rather exceptional collaboration of theologians whose thinking enjoyed great authority at that time in the area of relations between Church and world. Their exchange of ideas reflected their publications in the area, which were in everyone's hands or at least in the hands of the younger generation of 1960.[150]

The final version of the Malines text, which was finished, as anticipated, by the end of the meetings on September 17, was shorter.[151] Some sections of chapter II were sacrificed, while chapter III, based on Congar's contribution, remained unchanged. In the first part, on the proper mission of the Church, the emphasis was on the duty of proclaiming the gospel, the freedom of faith, and the evangelization of the poor. The quest for a Christian anthropology, which had been central to the first chapter of the Garrone-Daniélou schema (May 1963), likewise started with the human person as image of Christ.[152] The theme of building the

---

Rapport de la 3ème Assemblée, ed. W. A. Visser t'Hooft [Neuchâtel, 1962]). The World Council document is an appendix to *JCongar*, 279.

[149] Congar confirms that the group agreed to combine chapters III and IV into a single chapter. He notes also that some, among them Dondeyne, offered some interesting ideas on the modern world; he says, however, that these would provide material rather for an article and could not find a place in a dogmatic constitution (*JCongar*, 267). It seems to me that this remark applied also to Rahner. The realistic outlook that Congar and Philips shared made them aware of the limits necessarily imposed by a conciliar document. Rahner and Dondeyne would not be present for the final meeting on September 17.

[150] Here are some typical works by those who largely inspired the work being done at the beginning of September 1963: Y. Congar, *Jalons pour une théologie du laïcat*; idem, *Pour une Église servante et pauvre* (Paris, 1963); A. Dondeyne, *La foi écoute le monde*, 2d ed. (Paris, 1964); G. Philips, *De leek in de Kerk* (Louvain, 1952); idem, *Naar een volwassen Christendom* (1960); K. Rahner, "Grenzen der Kirche," *Wort und Wahrheit* 19 (1964), 249-62; G. Thils, *Théologie des réalités terrestres* (2 vols.; Paris-Bruges, 1946-49). The works of Philips were translated into various languages, especially French, German, English, and Italian.

[151] It contained thirteen pages and twenty-nine sections. The two versions have been published, in Latin, in J. Perarnau, *La formacio de "Gaudium et spes" 1962 — novembre 1963* (Barcelona, 1975), 106-28. This author had access to Tucci's archives. See also CLG, Prignon Archive, no. 243 ter.

[152] The second section dealt with the influence exerted by the Church on "the worldly

world, which was the subject of the second chapter, was developed in two sections: the autonomy of the world and the unification of the world. The third chapter, which bore the title "The Duties of the Church toward the World," was developed along the lines of the three aspects suggested by Congar:

a. *Witness* has to do with questions involving the dignity of the person. Even though the Church does not have a mission of settling secular and technological problems, its contribution can be indispensable to their solution.

b. The *service* of charity toward God and neighbor also includes relations between charity and justice and charity in everyday life.

c. *Communion* with all means the readiness of the Church to be at the service of all human beings, to listen to others, and to collaborate with them for the good of the human community.[153]

3) The Failure of the Malines Text

It has long been remarked that between September and the end of the second period of the Council the entire file for schema XVII seemed to have been covered by a thick fog. When the clouds lifted at a late plenary meeting on November 29, 1963, they revealed a mixed commission in a state of utter confusion and refusing to consider the Malines text. For a long time the more serious chroniclers have had the impression that the Malines text was regarded as more or less "private."[154]

The first thing that seems clear was the lack of communication between the CC and the competent mixed commission; the usual notification of the CC's decision to the mixed commission did not take place. Not only is this attested by A. Glorieux, the very active secretary of the mixed commission, but the expectation and uncertainty of that commission's members was also obvious.[155]

[secular] order," both through the teaching of the Church's magisterium and by the activity of the faithful, who make an effective contribution to the building of the world; created goods are to be received with gratitude, even if, as a result of sin, it is necessary to restore them in Christ.

[153] See also Tucci, "Introduction," 52-54.

[154] R. A. Sigmond, "Documentation historique sur la Constitution pastorale de l'Église dans le monde actuel," *IDOC-Bulletin*, no. 2 (1966), no. 2, 2; Glorieux, "Les étapes préliminaires," 402; Tucci says simply that many members of the mixed commission regarded the Malines schema as "undesirable and risky" ("Introduction," 56).

[155] Glorieux, *Historia*, 32. When the plenary meeting of November 29 began, many of the fathers had received the Malines text of September only a week before, and many had not had time to read it (see Tucci, "Introduction," 56). The decision of the CC had not been communicated to them.

As a result of these serious procedural obstacles and also of criticisms of the very content of the text (among others, that it was "too theological" and did not meet the expectations of people today) the Malines text was turned down, as was the schema that had been amended at Rome in May.

Although not part of the first intersession, the debate of November 29 is very instructive in regard to the course of the intersession.[156] The discussion was mainly about the content of the instructions that the CC had issued on July 4, 1963. Some of the participants argued that Suenens had been given a mandate to rewrite a first, doctrinal chapter (Browne, Cento, Charue, Hengsbach, Prignon, Rahner); others tried to reduce Suenens's job to a simple summary of all the chapters (Tromp); still others rebelled against the division between a doctrinal section and another with a lesser status, since the Council should take up all the questions with the same authority (Garrone, König, Häring).

This confusion makes it clear that the lack of communication between the CC and the mixed commission contributed to the failure of the Malines text. Who was responsible for the failure? On the one hand responsibility belonged both to Felici, the Secretary General of the Council, and to Cicognani, president of the CC,[157] who neglected to communicate the decisions of the CC to the mixed commission in due form at the beginning of July, as was customary. On the other hand, Suenens accepted the task of rewriting the first part of schema XVII without consulting the mixed commission on the matter. Yet this negligence was due, in a way, to the CC itself, which took the unusual step of asking Suenens "to develop a draft of this conciliar schema, which *will then be handed on to the mixed commission*, so that it may see to the redaction of the definitive text, using for the purpose specialists divided into sub-commissions."[158]

---

[156] There are accounts of this debate in Glorieux, *Historia*, 33-37, and in P. Delhaye, *Commission mixte novembre 1963*, CLG, Delhaye Archive.

[157] On the day after the CC's decision (July 5, 1963), Tromp was already spreading doubts about the decision of July 4, to the point that Glorieux felt obliged to write to Suenens in order to find out for certain what the situation was. But the doubt persisted when Glorieux received some copies of the new schema "for private use." The same Tromp who had refused to attend the CC's meeting on schema XVII, claimed at the meeting of the mixed commission on November 29, 1963, that Suenens had misunderstood the mandate given to him by Confalonieri (see Glorieux, *Historia*, first 32, then 33).

[158] *AS* V/1, 637. Italics added.

That was an unusual way of proceeding.[159] The idea of entrusting the revision of a first, doctrinal part to Suenens alone seems to have disappeared after September. If the Malines text had been presented rather as a limited part of the schema, it would probably have been easier to find some common ground with the mixed commission and fewer leaders would have been upset.

It is not difficult to imagine that the opponents of this schema XVII knew how to take advantage of their influence on procedure and strike at the promoters of the plan. But, in order to complete this panoramic view of the end of the intersession, we must also take into account certain tensions within the majority itself. The work done at Malines in September may have looked like a shortcut that directly threatened the authority of those in charge of the text at the end of May and, more especially, the prestige of Garrone, the person mainly responsible for a first chapter (which had been considerably amended). In other words, Malines was probably inconsiderate of the authors of the schema produced in May, who were probably already annoyed by Suenens's criticisms, on July 4, of their chapter I. In any case, the new draft from Malines in Septeber roused the wrath of Garrone,[160] who was not appeased by the active participation of a Frenchman such as Congar in the composition of the text. Daniélou was Garrone's regular expert in January 1963, and it was the Belgian College that had to take steps to have Congar appointed to the Doctrinal Commission at the beginning of February. It may be that in Garrone's eyes Congar was not representative enough of "French theology" to carry weight. We shall see later on that at the unexpected death of Msgr. Guano, a great organizer, the leadership of the schema (by now called schema XIII) passed increasingly into the hands of Garrone.

There still persisted a great concern not to disturb the self-esteem of those in charge of the preparatory schemas. This concern, which marked the first meeting of the CC, had led Suenens, in dealing with the schema on the Church, to offer a comparative list to show that the preparatory schema

---

[159] G. Turbanti has quite correctly pointed out that the assignment of a textual draft directly to an individual, even an influential one such as Suenens, was "an unusual action" of the CC, since it bypassed the authority of the mixed commission (see Turbanti, "La Commission mixte," 227).

[160] See Prignon's report to Suenens on October 4, 1962 (CLG, Prignon Archive, no. 514). Prignon remarked specifically: "Msgr. Garrone's bad mood is diminishing." Relations between Suenens and Garrone were not very cordial at Vatican II. Before the Council the clash between the Legion of Mary and Catholic Action had already created tensions, the memory of which did not fade at the Council. Later, at the beginning of 1964, all of Suenens's regular advisers, with the exception of Moeller, were excluded from the preparation of the schema in Zurich.

on the Church had not been labor lost. The approach to a new schema XVII showed the same procedure to try to convince people that the new text would take the various preparatory schemas as its starting point.

Thus chapter I, on the wonderful vocation of the human person (for which Liénart and Suenens were reporters), derived in part from the schema on the deposit of faith (chaps. II, III, VII-IX) and from the schema on the moral order (chaps. I and IV). Chapter III, on marriage and family (Spellman), used some elements of the discarded text on marriage and virginity. Chapter V, on the economic order (Suenens and Urbani), derived in part from the schema on the apostolate of the laity. Chapter VI, on the community of peoples (Suenens), derived in part from the schema on the international order.

It is obvious that such an attitude would not last. The road traveled in less than two months can be measured by comparing the turn taken by the group composing schema XVII at the beginning of March and the new atmosphere that permeated the CC at its meeting at the end of March.

B. The Launching of Two Other Projects

1. *Ecumenism*

Nothing illustrates more clearly the struggles of the second preparation of Vatican II than the slow and laborious emancipation of the schema on ecumenism between January and May 1963. It shows clearly how much skill, perseverance, and even combativeness the Bea-Willebrands team needed to cast off the tenacious mooring ropes of the Curia, steer their craft out of port, and reach open seas at last. If the operation would probably not have succeeded without John XXIII's very steady support of Bea, here again the CC's determination to forge ahead also had a decisive influence.

This long struggle, mainly, it seemed, over a question of procedure, was once again concerned with a fundamental issue, the proper competence of the Secretariat for Christian Unity. That this conciliar organ had been established without any connection with the offices of the Roman Curia was enough to make it suspect in Roman circles; and John XXIII took every means to see to it that the Secretariat's full competence was formally recognized.[161]

---

[161] The Pope's decision, October 19, 1962, confirmed that Bea's Secretariat was in every way equal in rank to the conciliar commissions. On November 30, 1962, the Council was told that, given the differences between the Orthodox and the Protestants, the Sec-

But at the beginning of the intersession the freedom of the schema on ecumenism was still burdened by the difficult link that had been established with the Commission on the Oriental Churches, which was itself a liege of the Curial congregation of the same name.[162] This situation had arisen at the close of the conciliar debate on ecumenism, shortly before the end of the first period. Of the three drafts on ecumenism before the fathers,[163] only the one on the unity of the Church bearing the title "That All May Be One" and coming from the Commission on the Oriental Churches, came up for discussion.

Because of its origin in a group that displayed little openness to the perspectives of the ecumenical movement, this schema had to endure a rain of criticism from the majority. One of the main faults found in the text was its complete lack of the spirit of dialogue. But when it was time to vote, some representatives of the majority were unwilling to inflict on Cicognani, the President of the Oriental Commission, a humiliation comparable to that which Ottaviani of the Doctrinal Commission had

---

retariat for Christian Unity would henceforth have two sections, both under the authority of the same president and the same secretary (*DocCath* 60 [1963], 36 and 634). On January 14, 1963, the Secretariat was formally put in charge of questions having to do with the Oriental Churches separated from Rome (official letter from the Secretariat of State to Bea, confirming that this had been within the competence of his Secretariat since its establishment; cf. Fr. Thijssen, "De geschiedenis van het decreet 'De Oecumenismo,'" in *Het decreet over de katholieke deelname aan de oecumenische beweging* [Hilversum, 1967], 15 and 23). By a decision of the CC at the end of March, 1963, the entire responsibility for the text on ecumenism (including the part on the Orthodox) was assigned to the Secretariat. Despite these official decisions some leaders of the Council continued to cast doubt on the competence of the Secretariat for, among other things, the difficult question of religious freedom, as was clear from the communiqué that Msgr. Felici issued October 9-10, 1964, in the name of Cicognani (see J. Grootaers, "Paul VI et la Déclaration conciliaire sur la liberté religieuse," in *Paolo VI e il rapporto Chiesa-Mondo al Concilio* [Brescia: Istituto Paolo VI, 1991], 111-17).

[162] At its root the conflict between the Secretariat for Christian Unity and the Congregation for the Oriental Churches could be traced back to the irreducible opposition between ecumenism and uniatism. This tension was all the more distressing because within the very group of leaders of the Oriental fathers at Vatican II there were dissensions that persisted and were still painfully evident toward the end of the journey of the schema on the Oriental Churches in October 1964. See also the statements of Msgr. Slipyi, of which we shall speak below, in chapter IX.

[163] The first text, chapter XI of the Theological Commission's schema on the Church, contained an explanation of several matters related to ecumenism. The second, the draft of a pastoral decree on Catholic ecumenism, prepared by the Secretariat for Christian Unity, was written in a spirit of openness to the separated brothers and sisters and was close to the Catholic ecumenical movement of which Willebrands had been one of the most important architects since 1950. The third was the schema "That All May Be One," presented by the Commission for the Oriental Churches and given priority by Cicognani (The texts were published in a special issue of *Istina*, 10 [1964], 407-92).

had to suffer; and Bea and Cicognani agreed on December 1 to a for-mula "that would give this schema a reverent burial."[164] The ambiguity of this agreement made it possible for both opponents and defenders of the text to join in a positive vote. It stated, first, that the fathers approved the text "as a document that brings together the shared truths of faith and as a manifestation of thoughtfulness and good will toward the separated brethren of the East." It then asked that the amendments be taken into consideration and that "this decree be combined" with the other two schemas "into a single document."[165]

This ambiguity, which made it possible for Cicognani to save face, would also enable the Commission on the Oriental Churches to block the will of the conciliar majority. A tripartite mixed commission com-posed of members of the Doctrinal Commission, the Secretariat for Christian Unity, and the Commission on the Oriental Churches was established on January 3, 1963, to recast the three schemas into one. But although this difficult collaboration was able slowly over some weeks to get underway, an unexpected tough line taken on February 5 by Welykyj, secretary of both the Oriental Commission and of the Oriental Congregation) put an end to the joint project.[166] The principal argument by which Welykyj and other leaders of the Oriental Commission justi-fied a return to the text criticized by the Council was precisely the first part of the ambiguous resolution passed on December 1. In their view the schema had been approved and the Oriental Commission alone was competent to make any amendments in it. Without going into the details of a battle over procedure that would not subside until the end of April, we may note that precious time was thus lost in struggles that later proved to be rear-guard actions of the Oriental Commission.[167]

---

[164] See O. Rousseau, always a well informed chronicler, who notes that the defects of the schema criticized at the Council had been pointed out long before by consultors dur-ing the preparatory period and that reports urging a recasting of the text had been sent at that time, in vain, to those in charge of the preparation for Vatican II (*Irénikon* 24 [1962], 530). This information was confirmed by the personal testimony of P. Stiernon, who had worked on the preparatory schema as the one "in charge of the theological section" (see his article "Concile et Unité Chrétienne," *La Libre Belgique*, December 4, 1962, 1-2).

[165] *AS* I/4, 7ff.

[166] Msgr. J. F. Arrighi, *Note sur la collaboration du Secrétariat avec d'autres Com-missions pour le schéma "De Oecumenismo,"* September 24, 1963, Dom E. Lanne Archive in the Monastery of Chevetogne. Many details of the meeting of Bea, Ottaviani, and Cicognani can be found in Alberigo, *Attese*, 207ff.

[167] The tough line taken on February 5 was followed by obstructive tactics at the beginning of March. When the tripartite collaboration of the experts could be resumed in February and when the drafts reached the level of the bishops of the mixed commission, the secretariat of the Oriental Commission refused to convoke the bishops over whom it

It goes without saying that in the opinion of the Council the responsibility for this procrastination was often assigned to the tactic adopted by Bea, whose gentlemen's agreements were not respected by the Oriental Commission. Chroniclers at the time (between January and May 1963) reported rumors of quiet agreements between Bea and Cicognani, and the historian can certify from various sources *in tempore non suspecto* that these agreements were made on January 3, at the end of February, and at the end of April.[168]

From all these facts it can only be concluded that, due to the tenacious influence that the Oriental Commission (and the Congregation of the same name) had on him, Cicognani constantly changed his mind and returned to conservative positions he had momentarily abandoned. His about-face before the CC on March 29, 1963, seems to confirm this fickleness, but, this time, in the other direction and after a probable personal intervention of John XXIII in person, as noted in the previous section. A combination of incompatible roles gave Cicognani a key position of great power at the Council but also certainly sapped his credibility.[169]

The bishops of the three mixed subcommissions, who met from February 23 on, were in fact working on newly edited texts. Behind this new redaction there were, to begin with, the authors of the three preparatory texts which were supposed now to be reduced to a "synthesis": Father J. Witte (chapter XI of the schema on the Church); Willebrands (schema on ecumenism); Welykyj (schema on the unity of the Church).[170]

---

had competence. The result was that the draft of chapter III, on the Oriental Churches, could not be validly approved until the final meeting, on March 9, 1963.

[168] I restrict myself here to sources belonging to the limited circle of the Secretariat for Christian Unity: (1) Arrighi's already cited note, 1, 2, 3; (2) the commentary of C. J. Dumont, "La genèse du décret sur l'oecuménisme," *Istina*, 10 (1964), 464 n.28; (3) the testimony of G. Thils, who, on May 1, 1963, attributed the unjamming of the situation to a recently concluded agreement that gave Bea freedom of action for the schema on ecumenism, in exchange for a series of amendments granted to Cicognani (see J. Grootaers, *Diarium*, Cahier 7; statements of É. Beauduin to the same effect are to be found in the same document, Cahier 9). An account of the meeting of the mixed commission on January 3, 1963, is given as Appendix II in Alberigo, *Attese*, 225-26).

[169] Even C.-J. Dumont, a very circumspect witness of these events, could not help but write of Cicognani combining the presidency of the Oriental Commission with the presidency of the CC: "This combination made him both judge and litigant, and that is always a very uncomfortable situation" (Dumont, "La genèse," 464 n.28).

[170] Witte, who taught ecumenism at the Gregorian University, would be called upon, some time later, to collaborate on the new section on Protestantism in chapter III. Welykyj, who belonged to the Order of the Basilians of St. Josaphat, was secretary of the Commission on the Oriental Churches and was to play a decisive role in the conflict with the Secretariat for Christian Unity.

In February, after the rejection of Thils's draft, recourse was had to a text by Witte, which was to be the basis of the first chapter. From this point on the main divisions of the material would be definitively set and would involve three chapters: I. The Principles of Catholic Ecumenism; II. The Practice of Ecumenism; and III. Particular Considerations on the Oriental Churches.[171] According to the directives given by the CC at the end of March, the last chapter was to have two sections: A. Reflections on the Oriental Churches; B. Separated Churches and Ecclesial Communities in the West.

As a result of the intransigence of the Oriental Commission, chapters I and II were assigned to a bipartite subcommission with representatives from the Doctrinal Commission (the most active being Léger, McGrath, and Witte) and from the Secretariat for Christian Unity (the most active being De Smedt and Thils), while the subcommission for chapter III was to have a tripartite composition that also included representatives from the Oriental Commission. However, as already noted, since the bishops of the Oriental Commission had not been convoked for a meeting, the draft of chapter III could not be approved at the final meeting on March 9.

Willebrands, who was the leader in this entire sensitive operation, then encountered a new obstacle thrown up by the Doctrinal Commission, and this at a time when the obstructiveness of the Oriental Commission had not yet been overcome. As we have seen, the Doctrinal Commission continued to demand direct control, at the plenary meetings, of texts from mixed commissions or subcommissions. Knowing of the conflict between Ottaviani and Cento on this precise point, Willebrands preferred to wait for the outcome of this crisis before deciding on his own strategy.[172] At its meeting at the end of March the CC backed Cento's position that further control by the Doctrinal Commission was superfluous. It may be supposed that this outcome made an impression on Willebrands. In any case, after sending chapters I and II of his draft to Tromp, secretary of the Doctrinal Commission (a gesture of deference but not of submission), Willebrands sent the schema to the Secretary of State and obtained the Pope's authorization to send it to the bishops on

---

[171] *AS* V/1, 464.

[172] In a note that is undated but can be placed toward the end of March 1963, Witte reported to Philips on the tensions between the Secretariat for Christian Unity and the Doctrinal Commission over the control the latter wanted to have over the mixed subcommissions. Witte stressed that Willebrands wanted first to see how the cardinals of the CC would settle the similar conflict between Ottaviani and Cento (see the Philips Archive, CCV, P025.07, 9-10).

April 22, that is, without waiting, as Tromp wished him to do, for the plenary meeting of the Doctrinal Commission on May 15.[173]

As a result of Bea's and Cento's steadfast defense of the autonomy of their Commissions, Ottaviani resigned himself to the emancipation of the promoters of the schema on ecumenism. Perhaps he regarded the stakes involved in the battle over the schema on the Church as more important.

Despite the authorization of John XXIII and his desire to speed up the proceedings, the text was not immediately sent to the fathers of the Council, as had been anticipated; a second section, dealing with the separated Churches of the East, still had to be added to chapter III. The plenary meeting of the Secretariat for Christian Unity had this on its agenda from May 18 to May 25.[174] This meeting of the Secretariat made its provisional final adjustments to the new schema on ecumenism that would be presented to the conciliar assembly on November 18, 1963, and would there be the subject of extensive debate.[175]

The schema produced during this second preparation differed radically from the unsuitable text that had been submitted to the fathers for a vote on December 1, 1962. During that first period the words *ecumenism* and *ecumenical* had quickly proved to be the passwords of this incipient Council. A preparatory schema from a commission that had no real sensitivity to the movement for Christian unity could not satisfy the thinking of the majority. As C. Dumont has written, the claim that the schema on ecumenism of May 1963 only brought a rearrangement of the material without touching the substance falls well short of the truth.[176] Although the redactors had used parts of the earlier schemas, the new text had adopted a completely different perspective. The reworked schema took as its starting point the real ecumenical movement as it had developed over the previous a quarter-century. If that movement had been ignored by the leading authorities of the Catholic Church, it was

[173] See Arrighi, *Note sur la collaboration du Secrétariat pour l'Unité avec d'autres Commissions*, 4. Not without some bitterness, Tromp wrote in his official report that the Doctrinal Commission had thus been faced with a fait accompli (*ante factum ut aiunt completum*)! (see the *Acta Commissionis de doctrina fidei et morum*, March 13 — September 30, 1963, 3).

[174] It is odd to see many chroniclers passing over in silence this phase in the redaction of the text. Fortunately, Msgr. Frans Thijssen, a close friend and collaborator of Willebrands, has left us a detailed account of it (see his "De geschiedenis," 22).

[175] Before the beginning of the second period of Vatican II, the Council fathers had the opportunity to send their observations to Rome, and several hundred such reached the Secretariat for Christian Unity.

[176] See Dumont, "La genèse," 466.

now being taken into account by this new Roman organization that John XXIII had established for the express purpose of renewing perspectives. The schema represented an effort — admittedly with a certain amount of trial and error, due to the novelty of the subject — to give expression to the vision of a Church that was opening itself to dialogue with the "separated brethren."

The first chapter included a description of the unity and unicity of the Church of Jesus Christ, an explanation of the relationship of the separated brethren and their communities to the Catholic Church, and a general approach to ecumenism itself. There was thus a shift from an abstract concept of the unity of the Church (as developed in the theology manuals) to the "mystery of the Church," and from the juridical idea of schism to the "mystery of division."[177] Many bishops of the Secretariat for Christian Unity and the experts, who had had to do their work very hastily, were not at all satisfied with the new section brought in at the last minute and dealing with the ecclesial communities born as a result of the Protestant Reformation of the sixteenth century.

2. The Apostolate of the Laity

It is undeniable that there is some likeness between the role the Commission on the Lay Apostolate filled at the Council and the role the Secretariat for Christian Unity took on at the same period. Both, although in different ways, were conciliar institutions outside the world of the Curia.[178]

---

[177] "The necessity of dealing (with the ecumenical question) arises from the new spiritual situation of our age. It is due to the fact that a centuries-long separation has in fact become scandalous to many Christians as well as to non-Christians. For separation is contrary to the formal will of Christ . . . and also paralyzes the evangelization of the world and the spread of the kingdom of God." These were the reflections of Msgr. Martin, Archbishop of Rouen, who had the duty of presenting the new text to the fathers. Cicognani's general introduction and Martin's report on chapters I and II were followed by a report entrusted to a bishop of the Oriental Commission, Msgr. Bukatko, who presented the first section of chapter III. This gesture, desired by Cicognani, was meant to ease the tensions that had accompanied the preparation of this chapter.

[178] The Commission for the Lay Apostolate was among the ten commissions established by the Motu Proprio *Superno Dei nutu* of June 5, 1960, to prepare the documents for the Council, whereas the Secretariat for Christian Unity appeared under a separate heading that supposed a more limited competence. Another difference between the two was that the composition of the Secretariat remained the same after the start of the Council, whereas the elections of commissions at the Council considerably altered the composition of the Commission on the Lay Apostolate. The "Conférence internationale d'oecuménistes catholiques" was founded in 1952 by Willebrands and Thijssen, who from the outset had contacts in the Roman Curia. It was in this Conference that John

The great debates that had gone on for several decades in the theology of the laity and in apostolic action, marked as they were by the awakening of a Christian laity within the Catholic Church, were the main sources of inspiration for the schema on the lay apostolate. In turn those debates had a direct impact on the positions taken by the Council in ecclesiology. The same was true to some degree for ecumenism, the pioneers of which had not only prepared the ground for a dialogue of the Catholic Church with the other Christian Churches but had also helped change the general image of the Church.

At the same time, however, the Commission over which Cento presided presented a profile very different from that of the Secretariat for Christian Unity. Although the Commission for the Lay Apostolate could not be regarded as one of the stars of Vatican II — as Bea's Secretariat could — neither could it be regarded as unimportant. The passage of time shows it to have had great qualities, the primary one being the sense it had of its own autonomy and proper authority as an organ of the Council. It was not inclined blindly to follow the directives of the General Secretariat, which told it to shorten its text (November 22, 1962) and to change the plan of the schema and introduce a section on "associations of the faithful" (beginning of December 1962).[179] At the preliminary meeting in mid-January 1963 a plea from Msgr. Pavan, who stressed the special character of social action in the apostolate, was enough to obtain the rejection of these official recommendations.

Despite this sense of its autonomy, which would find expression on several occasions, Cento's commission seems to have cultivated very flexible relations with Curial circles in general. This can be explained by the fact that well before the Council Cento and Glorieux had acquired personal experience of the Roman environment.[180] In addition, the

XXIII found the basis for building his Secretariat for Christian Unity (see the fundamental work of Ét. Fouilloux, *Les catholiques et l'unité chrétienne du XIXe au XXe siècle* [Paris, 1982]). COPECIAL (Comité Permanent des Congrès Internationaux pour l'Apostolat des Laïcs), founded in 1952, had Glorieux as its ecclesiastical liaison. John XXIII did not hesitate to increase the standing of this Comité as early as 1959 and to draw from it the men and ideas that would enrich the preparatory Commission for the Lay Apostolate (see J. G. Vaillancourt, *Papal Power* [Berkeley, 1980], 78-84; see also the communiqué on COPECIAL in *OssRom*, August 6, 1959).

[179] In the fascicle published at the beginning of December 1962, by authority of the General Secretariat, listing twenty schemas to be studied, the Commission for the Lay Apostolate was called upon to change its general argument, to combine the third and fourth parts of the preparatory schema, and to add a text dealing with "associations of the faithful" that was not familiar to it and came from the Commission for the Discipline of the Clergy and the Faithful. The Commission would refuse to carry out this request.

[180] Father R. Tucci seems to have been one of the Commission's principal figures; as

themes of the lay apostolate and Catholic Action had, certainly since Pius XII, become familiar to the officials of the Congregations and, in any case, had nothing in common with such risky innovations, regarded by some as close to heresy, as *ecumenism, religious freedom,* and *episcopal collegiality*. Furthermore, Italian Catholic Action, by reason of its proximity, was something that could be assimilated and was therefore reassuring.

One of the chief merits of the Commission's work would be that it reflected the great debates within the Church since the expansion of the apostolate of the laity, the polemics about the notion of Catholic Action and its "mandate," the question of groups of spirituality, and the need to find a way to organize the consulting of lay people in the Church.

And yet, as we reread today the successive versions of the schema out of which the Decree *Apostolicam actuositatem* emerged in 1965, it is hard to avoid the impression that those texts often did not represent the quality of the discussions and the participants within the Commission. The plan of the initial schemas lacked logic, and the texts seemed vague and repetitive.[181] In these respects the high level of the Commission was not always reflected in the texts it prepared.

On the other hand, one certainly has to take into account here the other activities of the Commission and, first of all, its important collaboration in the long and difficult redaction of schema XVIII. The fathers of the Commission for the Lay Apostolate played a leading role in the mixed commission for that draft. Many questions, among them a text on the family, that were on the table of Cento's Commission had to be handed over to the mixed commission — and not always with the expected results. Finally, collaboration with the Doctrinal Commission, always jealous of its birthright, was not easy when it came to the chapter on the laity in the schema on the Church. According to some testimonies, this collaboration had the negative effect of shifting the theological foundations of the lay apostolate from the Commission's schema to the chapter on the laity in the schema on the Church.[182]

---

director of *La Civiltà Cattolica* and close to John XXIII, he too had personal experience of the sensitivities of Curial circles; on many occasions he acted as intermediary between the "foreigners" at the Council and various Roman circles. This was especially the case in regard to information to be given to the press and, even later, in negotiations connected with the plan for the journal *Concilium*.

[181] See the commentary of Msgr. Streiff, himself a member of the Commission, in *Études et documents* (of the French episcopate), no. 14 (July 2, 1964), six pages.

[182] See Streif and M. de Surgy, in *Études et documents*, 1.

a. The Coordinating Commission

A decisive point in the genesis of the schema on the lay apostolate was the meeting of the CC on January 25, 1963. Even before that date, study sessions, first with some experts and then, from January 14 to 20, with some bishops and experts who were in Rome, had made it possible to shorten considerably the set of preparatory documents while retaining the titles of the four existing parts.[183]

Cardinal Urbani reported on this schema, printed at the urging of Tucci, at the January meeting. He emphasized the need to shorten the preparatory schema and also showed how to restructure the material.[184] A decisive part of the discussion at the CC was the report which Glorieux composed for Urbani's use and which was part of the official file submitted to the cardinals. In this report, dated January 20, 1963, Glorieux sketched the background of the text and justified the Commission's refusal to follow the instructions from the general secretary at the beginning of December 1962. The first part of the schema was retained, its purpose being "to explain some general ideas, once for all, and so avoid repeating them in each section." The three other parts were appreciably shortened. The Commission also said that it was impossible to merge the third and fourth parts, as it had been asked to do; such a merger "risked creating or maintaining serious confusions of two quite different spheres: the sphere of charitable activities . . . and the sphere of temporal activities." The major contribution of Glorieux's report was its insistent expression of the Commission's wish that a mixed commission be formed (from the Commission on the Lay Apostolate and the Doctrinal Commission) in order to prepare a single schema on the effective presence of the Church in the social order and in the community of peoples.[185]

Following upon these reports and an exchange of ideas, the CC decided to follow Glorieux and retain the division into four parts and also accept the recently revised text. Parts II and III could be shortened and could end up as "instructions," while part IV should be reduced to

---

[183] The four fascicles of the preparatory schema contained 166 large-size pages, a text which the conciliar authorities immediately judged to be an undigested mass. The four parts dealt with General ideas; Action tending directly to advance the reign of Christ; Charitable action; Social action (see *Schemata constitutionum et decretorum. Series quarta* [Vatican City, 1963], 45-176).

[184] *AS* V/1, 104-5, 194-5.

[185] *AS* V/1, 110-14.

a statement of some great principles for action while referring specific points to schema XVII.[186]

The three most important decisions reached by the CC in January marked the beginning of a new stage. The Cento Commission was asked to form a mixed commission together with the Commission on Discipline (to deal with associations of the faithful) and another mixed commission together with the Doctrinal Commission (with regard to the chapter on the laity in the schema on the Church and to schema XVII). Finally, the CC approved the proposal, "made orally," to organize a consultation with eminent lay persons as "experts" on this schema.[187]

b. The Plenary Commission on the Lay Apostolate

The day after the January meeting of the CC, the Commission began preparations for a plenary meeting that would have two phases, a meeting of the experts alone on March 1 and 3 and a meeting of all members on March 6 and 10.

The bishop-members of the Commission had not only received the reworked version but had also been asked to consult extensively but discreetly with the laity of their countries.[188] Their observations, synthesized in forty pages, were put at the disposal of the plenary commission. The latter decided, first, to modify the structure of the text, which no longer corresponded to the greatly shortened material; henceforth the text would be divided into two parts of more or less equal length: (1) the lay apostolate in general; and (2) the lay apostolate in particular.[189]

---

[186] Ibid., 117-18.

[187] This request and then the actual preparation of this consultation were shrouded in great secrecy; it is clear that people wanted, at any cost, to avoid stirring up certain sensibilities. They were thinking either of certain Roman circles or of the Council fathers themselves, who had not been consulted in due form and would face something like a fait accompli.

[188] The ecclesiastical liaisons of Catholic international organizations and the members of the management committee of COPECIAL also received the text so that they might give their reactions (see Glorieux, *Acta Commissionis Conciliaris "De Fidelium Apostolatu*, 27-29. See also idem, "Histoire du décret," especially 114-15).

[189] In March 1963 the Commission thought that it had produced a definitive work, but a year later the structure of the schema would be turned topsy-turvy once again. The division into two parts was criticized as illogical and very repetitious. The reworked schema of May 1964 had five chapters: (I) The call to the apostolate; (II) Communities of life and life settings; (III) Goals; (IV) Organizational forms; and (V) The order to be followed. In the schema promulgated in 1965 we find this division, except that a sixth chapter on formation has been added and the order of chapters II and III has been inverted (see Glorieux, "Histoire du décret," 122-23).

The draft, which the plenary group finished revising on March 10, was submitted again to the CC, which met at the end of that month. On this occasion Urbani expressed his entire satisfaction with the way in which Cento's Commission had followed the norms set down by the CC. He also supported the commission's refusal to introduce the text on associations of the faithful into its schema, and he said he was convinced that the schema in its present form deserved to be sent to the fathers, when one took into account "that this is the first time this subject will be discussed at a council," and in view, too, of the expectations existing among the laity.[190]

The schema on the lay apostolate was part of the batch of conciliar drafts approved by the Holy Father on April 22 and intended for immediate transmission.[191] The schema was a booklet of forty-eight pages and ninety-two paragraphs in two parts dealing with the lay apostolate in general and in particular.[192] During July and August the observations of the fathers reached Rome, and in September the Commission published a report that in general the opinions of the bishops were favorable, with the most frequent criticisms having to do with the length and wordiness of the schema. Countless improvements were suggested and were studied by the Commission.[193]

c. Lay People Associated with the Work of the Commission

More important, perhaps, than the inclusion of the subject of the laity in the agenda of Vatican II was the fact that "representative" lay persons shared in the redaction of conciliar texts. The beginnings of this historic experiment took place on February 26 and 27, 1963, and were directly concerned with the schema on the lay apostolate on the eve of its presentation to the full commission. A second consultation with lay people, fuller and more official, concerned schema XVII and took place at the end of April 1963. And the newly elected Paul VI, who in his time had

[190] *AS* V/1, 300-1.

[191] It is generally thought that the sending took place at the end of April or the beginning of May. According to Glorieux's chronicle, the schema was not sent until June (see *Acta Commissionis Conciliaris*, 52).

[192] Though the text was forty-eight pages in length in April 1963, it would undergo further changes: seventeen mimeographed pages in January 1964 and eighteen printed pages in June 1964.

[193] The full agenda of the second period of Vatican II (autumn 1963) did not allow for a discussion in the hall. There would only be a short presentation of the schema by Hengsbach on December 2, just before the end of this period (see, among others, Caprile, III, 410-11).

been a strong advocate of the laity in Italy, decided to invite lay auditors to the Council itself, a decision made public on September 14, 1963.

These events were of great historical interest because they shed new light not only on the antecedents of the Commission for the Lay Apostolate, but also, and more generally, on the antecedents of the role played by the laity at Vatican II.[194] As noted earlier, the first consultation of lay people took place in deepest secrecy. The leaders of the Committee for International Congresses of the Lay Apostolate met in Rome to discuss an ordinary agenda with no apparent connections with the work of the conciliar commission. The experts of the Commission "paid a visit" to the COPECIAL meeting in order to converse with its participants, and "everything went on as though any consultation had occurred incidentally."[195] But it is obvious that this first consultation in February 1963 did not spring from a void.

From the very beginning of the preparatory phase of Vatican II, a number of actions by international organizations for the lay apostolate made an active contribution to the preparation of the Council. The leaders of the Pax Romana — International Movement of Catholic Intellectuals sent a report to the authorities of the Council from their meeting in Fribourg on July 17, 1960. For its part, the Conference of International Catholic Organizations set up a Special Group with a view to the Council, and this sent a series of six reports to the authorities in charge (1961-62).[196]

---

[194] The indispensable study here is the article of Professor Rosemary Goldie of the Pastoral Institute of the Lateran University in Rome and an auditor at Vatican II, "La participation des laïcs aux travaux du Concile Vatican II"; as well as her article, "Lay Participation in the Work of Vatican II,"in *Miscellanea Lateranense* (= *Lateranum*, N.S. 40-41 [1974-75]. 505-25). Goldie's most important contribution to the Council in 1963 was the communication to the fathers of her panoramic view of the activity of the laity in the world (see R. Goldie, "Le panorama de l'Apostolat des laïcs," in *L'Apostolat des laïcs*, ed. Y. Congar [Unam Sanctam 75; Paris, 1970], 141-56). On the role of the international Catholic organizations at that period, see R. Sugranyes de Franch, *Le Christ dans le monde: les organisations internationales catholiques* (Paris, 1972); idem, "Die kirchlichen Weltverbände," in *Handbuch der Pastoraltheologie* IV (Freiburg, 1969), 659-71. Sugranyes himself played a key role in the international laity before, during, and after Vatican II.

[195] According to the testimony of J.-P. Dubois-Dumée, which was given at the time of the event. See Grootaers, *Diarium*, Cahier 9. According to Rosemary Goldie, in a letter which she kindly wrote to me on January 14, 1995, the only churchmen present were members of the ecclesiastical commission of COPECIAL.

[196] These reports dealt, among other things, with the activity of Catholics at the international level, the role of chaplains, women in society and in the Church, Christians in a technological world, and involvment in social life. Similar steps were taken by the Catholic Center connected with UNESCO, by Caritas International, by the international J.

It was, then, from this world of the international laity and more espe-
cially of the committee that had organized the World Congress of the
Lay Apostolate of October 1957 and was already preparing for the next
one that the lay people were chosen who were consulted by the conciliar
Commission for the Lay Apostolate.[197] Among the participants in the
"consultation" at the end of February we find the names of J.-P. Dubois-
Dumée (France), Marguerite Fiévez (Belgium), P. Keegan (Great
Britain), Prince Karl zu Löwenstein (Germany), Claude Ryan (Canada),
Ramón Sugranyes de Franch (Catalonia), Juan Vásquez (Argentina), and
Martin Work (U.S.A.). The COPECIAL committee was chaired by Sil-
vio Golzio, with R. Goldie serving as secretary. The summary of the
exchange of views at the meeting was sent to the conciliar commission.
The remarks made had to do, in order of priority, with the structure of
the schema, relations among hierarchy, clergy, and laity, coordination of
the lay apostolate, international action, and social action.[198]

On April 24-26, 1963, there was an official consultation in Rome, this
time in relation to schema XVII, between lay experts and the fathers and
experts of the mixed commission. The absence of any representation
from women's movements, which were so numerous and so active, was
regrettable. The concerns with method that surfaced on this occasion
would arise anew throughout the difficult course of this lengthy text.
The recurring question was: How can this schema be given a greater
unity in its development and style? Was it preferable to limit it to an
explanation of principles, or should it, on the contrary, lead to practical
applications?[199] The interventions of the lay persons highlighted what

O. C. (Jeunesse Chrétienne Ouvrière), in the form especially of "Reflections Submitted to
the Preparatory Commissions of the Council." I owe information on these documents to
the kindness of R. Goldie (letter of August 24, 1991). Some of these contributions were
published as supplements to the *Bulletin Lay Apostolate* in 1960-62. For more details, see
Goldie, "La participation des laïcs," 58-61.

[197] In this connection see the three volumes of *Documents du deuxième Congrès mondial pour l'Apostolat des laïcs* (Rome, October 5-13, 1957), I. *Les laïcs dans l'Église*; II.
Face au monde d'aujourd'hui; III. *Former des apôtres* (Rome: COPECIAL, 1958). Here
one will find most of the names that came up during the preparatory phase of the Council and during the work of Vatican II. During the audience granted to the leaders of the
Conference of International Catholic Organizations on November 11, 1963, Paul VI himself said that it was in recognition of the merits of the organizations that the first lay auditors were chosen from among their leaders.

[198] Glorieux's chronological survey says nothing about this consultation. Details are
given in Goldie, "La participation des laïcs," 63.

[199] Tucci, "Introduction," 42. Among the lay persons present were J.-P. Dubois-
Dumée, J. Folliet, J. Larnaud, J. J. Norris, R. Sugranyes de Franch, and V. Veronese; R.
Goldie and M. de Habicht were consulted by letter.

the world expected of the Council and, more especially, what the laity expected of the text on the presence of the Church in contemporary society. The participants also worked in subgroups on the individual chapters, along with theologians, many of whom had prepared the texts. These exchanges proved especially profitable.[200]

d. Salient Themes

I shall deal mainly with three major themes that arose at the full meeting of the Commission in March 1963: the question of Catholic Action and the meaning of a "mandate;" associations of the faithful; and the possible establishment of a permanent secretariat at the Holy See.[201] The resistance and occasional crises that marked the life of lay apostolate movements during the ten years before the announcement of the Council found a focal point in the debates over the idea of Catholic Action and its functions. The powder keg was lit, as it were, on the occasion of the World Congress of the Lay Apostolate in October 1957, when at the suggestion of Suenens, then a young auxiliary bishop of Malines, Pius XII expressed his readiness to re-examine the status of Catholic Action.[202] Lively opposition between movements, which had arisen at the national level, became international after the 1957 World Congress.[203]

An echo of this lively controversy was heard in the preparation for Vatican II. The chapter on Catholic Action in the preparatory schema on

[200] Glorieux, "Les étapes préliminaires," 397-98.

[201] The themes that held the Commission's attention in the spring of 1963 were not necessarily the same as all the salient points of the text that was promulgated on November 18, 1965. For the plenary meeting of March, 1963, I use the account of Msgr. A. Glorieux, *Acta Commissionis*, 29-52.

[202] Suenens was at that time the defender of the Legion of Mary and was endeavoring to end the monopoly on the mandate of Catholic Action enjoyed by a single form of the lay apostolate (see L.-J. Suenens, "L'unité multiforme de l'Action catholique," *Nouvelle revue théologique* 80 [1958], 3-21); and, at the same period, his preface to Jeremiah Newman, *What Is Catholic Action?* [Dublin, 1958], v-vi; see also idem, *Souvenirs et Espérances*, 40-41, 276-77; and idem, *Les Imprévus de Dieu* [Paris, 1993], 85-96, 171-75). In the passage written by Pius XII in 1957, the Pope denounced "an unfortunate and rather widespread disquiet" connected with the use of the term Catholic Action: "We are seeing the species seize hold of the genus" (see *Deuxième Congrès Mondial pour l'Apostolat des laïcs* I [Rome: COPECIAL, 1958], 21-22).

[203] At Vatican II Suenens continued to argue for an expansion of the idea of mandate, thus, according to Caprile, provoking a storm in the council hall. Twenty years later we find similar concerns in Suenens's contributions to the charismatic movement (see *Les mouvements dans l'Église* [Paris, 1983], 9-11, and *I movimenti nella Chiesa [2a Colloquio internazionale, 1984]* [Milan, 1987], 27-36).

the lay apostolate was a compromise among several tendencies. According to Glorieux, this text was strongly criticized in the Central Preparatory Commission: "On this occasion, His Eminence Cardinal Suenens, in particular, explained the suggestion he had submitted to Pius XII. . . . He asked for a reform in terminology that reserves the name 'Catholic Action' not to any particular movement but to the kind of apostolate that characterizes all the movements."[204] But members of the preparatory commission, stressing the reasons why it was not appropriate to follow Suenens's opinion, intervened with the Subcommission on Amendments to keep the text from being changed.

At the early meetings of the conciliar Commission on the Lay Apostolate some of the elected bishops reopened the debate. At the plenary meeting on March 3, 1963, Guano made the point that the intention of the prepared text was not to give a technical definition of Catholic Action but only to set forth some characteristics of it that, taken together, reflected the real state of affairs. But a number of English-speaking fathers brought up the fact that in many countries the term *Catholic Action*, because of pejorative connotations (suggestions of a pressure group) was not used at all; they also said that the expression was not a very happy one from the ecumenical point of view. Suenens's proposal to extend the name of Catholic Action to all apostolic movements, therefore, did not mesh with their pastoral situation. Speaking of the situation on the continent of Europe, Msgr. László (Austria) thought that where Catholic Action had developed according to the instructions of recent pontiffs, it had had a great value that ought not be imperiled by changes that would upset the situation.[205] Finally, some members of the Commission pointed out that in some countries where the organizations known as Catholic Action were still far from vibrant, the name might dissuade the best persons from getting involved in these associations.[206]

Guano undertook the defense of a text that would take account of these difficulties and strike a happy medium. He guided the plenary Commission toward a solution that was found acceptable; while the draft would retain what was said about Catholic Action, it would also speak in the same chapter of other forms of apostolate, whether individual or organized. Catholic Action would thus be seen as one form among

[204] A. Glorieux, "Introduction générale," in *L'Apostolat des laïcs* (Paris, 1966), 34. The French bishops at the Council, a large number of whom at that time came from Catholic Action, reacted sharply to Suenens's proposals.

[205] Glorieux, *Acta Commissionis*, 45-46.

[206] Glorieux, "Histoire du décret," 115.

others, since the "distinctive notes" of Catholic Action could be found, even in combination, in associations that did not bear that name. Finally, the schema would leave it to the bishops themselves to decide which associations corresponded best to the needs of their dioceses.[207] This new presentation of a chapter on "the various forms of organized apostolate" would win the support of a very large majority at the Council.[208]

The controversy should not make us forget that the main teaching of the decree was the fundamental assertion that every Christian vocation is by its nature a baptismally based call to the apostolate and to mission.[209]

Another very lively discussion arose when the great majority of the members of the Commission opposed the CC's decision that the text on associations of the faithful, which came from a different commission, should become part of the schema on the lay apostolate. The rejection was justified by various complaints: juridical language, confusion of two different subjects (membership in a Third Order is not sufficient grounds for speaking of an apostolate), and, finally, the responsibility of this Commission specifically for the lay apostolate. The exchange of opinions showed that the Commission wanted to keep the involvement of the laity in society from being devalued by appearing to be associated simply with "charitable works."

Finally, the possible establishment at the Holy See of a permanent secretariat for the lay apostolate was discussed at the plenary meeting of March 1963. The majority on the Commission had great reservations about a project whose need was not apparent; the lay apostolate was structured at diocesan or national levels and in in many and varied forms according to pastoral traits and local traditions. If such a secretariat were to become a reality, its role should only be consultative.[210]

For this intersession as a whole we may then distinguish three types of collaboration between the Commission for the Lay Apostolate and the Doctrinal Commission; in two of the three types lay people played an active part.

---

[207] Glorieux, "Introduction générale," 35.

[208] In the draft decree approved on April 22, 1963, no. 56 is on Catholic Action (pp. 33-34, with notes on 36), and no. 19 is on the "mandate" (p. 13, with notes on 16). In the document promulgated in 1965, the sections nos. 20 and 24.

[209] When Cento at last had the opportunity to present the schema to the conciliar assembly in 1964, he said: It is the heart of this text, and our deepest desire, that all the baptized may become aware that no one can be a genuine Christian until he or she thinks of themselves as an apostle; the manifestation of such an awareness would be the greatest triumph of Vatican Council II (see *Relatio super schema de Apostolatu laicorum* [Vatican City, 1964], 4).

[210] Glorieux, "Histoire du décret," 116.

1. The mixed commission for the chapter on the laity in the schema on the Church was still controlled by the Doctrinal Commission, which, still convinced that it should dominate,[211] saw the issue as establishing solid doctrinal foundations for more concrete applications that were the competence of the sort of pastoral commission over which Cento presided.[212]

2. The development of the decree on the lay apostolate was in the competence of Cento's Commission, but the mixed commission over which Cento and Browne presided jointly did have a right to inspect it. The consultation of the laity in the form of the Permanent Committee for International Congresses of the Lay Apostolate, at the end of February 1963, was another indirect operation in which the participation of the laity was hidden from the eyes of the Council fathers.

3. The proceedings of the mixed commission for schema XVII may be regarded as representing progress in terms of cooperation between two Commissions and of introducing the laity into the working of Vatican II. In April 1963 the mixed commission organized a direct consultation of the laity. This time the latter's contribution was much more explicit, and the lay people enjoyed the status of experts; but the deliberations on the final day of the meeting took place after their departure.

C. FAILURES IN THE SECOND PREPARATION

1. *The Schema on Bishops and the Government of Dioceses*

The pastoral and juridical aspects of the functions of bishops were a meeting point of the major concerns of Vatican II. While chapter II (soon to become III) of the schema on the Church was intended to establish the dogmatic foundations for the meaning of the episcopate in a

---

[211] One of the experts of the Doctrinal Commission said at the time that the mixed subcommission for the chapter on the laity had as its primary task to coordinate and revise a draft already composed by the Doctrinal Commission (testimony of Moeller, May 1, 1963 [see Grootaers, *Diarium*, Cahier 7]). In his personal impression of the meeting of the mixed subcommission on May 16, 1963, Congar wrote that he was very disappointed: Many bishops of the Cento commission were absent, and "I have seen nothing more woolly, nothing more discouraging. Everything is still at the stage of questions or of bare beginnings" (*JCongar*, 246).

[212] The lay "experts" did not participate in these discussions of the mixed group at the meetings on May 16 and May 25, when Florit, in the name of the subcommission, reported on the chapter on the laity (see Tromp, *Relatio Secretarii Commissionis*, March 13 — September 30, 1963, 30-32).

renewed ecclesial community, the schema on bishops was intended to derive applications for the concrete life of the Church. Both were regarded as a necessary complement to Vatican Council I (1869-70), which had promulgated the dogmas of the primacy and infallibility of the Roman pontiff, but had not had time to complete its program and take up its own draft documents on the episcopate.

This concern to complete the unfinished work of the preceding Council was very much alive on the eve and at the opening of Vatican II. Given the importance the majority attached to the updating of the exercise of the episcopal office, it was quite astounding to see the conciliar Commission on Bishops acting as though they were free to deal with the issue rather offhandedly. As a result, the reaction of the conciliar assembly in November 1963 would be ruthless, all the more so since the debate on this subject came at a turning point in the history of Vatican II — at the moment when the principles of episcopal collegiality had just been approved for the first time by an unexpectedly large majority.

The preparatory Commission on Bishops, chaired initially by Cardinal Mimmi and then by Cardinal Marella, had to draft a whole series of schemas on the functions of bishops, relations of the episcopate to the Roman Curia, the role of episcopal conferences, and so on.[213] Even during the preparatory phase people had realized that coordination was needed, and the task of achieving it was given to the Subcommission for Mixed Matters, which had been established by the Central Commission and began its work in June 1962.[214] At that time, one of its tasks was to unify and coordinate the fourteen different drafts dealing with the episcopate and with pastoral life.

When this Subcommission completed its work on December 3, 1962, it had sent on to the Secretariat of the Council two schemas meant for the new conciliar Commission on Bishops to study and develop: *On Bishops and the Government of Dioceses* and *On the Pastoral Office of Bishops and on the Care of Souls*. The first text summarized five schemas that had been approved by the Central Commission; it dealt with (1) relations between the bishops and the Curial congregations in Rome; (2) coadjutor and auxiliary bishops;[215] (3) episcopal confer-

[213] Among the seventy-three preparatory schemas printed on the eve of the opening of Vatican II, five came from the Commission on Bishops.

[214] The members of the subcommission for mixed questions were Cardinals Tisserant (President), Ferretto, Liénart, Rappouni, and Muench, with Suenens, Montini, and Coussa added later; the secretary was L. Governatori, who would take on the role of secretary of the conciliar Commission on Bishops (see Caprile, I/2, 533-34).

[215] R. Laurentin explains the meaning of the two terms (*Bilan de la deuxième session*

ences; (4) the division of dioceses; and (5) parishes, their merging and division.

The second schema combined in ten chapters the texts discussed by the Central Commission that, in order of priority, dealt with (1) the care of souls; (2) relations between bishops and parish priests; (3) the obligations of parish priests; (4) relations between bishops and religious; (5) the instruction of the Christian people; (6) the pastoral care of the working class; and (7) pastoral vigilance before the errors of materialism.[216]

These products of the preparatory phase had been composed under difficult conditions. The Commission had been constantly under the eye of the Theological Commission, and any member of it who was bold enough to propose some adaptation of the Roman Curia was immediately accused of arrogance. It even took an intervention of John XXIII to restore some freedom of speech. In addition, the final work of synthesis, completed in December 1962, accentuated the centralizing tendency of a document that ignored the proper role of the episcopate and the collegial aspects of this role.[217]

The wishes expressed by the Subcommission for Mixed Matters focused especially on two points: (1) that the schema be discussed at the Council only after discussion of the draft constitution on the Church, from which the doctrine on the episcopate should be derived; and (2) that explanatory notes be added to each chapter of the schema to draw attention to the changes that would have to be made in the existing law,[218] to assist an understanding of the themes and the general spirit that guided the composition of the schemas, and to highlight innovations "that meet some of the justified requests of the bishops."[219] To carry out this task Marella appointed a limited group of experts in Rome to proceed to this final phase of the preparatory schema at the end of which the

---

[Paris, 1964], 110). A *coadjutor* is an assistant of a residential bishop; he has only the authority given him by Rome or delegated to him by his bishop and may have right of succession. An *auxiliary* is an assistant without right of succession and for as long as his bishop is in office.

[216] See Caprile, I/2, 534.

[217] On this point see the personal testimony of Bishop Joseph Gargitter of Bressanone, Italy, in *Dekret über die Hirtenaufgabe der Bischöfe in der Kirche* (Münster, 1967), 6-7. When the conciliar discussion began at the beginning of November 1963, Gargitter was the first bishop to denounce the curialist centralization reflected in the proposed text (see *AS* II/IV, 453-55, and Caprile, III, 190).

[218] See *Relatio super schema decreti "De Episcopis ac de dioecesium regimine"* (Msgr. Carli, reporter) (Vatican City, 1963), 9. A brief history is given here of the different stages of the schema.

[219] According to a memorandum of Marella (February 23, 1963); *AS* V/1, 166.

text of the two schemas, provided now with notes, was presented to the CC.

When this text appeared on the agenda of the CC on January 26, 1963, it was accompanied by a lengthy memorandum in which Marella tried to protect his text against any criticism or at least against any fundamental alteration. (Given the importance of this document, I shall speak of it further on.) Döpfner, who was assigned to report on the text, does not seem to have been impressed by the argument of the president of the Commission on Bishops. He first gave a very critical report and then won approval of a series of guidelines that would be brought up again later, when a complete revision of the schema was finally undertaken. In Döpfner's view, the schema was too long and too detailed to be submitted to the Council. Many subjects could very well find a place in the revised Code of Canon Law and in a "handbook." The main point had to do with episcopal conferences; these were taken up in chapter III but ought to be made the subject of a special decree.[220] In proposals approved unanimously by the CC, the conciliar commission was required thoroughly to review the schema, chapter by chapter. Wherever there was question of faculties or "privileges" granted to bishops by Rome, it would be necessary first to state the general principle according to which residential bishops possess in an ordinary way all the faculties without which they would not be able to carry out their duties; they possess all except those which may be reserved to the Apostolic See.[221] This sensitive point was to remain a special bone of contention, as we shall see.

Finally, on the subject of episcopal conferences, it was necessary, according to the cardinals of the CC, to distinguish carefully between nonbinding consultations and binding decisions, which did not acquire the force of law until after approval by the Holy See.

The essential structure of the schema could be kept, but the various parts had to be amended and improved. It would also be necessary to take account of the observations of the fathers and, above all, of the theological foundations laid down in the schema on the Church and in its chapter on the episcopate.[222]

---

[220] See AS V/1, 140-41.

[221] A great number of bishops had mentioned this hotly debated question in their antepreparatory vota. Alfrink provided a good example of this trend when, as early as 1959, he asked for a change in the existing system of "granting dispensations to diocesan bishops," since the latter are not simply delegates appointed by the center of Christendom to rule a particular territory (see Grootaers, "Une restauration de la théologie de l'épiscopat," 802-3, 821-23).

[222] See AS V/1, 170-1.

The "Rump Commission"

The second stage of the journey began right after the Coordinating Commission's meeting of January 26, 1963. From then until the schema was presented to the Council in November, the full Commission on Bishops would be excluded from the work of revision, which instead was entrusted to what Klaus Mörsdorf, the well-known canonist at the University of Münster and a conciliar expert, dubbed the "rump commission" put to work by the leaders of the conciliar commission during this intersession.[223]

Several plenary meetings of the conciliar Commission on Bishops were announced, but each was cancelled;[224] and because no plenary meeting was held between December 1962 and November 1963 the whole Commission had no opportunity to examine, amend, or approve the schema before the discussion at the Council. Instead of convoking the full Commission, Marella followed a different procedure. Pleading lack of time and the difficulty of foreign bishops coming to Rome, he established a small subcommission composed, as Carli's official report would say, of "some of the nearby members of our Commission and some experts."[225] The subcommission was given the task of producing a new redaction of the schema in accordance with the recent guidelines of the CC while also taking into account the written *vota* that members of the conciliar Commission had meanwhile sent in.

In fact, the entire revision was managed by Bishop Carli of Segni, Italy, one of the strongest spokesmen for the minority that opposed a renewal of ecclesiology in general and of the theology of the episcopate in particular. The rump commission led by Carli, it should be noted, was working at the same time that the Doctrinal Commission was at work on a new schema on the Church; as long as this schema had not been approved by a majority at the Council, the game was not over and an opponent of the second preparation, such as Carli, could try to influence the outcome of the competition. He would constantly invoke this uncertain state of affairs as a reason to rein in every move toward renewal.

---

[223] See Mörsdorf's historical introduction to the decree on the bishops, where the term "rump commission" occurs, in *Commentary*, II, 167.

[224] Marella dispatched announcements of a series of meetings, each of which was cancelled when the time came: letter of March 21, 1963 (for a meeting on April 30); letter of April 1 (for a meeting at the beginning of September); letter of July 1 (for a meeting on October 1); letter of September 25 (for a meeting on October 7) (see the file of Msgr. Pierre Veuillot, Coadjutor Bishop of Paris, Archives of the Maison diocésaine de Paris).

[225] See *AS* II/4, 440.

The transition to a third stage occurred in connection with the second meeting of the CC, which found the amended text of the schema on the bishops on its work table at the end of March 1963. On the eve of that meeting Marella sent a letter of justification to Cicognani in which he said that although for lack of time and for practical reasons the recent revision of the schema had been done solely by some subcommissions, the Commission itself would have an opportunity to examine the text at a plenary meeting that was to meet at the end of April.[226]

But shortly after the March meeting of the CC, Marella changed his mind. In a letter to the members of his Commission, he reported on what had happened at that meeting and informed them that the April meeting was being postponed until September, that is, until after the schema would have been sent out to the bishops. Why the April meeting was postponed is an object of controversy. In his official report to the Council in November, Carli would say that the CC "heaped praises [on the schema] and did not think it needed to be discussed by the conciliar Commission, but ordered that it be printed immediately in order to be sent to the Council fathers as soon as possible."[227] Marella also attributed responsibility for by-passing the full Commission to the CC. In response to angry complaints of French bishops about their exclusion from the work,[228] the Cardinal said that "great emphasis was placed on not summoning the members to Rome, since we would thereby lose another month before the schema was printed and sent out to all the Council fathers."[229]

---

[226] This letter to Cicognani, dated March 20, was published in the report of the rump commission, which met on May 2, 1962 (see *Relatio facta in peculiari Commissionis coetu die 2 maii 1963*, 3 [CCV, W. Onclin Papers]).

[227] See *AS* II/4, 440.

[228] The patience of the members of the Commission, who had a great interest in the conciliar schema on the role of bishops, had already been severely tested. Among them the French bishops in particular were especially sensitive on this point. As early as December 1962, Veuillot had let Marella know of his complete readiness to come to Rome as part of the Commission (letter dated December 20, 1962). Liénart, Guerry, and Veuillot became indignant when they learned in February that Marella had brought together only a few nearby bishops. People in Rome tried to soothe the sensitivities of the French bishops. In his reports Marella noted the zeal of the French bishops, and his April 1 circular letter was accompanied by a handwritten and friendly personal letter to Veuillot, addressed as "Carissimo"! When, in April, Veuillot received new evidence of the policy of obstruction that was being followed by the leaders in Rome, he arranged a meeting of the bishops of the Paris Region; they, with the agreement of Feltin, declared the proceedings unacceptable (letter of April 11, 1963). Veuillot and Guerry decided to go to Rome despite the cancellation of the meeting at the end of April (for all this documentation, see the Veuillot files, Archives of the Maison diocésaine de Paris).

[229] See Marella's letter to Veuillot, April 2, 1963 (Veuillot papers, Archives of the Maison diocésaine de Paris).

But the testimony of two eyewitnesses to the March meeting of the CC, Msgrs. Villot and Glorieux, differs. Both men said that the CC gave rather resigned approval to the schema in general, but expected that it would still be reviewed and amended by the whole Commission before being sent to the fathers.[230] The CC, then, was not responsible for the postponement of the plenary meeting of the Commission.

This seems confirmed by the official report of the March meeting of the CC, which says that the schema was favorably received by Cicognani, Urbani, and Suenens, and finally by all. They appreciated the shortened form and the fact that the series of faculties granted to bishops were now listed in an appendix and in the order of the Code of Canon Law. But this official account expressly provided that the Commission on Bishops would be able to introduce amendments before the schema would be sent to the bishops.[231]

The problem of the relation between the Commission on Bishops and the rump commission arose again when debate on the text began at the second session of the Council. (Even though this incident took place in early November 1963, it has to do directly with the procedure followed during the intersession and thus has a place in this history.) On October 29, 1963, a week before the debate was to begin, Veuillot wrote a letter to Tisserant, chairman of the Council of Presidents. Noting that Msgr. Carli's official report to the Council was already prepared, Veuillot asked the Cardinal to assure that the conciliar regulations would be respected:

> According to article 65, paragraph 5, the report should be composed "in accordance with the mind of the commission or its majority; if a minority is opposed to the majority, a second reporter can be appointed by the minority." Well, not only have we had to complain during these recent months that the Commission has never met to discuss the text, but you must be told today that the report of His Excellency Msgr. Carli has never been submitted to the commission, whose members are ignorant of its content. I think, therefore, that it is in conformity with the letter and the spirit

---

[230] See Glorieux to Veuillot, March 27, 1963 (the day after the meeting of the CC), and Villot's letter [to Veuillot?], April 10, 1963 (Veuillot papers, Maison diocésaine de Paris).

[231] *AS* V/1, 321-23. According to Villot's account, only Felici was hesitant when Marella stated that the texts would still be reviewed at a plenary meeting. It is possible that the decision to cancel the April plenary meeting was the result of quiet consultation between Felici and Carli. When we realize the importance of regional patriotism in Italy and the solidarity to which it often led in Curial circles, it is not out of place to call attention to the personal friendship between Felici and Carli, both of whom were born in the city of Segni.

of the regulations, that the discussion of a schema not be on the agenda of a general congregation until the Commission has had an opportunity to know the facts and take a stand on the report composed by His Excellency Msgr. Carli.[232]

It does not appear that this letter had any effect, and on November 5 Carli gave the official report to the Council on the schema on Bishops. He began with a history of the text, which, as reworked by the small subcommission, he said had been so well received by the CC that it was not felt necessary to submit it to the planned April meeting of the full Commission.[233] A week later Carli would again have to answer criticisms of the procedures.[234] His remarks did not prevent complaints from being made that the whole Commission had not had an opportunity to vote on the schema or to examine the report Carli would present in its name.[235]

Perhaps the best insight into the conciliar philosophy that guided the president of the Commission on Bishops is gained from the note, dated January 23, 1963, that Marella addressed to the CC. His attitude can be summed up by saying that in his view the virtues marking the preparatory phase of the Council rendered any second preparation unnecessary and even dangerous. We also find in this note a self-justifying discourse that gives a detailed history of the preparatory phase of the schema on the bishops and stresses all the time given to the composition of the text (thirteen meetings) and all the care taken to have the draft examined by the Commission and approved by a vote. The note also deals with the fundamental revision effected in the Central Commission and in its Subcommission on Mixed Matters, work done under the presidency of Tis-

---

[232] See the Veuillot papers, Maison diocésaine de Paris.

[233] *AS* II/IV, 439-40.

[234] In his remarks on November 13, 1963 (see *AS* II/V, 72-73), Carli said that he had been elected reporter by secret ballot and that no member of the Commission had objected to the main lines of the report he was preparing to make to the Council. Then he went on the offensive and created a sensation at the Council by attacking the moderators for allowing the recent vote on preliminary questions on collegiality and by defending the invocation in the schema of the condemnation by Pius VI of the heresy of the Jansenists of Pistoia. This appears to have been a reply to the earlier speech by Msgr. Schäuffele, Archbishop of Fribourg, who had argued that the call to restore their original rights to bishops was essentially different from the claim at Pistoia that the pope has no right to reserve certain faculties to himself (see *AS* II/IV, 495-96). For the repercussions of Carli's remarks outside the Council hall, see Caprile, III, 262-63, and R. La Valle, *Coraggio del Concilio* (Brescia, 1964), 319-21.

[235] See the criticisms made at the very beginning of the discussion, on November 5, 1963, by Msgr. Correa León (Colombia), speaking in the name of 60 Latin-American fathers (*AS* II/IV, 462).

serant. This explanation, which was more than simply a *captatio benev-olentiae*, ended with the forthright conclusion that, given this lengthy history of the preparatory schema, it was unthinkable that it should be set aside or amended.

Marella even thought that the preparatory period put not only his Commission but the CC as well under obligation.[236] According to Marella, his preparatory commission had already carried out the measures that the CC had been instructed to take in order to facilitate the progress of the Council; any further intervention by the cardinals of the CC with regard to the proposed text could only damage it and deceive the bishops. As for the elected conciliar Commission, the eleven fathers who had not been members of the preparatory commission had a duty to go along with the preparation. Marella wrote: "According to some hints we have gathered, the latter [the newcomers] are inclined to take up the text from the beginning, as if they themselves had a duty to write a book and put their names on it. They have to be told that they can make observations and suggest improvements but not revise everything that has been prepared."[237]

These authoritarian views of Marella throw much light on the motives that led his Commission's leaders not to convoke plenary meetings, despite several promises to do so. This strategy, which was completely successful during the 1962-63 intersession, would not survive the discussion in the Council in November 1963. As a result of that discussion, a new limited group, with a mandate from the full Commission, would set to work in 1964 and begin the rejection of the tutelage imposed during the first intersession.[238] This work would be entrusted to Veuillot, who had long been interested in the question of the episcopate and had vigorously criticized the tactics of Marella and Carli.[239] The complete

---

[236] Marella did not like the control being exercised by the CC. Referring to a conversation with him, Villot attested to this attitude in a letter to Veuillot: "I have listened to a dressing down of the Coordinating Commission. . . . Cardinal Marella blames it mainly for existing" (letter of April 10, 1963, Veuillot papers, Archives of the Maison diocésaine de Paris).

[237] *AS* V/1, 164-67, at 167.

[238] This was the first subcommission that was appointed to draw up a new schema and was led by Veuillot and W. Onclin, canonist of Louvain; it was in Louvain that the first working sessions would be held in January 1964.

[239] Pierre Veuillot (1913-68) had worked in the Vatican Secretariat of State for ten years when he was made Bishop of Angers in 1959. In July 1963 he was named Coadjutor of Paris, with right of succession. While still in Angers he gave a talk (March 1960) in which he said: "The mission of the bishops, teachers, and pastors in their local Church, and also the mission of the episcopal college in union with the pope can be asserted with

revision of the material, which Marella's January note had excluded and which he had been able to prevent by refusing to convoke the full Commission, is precisely what would be done in the new schema of 1964. Then it was that the long delayed second preparation of the text on bishops could begin.

2. Schema on the Missions

Nothing could have been more conservative than the schema on the missions at the beginning of Vatican II. And nothing could have been more distressing than the atmosphere of suspicion and constraint that prevailed in the conciliar Commission on the Missions during the period of transition between 1962 and the reopening of the Council in October of 1963. The road traveled between the schema that was rejected at the beginning and rewritten at the end was strewn with ambushes, but it was also a path that made possible an openness of the document to the world and an enrichment of its teaching. In my opinion, we may see in this affair one of the most positive aspects of Vatican II.

I must note, first, that the Commission on the Missions, which was closely connected with the Curial Congregation for the Propagation of the Faith — whose prefect was its president, Cardinal Agagianian — did not hold a single plenary meeting during the first period of the Council. During the 1962-63 intersession a series of plenary meetings were held at the end of March 1963 at the College of Propaganda.

During the basic debate on the schema on the missions later in the Council, some fathers would complain about pressures brought to bear in the Commission that had prevented representatives of the majority from having their say.[240] According to the testimony of Father X. Seumois, the Curial Congregation regarded the members who, although part of the conciliar majority, were a minority in the Commission "as interlopers who were hindering the normal course of events."[241]

more clarity and forthrightness" (see *DocCath* 57 [1960], 676). Shortly after his arrival in Paris and with an eye on the council, Veuillot devoted an entire lecture to a description of the tasks and mission of a bishop (cf. *DocCath* 58 [1961], 1579-90).

[240] E. Louchez remarks: "Among the members of the commission there was to be seen, in fact, the usual division into majority and minority, but the inverse of what was to be seen in the conciliar assembly" ("La Commission *de missionibus*," in *Commissions*, 251-77, at 261).

[241] Ibid. Note that in the 1962-63 intersession the leaders of the Commission on Bishops had a similar attitude toward its members who represented the majority thinking at the Council.

The de facto leaders of the conciliar Commission on the Missions in 1962-63 all belonged to the administrative staff of the Curial Congregation and were completely devoted to the service of Agagianian. The main ones were S. Paventi, a minute-writer, N. Kowalski, general archivist, and L. Buys, a canonist, consultor to the Congregation.[242] Together they formed what was called at the time a powerful triumvirate.[243]

A rather accurate idea of why the leaders of 1963 were anxious to keep the conciliar Commission under the supervision of Propaganda is provided in Paventi's list of reasons for the refusal to convoke the Commission in 1962, reasons which also explain why the Commission, when it did meet in March 1963, was limited to innocuous activities. According to Paventi, the strong attacks on the Roman Curia and the bitter words spoken at the Council against the Congregation of Propaganda urged patience on these two bodies in the hope that time would restore minds to tranquillity. Another reason was some documents issued by certain bishops of French-speaking Africa that challenged the Congregation by calling for its limitation or even suppression.[244]

For example, a "memorandum" on the "problem of the decentralization of the Church in subsaharan Africa" proposed a "reform" of the Congregation of Propaganda. After having denied any personal competence in the clerks of the Congregation over steps taken by bishops, who are the "successors of the apostles," the document expressly proposed "the suppression of the Sacred Congregation for the Propagation of the Faith as an organ of pontifical government." The proposal was based on the argument that in the future the various tribunals of the Curia, having been internationalized, would be open "to the diversity of pastoral situations peculiar to each continent, instead of imposing a uniformity based on Mediterranean criteria. . . . It is natural that the business of the missions be handled by each tribunal concerned: Rites, Religious, Seminaries, Sacraments, Consistory, and so on."

This unfavorable climate weighed upon the leaders of the Commission,[245] which was torn by strong tensions from the very beginning of its efforts to draft a new schema on the missions.[246]

---

[242] *Annuario Pontificio*, 1961 (953-55), 1962 (881-83), and 1963 (907-9).

[243] See Louchez, "La Commission *de missionibus*." A new editorial leadership, under the innovative authority of J. Schütte, S.V.D., would take over only at the end of 1964, after the negative outcome of the debate in the hall.

[244] *Memorandum pour les réunions africaines antéconcilaires* (no place, no date); CCV, Onclin Archives.

[245] S. Paventi, "Le cheminement laborieux de notre schéma," *Rythmes du Monde* (Bruges), 15 (1967), 104-5.

[246] The preparatory Commission on the Missions had worked up seven schemas, from

After hearing Confalonieri's report at its meeting in January 1963,[247] the CC dealt rather quickly with the schema on the missions.[248] Its proposal was accompanied by a note that raised a series of rather explosive questions about the usefulness of the Congregation of Propaganda and suggested doing away with the division between territories governed by common law (and coming under the usual Curial tribunals) and those governed by missionary law (and coming under Propaganda alone). Were this to be done, it would mean the end of this Congregation.[249] This rather revolutionary "annotation" claimed to have for its purpose freeing the young Churches from a special status that was felt to be "colonialist." Obviously, the leaders of the Commission on the Missions were careful to reply to the annotation at great length and point by point, with many explanatory notes justifying the past and future activity of the Congregation.[250]

Out of a fragile and provisional agreement reached by the Commission in March 1963 there came a second schema that, like the preparatory schema, was divided into two parts: (1) the missions themselves (principles, ministry, status); and (2) missionary cooperation (missionary duty; cooperation of bishops, priests, and religious; and, finally, cooperation of the laity). In the exchange of views that led to this text we also sense the tensions that divided the Commission and led the supporters of a second preparation for the Council to draft alternative schemas that were circulated among the fathers for private use only.[251] In his report to the CC, Confalonieri would denounce "the self-styled schema on the missions composed by private individuals," which he saw as a deviant (or aberrant) draft issued by some members of the Commission who were dissatisfied with the official schema.[252] Döpfner replied that in

among which the Central Preparatory Commission selected two, which were combined into a single schema with two parts: (1) on the government of the missions; and (2) on missionary cooperation (see Caprile, IV, 376-77).

[247] AS V/1, 125-26, 133-34.

[248] Proposition 14 of this meeting specified that the Commission on Missions was to deal mainly with the general principles governing the status of the missions and missionary cooperation and urged that it contact the other commissions in order to help the latter when they would have occasion to deal with problems that had missionary aspects (see AS V/1, 199-200). Proposition 14 was mainly a response to the wish that Agagianian voiced to Cicognani on January 22 (see S. Paventi, "Étapes de l'élaboration du texte," in L'activité missionaire de l'Église, ed. J. Schütte [Unam Sanctam 67; Paris, 1967], 158-59).

[249] For this "annotation," see AS V/1, 136-37.

[250] Paventi, "Étapes de l'élaboration du text," 160-61.

[251] See Louchez, "La Commission de missionibus," 262.

[252] Notandum: de alio schemate extra-vagante (see AS V/1, 550).

his opinion the "wandering" schema contained some good principles and made some timely suggestions and that the official schema would not be accepted by the Council.

The Commission's schema would not go very far. On July 1963 the CC would not give it a wholly favorable rating, and we might speak here of a delayed rejection. Thus the schema on the missions would be constantly faced with one obstacle after another until 1965.[253]

When the CC met on July 3, 1963, it echoed within itself the deep disagreements that were still traumatizing the Commission on the Missions. Those who represented a majority in the conciliar assembly but a minority in the Commission found themselves in difficulty in the CC. The majority in the CC, following Confalonieri, the reporter, supported the Agagianian-Paventi text, while Liénart, Döpfner, and Suenens expressed clear reservations.[254] From the very beginning Cicognani opposed any questioning of the structure or the proper work of the Congregation of Propaganda, "which the Church still needs." Liénart thought it was necessary to give a clear definition of the concept of mission and that a revision of the text was required in order to set down pastoral guidelines geared to today's missionary realities. Döpfner's criticism was even stronger: the schema had no guiding thread; it did not define *mission*; and it did not provide any theological insight into this important reality. Oddly enough, the minutes of the discussion do not mention any formal, specific conclusion.

The letters subsequently exchanged by Cicognani and Felici show that the Secretary General of the Council, good lawyer that he was, was not disposed to be content with deliberations that were indecisive or at least reached no explicit conclusion.[255] The leaders of the Commission on the Missions were also in no mood to accept the criticisms of Liénart and

---

[253] After the delayed refusal by the CC at its meeting in July 1963, a new draft approved by the Commission on December 3, 1963, would run up against the requirements of the "Döpfner plan" and end up being completely recast, in May-June 1964, as a mini-schema containing a few short "propositions." These would provoke a general outcry during the discussion at a plenary session of the Council, despite the unfortunate and rather clumsy recommendation of them by Paul VI in the hall. This rejection by the Council would lead at last, in 1965, to a completely revised schema.

[254] *AS* V/1, 547-50, 566-67, 570-72.

[255] *AS* V/1, 679-83. A reading of these documents leaves the clear impression that in the face of fundamental criticisms from two "big names" like Liénart and Döpfner, Felici was somewhat frightened and anticipated failure for the schema when it should be presented in the hall, unless something were done to check the stubbornness of the leaders of the Commission on the Missions. In this respect, he showed a greater realism than did Cicognani, Confalonieri, and Agagianian.

Döpfner, and within ten days they sent Cicognani a lengthy memorandum replying point by point to the objections raised.[256]

When it quickly became clear that this refusal of the Commission meant that the schema would not be sufficiently revised, Felici consulted Liénart, Döpfner, and Suenens about what to do. The last two were of the opinion that the inadequately amended schema was not ready to be distributed; it would be better to call for a new version during the second period of the Council.[257]

At the meeting of the CC on September 25, 1963, it became clear that the version partly amended in July had been discussed by only a limited group of members of the Commission. Döpfner then made it a prime condition that the whole Commission re-examine the draft.[258] This suggestion, accepted this time by the entire CC, led the Commission on the Missions to revise its text in a series of plenary meetings from October 23 to December 3, 1963. Even Agagianian agreed with this step, but it should be kept in mind that some weeks later he became a moderator of Vatican II, as did Döpfner and Suenens.[259]

If the great debate on ecclesiology at Vatican II included a diffuse challenge to the improper procedures and actions of the Holy Office, the debate on the missions would give rise to another explosion of protests, aimed now at the Congregation of Propaganda. This discussion took place within the broader conciliar debate about reappraising the role of bishops and about episcopal collegiality and in favor of new structures for consultation, which would enable delegates of the local Churches to cooperate with the Bishop of Rome, who presides over the episcopal college.[260]

---

[256] *AS* V/1, 655-58.

[257] *AS* V/1, 679-883. Döpfner wrote that even though questions of missiology were difficult, the Council would have to make an effort to give good answers to them.

[258] *AS* V/1, 687-88.

[259] The schema thus revised now had the title "The Missionary Activity of the Church," which it would retain to the end. After receiving the approval of the CC at its meeting on December 28, 1963 (*AS* V/2, 96), this draft would soon fall victim to the draconian pruning measures of the "Döpfner plan" in the spring of 1964 and would therefore not be used.

The discussion in the hall at the beginning of November 1964 — the first general debate of the Council on the schema on the missions — would provide a hearing for the complaints of the Council fathers, who felt that they had not been able to speak their mind freely in the Commission in 1963. This belated debate thus revealed the full scope of the disagreement that had already been the issue in the tensions within the Commission on the Missions during the 1962-63 intersession.

[260] See the following in *L'activité missionaire de l'Église*: (1) the text of no. 6 of the decree, 24-29; and (2) the chapter by Congar, 185-221. Congar distinguishes, in particu-

But the defenders of the prerogatives of the Congregation of Propaganda would not readily release their grip on the schema; the complete revision of the schema (beginning in January 1965) would, in the end, be the work of Father Schütte and his team.

This quick glance ahead enables us appreciate better the distance that Vatican II would still have to travel at the end of this intersession. Our survey makes it sufficiently clear that the second preparation for the Council was not a comfortable affair in a number of specific cases and also that the schema on the missions has to be regarded as among the failures of the first intersession.

3. *The Schema on the Oriental Churches*

The evolution of the conciliar Commission on the Oriental Churches did not resemble that of any other commission during the 1962-63 intersession. Its trajectory was not comparable to that of the commissions that tried to begin a second preparation in the first months of 1963 (for example, the commissions on the Church or on ecumenism) or to that of commissions whose renewal would not be able to get off the ground until after the second or third period of the Council (for example, the commissions on bishops or on the missions), a late start that, generally speaking, could not take place until after the team directing the composition of the schemas in question was changed.

It is true that for a long time the conciliar Commission on the Oriental Churches, like other commissions, had to carry the burden of the preparatory phase. It is also true that during the months of the 1962-63 intersession it was paralyzed by the refusal of its leaders to summon it to a plenary meeting; and in this respect it shared the lot of the Commission on Bishops.

But from the outset and until the final vote, the activities of the Commission on the Oriental Churches were determined by the inability of the Orientals to reach a minimal consensus among themselves, a problem peculiar to this Commission. This fact did not limit the outstanding role

---

lar, several modern "schools" of missiology, among them that of T. Ohm (Münster), A.-M. Henry (Paris), and P. Charles (Louvain). It was the last named who had best developed the idea of mission as implantation of the Church (201-3). For more details on the different currents of thought on the eve of Vatican II, see E. Loffeld, "Convergences actuelles en théologie missionaire," *Église vivante* 15, no. 1 (January-February 1963), 44-58. In a biographical note on Father Charles, J. Masson writes that the concept of mission as the implantation of an indigenous Church, which Charles developed and maintained in the 1920s, "entered the texts of the Second Vatican Council in 1965" (see *Biographie Nationale* 35 [Brussels, 1970], cols. 108-9).

that the bishops of the Oriental Churches united to Rome played in the Council generally, a role disproportionate to the smallness of their numbers and the modesty of their means.

Congar stressed the difference from what happened at Vatican I, where the Melkite Patriarch Gregory Yussef had met with an almost complete lack of understanding. If the Orientals exercised a considerable influence at Vatican II, this was in great part due to the encouraging attitude of John XXIII and Paul VI, as well as to the ecumenical openness of the majority among the Council fathers.[261] "The Orientals were no longer thought of as simply folkloric or outdated vestiges of the past; despite their weaknesses and deficiencies, they had something to say to the Church as a whole. Their voice was generally heard."[262] This is true especially of the contributions made by the representatives of the Melkite and Maronite Churches, and, among these, by the great Patriarch of the Melkites, Maximos IV Saigh. He was a venerable old man, but had a young heart and a sharp mind and quickly became one of the most heeded authorities in most of the important conciliar debates.[263]

The contribution of those Orientals who were most open to the conciliar renewal and at the same time the most emancipated from Curial supervision had to do with essential points in the ecclesiological work of Vatican II. The witness of their liturgical life, the contribution of a theology based on the patristic tradition, and their actual experience of the idea of the local Church were so many "stones" with which to help build an image of the Church derived from the sources. Their contribution made it clear that the Latin Church, even with its great numbers, was not itself the Catholic Church. As I. Dick pointed out, the best of the Oriental speakers showed that the truly Catholic Church is not a monolith and is by no means limited to a particular culture but can embrace all cultures.

This having been said, it must be recognized that the contribution made by the decree prepared by the Commission on the Oriental

---

[261] Y. Congar, "Préface," in Les Églises orientale catholiques, ed. N. Edelby (Unam Sanctam 76; Paris, 1970), 13-14.

[262] I. Dick, "Vatican II et les Églises orientales catholiques," in Deuxième, 623.

[263] Scholars have often stressed the regular contacts that the Melkite hierarchy cultivated at Vatican II with the most dynamic western bishops and the best known theologians. They have often overlooked the fact that this rapprochement began well before Vatican II and constituted a kind of preparatory phase. Before Vatican II opened, the Patriarchate of the Melkite Church had published in the West a collections of texts by Maximos IV and his bishops under the title Voix de l'Église en Orient (Paris-Basel, September 1962). See J. Grootaers, I protagonisti del Vaticano II (Milan, 1994), 174.

Churches and completed amid the pains of a "difficult childbirth" was not on the same level as the overall contribution of the Melkites and Maronites to Vatican II. One might almost be tempted to say that their most beneficent influence was to be seen elsewhere, in other and more important conciliar texts.[264]

Another striking peculiarity is perhaps to be seen in the composition of the Commission. More than in other cases, the nine members appointed by John XXIII to complement the elections seem to have been chosen for their membership in small Oriental communities not yet represented on the Commission. In a way, the principle of "administrative" representation took precedence here over their ability to get elected; an effort was made to have representatives from the entire range of the "Oriental Churches" in communion with the Roman See.

A final characteristic is to be seen in the fluctuating divisions within Oriental opinion, divisions that often caught the attention of observers. The dividing lines that separated the Oriental bishops among themselves at Vatican II changed several times, depending on the stakes in the debate. Among the key questions that were recurring causes of division among the Orientals, both in the Commission and in the hall, were (1) the expression "local Churches"; (2) the obligation in principle to remain in one's original rite; (3) the promotion of the institution of patriarchates;[265] and (4) the problem of *communicatio in sacris* or shared

---

[264] The already cited article of Ignace Dick says that the Melkites were the "principal crafters" of the decree. It seems to me that the minutes of the meetings of the conciliar commission in 1963 show just the opposite. The base text did not come from the Melkites; the latter, on the contrary, defended the most important amendments that were to improve it.

[265] The existence of patriarchates was constantly at the center of more or less impassioned controversies at Vatican II. The status of the patriarchs had evident implications in ecclesiology, in ecumenism, in canon law, and even in the matter of precedence in the council hall. The appointment of the Oriental patriarchs (in union with Rome) as "adjunct members" of the Congregation for the Oriental Church in March 1963 gave rise to sharp criticism, and the "promotion" of a great Oriental personage such as Maximos IV to the cardinalate in February 1965 caused a real crisis that had repercussions at the Council (see *DocCath* 60 [1963], 570-72 and 62 [1965], 513-15; also see the statement of Maximos IV in *La Croix* for February 7, 1965). According to *Irénikon* 38 (1965), 246-52, the decisions which the Council took in order to strengthen the institution of the episcopal college and the importance of the local Churches were directly challenged by the revival of curialism and the "promotion" of patriarchs to the cardinalate, a juridical and specifically Roman institution that can in no way replace the episcopal college with its apostolic origin. The cardinalate, which had found no place in the Constitution *Lumen Gentium*, seemed here to have won a real revenge. After resigning as patriarchal vicar for Egypt, Msgr. E. Zoghby circulated an *Étude sur "l'élévation" des patriarches au cardinalat* (March, 1965).

worship. Down to the final vote to save or reject the schema the Orientals were divided, and in the face of this lasting confusion many Latin bishops, for whom the issues were often elusive, found themselves helpless to decide which side to take. Those who wanted to reject the schema had varied motives and concealed divergent intentions. Ecumenists found it too "Uniate," Latinizers found it too "Byzantine;" Latins found it too "Oriental."[266]

Behind these disagreements among united Churches there was usually the history of various unions with Rome in the course of the centuries, unions that at times had no elements in common. The gathering of all these unions under the common rubric of uniatism concealed this long and complicated history; as a result, the oppositions between these Churches was incomprehensible to Western observers.

The schema was saved in October 1964 when the Melkites intervened in force and finally stated that a schema that was imperfect but could be improved in the future was better than a negative vote that might only lead to the loss of the good things in the schema.[267]

a. The Conciliar Commission on the Oriental Churches

In the Commission's deliberations, the spokesmen for the conciliar majority were in the minority, even though the active element among the Oriental bishops (chiefly the Melkites and the majority of the Maronites) made common cause with the Latin bishops who were open to ecumenical viewpoints.[268] Among the Orientals less open to the major concerns

---

[266] N. Edelby, "Discussion du schéma par le Concile," in *Les Églises orientales catholiques*, 90. I. Dick, for his part, wrote: "The proposed schema was resisted on the right by those who found too many 'privileges' being given to the East, and on the left by picky ecumenists who feared that the Orthodox would be offended if the Council were to legislate for the East and give recognition to a detested uniatism" ("Vatican II," 621). Some Oriental communities that do not have an Orthodox branch said they were disappointed by the conservatism of a text that did not address relationships among the different Oriental Catholic Churches that live in the same territory.

[267] Another incident that illustrates the fluctuations in tendencies within the Oriental Churches was the rejection, expressed in 719 *modi*, of the text that established in principle the obligation to remain in the same rite. The principle was rejected by those who wanted to respect individual freedom and keep the door open to Latinization, by others who leaned toward proselytism, and by still others in the United States who wanted to facilitate passage to the Latin rite. The rejection forced those in charge to find, in the end, a compromise formula (cf. Edelby, "Discussion du schéma par le Concile," 79).

[268] Among the most active speakers in the Commission were Patriarchs Maximos IV (Melkite) and Paul-Pierre Méouchi (Maronite), Melkite Bishop N. Edelby, and Abbot Hoeck (German Benedictine), all of whom were the leaders of the open tendency, as well as Msgr. de Provenchères (France) and Msgr. Baudoux (Canada).

of Vatican II and less sensitive to the requirements of the ecumenical movement were the delegates of the Chaldean and Armenian Churches, along with some Maronites. These were the closest to Roman centralism and were radically opposed to the proposals of Maximos IV and Abbot Hoeck.

But other burdens also weighed heavily on the Commission. I am referring to its president, Cicognani, and to its secretary, Athanasius G. Welykyj, a man very typical of the Ukrainian Church with its well-known Uniate tradition, anchored in a harrowing past and strongly opposed to Russian Orthodoxy.[269]

There was, finally, the apparently decisive role of a group of "Roman experts." These remained attached to preparatory schemas whose ecclesiological unionism was clearly opposed to the ecumenism that was one of the inspiring sources of the conciliar renewal.[270] The more dynamic wing of the conciliar commission was very conscious of the braking efforts being made by the hard core of Roman experts whom eminent members of the Commission held responsible for their not having been called to meet during the intersession. Edelby, a spokesman for the active group in the Commission, attacked the role of "experts living in Rome;" he openly stated that they should keep to their place and had no right to substitute themselves for the bishops, whose views they did not represent.[271]

---

[269] The work Welykyj did as a historian in Rome over the course of thirty years bore witness to his deep attachment to the person of St. Josaphat, to the special role of the Ukrainian and Byelorussian episcopates since the Union of Brest, and, in short, to the national past of his Ukrainian homeland. At the time of his appointment in the preparation for the Council, Welykyj was pro-rector of the Ukrainian College in Rome and editor of the *Analecta Ordinis Sancti Basilii Magni*. He was a skilled archivist whose patience met every test.

[270] The list of the members and consultors for the preparatory commission had been drawn up by the Congregation for the Oriental Church in the Roman Curia, which tried to satisfy everybody by mixing in various communities. The conciliar commission inherited, in large measure, this sometimes cumbersome legacy (see Edelby, "Discussion du schéma par le Concile," 73-75).

[271] *Commissio "de Ecclesiis orientalibus," IIIa Sessio plenaria*, 19: a report by the secretariat of the conciliar commission (CCV, C. Declercq Archive). As for the braking role played by some experts on the conciliar commission, Edelby would tell of a typical incident that occurred later on. The chance absence of the Roman experts from the Commission enabled him, one day in October 1964, to introduce into the texts three amendments in favor of the power of patriarchs that were among the most daring of the Melkite proposals and among those he despaired of having accepted. This was a miraculous opportunity made possible only "by taking advantage . . . of the absence of certain Roman experts, who were certainly well-intentioned but who because of their training and what they believed to be their mission in the Commission on the Oriental Churches,

Among the many schemas that originated in the very active preparatory commission on the Oriental Churches, only the last was on the agenda for the first period of the Council,[272] a draft on the unity of the Church entitled "That All May Be One." After the very critical examination of this schema by the conciliar assembly at the end of November 1962, it was expected that the text would be rejected. But on the initiative of Bea and Cicognani and to avoid an impasse, the Council accepted a resolution that demanded and obtained a combining of the three drafts dealing with the unity of Christians.[273]

The reader will recall that the somewhat ambiguous text of this resolution allowed Cicognani not to appear as the great loser in a debate that had not spared the work of his Commission. The two-part resolution first gave approval to the schema as a pledge of good will toward the Orthodox, but then required that it be combined with that of the Secretariat for Christian Unity and with the chapter in the Theological Commission's schema on the Church.

From the very start of the intersession this resolution was to be given two entirely opposed interpretations and to reveal the latent conflict between the positions of the Secretariat for Christian Unity and those of the Oriental Commission. An effort would nonetheless be made for several weeks to reconcile these two incompatible positions. In the eyes of the leaders of the Commission on the Oriental Churches the conciliar resolution meant that their preparatory schema had been approved by the Council and therefore retained its full value in the discussions that were to come. This view erased from memory the fundamental objections that the conciliar majority had expressed over the course of several days, and

---

imposed themselves and had thus far served as a brake on any at all 'progressive' improvement of the text'" (see Edelby, in *Les Églises orientales catholiques*, 291-92).

[272] Between November 1960 and the end of October 1961 the Oriental commission had prepared a series of fifteen schemas, which were submitted to the judgment of the Central Commission; on the initiative of the latter, the number, judged to be excessive, was reduced to nine, which dealt, among other things, with rites, the patriarchs, the permanent diaconate, mixed marriages, and the celebration of Easter. This material was later distributed differently, and some subjects, such as the patriarchs and *communicatio in sacris*, were reserved to the pope or to departments of the Curia (see Edelby, "Historique," in *Les Églises orientales catholiques*, 71-72).

[273] Just before the debate on the Oriental Commission's schema on unity began, Bea and Ottaviani had gone to Cicognani and suggested that he submit the three different texts on ecumenism for discussion at the same time (see Caprile, II, 203 n.9). Not anticipating the difficult debate that his Oriental Commission was to face, Cicognani rejected the suggestion. A week later the same proposal provided him with a neat way out, which he was quick to accept.

it also distorted the meaning of the second part of the resolution, which called for a recasting of the three texts.[274]

It was in this difficult setting that the mixed commissions charged with composing a single schema on ecumenism began their work.[275] Since I have already dealt with the failure of this phase of the work in my section on the genesis of the schema on ecumenism, I shall here summarize this failure from the viewpoint of the Oriental Commission.

The refusal of the representatives of the Oriental Commission to abandon the preparatory schema to the mixed commission and their opposition to the composition of a new text, as desired by the experts of the other two commissions, show that a second preparation was unacceptable to them.[276]

While the failure to cooperate with the Secretariat for Christian Unity in February and March, 1963, had already been a difficult trial for the Oriental Commission, the decisions of the CC at the end of March, 1963, were experienced as a disaster. At the first meeting of the CC, at the end of January, 1963, Cicognani had managed to bring out the "ecumenical" character of the schema on the Oriental Churches and to keep the schema completely under the control of the Oriental Commission. For the schema on ecumenism, however, the CC was still bent on an illusory reworking of the three texts by a tripartite commission.[277]

At the next meeting of the CC, in March 1963, Cicognani tried again to argue the case for the ecumenical character of the schema on the Ori-

---

[274] The one-sided interpretation of this document by the leaders of the Oriental Commission made Bea appear to be the victim of a fool's game. In ecumenical circles at the Council he was blamed for having accepted a resolution whose ambiguity was now being turned against the Secretariat for Christian Unity.

[275] See the *Note sur la collaboration du Secrétariat pour l'Unité des chrétiens avec d'autres Commissions conciliaires pour l'élaboration du schéma "De Oecumenismo,"* by J. F. Arrighi, dated September 24, 1963, and intended for the full Secretariat. The author gives the context of the tough line taken by the representatives of the Oriental Commission during the first two weeks of February, 1963 (see Lanne Archives, Monastery of Chevetogne, 2).

[276] In Welykyj's report on this subject, he rejected the "complete destruction" of his decree and insisted on fidelity to the Council's resolution, which in his interpretation had approved the text he proposed. He later rejected as baseless all the accusations of "sabotage" (Italian *sabotaggio* — in a Latin document!) that were being made against the Oriental Commission. One of the bitterest discussions in the mixed subcommission had to do with two phrases: "the means of achieving union" (according to the decree of the Oriental Commission) and "the practice of ecumenism" (in the terminology of the Secretariat for Christian Unity). After this session, it became clear that the difficulties were becoming insurmountable (see *Praeparatio Schematum Decretorum: relatio Secretarii in sessione plenaria* [September 19, 1963], 1-4 [CCV, C. Declercq Archive]).

[277] *AS* V/1, 180-81.

ental Churches, but this time he met with considerable opposition. In the presence of Welykyj, who had written Cicognani's report, and in the absence of the leaders of the Secretariat for Christian Unity, the draft on the Oriental Churches at first seemed to have been accepted, but the examination of the schema on ecumenism soon led Cicognani to demand that the chapter on ecumenical relations with the Orthodox Church be taken from the Secretariat for Christian Unity and left to the Oriental Commission. He did not think it was possible to speak of the Protestants and the Orthodox in the same schema, since the Church's relations with these two groups were inherently different, a view he had already defended at the plenary meeting of the Oriental Commission in November 1962.[278] Despite the opposition of numerous members, Cicognani's thesis seemed unshakable.[279]

This discussion took place in the presence of John XXIII, who was paying an unusual visit in order to encourage the CC. This fact had a special significance for the debate at that meeting, for the next day Cicognani issued a surprising retractation. He stated formally that his proposal to remove chapter III and include it in the decree on the Oriental Churches was for him a matter of secondary importance, and he now said he was ready to leave it in the decree on ecumenism, provided it deal also with relations with the heirs of the Protestant Reformation.[280]

It was not in Cicognani's character to make such an about-face. Although we have no formal proof — nothing, after all, is more elusive and therefore more fleeting than a conversation between a pope and his secretary of state! — John XXIII's intervention in this affair seems to me more than probable.[281] An intervention of Bea with his friend John XXIII was not possible, since he was in the United States at the time. When Cicognani was to make his entrance into the next plenary meeting

---

[278] Cicognani said: It has to be stated openly that the Oriental dissidents cannot be mixed in with the Western (*Series Actorum Commissionis de Ecclesiis Orientalibus. Sessio plenaria* [dated November 27, 1962], 3 [CCV, C. Declercq Archive]).

[279] Liénart, Döpfner, and Suenens defended the Secretariat for Christian Unity. Urbani, a veritable Solomon, proposed devoting an independent schema to the Orthodox. Confalonieri, Morcillo, and Felici were in favor of Cicognani's thesis (see *AS* V/1, 512).

[280] See *AS* V/1, 512

[281] In the report for internal use that Welykyj composed on September 19, 1963, we find a perhaps revealing slip of the pen. In mentioning the assignment of the question of unity to Bea's Secretariat, the author indicates that this arrangement was due to "higher authority," immediately explained as "the CC, with the permission of His Holiness." To describe the seven cardinals of the CC as a "higher authority" (*auctoritas superior*) was unprecedented and contrary to Roman practice. There was here a bit of confusion that may have been deliberate, and it would in my opinion confirm the fact of John XXIII's intervention (see *Praeparatio Schematum Decretorum*, 19).

of the Oriental Commission, he heaped praise on the schema and conveyed the personal encouragement of the Pope himself; but this was in
September 1963 and the Pope was Paul VI.

While this decision of March 29, 1963, which caused a sensation, marked
a turning point for the Secretariat for Christian Unity, which saw full supervision of the schema on ecumenism restored to it, it was felt as a defeat and
even a disaster by the Commission on the Oriental Churches. Its own draft
had lost all authority in the area of relations with the Orthodox Church and,
with its field of application now limited to the Churches united to Rome, it
seemed to have become of merely disciplinary significance.

The step thus taken was very important for the future of the ecumenical dialogue. The "unionist" school of interconfessional relations, which
regarded the Uniate Church as a bridge between Rome and Orthodoxy,
lost the privileged position that official or quasi-officials circles in Rome
gave it at that time, while the truly ecumenical view of dialogue won a
new authority in keeping with the prevailing wishes of the Council.[282]

---

[282] The difference here was between those who advocated individual "conversions" as
the way of obtaining a union with Rome as the center, and those who wanted a dialogue
among communities with a view to reconciliation among Churches. This difference in
viewpoint had already been the cause of lively controversies under Pius XI between 1925
and 1930. The uniatism of the first group was an obstacle to the ecumenism of the second. At that period, traces of the controversy were to be found in the early issues of
Irénikon, which for the first time advocated a fraternal dialogue with the Orthodox and,
by doing so, elicited keen hostility in some Uniate circles. The serious difficulties which
Dom Lambert Beauduin met at the birth of this movement for a Catholic ecumenism have
often been attributed to his very reserved attitude toward a systematic policy of "individual conversions," which in the long run would hinder a rapprochement between Christian
Churches (see Dom Beauduin in *Irénikon* 5 [1928], 481-92 and 7 [1930], 385-93; on the
other hand, see C. Korolevsky, *L'Uniatisme* [Irénikon-Collection 5-6; 1927], 48f.).
When Welykyj reported on this painful episode to the Commission, he was careful to
play down the traumatizing element in it. According to him, the decision of the CC was
a compromise solution which provided that the Secretariat's schema on ecumenism could
retain its chapter III provided that another section were added in which the Protestants
were treated in the same way as the Orientals had already been treated. As for the schema
on the Oriental Churches, it retained its second part, which dealt with unity from the
viewpoint of the particular Churches, both Catholic and non-Catholic. Welykyj also
recalled that the Oriental Commission had already decided at the end of January that
Bea's Secretariat should deal with "the dissident Orientals," but the Secretariat had
refused, saying that the first two chapters of its schema already spoke of them in a general way (cf. *Praeparatio Schematum Decretorum*, 7). In a less confidential report than
the one for internal use, the Secretariat of the Oriental Commission failed to mention the
failure of the mixed commission in February 1963 and said nothing of the instructions
given by the Coordinating Commission at the end of March (see "De labore a Commissione peracto," in *Schema decreti de Ecclesiis orientalibus [27.04.1964]* [Vatican City,
1964], 19).

b. Another Rump Commission?

We have already seen how the refusal to convoke the full Commission on Bishops during the 1962-63 intersession had elicited protests and given rise to controversy. History was to repeat itself, although less spectacularly, in the case of the Commission on the Oriental Churches. After December 5, 1962, it would not hold another plenary meeting until September 20, 1963, only eight days before the beginning of the Council's second period.

To justify the failure to call a plenary meeting Welykyj would appeal to the intense labor of the Roman working group, whose documentation was at the disposal of the members and the other experts. But these explanations would not satisfy a good many bishops, among them Hoeck and Edelby. Edelby found it unacceptable that the Secretariat of the Commission had simply refused to associate the bishop-members of the Commission with the mixed commission of February, whereas the bishops of the other commission did take part in it. He also found it unacceptable that neither the text of the schema sent to the fathers nor the official report intended for the Council had been submitted to the plenary commission, which alone was competent in the matter. It was not individual persons but the very authority of the bishops that was not acknowledged.

Welykyj's attempt to justify himself sheds a great deal of light on those who refused to consider the possibility of a second preparation. He argued that (1) the Oriental Commission was not the only one in which the full body was not called together (see the case of the Commission on Bishops); (2) the results of the work of the preparatory commission were still valid and could be amended but not rejected; and (3) the range of opinions had been respected in it. No commission had developed a new schema.[283]

The plenary meetings held later by the Commission during the days before the reopening of the Council and then during the second period (from September 23 to December 3) would be devoted mainly to the study of the many amendments sent in writing to the secretariat of the Commission.

According to a poll taken by Hoeck, the great majority of a hundred or so bishops of northern Europe had no knowledge of the schema in question. A third of them had sent responses, almost all of them calling

---

[283] When Welykyj invoked the precedent of the Commission on Bishops, in which only the subcommissions did the work, Hoeck replied by giving the example of G. Philips, who had composed a new schema, the text of which was approved by John XXIII.

for a confirmation of the privileges of patriarchs and a halt to a danger-ous Latinization. The bishops said they were convinced that greater autonomy for the Oriental Churches could contribute to surmounting the schism.

The leaders of the Commission tried as much as possible to give prominence to the study of the amendments received from the conciliar fathers, an effort to increase the importance of the plenary meetings that had been so tardily organized. This work was nevertheless felt to be of little use, since the text of the schema that was to be examined at the Council had already been established and sent to the Council fathers back in April-May 1963. The draft, whose sending was approved by the Holy Father on April 22, 1963, comprised a first part "on the discipline of the Oriental Churches" (nos. 1-44), and a second "on the union of Oriental Christians" (nos. 45-54).[284] Maximos IV and Edelby had offered forty pages of amendments, with abundant justifications for them, and these were put on the agenda of the conciliar commission.[285] Maximos put the weight of his authority in the balance. He rejected the use of the concept "particular Church" solely for the Orient, since the Latin Church, too, was a "particular Church." He regarded it as "unac-ceptable" that no. 9 of the schema already distributed would allow that Orthodox who came over to Catholic unity could sometimes abandon their Oriental rite. That text had been substituted for a different section approved by a large majority and after lengthy discussion on April 21, 1961. This very serious change had been made without the knowledge of the Commission; "to hide this way of acting they were careful not to convoke the conciliar commission, so that they might face the Council fathers with a fait accompli."[286]

In regard to mixed marriages, the Oriental Commission had voted for a text that facilitated the discipline in force in the Orient. In the new schema this passage was preceded by an introduction that was offensive to non-Catholics and contradicted the text itself. As for the institution of

---

[284] *Schema decreti de Ecclesiis orientalibus* (Vatican City, 1963). At the meeting on September 20, 1963, Welykyj denied that this second part was not favorable to the Chris-tian Orient; the text was derived as much as possible from the documents of the prepara-tory period and therefore reflected not the opinion of experts but that of many bishops now sitting on the benches of the Council.

[285] The original text of this lengthy series of remarks may be found in the collection entitled *L'Église grecque melkite au Concile* (Beirut, 1967), 290-307. It should be noted that these observations of Maximos IV were the result of a critique done in collaboration with his Holy Synod in August 1963.

[286] Ibid., 293.

the patriarchate in the Orient, Maximos IV insisted that it was historically false to describe the four great patriarchates of the Orient as if they had been created by the popes or by a council; on the contrary, this institution had its roots in the apostolic age. Yet "in the Catholic Church the institution of the patriarchates is regarded by supporters of centralization as the chief enemy."[287]

According to Maximos, the Latin West's incomprehension could be gauged by this brief passage that traced the origin of patriarchates to privileges granted by the pope. He emphasized that the Bishop of Rome is himself Patriarch of the West. In his eyes this was undeniably the most defective part of the schema on the Oriental Churches, although the idea of the patriarchate was indispensable to any tranquil dialogue with the Orthodox Church.[288]

It seems obvious to us that the new appreciation of the episcopate at Vatican II should have provided a point of reference for dialogue with the Orthodox. In addition, the lack of any theological status for the cardinalate (which was never mentioned in the schema on the Church) should have helped restore balance to Catholic ecclesiology in the eyes of the other Churches.

The moments of acute crisis through which the Oriental Commission passed during this intersession were thus accompanied by controversy about the status of the ancient patriarchates of the Churches united to Rome.[289] Even though this painful controversy concerned other schemas of the Council as well, among them those on the Church and on bishops,

---

[287] Ibid., 301.

[288] The local court (Curia) of Rome, which belonged to the Roman Diocese and included the college of cardinals, should not try to substitute for the college of apostles, who live on in their successors, the bishops. This was the opinion expressed by the Melkite Patriarch in the hall at the beginning of November 1963. For the same thought, see the memorandum of Archbishop Elias Zoghby, *Étude sur "l'élévation" des Patriarches au cardinalat.*

[289] When there was question, later on, of "promoting" the Oriental patriarchs to the cardinalate, the controversy turned dramatic. After the promulgation of the decree on the Oriental Catholic Churches, the Curial side in Rome got its revenge. Patriarch Maximos IV was obliged to accept the cardinalatial dignity in February 1965; he described it as "the hardest trial of my life." It was also a blow to the future "synod of bishops," of which Maximos IV and others wanted to become members in virtue of their being patriarchs (see *DocCath* 62 [1965], 482-93, 505, 514-16); *Irénikon* 38 [1965], 246-52, in a bulletin entitled "Autour de la question des 'Patriarches-Cardinaux'"; see Maximos himself on the incompatibility between patriarchate and cardinalate in *L'Église grecque melkite au Concile*, 179-96; and see the address of Hoeck in the hall on October 19, 1964 [*AS* III/5, 45f.]).

it interfered directly in the tensions within the Oriental Commission of that period.[290]

But during this intersession criticisms of the schema on the Oriental Churches were not confined within the walls of the competent Commission. The most active minds of the Oriental Churches expressed their often harsh criticisms in appeals to the general conciliar opinion. An example is the reports which the Coptic Catholic bishop Isaac Ghattas (Sohag in Upper Egypt) sent annually to a great many of his fellow bishops in booklets entitled *A propos du Concile Vatican II.*[291] Since he was not a member of the Oriental Commission, Ghattas spoke more freely and more sharply than other critics.[292] We shall see later that Maronite Bishop Michael Doumith (Lebanon) would declare that the great hopes which the Oriental Churches had placed on the Council had vanished at a reading of the schema presented.[293]

---

[290] *Lumen Gentium*, which was promulgated on the same day as the Decree on the Oriental Catholic Churches, contained in its famous nos. 22-23 on the college of bishops a paragraph that heightened the importance of the institution of the patriarchates by interpreting it in terms of structural pluralism. For the origin of that paragraph (in no. 23), which begins *Divina autem providentia* ("By divine providence"), see Dom O. Rousseau, "Histoire d'une phrase de Vatican II," in *Ecclesia a Spiritu Sancto edocta. Mélanges Mgr. Gérard Philips* (Gembloux, 1970), 281-89.

[291] These reflections were the fruit of the labors of a commission of priests in the service of the Oriental Churches. The report sent on the eve of the opening of the Council reviewed the schemas that had been received. On July 30, 1963, Msgr. Ghattas examined mainly the schemas that had been prepared for the second period, among them the draft on the Oriental Churches. The third booklet was dated August 15, 1964, and returned once again to the that schema.

The main faults that the Coptic Catholic bishop found had to do with the ambiguity that was at the basis of the schema and hampered the entire exposition: Was this decree speaking also of the Orthodox Churches or only of the Uniate Oriental Churches? The dogmatic statements made in the schema would have their proper place in the schema on the Church (report of July 30, 1963).

The amendments made in the schema by the Oriental Commission in the autumn of 1963 did not satisfy Msgr. Ghattas: "We are still caught between two stools." Juridicism and immobilism still controlled the schema. In his view the schema should be abolished because it treats the Oriental Churches as an "appendage to the Catholic Church" instead of as integral parts, and it fails to remedy the "pastoral anarchy" in many jurisdictions (report of August 15, 1964).

[292] The writings of the Coptic Catholic bishop displeased the leaders of the Oriental Commission. At the plenary meeting on September 20, 1963, Welykyj said that Ghattas's pamphlet had never been filed with the secretariat of the Commission and for him, therefore, did not exist (see *Commissio "de Ecclesiis orientalibus." IIIa Sessio plenaria*, 17).

[293] For the further history of the schema, see especially the collection of essays edited by N. Edelby and I. Dick, *Les Églises orientales catholiques*; Johannes M. Hoeck, "Decree on Eastern Catholic Churches," in *Commentary*, I, 307-31, and Wilhelm de Vries, "Il decreto conciliare sulle Chiese orientali cattoliche," *CivCatt* 116, no. 7 (April 17, 1965), 108-21.

4. *Schema on the States of Perfection*

For reasons both of procedure and of content it is difficult to summarize the discussion at the Council on the schema on the adaptation and renewal of religious life. A great many conciliar texts dealt with intertwined areas and required collaboration among commissions. The Roncallian solution was to multiply mixed commissions (involving two or three commissions) in order to avoid battles, a method that was not completely satisfactory in many instances. We have already discussed the sometimes lukewarm cooperation between the Commission on the Lay Apostolate and the Doctrinal Commission and between the Secretariat for Christian Unity and the Commission on the Oriental Churches, as well as the tensions between the Commission on Religious and the Doctrinal Commission in preparing chapter IV, on the religious vocation, in the schema on the Church. The latter again concerns us now, but this time from the perspective of the Commission on Religious.

Here we see a kind of hide-and-seek game going on. In March 1963 the mixed commission (representing the commissions on religious and on doctrine) that worked on chapter IV of the schema on the Church composed a revised text that was supposed to be approved by the full Doctrinal Commission. But the text was instead submitted directly to the CC. This by-passing of the Doctrinal Commission prompted the latter to reject the revised chapter and to appoint, on its own authority, a new writing group chaired by Bishop Charue and with the collaboration of some religious. It later became clear that the group had no mandate from its own Commission.

At the end of May the full Doctrinal Commission gave its approval to the new Charue draft, which had been done hastily and then accepted without passing through the Commission on Religious. On July 4, 1963, the newly elected Paul VI accepted the decision of the CC and ordered the immediate sending out of the Charue version of the chapter, which signaled its new approach in its title: "The Call to Holiness in the Church."

The Commission for Religious felt wronged by these proceedings and denied that it had been represented by the few religious who had, unknown to it, worked with Charue. The content of the new draft also seemed unacceptable to the Commission, which immediately alerted many bishops from religious orders.[294] The group of religious bishops

---

[294] The count of religious bishops at the Council varied widely according to the criteria used. While Schütte counted 1050 Council fathers, Dom Reetz spoke of 800 bishops

immediately organized a radical opposition to the chapter in the form in which it had been officially distributed.

Chapter IV, the chapter in question, had two subjects: the universal call to holiness and the religious state. To the religious this meant that the special chapter on religious life had disappeared from the Council's agenda and that its content would be included in a chapter of a more general kind. The specific nature of the religious state was thereby threatened to some extent.[295] While many fathers in the other camp and the members of the Commission on the Lay Apostolate wanted to have the call of every baptized person to holiness put in the foreground, religious at the Council reacted strongly and called for a separate chapter on their state of life in order to safeguard the special place which religious have in the Church in virtue of its constitution.[296]

These tensions with regard to the chapter in the schema on the Church to some extent embittered the work on the schema for a separate decree on the renewal of religious life. Two different kinds of text were under consideration; in principle, the chapter in the constitution on the Church would state doctrinal principles, while the decree on religious was to make applications inspired by them. But this fine logic did not really work out in practice, for while the decree would refer to the text on the Church, it would not in fact be inspired by it. The redactional genesis of the draft decree would involve other kinds of cooperation than that which been used for the schema on the Church. The decree would require collaboration with the Commission on Bishops (for the sometimes ticklish relations between religious and bishops) and the Commission on the Missions (for the special role of religious congregations in mission countries).

who were religious. The latter counted only bishops in the strict sense, whereas Schütte included in his total the superiors general and also the prefects apostolic, most of whom were religious (see A. Wenger, *Vatican II: Deuxième session* [Paris, 1964], 120). See above, chapter IV.

[295] See especially J. Galot, *Les religieux dans l'Église* (Gembloux, 1966), 6-8.

[296] If we may judge by a document signed by 680 fathers in favor of a separate chapter on religious life, the Christian vocation lived out by lay people in the bonds of marriage (the spirituality of involvement in temporal activity) threatened the superiority of the state of virginity or celibacy, as taught by the Council of Trent. One of the main spokesmen for this view was Jean Daniélou; see the article he published in February 1964, at the time when the movement in favor of a separate chapter was taking form in conciliar opinion ("La place des religieux dans la structure de l'Église," *Études* 320 [January-June 1964], 147-55).

a. Uneasiness and Tensions

The redactional history of the schema that would become the conciliar text *Perfectae caritatis* was a tumultuous one. I must call to mind here, in a summary way, the vague feeling of uneasiness some religious must have felt in face of the directions being taken by the Council. The prevailing trend to emphasize the episcopate and the local Church, the general interest in the lay apostolate, the previously unknown attitude of openness to the world with its advocacy of involvement in so-called temporal tasks: these were new tendencies that broke into the open in the Council hall and could threaten, directly or indirectly, the very status of the religious orders. "Religious entered the Council suffering from a bit of a 'complex,'" wrote Msgr. A. F. Le Bourgeois, Superior of the Eudists and, during the Council, called to be adjunct secretary of the conciliar Commission.[297]

A further difficulty came from the endless variety of approaches, statutes, organizational forms, and life styles into which the world of religious was broken up. In the background, among things left unsaid, was the major difficulty of the degree of solidarity that had been created between religious and the Curial administration in Rome. Over the centuries some large religious orders had acquired a structural unity — not always conformed to the spirit or the instructions of the founder — that had sometimes become a tool in the service of the centralizing role of the Roman Curia. This underlying tendency was incompatible with the mobility of Vatican II, which was looking to restore the local Church, heighten the authority of bishops, and revive collegiality and synodality both in the Church and in its institutions.

In any case, the close connections between the Commission for Religious and the Curial Congregation of the same name were obvious. This solidarity counted heavily in the preparation of the decree. Thus the subcommission of seven appointed by the Commission on Religious at the beginning of December 1962 to revise the draft of the text hardly represented the *aggiornamento* that had marked the first period of Vatican II and was supposed to animate the second preparation. President of the subcommission was Msgr. Paul Philippe, a Dominican and secretary of the Curial Congregation for Religious; its vice-president was Msgr. Compagnone, a Discalced Carmelite and strong defender of the schema

---

[297] See A. F. Le Bourgeois, "Introduction," in *Documents conciliaires* 2 (Paris: Centurion, 1965), 77.

of the preparatory commission.[298] The "limited commission" (February 1963) and the "writing committee" were made up of experts who themselves were often in the service of the Roman Curia. The chief of them was Father Rousseau, O.M.I., who had been appointed secretary of the conciliar commission.[299] On several occasions some bishops complained of the dominant role played by certain experts whose activity in the proceedings they felt went beyond the bounds of their competence.[300]

A final indication of the difficulties that the schema on religious life would encounter on its course was the progressive diversification of tensions. The simple polarity between promoters and opponents of a second preparation was in a way left behind by the birth of another polarity, namely the tension between the leadership of the majority trend and the organized collaboration of many bishops from the religious orders. The latter succeeded in defending the values peculiar to the religious orders against what they regarded as the extreme positions of the innovators. I have already made reference to incidents involving procedure at the end of May 1963; the movement of the religious arose out of those and out of the debate in October 1963, but it acquired its full scope only in 1964, when it would emerge victorious in some important votes (especially that of November 14, 1964).

A new organ for collaboration among the religious bishops at the Council was called the Secretariat of Bishops; it was to play an influential role beginning in November 1963.

b. Stages in the Development of the Text

Three stages in the development of the schema are usually distinguished during the period we are discussing here. The first had to do

---

[298] The majority of the members were religious, among them, Father Sepinski, Superior of the Franciscans (O.F.M.) and Father Kleiner, Abbot General of the Cistercians. Present as "bishops in the strict sense" were Msgr. Huyghe (Arras) and Msgr. Urtasun (Avignon). The latter said that he was the only nonreligious bishop on the Commission (see Wenger, *Vatican II*, II, 116).

[299] The makeup of these very active editorial groups is given in N. Hausman, *Vie religieuse apostolique et communion d'Église* (Paris, 1987), 74. See also Friedrich Wulf, "Introduction," in *Commentary*, II, 303-4. Fathers Abellán, Gutiérrez, Gambari, and Joulia, who were among these experts, were regular collaborators of the Roman tribunal (see *Annuario Pontificio*, 1963, 901-3).

[300] See Wulf, "Introduction," 319; R. Wiltgen, *The Rhine Flows into the Tiber* (New York, 1966), 214-15. The reporter for the German episcopate was not satisfied with the procedure in this respect, and Huyghe complained, among other things, that the plenary meeting of May 1963 was cancelled without any prior consultation; see also G. Huyghe, "Vie religieuse et apostolat," in *L'adaptation et la rénovation de la vie religieuse*, ed. J. Tillard and Y. Congar [Unam Sanctam 62; Paris, 1968], 178-79).

with the draft text of the preparatory commission, which was entitled *Schema constitutionis de statibus perfectionis adquirendae*.[301] But the conciliar Commission first saw this schema only as the Council's first session was coming to an end. In the weeks that followed, a series of restrictive instructions compelled the Commission on Religious to go back to and revise the preparatory schema; this was a stage marked by frustrations. The directives from the Council of Presidents (early December 1962), the new agenda that came from the Secretary of State, and the specific guidelines of the CC, all of which aimed at reducing the undigested mass of drafts prepared for the Council, required the Commission on Religious to take stringent measures to reduce the size of its preparatory schema.[302]

The Commission began by appointing a subcommission of a few members that took over the direction of the entire operation. This was the subcommission of seven chaired by Paul Philippe, secretary of the Curial Congregation for Religious. This limited commission included the experts of the writing team.[303]

Two mixed commissions were to be established to deal with material shared with other schemas: one on relations between religious and the missions and the other on relations of religious with bishops. The plenary meeting at the end of February 1963 made it possible to complete an abridged version of the schema, which was submitted to the CC on March 27, 1963. It had shrunk from 100 pages to 35. Before official approval was given at the end of April 1963, alterations would be made by a small team of five members.

In the view of the majority of the Commission on Religious the text did not sufficiently reflect the tendencies toward renewal that were already at work in some religious orders. The juridical approach taken

---

[301] This was the product of thirty-five plenary meetings of the commission from February 1961 to June 1962, and of thirty-six other meetings from November 1961 to April 1962, and took up about a hundred pages in the large-format volume of the *Series tertia* in the collection of preparatory documents. The material in the draft was divided into two parts: (1) a description of the states of perfection; and (2) renewal of the practice of religious life.

[302] See Caprile, IV, 403-6; Wulf, "Introduction," 303-21; Le Bourgeois, "Historique du décret," in Tillard and Congar, *L'adaptation et la rénovation*, 52-61.

[303] It is noteworthy that the leaders of the Commission on Religious felt the need to send a justificatory note to the CC after the first instructions of the latter had been received (end of January) and with an eye on the second meeting of the CC (end of March). The point of interest about this note of March 9, 1963 is that it contained a detailed description of the procedures and the different levels of the limited commissions (see *AS* V/1, 422-24).

by the schema and its static conception of the "states of perfection" were the objects of strong criticism. Its prevailing idea of the "world" reflected an outdated pessimism, whereas an attitude favorable to an active apostolate was possible only where there was openness to the changes in contemporary society. According to the testimony of Huyghe, the bishops on the Commission succeeded only rarely in having glimmers of light shine through: "The apostolate is now regarded as a value and no longer as only a danger."[304]

At the meeting of the CC at the end of January 1963, Döpfner, reporter for the schema on religious, suggested that important parts of the text be included in the schema on the Church; the remainder could be remanded to a directory or to a revised Code of Canon Law. In his view, the primary need was to root the religious vocation in Christ and in the life of the Church and to move beyond the perspective simply of personal salvation.[305] In response to these proposals, the CC maintained the necessity of a short decree on the "states of perfection" (a title that was likewise criticized).[306]

When the pruned version of the schema was submitted to the CC at the end of March 1963, Döpfner praised the stringent reduction in size, but he continued to oppose the terminology of "states of perfection." His objections to the content of the schema were more serious. It lacked, he said, theological and biblical foundations. Even though it was still necessary to guard against the prevailing activism, a more positive vision of the world was very desirable. (Here we can see signs pointing ahead to the debate on schema XVIII when Döpfner insisted that the world is not simply a place infected by sin but is also a creature of God and redeemed in Christ.[307]) But the CC gave approval in principle to the revised draft, with the understanding that account would be taken of the remarks that the reporter had made on it. A small editorial group would immediately turn to this task.

Once the schema in its shortened version had been sent to the members of the Council, many varied observations poured back to Rome.[308] The text was praised by some, criticized by others. The harshest reactions came from the English and Dutch bishops. In the camp of the conciliar majority the general view was that the schema contained mainly

---

[304] Huyghe, "Vie religieuse et apostolat," 179-80.

[305] See *AS* V/1, 127-31, 134, 137-39.

[306] See ibid., 192-93.

[307] See ibid., 424-26.

[308] All the observations covered 243 mimeographed pages (see Caprile, IV, 404).

commonplaces and repeated official statements while passing over the essential questions of contemporary religious life. There was nothing about what religious consecration essentially is or about its connection with the gospel; the pastoral character of the religious orders was disregarded; the distinction between the contemplative and active lives was not clearly drawn; the sometimes difficult collaboration between religious and bishops was not discussed.

But in the eyes of clear-minded observers these criticisms themselves remained too general and even superficial. Father Wulf found very few constructive points in them that could be useful for a contemporary renewal of the religious orders. The criticisms had insufficient depth.[309]

The study of the observations sent in by the bishops was entrusted to four subcommissions following the fourth plenary meeting of the Commission at the end of September and the beginning of October 1963. But the fate of what had become a text of eighteen pages was no better than that of the draft of April 1963. Never discussed at the Council, the schema was later condemned to a complete revision. According to new instructions from Cicognani, issued on November 29, 1963, the Commission on Religious was required to reduce its schema to a few short propositions. This marked the beginning of a new stage in its history, which occurred outside our timetable.

If it is hard to deny, then, that efforts at the renewal of religious life ended in failure during the second preparation, it is not easy to determine the meaning of this failure. Beginning in November 1963, Vatican II would gradually enter another phase, that of the "Döpfner plan," instituted in order to accelerate without too much fuss the conclusion of the Council. Some of those whom I have called opponents of the second preparation shifted to another aspect of the conciliar event and became "promoters" of a hasty conclusion of Vatican II. The circumstances in which this change of course was prepared and the real meaning of the failure with which it finally met are subjects I will take up at the end of the chapter.

D. Latecomers

Among the drafts sent to the fathers for their judgment in May and July of 1963 were six that I shall here call latecomers. Due to a combi-

---

[309] See Wulf, "Introduction," 320.

nation of circumstances these schemas were taken up only belatedly by the conciliar assembly: (1) The Blessed Virgin Mary; (2) The Care of Souls; (3) The Sacrament of Matrimony; (4) Clerics; (5) The Formation of Candidates for Orders; and (6) Catholic Schools. (The last three of these were to see their titles change several times.)

The first three of these schemas disappeared as such from the agenda, either through complete (Blessed Virgin Mary) or partial (Care of Souls) absorption into another schema, or because they were left to the care of the sovereign pontiff (Sacrament of Matrimony). If the last three ended up at the end of the Vatican II calendar, this was also because they suffered a common fate, that of being included in the list of the "Döpfner Plan" (spring of 1964), which was meant to hasten the proceedings at the Council for the unstated purpose of having it close at the end of the third period. This meant that the schemas on the clergy, seminaries, and Catholic education were to be reduced to very short texts containing only a few propositions; this won them the name "short schemas."[310]

1. Schema on the Blessed Virgin Mary

The antepreparatory commission for Vatican II received almost 600 *vota* from bishops asking that the Council compose a document that would clarify the standing and role of the Virgin Mary.[311] The desired schema was composed from July to November 1961 and sent to the Central Preparatory Commission in June 1962.[312] Although distributed to the fathers on November 10, 1962, it was not discussed during the first period of the Council. At the end of January 1963 the CC decided that the text should remain distinct from the draft of the constitution on the Church and be sent separately to the fathers. (This schema would become an integral part of the schema on the Church as the result of a vote in the Council on October 29, 1963.) The schema sent out on April 22, 1963, was unchanged except in title, which had become "The Virgin Mary, Mother of the Church."[313]

---

[310] For a short description of this temporary phenomenon see R. Laurentin, *Bilan de la troisième session* (Paris 1965) 306-8.

[311] See *ADA*, II/1, 131-42.

[312] See the defense Father Balic wrote in the form of a pamphlet in May 1963, *Circa Schema Constitutionis Dogmaticae De Beata Maria Virgine Matre Ecclesiae* (Vatican City, 1963), which includes a history of the text, almost half of which was devoted to his defense of the titles "co-redemptrix" and "mediatrix."

[313] The title "Mother of the Church" remained a point of contention at the Council. Rejected by the majority in the Doctrinal Commission because it lacked any theological

The authors of the schema submitted in 1963 made an effort to be objective by opposing both maximimalist and minimalist errors in Marian devotion.[314] They also sought to give proof of ecumenical openness by assuring the reader that they had omitted expressions and terms that, though valid, could be difficult for the separated brethren to understand; for example, the mediation of the Virgin, far from being an obstacle to the mediation of Christ, honors it instead.

No part of the constitution on the Church gave rise to as many commentaries or elicited such a flood of publications as what the Council said about the Virgin Mary. Philips distinguished two opposed and irreconcilable approaches at work in this area: on the one hand, the adherents of positive theology started with the earliest documents and traced the gradual development of the history of salvation; on the other hand, the defenders of the "privileges" of our Lady began at the other end and mainly analyzed the glorious titles of the Virgin as described in the encyclicals of the recent popes.[315] The March 1963 schema on the Blessed Virgin reflected the second approach. The Council fathers who defended the insertion of the statement of doctrine on Mary into the constitution on the Church, and who were to win the point in October 1963, took the first approach, which located the Mother of God in the history of salvation. The road Vatican II would have to travel in order to move from the one approach to the other would be long and strewn with ambushes.[316]

2. *The Schema on the Care of Souls*

Among the schemas approved on April 22, 1963, and immediately sent to the Council fathers was a bulky schema of 126 pages on general problems of pastoral care. As submitted at the first meeting of the CC in January 1963, it had two distinct parts: the first devoted chiefly to the responsibilities of the episcopal office, and the second dealing with catechesis and specialized forms of pastoral care (migrants, sailors, pilots, nomads).

basis, it was nonetheless proclaimed, at the end of 1964, by a formal act of Paul VI (see *OssRom*, December 6, 1964; *DC* 62 [1965], 18 n.1; see ibid., 2051).

[314] See the introductory notes to the *Schema Constitutionis Dogmaticae De Beata Maria Virgine Matre Ecclesiae* (Vatican City, 1963), 13-15.

[315] G. Philips, *L'Église et son mystère au IIème Concile du Vatican* (Paris, 1968), II, 207-11.

[316] The final reintegration of the schema in *Lumen Gentium* would respond to the ecumenical concerns of Vatican II: veneration of the Blessed Virgin Mary would receive a christological foundation.

The main concern of the CC was to dismantle the schema by steering the various chapters to different destinations: to a revised Code of Canon Law, to "handbooks"for bishops or for parish priests," to a "directory of catechesis," or to the schema on the lay apostolate. The CC expressly asked that a short resolution be submitted to the Council at a general congregation, ordering the Commission for the Discipline of the Clergy and the Christian People to compose a "handbook" or "directory" such as those suggested.[317]

In fact, this schema was never discussed or voted on in the hall. The text sent to the bishops in the spring of 1963 had been restructured. It now contained five chapters dealing with principles and guidelines for various aspects of pastoral care: the responsibility of bishops, the duty of parish priests, relations between bishops and religious, the catechetical formation of the faithful. In addition, the schema had seven appendixes, all of which referred the formulated guidelines to some nonconciliar addressee, either the Code of Canon law or a general directory.

Although no longer on the agenda of Vatican II, the schema was not therefore lost. Important parts were "retrieved" by the Commission on Bishops and Dioceses. When the plan of this latter schema was entirely revised in January 1964, many themes of the schema on the care of souls fitted into it quite naturally.

3. *The Schema on the Sacrament of Matrimony*

What had been a "mountain" of six different schemas on marriage on the eve of Vatican II brought forth a "mouse" of a two-page mini-document in February 1964. The six preparatory schemas dealt with preparation for marriage, impediments, consent, the celebration, trials in a marriage court, and mixed marriages. In the end only this last topic would remain.

Already reduced to a single decree in January 1963, it was then studied by the CC which decided that it should contain only general principles and that other aspects should be left to a revised Code of Canon Law. For the chapter on mixed marriages, it would be appropriate to form a mixed commission with three participants: the Secretariat for Christian Unity, the Doctrinal Commission, and the Commission on the Discipline of the Sacraments. An instruction on the preparation of engaged couples was to be appended to the decree.[318] After approval by

---

[317] See *AS* V/1, 142-44, 172-73, 399-401.
[318] *AS* V/1, 198.

the CC on July 3, 1963, the text, now reduced to twenty pages, was sent to the bishops.[319]

4. *The Schema on Priestly Ministry*

During the preparatory phase of the Council, the Commission on the Discipline of the Clergy and the Christian People, with Cardinal Ciriaci as its President and Father Berutti as its secretary produced four schemas of a primarily disciplinary kind. In December 1962 the conciliar Commission undertook a revision of the first three (which dealt with the clergy) and transferred the fourth (on associations of the faithful) to the Commission on the Lay Apostolate.

But at its meeting in January 1963, on hearing the report of Urbani, the CC decided to tell the conciliar commission to produce a single schema with three chapters: (I) on the perfection of priestly life; (II) on the study of pastoral practice; and (III) on the proper use of ecclesiastical possessions. The first of these chapters was to be revised to bring out the principles governing the life of priests. The second chapter should explain the methods of pastoral care in light of the experience of our age. Among other things, the third chapter should claim adequate material support for priests and stress that they should avoid commercial activities.[320] Questions about ecclesiastical benefices should be passed on to the Commission for the Revision of the Code, while "the distribution of the clergy" should be the subject of an "exhortation" appended to the decree on clerics.

Thus began the first stage of a lengthy process that would have three stages in all and would last to the end of Vatican II.[321] The four subcommissions that saw to the carrying out of these instructions in February and March 1963 had the satisfaction of seeing their new schema approved by the CC on March 25, 1963, except for a few minor points. In April 1963, after the usual formalities, this text was sent to all the

---

[319] The approval was not given without serious reservations, especially on the part of Liénart, who deplored the fact that in speaking of the sacrament the schema said nothing about the state of life in which marriage places Christians. He thought that the schema should have spoken of marriage as a union not only between two individuals of different sexes, but also between two persons who love one another, between two Christians who are to help each other through the gift of themselves (see Liénart, *Vatican II*, 94).

[320] *AS* V/1, 191.

[321] There is a sketch of these three stages in Jean Frisque, "Le Décret *Presbyterorum Ordinis*," in *Les prêtres, formation, ministère et vie*, ed. J. Frisque and Y. Congar (Paris, 1968), 126-28. See also R. Wasselynck, *Les Prêtres: élaboration du texte de Vatican II* (Paris, 1963), 17-34.

bishops of the world with a request to send in their remarks on it to the General Secretariat of the Council.

It may be asked what circumstances and factors led to this schema's being relegated to the batch of schemas that were the last ones taken up by Vatican II, even though priests were the closest collaborators of the Council fathers and, in the final analysis, the principal intermediaries in the application of the major documents of Vatican II. Preoccupied with the restoration of the episcopal function and with the emergence of a new kind of lay involvement in the apostolate, the bishops did not realize that in a time of *aggiornamento* the priestly ministry required a doctrinal approach that transcended the level of mere disciplinary matters. In this respect the mind of the Council reached maturity only as the result of a series of events, among them the failure of a planned message to priests; the promulgation of *Lumen Gentium*, some numbers of which provided the basics on priests;[322] personal contacts with diocesan priests during the second intersession, and, finally, the consciousness of the pastoral goals of the Councils. Some of those involved, Jean Frisque among then, even spoke of a "full maturity" reached only in 1965![323]

5. *The Schema on Seminaries*

The closely related schema on the formation of priests aroused no less interest at Vatican II than the schema on the priestly ministry. The question of seminaries continued to enjoy the importance that the Council of Trent had assigned to that solid institution. At the middle of our ever more rapidly evolving twentieth-century it was clear that the formation of priests, which had been the subject of a preparatory schema, also had to be appropriately updated. It is striking that the leaders of the majority current at Vatican II made this updating one of their major concerns at the Council.

The draft of a Constitution *De sacrorum Alumnis Formandis* (On the Training of Candidates for Sacred Orders) that was sent to all the bishops of the Church on April 22, 1963, was a text already reduced in size (twenty-seven numbers, sixteen pages) as a result of the decisions of the

---

[322] On this point see Y. Congar, "Le sacerdoce du Nouveau Testament, mission et culte," in Frisque and Congar, *Les prêtres*, 249-51.

[323] Frisque, "Le Décret," 129-32; see also J. Lécuyer, "History of the Decree," in *Commentary*, III, 183-209.

CC in January 1963.[324] This schema was later reworked in light of the many criticisms the bishops sent to Rome.[325]

Such leaders as Döpfner, Suenens, and Lercaro, and such authoritative speakers as Charue, Garrone, Hurley, and Weber, all addressed this need of updating in their interventions in the hall. Their remarks were usually based on their personal experience of directing the formation of priests in their own dioceses.[326] But here again, as in the case of the schema on priestly ministry, we are speaking of a late phase of Vatican II.

6. *Declaration on University Studies and Catholic Schools*

This draft, which was one of the batch of schemas sent to the fathers of the Council in April-May 1963, would still have a long journey before it, but, unlike other texts in the same category, it survived the journey.

In the beginning the preparatory Commission for Studies and Seminaries, which was under the authority of the leaders of the Roman dicastery of the same name, completed a first draft of seven chapters that focused mainly on Catholic schools (March 1962). After receiving the observations of the Central Preparatory Commission (June 1962), the Commission offered an amended version, which was approved by the Subcommission for Amendments. In mid-December 1962 this approval reached the conciliar commission, which had replaced the preparatory commission but was still under the authority of the leaders of the dicastery.

In January 1963, after hearing Confalonieri's report, the CC issued its instructions: a shorter schema should be composed that would follow the order of the material in the Code of Canon Law and would also match its pastoral guidelines with the Code. As for the applications of principles, it was recommended that these be turned into "Instructions"; canonical material should be used for the revision of the Code. As for the second schema, which dealt with obedience to the magisterium,

---

[324] See *AS* V/1, 198. For the texts and commentaries see *Vocation*, no. 233 (January 1966), a special number entitled *Les prêtres dans la pensée de Vatican II*.

[325] When, in November 1964, the schema was presented to the fathers in the reduced form of twelve propositions, it was given a favorable reception, although there was continued disagreement on the importance of teaching St. Thomas. The Decree *Optatam totius* was promulgated at the end of October 1965.

[326] The notable address that Msgr. Garrone (November 17, 1964) delivered on the need of renewing the outdated methods still in use in the Curia's Congregation for Seminaries resulted in his appointment as Pro-prefect of that Congregation at the beginning of 1966.

some of its general principles should be used in the schema on the Church.[327] At the second meeting of the CC, in March 1963, Confalonieri acknowledged that the Commission had carefully followed these recommendations. The text would gain in persuasive power if it eliminated all polemical tonalities, which were not appropriate in a conciliar text with a pastoral purpose.[328]

The schema on Catholic schools was to undergo a radical change of approach when in 1964 it became a Declaration on Christian Education. Meanwhile, the schema, in the form in which the bishops received it in the spring of 1963, included an introduction that stressed the duty and right of the Church in the matter of education. The three parts of the draft dealt successively with: (1) the fundamental rights of the person, the family, the state, and the Church; (2) schools in general and Catholic schools in particular; and (3) the importance of Catholic universities.

IV. RESULTS ACHIEVED AMID TENSIONS

A. SOME LEADERS WHO INTENDED TO "MODERATE"

It can be said without exaggeration that during the phase of preparation for Vatican II the leaders of the Holy Office regarded themselves as invested with special and sovereign authority to prepare for the Council.[329] After exercising this Curial authority over the preparatory commissions, which themselves were under the supervision of the Curia, these leaders tried to transfer their precedence to the Council as it began. But there they were quickly resisted by a conciliar current of critical and independent mind.

During the first period of the Council, Bea and De Smedt, speaking in the name of the Secretariat for Christian Unity, were the first to become the interpreters of an assembly that was still in search of itself but already clearly wished to resist any external tutelage, especially one that

---

[327] See AS V/1, 199.

[328] Ibid., 243-46.

[329] Drawing upon the memoirs of Confalonieri, *Momenti Romani* (1979), Andrea Riccardi reports that after the first announcement of the Council in the Church of St. Paul Outside the Wall, Cardinal Canali asked John XXIII whether "this time again the Holy Office would be in charge of the preparation." The Pope, who seemed surprised, answered after a brief pause: "The pope is the president of a council" (see A. Riccardi, "De l'Église de Pie XII à l'Église de Jean," in *Jean XXIII devant l'histoire*, ed. G. Alberigo [Paris, 1989], 150).

was conservative. But, as Father Dossetti noted in a working document from that period, the polarity between Ottaviani and Bea did not entirely correspond to the problem that had to be resolved as the first intersession began. For, if the course of the first conciliar period had revealed the Holy Office's inability to satisfy the criteria for the work of a council, it was also clear that the Secretariat for Christian Unity, because of the specific character of its important but inevitably limited ecumenical tasks, was not adequate to handle the entire range of the Council's problems.[330] John XXIII solved the problem by making the Secretary of State the president of the CC and choosing as its members a small number of cardinals that did not include Ottaviani and Bea. Cicognani was thus called upon to represent the Sovereign Pontiff himself and to exercise authority in his name.

At the Council itself a great many fathers, whether in the council hall or in the corridors of the assembly, had wanted a chief commission to be established that would direct the continuation of the Council's work.[331] Some bishops had hoped that the CC would have more members and might be a kind of "council in miniature." Some were disappointed at its small membership and its "elitist" character, that is, the exclusion of simple bishops.[332]

In this setting the decision of John XXIII to appoint his Secretary of State president of the CC was quite significant. The Pope meant to be represented at the head of the new organization, which would thereby be "above the battle." Unfortunately, Cicognani had been and remained also president of a conciliar commission that had been roughly handled by the conciliar assembly at the end of the first period. Given this painful and unexpected experience, Cicognani could only feel a certain solidarity with the schemas of the preparatory period. In other words, it would be difficult for him, wholeheartedly and without second thoughts,

[330] Dossetti Archive I, 7 (ISR).

[331] Besides the major interventions by Suenens, Lercaro, Montini, and Döpfner, see also the addresses by Léger and Hurley on December 3, 1963, and many informal documents circulating at the end of the first period: a memorandum of the Council of the French episcopate, a series of "Remarks and Proposals" on the subject of procedure, a document of Hurley's entitled "Council Procedure," and still others (see *AS* IV/1, 163f., and Caprile, II, 265-67).

[332] The idea of a "council in miniature" was current at the time and even showed up in some newspapers, for example, *La Libre Belgique* (December 4, 1962) and *De Tijd* of Amsterdam (December 5, 1962). It is not impossible that a confusion of the terms *consilium* and *concilium* gave rise to this rumor. Léger had spoken of the former, but some may have thought he meant the latter! Note that in English the term *council* has both senses, and this has often contributed to a misunderstanding.

to guide a second preparation that the majority group at the Council
wanted and expected but that Cicognani himself felt rather as a threat. In
addition, Cicognani found himself at the head of a CC that had been
conceived and established without his knowledge! For Felici, too, whom
the Pope called on to continue his work as Secretary General and now
also for the CC, the establishment of this Commission was an unpleasant surprise. The testimony of Msgr. V. Fagiolo leaves no doubt that he
had not been consulted about it.[333]

With Ottaviani and Bea not members of the CC, Cicognani and Felici
took over the role of leaders. In their view, to undertake an entirely new
preparation would clearly represent an unthinkable rejection of the work
done during the preparatory phase.[334] On the other hand, their appointment to the CC could be given a positive interpretation. It meant that
John XXIII, while favorable to a more open Council, did not intend to
leave the way completely open for the supporters of a new (and dangerous) direction: "He [the Pope] intended to exercise a moderating role
through Cardinal Cicognani and Msgr. Felici."[335]

Cicognani's intention of "moderating" the French-German wing's
trend toward openness had rather mixed results. As I have already noted,
in the case of the most important schemas, such as the ones on the
Church and on ecumenism, and some others, the Liénart-Suenens-
Döpfner group finally prevailed. With regard to some other schemas, the
opponents of a second preparation temporarily succeeded in preserving
them in their preparatory form. Absent from the list of members of the
CC,[336] Ottaviani and Bea were also occasionally absent when their own
schemas were on the table. When the CC invited the leaders of the Doctrinal Commission to its meeting of March 1963 on schema XVII, Ottaviani and Tromp refused to have anything to do with the meeting; when

[333] Msgr. (now Cardinal) Vincenzo Fagiolo, Felici's right hand man at Vatican II, provides a valuable testimony for this period, based on his own experience, in "Il Cardinale
A. Cicognani e Mons. P. Felici," in *Deuxième*, 229-42. According to Fagiolo, some
fathers from French-German circles, supported by some Italian cardinals (Lercaro and
Montini), wanted to reorient the Council of Presidents and the Council itself; the impact
of this influence (he says) found expression first of all in the closing address of John
XXIII, which gave the Council a new direction, then in the establishment of the CC, and,
finally in the appointment, later on, of the moderators (235-36).
[334] Ibid., 236.
[335] Ibid., 237.
[336] There were, obviously, other persons whose non-membership in the CC was
remarked on: during the intersession Montini was a member of the Commission for Technical and Administrative Questions; as for Lercaro, he would be appointed a moderator
on the eve of the reopening in September 1963.

Bea and Willebrands were invited for the discussion of the schema on ecumenism, they were abroad.[337]

When all was said and done, it was understandable that the Holy Office, which had already been humiliated during the first period of the Council, should think that the authority it claimed over the mixed commission on schema XVII had been taken from it by the CC. In its eyes, this represented a new defeat. The schema on the Oriental Churches, which Cicognani wanted to remove from the authority of the Doctrinal Commission, was another apple of discord; but he managed to eliminate an interposition of Ottaviani regarding it. An appreciation of the results achieved by the CC during the first semester of 1963 is possible only when we take due account of these institutional and personal factors.[338]

B. The Opponents of the Second Preparation

An assessment of the work accomplished by the CC and by the conciliar commissions requires a rapid glance at the activity of the opponents of the second preparation within these commissions. During the opening period of Vatican II, the defenders of the preparatory schemas and of the positions those texts implied were subjected to increasingly heavy fire from a critical group whose real power was not realized until mid-November, at the turning point represented by the vote on the schema on the sources of revelation (November 20, 1962) and the appointment of a mixed commission. During the 1962-63 intersession the defenders of the preparatory texts phase became the opponents of a second preparation.

The distinction used above between, on the one hand, "important schemas" and others being "launched," and, on the other, the "failures" of the second preparation is a summary classification of the various schemas being handled by the conciliar commissions during the intersession. That classification calls for some comment. The first category seems to me to have come into being mainly through the efforts of those who, in obedience to the instructions given in December 1962, sought to

---

[337] We do not know what Bea's attitude was toward his "exclusion" from the CC. He may have felt some disappointment, but his closeness to John XXIII would have given him great confidence for the future. His lack of membership did not harm his cause very much; we saw earlier that Cicognani was obliged to retract the schema on ecumenism, probably under direct and very firm pressure from the Pope.

[338] The work of the CC was done in an entirely different setting after the election of Paul VI. I shall speak of this at the proper time.

effect a successful second preparation for the Council, so that the latter could make progress during the second period. These efforts failed when, in any given commission, the direction taken remained in the hands of those who thought that the schemas of the preparatory period retained their full value and that a second preparation was unnecessary and perhaps even harmful. As described in each instance, the "failures" came in commissions whose leaders or dominant trend remained in one or other fashion under the supervision of the dicasteries of the Roman Curia.[339] Liberation from this supervision would come later, either after the changing of the writing team within a commission or as the result of a negative vote in the hall that punished the inertia or stubbornness of a commission.

When I speak of opponents of the second preparation, I am not by any means speaking metaphorically. This is the place to be a little more specific about the position taken by this influential fraction of conciliar opinion.

The opponents of a second preparation regularly stressed that the texts of the preconciliar phase had been prepared with the greatest care and at the cost of ceaseless labor,[340] had been closely examined by the Central Commission and, usually, further improved by the Subcommission on Amendments, and finally, had been approved by John XXIII himself. For these reasons they thought they deserved a better fate than the criticism or scorn which too many Council fathers had expressed regarding them during the fall of 1962. Thus, in a note to the CC in January 1963, after reminding it that the preparatory schema on bishops had already undergone critical revision by the Central Commission, Marella expressed his conviction that a second preparation would be not only unnecessary but even dangerous; it was unthinkable to rearrange a schema so well prepared!

---

[339] While this was the case with the four schemas listed as failures, it must be said that they were not alike in every point. The divisions in respect to the schemas on the Oriental Churches and on the states of perfection were marked by nuanced and changing polarities. There was not the same scattering of forces for the schemas on the bishops and on the missions. As for the "latecomer" schemas, some, like those on priests and on seminaries and Catholic schools suffered from Curial supervision. The case of the schema on revelation is special; its belated failure was due to the ambiguous situation in a mixed commission paralyzed by conflicts.

[340] In the countless interventions within the commissions, some speakers never tired of harking back to the volume of work done during the preparatory phase. So too, twenty years later, we find Fagiolo still listing the number of meetings held by the preparatory commission on the Oriental Churches and by its subcommissions, the number of hours of work, and the number of draft decrees that were composed — all this under the active presidency of Cicognani (see Fagiolo, "Il Cardinale," 236).

Father Welykyj, for his part, justified his action in not calling the Commission for the Oriental Churches to a plenary meeting by reminding his hearers that the results achieved by the preparatory commission were still valid; in addition, the preparatory schema had been approved by many bishops who now had become Council fathers. In short, he rejected "the complete destruction" of his decree!

Msgr. Paventi in turn was anxious to explain that if he had not judged it opportune to convoke the conciliar Commission on the Missions in 1962, it was in order to allow the squall of attacks on the Roman Curia and the Congregation of Propaganda to blow over. This brings up the fact that the attitude of the opponents of the second preparation was sometimes reinforced by the radical hostility of some "progressives" toward the Curia. In the particular case of the all-powerful offices of Propaganda, there was the manifesto of a group of bishops from French-speaking Africa, who, in order to put an end to the "colonialist" discrimination practiced by Rome, called for a downsizing or suppression of the dicastery that dealt specifically with the missions. The missions (they claimed) should be the concern solely of the ordinary dicasteries.

As for the schema on the bishops, people in Rome had not forgotten the statements of Alfrink, the proposals of Karl Rahner, and the Dutch bishops' pastoral letter, all of which wanted to reduce the agencies of the Curia to a subsidiary role. From the moment when the collegiality of the bishops was invoked at the opening of the CC, Cicognani immediately warned against the threat of episcopalism. The reader will also recall the critical commentaries published during the intersession by Msgr. Ghattas (a Copt) and Msgr. Doumith (a Maronite), who called for the suppression of Welykyj's schema on the Oriental Churches. Finally, it seems clear that the radicalism of the draft produced by the Charue-Thils team on the "call to holiness" in May 1963 gave the opponents of a second preparation an opportunity to sound the alarm.

A familiar method used by the opponents of a real revision of texts was that of the "rump commissions." Thus, despite the protests of some member bishops and the steps taken by Patriarch Maximos IV, ten months went by before a plenary meeting of the Commission on the Oriental Churches was called. To justify himself, Welykyj invoked the precedent of the Commission on Bishops which had several times announced a plenary meeting but each time had cancelled it without prior consultation, with the result that Marella's Commission held no plenary meeting between December 1962 and November 1963! Similarly the scheduled plenary meeting in May 1963 of the Commission on Religious was cancelled without any real justification.

Among similar phenomena we should recall the distrustful reception some members elected by the conciliar assembly received in certain conciliar commissions. In his note of January 23, 1963, Marella wrote that the "newcomers" must not think that they could take the schema back to point zero and recast all the material prepared. One witness, Father X. Seumois, notes that the elected members of the Commission on the Missions were regarded as "intruders."

The stubbornness with which defenders of the preparatory schemas in some conciliar commissions refused any fundamental reorientation, despite general and specific instructions from the CC, had a result some had not expected: it led to the production, in the shadows, of alternative schemas reflecting the wishes of the conciliar majority.

In the course of the first period, the difficulties in getting the Doctrinal Commission to meet and then to translate into worthwhile propositions what the conciliar assembly had said, were already the reason for the preparation of many more or less unofficial schemas dealing with biblical revelation, episcopal collegiality, and the Church. Similarly, when some commissions reached an impasse, thus frustrating the hopes placed in their work during the intersession, alternative schemas were prepared, for example, on missionary renewal, the Oriental Churches, and other subjects. It is obvious that these initiatives were strongly disapproved of by the leaders of commissions that remained in the grip of the opponents of a second preparation for Vatican II.

C. THE DECISIVE CONTRIBUTION OF THE COORDINATING COMMISSION

My earlier description of the establishment of the CC and the procedure it was to follow was limited to a general view of the second preparation as seen in its beginnings. Having followed the work the conciliar commissions did under the authority of the CC during the ten months of the intersession, I think it worthwhile to describe briefly once more the main results achieved amid the tensions of a "battlefield" on which supporters and opponents of the second preparation were in constant conflict.

It cannot be denied that the CC had the decisive influence on the success of the preparation for the second period of the Council. Its principal contribution in this respect was to impose an accelerated rhythm of work on the conciliar commissions in order to get through a very tight calendar. In many instances the CC also forced the commissions to take into account the gains made in the fall of 1962. At times the CC also served as a court of appeals when the spokesmen for the majority trend felt reduced to a minority in one of the conciliar commissions. While it was true that the CC was itself divided, it was no less true that its overall influence was a dynamic one and enabled Vatican II to get a new start at the end of September 1963.

There were, of course, other positive influences besides that of the CC. We must bear in mind the influence of John XXIII, who, himself pressed by illness, constantly emphasized the need of getting the revised schemas to the fathers. Finally, within the conciliar commissions small redactional teams played the part of movers who finished the second preparation in record time and overcame the braking efforts of the opponents of the new preparation.[341]

What were the concrete results achieved after ten months of varied activities that had begun in an atmosphere heavy with uncertainties and that had been carried on in the midst of serious tensions?

1. *Texts*

In April-May 1963 the Council Secretariat sent the fathers a first set of schemas. I list them according to the sequence in the pontifical rescript of April 22, 1963: (1) seminaries; (2) Catholic schools; (3) priests; (4) the lay apostolate; (5) bishops and dioceses; (6) the care of souls (pastoral practice); (7) the states of perfection (religious); (8) the Oriental Churches; (9) revelation; (10) the Church; and (11) ecumenism.[342] This mailing was accompanied by a recommendation to send in, in July at the latest, the observations, amendments, and suggestions that the bishops might think useful. At the end of July 1963 two other schemas were sent to the fathers: (1) the schema on the sacrament of marriage, and (2) the second part (chapters III and IV) of the constitution on the Church.[343]

---

[341] We must recall here the dynamic role of small teams like those, among others, of De Smedt-Hamer, Charue-Philips, Bea-Willebrands, Cento-Glorieux, Veuillot-Onclin, and even Garrone-Haubtmann, which often became driving forces at the Council.

[342] *AS* V/1, 522, to which should be added the schema on the Blessed Virgin Mary.

[343] Pontifical rescript of July 19, 1963, in *AS* V/1, 642.

2. *An Agenda*

On June 27, 1963, a few days after his election Paul VI decided that the second period of the Council would begin on September 29, 1963. Following deliberations of the CC at the end of August 1963, the agenda for the coming assembly was set as follows: (1) the Church (first four chapters); (2) the Blessed Virgin; (3) the bishops; (4) the lay apostolate; (5) ecumenism. This agenda is relatively homogeneous, reflecting the axis of ecclesiological renewal. Given the confusion with which the inter-session began, the work of the CC now appears to deserve praise. Except for the schema on the role of bishops, one of the "failures" of this inter-cession, these texts stand within the movement of the second preparation. When the draft on the Blessed Virgin was rejoined to the text on the Church (late October 1963), it too would enter into this dynamic.

As for the "volume" of this agenda, one must realize that the CC had made a reasonable assessment of the time that would be available during the second period. Despite difficult debates, the only one of these schemas that would not be discussed in depth would be the one on the apostolate of the laity, which would be reported to the assembly but a discussion of which would be postponed.[344]

3. *A Revised Procedure*

On August 31, 1963, the CC established a new organization of the groups guiding the Council. This reorganization received the official approval of the Pope, but it obviously arose out of prior suggestions and meetings that had the Pope behind them. The master stroke among these new structures was the appointment of four moderators or legates of the Council, mandated to direct the conciliar discussions. Other important innovations were the announcement of a new set of Regulations for the Council and the establishment of a special committee of Council fathers to handle press matters. I shall return to these later.

4. *Participation of Lay Representatives*

One of the principal merits of the CC was that at the very beginning it brought representatives of the Catholic laity into the work of two com-

---

[344] *AS* V/1, 649-50. During this discussion Döpfner urged that the discussion of the draft on revelation be postponed because it was not yet ready for the Council. Lercaro endorsed the proposal to put the text on the Church at the top of the agenda, since it treated the Council's main topic.

missions: the Commission on the Apostolate of the Laity and the mixed commission that was composing schema XVII. Thus the way was opened for the more active and more formal participation of the laity that would begin in the second period of the Council. Pope Paul VI would see to that by appointing in 1963 a series of auditors who were called to take an official seat on the conciliar commissions.

V. FROM COUNCIL TO CONCLAVE

Many thought, and some said, that the somewhat chaotic way in which the proceedings of the first period of the Council were conducted[345] was due in large measure to the passivity of John XXIII, who was inclined to "do nothing and let things ride," but also, in some degree, to the lack of perceptiveness on the part of the Council of Presidents. Very respectful of the freedom of others, the Pope wanted the bishops to find their way by themselves, the leaders of the Curia to learn by experience, and, above all, the Holy Spirit to act in depth during this phase when the fathers' self-consciousness was maturing.

The disorder of the fall of 1962 inevitably produced the uncertainties and confusion that marked the beginning of the intersession. But John XXIII knew that the transition that would begin in December 1962 would be of decisive importance, and his important interventions, running from December 5, 1962 (his "Agenda for the Period between the End of the First Period of the Ecumenical Council and the Beginning of the Second"), to January 6, 1963 (the letter *Mirabilis ille*), showed even more clearly the direction he wanted to give to this Council, the bold plan for which had sprung from his pastoral heart.

During the month of December the Pope returned unceasingly to the same theme: the need of successfully concluding a Council begun in a spirit of renewal. On December 12 he stressed the importance of the experience acquired that fall: "It took only a few weeks . . . to see that the light of the Lord was visibly manifested."[346] Some supporters of the

---

[345] The facts are well known: the change in the quorum for election to commissions; the assimilation of Bea's Secretariat to the commissions; the unjamming of the paradoxical vote on the schema on the sources of revelation; the establishment of a mixed commission, something not provided for in the Regulations; the slowness in announcing each subject on the daily agenda of the Council; etc. (see G. Alberigo, "Jean XXIII et Vatican II," in *Jean XXIII devant l'histoire* [Paris, 1989], 193-95).

[346] *DMC* V, 318; *DC* 60 (1963), 168-69.

preparatory schemas were of the view that this represented an abrupt change in the Pope's orientation; they had not noticed the stand in behalf of renewal that was already present in the Pope's opening address, a stand he later repeated several times.[347]

The turning point of December 1962 was thus decisive less in its content than in the establishment of new roles and of a different team in charge. John XXIII judged that the period of maturation, which ran parallel with the disorder of the first months, was over and that it was now necessary to go beyond that kind of confusion. The pressure of time was undoubtedly in the background of this turning point. We know that the seriousness of the Pope's illness became suddenly clear toward the end of November 1962.[348] It was then that the Pope, on being informed of the diagnosis of death, decided to push back the second period of the Council from May 1963 to September 1963.[349] It was then, too, that the group of cardinals who had met several times at the Belgian College prepared together their "programmatic" addresses for the beginning of December.[350] A few days later the two allocutions of Pope John that ended the first period of the Council gave a glimpse of the feelings of the old man who, like Moses, saw the promised land from afar but knew now that he could not enter it himself. In these special circumstances the period from Epiphany to Pentecost 1963, was for John XXIII personally much more than an "intersession." It was a time of personal trial and of sacrifice accepted for the success of the Council's work.

From the historical viewpoint it is obvious that the steps taken by the Pope for the sake of a second preparation would have a dominant influence on the intersession. The letter *Mirabilis ille* of January 6, addressed to each member of Vatican II, was the charter of the transition to the second period of the Council's activities. Among the most important themes of this document there were three that John XXIII wanted to put in the forefront: (1) the effective cooperation that all those who had returned home should continue by maintaining contact with the central leadership of the Council; (2) the need on the part of clergy and laity of a growing readiness and constant concern to contribute to the success of the Council; and (3) realization that the program of the Council must be

---

[347] Fagiolo was in this group. He thought it was at the close of the first period that the Pope decided to give a new orientation to Vatican II (see "Il Cardinale," 236).

[348] See the memoirs of Suenens, *Souvenirs et espérances*, 69-71.

[349] Alberigo, "Jean XXIII et Vatican II," 189.

[350] L. J. Suenens, "A Plan for the Whole Council," in *Vatican II Revisited*, 88-105. To gauge the impact on public opinion at the time, see Jean Pélissier in *La Croix*, December 6, 1962, 4.

given as broad as possible a scope and embrace the whole of Christendom and the whole of humanity.

The desire to keep in a state of alertness the bishops who had left Rome to take up again the business of their dioceses and the desire to associate the "periphery" as much as possible with the work being done at the "center" gave eloquence to this charter, which the Pope addressed to his "brothers in the episcopate." Even though not everyone at the "center" would be inspired by these sentiments of brotherhood, the attitude of John XXIII in this respect would be a source of inspiration.[351] The letter *Mirabilis ille* had at least one very clear and very important result: it "made explicit and definitive the symbiosis between the pope and the great majority at the Council."[352]

As for the second preparation for the Council, Pope John, knowing that his own days were numbered, became increasingly impatient to see the revised schemas, approved by him on April 22, sent to the Council fathers. A week later Cicognani announced to the bishops that he would do everything in his power to get the twelve schemas now ready to them as quickly as possible. The month of May had barely begun when John XXIII learned that the promised dispatch had still not taken place, and he ordered Cicognani to send a new message to the bishops (May 9). In fact, only on May 21 did Felici send the first six schemas.[353]

A. THE LAST THREE MONTHS

The events that marked the last three months of John XXIII's pontificate would have a direct impact not only on the conclave of June 1963 but also on the remainder of Vatican Council II. In the foreground of this evolution were, first of all, the turn taken by Italian political life at the beginning of 1962 due to the adoption of the "center-left" line,[354] and

---

[351] An incident involving the press illustrates this point. When the Conference of German-speaking and Scandinavian bishops studied the schemas of the second preparation at Fulda in August 1963, some Italian newspapers provided unpleasant commentaries that threw doubt on the intentions and loyalty of the participants at Fulda, as though they were engaged in a conspiracy. Frings immediately issued a public statement that denied the accusations and said that the work done by the bishops reflected exactly the instructions the Pope had given them on several occasions and was therefore inspired by him (see *Katholiek Archief* 18 [1963], 1007-10).

[352] Alberigo, "Jean XXIII et Vatican II," 199.

[353] Wiltgen, *The Rhine Flows into the Tiber*, 70-72; Caprile, II, 417-19.

[354] There is a detailed chronicle of these events in "Les catholiques italiens à l'épreuve de la politique," *ICI*, no. 192 (May 15, 1963), 15-23.

then the Italian elections of April 28, 1963. In the background was John
XXIII's disengagement from Italian political life generally and from the
Christian Democrats in particular. However his attitude was interpreted,
the consequences of his action were considerable.[355] In a letter of July 9,
1962, we find the Pope confiding to Msgr. Capovilla:

> In the four years since Pope John has been carrying out his responsibilities,
> he has never had, nor taken, nor profited from a single opportunity to meet
> with those in government on the right or on the left, or with any of the chief
> actors in the quarrel, or to abandon his own reserve; he has acted accord-
> ing to the ancient example of Jacob the patriarch who, surrounded by his
> sons on the right and the left, was content to look, to suffer, and to be
> silent: "But the father reflected on the matter in silence" (Gen 37:11).[356]

It was in this context that one of the high moments of Roncalli's pontificate occurred. The international Balzan Foundation, with support
from its Soviet members, decided, on March 1, 1963, to bestow its Peace
Prize on John XXIII. A few days later the Pope received the President of
the Italian Republic as the representative of the Balzan Foundation and
told him that he would be happy to accept the prize as a tribute to the
activity of the Church on behalf of peace. The general tenor of his
address on March 7, in which he came out in favor of the Church's
"political neutrality," caused a sensation, as did also the personal audience he gave that same day to Alexis Adzhubei, editor of *Izvestia* and
son-in-law of N. Khrushchev.[357] These two events not only surprised
public opinion but also caused consternation in Roman Church-circles in
Rome, which are always obsessed by Italian politics. In Curial circles
connected to conservative forces in Italy, there was general condemnation. This could be seen especially in the efforts made by *L'Osservatore
Romano* and Vatican Radio, first simply to ignore the audience for
Adzhubei and then to make it disappear (to use R. Rouquette's description).[358]

---

[355] In a quite remarkable historical sketch, Andrea Riccardi detects in the choice of
Cardinal Tardini as Secretary of State a return to the line of Gasparri, who sought to
remove the Church from politics; the appointment of Father Tucci to the editorship of *La
Civiltà Cattolica* and the upheaval that followed this were a move in the same direction
(see Riccardi, "De l'Église de Pie XII à l'Église de Jean XXIII," 138-40).

[356] Ibid., 141.

[357] *DC* 60 (1963), 420-25; for the presentation of the Balzan Peace Prize on May 10,
followed by a visit of the Pope to the Quirinal, see ibid., 713-24.

[358] R. Rouquette analyzed the signs of change in the attitude of the Kremlin, which
had become less hostile toward the Catholic Church: "It really seems that the Kremlin
has realized that Catholicism is not in favor of international war and can, to some degree,
help in limiting the unimaginable dangers of an atomic conflict" ("Chronique," *Études*

Some weeks later came another important event: the publication of the encyclical *Pacem in terris*, promulgated on Holy Thursday 1963. In it Pope John taught that Christians were not to look to human institutions for salvation and protection but were to be active in them as the incorruptible leaven of Christian life. Desirous of moving forward, the Pope reminded his readers that the "signs of the times" could signify the twilight of an era left behind by more radical demands for justice.[359] The encyclical helped update the language of the Church's social teaching and broaden its horizons to the international sphere. When the commission for schema XVII took up its work again, it quickly became clear that the draft to be submitted to the Council would have to be revised in order to take *Pacem in terris* into account.

Finally, the results of the Italian elections on April 28, 1963, a setback for the Christian Democratic Party and a gain for the Communist Party, brought the dissatisfaction of the most influential Curial circles to a climax.[360] They faulted John XXIII for playing into the hands of the Communist Party both by his addresses and by his silence. Thus a campaign of outright criticism of the old Pope was aimed both at his speech on March 7, which was blamed for inviting an interpretation of softness toward Marxism, and at his silence when he failed to support the interventions of the Italian episcopate during the electoral campaign; and certain Curial cardinals thought his silence may have done more harm than his addresses had! Suenens would later comment: "John XXIII suffered much from the accusation in Curial circles that he was responsible for the electoral success of communism in Italy."[361]

316 [May, 1963], 240-44). Rouquette thought that the sending of Russian Orthodox observers could not have been done without Kremlin approval. The mediatorial role of those observers was not negligible.

[359] The attention and praise this document elicited everywhere gave the Roman pontiff an audience that now included the governments of all the major countries and the representatives of the world religions; at the same time the encyclical provoked hostile reactions from conservative circles in the West (Germany and Italy, among others).

[360] The Italian episcopate had thought it necessary to descend into the political arena and on March 12, 1963, had published a statement urging Catholics — in veiled but clear language — to vote for the Christian Democratic Party. The statement was picked up by *OssRom* (March 14, 1963) and accompanied by commentaries in favor of its political outlook; one article, among others, signed with the initials of R. Manzini, editor of the Vatican newspaper, advocated a "spirit of crusade" — in the good meaning of this word! The Christian Democrats lost thirteen seats in the Chamber, and the Communist Party gained twenty-six (see the *OssRom* for March 30 and April 7, and the French edition for April 5).

[361] Suenens, *Souvenirs et espérances*, 94.

Foreign observers and chroniclers of the Council were struck by the influence which the domestic political situation had in Rome not only on the positions taken by certain parts of the Curia during Vatican II, but also on the surprising interpretation they gave to the directions being taken by the ongoing Council. For this reason, historians of Vatican II who pay attention to Italian politics at that period cannot be accused of being on the wrong track.

In the past and even during the time of the Council, it very often happened that Roman interventions meant for Italy were unduly echoed in the universal Church. John XXIII's intention was precisely to restore the credibility of Rome's universal vocation. In this respect the Council had a direct impact. Italy, once regarded as "the papacy's stool," now had to take its place in a more international landscape.[362] The conservative wing of the Italian press and episcopate and of the Curia tended to interpret certain directions taken by the Council in the narrow terms of issues of domestic politics. On the contrary, the preparation for Vatican II and the first period of the Council's activity expanded the attention of open Catholics beyond Italy, in a perspective that would increasingly embrace the dimensions of the world.

B. THE PLEBISCITE

On June 3, 1963, the morrow of the celebration of Pentecost 1963, good Pope John succumbed to the illness that had been threatening him for so long.[363] Throughout his pontificate the Feast of Pentecost had had special meaning for him.[364] On May 20, 1963, the Holy Father had

---

[362] See the article by the editors of the Venetian journal *Questitalia*: "En Italie, l'ouverture à gauche," in *Esprit* 31, nos. 7-8 (July-August, 1962), 142.

[363] The suffering Pope appeared in public for the last time at the window of his office on May 22 and recited the *Salve Regina* with the crowd. The first health bulletin was published in *OssRom* for May 28; it spoke of a "gastric heteroplasia" (cancer) from which the Holy Father had been suffering for a year. On the evening of May 29 his condition seemed to be noticeably improved, but during the night of May 30-31 it suddenly deteriorated. On the morning of May 31 the pope received the sacraments of the sick; in a clear and firm voice he renewed the offering of his life for the success of the Council, whose great work begun would certainly be crowned. John XXIII died on Monday, June 3, at 7:49 P.M., a few minutes after the end of a Mass celebrated for his intention on St. Peter's Square in the presence of a large crowd. His reign had lasted four year, seven months, and one week.

[364] Thus at Pentecost 1960, the Motu Proprio *Superno Dei nutu*, marked the opening of the preparatory phase of the Council; in an apostolic letter, Pentecost 1961, John XXIII asked for prayers for the Council; and in 1962 he reminded Catholics that the Council would be a new fulfillment of the promises of Pentecost.

addressed to the Catholic episcopate the Apostolic Exhortation *Novem per dies* to mark the beginning of the novena before Pentecost and to express his joy at the progress made in the preparation for the coming reopening of the Council.

The mortal agony of John XXIII over three endless days was followed, hour by hour, by the news on the radios of the world. The loving reception of a lovable Pope had broadened from *urbs* to *orbis*, from Rome to the world, in a tidal wave of sympathy as the whole world, without distinction, attended the final phase of the Pope's mortal illness. The televised funeral celebration moved both believers and nonbelievers.

This unprecedented plebiscite stunned the Roman Curia. Three weeks before, its right wing was still campaigning against the Pope's policy of detente, which in their view could only favor the forces of the "left." Opposition, whether muffled or open, had also been aroused by John XXIII's openness to the non-Catholic Churches and his desire to associate the bishops with the exercise of authority in the Church. These Curialists were most disconcerted by the unanimity of the homage paid by both the most conservative and the most progressivist circles.

Vatican circles had not anticipated that this man with his friendly straightforwardness, who did not hide his peasant origins or his intellectual deficiencies, would have such influence. The openness of every kind that Pope John advocated could only mean, to them, the Church's abandonment of a politics of power. Thus for certain Roman leaders the hour had come for an examination of conscience: How were they to explain that an attitude of "weakness," such as that of John XXIII, could reap such successes? According to testimonies from that time, John XXIII spoke more strongly and more loudly by his death than he had ever spoken in his lifetime.[365] It became very quickly clear to the entire world that this plebiscite was a major event and would have great influence at the conclave and then on the continuation of the Council.

Another important factor on the eve of the conclave was the eulogy for the dead Pope that Montini immediately delivered in the cathedral of Milan. In particular, these words became famous: "With an eye on his now sealed tomb, we can speak of his heritage, which the tomb can

---

[365] The expression was that of an expert at the Council upon his return then from Rome (see J. Grootaers, *Diarium*, Cahier 9, 1183-83). The *JCongar* described the immense echo of John XXIII's death: "A kind of extraordinary unanimity was created." In Congar's view it was clear "that the most important thing is not ideas but the heart."

never lock away, of the spirit which he instilled into our age and which death can never stifle."[366]

C. FROM COUNCIL TO CONCLAVE

Council and conclave are two examples of dialogue which, despite essential differences, have aspects that are comparable. They are both privileged moments for free expression and collegiality in the midst of rigid, monarchical structures. Every conclave is preceded or accompanied by an exercise in assessment, when people try to draw up a balance sheet of gains and losses for the pontificate that has just ended.

At the death of John XXIII no one knew whether this assessment would take its cue from the conciliar dynamism that was, obviously, present to all minds. In his address "on electing a pope," Msgr. A. Tondini explicitly came out against the optimism of the deceased Pope and suggested postponing the remainder of the Council to a later date in order to leave time for questions raised to ripen.

In the conclave the normal continuation of Vatican II was the principal issue in the tension between the "conciliar party," which included, among others, the cardinals from the periphery, and the conservatives, who wanted a pontificate that would "turn the page." On the eve of the conclave some were afraid that the difference in emphasis between this conclave and the now temporarily suspended Council represented a threat to Vatican II.[367] If Montini managed to gain the required two-thirds majority at the sixth vote, it was only at the price of concessions made to some renegades from the "Curial bloc" and with the support of a majority that was temporary and hybrid in character.[368]

---

[366] G. B. Montini, *Discorsi e scritti sul Concilio (1959-1963)* (Brescia, 1983), 218; *DC* 60 (1963), 848. At the time, people recalled the position taken by Montini on December 5, 1962, at the end of the first conciliar period, in a much-noticed address that many listeners at the time understood as a program for the coming conclave (see *AS* IV/1, 291-94).

[367] The great difference in "tone" between Council and conclave must be emphasized here: whereas the conclave included fifty-five European cardinals (out of a total of eighty-two), only a third of the Council's members were of European origin. It could therefore be said that the Council was less removed from the realities of the contemporary world than the conclave was. Furthermore, almost a third of the cardinals at the conclave were Italians, while at the Council Italians were only a fifth of the whole assembly. Not to be forgotten in this context is that in 1962-63 the proportion of Italian bishops really involved in the conciliar event was minimal.

[368] I am here following G. Zizola, according to whom Cicognani and Ottaviani helped win the support of conservative voters, who in the final analysis played a decisive role in favor of Montini (*Quale Papa?* [Rome, 1977], 160-72).

If it was true that Montini's election was the result more of a compromise than of bold efforts to find someone new, it is clear that the conclave of June 1963 could bear upon the tenor and level of the continuation of the Council. This view is summed up by G. Zizola when he says that there would be question of a modernization (of structures) rather than of a reform in depth.[369]

The positive aspects of Montini's election were evidently to be found, first, in the intellectual openness of the new Pope to the great movements of liturgical, ecumenical, and theological renewal, which were being called on to supply inspiration for the major documents, now in gestation, of Vatican II. Second, there was Montini's willingness to examine and to repair the deficiencies in the operations of the Curia. A final "constructive" influence exerted by this conclave on the further evolution of the conciliar meetings was the strategic reorganization that Paul VI undertook even before the end of the intersession, especially by establishing a college of four moderators, which was meant to solve the problem of the multi-headed authority at the Council. But the "scars from the conclave" would not be healed for quite some time.[370]

VI. From Conclave to Council

A. The Beginning of the Pontificate of Paul VI

The special role of Montini during the first year of Vatican II is also to be understood in light of his peculiar situation in the Italian Church, where at the end of Pius XII's reign his position had become marginal.[371] But Montini then became John XXIII's first cardinal and was called on to be a member of the administrative committee of the Italian Episcopal Conference. While he played an active role in this committee in its preparation for Vatican II, he was excluded from the official preparatory phase.

[369] Ibid., 169-70, where Zizola suggests that the abandonment of Lercaro's candidacy to the profit of the reformist outlook of Suenens may have meant a reduction in the plans of the "Roncallian revolution."

[370] "The conflicts that made their appearance during and after the Council between Paul VI and Cardinals Lercaro and Suenens would show the precarious nature of the electoral compromise and the power which this had given to the Curial party" (ibid., 172).

[371] In four years Montini participated in only two meetings of the Italian Episcopal Conference, over which Siri presided (see J. Grootaers, "L'attitude de l'archevêque Montini au cours de la première période du Concile," in *G. B. Montini, arcivescovo di Milano e il Concilio ecumenico Vaticano II. Preparazione e primo periodo* [Brescia, 1985], 264-66).

At the beginning of the Council, Montini and Lercaro were almost the only Italian prelates who were well known to the foreign bishops arriving in Rome. Montini was also one of the only Italians to have been personally involved in the ecumenical movement and in the preconciliar renewal of ecclesiology.[372]

During the first period of the Council Montini played a very unobtrusive role, except for his intervention in the debate on the liturgy and the speech in which, in December 1962, he joined Suenens, Lercaro, and Döpfner in proposing a revision of the program for the Council. On the other hand, during the first six months of the 1962-63 intersession, the Archbishop of Milan spared no effort in associating his diocese as closely as possible with the conciliar event.[373] He took every opportunity to address his clergy and faithful on the subject: the Week of Christian Unity (January 1963), a study session for priests (February, in Varese), priestly ordinations (March 10), the celebration of Palm Sunday and the day of ecclesiastical vocations (both in June), and, finally, the famous tribute he paid to the memory of John XXIII in the cathedral of Milan.[374]

Like Lercaro, Montini found himself excluded from the official preparation for the Council, except for his participation in meetings of the Central Commission, where he found an audience better disposed toward him, precisely because it was international in composition. The Roman Curia, which was mainly in control of the preparatory phase of the Council, had turned its back on the forces of renewal in Italy.[375]

[372] One should remember the disproportion between the number of Italian bishops at Vatican II (400, more or less) and the part they took in activities at the beginning of the Council; on all the commissions in existence in October 1962, there were only nineteen Italian members among the hundreds elected.

[373] See especially *Rivista Diocesana Milanese* (1963), 117-19, 368-69, 388-89, and 467-71, as well as *DC* 60 (1963), 1090-91, which reprints a text that had appeared in the newspaper *L'Italia,* June 30, 1963.

[374] Montini's address on March 10, which was devoted to "the indispensable role of the priest," and the text of which was tape-recorded, shows better than any other text the deep meaning Montini saw in the great conciliar event: "You see the Church in search of herself, seeking with great and touching effort to define herself, to understand what she is. . . . Not only is the Church in search of herself, she is also in search of the world." The Church wants to recover her prophetic power so that she may speak to the world words that should put the world right. She does this "by fathoming the world's needs, by observing the inadequacies, necessities, aspirations, sufferings, and hopes that are at the heart of humanity" (see *Discorsi dell'arcivescovo di Milano: al Clero (1957-1963)* [Milan, 1963], IV, 73-80). This major text with its passionate but controlled tone made a deep impression at the time. It was echoed in the lecture Father Chenu gave in Rome in 1965 on schema XVII, published in M.-D. Chenu, *Peuple de Dieu dans le monde* (Paris, 1966), see 12-13.

[375] It was no small paradox to see two eminent archbishops of Italy, Lercaro and Mon-

In this context, the last of the seven "letters" that Montini addressed to his diocese at the end of 1962 is instructive. It was published on December 2, only a few days before the major address he delivered in the council hall. Despite his usual reserve, Montini did not hesitate to give in this letter a very critical list of the errors committed during the preparation for Vatican II. While some people might be fearful that a confused discussion would be fruitlessly prolonged, he expressed his confidence in the coming redirection of the Council: "The second session will move along much more expeditiously," because the material will be concentrated in a few short schemas, motivated by present, pastoral needs. "Thus the Council, full of energy, will reach the threshold of its primary subject, the Church."

Given the important role that Montini took in the redirection of Vatican II on the eve of the intersession, we might have expected to see him working on the CC, which made its debut in January of 1963. Nothing of the kind. I have cited the circumstances in which John XXIII placed this new "supercommission" under the authority of the Secretary of State. Several explanations are possible of why Montini and Lercaro remained so unobtrusively in the background. Since solidly based evidence is lacking, we may suppose that this reserve may have been connected with the coming conclave. It is certain that in majority circles of the Council Montini was generally regarded as John XXIII's "dauphin" or heir apparent. As for Lercaro, we must bear in mind that during the intersession the Archbishop of Bologna was very active on the conciliar Commission on the Liturgy and served as one of its presidents; but one may doubt that this was the real reason why he was excluded from the CC.

In any case, the fact is that in the conclave of June 21 and 22 they were the two candidacies who received a large number of votes. When Montini was finally elected on June 21, the event gave rise to high hopes among the conciliar majority and to fears or even real consternation among the leaders of the minority and of the Roman Curia.[376]

Two burdens seemed to weigh on this pontificate as it began during the intermission of this difficult council. First, the universal popularity

tini, who enjoyed great prestige abroad, quarantined by the leaders of the Italian Episcopal Conference and by those who were preparing for Vatican II, but then soon becoming leaders at the Council once it opened.

[376] In the view of the "right" in the Curia, Montini was a kind of leftist; the Archbishop of Milan had been raised in an anti-fascist family and had publicly taken positions hostile to the Franco regime in Spain.

of the deceased John XXIII had become so great that it seemed to "crush" his successor, who was an intellectual. Second, it was known that Montini, who had spent over a quarter of a century in the Secretariat of State in Rome, was going to have to reform the Curia and convert it to the Council by somehow removing it from the heritage of Pius XII, an eminently paternal figure to whom, despite everything, he himself remained deeply attached. Montini was going to have to dissociate himself from his former colleagues.

It has been repeatedly said that Paul VI was inclined by temperament to seek "the happy medium" of compromise solutions. If his whole pontificate perhaps does not deserve that judgment, it seems to me certain that the first months of his pontificate were indeed marked by indecision and compromise. This seems clearer to us today than to witnesses at the time. In this matter we may suppose that the fallout from a very difficult conclave and the more or less formal commitments made to the two parties in the field, with the Council as the stakes, contributed to the hesitations of the new Pope and perhaps reduced his freedom of movement.

In any case, the "state of grace" which the new pontiff enjoyed was to be of short duration, certainly with regard to the radical reorganization of conciliar structures that leaders of the majority expected from him, very probably as a result of the conclave. The first ten days that followed the election of Montini on June 21, 1963, were dazzling. On the very next day, the new pontiff addressed a first message to the world, in the Sistine Chapel and in the presence of seventy-nine cardinals. He clearly committed himself to make the continuation of Vatican II "the most important part" of his pontificate: "This will be the chief work to which We intend to devote all the energies the Lord has given Us."[377]

As early as June 27, Paul VI set September 29 as the date for the resumption of the Council, a date considered rather near. Then, at his coronation on June 30, he prayed God that the great event of the ongoing Council might strengthen the faith of the Church and show the separated brethren a rejuvenated Church that would be attractive to them and make easier their heartfelt reunion with the Mystical Body of the one Catholic Church.[378]

This initial period also included the third meeting, on July 3-4, of the CC, which was still conducting its sessions in the style of John XXIII's CC, with an agenda still concerned entirely with the activities of January

[377] *Insegnamenti*, I, 13; *DC* 60 (1963), 835.
[378] *Insegnamenti*, I, 38.

and March. At the same time, plans were coming into existence for the reform of Vatican II, about which we will speak later.

The apparent calm that followed upon the euphoria of these two weeks ended during the second half of August. September was marked by a whole series of decisive measures with regard to the reopening of the conciliar assembly: the establishment of a press committee for the Council (announced on September 8 in *L'Osservatore Romano*), the letter *Quod apostolici muneris* addressed to Tisserant and listing all the steps in a reorganization of the organs directing Vatican II (September 12), the publication of the revised conciliar Regulations (September 13), the letter *Horum temporum,* which Paul VI sent to each bishop reminding him especially of the main purposes of the Council (September 14), and, finally, the address of the Pope to the Curia shortly before the reopening of Vatican II, in which he spoke of the reform of the Curial agencies and of bringing diocesan bishops to participate in the government of the Church (September 21).[379]

On September 29, as crown of this period of great activity and marking the end of the intersession, Paul VI gave a programmatic address at the opening of the second period of the conciliar assembly. After recalling the path laid out by John XXIII, the Pope dwelled on the more important goals of the Council, the main subject of which was to be the Church, its self-awareness, its program for renewal and unity, and its dialogue with the contemporary world.[380]

The letter of September 12 to Tisserant contained a detailed reorganization of the structures of Vatican II: the CC, the role of the lay auditors, the Secretariat for Extraordinary Affairs, the Council of Presidents, and the new board of moderators. Within this set of instructions, the preparation and promulgation of which marked the beginning of Montini's pontificate, there was one new structure that especially caught the attention of the bishops and of public opinion: the appointment of moderators of the Council, four in number, who were called upon by Paul VI "to organize the discussions at the general congregations, while always safeguarding and ensuring the freedom of the Council fathers and having it in mind to make each intervention and the collection of interventions emerge in a clearer and more organized way."[381]

---

[379] *Insegnamenti,* I, 164-65, 167-69, 181-83.
[380] *Insegnamenti,* I, 197-219.
[381] *Insegnamenti,* I, 165.

The selection of Cardinals Suenens, Lercaro, and Döpfner as moderators clearly gave representation to the conciliar majority. The appointment of Agagianian, the influential Prefect of the Congregation of Propaganda and a representative of the Curia, served as a counterbalance. One may recall the four major speakers of December 1962, who in turn suggested routes to be followed in releasing the Council from its impasse. Suenens had outlined the reorganization to be undertaken; Lercaro had called attention to the need for evangelical poverty; Döpfner, the youngest, had recalled the demands of the gospel in relation to the realities of life;[382] Montini, the last of the four at that time, had now been elected Bishop of Rome.

It is in the genesis of this innovation, which was, indeed, part of the whole reorganization, that one can detect half-measures and compromises. This was an institution whose purpose, in the beginning, was to make the entire procedure at the Council more effective and transparent, but also to give Vatican II a new and more "conciliar" face. It is not easy, as others have already noted, to establish with certainty the calendar of the genesis of this innovation.[383] According to some consistent evidence from that period, a single moderator had originally been planned, who would be the pope's "legate" at the Council, a title that would have given him precedence over the Curial agencies. But afterward there was question of two, then three, and finally four "moderators."[384]

In the view of Suenens, who seems to have been the first one sounded out, the "control" (moderamen) was to be that of a brain trust that would think out and implement the general procedure to be followed by the large and sometimes disorderly assembly. The group around Lercaro in Bologna also had the sense that while the Council of Presidents was responsible for the good order of the work, the "political guidance" should be entrusted to the moderators.[385]

---

[382] Laurentin, *Bilan de la deuxième session*,18-19: "Three men of caliber and breadth, whose interventions had been very important for the direction taken in the first session."

[383] G. Alberigo, "Concilio acefalo? L'evoluzione degli organi direttivi del Vaticano II," in *Attese*, 214.

[384] J. Grootaers, *Diarium*, Cahier 27, citing Laurentin (October 6, 1964). According to Suenens, Paul VI wanted the Council to be run by two "legates," Agagianian and Suenens, which meant in fact two orientations; if a third were added, it would be Döpfner; the Pope did not mention the fourth, Lercaro, who would be added later (Suenens, *Souvenirs et espérances*, 110).

[385] Grootaers, *Diarium*, Cahier 83 (September 16, 1969); and Suenens, *Souvenirs et espérances*, 110.

During the preparation for the second period, the main concern of Suenens and also of Lercaro's entourage was to obtain at all cost a set of regulations for the college of moderators itself.[386] Such regulations were regarded as the only firm guarantee of direct and assured relations with the Supreme Pontiff and as the principal means of ensuring an autonomous interaction with the conciliar assembly.[387] This somewhat "ideal" conception of the role of the moderators was not realized during the second period of Vatican II. Paul VI never promulgated a set of regulations for the moderators; in the end, he gave the impression that he preferred to leave somewhat vague the relations between the different organs whose function it was to direct the Council.

The original plan for a college of moderators was made at the very beginning of July.[388] But between July and September Paul VI found himself compelled to "deal considerately with other individuals" and to limit the competencies at first envisaged.[389] The first step back was the argument of canonists that the term *legate* could be allowed only to a representative of the pope outside of Rome. The word was therefore replaced by *moderator*, which signifies someone who leads an assembly.[390] It seems that during August Paul VI was at first on the point of completely dropping the plan. He seems later to have decided to establish this leadership, but with clearly limited powers.[391]

---

[386] Suenens, *Souvenirs et espérances,* 111; and G. Alberigo, "Dinamiche e procedure nel Vaticano II. Verso la revisione del regolamento del Concilio (1962-1963)," *CrSt* 13 (1992), 146-49.

[387] One of the most well-informed experts of that period, G. Alberigo, adviser to Lercaro, wrote at the time: "The aim was to establish an organ which, in addition to its formal functions, would be a flexible link . . . between the head of the Council, that is, the pope, and the body of the assembly, that is, the universal episcopate, so that the dialogue would be as orderly, free, and fruitful as possible" (*L'Avvenire d'Italia*, September 29, 1963, cited in Laurentin, *Bilan de la deuxième session,* 21).

[388] Testimonies that are in agreement in Grootaers, *Diarium,* Cahier 24, citing A. Prignon (September 24, 1964), who adds a detail, "shortly after the CC meeting of July 3," and Cahier 83 (September 16, 1969). Archival confirmation may be found in the documents that G. Dossetti composed either before or after a papal audience during the first two weeks of July (see *Inventorio dei Fondi G. Lercaro and G. Dossetti* [Bologna, 1995], 101-2, under references FD 76, FD III 258, and FD II 107).

[389] Grootaers, *Diarium,* Cahier 24, citing A. Prignon (September 24, 1964) and Cahier 83 (September 16, 1969).

[390] Laurentin rightly observes that the French word *moderateur* calls to mind the function of one who restrains (*Bilan de la deuxième session,*17); in good Latin, however, it signifies a more active function; the *moderator* of a ship is its pilot, the one who holds the helm.

[391] Grootaers, *Diarium,* Cahier 24, citing A. Prignon (September 24, 1964); Cahier 40, citing A. Prignon (October 14, 1965); Cahier 83, (September 16, 1969); Suenens, *Souvenirs et espérances,* 113.

If we track the strategy developed by Cicognani, whom Paul VI confirmed in his role of Secretary of State, I think we will have one of the keys that give us access to the background of the event. Cicognani's strategy was to persuade the Pope to forestall possible competition in the reorganization of the Council. Cicognani succeeded, first of all, in prolonging the role of the CC, of which he was president, for the entire duration of Vatican II and in suppressing the Secretariat for Extraordinary Affairs.[392] Next, the CC was expanded by the appointment of three new members, Agagianian, Lercaro, and Roberti. This expansion, took place three weeks before the appointment of the four moderators was made known on September 12. Thanks to this expansion, the four future moderators found themselves included in the CC before they were appointed as moderators! Finally, on August 31, there was a surprise meeting of the now expanded CC.[393]

This meeting was a key moment, since it gave rise to a closely argued debate on the status of the future moderators, who had not yet been named.[394] In a very revealing confrontation two conceptions of the role of the future moderators clashed. While Cicognani described them as "delegates of the Council of Presidents or of the CC," Lercaro said that "the four are the spokesmen of the Holy Father."[395] Lercaro believed, and Felici agreed, that the effective leadership would belong to the moderators, but Roberti defended the thesis that they would have to function as "delegates of the Council of Presidents."[396] The Archbishop of

---

[392] At the first meeting of the CC under the new pontiff, on July 3, 1964, Cicognani mentioned in passing that the life of the CC had been extended. This decision, which elicited no reaction at the meeting, meant in fact a radical change in the organization as planned in January 1963, when it was intended to serve as a watchdog in the absence of the bishops during the intersession. As for the members of the Secretariat for Extraordinary Affairs, they either joined the Council of Presidents (which was expanded to twelve members) or the CC in its new form (see AS V/1, 566).

[393] Of the ten members belatedly summoned, half would be absent. It is not unthinkable that Suenens kept away from the meeting in order not to be submitted to the authority of the Secretary of State at a time when the status of the moderators had not yet been clearly established. It seems to me remarkable that at the meeting of the CC on September 26, if we can believe the report of the meeting, Suenens took no part in the exchange of views on the competencies of the moderators; at that point he was the only moderator to remain silent on a subject that would affect him very closely.

[394] It was surprising and, in all probability, contrary to the habits of the Curia, to see the Secretary of State organizing an exchange of ideas on measures still in preparation and not yet promulgated by the sovereign pontiff! In a letter of September 6 to Tisserant, Cicognani announced the institution of the moderators, and on September 9, he told Msgr. Felici. The official notification came on September 12 (see AS V/3, 693-94).

[395] AS V/1, 647-49.

[396] There is something surrealistic about seeing Cicognani listing "possible" candi-

Bologna asked in vain for a clarification of the relationship between the Council of Presidents and the four moderators. The distance between the two perspectives at issue was great. Paul VI would choose neither of them; he seems to have decided on a vague intermediate definition by describing the four as "delegates or moderators of the Council."[397]

Cicognani's final movement on the conciliar chessboard came three days before the reopening on September 29 and consisted in calling a joint meeting of the Council of Presidents, the CC, and the moderators for a common study of the norms recently introduced into the Regulations for the Council and of questions having to do with the resumption of the Council's activities. This manner of proceeding corresponded very closely to the vision that the Secretary of State had defended on August 31, according to which the activity of the moderators was carried on within the CC, whose "delegates" they were.[398] It is noteworthy that of the four moderators Lercaro was the only one new to the CC. Thus the situation came about that Suenens and Lercaro had done everything they could to avoid,[399] the ambiguity of which was to weigh heavily on the authority of the new moderators.

May it not be said that Cicognani obtained a firm grasp on the tiller by winning, at the right time, a change in the CC, on which his authority within the Council was based? He won a change in the function of the CC, which henceforth was no longer limited to the intersession, an

dates for the new body (Suenens, Döpfner, Lercaro, Liénart, Agagianian, Ruffini, Roberti), when, if we believe Lercaro, it was clear that the four names were already known behind the scenes.

[397] See Cicognani's letter to September 6 to Tisserant (*AS* V/3, 693).

[398] Meeting of September 26 (*AS* V/1, 685-94). That meeting may be understood as an anticipatory sign of the "summit" that would be held on October 23 to discuss the five preliminary questions the moderators wanted to place before the assembly; it would be a "summit" at which, it was hoped, the four moderators would find themselves in a minority. Instead of being the "legates" of the Pope, as an initial draft had called them, they would become, at least in Cicognani's mind, the delegates of the CC.

[399] In his letter of forewarning on September 19, Suenens begged Msgr. Dell'Acqua to obtain direct instructions from the Holy Father before the meeting of the CC on September 25: "Otherwise we will be swamped within this CC which is likely to settle *in obliquo et ab extrinseco* [indirectly and extrinsically] vital pastoral problems that must first be studied by the group of four *in recto et ab intrinseco* [directly and intrinsically]." The impression must not be given that the four are "a product of the CC" (*Souvenirs et espérances*, 11-12). At the request of Paul VI, on September 6 Lercaro had sent the Pope a draft, composed by Father Dossetti, of internal regulations for the group of moderators. On September 25, at the audience the Pope gave to the moderators, the question was once again raised of a pontifical instruction concerning their task (see Alberigo, "Concilio acefalo?" 214-16). The promise to have a set of internal regulations drawn up was never fulfilled.

expansion of its membership by including in it the future moderators, and a direct interference in the definition of the functions of the other organs that were directing the Council. The combination of his conciliar role with the highest office in the Curia obviously allowed Cicognani to forestall others in the reorganization of Vatican II in the fall of 1963.

B. THE COORDINATING COMMISSION

During the last part of the intersession, after the election of Paul VI, there were four meetings of the CC, the last three of which differed from the first. The meeting of July 3-4 was still in continuity with the activities of the spring and followed the same style. On the agenda were the study of the schema on the missions and the draft on the sacrament of matrimony. This latter was the subject of a mixed commission (combining three commissions) and was finally approved for sending to the bishops. This was not the case with the schema on the missions, the text of which was to be the subject of a new debate at the meeting of the CC on September 25.[400]

The next meeting of the CC, held on August 31, 1962, marked a turning point in its evolution, not only because of the expansion of the number of its members but also because of the increased authority the Commission was to enjoy by reason of the prolongation of its mandate. It was at this meeting that the decisions were made to delay the presentation of the schema on revelation to the fathers because it was not mature enough (Döpfner) and to put the schema on the Church on the agenda as the central theme of the Council (Lercaro). Another decisive step was the determination of the program for the second period; it included the schemas on (1) the Church; (2) the Blessed Virgin; (3) the bishops; (4) the laity; and (5) ecumenism.[401]

The CC's meeting on September 25, 1963, again took up the study of the schema on the missions. Some cardinals insisted that the entire commission on the missions be put to work revising the text (Döpfner and Suenens). As a result, the schema was not included in the Council's agenda. One part of the meeting was also devoted to a study of the revised regulations for the Council and, more especially, of the sections dealing with the moderators.[402]

---

[400] AS V/1, 565-69.
[401] Ibid., 646-50.
[402] Ibid., 688-89.

This same point occupied a good deal of the Commission's attention at its next meeting, on September 26; this time the participants included the Council of Presidents and the moderators. The tricky point remained the question of relations between the moderators and the Council of Presidents. The latter was regarded rather as guardian of the Regulations and a court of appeals in case of doubt. The direction to be taken in the "internal" development of the Council was the responsibility of the college of moderators. The Regulations also gave them the power to appeal to the fathers in order to cut off repetitive interventions.[403]

C. First Deliberations of the Moderators

On the basis of the pontifical audience on September 25, the three moderators who represented the thinking of the majority agreed to continue the active conception of their responsibilities and to regard their operation as independent of the General Secretariat of the Council. As secretary they had appointed Father Dossetti, a member of the Cardinal of Bologna's immediate entourage.[404] On the basis of the latter's work notes, it is possible to state that at the end of September the three moderators still counted on setting up their own infrastructure with an autonomous headquarters, archives, and their own group of experts; they were prepared to consider how to provide for direct contacts with the Sovereign Pontiff and how to prepare the subjects to be dealt with at the general congregations.[405] At the same period Dossetti drew up a memorandum for the moderators in order to clarify their responsibilities and their role as representatives of the papal authority in directing the work of the Council.

This active viewpoint would be unable to survive the tensions of the second period and, in particular, the conflict at the end of October, when Dossetti withdrew from his role.[406] When Felici was received by Paul VI for the first time, on July 5, 1963, he left the audience with the satisfaction of having been confirmed in his office as Secretary General of the

---

[403] Ibid., 691-94.

[404] Suenens, *Souvenirs et espérances*, 112-13.

[405] I owe these data to the analysis of some points in the Dossetti archives by G. Alberigo, *Attese*, 214-16.

[406] Felici would later threaten to resign if he did not replace Dossetti as secretary to the moderators (see Suenens, *Souvenirs et espérances*, 113); Suenens's disabused tone reflects the disappointment he felt at the time.

Council by a prelate, newly elected to the See of Rome, whose opponent he had always been before. Just as Cicognani was threatened by the institution of the moderators, so Felici felt endangered by Dossetti's role.[407]

---

[407] I have located the first rapprochement of Cicognani and Felici at the beginning of the intersession. A second was caused by the appointment of the four moderators and Dossetti. A third would take place on the occasion of the election of additional commissions in November 1963. In outlining the course of Vatican II, which he witnessed, German journalist David Seeber noted the growing influence of the conservative wing among the leadership of the Council.To the degree that the leaders were prevented from making decisions or showed themselves incapable of doing so, the importance and the influence of the Secretary General were strengthened (David A. Seeber, *Das Zweite Vaticanum* [Freiburg, 1966], 328-29).

CHAPTER IX

EBB AND FLOW BETWEEN TWO SEASONS

JAN GROOTAERS

As a privileged moment in the life of the Church, the Council had two dimensions. Vertically it was in continuity with the patrimony of preceding councils; horizontally, the *urbs* (the city of Rome) was for a moment occupied — besieged? — by the *orbis* (the world). Before Vatican Council II, the Church's discourse was generally monopolized by the Roman authorities (the *urbs*), but thanks to the Council the local Churches (the *orbis*) were able to speak.[1]

Even before the conclusion of the Council, however, there ware already movements of ebb and flow during the four years of its course. The movement of "flow" was represented first by the *vota* sent to Rome by the bishops of the entire world and then by the arrival in St. Peter's square of the long procession of Council fathers come from the four corners of the world for this vast assembly. Part of the flow was also the presence of countless theologians and experts, journalists and editors (as well as some "tradesmen in the temple"), all of whom, like an ancient dramatic chorus, surrounded the vast nave of the basilica with their babble and their voices in a constant and at times deafening buzz.

The "ebb," on the other hand, occurred when this tide withdrew and carried the deposits left by the assembly to other shores under other skies. Temporary each time the work was interrupted, the conciliar ebb became definitive at the close of the Council. This shuttle movement was especially important during the first intersession, which gave the now scattered bishops time to take stock and opportunity to intensify the flow when they returned to Rome the following fall.

Any attempt to outline the main repercussions that the movement of Vatican II had after its first period would be not only too ambitious but even rash. I shall, however, try to identify some obvious trends and some revealing events, especially in the area of ecumenical relations. These will be only summary items of information.

---

[1] See Y. Congar: "A horizontal [dimension]: a kind of shifting of the center from the *urbs* to the *orbis*, because the *orbis* took possession of the *urbs*. The Church was going to speak" (*Le Concile Vatican II* [Paris, 1984], 54).

I. AN EBBING IN CONCENTRIC CIRCLES

When a stone is thrown into a pond, it creates concentric circles that become ever wider toward the edges.

A. STARTING FROM THE CENTER: A FIRST CIRCLE

At the center of this ebbing movement we must refer, to the extent that their activity left legible traces, to the activity of the Council actors themselves: the bishops, the non-Catholic observers, and John XXIII. One of the first consequences of the conciliar meeting was a clear change in the relations of bishops among themselves. After discovering one another, they established a network of lasting and previously unthinkable fraternal relationships. This meant a change of style and a new quality of life in the Church. During the 1962-63 intersession these mutual relations were strengthened by exchanges of letters and private meetings or semi-official encounters. The change was not spectacular, but took place at deep levels and only revealed itself on occasion.Thus, for example, the conclave of June 1963 had a hitherto unparalleled dimension simply because many of the cardinals assembled for the election of a pope had come to know and to appreciate one another personally during the first period of the Council.

1. *Pastoral Letters*

We will consider, first, the pastoral letters of Council fathers and the testimonies of the Council observers, the two main ways in which the ebbing tide of 1963 flowed out. The first pastoral letters published during the 1962-63 intersession provided a valuable appraisal both of the beginnings of the conciliar event and of the degree of personal involvement of individual bishops who were now taking public stances. There were so many such letters addressed to the faithful of dioceses that any description of them all is impossible. The trends expressed in them cover a wide range of attitudes that vary from enthusiastic commitment to critical, more or less veiled negative reactions.[2]

---

[2] The historiography of Vatican II would require inventories of these letters by continent or region of the world. For the Italian bishops in 1963, the reader will find an interesting initial list for our period in Caprile, II, 362-65. Inventories of pastoral letters for some regions of Italy were published in *Fonti e materiali per la storia della Chiesa italiana*, edited by D. Menozzi.

If we limit ourselves to some examples from western Europe, we can get a general idea of this region, which is restricted to a few countries many of whose bishops had been the spokesmen for the nascent "majority" at the Council.[3] The collective letter of the Dutch bishops in September 1963 emphasized the importance which the Council had attached to the liturgical movement, the biblical renewal, and ecumenical openness.[4] There was a sharp contrast between the Dutch episcopate's praise of the work of journalists at the Council and the reaction of Msgr. Pelaia, Bishop of Tricarico (Italy), who sharply attacked the press, accusing it of dwelling on the political or trivial aspects of the Council and hiding the true face of the event.[5] Many of the Italian bishops chose to highlight the ecumenical dialogue the Council had decided to open.[6] Although not a pastoral letter, the statements Cardinal Siri made in the U.S. weekly *America* captured attention, especially when this president of the Italian Episcopal Conference called for an end to the ambiguities that burdened the question of collegiality: "The pope is also the Vicar of Christ on earth, and he would be this even if there were no episcopal college."[7]

Some letters reflected the new perspectives of the Council less in their content than in their method of composition. Thus the pastoral letter that Msgr. De Smedt devoted to the family in April 1963 was the product of an active collaboration of several thousand lay people who shared in the composition by sending in their suggestions.[8]

Another instructive aspect of this phase of Vatican II was the changes in bishops' attitudes depending on whether they were in Rome or back in their dioceses, an aspect of the ebb movement that deserves the attention of historians because it was a sort of precursory sign of the difficulties and even tensions that would be seen during the postconciliar "reception." (It perhaps suggests the need to distinguish between renewal in theory [in the council hall] and renewal in practice [in a bishop's own local church].) This difference can be seen in certain bish-

---

[3] We will find in *DC* 60 (1963) important pastoral documents by Guerry (175-90), Florit (191-94), Liénart and Frings (455-66), Siri (819-22), van Cauwelaert (1155-62), Liénart again (617-19 and 830-31), Duval (267-69), and, of course, Montini (1077-91). Other journals that published such documents are *Herder-Korrespondenz* and *Katholiek Archief*. For the French bishops see also *OssRom* (French edition), April 5, 1963, 7.

[4] *Katholiek Archief* 18, no. 40 (October 4, 1963), 999-1002.

[5] Caprile, II, 364.

[6] See especially Jannucci (Pescara), Nicodemo (Bari), and Piazzi (Bergamo) (Caprile, II, 363-65).

[7] G. Siri, "Truth First and Always," *America* (March 30, 1963), 434-35.

[8] See *Katholiek Archief* 18, no. 21 (May 24, 1963), 504-17.

ops when they went home and had to overcome hesitations and confusion in order to practice an openness to the laity, a spirit of brotherhood toward their priests, and collegiality in the episcopal conference. When such difficulties manifested themselves among key figures of the majority, they attracted even more attention in conciliar opinion after the "return" in the fall of 1963.

The letter of the German episcopate published at the end of September 1963 was an eloquent example; it gave rise to a hue and cry in the section of Christian opinion in Germany that was most in favor of the conciliar renewal. The most famous attack on this pastoral letter came from Walter Dirks, spokesman for German Catholic intellectuals, in an article entitled "In Rome and in Fulda."[9] The writer began his article by praising the vigor and boldness of the German Council fathers in Rome, whose attitude went far beyond what lay people who favored openness in the Church had dared hope for beforehand. But Dirks was offended by the suspicion the bishops voiced about false and even heretical conceptions of the Church allegedly widespread among German intellectuals. Dirks described the criticism voiced in the letter as "destructive," for, since no particular person was denounced in the bishops' letter, all kinds of hypotheses were beginning to circulate.[10]

Similar warnings were published elsewhere in Western Europe. One example involved the diocese of Malines-Brussels, in which a whole series of ecumenical undertakings, some of which had already existed in the past, were formally banned by authority of Cardinal Suenens.[11] Similar complaints arose among the laity of Holland. Michel Van der Plas, a well-known writer and journalist, expressed his deep disillusionment at the reserved attitude of the Dutch bishops when they returned to their country after their honeymoon in Rome.[12]

In an effort to interpret the phenomena he was attacking, Dirks remarked that while in Rome the bishops were free of their habitual setting, but once they returned home to Germany they again felt the weight

[9] W. Dirks, "In Rom und in Fulda. Der deutsche Katholizismus auf dem Konzil und zuhause," *Frankfurter Hefte* (January 1964), 27-36.

[10] Dirks hypothesized that C. Amery, F. Heer, H. Böll, and R. Hernegger were possible targets.

[11] Telemachus, "Meer vertrouwen gevraagd," *De Maand* VI, 3 (March 1963), partially reprinted in *ICI*, March 15, 1963, 6.

[12] M. Van der Plas, "De verslaggevers tussen twee zittingsperioden," *Ter Elfder Ure* X, 6-7 (June-July, 1963), 212-14. This journal, an organ of Catholic intellectuals, devoted this special summer issue to disillusioned reflections "between two phases of the Council."

of their administrative machinery. Another hypothesis cited by Dirks referred to the close bonds between the episcopate and the confessional party in Germany, bonds that barred the freedom of movement that bishops elsewhere, in France for example, enjoyed.[13]

One particular sentence in the Fulda pastoral letter may yield the explanation of this increased caution on the part of the German bishops. It was a self-justifying reference to what other Council fathers might think: they might begin to doubt the validity of the German bishops' efforts to update the Church if at the same time some German lay people were to start voicing claims of a heretical kind.[14]

But opposite cases also occurred: conservative reactions that accused the local bishop of committing himself thoughtlessly to radical changes and of paying too little attention to what British writer Evelyn Waugh described as "the most important but least noisy section of the faithful."[15] Some literary works that appeared at that time, such as those of Michel de Saint Pierre (France) and Alexis Curvers (Belgium), expressed their authors' indignation at the abandonment of traditional values.[16] In Holland mail from readers to the newspapers showed the uneasiness that was arising in conservative circles.[17]

The positive manifestations of which I have spoken showed clearly the spread of the Roncallian and conciliar *aggiornamento* and the progress that had been made in a very short time. If the attitude of some

[13] Dirks, "In Rom und in Fulda," 33-35.

[14] Under the surface, this could mean that to be acceptable in conciliar and Curial circles, the German bishops would have to show how strict they were in their own dioceses, a strategy that at one time was often attributed to some "progressive" bishops.

[15] As early as December 1962, Evelyn Waugh wrote: "I think that I am rather typical of the rank and file of the Church" (*ICI*, January 15, 1963), 6-7. Some time later, in his personal journal, the great British writer described the repugnance he felt at a Mass that had become a kind of "communal meal" without poetry or dignity; he accused Cardinal Heenan of having two faces, one agreeing with the conservatives, the other pushing for reforms (see *The Diaries of Evelyn Waugh*, ed. M. Davie [London, 1976], 793). As he made explicit in his correspondence, Waugh and his close friend Msgr. Ronald Knox felt the liturgical reform issuing from Vatican II to be a catastrophe; they saw in it a "loss of substance" that disfigured the face of a Church that had become unrecognizable to them.

[16] On the other hand, a master of contemporary literature such as François Mauriac greeted the pontificate of John XXIII with joy: "Peter is no longer an old man isolated if not confined by his servants. I see him surrounded by all his children, even by those who had asked for their part of the inheritance. And, look! he is no longer uttering anathemas . . . and all the nations are turning their gaze to the prow of the ancient ship" (*Ce que je crois* [Paris, 1962]).

[17] In July 1963 J. Van der Ploeg, a Dominican confrere of Schillebeeckx, published a defense of the "two sources of revelation," following the viewpoint defended by the minority group at the Council ("Belangstelling van de Hl. Schrift," *De Tijd*, July 17, 1963).

bishops was different at home than in Rome and if, on the other hand, they found themselves faced with opposition from both the "left" and the "right," the significance of these perilous divorces was not yet seen in its true meaning. It is possible today to make out the precursory signs of polarities and conflicts that would characterize future developments.

If these contradictions did not remain hidden, this was due in large measure to the experts and religious journalists who were in Rome during the 1962-63 intersession and established an unforeseen link between Rome and home. The ebb of the intersession would change into a new flow, that of the second period of the Council, when the *orbis* once again took possession of the *urbs*, but in circumstances no longer the same.

2. *Appointments and Promotions*

Besides in the publication of texts, the fallout in the local churches from the first period of the Council was felt also in the appointments of individuals, two exemplary instances of which can be cited. The first was the appointment early in 1963 of Msgr. John Heenan to the Archdiocese of Westminster to succeed Cardinal Godfrey, who in 1962 had belonged to the conciliar wing opposed to ecumenism and to the biblical renewal.[18] Heenan, bishop of Liverpool and a member of the Secretariat for Christian Unity, cultivated a friendly relationship with Archbishop Michael Ramsey, Primate of the Church of England, who had hosted Cardinal Bea for a day of cordial dialogue.[19]

The second instance was in Poland. Early in 1963 a new archbishop had to be appointed to the vacant see of Cracow. At first glance the candidacy of Msgr. Karol Wojtyla was far from certain. Cardinal Wyszynski, who had little sympathy for the very intellectual environment in Cracow, gave the political authorities a list of six candidates, Wojtyla's name being the last. But in the end the slowness of the process and various steps taken worked in favor of the least well-placed candidate. The appointment of Karol Wojtyla as Archbishop of Cracow must also be attributed to his participation in the Council! Initially, Wojtyla was little known to the "leaders" of the Polish episcopate; it was in Rome that

[18] The influence of Cardinal Godfrey in the Roman Curia was still such that his negative advice caused Rome to prohibit the University of Nijmegen from conferring a doctorate *honoris causa* on the great Anglican theologian Eric Mascall, a man of "Catholic" tendencies (see *De Tijd*, September 17, 1963).

[19] In an article in the *Catholic Herald* for January 18, 1963, Heenan attested to the fact that formerly it was the Catholic ecumenists, few in number, who were thought poorly of, but now it was those hostile to ecumenical work who were looked at askance.

they discovered him and were favorably impressed by the personal involvement of the young auxiliary bishop in various activities of the nascent Council.[20]

But in the "other" Churches also the tendency to greater openness to reconciliation with Rome was strengthened. In August 1963 Archbishop Nikodim was raised to the rank of a metropolitan and appointed president of a new "Ecumenical Commission" of the Russian Orthodox Church. He was known at that time as an admirer of the Catholic Church and supporter of a rapprochement with it.[21] It was in 1962-63 too that Dr. Ramsey, quite favorable to dialogue with the Roman Church, succeeded Lord Fisher as Archbishop of Canterbury and Primate of the Church of England. After a visit from Cardinal Bea, Archbishop Ramsey announced publicly his intention to visit Rome soon.[22]

B. Testimonies of Observers (Second Circle)

The testimonies and reports that the non-Catholic observers gave after the first period of the Council helped both to spread and to accelerate the force of the ecumenical movement. The observers at the Council felt the need not only to report to the authorities of the churches that had appointed them but also to give an account to public opinion in their own religious confessions. This concern arose all the more spontaneously because their experience in Rome during the fall of 1962 far surpassed what they had expected.

The first point that emerged in their reports was obviously the increased role of the observers at the Council. Initially meant to be merely passive, their role had quickly developed into one of true dia-

---

[20] See Tad Szulc, *Pope John Paul II* (New York, 1995), 227-28. The chapters of this monumental biography are not all of equal value, but the passages that tell of the appointment of Karol Wojtyla to the See of Cracow are based on testimonies, the solidity of which I have been able to verify.

[21] See *ICI*, no. 199 (September 1, 1963), 14. Metropolitan Nikolas, who had preceded Nikodim as head of the foreign relations service, had died in December 1961 (see ibid., January 1, 1962, 16).

[22] See *ICI*, September 1, 1962, 5. In the spring of 1963 Dr. Ramsey traveled to the continent and was received by the University of Louvain (Belgium), where he had a meeting with some conciliar experts, especially those of the Secretariat for Christian Unity, and also gave an important lecture on Christian spirituality (see M. Ramsey, "Christian Spirituality and the Modern World," *Eastern Churches Quarterly* 15 [1963], 15-24).

logue and trustful collaboration, one of the most decisive changes
brought about by the ecumenical dynamic at work in Vatican II.[23] In
addition, the simple fact of their always attentive presence greatly influenced the tone of addresses at the Council.[24]

Dr. E. Schlink of the Evangelical Church in Germany (EKD)
reminded people of the fundamental theme of the Council, namely, the
Catholic Church's conception of itself and of the other Churches. This
theme had been tackled, at the end of the session, "from a new point of
view and with surprising fairness toward other Christians: this has given
a powerful impulse to the ecumenical spirit."[25] It was possible, said Pastor Hébert Roux of the World Reformed Alliance, that juridical minds
could only feel mistrust of the Council's work,

> but those who take the gospel seriously and have been welcomed as broth-
> ers in Christ . . . to whom have been given, in a spirit of complete trust, the
> means of following the discussions . . . such people can and ought to bear
> formal witness to the remarkable effort at spiritual understanding, humility,
> and honesty that this first internal step taken by the Church of Rome repre-
> sents."[26]

The first impressions of Dr. Lukas Vischer, an observer at the Council from the World Council of Churches, were also positive: "We were
surprised to see how much the bishops were endeavoring to understand
the convictions we represent. This was a great experience for us on the
religious level."[27] Orthodox Archpriest V. Borovoi, appointed an
observer for the Patriarchate of Moscow, abstained from any indiscreet
remarks but felt compelled to call attention to "an atmosphere permeated by good will and fraternal sentiments toward other, non-Catholic
Christians . . . and a very friendly attitude . . . to us personally."[28] Msgr.

---

[23] See "The Vatican Council and the Ecumenical Situation," *The Ecumenical Review*
16 (1964), 213-14. This commentary by the editors of this authoritative review noted, in
particular: "The Roman Catholic Church is in the process of working out its own form of
ecumenism. This means that new opportunities are appearing in the realm of ecumenical
conversation and cooperation. It means at the same time that the ecumenical situation is
becoming more complicated" (214).

[24] The Council fathers had to be careful to explain their thoughts in a way that would
be intelligible also to the "separated brethren"; this effort to avoid taking refuge in more
or less fuzzy positions and to find formulations as precise as possible was an excellent
exercise in ecumenism. Such was the testimony of Msgr. Thomas Holland, "Ecumenism
at the Council," *Eastern Churches Quarterly* 15 (1963), 13.

[25] *DC* 60 (1963), 392.

[26] Ibid., 391.

[27] Ibid., 390.

[28] Ibid., 386-89.

Cassien, Rector of the Institut Saint-Serge in Paris, said that he had left Rome with great hopes: "What they had told us was only an internal matter for the Roman Church has taken on a great importance for us. The life, the public opinion, the voices which the Council has uncovered give it dimensions that transcend the Catholic Church."[29] Anglican bishop John Moorman gave a positive appraisal of the repercussions of the beginnings of this Council: "Whatever the outcome of the event, we must believe that honest and basic reforms are becoming inevitable for the Catholic Church." As for the future of the papacy, he had no doubt that John XXIII and Paul VI were giving it a new direction.[30]

C. The Rearguard Begins to Move (Third Circle)

The most eloquent witnesses to the spread of the conciliar spirit were to be found in countries whose tradition was fundamentally Catholic but in which public opinion was least prepared for Roncalli's openness and the conciliar renewal. Thus the most obvious and most important growth in awareness at this time was to be detected in two extensive "rearguard" areas, if I may be permitted this somewhat brusque description. I am referring to the spheres of Spanish or Spanish-American influence and tradition, on the one side, and Catholicism imbued with the Irish spirit, on the other. Between these two I will discuss the awakening in Italy, which presented rather different characteristics.

1. *Areas of Spanish Tradition*

On the eve of the Council the Church in Spain was often accused of persecuting the Protestant Churches in its territory, a reproach also leveled at the Catholic Church in Colombia, especially by the authorities of the World Council of Churches.[31] But early in 1963 it was within Spanish and Latin American Catholicism itself that intolerance and the abuse of the laws in force began to be attacked. Ecumenical concerns began to

---

[29] Ibid., 384.

[30] *Herder-Korrespondenz* 18 (1963-64), 156.

[31] In a press conference in Rome at the end of 1963, Father Gustave Weigel (Woodstock, Maryland) showed how the inadequacy of the Catholic clergy had caused Protestant groups to send to Latin America missionaries who wanted to bear witness to their faith, many of whom displayed no ecumenical interests. He mentioned Adventists, Pentecostals, and Southern Baptists (see a document of the U.S. Bishops' Press Panel, November 19, 1963).

make their way,[32] and on behalf of the government the Spanish bishops and metropolitans were studying a statute aimed at the legal emancipation of the Protestants of the country.[33] At a conference on "Protestant Churches in Latin Countries," held in Leysin in October, 1963, when the "minority Churches" of southern Europe took stock of their situation, they had to acknowledge that even in Spain a dialogue, still timid indeed, was beginning.[34]

On the vast Latin American continent the "thaw" took countless forms, some of which were a direct result of the personal contacts, not previously experienced, that many Latin American bishops had in Rome with the non-Catholic observers. On the other hand, intellectual circles among the laity and young theologians were opening themselves to the influence of Vatican II and thereby to the interconfessional problem; this opening was perhaps less difficult for Catholic opinion in the countries of the "southern cone," where the partner in dialogue was more the classical Protestantism of Churches with ecumenical ties. A typical instance of this openness to the Council among Catholic intellectuals can be found in the periodical *Criterio* of Buenos Aires.

> We wanted to explain to our readers, as clearly as possible, the situation at this great assembly (on the eve of its second session), its present direction, its difficulties, and its perspectives. In doing so, we want each Christian, each person, whom we reach, to feel present, in a way, to what is going on in Rome; we are thinking of our brothers and sisters, whether united with us or separated from us, who, according to their abilities, are helping to make the Council be responsive to God's plan. We are thinking also of non-Christians, who constantly remind us that in the final analysis the Council is for them, and who require of us the witness they expect.[35]

[32] A few of the other examples: (1) Roger Schutz, Prior of Taizé, was called to Seville to give the opening public lecture at a colloquium of Catholic intellectuals (see the interview with Brother Roger in *La Croix,* April 9, 1963); the brothers of Taizé played a crucial role in introducing the Catholics of southern Europe to ecumenism; (2) the reopening of ten Protestant churches (see *ICI,* February 1, 1963, 12); and (3) the public stand taken by Msgr. Cantero, Bishop of Huelva, on behalf of the religious freedom of Protestant children (see *De Tijd,* February 5, 1963, and *ICI,* March 15, 1963, 12).

[33] See *La Croix,* January 22, 1963; *ICI,* February 1, 1963, 11.

[34] Protestant theologian G. Crespy also wrote: "Almost all reports have noted a change in the climate of relations with the Catholic Church. . . . It seems that henceforth Catholicism will no longer be regarded, by all without exception, as the supreme adversary" ("Moins de complexes," *Réforme* [October 12, 1963]).

[35] "El Camino del Concilio," *Criterio,* September 26, 1963, 646. This unsigned editorial was written by a young theologian, Jorge Mejia, who at the time was very much involved with the journalists and experts of the Council. As a result of this involvement he expressed his sentiments in a way that would become famous: a pamphlet opposing the schema on the communications media that was distributed at the entrance to the coun-

Along similar lines, at a meeting in April 1963 a number of Argentinean bishops and experts formulated *vota*, practical but with doctrinal importance, with reference to the second period of the Council.[36] For his part, Msgr. Larraín, Bishop of Talca (Chile), vice-president of CELAM, and one of the most authoritative spokesmen of the continent at Vatican II, lamented the fact that a pessimistic vision of Latin America was being communicated. He believed in a pastoral renewal in the direction of social justice and an expansion of the laity's role.[37] Ecumenical meetings at the university level were reported in Chile and Argentina.

If in the past, any openness on the Catholic side had been held in check above all by the rejection of the idea of a pluralist society, now, from 1963 on, it could be seen that "the Council announced and begun has had tremendous ecumenical effects."[38]

2. *The Awakening in Italy*

Catholic public opinion in Italy had certain features not common elsewhere in Europe. Subject as it was to the crushing authority of an episcopate itself under Roman supervision and faced with a clergy ill prepared to accept the conciliar *aggiornamento*, Italy had also had the experience of numerous small communities that were coming into existence at the initiative of lay people and young clerics in search of a renewal of the faith.[39] These groups and currents had suffered greatly

cil hall on November 25, 1963. This move was immediately attacked and condemned by Cardinal Tisserant in the council hall (see John Cogley, "Grounds for Hope," *Commonweal* [December 27, 1963], 399). In the same article, the editor announced that *Criterio* would henceforth have a permanent section on the Council: "But we think, at the risk of seeming obsessed, that the Council is, properly considered, the life of the Church as revealed to itself and to others. It is the consciousness of the Church finding expression, and we express ourselves in it" (643).

[36] These *vota* dealt with episcopal collegiality, the canonical establishment of episcopal conferences with power of jurisdiction, the diaconate, a real theology of the laity, and concern for the evangelization of the poor (see "Voeux pour le Concile," *ICI*, July 15, 1963, 20, and an undated document of the Centrum Coordinationis Communicationis del Concilio, "Conclusion de la rencontre des évêques et experts" [Villa Marista, April 24-26, 1963, Grootaers papers]).

[37] Statement published in *La Croix*, January 1, 1963.

[38] J. Mejia, "La situation oecuménique en Amérique latine," *Lumen Vitae* 19 (1964), 56-57 and throughout; the main positive factors listed in this article were (1) the creation of the Secretariat for Christian Unity and the invitation of observers to the Council; (2) the ecumenical attitude of John XXIII; and (3) news about the Council in Latin America.

[39] Without trying to give a complete list of publications from these "catacombs," it will be useful to mention here some important journals that represented a spiritual, theological, and ecclesial renewal: *Testimonianze* (Florence), *Il Gallo* (Genoa), *Questitalia*

526 CHAPTER IX

from having to live in the "catacombs" of a clerical and often triumphalistic Church.[40]

When Vatican II began in Rome, the unstable situation of these "points of contact" was radically altered. The inspiration these small Italian groups had generally derived from abroad suddenly acquired a human and friendly embodiment as the great masters of the theological renewal in France and Germany, previously venerated from afar, now began meeting in Rome. Among the foreign theologians who quickly acquired an extraordinary influence on the Italian laity I must mention at least Father M.-D. Chenu, who always made himself available to informal groups and had a gift for friendly encounters. The experience of the first period of the Council in their midst transformed these lay people by giving them a sense of their own responsibility and opening them to cooperation with others.[41]

3. *Areas of Irish Tradition*

Irish Catholicism had long influenced the Catholic Church in the English-speaking countries. The massive emigration of the Irish to North America enabled them to have a dominant impact on Catholicism in the United States (it was not until the pontificate of John XXIII that the first American prelates not of Irish descent reached the cardinalate).[42] In addition, a vast Irish missionary movement ensured a

(Venice), *Adesso* (Milan), *Il Mulino* (Naples). Differing greatly among themselves, these periodicals were traces of a current of thought at the margins. Other expressions of the same current could be found in books such as that of M. Gozzini, *Concilio aperto* (Florence, 1962) or in the bulletins that Mario Rossi published regularly in the French weekly *Témoignage Chrétien*. It was there and elsewhere that the seeds were sown of a harvest that would be abundant after the Council and, at times, even richer in Italy than in the countries of northern Europe.

[40] As late as 1962-63 the bimonthly *Adesso*, published by a team of young lay people, had to shut down due to pressure from the hierarchy, while Father Balducci, of *Testimonianze*, was condemned by ecclesiastical authorities for having defended a conscientious objector (see *ICI*, January 1, 1963, 14, and November 15, 1963, 20). The aim of *Adesso*, "to be open to the problems of the world, while shrugging off an infantile submissiveness," could only render it suspect, especially in the eyes of the Holy Office.

[41] An eloquent description of the influence of the Council, at its beginning, on groups of laity in Rome is found in Nicoletta Riccio, "Brief uit Rome," *De Maand* 7 (March 1964), 148-56. This is the place to mention the holding of friendly meetings with the Italian Waldensian Church.

[42] The Irish exerted the same influence on Catholicism in England and in other geographical areas to which the Irish immigrated, such as Australia, South Africa, and English-speaking Canada. Between the independence of Ireland in 1922 and 1964, a million Irish had gone to live in Great Britain.

worldwide influence out of proportion to the population of the home country.[43]

The progressive and relatively rapid "thaw" in this Irish influence in the Catholic world of the United States was one of the most visible consequences of Vatican II. It was all the more startling because the religious culture that marked that influence was at the opposite end of the spectrum from the conciliar renewal; that particular Catholicism was very unprepared for an ecumenical openness, a declericalized ecclesiology, the active participation of the laity in the liturgy, and a more balanced devotion to Mary.[44]

Part of the fallout from the first period of the Council, which had been anticipated by the liberating outlook of Pope John XXIII, was that a new ecumenical spirit arose in North American Catholicism.[45] An outside observer such as Hans Küng spoke at the time of "an ecumenical springtime in America,"[46] and the publication of a series of periodicals with ecumenical tendencies seemed to prove the truth of the observation.[47] This period also gave rise to exchanges of ideas between Catholics and Protestants at a high theological level. Even if at the time it was thought that the United States had to do a lot of catching up with Europe in this respect, it could at least be said that the dialogue had really begun.[48]

---

[43] Along with Holland and perhaps Belgium, Ireland has been one of those little countries whose very numerous Catholic missionaries built a kind of "universal Church"; this strength, so disproportionate to the size of Ireland, was clearly manifested when the bishops of the five continents gathered in Rome for Vatican Council II.

[44] It must be noted, however, that the election to the U.S. presidency at the end of 1960 of John Fitzgerald Kennedy, a Catholic from a typically Irish milieu, symbolized a degree of emancipation and an openness to pluralism; his assassination in November of 1963 was tragic confirmation that a Catholic could give his life for his country at the highest level of office, from which Catholics had until then been excluded (see John Cogley, "Kennedy the Catholic," *Commonweal* [January 10, 1964], 422-23).

[45] Presbyterian theologian Robert McAfee Brown, himself a Protestant observer at Vatican II, referred to the silence of American Catholics, who under Pius XII had been afraid to express any ecumenical openness, with the exception of the avant-garde figure of Father Weigel (see Brown, "Situation sociologique aux États-Unis et perspectives oecuméniques," *Lumen Vitae* 19 [March, 1964], 43-55 at 47).

[46] H. Küng, "Oekumenischer Frühling in Amerika," *Rheinischer Merkur*, June 21, 1963, 20. The young theologian conducted a successful lecture tour in Boston, St. Louis, Chicago, Los Angeles, and Houston, but the rector of Catholic University in Washington barred him from that institution.

[47] I am referring especially to periodicals that became interconfessional in their editorship, such as the *Journal of Ecumenical Studies*.

[48] Even if it seemed that relations between theologians had to be the basis for other relations, Brown believed that "relations between Catholics and Protestants at the practical level facilitate relations at the theological level, and vice versa" (Brown, "Situation sociologique," 49).

During the Week of Prayer for Unity, Catholics and Protestants were still praying *for* one another, but some were beginning to pray *with* one another.

It would be difficult to find a better illustration of this rapid development than the great interconfessional colloquium organized at Harvard University, March 27-30, 1963, with more than 150 university professors and specialists participating, half of them Protestants, half Roman Catholics. According to the organizers, this meeting revealed "a radical change in the religious climate of the world."[49] The active participation of Cardinal Bea in these discussions gave them a special standing; the three lectures of the President of the Secretariat for Christian Unity dealt with the role of universities and the cause of Christian unity, non-Catholic Christians and Vatican II (first period), and, finally, an appraisal of the ongoing Council and its prospects.

In Ireland itself Vatican II did not go unnoticed. According to a very provisional assessment published at the time by John C. Kelly, account has first to be taken of the general change in Irish society since its economic expansion, the increase in contacts with Europe, and the invasion by British television. Ireland's traditional isolation was being breached everywhere. This change often entailed a positive attitude that tended to confront the faithful with their responsibilities. Although efforts to promote ecumenism were still sporadic, the liturgical reform was beginning to find an extensive response among the laity and the younger generation of priests. Familiarity with the Bible and a formation in theology were beginning to be taken seriously.[50]

As for Catholicism in Great Britain, the 1962-63 intersession represented an important stage characterized by the awakening of lay Catholics and their receptivity to the liturgical and theological renewal. The awakening of the English laity was linked to a new generation of the faithful, the first to have received a university education and to have climbed the social ladder. These experiences were incompatible with submission to a clerical and authoritarian Church. This emancipation extended also to the young clergy, but since the latter did not yet enjoy the freedom of opinion that the laity had, they found themselves muz-

---

[49] See the proceedings of the colloquium in *Ecumenical Dialogue at Harvard*, ed. S. H. Miller and G. E. Wright (Cambridge, Mass., 1964), preface, VII. The principal subjects were scripture, tradition, and authority; worship and liturgy; the concept of "reform."

[50] John C. Kelly, "Le catholicisme en Irlande à l'heure du Concile," *Études* (May 1964), 692-700.

zled. The Roncalli pontificate and the conciliar event encouraged this intellectual elite to raise its voice. As in Italy and the United States, the laity found a source of constant inspiration in the "new theology" of Western Europe.[51]

Figures such as John Coulson and J. M. Todd exercised lay leadership, the former by prompting a series of theological study weeks in close collaboration with Abbot Butler and the Abbey of Downside, the latter by launching a publishing house geared to ecumenism and theological renewal.[52] To these two names must be joined those of Michael de la Bedoyere, editor-in-chief of *Search*, and Tom Burns, editor of the weekly *Tablet*.

Conflicts with members of the Catholic hierarchy, who were accustomed to exercising an unquestionable authority, were not lacking. As a result, one of the main focal points for the thinking of this new generation quickly became the exercise of authority in the Church and the role of the *sensus fidelium*. A prominent concern was for an open theological formation, especially by having Catholics attend the theological faculties of the British universities.[53] For the laity and young priests who made up the avant garde of the renewal, Vatican II thus accelerated the emergence from the Catholic ghetto in England. For the first time since the Reformation, Catholics took part in interconfessional dialogue as full partners.[54]

[51] The prestige of the renewal on the continent was such that some leaders of the English laity organized an Anglo-French symposium at the Abbey of Our Lady of Bec in Normandy, on the eve of Vatican II and with an eye on the opening of the Council, which they regarded as "a primordial manifestation of the Church's life" (see *Problems of Authority* [London, 1962]).

[52] In 1963 lay theologian Brian Wicker wrote that the time was past when the "doctrinal" formation of the laity consisted in having them swallow Scholastic manuals with a view to "social action." That approach completely neglected the dimension of salvation history and the personal undertakings to which it gave rise (see Brian Wicker, *Culture and Liturgy* [London, 1963], 187-89).

[53] This was the theme of the symposium organized in 1963 by John Coulson; it was taken up again at the Leicester Conference in April of 1964, whose papers may be found in *Theology and the University* (London, 1964) and *Theology in Modern Education* (London, 1965). (Brian Wicker's contribution was inspired by the debates on liturgical reform at Vatican II.) It was as though, after a century, John Henry Newman finally had his "revenge"!

[54] When Michael de la Bedoyere made a selection of texts by Catholic writers who advocated freedom of opinion and published it under the somewhat provocative title of *Objections to Roman Catholicism* (London, 1964), the writer of the Preface greeted the appearance of the book as a historical event. Until then, no one in Protestant or humanist circles could have thought it possible for committed Catholics to acknowledge publicly the difficulties they met with in their faith; now, however, it was necessary to salute the emergence of an informed and courageous laity.

4. *Two New Questions Emerge*

In this special atmosphere of 1963, two other burning questions surfaced, first in Great Britain, and then in the United States, questions on
which Catholics often engaged in passionate debate. The connection
between these questions and the ongoing Council was not always
explicit but would soon become clear.

The first of these questions was the need for a moral assessment of a
new means of birth control. After having been the subject of scientific
articles for about ten years and having been available in the U.S. since
1960, the pill that inhibits ovulation in women and can be used either to
prevent ovulation (Pincus) or, on the contrary, to remedy certain kinds of
sterility (Rock), came on the pharmaceutical market in Europe beginning
in 1962-63. Some Catholic moralists thought that the pill represented a
new fact unknown at the time of the encyclical *Casti connubii* (1930)
and that it therefore required a new moral evaluation of the means of
birth control. They found confirmation of this view in the favorable attitude of the magisterium under Pius XII with regard to "periodic conti-
nence" (the Ogino-Knaus method).

The first interventions of bishops, at least in Western Europe, in
regard to a possible reassessment in an area of morality particularly sensitive to public opinion, occurred in 1963 and 1964. If the establishment
of a Pontifical Commission on Questions of the Birth Rate in the spring
of 1963 was not known by the bishops or public opinion at the time, it
was well known that conjugal morality was to be an important point on
the agenda of Vatican II. In fact, it had already been an object of controversy in the Coordinating Commission (CC) as it discussed the problem of the hierarchy of ends in marriage in connection with the chapter
on marriage in schema 17. In a televised discussion in March 1963,
Msgr. Bekkers, Bishop of Bois-le-Duc (Holland), was the first to take a
position in favor of a new conception of the life of the married couple,
whose conjugal love finds a special, and necessary, expression in sexual
intercourse. This view implied a revision of the general line taken in
Casti connubii. This statement was followed by a pastoral letter of the
entire Dutch episcopate (August 1963), which pointed to the new means
of regulating human fertility as an indication that discussion of the matter was necessarily open in the Catholic Church.[55]

In the discussion that was thus started in the Catholic world, the issue
was not so much the negative one of contraception as the positive one of

---

[55] See *Katholiek Archief,* no. 18 (1963), 347-49 (Bekkers) and 928 (pastoral letter).

regulation. This meant an important shift of emphasis. In the more "open" view defended by bishops and moralists we can see also the influence the new "Christian family" movements had on their surroundings. At the time these movements were helping to promote in the faithful a new awareness of their own responsibilities as lay people, spouses, and parents. This was one aspect of the awakening of the laity at Vatican II, and it marked the end of the interference of some clergy in "what goes on in the bedroom."

A short time later the Dutch pastoral letter was referred to by the Episcopal Conference of England and of Wales in a joint statement (May 1964), the principal purpose of which was to support the encyclical of 1930: "The bishops consider themselves obliged to proclaim the immutability of the law of God. If we remain silent when so many voices are trying to lead our people astray, we would fail in our duty as pastors of souls." The passage Msgr. Heenan cited from the Dutch letter had been cut short in the English translation; the translator had omitted the concluding clause in the sentence which declared the discussion still open. A few weeks earlier Msgr. T. D. Roberts retired Archbishop of Bombay, had caused a stir by taking a "liberal" position that was reported in the widely circulated *Sunday Times on* April 19, 1964. At the same period Msgr. Reuss, Auxiliary Bishop of Mainz in Germany, in an article, and Cardinal Suenens of Malines-Brussels, in a press conference in Boston, said they were in favor of a reevaluation of the morality of birth control. A reply of B. Häring (secretary of the conciliar commission on schema 17) to the pastoral letter of the English and Welsh episcopate would appear in the *Guardian,* May 15, 1964, and would arouse in Msgr. Heenan a profound resentment which he would later express publicly in the council hall.[56] Meanwhile, the joint statement elicited numerous reactions in the British press as a whole. It must be noted, however, that the tone on the Catholic side was often more critical than among the non-Catholic commentators, who, without saying they agreed with the Catholic episcopate, nonetheless expressed their appreciation of the courage shown by the bishops. The distance between the preparatory schemas on morality and the new concerns of many bishops at the Council was only becoming greater and would soon appear to be insurmountable.[57]

[56] See *AS* III/5, 315f.

[57] Among the works by Catholic authors that appeared in 1963 and 1964 and became time points of reference in the new discussion of are: *Books:* John Rock, *The Time Has Come (to End the Battle over Birth Control)* (New York, 1963); Leslie Dewart, *Contra-*

The other question was the controversy over "secularization" that was brought to public attention by the publication of *Honest to God*, a seemingly commonplace little work by Anglican Bishop John Robinson, which, to the surprise of the author himself, sold a half-million copies within a year.[58] The originality of the book was that it addressed to the person in the street some simple thoughts on a very pertinent religious theme that had been dealt with by great theologians but had never been raised with the general public: the confrontation of contemporary men and women, immersed in a secularized world, with questions about the existence of God and a next world. In dealing with these questions the author appropriated some basic tendencies of Rudolf Bultmann (the rejection of all "mythology"), Paul Tillich (opposition to any "supernaturalism"), and Dietrich Bonhoeffer (distrust of things "religious").

When other theologians said that Robinson was not saying anything new, they were losing sight of the fact that, thanks to his great pastoral sensitivity, the author had discovered how to touch the hearts of persons in the street — whatever they might be, atheists, half-believers, or Christians in difficulty — who recognized themselves in the malaise the author laid bare. In less than two years, 750,000 copies were sold of a book that spoke of nothing but God!

The unassuming pocketbook had an effect like a bomb and gave rise to widespread uneasiness among the ecclesiastical authorities not only of the Church of England but also of the other Churches, including the Catholic Church in Europe. These Church authorities were made nervous by the dangers of a theology that did not respect established terminology and was, in addition, broadcast far and wide, and they looked for ways to give their faithful some "pastoral" protection. Some Catholic

---

ception and Holiness (New York, 1964). *Articles:* C. Mertens, *Nouvelle revue théologique* 85 (1963), 176-88; P. Antoine, *Etudes* (1963), 162-83; L. Janssens, *Ephemerides Theologicae Lovanienses* 39 (1963), 787-826; J. M. Reuss, *Tübinger Theologische Quartalschrift* 143 (1963), 454-76; W. Van den Marck, *Tijdschrift voor Theologie* 4 (1964), 738-413; H. and L. Buelens-Gijsen, *De Maand* 7 (1964), 129-40; B. Häring, *Theologie der Gegenwart* 7 (1964), 63-71; L. Dupré, *Cross Currents* (1963-64), 63-85.

[58] John A.T. Robinson, *Honest to God* (London, 1963). The personality of the author was a very complex one. He was at once a recognized New Testament exegete, a good administrator of the Church of England, and a bishop very aware of the spiritual needs of his ordinary faithful. His pastoral work as Bishop of Woolwich (1959-69) was preceded and followed by a university career at Cambridge, first in Clare College (1951-59) and later at Trinity (1969-83). The scientific works he published before 1962 had not won him any exceptional fame.

leaders were especially distrustful of the theologians, hardly known to the general public, whom Robinson cited as authorities and whom they regarded as questionable and dangerous.

Three categories of readers may be distinguished, in order of mounting importance: those who thought the Anglican bishop was not saying anything new; shocked believers, who had no difficulty in localizing God "up there" or "down here" and felt no need to update their education (as Robinson wanted them to do); and, finally, the great mass of readers who were moved at discovering an author, and a bishop at that, who at last expressed what they had long felt deep down inside, often with an uneasy conscience. The Bishop of Woolwich argued on behalf of a religious outlook that had no need of a "supernaturalist" superstructure, but in which faith in God was based on a radical trust in the power of love.

The *Honest to God* movement was no passing phenomenon, and the problem of "secularization" remained on the agenda of theological research; this was true also in the Catholic world at the time of Vatican II and well after the Council. The names of some Roman Catholic authors were already to be found in the review of the initial discussions that appeared some months later as a book.[59] Some conciliar theologians realized the importance of the nascent theological debate on the subject of "secularization." In 1963 and 1964 E. Schillebeeckx devoted two substantial articles, first to Robinson's book and then to *The Honest to God Debate*. While this adviser to the Dutch episcopate at Vatican II observed that *Honest to God* had raised expectations its author was not able to satisfy, he recognized that the question raised was a real one and in tune with his own concerns.

The themes of *Honest to God* did not, however, really touch the ongoing conciliar assembly. The agenda of a general council such as Vatican II could only raise questions that had reached a degree of "maturity for a council." This was not the case with the stir created by the little book of the Anglican bishop. But the "reception" of Vatican II would be stubbornly faced with it. Supporters of Robinson would criticize the Council for having passed over a problem of the first

---

[59] See *The Honest to God Debate* (London 1963), a work useful for gauging the intensity and extent of the discussion. After Bishop Robinson's death in December 1983, his colleague Dr. M. Stockwood noted that Robinson himself liked to point out that he had often been given a more "constructive" and "sympathetic" reception in Catholic theological circles than in his own Church (see *The Catholic Herald*, December 16, 1983, 7).

importance for contemporary men and women, whom Vatican II had hoped to address. The conservative opponents of the Council would call attention to the excesses of the debate on "secularization" in order to show the need to stay with the thought structures of the time before John XXIII and the Council.[60]

Neither birth control nor the problem of secularization would receive a satisfactory answer at Vatican II, and both were destined to burden the reception of the Council in some degree, at least in Western Europe and North America.

What I have described as the first movement of "the rearguard" had some common traits in 1963 that marked the development of Catholicism in such countries as Great Britain, the United States, and Holland. In each of these diverse national situations a Catholic population that was a sociological minority confronted a cultural model that was either Protestant or secularized.[61] Opinion polls at first and studies in religious sociology later on — both of which were beginning at that time to be very much the vogue in Catholic faculties — showed how the Catholic world was deeply marked by its situation as a cultural minority. At the same time, however, the surmounting of this situation through social improvement, access to university studies, and the acquisition of an adult outlook in religious matters, among still other factors, coincided more or less with the pontificate of John XXIII. In any case, the intellectual emancipation was accelerated by the conciliar renewal and became obvious after the close of Vatican II.

---

[60] Some titles: John A. T. Robinson, *Honest to God* (London, 1963); idem and David L. Edwards, *The Honest to God Debate* (London, 1963); idem, *The New Reformation?* (London, 1965); Albert H. Van den Heuvel, "The Honest to God Debate in Ecumenical Perspective," *The Ecumenical Review* 26 (1964), 279-94 (Dr. Van den Heuvel represented the new theological wave in Geneva; his article irritated the leaders of the World Council of Churches); 5) E. Schillebeeckx, "Evangelische zuiverheid en menselijke waarachtigheid," *Tijdschrift voor Theologie* 3 (1963), 283-315, and "Herinterpretatie van het geloof in het licht van de secularisatie," ibid., 4 (1964), 109-50 (ET in *God and Man* [New York, 1969] 85-209); R. Rouquette, "Tempête dans l'Église d'Angleterre," *Études* (March 1964), 402-7.

[61] The world of the "civilized pagan," of art, literature, music, and philosophical discourse, was almost completely strange to Catholics in England: "Either we have ignored it or we have preferred to regard it as hostile" (Brian Wicker). "Civilized pagans," for their part, could not take the Church seriously, or if they did, they saw it as a dangerously anachronistic and negative force. "Yet in England we are living in the same society;" that is how Brian Wicker introduced his plea for a "cross fertilization" of religion and the world in the realm of culture (see the cover of his book *Culture and Liturgy*).

II. THE ECUMENICAL MOVEMENT: A PROMISING DISORDER[62]

The 1962-63 intersession was marked by a series of ecumenically important events that made it possible to assess with some accuracy the immediate results of Vatican II as far as the improvement in relations among Catholics and among Churches was concerned. These results were also often attributed to the special influence exerted by the open attitude of John XXIII. I shall speak, first, of deliberations within the World Council of Churches (WCC) and its affiliated organs and, second, of statements issuing from the great confessional families, the latter sometimes leading to more positive evaluations of Vatican II than did the deliberations of the WCC.

A. THE WORLD COUNCIL OF CHURCHES

The meeting of the executive committee of the WCC in Geneva at the end of February 1963 was its first opportunity to take an official position on the first stage of the conciliar event.[63] In his address Dr. Visser t'Hooft's assessment included three points:

1. Will the Roman Catholic Church in council limit itself to adopting a suitable terminology or will it be ready to enter on a real dialogue that takes seriously the questions raised by the other Churches?

2. The Roman Catholic Church is in the process of becoming aware of its true situation in the contemporary world.

3. The Roman Catholic Church has become, in its turn, a "center of ecumenical initiative," with the risk that some elements of the Catholic

---

[62] This title, "A Promising Disorder," is an effort to capture in a few words the special atmosphere of the transition from 1962 to 1963, which was a compound of the joy caused by ecumenical meetings and an abundance of initiatives in different directions and at all levels. The words were inspired by the phrase "promising chaos," which Anglican Bishop Oliver S. Tomkin, President of the World Conference of Churches meeting in Montreal in the summer of 1963), used at the time to sum up the conference (see Lukas Vischer, *The Ecumenical Advance,* History of the Ecumenical Movement 3, ed. Harold E. Fey [London, 1970], 333).

[63] A few weeks before the meeting of this committee, the Secretary General of the WCC had met in Geneva with an international group of editors of periodicals. Statements made on that occasion by Dr. Visser t'Hooft attested to a softened attitude and a greater tactical prudence in regard to the ecumenical "springtime" that was dawning at Vatican II. The speaker expressed his distrust of a dangerous euphoria, since real dialogue had not yet begun and since the two questions that would test the sincerity of the Catholic Church had not yet been discussed: mixed marriages and religious freedom (see J. Grootaers, "Gesprek met Dr W. A. Visser t'Hooft," *De Maand* 6 [1963], 99-104; see also, along the same lines, *DC* 60 [1963], 404-5).

press are advocating a "triumphal ecumenism" in which Rome is the only valid center in the search for unity.[64]

The Central Committee, the chief permanent organ of the WCC, met for the first time since the opening of Vatican II in Rochester, New York, at the end of August 1963.[65] This meeting included two important elements: the general report of the secretary and a review of the first period of Vatican II by Dr. Lukas Vischer, who had been an observer at the Council. The latter raised four main questions to which the Council would have to give a satisfactory answer in the near future: the common profession of faith in the same Lord; the ecclesiological significance of non-Catholic Churches; religious freedom and mixed marriages; and common witness in today's society.

Vischer's overall assessment of the Council was nuanced. The new situation created by the Catholic Church would have sure repercussions on the other Churches, but every period of transition is inevitably a time of confusion which can only hold back the advance of the true ecumenical movement. Despite the openness shown by the Roman Catholics, it would be necessary to be on guard against juxtaposing two movements representing different conceptions that were in danger of becoming competitors.[66]

Visser t'Hooft mentioned the exceptional merits of the WCC in the pioneering role it had played since it was founded in Utrecht twenty-five years before (May 1938). Wanting to be neither skeptical nor romantic, the Secretary General gave it as his view that in the present state of affairs the fundamental questions separating Christians remained inflexible realities. The vital question "is therefore not whether we can unite, but whether we can undertake a real dialogue."[67]

---

[64] Visser t'Hooft's report was published in *ICI* for March 22, 1963, 5f.; see also the Geneva Communiqué in *DC* 60 (1963), 401-3. Visser t'Hooft attributed one expression of the ecumenism of "conquest," which he was attacking here, to the editors of *Herder-Korrespondenz* (meeting of February 2, 1963, with religious newspersons).

[65] The Central Committee is the authoritative body in the interim between general assemblies of the WCC, which are held only every six or seven years. At the New Delhi Assembly (1961), the membership of the Central Committee was increased from 90 to 100. From the viewpoint of the member-Churches represented on the Committee, the most sizable increase in membership went to the Orthodox (who went from 12 to 17 members when the Russian Orthodox Church joined the WCC). The other traditions were represented by 16 Lutherans, 15 Anglicans, 11 Methodists, 10 United Churches, 5 Baptists, 4 Congregationalists, 2 Syrians, 2 Copts, etc.

[66] Lukas Vischer, "Report on the Second Vatican Council," *The Ecumenical Review* 46 (1963-64), 43-59.

[67] "Report of the Secretary General," *Istina*, no. 4 (October-December 1963), 445-52.

The apprehensions expressed in 1963 by the representatives of the WCC[68] were not the only guarded reactions expressed at the time in non-Catholic circles. When the relic of St. Andrew was restored to the Ecumenical Patriarchate by a delegation from the Holy See, the authorities of the Orthodox Church in Greece saw in this action only a trap set by the Church of Rome. For their part, some representatives of the French-speaking Reformed Churches thought that a return of the Roman Church to "the common faith of the early Christians" was quite unlikely despite the openness of Vatican II.[69] The response of Karl Barth, one of the founding fathers of the WCC, was quite different. The first period of the Council led to a "thaw" on the part of the great Reformed dogmatic theologian, who, in contrast to his friends in Geneva, gave a very positive greeting to the ecumenical openness shown in the early conciliar debates.[70]

Among the "subsidiaries" of the WCC that took a position on the first period of the Council, a special place belongs to the Fourth Faith and Order Conference, held in Montreal, July 12-26, 1963. This conference was the major event of the period being studied here, not only because of the active participation of a Catholic delegation officially appointed by the Secretariat for Christian Unity,[71] and not only because of the rather extraordinary and pervasive feeling of rediscovery on the part of brothers and sisters who had been separated and were at last reconciled,[72] but also because of its ecclesiological program, which was of

---

[68] It would not be until the meeting of the Central Committee in January 1965 at Enugu, Nigeria, that the WCC expressed a relaxed attitude regarding Vatican II; at that time, the decree on ecumenism, which had just been promulgated by the Council, and the agreement to set up a joint working group were judged to form a useful basis for a genuine rapprochement (see J. Grootaers, "Etappen der Ökumene," *Herder-Korrespondenz* 39 [1985], 419-25). The then recent visit of Bea to the headquarters of the WCC greatly contributed to this detente.

[69] See *Christianisme au XXᵉ siècle*, January 3, 1963, reprinted in *DC* 60 (1963), 397.

[70] Barth had given one of the most anti-Catholic addresses at the founding Assembly of the WCC in Amsterdam in 1948. For his statements in 1963 see the interview reprinted in *DC* 60 (1963), 403-4, and especially his article written at the express request of W. Visser t'Hooft, "Thoughts on the Second Vatican Council," *The Ecumenical Review* 25 (1963), 420-31. Later, a visit of Barth to Vatican II and Paul VI confirmed the great old man's attitude of welcome and enthusiasm, which would be crowned by the publication of a little work that caused a sensation at the time: K. Barth, *Ad limina Apostolorum: An Appraisal of Vatican II* (Richmond, 1968). In it we read: "I gained a close acquaintance with a church and a theology which have begun a movement, the results of which are incalculable and slow but clearly genuine and irreversible. In looking at it we can only wish that we had something comparable" (17).

[71] The five appointed observers were joined by a group of Catholic theologians attending as journalists.

[72] Some non-Catholic commentators issued warnings to those Protestants who had let

major interest to all the authorities of Vatican II, whose second session would open two months later.

Father Gregory Baum, an official Catholic observer in Montreal, emphasized the remarkable progress made by two sections of the conference. The second of them developed an idea of "tradition" in which Protestant and Catholic positions were obviously close (not only the individual believers but the entire community is assured of the assistance of the Spirit in dealing with scripture), while the fourth presented an image of the Church that was in harmony with this conception of "tradition."[73] These were ideas at the heart of the controversy still dividing the mixed commission at Vatican II that had been assigned to rewrite the schema on revelation.[74]

The repercussions of the Montreal Conference were very important at the local level because they inaugurated a new era of rapprochement among the Churches. In this respect, a charismatic address of Cardinal Léger was a milestone.[75] But at the same time, a change was beginning on the level of structures, for the Roman Church at last agreed to cooperate in some measure with the ecumenical movement it had for so long regarded as suspect.[76] The generous spread of information about the positive aspects of the Conference by very many correspondents of the Catholic press at Montreal certainly helped to increase awareness of the ecumenical advance the Council was prompting.[77]

The second wind the Council's mixed commission for the schema on revelation displayed after 1963 has been attributed, in some degree, to the influence of Montreal on Vatican II. Thus the ebbing movement

themselves be carried along by the atmosphere at Montreal and thus risked losing sight of the fact that no concession had as yet been made regarding the formulations of the Council of Trent (see especially *The Church Herald*, cited in *The Ecumenical Review* 16, no. 2 [January, 1964], 164).

[73] G. Baum, *Commonweal* (August 23, 1963), 505-11, especially 509-10.

[74] See on this subject the reflections that M. Villain wrote on his return from Montreal, in *Nouvelle revue théologique* 85 (1963), 819-46, especially 834-36.

[75] Following the Reverend G. Johnston and Greek Orthodox Metropolitan Athenagoras (of Canada) on the platform at a public meeting, the Catholic Archbishop of Montreal devoted his address to the theme "We Are One in Christ" (see *DC* 60 [1963], 1215-20).

[76] See the excellent report, one of the few published at the time, by R. Aubert, "L'évolution des tendances oecuméniques dans l'Église romaine depuis l'ouverture du Concile," *Irénikon* 37 (1964), 359.

[77] Limiting myself to a few French newspapers, I may mention the series of articles by H. Fesquet in *Le Monde* (July 23, 28, and 30, 1963) and the six reports by A. Wenger in *La Croix* (beginning on July 31, 1963). For Fesquet, Montreal contributed "to the improvement of psychological and doctrinal relationships between the Churches" (*Le Monde*, July 28, 1963); according to Wenger, the meeting confirmed "the existence of ecumenism in the Catholic Church" (*La Croix*, July 31, 1963). A general survey of the press is given in *The Ecumenical Review* 16 (January, 1964), 182-95.

toward the periphery changed, once again, into a new flow toward Rome. The influence of Montreal was discerned in some addresses in the Council hall, among them that of Léger who asked in particular that the text make clearer the transcendence of the word over later formulations.[78] But, in my opinion, it was in the conciliar Commission that the rapprochement effected at the Faith and Order Conference bore its most lasting fruits.[79]

Another meeting, likewise organized by the WCC, took place some months later in Mexico City. This meeting, sponsored by the WCC's Commission on Missions and Evangelization (which replaced the International Missionary Council), was the first to be held in Latin America, which was "prime ground for missionary conflicts between Catholics and Protestants (and others)."[80] It was thus an occasion for bringing the WCC, an organization often misunderstood by Latin American Catholics, into contact with a Catholic milieu that was being awakened by Vatican II.

B. The Confessional Families

By a remarkable combination of circumstances, several large "confessional families" held their assemblies in August 1963 and reacted more or less explicitly to Vatican II.[81] All these assemblies took care to

[78] *AS* III/3, 182-85. Léger said that the text should make a clearer distinction between apostolic and post-apostolic traditions and that it differentiate between the authority of revelation itself and the lesser authority of the magisterium.

[79] Pastor J. L. Leuba made a close study of this influence, which can be detected mainly in nos. 9-10 of the Constitution *Dei Verbum*. Here can be seen a striking basic agreement with Montreal on the relationship between scripture and tradition (see J. L. Leuba, "La tradition à Montréal et à Vatican II," in *La Révélation divine*, ed. B. D. Dupuy [Unam Sanctam 70B; Paris, 1968], 475-97. See also A. Wenger, *Vatican II: chronique de la quatrième Session* [Paris, 1966], 355-56).

[80] See the article by J. Mejia, an official observer for the Catholic Church at the Mexico City meeting: "La Mission exige l'unité" (*ICI*, February 1, 1964, 29-30); see *Irénikon* 37 (1964), 122-28; for the report of the Mexico City Conference see *Witness in Six Continents*, ed. Ronald K. Orchard (Edinburgh, 1964).

[81] The vague term *confessional family* covers quite different forms of linkage between (often national) Churches that belong to the same confessional tradition, whether Anglican ("communion"), or Lutheran ("federation"), or Reformed ("alliance"), or Methodist ("council"), and so on. Since the origin of the WCC in 1948, membership had been through Churches (often national), which in turn awakened the awareness of confessional characteristics and values. Thus, during recent decades the large federations had increased their influence and authority, and when the Secretariat for Christian Unity decided to invite observers to Vatican II, it was through the confessional federations that specific invitations were given (see Vischer, *The Ecumenical Advance*, 328-29).

invite observers from the Roman Catholic Church, obviously a result of the first period of Vatican II. Among these observers were some conciliar experts who represented the movement for renewal; sometimes they were even from the editorial team for the new schema on ecumenism, which was still in gestation. These assemblies also had an opportunity to hear their own observers at Vatican II, who gave their testimony regarding the ongoing Catholic Council.

When the Lutheran World Federation held its fourth General Assembly in Helsinki at the beginning of August 1963 (with representatives from sixty-three Lutheran Churches), it placed the concern for Christian unity in the foreground. The main preoccupations were close to those of the Council, among them the question of how to present the Christian faith to contemporaries who were unbelieving, individualist, and rootless in the midst of an industrialized society.[82]

The Toronto Congress (August 13-20, 1963) was the first Anglican assembly since 1954. With over a thousand official delegates, this congress represented a fellowship of eighteen ecclesiastical provinces containing 340 dioceses in all, united chiefly by their liturgical order and inheritance from the original Church of England. The central theme, "The Church's Mission to the World," gave this world assembly a pastoral character very similar to that of the Helsinki meeting and often similar to Vatican II. Many participants said that Anglicanism "is not an end in itself" and might be called upon to disappear into a large communion.[83] On his return from Toronto, Archbishop Ramsey, Primate of the Church of England, said that "the ultimate goal of the ecumenical movement was a reunion with Rome, but, indeed, not with the Roman Church in its present form." He did not think, however, that he would see such an organic integration in his own lifetime.[84]

---

[82] See *ICI*, no. 199 (September 1, 1963), 13-14. George Lindbeck, a Lutheran observer at the Council, the Helsinki Assembly, and the Faith and Order Conference in Montreal, made a lengthy comparative study of these three events, which is still of interest today ("Helsinki, Rome et Montréal: impressions sur l'Église en concile," *Istina* [1963], 480-92).

[83] R. R[ouquette], "Les assemblées de Toronto et Rochester," *Études* (October 1963), 120-21, and É. Lamirande, "Solidarité interne et oecuménisme," *Irénikon* 36 (1963), 476-506. A spokesman at Toronto stressed the fact that the fraternal welcome given to the Anglican congress by Cardinal Léger (Montreal) and Catholic Archbishop Pocock (Toronto) was in contrast to the hostile attitude of the Catholic hierarchy at the time of the previous Anglican congress held in Minneapolis in 1954 (Lamirande, "Solidarité interne et oecuménisme," 496).

[84] See *Le Monde*, September 15, 1963.

The first Methodist World Conference since the ecumenical movement had begun to accelerate was held in August 1963 at Lake Junalaska in North Carolina. The presiding officer, Bishop F. P. Corson, also an observer at the Council, said at the time: "The crucial period in relations between Catholics and Protestants will come after the Vatican Council and will be located at the diocesan and parochial levels." Methodist Bishop Emsley said that the present ecumenical movement was for our century what the great Protestant revival had been in the eighteenth century.[85] Among the Catholic personalities who attended the work of the assembly were Archbishop Hallinan (Atlanta) and Bishop Wright (Pittsburgh), who were among the most active fathers of the Council.

C. The Orthodox Church and Its Meetings

Among the effects of Vatican II must be counted the new phenomenon of inter-Orthodox meetings and the establishment of links with the Catholic Church. But these events reveal their full meaning only in the context of the visible acceleration of the ecumenical movement as a whole from 1959 to 1962. This had become a multilateral and dynamic phenomenon of increasing complexity, with Vatican Council II being one of the important movers but not necessarily the main center of gravity. Thus when John XXIII in January 1959 announced a general council that would adopt an ecumenical perspective, Russian Orthodoxy had already been preparing for membership in the WCC since 1955-56.[86]

The exciting activities of those years included in particular:

- The decisive meeting of Dr. W. Visser t'Hooft (WCC) with delegates of the Russian Orthodox Church with a view to the membership of the latter in the WCC (Utrecht, August 1958).
- The announcement by John XXIII of the convocation of a general council of the Catholic Church with a view to promoting Christian unity (Rome, January 1959).
- The establishment of a Secretariat for Christian Unity in Rome and the installation of the Bea-Willebrands team (Rome, June 1960).

---

[85] See *ICI*, no. 299 (January 15, 1963), 7. On February 8, 1963, the Rev. L. Davison was the first Methodist President to be received in a private audience by Pope John XXIII (see *Katholiek Archief* 18, no. 10 [March 8, 1963], 254).

[86] See the detailed timetable in *ICI*, January 1, 1961, 24, under the title "Le patriarcat de Moscou entre au C.O.E."

- The General Assembly of the WCC with the official membership of the Russian Church (Patriarchate of Moscow) in the WCC (New Delhi, November-December 1961).
- A stream of leaders of non-Catholic Churches who wanted to be received by John XXIII (a phenomenon without precedent).
- The official announcement of the invitation to Protestant, Anglican, and Orthodox observers to the Council (spring 1962).
- Repeated friction between Moscow and the Ecumenical Patriarchate, especially in regard to sending observers to the Council (summer and autumn 1962).
- The opening of the Second Vatican Council of the Catholic Church, with non-Catholic observers (among them two delegates from the Patriarchate of Moscow) playing an especially important role (Rome, October 1962).

This background illustrates the multiplication of centers of activity that were either hastening or slowing ecumenical initiatives and that were obviously in competition. This element of competition was evident especially in relations between Geneva and Rome (the "Rhodes incident" in August 1959), between Moscow and Constantinople (in regard to the invitation to send observers), and between Geneva and the confessional federations (along with the group of observers at Vatican II).

Father C.-J. Dumont, a principal player on the Catholic side in the regrettable case of friction with the Central Committee of the WCC, the so-called Rhodes incident (in August 1959), himself lifted a corner of the veil when he attributed the anti-Roman nervousness shown in the Central Committee at Rhodes to the WCC's fear of seeing its plans turned upside down by the unexpected entrance of Rome into the game. "Such a sentiment, combined with such an [anti-Roman] complex," was hardly ecumenical, Dumont said; it was one of those "moments in which the depths of the soul rise to the surface despite the face one tries, however resolutely, to show."[87]

As for Dr. Visser t'Hooft, I have reached the conclusion that his statements at the beginning of Vatican II generally revealed the outlook of the "older brother" who really did not understand why it was necessary to give such a festive welcome to the "prodigal son." While he, the

[87] C.-J. Dumont, O.P., "Rome, Constantinople et Genève: l'oecuménisme au tournant," *Istina* (1959), 415-32, especially 431. The title of the article brings out nicely the complexity of the acceleration of ecumenism at that time. On the Rhodes incident, see the bulletin edited by Dumont, *Vers l'Unité chrétienne* 12, no. 8 (September-October 1959), 73; 13, nos. 1-2 (January-February 1960), 1-4 and 4-15.

elder, had worked so long and so unceasingly in the "house" of the ecumenical movement, the other, the younger, after turning his back for half
a century, now suddenly underwent a belated conversion and was winning the full favor of public opinion! The Secretary General himself
listed the WCC among the "workers of the first hour" and compared the
belated ecumenism of Rome to the work of "the laborers of the eleventh
hour," who had not borne the heat of the day. In the Gospel parable, of
course, that the latecomers receive the same day's wage is resented as a
serious injustice by the all-day workers, who are read a lecture by the
owner.[88]

The sending of observers by the Patriarchate of Moscow at the opening of Vatican II gave the impression of a "honeymoon" with Rome.
The situation continued during the 1962-63 intersession, but with two
very different consequences: on the one hand, the intensification of the
signs of brotherly feelings between Rome and Moscow and, on the
other, and paradoxically, the renewed zeal with which Constantinople
would try to send its own representatives, but without at this time succeeding.

As early as January 1963, in a study devoted to the beginnings of Vatican Council II, the *Revue du Patriarcat de Moscou* acknowledged the
positive aspects of the Council and expressed the hope that "the fathers
of the Council will enter even more fully into the ecumenical atmosphere."[89] The participation of the Catholic Church in the jubilee of Patriarch Alexis of Moscow, who celebrated the fiftieth anniversary of his
priesthood in July 1963, showed Rome's desire to strengthen ties with a
sister Church. A Roman delegation led by Msgr. Charrière, Bishop of
Lausanne-Geneva, was the first in several centuries to take part in a
Russian Orthodox ceremony.[90] Along the same lines, on September 15,

[88] Another manifestation of the agitation felt by the leaders in Geneva at the unexpected ecumenical initiatives of Rome was to be seen in December 1963, when news of
a planned meeting between Paul VI and Athenagoras I in Jerusalem burst like a bomb on
the Conference on the Missions, which the WCC was conducting in Mexico City. Visser
t'Hooft immediately had one of the Catholic observers present telephone the Vatican to
receive assurances on the exact scope of this sensational plan for a "summit" between
two major Churches.

[89] See *ICI*, April 15, 1963, 5. Not to be forgotten is the critical attitude of the same
periodical and its *non possumus* position in 1961. In an interview published in the Greek
newspaper *Ethnos* for February 16, 1963, Patriarch Alexis of Moscow stressed the point
that the Russian Church had accepted the invitation to send observers to the Council "in
an ecumenical spirit," the same spirit that had also impelled it to join the WCC (see *DC*
60 [1963], 406).

[90] Speaking in the name of Paul VI, Msgr. Charrière assured the Patriarch that "after

1963, Pope Paul VI gave a lengthy audience to Metropolitan Nikodim, who was in charge of "foreign relations" for the Russian Orthodox Church; the visit was unprecedented in the history of the Church and furthered the rapprochement between Rome and Moscow. The Orthodox prelate laid flowers at the tomb of John XXIII.[91]

The most important ecumenical event of 1962-63 was undeniably the second Panorthodox Conference held in Rhodes in September 1963.[92] The principal issue at this meeting was a direct consequence of the ecumenical openness of John XXIII and the first period of Vatican Council II. The issue was to determine a joint response to the crucial question whether the representatives of the Orthodox Churches should agree, in principle, to official conversations with the Roman Church. In addition to lasting disagreements between Moscow and Constantinople, there were many divergences within Orthodoxy. While the autocephalous Church of Greece even refused to go to Rhodes, within Greece itself the ecumenical spirit of major theologians contrasted with the closed attitude of the local hierarchy.

In Rhodes, disagreements crystallized around several points. Did the question of observers at Vatican II have to be linked to the more important question of opening an official dialogue with Rome? Did the sending of observers have to be a joint decision or was each Church free in this regard? Was an official dialogue with Rome to be begun without delay or was it to begin only after the end of the Council? The delegates from Constantinople and Alexandria preferred to begin the dialogue on a footing of equality, since the mere sending of observers was ineffective. The Churches of Europe and the East that advocated the sending of observers wanted to wait for the end of the Roman Council before moving on to a dialogue with the Roman Church.

At the conclusion of the Panorthodox Conference, the twenty-two official delegates came to an agreement. On the one hand, each Church

centuries of separation, new fraternal relations were beginning. . . . This rapprochement cannot be directed against anyone or directed toward anyone." See *ICI*, August 1963, 3, under the title "Rediscovery in Moscow."

[91] The newspaper *Le Monde* for September 17, 1963, wrote: "Msgr. Nikodim will probably attend the coming Panorthodox meeting in Rhodes and will thus be able to argue for an increased representation of Orthodoxy at the second session of Vatican II."

[92] The first Panorthodox Conference had been held in Rhodes in September 1961, its principal purpose being to decide on the list of subjects to be discussed at the prosynod before the Orthodox Synod could set to work (see C.-J. Dumont, O.P., "Une grande date pour l'Église orthodoxe," *ICI*, November 1, 1961, 39-42). A fact not to be forgotten is that the millennium of Mt. Athos, celebrated in June 1963, had been the occasion of an unprecedented gathering of worldwide Orthodoxy.

was allowed to send observers to Vatican II, but they were to be chosen from among priests or the laity and not from among bishops; on the other, an official dialogue with the Roman Church was accepted in principle, but under two conditions: that it be on a footing of equality and that it involve the whole of Orthodoxy. It would be up to the latter to decide how it would speak with a collective voice.[93]

The Ecumenical Patriarch took the occasion of his Christmas message to praise the initial work done at Vatican II. In response to this message Rome sent him the files of conciliar documents.[94] In January 1963 Patriarch Athenagoras had announced his firm intention of sending Orthodox observers to the next session of the Council, but at the Conference in Rhodes the position of the delegation from Constantinople seems to have been more nuanced regarding the usefulness of observers at the Council. After the Rhodes Conference the official organ of the Patriarchate of Constantinople published the letters of good wishes that Paul VI and Athenagoras had exchanged at that time.[95]

Having summed up the ecumenical movement at the time as a "promising disorder," I ought at this point compare the disorder and the promise. Truth compels me to acknowledge that everyone did not see promise in the disorder in 1963; some of the veterans and pioneers were claiming their "birthright"; some others, instead of celebrating the "engagement," were fearful of competition. The representatives of organized ecumenism were fearful that a feverish atmosphere might rock institutions they had patiently built up and for which they felt responsible. Within Catholicism itself, some were afraid of results pointing to a transition, the direction of which was not always clear or reassuring to them.

It was no less true, however, that the great majority of those playing an active part in the acceleration of ecumenism in 1962-63 felt that the "promises" were greater by far than any elements of "disorder." Were

---

[93] On his return from Rhodes, Msgr. Basil (Krivochéïne), Russian Orthodox Bishop of Brussels, gave a nuanced and detailed personal report: "La IIe Conférence panorthodoxe de Rhodes," *La Libre Belgique*, December 31, 1963. See also the articles of E. Stephanou, "Une étape vers le dialogue oecuménique," *La Croix*, November 15 and 16, 1963. The question of the date for beginning an official dialogue with Rome would not be settled in 1963 but would be put on the agenda of the 1964 Conference.

[94] See *ICI*, March 1, 1963, 7.

[95] Paul VI wrote, in particular: "We have been grasped by Him, by the gift of the same baptism, of the same priesthood, celebrating the same Eucharist, the one sacrifice of the one Lord of the Church." These documents appeared in *Irénikon* 36 (1963), 541-45.

not people everywhere speaking of reconciliation and a rediscovery of themselves as brothers and sisters? This latter view is the one that imposes itself on anyone who closely examines the documents and literature of that eventful intersession.

III. JOURNALISM AND THE "BOOMERANG" EFFECT

A. THE ECHO OF VATICAN II

At the outset, chroniclers and journalists who were covering the first period of Vatican II did not accurately assess the response that news about the Council was eliciting from public opinion. It was only after they had returned home that they were surprised to discover the breadth of this response. It soon became clear that the phenomenon was universal in Western Europe and North America. It also became clear that, paradoxically, the great non-Catholic newspapers (often belonging to the liberal tradition) in Germany, Switzerland, Italy, the United States, and elsewhere were showing the greatest interest in the Council and had invested their money by delegating permanent correspondents.[96]

It was, then, rather odd that the Catholic press was generally not in the forefront with news about the Council, whether because of a tendency to sermonize about the Council (Germany) or because of overly close ties with the episcopate (Italy and England), or because of intellectual laziness in the presence of an unexpected Church event (Spain and Belgium). Among the exceptions mention must be made of the great Catholic newspapers of Canada and Holland, which, thanks to good contacts with a local, open-minded episcopate and to a serious theological preparation, soon appeared, including in Rome, as in the avant garde.[97]

---

[96] Among these large-circulation nonconfessional dailies I may mention the following: in Switzerland, the *Neue Zürcher Zeitung* (on a high level) and the *Nationale Zeitung*; in Germany, the *Frankfurter Allgemeine* and *Die Zeit*; in France, *Le Monde* (in which the very lengthy articles of H. Fesquet enjoyed the privilege of never being shortened); in the United States, the *New York Times*; in Holland, the *Nieuwe Rotterdamse Courant*; and in Italy, the *Corriere della Sera*, among others. In Italy, the interpretation of the Council often created a distorted perspective (leaning to the right), but, on the other hand, news about the Council met with a deep and unexpected interest in the great weeklies that were widely read (on the left), especially *L'Espresso*. (This information and that which follows comes in great part from my own files: J. Grootaers, Cahier 6.)

[97] So, too, it was in (French-speaking) Canada and in Holland that news about the Council on radio and television was most extensive. Radio Canada devoted a daily broadcast to the Council. The Dutch Catholic radio and television stations heavily subsidized

Another surprising fact: there were even many instances in which demand outstripped supply, and newspaper readers found fault with the newspapers for giving them insufficient news about the Council in Rome.[98] A great unsatisfied public curiosity soon made a success of the many lectures given by the "front-line combatants" on temporary home-leave, who used them to fill in the blanks in information given in the newspaper.

Some of these ventures went further, already seeking to go more deeply into the message of Vatican II, and the first precursory signs of the "reception" that would follow. A model case was the International Study Days that *Informations Catholiques Internationales* (Paris) organized in May 1963 for packed audiences; the general theme was "The Mission and Freedom of the Laity in the World."[99]

The most lasting expression of the "ebb" of 1963 was probably the publication of works devoted to the events of 1962 and of specialized periodicals by which the way was prepared, in a very dynamic atmosphere, for a deeper understanding of the themes of Vatican II and for the spread of its impact. I am referring not only to the very useful collections of the articles of chroniclers, such as those of R. Kaiser, R. Laurentin, X. Rynne, A. Wenger, and many others,[100] but also to theological readings of the ongoing event, with Y. Congar, J. Ratzinger, E. Schillebeeckx, and H. Küng providing models of the genre.[101] Names of the

the conciliar Centre de Documentation, which had been set up in Rome at the opening of the Council. The special merits of news about the Council in Canada and Holland would be acknowledged by the Roman authorities later on, when these two countries were each given the right to have a representative on the conciliar press committee set up in September 1963.

[98] This was especially the case in Spain, where newspaper editors were convinced that the public was not interested in news about the Council and where some readers protested at being given only the meanest share. The simple inability of some editors to sort out the complex news about the Council contributed to their neglect of this category of news.

[99] The breadth and ambitiousness of this project may be judged from the names of the speakers during these two days: A. Vanistendael, T. Mazowiecki, John Todd, Joseph Folliet, R. Sugranyes de Franch, G. La Pira, Msgr. Blomjous, Jan Grootaers, and P. Liégé, O.P. The papers of this meeting circulated in book form under the title *Mission et Liberté des laïcs dans le monde*, ed. G. Hourdin (Paris, 1964).

[100] Robert Kaiser, *Pope, Council and World* (New York, 1963); René Laurentin, *Bilan de la première session* (Paris, 1963); X. Rynne (a pseudonym of F. X. Murphy), *Letters from Vatican City* (New York, 1963); Antoine Wenger, *Vatican II, première session*; M. Descalzo, *Un periodista en el Concilio* (Madrid, 1963).

[101] Y. Congar, *Vatican II: le Concile au jour le jour* (Paris, 1963); J. Ratzinger, *Die erste Sitzungsperiode des Zweiten Vatikanischen Konzils: eine Rückblick* (Cologne, 1963); E. Schillebeeckx, *Vatican II: A Struggle of Minds, and Other Essays* (Dublin, 1963); idem, *L'Église du Christ et l'homme d'aujourd'hui selon Vatican II* (Le Puy-

first importance were still missing from this list for the simple reason
that many authoritative chroniclers published their work in book form
only after 1963 or began only with the second period of the Council.[102]
Finally, there were some collective volumes that published theological
assessments made in 1963.[103]

The final point here is the sudden development of specialized periodicals: either older periodicals whose circulation shot up, for example, the
ecumenical review *Irénikon* and the religious news journal *Informations
Catholiques Internationales;* or new periodicals that came into existence
in 1962-63.[104] Two journals born of the Council and devoted exclusively
to it found a sufficiently large readership to make them great successes.[105] A final way of spreading news was works of introduction to
the ecumenical problems faced by the Council.[106]

Lyons, 1964-65); H. Küng, *Kirche im Konzil* (Freiburg im B., 1963); Y. Congar, *Pour
une Église servante et pauvre* (Paris, 1963) (which includes, among other things, a lecture
to a group of bishops in Rome in November 1962); B. Häring, *Das Konzil im Zeichen der
Einheit* (Freiburg im B., 1963).

[102] This is true especially of the publications of G. Caprile, L. Dom and W. Seibel, R.
La Valle, M. Novak, M. Plate, R. Rouquette, D. Seeber, M. van der Plas, M. von Galli,
and R. Wiltgen.

[103] Two examples: *La collégialité épiscopale: histoire et théologie* (Paris, 1965), with
an introduction by Y. Congar, contained, among others, studies presented at the collo-
quium organized at the Monastery of Chevetogne in September 1963; *Das Zweite
Vatikanische Konzil* (Würzburg, 1963) published lectures given at the Katholische
Akademie von Bayern after the first period (contributions from W. Kampe, J.
Hirschmann, J. Ratzinger, J. Pascher, and K. Rahner).

[104] Among both kinds of periodicals that devoted themselves to the progress of the
ecumenical movement as a result of the ongoing Council, these may be mentioned: *The
Ecumenist* (United States and Canada), due to the initiative of G. Baum; *The Ecumenical
Catholic Quarterly* (previously *The Eastern Churches Quarterly*), which at the beginning
of 1963 announced its intention of devoting itself completely to ecumenism and which in
the following year became *One in Christ* (Great Britain); *Oecumene* (formerly *Het
Schild*), which in 1963 ceased to be a narrowly confessional journal of apologetics and
became, under its new title, an organ of ecumenical thought open in all directions (Holland); *Sjaloom*, a new journal that was the product of an interconfessional group for the
street apostolate in The Hague and soon became the voice for social and pacifist ecumenism (Holland). It was not by chance that the most typical periodicals, the ones listed
here, all came from Catholic circles, which (as I noted earlier), thanks to John XXIII and
Vatican II, very quickly "took the initiative."

[105] I am referring to *Concil Aviu* (in Catalan) and *Vaticanum Secundum* (in Dutch).
The latter had 6,000 subscribers after four months of existence. I may note, finally, that
the French daily, *La Croix*, gained 50,000 subscribers when Vatican II began.

[106] A few examples from among many: Bernard Lambert, *Le problème oecuménique,*
2 vols. (Paris, 1962); S. Martineau, *Pédagogie de l'oecuménisme* (Paris, 1965); G. Thils,
Histoire doctrinale du mouvement oecuménique, new edition (Louvain, 1963).

B. Preparation for a New "Flow"

During the preparation of the Council, an international group of editors of reviews directed by lay people, known as "Rencontres Internationales d'Informateurs Religieux" (RIIR), had tried to pass on to the Pope and the chief authorities of the Council the wishes of the press generally and of religious journalists in particular.[107] After the conciliar assembly had taken its first steps in October 1962, this informal network concerned itself with seeing that the stream of information flowed in the other direction, that is, from conciliar Rome to the public. This "ebb" of the results of Vatican II toward the periphery during the 1962-63 intersession would soon be replaced by a new "flow" toward the center.

During the intersession, religious reporters and the editors of journals were led to reflect on their experience during the first period of the Council and to draw conclusions for the future, that is, in view of preparation for the second period of Vatican II. The RIIR organized a large meeting in Geneva, February 2-3, 1963, for the purpose mainly of improving the press services after the return of the Council fathers. Just as some bishops met during the 1962-63 intersession and many theologians held colloquia during that period, it was natural that the leading newsmen at Vatican II should organize their own international meeting in view of the resumption of their activity at the Council.[108]

In the very special atmosphere of spring 1963, amid the "promising disorder" of which I spoke earlier, there was a euphoria that sometimes stirred dreams but did not prevent people from feeling a vague apprehensiveness about the unknown future. This "high temperature," which the following intersessions would experience in far less degree, was not missing at the meeting in Geneva. The general survey with which the meeting began made clear the success that news from the Council

---

[107] For more details, see Jan Grootaers, "Informelle Strukturen der Information am Vatikanum II," in *Biotype der Hoffnung (Ludwig Kaufmann zu Ehren)*, ed. N. Klein (Olten, 1988), 268-81; idem, "L'information religieuse au début du Concile," in *Vatican II commence*, 211-34.

[108] In addition, these three "levels" at Vatican II (bishops, theologians, newsmen) were not separated into watertight compartments. At the Geneva meeting in February 1963, such theologians as R. Tucci and E. Schillebeeckx played an active part, and a bishop, Msgr. Blomjous (of the Secretariat of the Pan-African Episcopate), was closely involved in the meeting of review editors. Among the forty-eight participants, the largest group was the representatives of twenty-four editorial boards of reviews; some centers for conciliar documentation, five dailies, some press agencies, and the WCC completed the picture. A dozen countries were present but not "represented." Tucci (of *Civiltà Cattolica*) chaired the meeting, and J. Grootaers (of *De Maand*) served as secretary.

enjoyed among the public. While this fact contributed to the euphoria, it also caused the participants to become aware of the importance of their role in the spread of Vatican II as a renewal of the Church's presence in the world.[109] The exchanges confirmed the certainty of the participants that people today wanted to be, first and foremost, *informed*: "If our contemporaries have not been suitably informed about the Council, it will not be possible for them to live the Council later on" (Francis Mayor).

This meeting occurred at a pivotal moment. It was known that, after the departure of the Council fathers from Rome, certain opponents of the *aggiornamento* once again had a clear field for their activities, but it was also known that the new CC, at the beginning of its work, was showing a greater receptiveness to more open tendencies. It was thus to this CC that the RIIR in Geneva could address a series of concrete proposals.

The first thing on the agenda was an introduction to the methods the WCC had developed for establishing good relations with the press. To this end, Dr. Visser t'Hooft and Pastor Philippe Maury addressed the group and took part in an exchange of views. The experience of Maury, who had been in charge of press relations at the General Assembly of the WCC in New Delhi (1961), where he had to deal with 375 journalists, provided a recent point of reference.[110]

The exchange of views led to some proposals to improve the deficient news given out during the first period of the Council and to relieve the strong tensions connected with the rule of conciliar secrecy. 1) A cardinal from the CC should take charge of the Council's press office and of the general policy about news; this responsibility should not belong to the Secretary General of the Council. 2) A limited group of journalists should have access to the council hall itself. 3) Within each conciliar commission a bishop and an expert should act as liaisons with the press bureau.

The principal subject, however, of the meeting quickly became the question of national centers, in Rome, for news about the Council. Real cooperation among these centers should avoid duplicating effort and wasting energies, and all competition should be avoided between these

---

[109] L. S. Chiale, "Gli orizzonti del Concilio sono quelli del Mondo," *Rocca* 22, no. 2 (February 15, 1963), 16-17.

[110] Maury, director of the WCC's Department of Communications, emphasized the primary importance of distinguishing carefully between news and commentary. In his view, the former should be brief, while the latter had for its purpose to situate the news in a broader setting that could reveal its deeper significance (see Lindbeck's criticisms of the WCC press service, below, n. 133).

national undertakings and the official press service of Vatican II.[111] Tucci reported on the subject of his own tireless activity as intermediary between the press office of the Council and the national centers. Meanwhile, Schillebeeckx offered a theological reflection on the complementarity between the two types of press centers for news and documentation.[112]

The key result of the meeting was a resolution to create in Rome a flexible but well-equipped structure, whose purpose would be to provide coordination among the national centers, while not, of course, imposing anything on organizations that wanted to retain their autonomy. This resolution led, not without some difficulties created precisely by this respect for autonomy (especially of the American and German centers), to a new center with the rather lengthy name of *Centrum Coordinationis Communicationum de Concilio* (Center for Coordinating News about the Council), usually referred to as CCCC.[113]

Following the example of Geneva, the directors of the national centers and the representatives of some religious orders held still other meetings in order to decide on the functioning and financing of the CCCC.[114] When the Council resumed, the CCCC would tackle many jobs of translation, the distribution, even abroad, of the documents of the various

[111] According to a document from the beginning of the second period of the Council, there were in Rome eight national centers for news and documentation that had been established or at least were patronized by national episcopates and were prospering; these were for Germany, the United States, Canada, Brazil, Spain, France, Holland, and Italy, with, in addition, a Latin American center and a Pan-African center. This important phenomenon, unknown at Vatican I, contributed to preventing any monopoly on news. In preparation for the February 1963 meeting, the Secretariat of the RIIR had prepared a dossier (seventeen typewritten pages) of reports on five of the national centers: Holland, Spain, the French-speaking countries, Canada, and the United States.

[112] The theologian from Nijmegen saw a fruitful complementarity between the ordinary news given out by the official press service and the historical and theological light shed by the independent centers of national origin. In his view, this complementarity even had ecclesiological significance: an official press bureau recognized the legitimacy of hierarchical authorities, while the national-level centers were justified by the experience of the faithful throughout the Christian world (see E. Schillebeeckx, *Quelques malentendus à la première session du Concile*, a mimeographed text of seven pages, distributed by the Secretariat of the RIIR on March 27, 1963).

[113] The religious journalists who met in Geneva were not the only group to propose improvements. The Geneva resolutions found a favorable response at the annual meeting of Catholic journalists in Austria; see *Katholiek Archief* 18, no. 22 (May 31, 1963), 540.

[114] These meetings, administrative and technical in character, were held in Rome on March 24 and May 19, 1963. The minutes of the first meeting were not accepted by either the American or the German center. In contrast, there was general agreement at the second meeting, which even proceeded to appoint the Director of the CCCC, sociologist J. Grond (Holland), Director of FERES in Fribourg (personal files of J. Grootaers).

centers, and the organization of some fifty international press conferences in 1963. Fifteen individuals worked full-time for the CCCC and
four half-time during the second period of Vatican II.

C. The Special Role of the Coordinating Commission
When everything is secret, nothing is kept secret.
(F. X. Murphy, July 1963)

From the very beginning of the Council in October 1962, the attitude
of the Roman authorities toward news was based on a glaring contradiction: on the one hand, the very strict obligation to preserve secrecy that
was imposed on the fathers of the Council (article 26 of the Regulations
for the Council), and, on the other, the establishment of a press office,
the obvious purpose of which was to serve as a source of news.[115]

But in 1963 the negative results of this contradiction and the strong
tensions to which it had given rise finally yielded their fruits. Thus there
was what might be called a boomerang effect, as the rule of secrecy and
silence contributed to an explosion of unrestricted news. Some defenders of the rule began to experience the disadvantages it had for themselves. Thus the stubborn refusal to grant an interview, useful though
this would be for personal justification, could not be maintained by
someone like Cardinal Ottaviani, who finally agreed to receive some
journalists. Thus, too, the defenders of secrecy about the Council soon
learned, at their own expense, that denying stories that were only partially true wound up costing them dearly. This too was part of the
boomerang effect, which no participant in the Council escaped, whether
he was a prelate of the Curia or the Secretary General of the Council.[116]

As noted above, many episcopates expressed satisfaction with the
news given by a press that was generally interested in the real meaning
of Vatican II as an ongoing event, a press that was often responding to
the demands of an awakening public opinion. It may be that the steps
taken by the spokesmen for the religious newsmen and by the national

---

[115] See R. Laurentin: "To journalists the secrecy seemed hypocritical; to the Roman
Curia, news, even if accurate, seemed an indiscretion or a sour note, even defamation"
("L'information au Concile," in *Deuxième*, 365). In the past secrecy had served to intim-
idate individuals and destroy reputations, but in the Council's climate of freedom of
thought established by John XXIII and desired by many bishops, this state of affairs was
no longer tolerable (see Francis X. Murphy, "Secrecy at the Council," *America* [July 27,
1963], 97).

[116] For examples, see Murphy, "Secrecy at the Council," 97.

centers for news about the Council (centers sponsored by some bishops or an episcopal conference), as well as the steps taken by the press agencies, which Bea urged to cooperate must have had a direct influence on the measures being considered. The direct contact of these various groups with Msgr. Fausto Vallainc, head of the official press office, signified a de facto solidarity that renewed the activity undertaken during this 1962-63 intersession.

But the reorganization of the general policy regarding news during the second period of the Council supposed one other step. The official press office had to be freed from its feudal connection with the Secretary General of the Council, and news about the Council had to be placed under the authority of representatives of the assembly itself. The CC would try to achieve this goal while at the same time studying how to ease the law of conciliar secrecy.

This process, which would go through several stages, was begun at the second meeting of the CC on March 29, 1963, when Felici presented a lengthy report "on releasing news."[117] This document breathed a spirit of openness that was completely new on the part of the Secretary General. The report had been composed by Msgr. Vallainc and contained suggestions coming from the religious journalists of whom I spoke earlier.[118] The report argued in favor of easing the conciliar secrecy, which had, in fact, been bypassed in "more or less authorized" indiscretions (press conferences given by the fathers; communication of the results of votes; complete reports of meetings in certain newspapers; activities of the national centers for documentation). The secrecy had, in fact, put the more "obedient" Catholic newspapers in a position of inferiority and had in the end made them victims of unfair competition.

The report listed three possible solutions: open a tribune for the press (in the council hall); commission a Council father to give oral comments to his own language group, after the fashion of the American "panel" that had operated in 1962;[119] or officially appoint one or more bishops,

---

[117] Felici, *Relatio de nuntiis dandis*, in *AS* V/1, 508-11.

[118] The unusual presence of Vallainc at the CC meeting points to his participation in drawing up the report (see the official communiqué in *OssRom*, March 31, 1963). Some sources suggest that Vallainc himself delivered the report to the Commission (see the chronicler in *Études* [May 1963]), which seems rather improbable. On the other hand, *Katholiek Archief* 18, no. 22 (May 31, 1963), 15, states that Vallainc's report was delivered in the name of the many press organizations that had been active during the first period of the Council.

[119] Under the aegis of the bishops of the United States and in particular of Bishop

assisted by experts, who would daily comment on the press communiqués to all of the journalists (with simultaneous translation). As for the Press Office, a Council father from the General Secretariat might take charge of inspecting and revising the daily communiqué.

From the very beginning of the exchange of views on the report given by Felici, Cicognani, president of the CC, took a definitive position, rejecting the idea of a tribune for the journalists and expressing his preference for the third possibility.[120] But within the CC itself opinions were divided. At the end of the meeting Cicognani announced simply that a new summary of the question was to be submitted at the next meeting.[121] As a result of the death of John XXIII, the third meeting of the CC could not be held until the beginning of July 1963.

The plan for a central organism that would have authority over news about the Council and on which the Council would be represented to the press was the main subject of the proposal that Felici submitted to the CC at its meeting on July 4, 1963.[122] The proposed agency corresponded, in fact, to the press committee for which many organizations of newspersons and journalists had recently been calling; it would be headed by a cardinal, be made up of Council fathers already interested in press-relations, and would be aided by a secretary, who would also be director of the official press office. This standing committee would have for its task to give any useful instructions to the press office on the sub-

---

Wright, at three o'clock every day a dozen or so American experts — theologians and canonists — met with the journalists in a "basement" on the Via della Conciliazione to comment on recent events and in particular on the general congregation that had ended an hour before. During the first session of Vatican II this informal panel was the only quotable source available to the editors of the great English-language dailies. Without that daily meeting they would long since have returned home (see the testimonies of journalists at that time, and especially that of Bernard Daly, who was in charge of the News Service of the Canadian Catholic Conference, in Report no. 5 in the RIIR file for the meeting in Geneva on February 2, 1963).

[120] Msgr. Fagiolo, who studied the Cicognani documents, observed that the Cardinal complained bitterly of the attitude of bishops who gave the text of their interventions to journalists; he also lamented the establishment by some episcopates of centers for documentation that even went so far as to organize press conferences, thus violating conciliar secrecy (see V. Fagiolo, "Il Cardinale A. Cicognani e Mons. Felici," in *Deuxième*, 238-39).

[121] See *AS* V/1, 515-16. The procedure adopted would necessitate dealings that lasted beyond the planned delay. As a result, some witnesses neglected the difference between the report read by Felici (in March), which had to do with proposals, and the report (in August), which had to do with decisions (see, e.g., the report, lacking in these nuances, that would be published by Msgr. Morcillo (Saragossa) in the bulletin of his archdiocese and reprinted in *DC* 60 (1963), 807-9).

[122] See *AS* V/1, 634.

ject both of the daily communiqués and of the press conferences meant for the entire group of journalists.[123]

The new discussion showed that the idea of putting a cardinal at the head of the press committee did not displease the majority of the CC (Cardinal Döpfner even proposed appointing Cardinal König to the post), but another idea soon came up, that of shifting the entire responsibility for the committee to the Council of Presidents (Confalonieri's proposal). This idea was picked up by Felici, whose final report was accepted.[124]

Finally, during the fourth meeting of the CC on August 31, 1963, the matter of the press committee was finally settled: the chairmanship was given not to a cardinal but to Msgr. Martin J. O'Connor, who was vice-president of the conciliar Commission for the Lay Apostolate and was regarded as a specialist in the communications media.[125]

A few days later the decision to establish this Press Committee of the Council was made public.[126] Its main tasks would be to supervise the official press releases and press conferences and also to provide "doctrinal assistance to the various Centers for Documentation." The makeup of the Committee showed that it brought together bishops representative of the major linguistic groups and of geographical areas (Oriental Church, Africa, Asia, and Latin America), as well as a bishop representative of the missionary press. That Holland and Canada were represented reflects an acknowledgment that they were countries in which news about the Council had become especially abundant.[127]

The most sensitive problem remained that of easing the conciliar secrecy. Only a week after the solemn reopening of the Council, at the end of September 1963, Cicognani, writing in the name of the Holy

---

[123] Felici's plan, it should be noted, provided that the members of the committee should get in touch with the different national centers for documentation, in order to prevent these from calling on "unqualified persons" for their own press conferences. This point left no doubt about the desire to have some supervision over the activity of the centers sponsored by the bishops.

[124] In proposing the Council of Presidents as the ultimate authority, it may be supposed that Confalonieri and Felici wanted to avoid the risk of seeing a cardinal of the CC at the head of the press committee, a solution suggested by the religious newsmen. Some cardinals, such as Döpfner and Suenens, had agreed to give press conferences in a spirit of independence that had not always pleased Roman circles.

[125] See *AS* V/1, 648-59.

[126] See *Oss Rom*, September 8, 1963, reprinted in *DC* 60 (1963), 1251-52, and in Caprile, II, 538.

[127] See the detailed analysis of the makeup of the Press Committee in the lecture which Bishop Pangrazio (Goriza), himself a member of the committee, gave in Padua (the text is given in Caprile, III, 301-5, see especially 302).

Father, passed on to Felici the new conditions: henceforth secrecy
was to be maintained about the schemas and the work of the commissions, while "necessary discretion" was to be observed about the discussion at plenary meetings.[128] This indirect way of announcing that
secrecy was lifted for discussions in the hall makes it sufficiently
clear how much Cicognani himself wanted to restrict any easing of the
rule of secrecy. The same desire became clear some days later when
Felici, answering a question of Msgr. O'Connor, said that while the
CC and the Council of Presidents thought it appropriate to publish a
complete list of the names of those who intervened, whether orally or
in writing, on the day being reported, it was not advisable that the
name of each speaker should accompany the summary of his intervention.[129]

At the beginning of the second period of the Council the names of all
interveners on a given day were listed together at the beginning of the
press office bulletin, with the result that it was impossible to identify
with certainty the authors of the interventions that were then summarized. However, on the initiative of Msgr. Pierre Haubtmann, spokesman
for the French-language press group, the names of the speakers were
soon listed in such a way that each intervention could be attributed to its
correct author. The other linguistic groups had no choice but to follow
the example of this courageous innovation.[130]

---

[128] See AS V/1, 696.

[129] See ibid., 695.

[130] During the 1962-63 intersession the Assembly of the Cardinals and Archbishops of
France decided to put theologian Pierre Haubtmann in charge of the daily news to be
given to the French-speaking group of the Council's press office. Msgr. Stourm then
became head of the French episcopate's committee on news. In Rome, Haubtmann
believed that in conscience he must make known the names of the speakers, unless
Stourm forbade it. The latter answered that Haubtmann must act according to his conscience. Once the general congregations resumed, Haubtmann gave the name of each
intervener in his daily oral bulletin. Beginning on October 8, the mimeographed communiqués of the Council in English and German also gave a report of the meeting that
enabled readers to identify the speaker. The mimeographed communiqué in Italian followed suit beginning on October 9. In contrast, OssRom declined to follow Haubtmann's
example throughout the entire second period of the Council.

The courageous undertaking of the French theologian marked a turning point in the
removal of secrecy from Vatican II; it drew the other linguistic groups into an irresistible
movement to reject the restrictive interpretation Cicognani had given of the Pope's
instructions. The event also illustrated the influence a national initiative could have on an
international galaxy of individuals such as a council (see the Jan Grootaers archive,
Cahier 38).

If for ecumenism the 1962-63 intersession seemed a time of joyful and promising disorder, for the press it was a euphoric time when "all possibilities" seemed to be open. It was certainly a time of decisive progress. At the level of informal structures there was the establishment of broad coordination among the national centers for documentation in Rome and, at the level of official structures, there was an easing of conciliar secrecy and the establishment of a conciliar press committee under the authority of a group of bishops already experienced in press matters.

The fallout from the first period of Vatican II and the boomerang effect of its strong tensions in regard to news ended up proving salutary. Through a surprising combination of positive attitudes a kind of consensus took concrete form during the first six months of 1963: the open attitude of a large number of bishops and episcopates in regard to the serious work done at the Council by newsmen and by journalists who to some degree became *their* news men and journalists. Thanks also to the moderate way in which the newsmen presented their claims and to the tenacious steps and diplomacy of such intermediaries as Tucci and Vallainc, the atmosphere became much more peaceful. Finally, the more positive attitude of the Council authorities also contributed to progress; here the role of the CC as a place for meeting and the exchange of views seems to have had a major influence.

This happy combination of circumstances did not yet explain the fundamental cause that made it possible, in so short a time, to reassert the value of the role of news at Vatican II; namely, the increasing awareness that the very existence of a Church-gathering that intended to be pastoral depended in large measure on the transmission of its message to the public. But if public opinion had become so widely attentive to the message of Vatican II, it was because it discovered authentic opinions being voiced there and a freedom of discussion people had thought incompatible with a seemingly monolithic clerical organization. This freedom of thought in a Church previously regarded as intolerant and authoritarian was the first and very clear message that had drawn the attention of the general public, and it became known only thanks to the unsupervised news distributed by the press.

People who reflected at the time on the role of the media were quick to stress the importance of this occurrence. According to Professor Otto B. Roegele, "few things contributed as much to making the Church and the Council credible in the world's eyes as the admission that there was no prefabricated agreement on all questions, the admission that an honest conflict was underway in which participants were serious about having their cause prevail."[131] For that reason, those who felt responsible for honest reporting wondered why the official press service still felt obliged to conceal the existence of divergent tendencies, which represented diversity in unity and were a sign of health.[132]

The non-Catholic observers present in the fall of 1962 had been reassured by the honesty of this genuine debate. One of them, Dr. George Lindbeck of the Lutheran World Federation, carried his approval even further.[133] According to his testimony, the deficiencies and incompetence of the official press office in Rome had compelled journalists to push their investigations further than if the authoritative spokesmen had been helping them, as was customary at the WCC and some Protestant or Anglican assemblies.[134] According to Dr. Lindbeck,

> Thanks to these criticisms that were published for the first time, Catholic Christians, Roman or not, have had to acknowledge that the Church of Rome possessed a greater dynamism and a greater zeal for reform than they had thought. . . . The press office of the Council was incompetent beyond expectations, but the secular press agencies ensured accurate, extensive, and favorable reporting.[135]

The dissensions in the council hall that the meaningless and sometimes even infantile press bulletins of 1962 were still trying to conceal were precisely the things that expressed the new life of the Catholic Church gathered in council. What the leaders of the Council as it began regarded as intolerable indiscretions that were defaming the Church were, on the contrary, in the eyes of world opinion, a reason for genuine sympathy and, among Christians, a reason for hope. Great indeed was the gap between the views of some conservative circles (and not just in Rome) and the realities of public opinion, between clerical tradition and the perspectives of Church renewal. It was this gap that the journalists at the Council had tried to bridge with their own special tools. The effort to come to grips with this state of affairs was the background that during the 1962-63 intersession inspired the steps taken to provide better news.

---

[131] O. B. Roegele, "Entscheidungen in Rom," *Rheinischer Merkur*, October 2, 1964.

[132] Bernard Daly, in charge of the press service of the Canadian episcopate, in Report no. 5 of the RIIR file (note 116, above), 17.

[133] Lindbeck, "Helsinki, Rome et Montréal," 480-92.

[134] According to this not unparadoxical interpretation, the press services of the great assemblies in Montreal (of the WCC) and in Helsinki (of the Lutheran World Federation) had been skillful in provided edifying reports that had satisfied the curiosity of the press and at the same time had anesthetized the press to the more fundamental controversies that had been going on.

[135] Lindbeck, "Helsinki, Rome et Montréal," 487.

IV. A New Eastern Policy

The 1962-63 intersession was marked by an intensification of the policy of making contacts with the communist regimes of Eastern Europe. What was called the new eastern policy (*Ostpolitik*) of the Holy See began to emerge during the first years of the pontificate of John XXIII.[136] In the obviously different cases I shall cite, we can see in that policy as a whole the influence of Roncalli's pontificate and of the openness shown by the conciliar assembly during its initial period.[137]

It must be noted, by way of preface, that historians have often highlighted the year from the resolution of the Cuban crisis in October 1962 to the death of President John F. Kennedy in November 1963, because a new spirit of hope and detente was at that time alive on the international scene. Three key figures symbolized the new perspectives adopted during that short period: President Kennedy, Chairman Khrushchev, and Pope John.[138]

During the 1962-63 intersession several generally unexpected events came in rapid succession: the release of Ukrainian Metropolitan Slipyi, the visit of Rada Khrushchev and Alexei Adzhubei to John XXIII, and the attempts to settle the fates of Cardinal Mindzenty in Budapest and Msgr. Beran in Prague.

---

[136] Among the first manifestations of this new policy we may note the call for negotiations John XXIII issued at the height of the Berlin crisis (summer 1961), his appeal to all governments when war threatened in Cuba (October 1962), and his message to believers and nonbelievers that they should oppose nuclear armament. These initiatives made a strong impression on the leaders and public opinion of the Soviet Union. Khrushchev began to think that the Vatican was henceforth no longer controlled by the American State Department and that the line taken by Pope John could mean support for his own foreign policy, which at the time was already being sharply challenged in the Central Committee of the Communist Party by supporters of an increased Soviet arms buildup.

[137] It must not be forgotten, however, that history does not readily allow itself to be divided into periods. H. J. Stehle has shown that the first signs of a thaw between Rome and Moscow were perceptible as early as 1955, at the end of the pontificate of Pius XII (see the chapter "Mühsame Wende zur Koexistenz 1955-1964," in his now classic book, *Die Ostpolitik des Vatikans* [Munich, 1975], 316ff.). It must also be noted that the first steps taken by the Patriarchate of Moscow toward the WCC dated from 1956. Because of Western anger at the repression of the revolt in Budapest, these steps were momentarily halted, but then resumed, to be completed in 1958.

[138] Norman Cousins, who himself carried out a key mission at the time, defended this thesis in his personal memoirs, *The Improbable Triumvirate Kennedy — Khrushchev — Pope John. An Asterisk to the History of a Hopeful Year, 1962-1963* (New York, 1971). It is to be noted that Khrushchev's political decline began in 1962 and that his resignation came in October 1964. Pope John was elected at the end of 1958 and died on June 3, 1963. Kennedy, whose presidency was inaugurated in January 1961, fell before the bullets of his assassin in November 1963.

The release of Msgr. Slipyi, representative of the Ukrainian Church, after eighteen years in Soviet detention, occurred at the beginning of 1963. It was the result, first and foremost, of the negotiations carried on by American journalist and pacifist Norman Cousins during a heart-to-heart conversation with Nikita Khrushchev in Moscow on December 14, 1962. Cousins had been given this mission by Cardinal Bea and Msgr. Dell'Acqua, and on his return he reported personally to John XXIII.[139] At the beginning of that same month, the two Council observers from the Patriarchate of Moscow had a confidential talk with Cardinal Testa in the presence of Msgr. Willebrands; the observers promised their support of Metropolitan Slipyi. Early in February 1963 Willebrands and Father Borovoi were in Moscow to welcome the Ukrainian prelate on his arrival from Siberia.[140] The press later learned that the observers from the Patriarchate of Moscow had sent a report to the Synod of their Church in which they recommended that it intervene with the Soviet government on behalf of Msgr. Slipyi.[141]

The personal audience that John XXIII granted to Rada and Alexei Adzhubei, the daughter and son-in-law of Khrushchev (Adjubei was the editor of *Izvestia*) on March 7, 1963, was an event of considerable importance during the intersession. The pre-electoral climate in Italy and the sharp criticism of the rightist press gave this audience a significance mainly in the realm of domestic Italian politics.[142] What Western opinion generally underestimated at the time was the power of the personal-

---

[139] After reaching Rome on December 1, on his way to Moscow, Cousins had a series of conversations in the Vatican. The question regarding international order, which the Pope put to the Soviet leader by way of Cousins, was whether the Soviet Union would welcome interventions by the Holy See in the area of peace. Khrushchev's reception of this idea was evidently a very positive one. As for the petition to release Slipyi, the Communist leader, who was himself of Ukrainian origin and fully aware of what had happened in 1945-46, showed himself initially to be very skeptical and even negative, and he asked for time to think about it. During the lengthy conversation between Cousins and Khrushchev, the Communist leader clearly showed great personal sympathy for the elderly Pope, who, like himself, "has kept his ties to his peasant origins." Cousins' mission included a message from President Kennedy (see Cousins, *The Improbable Triumvirate*, 21-29).

[140] Personal conversation of the present writer with Father V. Borovoi on August 31, 1995; see also *ICI*, March 1, 1963, 10.

[141] See *ICI*, November 1, 1963, 14.

[142] The entire European press devoted countless commentaries to the subject without achieving adequate explanations. See the survey of the French press in *ICI*, where, under the meaningful title "Clovis ou Attila?," Helène Peltier-Zamoyska and Bernard Feron (of *Le Monde*) commented on the swirl of public opinion; Feron noted that "others blame the pope for weakening the coalition of the free world by permitting himself to approach Attila" (*ICI*, April 1, 1963, 3-5).

ity of Adzhubei, who at that period formed, along with two or three others, the all-powerful "personal cabinet" of Nikita Khrushchev. It was this personal cabinet that was strongly criticized in the USSR for short-circuiting the normal processes of government and especially for encroaching on the areas of competence proper to the ministers. In the end these criticisms helped hasten the fall of the Soviet leader and his son-in-law in 1964.[143]

In the spring of 1963 a series of steps was taken in the hope of resolving the impasse in the matter of Cardinal Mindzenty in Hungary and of the persecution of which Msgr. Beran was the victim in Czechoslovakia. Some weeks after a lightning trip of Cardinal König to Budapest, Msgr. Casaroli, Undersecretary for Extraordinary Affairs, also went to the Hungarian capital and had a conversation with Mindzenty (April and May 1963). Next came the steps that Casaroli took in Prague with a view to the release of Msgr. Beran and other bishops who had fallen victims to condemnation by the Communist regime (May 1963). During his visit to Poland in 1961 König had already been in contact with the Vice-President of the Council of State (a move against which both Wyszynski and Wojtyla advised him). On April 10, 1963, König visited Mindzenty in Budapest as a personal messenger from John XXIII, who sent word that people were concerned about him and that they would send him news of the Council.[144]

The Roman initiatives followed at least three different lines, which, though parallel, were nonetheless formally independent of one another,

---

[143] Although Nikita Khrushchev had been the one who "destalinized" the government in 1956 and had promised a return to "collegial decision-making," his enemies were able later to point to his abuses of power and the operation of an unofficial "personal cabinet" in which Adzhubei, his son-in-law, who accompanied him on almost all his travels abroad, made foreign policy decisions without even consulting a very angry Gromyko (see R. and J. Medvedev, *Khrouchtchev, les années du pouvoir* [Paris, 1977], 153-58, and W. Hyland and R. N. Shryock, *The Fall of Khrushchev* [New York, 1968], especially 12-15 and 100-6).

[144] König, in an interview with R. Giacomelli, in *San Pietro e il Cremlino* (Casale Monferrato, 1991), 81. There is a slightly different version of the facts in the conversation of König with G. Licheri, *Where Is the Church Heading?* (Slough, 1986). According to this account, it was before the beginning of Vatican II that John XXIII sent König to Mindzenty to invite him to the Council; subsequently the Archbishop of Vienna was sent regularly to Mindzenty by Paul VI, but the Hungarian Cardinal showed very little interest in the conciliar documents that were brought to him at the time (67-69). However, in an interview with Yvonne Chauffin, König confirmed that it was indeed on April 10, 1963, that he visited Mindzenty for the first time (in *L'Église est liberté* [Paris, 1980], 100). See also Thomas Weyr, "The Mindzenty Tragedy," *Commonweal* (January 17, 1964), 454-57.

although we may suppose that there was some coordination, if not orchestration, at their origin. The three approaches, far from being incompatible, had their origin in the same person, John XXIII, who liked to have several irons in the fire at the same time.

In the first place, there were the steps taken by Willebrands, of the Secretariat for Christian Unity, who went to Moscow (in September 1962) to pave the way for inviting Russian Orthodox observers to the Council. The success of this mission made Willebrands the natural intermediary, later on, for completing the negotiations so successfully begun by Cousins for obtaining the release of Slipyi. The good results of this operation were directly tied to Vatican II, since it was the Russian observer Borovoi who "received" the Ukrainian prelate in Moscow when he left prison. And it was also at the Council that the freed Metropolitan was welcomed as a pledge of a thaw that was indeed political but principally ecumenical. The religious aspect of the steps taken by the Secretariat for Christian Unity seems to have been predominant. Nonetheless the approval of Secretary of State Cicognani remained essential. Willebrands, who stressed the religious character of the event, defended himself against having acted without the knowledge of the Secretary of State. But the negotiations for Slipyi were, in fact, supported by Bea and Testa, two close friends and collaborators of John XXIII, who himself was responsible for this sensitive operation.[145]

The second "parallel line" was that of Cardinal König, who as Archbishop of Vienna had inherited a see that had been at the center of the Austro-Hungarian Empire and whose lot had long been shared by Budapest, Prague, Zagreb, Cracow, and Lwow,[146] all of the latter then under the Soviet empire. Despite his many diplomatic missions, which began with a journey to Yugoslavia as early as 1960, König liked to

---

[145] In an interview with R. Giacomelli, Jan Willebrands noted that at that time the Secretariat for Christian Unity was not a dicastery of the Roman Curia but an organ of the Council (see D. del Rio in Giacomelli, *San Pietro e il Cremlino*, 158-62). He also added: "When we speak of *Ostpolitik*, we are on a different and much larger ground than that of meetings at the religious level" (162).

[146] Austrian national sentiment liked to emphasize the peace-making role of a small country whose vocation was to be neutral and which had an authentic experience of "empire," there at the heart of Europe. That is pretty much what Cardinal König was saying when he told Yvonne Chauffin: "I am Archbishop of Vienna, that is to say, the head of the diocese that is geographically closest to the eastern countries. . . . I am in a better position than any of my colleagues to respond to Christians who are cut off from any connection with Rome" (*L'Église est liberté*, 97). Austria was, as it were, "a beacon of freedom on the frontiers of the vast Slavic empire of the Soviets," a description we find at that time in Henry C. Wolfe ("The Austrian Revival," *America* [March 2, 1963], 297).

stress the independence of his undertakings and to play down his role in order to distance himself from the Roman Curia. On several occasions he absolutely refused to be regarded as a diplomat of the Vatican.[147] The Austrian Cardinal openly acknowledged that at the beginning the Roman Curia had undoubtedly had distinct reservations about his undertakings in the East,[148] but he never failed to report to John XXIII (and later Paul VI), who gave the impulse to his various travels.[149]

The third and last of the "parallel lines" was the most specific and therefore the most important one when dealing with the new Eastern policy in 1962-63. The activity of the Secretariat of State was aimed at giving greater importance to relations between the Holy See and the political regimes of Eastern Europe. The activity was predominantly political in character, despite the official denials on this point that were issued by Casaroli.[150] In May 1963, when John XXIII formally gave Casaroli the task of establishing contact with the governments of Hungary and Czechoslovakia, he was told he should take measures, cautiously and without illusions, anytime there was a possibility of easing living conditions in the oppressed Churches.[151]

The remaining question is how this ebb movement of the first conciliar period was perceived by the people for whom it was intended, in this case in the countries under Communist rule. While in general the Catholic populations in Hungary and Poland rejoiced at having visits "from the West," especially those of König, which people saw as proof that the outside world had not completely forgotten them,[152] the leaders of the Catholic Church in Hungary and Poland often voiced more mixed feelings on this point. Mindzenty and Wyszynski were afraid that the

---

[147] Interview with Y. Chauffin in *L'Église est liberté*, 97. See also the interview with G. Licheri, where we read: "My mission was strictly pastoral and not diplomatic. The *Ostpolitik* of the Holy See was initiated, developed and concluded by Casaroli under the authority of Paul VI" (*Where Is the Church Heading?*, 69).

[148] See Giacomelli, *San Pietro e il Cremlino*, 94.

[149] "Each time I informed the Holy Father of the results of my actions, whether the pope was John XXIII or Paul VI, with whom I have always had the most cordial relations" (König, in *L'Église est liberté*, 95).

[150] In his conversation with D. del Rio, Casaroli said that it was for linguistic convenience that this *Ostpolitik* was described as "political," "but in the sense in which the term can be applied to the activity of the Holy See, it describes an activity that is strictly religious and ecclesial. Pope John's concern . . . was with the situation of the Church and religion in the countries under Communist rule" (in Giacomelli, *San Pietro e il Cremlino*, 61).

[151] Casaroli, conversation with D. del Rio (Ibid., 62).

[152] See what König had to say on this point in Giacomelli, *San Pietro e il Cremlino*, 81 (Hungary) and 88 (Poland).

emissaries of the Vatican might begin negotiations with the Communist government without the knowledge of the local episcopate.[153] The Polish episcopate always claimed to act with real autonomy as far as negotiations with the political authorities were concerned.[154]

As for Msgr. (later Cardinal) Slipyi, he had to wait many years before he could express his feelings. In October 1971, at the Synod of Bishops in Rome, the Ukrainian Metropolitan, speaking in the name of the Ukrainian bishops, complained openly of Vatican diplomacy and the attitude of the Secretariat for Christian Unity.[155] A good while later, when recalling contacts between Rome and Moscow at the time of Vatican II, the new Ukrainian archbishop, V. Sterniuk, complained about ecumenical initiatives at that time; it seemed to him that Rome preferred good relations with the Orthodox Patriarchate of Moscow and neglected the interests of the Ukrainian Catholic Church.[156] The bitterness felt toward Casaroli was long lasting. Ten years after the Council, Wyszynski told the Synod of Bishops in 1974: "I am not a Casaroli man."[157]

---

[153] When König was sent in haste to Budapest to allay the anger of Mindzenty, the latter remarked that he was not obliged to obey a Roman Curia that was cultivating contacts with Kadar's government. When König was in Poland, Wyszinski did not hide his satisfaction on learning that the meeting of the Austrian archbishop with a member of the Polish government had ended in failure (see Giacomelli, *San Pietro e il Cremlino*, 84 and 89).

[154] These circumstances shed a special light on the support Wyszinski and the Polish bishops gave to the conciliar trend that favored a renewed promotion of episcopal conferences. For more details see Jan Grootaers, *I protagonisti del Vaticano II* (Cinisello Balsamo, 1994), 248-49.

[155] On this occasion the Ukrainian prelate directly attacked the Vatican diplomats who regarded the Ukrainian Catholics as an embarrassment and remained silent about the six million persecuted Ukrainians. He attacked the delegates of the Secretariat for Christian Unity who, when present in Moscow at the Russian Synod, did not respond to the viewpoint of Patriarch Pimen when he declared the union of the Ukrainians with the Roman Church to be null and void. He also attacked Catholic and Communist Poland for not intervening on the side of a half-million Ukrainians who were deprived of the most basic rights (see the summary in the press release of the Sala Stampa on October 23, 1971, reprinted in the French edition of *OssRom*, November 19, 1971, 6. G. Caprile supplies important corrections of the allegations made in that address, in his *Il Sinodo dei vescovi* [Rome, 1972], II, 826-27).

[156] Volodymir Sterniuk in an interview with R. Giacomelli, in *San Pietro e il Cremlino*, 184. On his arrival in Moscow after just being released from a detention camp, Slipyi wanted to telephone some friends in the Uniate Church but was formally forbidden to do so by Borovoi and Willebrands. The latter's mission was to bring Slipyi straight to Vienna, without any contacts in the Soviet Union (from a conversation of this writer with Borovoi, August 31, 1995).

[157] A. Casaroli, conversation with D. del Rio, in Giacomelli, *San Pietro e il Cremlino*, 70.

CHAPTER X

THE CONCILIAR EXPERIENCE
"LEARNING ON THEIR OWN"

GIUSEPPE ALBERIGO

When Vatican II began in St. Peter's Basilica on October 11, 1962, almost four years after it was first announced, it was not easy to predict what would happen. The best known council, that of Trent, was four centuries in the past and had been held in difficult ecclesiastical, political, and geographical circumstances quite different from those of the 1960s. The memory of Vatican Council I was much less remote, of course. A good number of people thought that the new council should bring it to completion, but if so, would there not be a repetition of the tensions that had then marked the debate on papal prerogatives? Had not the Catholic memory, especially in Rome, interiorized a troubling sequence: *council — conciliarism — antipapalism*? If, this time, the lengthy preparation had been designed specifically to avoid "the unexpected," might not the "foreigners," as the transalpine bishops were called in Rome, for all their good intentions, have some unwelcome surprises in store?

In fact, as the thousands of *vota* in the antepreparatory period had shown, the spiritual and cultural state of the "foreigners" was much different from that of the episcopate that attended Trent in the sixteenth century and from that of the bishops called to Rome in 1869. Gallicanism and episcopalism were now hardly anything more than ideas mentioned in the classroom, without contemporary relevance.

Very few bishops consciously related the now opening council to the changed conditions of a planet that had shortly before emerged from a destructive conflict and was still divided by opposing ideologies and living under the threatening shadow of a nuclear war. Humanity wanted peace but was incapable of attaining it; it was caught up in an exciting period of scientific, economic, and technological development, but troubled by formidable social imbalances. Councils had traditionally had for their purpose to pass judgment on preceding situations of Church-conflict, that is, they were motivated essentially by problems that had arisen in the past and for which no solution had been found. But the context of Vatican II was of a quite different kind.

The result was a period of waiting that was marked by great uncertainty and perhaps by suspense. Only slowly would the realization dawn that the real element of novelty here, in comparison with previous councils, was the Pope.

I. ACCEPT THE PREPARATION?

The transition from the lengthy preparation for the Council to its actual celebration found almost everyone unprepared. A great many people believed that the Council would be short and would consist of approving the many texts presented by the Central Preparatory Commission. In fact, the dispatch of a "sampling" of schemas to the bishops in the summer of 1962 had stirred a great deal of dissatisfaction, tempered only by pleasure at the proposed liturgical reform. Harsh criticisms of the results of the preparation had begun to circulate as the tenacious "secrecy" that had curbed all preconciliar discussion began to break down.

The group who had controlled the preparation aspired to continue their operation during the Council; and, even after the conciliar commissions had been freely elected, the preparatory commissions resisted leaving the field, some of them continuing to assemble their "old" members. The Central Commission's Subcommission on Mixed Matters also thought of itself as still in existence, and it continued to work until December 1962. This tenaciousness was also illustrated by the Secretariat for Christian Unity, in the composition of which the Council had no say at all, and by the Liturgical Commission, which, backed by the consensus of the fathers, was asking that its preparatory schema be respected in its entirety.

The great majority of the bishops who came together in Rome had little awareness of themselves as a council and, with regard to both the decisions and the duration of the Council, preferred to ask "What does the pope want?" The difficulty, reflected in the antepreparatory *vota*, in achieving a global vision of the Church and of the historical situation had not yet been overcome, even though the expectations raised by the announcement of the Council had affected many bishops.

The atmosphere as the Council began its work was one of pious subordination on the part of the vast majority of the bishops to the Roman Curia and therefore to the results of the preparation, which the Curia had controlled. In particular, the bishops of the Latin world were conditioned by their geographical and cultural closeness to Curial congregations composed almost completely of Italians. On the other hand, the episcopates of other cultural areas tended to underestimate the weight of Curial influence. Both groups would realize, more or less quickly, that the Council could not get under way without coming to terms with the Curia.

That the first period ended without any decrees having been approved could be seen as an unmistakable rejection of the preparation and as evidence that the Council had become aware of its own historic role. Only slowly and gradually would it be seen that the conditioning created by the preparatory period retained its force and that the Council had overcome it only partially and less radically that many seem to have thought.

II. In Search of an Identity

Enthusiasm, bewilderment, eager study, boredom, and disappointment alternated and overlapped during the weeks between October 11 and December 8. The idyllic image of the Council faded away as the assembly began the complex process of constructing its identity. The lack of group experience in the Catholic episcopate and, even more, the lack of familiarity with working as an assembly necessitated an accelerated apprenticeship and a period of wearisome adjustment. Cardinal Gracias of India expressed this nicely when he said at the beginning of December that "we have learned to walk on our own feet." He was echoed by Dominican theologian M.-D. Chenu, an expert for a bishop from Madagascar, who wrote:

> From the very first exchanges I received the happy impression that the isolation of the individual bishops, each in the service of his local concerns, was giving way to a lively sense of solidarity in the face of problems felt by all. This solidarity very quickly found expression in active contacts with other African groups that spoke French, English, or even Portuguese, and led to the formation of working groups. . . . The same phenomenon occurred among the "episcopal conferences" as a whole. . . . This rather impressive "consensus" was also found at the level of pastoral sensibilities.

The allocution of John XXIII on September 11, together with the message approved by the fathers on October 20, and then, and above all, the perspectives opened by the papal allocution *Gaudet Mater Ecclesia* — which once again were unexpected and were assimilated only slowly and not without effort — gave the assembly a very substantial common denominator.

Their success in postponing the election of members for the conciliar commissions — an election planned, with incredible casualness, as a conciliar reconfirmation of the members of the preparatory commission — generated among the fathers an intoxicating leap in self-awareness. The debate on the liturgy provided a beginning with a subject that was very concrete and not too difficult so that the dialectic began without harsh tensions. Many found themselves at ease with a set of familiar problems, and this helped them overcome initial timidity. Some had perhaps not been entirely aware of the doctrinal significance of some crucial passages in the schema on the liturgy (the liturgical celebration as "source and summit" of the Church; the central place of the local church; the importance of episcopal conferences; the equal emphasis placed on the liturgy of the word and the liturgy of the Eucharist), yet these were gains that, as would be seen later on, constituted meaningful guidelines for ecclesiology and had the potential to condition all the subsequent work of the Council.

In any case, the demands for renewal that had been promoted for a century by the liturgical movement, especially in central Europe, were at last being given full recognition. Many, however, were disappointed that it had not been possible to obtain definitive approval of a decree before the suspension of the Council's work. Already becoming evident was the thorny problem of reaching agreement between the conciliar majority and the working commissions, all under Curial management and less interested in the maturing of a conciliar climate.

In less than three days the assembly got rid of the schema on the social communications media, regarding it as a waste of time when all were waiting to discuss the schema on the Church. Now, several decades later, we may ask whether, due in part to the inadequacy of the schema itself, the Council was not myopic in its failure to grasp the enormous expansion, already imminent, of the cultural and spiritual importance of the media.

In the second half of November the existence became clear of a powerful majority that rejected the first dogmatic schema, on the question of the relation between the Bible and tradition, a burning question among Catholics and of great importance for relationships with Reformed Christians. This majority was confirmed and endorsed by the resolute decision of the Pope to remand the schema to a mixed commission, a possibility that Ottaviani's Commission had always refused during the preparatory period, in effect burying the text and initiating its complete revision. All this revealed a growing self-consciousness on the part of the episcopate; it shook off its worry that the preparatory schemas, because they had been sent to the bishops with the Pope's authorization, might be covered by his authority and therefore could not be rejected or replaced. As early as November 14 Cardinal Alfrink had openly asserted at the general congregation that a preparatory schema could be rejected without offense to the Pope. But during those same days the theologian Gagnebet was telling his colleague Labourdette that there were lawyers who claimed a preparatory schema could not be replaced by a new one without an intervention of the Pope.

Ten days later the interventions on the schema on the Church would attest the existence of a movement to leave behind the opaque and obsolete securities provided by the preparatory material and to commit the Council to the perspectives of renewal that John XXIII had outlined on October 11, although as late as December 1 Msgr. Marcel Lefebvre, harking back to the Tridentine distinction between faith and morals, was still insisting that on every subject the Council should work up two texts, one doctrinal and the other disciplinary. While these surprising developments confirmed and reassured some fathers, many others experienced these weeks as a time of schooling, of listening in order to learn; finally, many others were frustrated that the preparatory material was being set aside, an action that to them seemed hasty and superficial, if not dangerous to the authenticity of the Catholic tradition.

The delay in distributing the schema on the Church, which was the one most awaited and even, for many, the only one that merited the celebration of a new council, caused surprise and apprehension. Was this not the text that was to provide a balance to the "papal" decrees of Vatican I on primacy and infallibility? Was this not the subject for which all were waiting, the main subject in the *vota* of the preceding years, the subject that had received the greatest attention in the theological research of recent decades? At this point there was a fear that even the important trends that had emerged in the debate on liturgical renewal could still be contradicted and lost.

As the suspension of activity on December 8 drew closer, the worry grew that the spiritual climate and the new directions so laboriously developed during these first months might be lost during the lengthy interval, during which there might be a revival of the "Roman" and Curial influence that had left its mark on the years of preparation. The fragmentary but alarming bits of news about the pope's health did nothing to dissipate these worries. They were expressed with keen sensitivity and gravity by, among others, Cardinal Léger, who proposed the creation of a new commission that would have authority over all the other organs of the Council and would be charged with coordinating and accelerating the work of the commissions and thereby safeguarding and developing "the great gift which God has given to his Church" in the Council. John XXIII's timely creation of a Coordinating Commission was an answer to these petitions and filled a gap in the organization of the leadership of the Council, which had repeatedly given the impression of lacking a clearly defined leadership.

In the new climate that emerged in Vatican II, the irruption of preconciliar movements was one of the more important novelties. The liturgical renewal, ecumenism, the return to the sources, the return to the Bible — movements that for decades had led a sad life, often suspected or merely tolerated — unexpectedly became the lode-stars of the *aggiornamento*. Some bishops were gratified by this turn of events; others feared a revival of modernism; the majority were surprised and amazed. These movements had been, even if unwittingly, the breeding ground for the Council, and now they were unexpectedly exercising a directive role. It was true that they had built up a patrimony of hopes, spiritual experiences, and pastoral impulses, but when faced with the need of supporting the development of complex conciliar documents they would also display a certain weakness. The supremacy of traditional theology, which had often been confirmed by decree (we need only recall *Humani generis* and the campaign against the "new theology"), had been so oppressive as to hamper the leaven of theological renewal, which had too often remained in an embryonic stage.

The corpus of decrees of Vatican II would not be completely free of this weakness. Despite the collaboration of many first-rate theologians, the Council's elaboration of the doctrinal lines of the renewal and its textual expression of them would create major problems. Enjoying the perspective of history, however brief, we have attempted to go beyond merely providing information on the laborious steps taken day by day and to clarify the "red threads" that it is possible today to see running throughout the Council's work. Of course we cannot ignore the fact that the Council's activity engaged an ever vaster range of topics and that many problems were addressed simultaneously by various bishops and theologians; thus it is often impossible to compare and to coordinate "parallel" developments. One has the impression that the Council found itself having to address new problems or new perspectives on old problems as a "work in progress."

To transcend the scholastic anthropology, to reintegrate pneumatology into ecclesiology, to go beyond the Church-State problematic, and to promote the unity of Christians without uniformism or "return" — these were the great challenges that appeared already in 1962-1963. Anyone who imagined that Pope John XXIII's call for the Council to realize "a leap forward toward a doctrine penetration . . . in more perfect correspondence with fidelity to authentic doctrine, studied and presented in the forms of inquiry and literary expression of modern thought" was reductionistic was mistaken. Vatican II was not able to draw upon pre-existing and mature doctrinal statements, in part because of the climate of distrust that had limited and hindered so many Catholic theological circles.

The Church of the Poor Group, which represented experiences and demands that were more complex than Father Gauthier's original inspiration, became active on the periphery of the great assembly. Attention to the Church-world problematic also began to ferment, a matter on which the conciliar preparation had followed obsolete paths. The nuclear threat, which had proved real during the Cuban Missile Crisis and which had been avoided in part because of the Pope's intervention, also urged minds in this direction. Congar recalls that a projected text on the international order was circulating informally, an effect of the Cuban crisis. John XXIII had recently developed contacts with the USSR, taking advantage of Msgr. Lardone and of Bea's Secretariat, to whom he had also entrusted the mission of establishing a direct channel to President Kennedy.

Even more significant was the effect of the participation of many Christian observers in the work of the Council; this group entered unobtrusively, but more quickly than many bishops, into the dynamics of the assembly. This fact helps us understand the growing importance that attention to ecumenism had in the Council's work, beginning with the liturgical constitution. We must recognize, however, that during these months there was a continued lack of understanding of the concrete and immediate terms of Christian unity as Pope John had described them in his announcement of the Council and in the months immediately after. The conciliar assembly understood and assimilated to a much greater degree the perspectives the Pope had formulated in *Gaudet Mater Ecclesia*: the urgency of an *aggiornamento* of the Church to be effected by giving priority to the "pastoral." The intervention of Bishop De Smedt on November 19 marked a crucial step forward in the formation of a conciliar consciousness; his purpose was to activate an awareness among the bishops of the ecumenical dimension of the problems the Council had before it, an awareness completely alien to a large number of Council members. The feelings and, in several cases, the powerful emotion that his intervention roused were a testimony to the widespread lack of preparation, but also to the great freedom that reigned henceforth in the Council. The Catholic ecumenical movement passed beyond the pioneer stage as a matter for "experts" and became a "catholic" problem.

During the intersession an intense exchange took place between Rome and Constantinople in an attempt to permit the latter to send observers to the Council and to go beyond this problem by instituting other forms of relationship. In the spring of 1963 the possibility was considered of re-establishing *apocrisiaries*, that is, representatives of the Pope at Constantinople and of the Patriarch at Rome, in accordance with custom in the first millennium. At the same time the Oriental section of the Secretariat for Christian Unity came to life and marginalized the Oriental Congregation and corresponding conciliar commission. For his part Athenagoras was inclined to forego sending observers to Vatican II in favor of direct theological encounters between Roman Catholics and the Orthodox of Constantinople. And Rome was not forgetting the other pole: Moscow. In July an official delegation took part in the celebration of the episcopal jubilee of Patriarch Alexis.

All this activity caused some concern among the leaders of the World Council of Churches in Geneva, who feared being marginalized by Rome's new ecumenical dynamism. The man who committed himself to maintaining the connection between the various facets of this problem was Bea, who advanced unchallenged to the footlights as a protagonist second only to John XXIII.

But the Council did not live in isolation; it was an epicenter of contemporary life, starting with Rome, which had been "invaded" by thousands of participants from every part of the world. Despite the *extra omnes* ("everyone outside") that marked the beginning of the conciliar sessions, Vatican II was not isolated either from Rome or from life. There were ongoing contacts at various levels: from the correspondence many fathers kept up with the faithful at home, to the pastoral letters sent periodically to the dioceses, to the countless number of written and oral bits of news that bombarded the members of the Council, and, finally, to the media, which were anxious to obtain and pass on news and which at times unexpectedly influenced events in the Council. We may recall, for example, the statement of lawyer Costantino Mortati, a member of the Italian Constitutional Court, on the TV/RAI program aired November 10, 1963. When asked for an opinion on the Regulations of the Council, Professor Mortati stressed the lack of provision for a vote that would serve as a guide at the end of the general debate on a schema; it appears that this authoritative opinion influenced the decision of the Council of Presidents to ask for a vote on the liturgical schema on the following November 14. Just as significant was an intervention of quite different character, the article published by Msgr. Philips in the March 1963 issue of *Nouvelle Revue Théologique*, "Two Tendencies in Contemporary Theology: At the Margins of Vatican II." Philips's bipolar description was rapidly taken to be exhaustive and contributed a great deal to crystallizing the distinction between majority and minority.

During those weeks information-centers, such as the Dutch DO-C and the Canadian CCC began to operate. During those same weeks Dutch editor Paul Brand renewed earlier contacts with K. Rahner, E. Schillebeeckx, and other theologians, with a view to starting a planned international theological journal, to be called *Concilium*. This was a sign of the fruitfulness of the new kind of collaboration to which the conciliar event gave rise and that people wanted to continue after the Council.

Along with the Council fathers, the Pope, too, developed through contact with the conciliar experience. Interiorly convinced as he was of the rightness of the path he had started on with his convoking of the Council in 1959 and had confirmed in his Allocution *Gaudet Mater Ecclesia*, John XXIII, despite the progress of his illness, followed the work of the Council without interruption and reinterpreted in creative ways his responsibility as head of the Council. He succeeded in balancing his own personal convictions, the tumult of directions that were emerging in the Council hall, and the pressures brought to bear on him as he sought to exercise his responsibility in a way that, far from humiliating the bishops, would promote their freedom. This outlook is attested to by his repeated, timely, and liberating interventions against constricting or unsuitable Council Regulations, and, even more, by the way in which he gradually brought into focus both his own role vis-à-vis the gathered episcopate and the very purpose of the Council. His material absence from the Council hall did not signify a lack of interest or attention on his part but rather his concern not to limit the debate. It is significant that on December 13, 1962, he responded quickly to a memorandum from Bea and authorized the restoration of the scheme on the Jews to the Council's program.

The norms for the intersession, the concluding discourse on December 8, and, above all, the letter to the bishops on Epiphany 1963 were so many stages in an increasingly perceptive awareness. A short time later, after a meeting with the Coordinating Commission, the Pope noted: "It has been on my conscience, I confess, that *contrary* to what happened in the first two months, from October 11 to December 8, the pope should take his proper place, discreetly indeed but as the real president by supreme right, as head of the Catholic Church." A comparable manifestation of intentions by the Pope found expression in the meeting of the Coordinating Commission on March 28. On February 9, during an audience for the editor of *La Civiltà Cattolica*,

> he [the Pope] said that he was fully satisfied with the Council; true enough, the Council had entered fully into its work only during the final weeks, when it began to grasp the implications of the message in September and of the inaugural address on October 11. . . . During the first session he preferred not to intervene in the debates, so as to leave the fathers their freedom of discussion and the chance to find the right way on their own; on the other hand, since he himself did not have the required competence in the various questions, an intervention of his might disturb things more than help them; the bishops had to learn on their own, and they had done so.

The Council also underwent a breaking-in period at the level of its everyday operation. It learned from experience the effective help that young clerics from the Roman colleges provided as ushers (*assignatores locorum*); the bars within the basilica became places not only for relief from the boredom induced by the repetition of the same ideas and from the fatigue caused by Latin spoken with as many pronunciations as there were bishops (only the observers enjoyed the privilege of translations), but also occasions for contacts and exchanges. The running of the conciliar machine meant financial costs that became more worrying as time passed. After the wearying experience of the vote for elections to the commissions, when it took days to count the ballots, the mechanics of voting were gradually improved to the point that they became a model for so complex an assembly. The General Secretariat, headed by Pericle Felici, who was becoming "the man of the Council," effectively oversaw everything and often filled in for others. For his part, Cicognani, the Secretary of State, did not give up trying to influence the Council, even if only indirectly, through contacts with the Pope and by means of his office as president, first of the Secretariat for Extraordinary Affairs, and later of the Coordinating Commission. With his soft style and without allowing himself to be identified with the intransigent positions of many of his Curial colleagues, Cicognani quickly became the real leader of the group that wanted the Council to continue along the line of the preparation by skillfully reining in the impulses to renewal.

It took only a few weeks for the conciliar assembly to recognize the real protagonists: from Bea and Ottaviani, who were already known, to Ruffini, Frings, Léger, Suenens, Lercaro, Liénart, and, less openly, Montini. But there were also Larraín of Chile and Malula of Africa. No less important were such experts as Tromp, Schillebeeckx, Congar, Ratzinger, K. Rahner, and Daniélou, to name only a few, and such organizers as the Jesuit Greco, creator of unity in the African Episcopate, or the Rector of the Belgian College in Rome, Prignon, Suenens's indefatigable shadow.

The enormous size of the conciliar assembly was a stimulus to regional meetings of bishops, an activity over which the Holy See had traditionally kept careful watch. Even the Italian bishops emerged from their age-old dispersal and began to hold periodic meetings, but, more important, the Council provided Latin American prelates with the possibility of meeting frequently and allowed the African prelates to meet across colonial and linguistic barriers. Still more surprising was the meeting of the German bishops from the Federal Republic of Bonn and those of the Democratic Republic of Pankow. Various experiences could be compared and exchanged, something that would otherwise have been difficult, if not impossible. These meetings were fruitful for the life of the Council, but they were destined also to be continued after Vatican II — an anticipation of the reception of the Council.

On a different level there were typically conciliar associations, such as the *Coetus* that gathered some Argentine bishops or the one that saw a growing number of periti gathering at the Belgian College and, above all, around the "Belgian squad," thereby giving rise to an exceptionally influential source of development.

After more than thirty years, it is still possible to agree with the observations Congar wrote in the heat of events:

> The episcopate has discovered itself. It has become aware of itself. Given that, the formulas will emerge. They will come spontaneously, because the way has been cleared for them. I have already said, having strongly experienced it, as have so many others, what an original and irreplaceable reality is the very fact of the assembly as such. As a result, each of the participants becomes, in many respects, another person: he sees things differently; tendencies asleep within him come fully alive, while others that had been dominant quietly withdraw; he is excited at sharing in other types of humanity, in other horizons; finally, he realizes fully the world-

wide solidarity and responsibility of the episcopate. Gone are the trite
images of the life of a bishop in his see, alone there at the head of a diocese with its daily and sometimes petty problems. Each bishop feels himself to be a member of a body not limited by place or time: the body of the
apostolic pastorate of which Jesus Christ is the invisible head, the one
whose universal pastoral office is reflected in that of the successor of Peter.

III. FROM THE FIRST TO THE SECOND PREPARATION

It was not without regret at the lack of a definitive decision, at least on
the liturgy, that the Council suspended its work on December 8. While
bishops and experts were glad to return home, the more alert among them
were aware of the danger that before the resumption of work in September
1963 the autonomy the Council had won, not without traumatic moments
and despite the encumbrance of the preparatory schemas, might be lost. All
of them had been changed or were being changed. It was incumbent, especially on the leaders whom the assembly had put forward, to avoid this
danger and even to ensure that the directions the Council had begun to take
and the shape it was assuming be consolidated and strengthened.

The epicenter of the "second preparation" was the Coordinating
Commission, which John XXIII supported with constant and close attention. In this Commission, to a greater degree and more effectively than
in the Secretariat for Extraordinary Affairs, the members bent on
renewal succeeded in voicing the proposals that guided the re-examina-
tion of such texts as had survived the collapse of the first preparation.
Knowing that they could rely on a broad consensus, Liénart and Suenens, along with (despite some wavering) Döpfner, Urbani, and Confalonieri and despite the resistance of Spellman, promoted guidelines for
the conciliar commissions, which were being reined in by Cicognani, the
authoritative, skillful, and stubborn patron of the preparatory work. The
conviction that they had to proceed in such a way as to avoid any overly
sharp contrasts and conflicts resulted almost always in the preservation
of substantial elements from the preparatory texts. The leaders under-
rated the costs of such a strategy from the viewpoint of doctrinal clarity
and of response to the expectations of renewal that had been raised.

The man who inspired this approach and worked tirelessly for it was
Msgr. Philips of Louvain, who, flanked by the "Belgian squad" and
backed by Suenens, played a role that was at least as important as the
one that Tromp had played in 1960-62. During the years of preparation
the Theological Commission had pursued the mirage of a doctrinal

monopoly, while leaving "disciplinary" matters to the other commissions. Now, on the contrary, Suenens and Philips chose a more respectful course of influencing the ongoing work within the complex constellation of commissions, subcommissions, and mixed commissions, both through guidelines issued by the Coordinating Commission and by direct participation in the various working groups at crucial moments. Bea, for his part, continued to be a basic point of reference through the many-sided undertakings of the Secretariat for Unity.

Roman circles trusted the Secretary of State to protect their viewpoints; on the other hand, the now imminent change of pontificates might bring new scenarios.

The impulse received during the weeks of the Council continued to manifest itself even outside of Rome, in regular exchanges of news and thoughts among bishops and especially among theologians, and in numerous meetings of entire episcopates. The conciliar spirit was spreading throughout Catholicism and feeding new waves of expectations in general public opinion; in the latter, the encyclical *Pacem in terris* and then the death of John XXIII brought an involvement of hitherto unknown intensity and extent.

Could the turbulent and inebriating experience of the eight weeks of the first period survive the dispersal of the bishops and their return to "ordinary life"? It is of interest that more than one of the fathers became the object of the criticism that the "open" attitudes they showed during the work of the Council was not matched by corresponding openness when they conducted the ordinary business of their dioceses. In some cases the end of the intense experience of "becoming a council," together with the repercussions of the disappearance of the encouraging presence of Pope John, even left room for an incipient disaffection, as seems to be true of an especially perceptive person such as Léger of Canada.

IV. A BREAKING-IN PERIOD FOR THE CONCILIAR EXPERIENCE

While these first eight weeks of uninterrupted presence in Rome were a new experience for many bishops, participation in a council was a new experience for them all. If only gradually, they were affected by now "counting" for something, by the realization that they were supposed to do something more than simply put in an appearance and follow an already fulled worked out script. In varying degrees the orientations each bishop was led to form for himself, at least in deciding how to vote, required tiring effort but also kindled a sense of satisfaction.

It was easy and not uncommon for bishops to hide behind acceptance of a leader's opinion and to shirk the task of reaching a personal conviction, especially when the subject of debate was questions and problems on which their knowledge had not advanced since their long-past years of seminary studies. Gradually, however, the opportunities for getting information and making comparisons allowed many to acquire personal convictions, at least when it came to major choices. The very fact that the commissions, that is, the centers where sophisticated technical developments were taking place, remained almost inactive during this first session made it easier for the assembly members to make the work done their own at a level sufficiently general to be accessible to very many of them.

The need to escape from the anonymity generated by the great number of members of the Council led to a movement, starting with the initial election of commissions, to take advantage of the episcopal conferences as bodies intermediate between the individual bishops and the full assembly. The effort at a coordination of the episcopal conferences, which was promoted, unobtrusively but with great effectiveness, by R. Etchegaray and H. Câmara, had a similar purpose. This was a true and proper choice among ecclesiologies that was also peacefully accepted and shared in as a functional necessity.

The confrontations for which the Council provided the occasion produced a freedom hitherto unknown in Catholicism, something that happily surprised the observers more than anyone else. It was also very quickly realized that, beyond and apart from the themes that were the subjects of debate, the way had been opened for a radical and apparently unconditioned reshuffling of the "certainties" that had still been the background of the preparation for Vatican II. Efforts at "resistance," such as that of the International Group of Fathers, took the limelight. There were even signs suggesting the danger that the room for doctrinal "mobility," which had been gained during these weeks over against the monopoly of the Roman schools, might be just as quickly absorbed by a new and different "orthodoxy," no less demanding even if less arrogant than its predecessor.

V. FROM JOHN TO PAUL

The change of pontificate, which traditionally causes important discontinuities, did not undermine the conciliar atmosphere; in fact, the conciliar event clearly conditioned the conclave. The new pope, Paul VI, had participated in both the preparation and the first period, although he preferred to stay out of the limelight. He had hardly been elected when he announced the resumption of the Council and determined the date for it, postponing the previously set date by the exact number of days during which the Roman See had been vacant.

The differences between Pope John and Pope Paul were very substantial and were not slow to show themselves, even in regard to the conduct of the Council. Above all, a different atmosphere quickly became perceptible, one determined not only by the character of the new pope but also by his training, his long experience of service in the Roman Curia, and, finally, by his keen concern to ensure the greatest possible consensus on the decrees that the Council was beginning to prepare.

The deep feeling that the death of John XXIII aroused throughout the world, and the widespread impression so many had of having been left orphans, could not but affect the first hundred days of his successor. Pope Paul lacked both the element of surprise in an election that had in fact been only too often "predicted" and the tranquillity usually characteristic of a newly elected pope that would allow him to feel completely free in relation to his predecessor. It was impossible for Paul VI not to feel the weight both of the Council, which *had* to continue, and of the increasing identification people felt with John XXIII. It would be several months before he could really begin *his* pontificate.

In the period studied in the present volume the most important intervention in the life of the Council was the repeatedly requested decision to put in charge of the work of the assembly and of its commission a collegial group of directors (the *moderators*), with the intention of putting an end to continuing uncertainties about the direction of the Council.

VI. THE CHURCH IN A STATE OF COUNCIL

The conciliar assembly was not cut off from the conditions and events of contemporary society, much less from events in the Christian Churches. But neither should we neglect the opposite phenomenon, that is, the impact of the Council both on a large sector of world society and, above all, on the Churches. Although the first period of work ended without anything being definitively approved, the effects of the atmosphere at the Council were substantial and perhaps even greater than those which the approval of a decree would have produced. In fact, during these months from the fall of 1962 to the fall of 1963, the conciliar phenomenon could be read and interpreted with the highest degree of creativity, precisely because it was still made up solely of general impulses to conciliarity, *aggiornamento*, and the pastoral spirit, or, in a word, to renewal.

The Council was not only an institutional phenomenon, reserved to those at the top of the ecclesiastical pyramid, a manifestation of the "teaching Church." From the time of its announcement on January 25, 1959, it involved all of Catholicism and, gradually, the other Christian communities as well. The conviction, and even prior to that the feeling, spread that the entire community of believers was "called to a council." The assembly that actually met in Rome beginning on October 11, 1962, was seen as an "icon" of the "state of council" in which the entire community of Christians was now participating.

It is not possible here to give even a summary description of the reception of these impulses, but I cannot fail to mention at least the impact they had. Events at the Council, although still known only in very general and often distorted terms, generated the conviction that a historical turning point was at hand. This conviction urged and accelerated the process of surmounting the Cold War and the corresponding climate of frontal opposition between the two politico-ideological blocs: the West and the Soviet Union. This lessening of tension affected both international relations and the internal political attitudes of many countries, above all in Europe, but also in Latin America and Africa.

But the turning point was perceived with even greater intensity in the world of the Churches and, above all, of the Catholic Church. It was a turning point that rendered obsolete the recent past of the Cold War, which, especially in the 1950s, had been experienced increasingly as oppressive and suffocating. The thesis of "the end of the Constantinian era," which had been started by Archbishop Jaeger and taken up in authoritative fashion by Father Chenu, gave a cultural dimension to this climate of opinion and, at the same time, received very considerable confirmation of a kind unthinkable a very short time before, from the lines of thought that emerged in the two months of conciliar activity. It seemed the end of the era of a threatened and self-absorbed Catholicism, the era in which it had magnified the elements of its self-identity even at the cost of aggravating separations and contrasts.

The conciliar effect was thus manifested with a disruptive energy that was unexpected and contagious. Problems that had been dismissed in preceding decades moved, sometimes rather virulently, into the foreground. Mechanisms to preserve balance and retain control unexpectedly proved inadequate under the weight of a worn-out authoritarianism and outdated methods now being commonly rejected. The Holy Office and the Congregation of Propaganda in particular would pay the price.

Hopes and expectations long hidden burst forth into the light of the sun; repressed longings found room that had not even been dreamed of. The primacy given to rote-repetition, preservation, and passive obedience was replaced by new tendencies to independent investigation, creativity, and personal responsibility.

VII. TOWARD WHAT KIND OF FUTURE?

The creation of the Coordinating Commission had avoided the dreaded vacuum between the first and second period of the assembly's work and, even more, a return to the atmosphere of the preparatory period. But the death of John XXIII was a traumatic blow. The continuation of the Council was not in doubt, but when the work began anew there would be unknown quantities. The change of popes in the Catholic Church plays too determining a role not to be felt at every level and, all the more by a council, which has the pope as its natural president. This was the case here, even though the new pope had taken part in the work of the first period, had proclaimed his complete loyalty to the Council, had promptly set the date for the resumption, and had introduced important changes in the Regulations. John XXIII did not leave behind a "Roncalli party." What, then, was his heritage to be? The Council would find it difficult to assimilate that heritage in a more than nominal way.

What would be the thoughts and feelings of the bishops as they returned to Rome? The naive ignorance of October 1962 was behind them, but how had the experience of two months of work at Council and then of their return to diocesan routine changed them? Would they feel constrained by Paul VI, who in his long service at the Secretariat of State had been behind the appointment of many of them? No less important were the changes on the great world stage, among which I need mention only the acceleration of African independence, the weakening of Khrushchev in the Soviet Union, and the (imminent) assassination of John Kennedy.

From many points of view there would be a new beginning, marked, this time, more by the experience of the first period than by the preparatory work, a new beginning in which the bishops would surely be more aware of the mechanics of the assembly and more insistent that its work be done efficiently. Above all, Vatican II had begun to take on a much richer and more complex identity than that given by the initial expectation of the "need" to complete the ecclesiology of Vatican I. On the eve of his death Pope John had persuaded it with gentle firmness to adopt the perspective of

> serving humanity as such and not just Catholics; defending, above all else and everywhere, the rights of the human person and not just those of the Catholic Church. Present-day circumstances, the demands of the last fifty years, and a deeper understanding of doctrine have brought us before new realities. It is not the gospel that changes; it is we who are beginning to understand it better. The moment has come to recognize the signs of the times, to seize the opportunities offered, and to look far ahead.

The pastoral outlook and *aggiornamento* would gradually take on new dimensions and interconnections that would broaden the horizons of the Council and the expectations it was raising. Interest in schema XVII would grow out of all proportion. This also led to two difficult challenges. First of all, did the Council have at its disposal a patrimony of thought such as would adequately sustain a conciliar formulation that would carry it beyond the habitual limits of theological inquiry? The especially laborious and tortuous history of the future pastoral constitution *Gaudium et spes* would evidence a weakness that would emerge clearly only as the Council progressed. Second, would not the distrust that had already shown itself toward initiatives for renewal find new sustenance in the tendency of the Council to abandon the habitual formulation of Church-state relations and to attempt a new understanding of the situation of the Church in the midst of modern pluralistic and secularized societies? The goal of ultimate unanimity in the Council became thereby more difficult to achieve but also more desirous.

VIII. EIGHT USELESS WEEKS?

How are we to evaluate the fact that the first period ended without a single document having been approved? What meaning is provided by the careful historical reconstruction of these first thirty-six general congregations over fifty-nine days? From the standpoint of a hermeneutics of the corpus of conciliar texts, was the first period only a remote premise, a break-in period not worth much attention?

Here is the point at which the methodological choice that inspired the concept and realization of this *History of Vatican II* is put to the test. That choice rested upon the view that to equate Vatican II with the corpus of its texts not only impoverishes the hermeneutics of those texts themselves but is also fatal to the image of the Council. Vatican II has often been known a little too abstractly as if it were only a set of texts — many texts, even too many texts! But to understand the conciliar event one cannot prescind from that generative phase that was the first period.

Going beyond the already known chronology of those two months, the reconstruction offered in this volume brings to light the evolution of the conciliar assembly and the shape it took. If certain crucial steps had, of course, to be stressed, steps that were to be completed in the structure and contents of texts approved long afterward, even more important for a knowledge of Vatican II was the journey by which the assembly gained its own identity. As we have seen, it was a journey that was often stormy and by fits and starts, made more difficult by the lack of a "program," but for this very reason also much freer and significant in its results.

That the bishops, and their "experts" with them, gained an almost totally new awareness of their concrete and common general responsibilities for the universal Church would be enough by itself. But during this first period many of them discovered new dimensions of their communion with each other, gained the experience of exercising effective responsibility by the use of the vote and then also by gathering in groups of marked doctrinal orientation (majority-minority), and came to recognize themselves as protagonists (or, better, co-protagonists) rather than as the obedient representatives, at the periphery, of higher authority.

All this is indispensable for understanding how the first period, despite its "sterility" when it came to approving final texts, was later to constitute the paradigm of Vatican II. To some degree it would remain the "magic moment" by which to measure greater or lesser successes of the succeeding stages of the Council's work.

In the course of the three years during which the celebrations of Vatican II took place, the alternation of conciliar fathers was to be insignificant and for that reason the memory of its various phases was particularly constant and lively. When they looked back to the autumn of 1962, it would not be the uncertainties, the weariness, the annoying repetitions that would appear pertinent, but instead and above all the assembly's growing self-awareness as it discovered it could master its own destiny, could frustrate predictions that it would be an assembly of "yes men" called together only to approve a synthesis of what they had learned thirty years earlier during their theological studies. It had become a Council that knew how to construct a life of its own, departing from a season of Catholicism in which liberating ferments had been in constant danger of being suffocated by a uniformity inspired more by ideology than by the gospel. This rejuvenation echoed the flourishing hopes aroused among the common people by the 1959 announcement and gave them even greater force with the mythic authorization of a council.

In its later phases of work Vatican II would come to make many particular decisions possible because of the start it had made in 1962. Perhaps it also raised, at least in some minds, a doubt whether such necessarily concrete decisions about texts were not purchased at the cost of a blurring of the fascinating and perhaps unrepeatable experience of a "new Pentecost" during the first period. In any case, those eight weeks have a unique place in Vatican II and thus in its history as a great event of the Spirit.

INDEX OF NAMES

INDEX OF SUBJECTS

PRINTED ON PERMANENT PAPER • IMPRIME SUR PAPIER PERMANENT • GEDRUKT OP DUURZAAM PAPIER - ISO 9706

ORIENTALISTE, KLEIN DALENSTRAAT 42, B-3020 HERENT